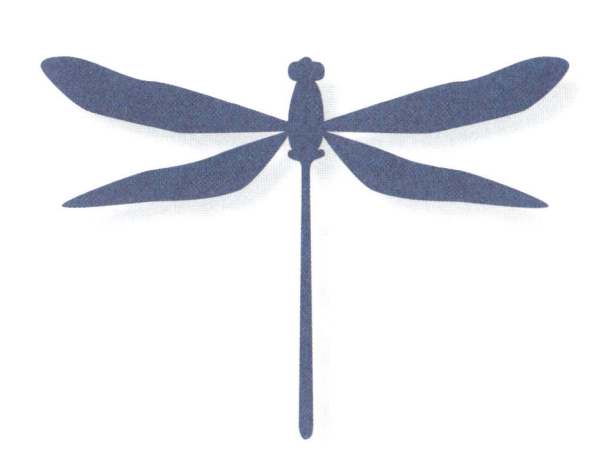

SPECTACULAR
MODERN
HOMES
TEXAS

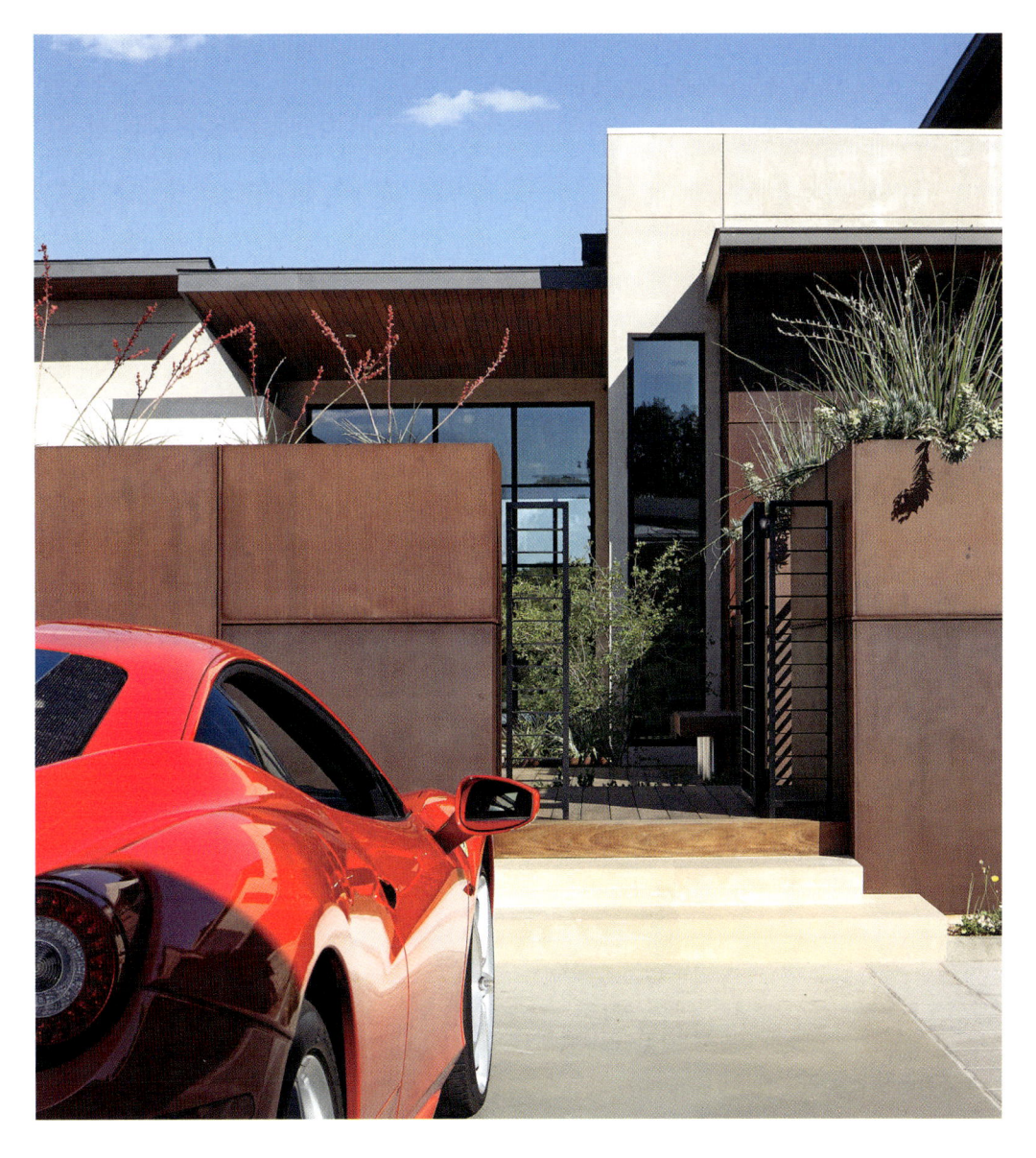

A STUNNING COLLECTION OF FINE RESIDENTIAL DESIGN

Jolie Carpenter Berry

Benefiting CancerBelowTheBelt.com | Spreading Awareness | Helping Patients | Uniting Survivors

Published by

Signature

www.signatureboutiquebooks.com
Publisher: Jolie Carpenter Berry
Publishing Coordinator: Lynne Traugott
Editor: Rachel Watkins
Collaborating Partner: Brian Carabet
Senior Art Director: Donnie Jones
PR | Architectural Publicist: Diane Purcell

Copyright © 2021 by Signature Boutique Books
All rights reserved.

No part of this book may be reproduced or transmitted in any form or by any means, electronic or mechanical, including photocopying, recording, or by any information storage or retrieval system, except brief excerpts for the purpose of review, without written permission of the publisher.

All images in this book have been reproduced with the knowledge and prior consent of the professionals concerned and no responsibility is accepted by the producer, publisher, or printer for any infringement of copyright or otherwise arising from the contents of this publication. Every effort has been made to ensure that credits accurately comply with the information supplied.

Printed in the United States

Distributed by Independent Publishers Group
800.888.4741

PUBLISHER'S DATA
Spectacular Modern Homes of Texas
Library of Congress Control Number: 2021939472

ISBN-13: 978-0-9964240-73
First Printing 2021
10 9 8 7 6 5 4 3 2

PREVIOUS PAGE AND RIGHT: LaRue Architects. Photography by Dror Baldinger FAIA.

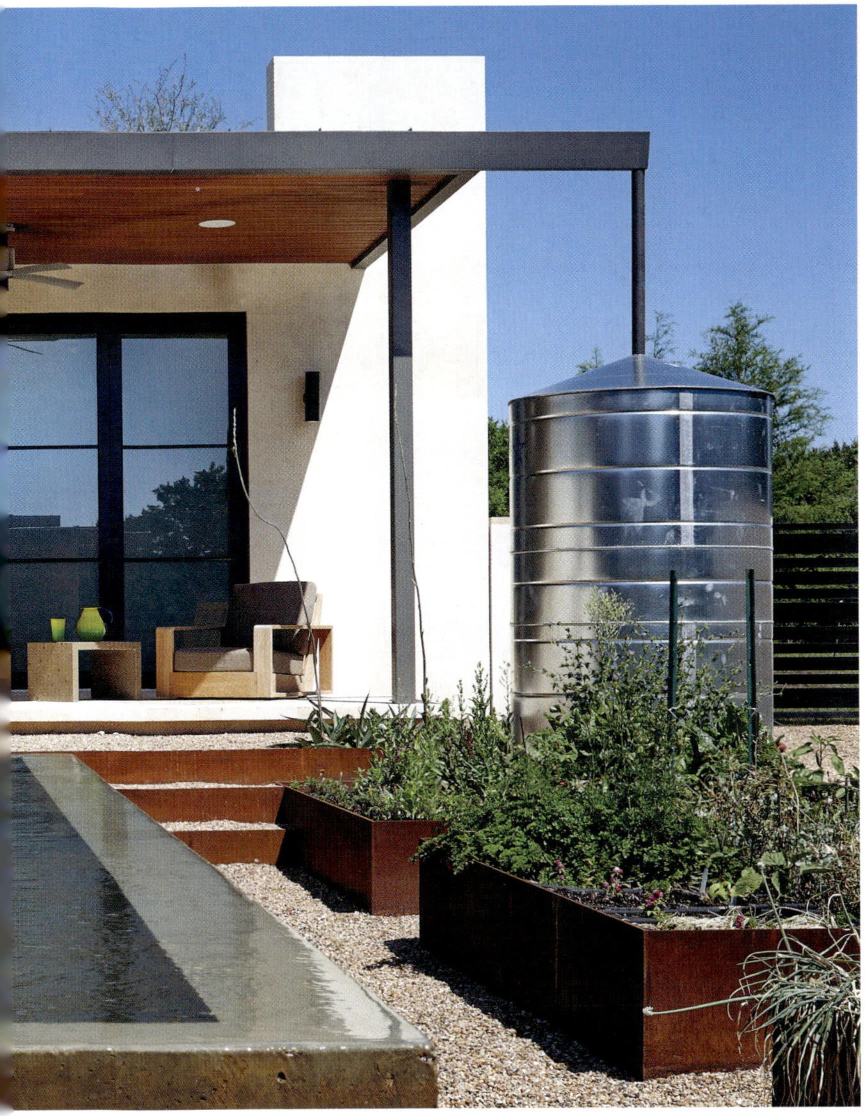
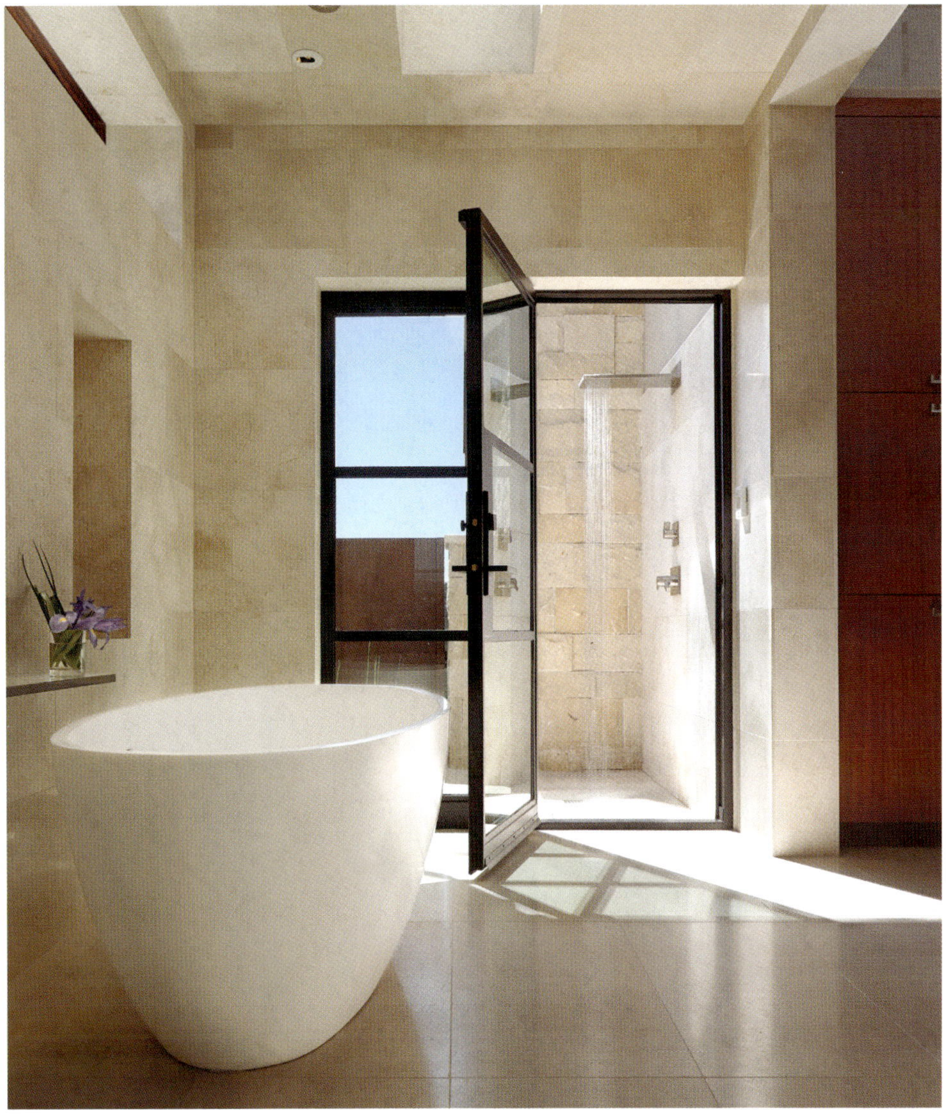

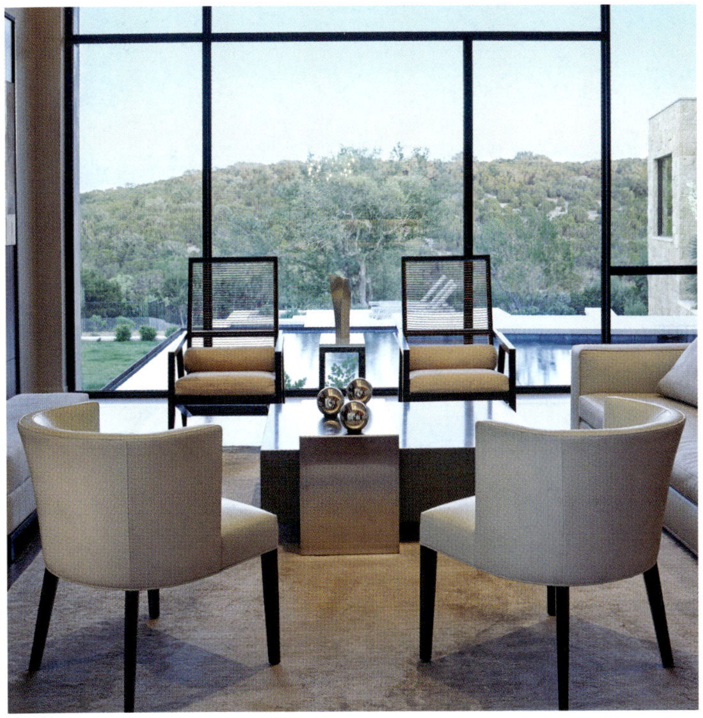
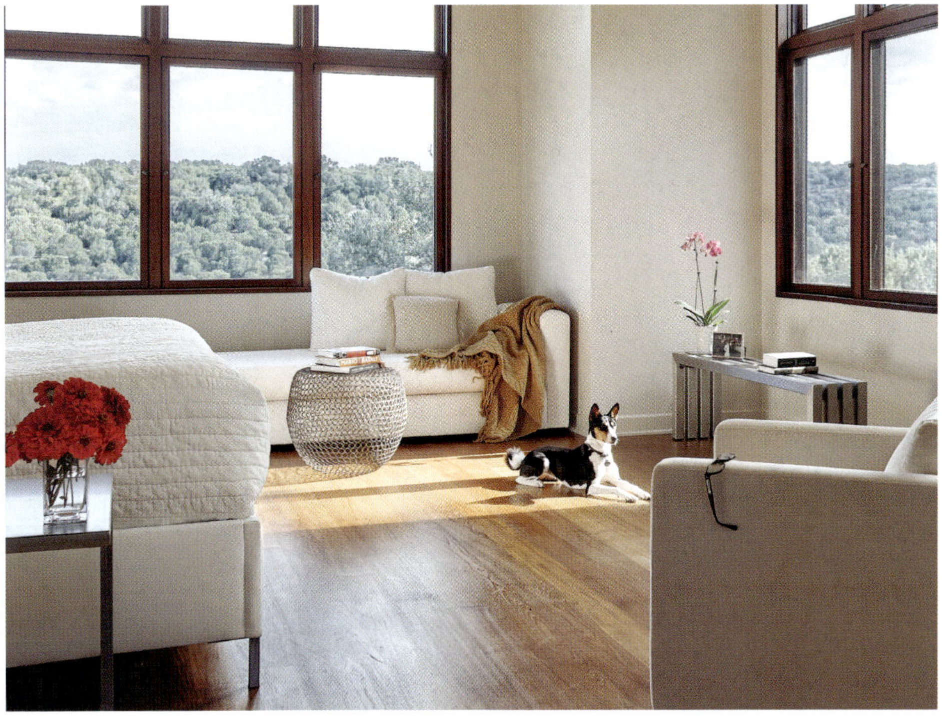

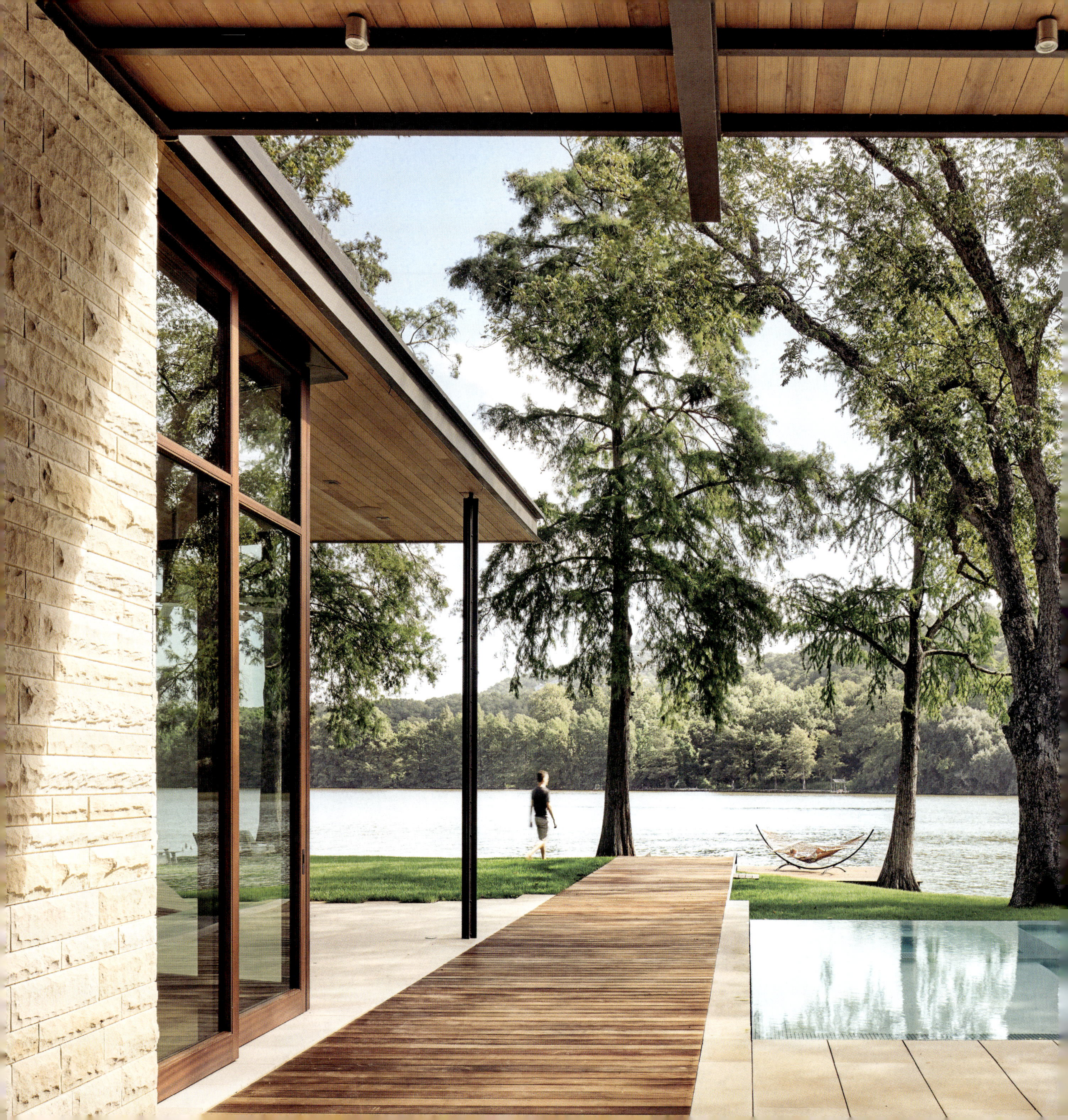

INTRODUCTION

When I set sail on this book project, I could have never imagined the storm I was going to run into. Every book project comes with its challenges, but this was a tsunami in the form of a global pandemic. Photo shoots were cancelled, installations were pushed back, showrooms were closed, and the interior design and architectural industry was on standby, wondering what would happen with their businesses. I was wondering if my book was going to be put on hold indefinitely. Luckily, the industries bounced back quickly into full operating mode. Our photo shoots resumed and it was business as usual with the addition of masks and hand sanitizer on every countertop. Everyone felt fortunate to live in Texas and to be working in a thriving industry, while at the same time, in shock at what was happening in our world with Covid-19.

I think one thing we can all relate to is that we were forced to make the best of staying at home, which meant beautifying our environments. Our homes became our sanctuaries, our staycations, and our offices. Residential design became a topic of conversation and more popular than ever. We were all looking for ways to reinvent our spaces where we were spending more time than ever. It turns out, this book was created in the perfect timing and I hope it inspires everyone who lays their eyes on the beautiful projects featured in this collection of stunning modern residential design.

Since there is no one singular modern style in Texas, you will find a variety of approaches to modern design on the forthcoming pages from a talented and visionary group of architects, designers, and builders. And you'll find that every region of Texas has its own unique influences on design, depending on the topography, climate, and local culture.

For example, only in Austin, would you find a bachelor pad penthouse with 180-degree views of downtown, decorated with a mirrored steer and a neon sign that says "live music." You'll also see sprawling Hill Country homes with resort-style amenities, swimming pools, and outdoor living spaces that represent a casual lifestyle (and a never-ending vacation mindset!). You'll get a peek inside lakefront homes with postcard-worthy views. And, you'll be impressed by Dallas and Houston's glamorous, modern residences with museum-quality art collections and custom furnishings.

There is something for everyone among the vast array of approaches to modern design. As you flip through the pages of this collection of houses, you'll understand the connection to the environment and appreciate the sense of place that radiates within each city chapter.

Enjoy,

Jolie

LEFT: A Parallel Architecture. Photography by Casey Dunn.

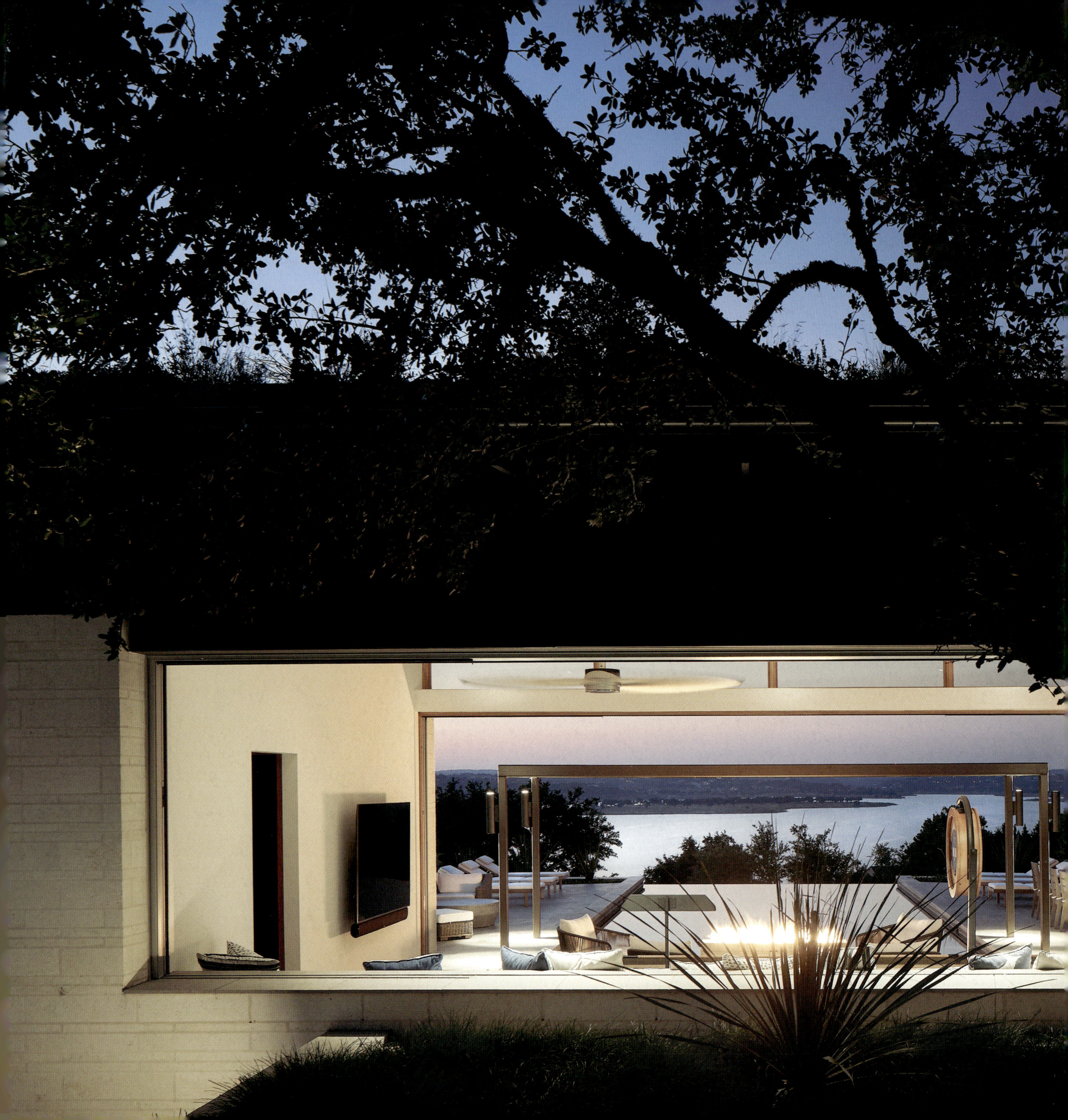

FOREWORD

A home is not just a house, it is an embodiment of the people who dwell within it – an extension of their personalities and expressive of their passions. It provides engagement with its surroundings and an intuitive sense of belonging. Good modern homes do this in recognizable ways. Great modern homes also do this in unexpected ways. *Spectacular Modern Homes of Texas* does this in ways that speak to us of place.

A solid concept and disciplined editing of extraneous information are some of the recognizable aspects of a good modern house. The parti, or organizing concept, is apparent in siting, in plan, in form, and even in furnishings. From the big idea to the execution of the smallest detail, the evolution of the design builds in strength by testing the design decisions against the initial premise.

Good modern houses reach into the landscape with skinny, exaggerated planes of roofs, ceilings resting on clerestory windows and expanses of glass that invite the outside in. They glow at night like Japanese lanterns, spilling their light softly. Detailing is always spare and taut. The resolution of details, without the cover up of moldings and trim requires better craftsmanship at every level. That is not to say that there is no whimsy or humor or inventiveness in great modern houses. Just check out the flue in the Jobe Corral fireplace in this book as an example of an unexpected twist.

However, there is an extra element of design that occurs in the best Texas modern houses and that is the sense of rootedness. Our shared architectural heritage is one of dogtrots and breezeways and summer kitchens and deep porches. We revere the ancient trees in our state and position our houses delicately around them to shelter under their massive limbs and broad canopies. We are adept at creating those spaces "in-between," where we can attain repose and watch the weather roll in.

Heather McKinney

LEFT: McKinney York Architects. Photography by Dror Baldinger FAIA.

CONTENTS

AUSTIN
- A PARALLEL ARCHITECTURE 12
- COXIST STUDIO 16
- DARWIN HARRISON ARCHITECT 20
- DICK CLARK + ASSOCIATES 28
- DK STUDIO 32
- ELIZABETH BAIRD ARCHITECTURE & DESIGN 36
- JAY CORDER ARCHITECT 40
- JAY HARGRAVE ARCHITECT 46
- JEI DESIGN 50
- JOBE CORRAL ARCHITECTS 54
- KASEY MCCARTY INTERIOR DESIGN 60
- KELLE CONTINE INTERIOR DESIGN 64
- LARUE ARCHITECTS 68
- LEVESQUE & CO. 76
- MATT GARCIA DESIGN 80
- MCKINNEY YORK ARCHITECTS 84
- MERZBAU DESIGN COLLECTIVE 88
- MIRÓ RIVERA ARCHITECTS 92
- MOONTOWER 96
- NICOLE BLAIR ARCHITECT 100
- ROOST CUSTOM HOMES 102
- STUDIO STEINBOMER 106
- TOM HURT ARCHITECTURE 110
- VANGUARD STUDIO 114

DALLAS FORT WORTH
- A GRUPPO ARCHITECTS 122
- ELEMENTS OF DESIGN 126
- ERIC LAPOINTE ARCHITECT &
- SUSAN SMITH DESIGNS 132
- IBAÑEZ SHAW ARCHITECTURE 136
- JEAN LIU DESIGN &
- CLINTON + COMPANY ARCHITECTS 140
- LINDA FRITSCHY INTERIOR DESIGN 146
- L. LUMPKINS ARCHITECT 150
- MAESTRI STUDIO 158
- NORMAN WARD ARCHITECT &
- GEARHEART CONSTRUCTION 162
- RGD+B 170
- RICHARD TRIMBLE & ASSOCIATES 174
- SEBASTIAN CONSTRUCTION GROUP 176
- STARR CONSTRUCTION 184
- SUSAN SEMMELMANN INTERIORS 188
- TEN PLUS THREE 194
- URBANOLOGY DESIGNS 202

HOUSTON
- 2SCALE ARCHITECTS 206
- BORDELON DESIGN ASSOCIATES 210
- DILLON KYLE ARCHITECTS 214
- ROTTET STUDIO 222

SAN ANTONIO
- A-DESIGN BY GUSTAVO ARREDONDO 230
- CRAIG MCMAHON ARCHITECTS 236
- ELIZABETH HAYNES ARCHITECT 246
- JOHN GRABLE ARCHITECTS 252
- LAKE | FLATO ARCHITECTS 260
- LORI CALDWELL DESIGNS 264
- NR INTERIORS 268
- OVERLAND PARTNERS 272
- PALMER TODD 282
- T . A . D . A 286
- TOBIN SMITH ARCHITECT 290
- TODD GLOWKA BUILDER 298

WEST TEXAS & THE HILL COUNTRY
- RHOTENBERRY WELLEN ARCHITECTS 310
- KELLY HALLMAN DESIGN 316
- BORNE DESIGNS 322
- LAUGHLIN HOMES + RESTORATION 326
- MABERY CONTRACTING 330
- R. GLADWIN DESIGN - TILE 334

ABOVE: Pool built by Aqua Builders. Photography by Jake Holt Photography.
FACING PAGE: Design by Jay Corder Architect. Photography by Andrea Calo.

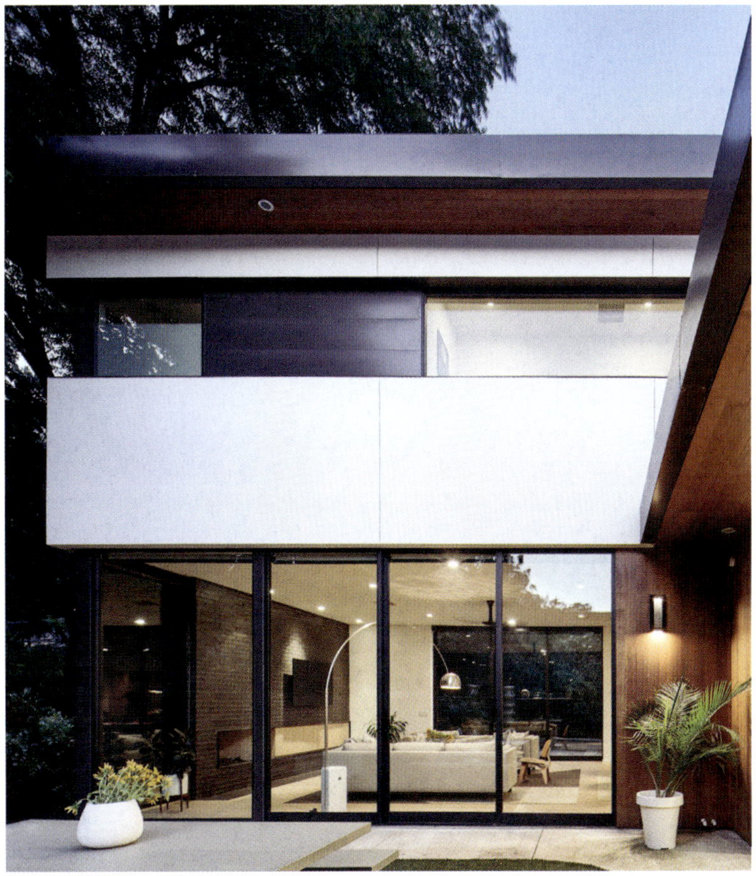

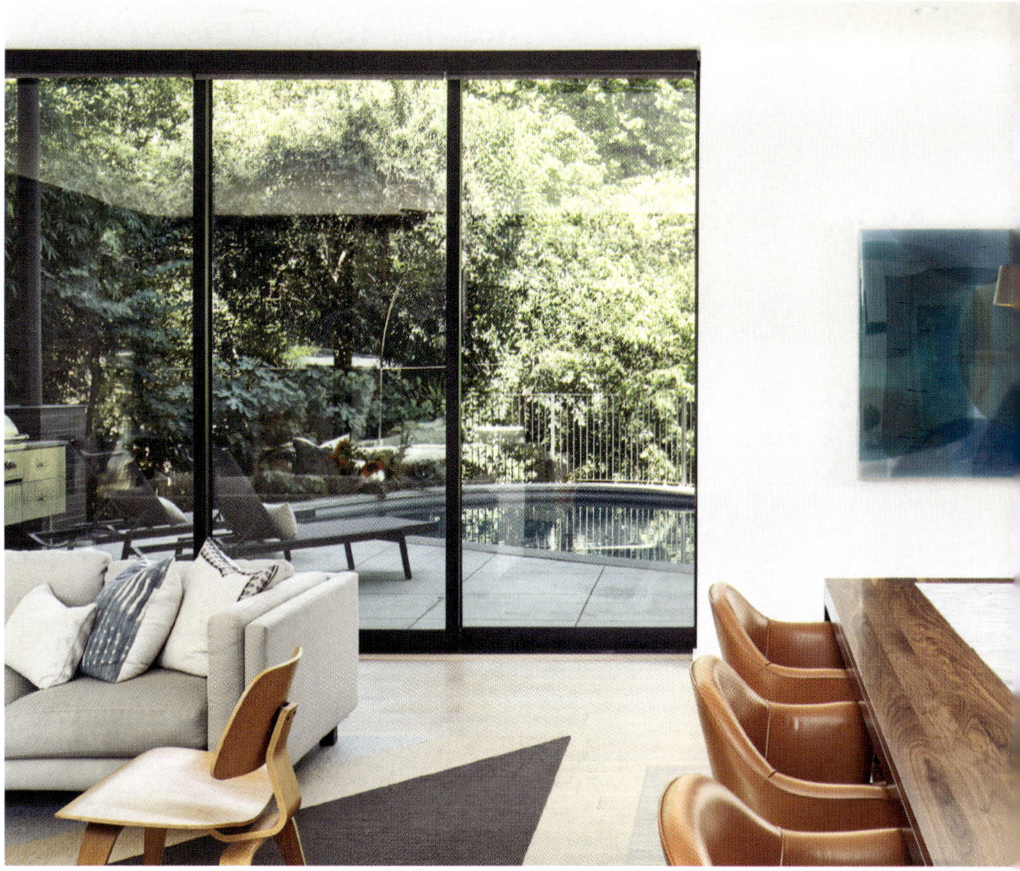

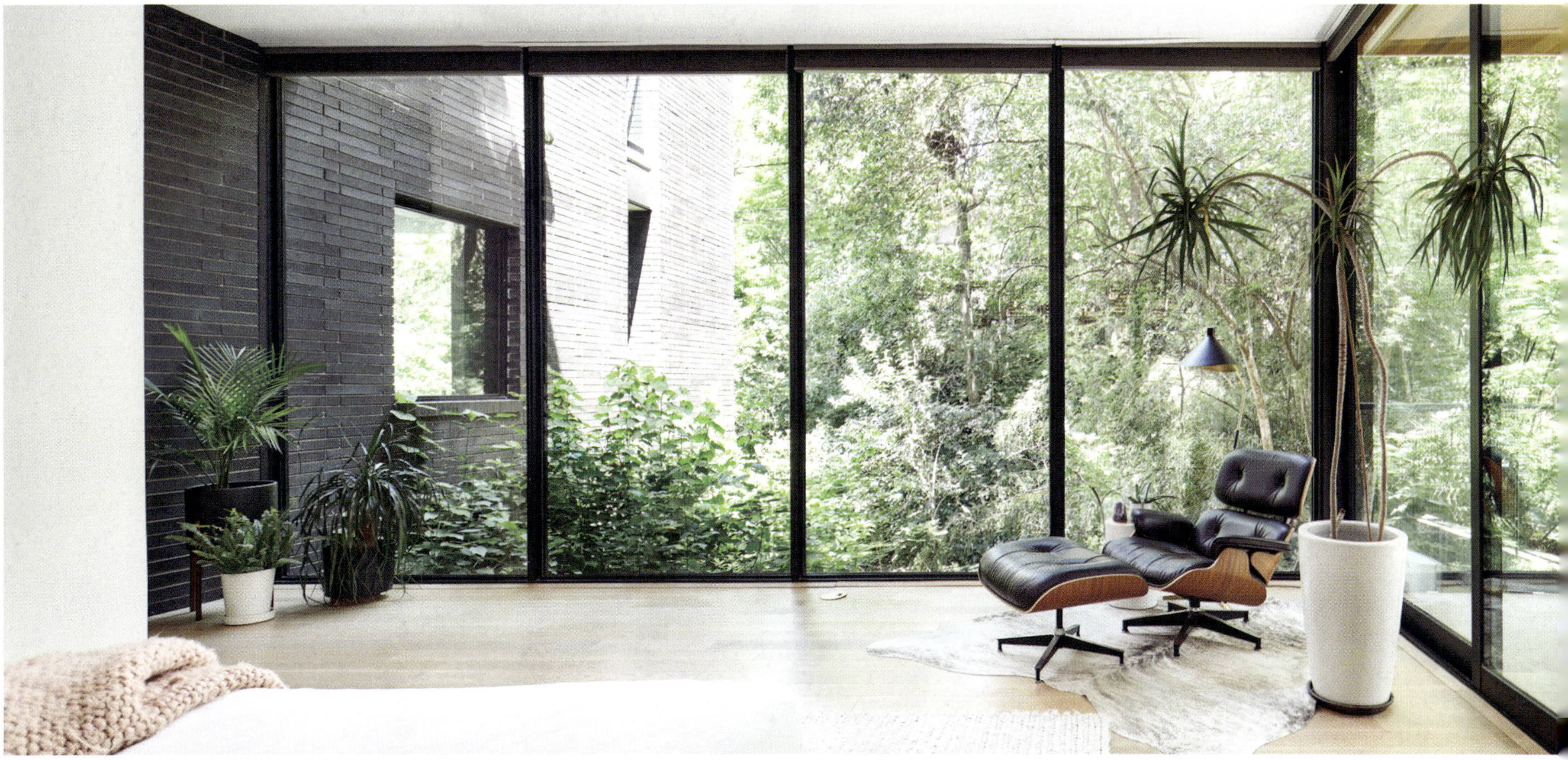

Designed by LARUE ARCHITECTS

Photography by Casey Dunn

AUSTIN

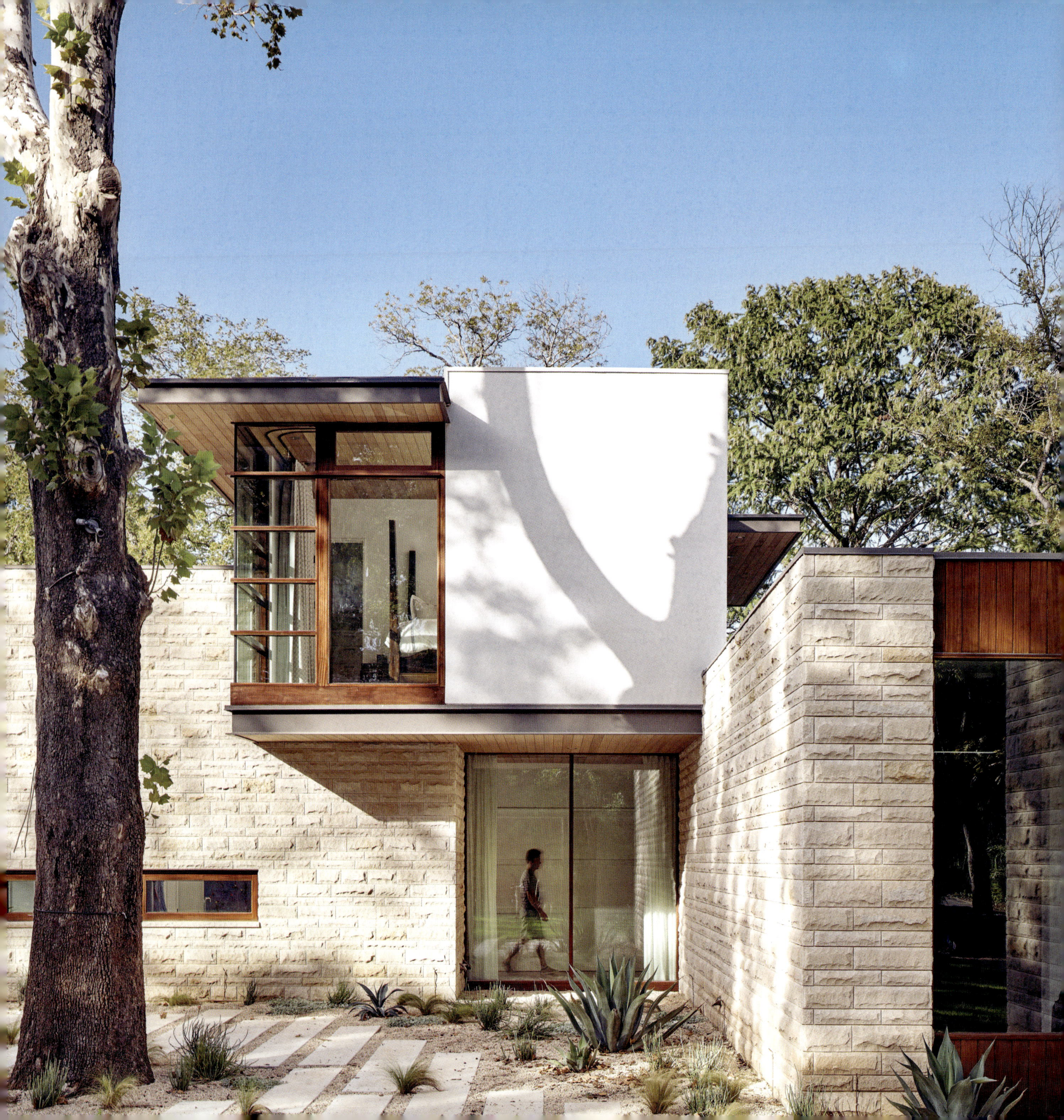

A PARALLEL ARCHITECTURE

Partners Ryan Burke and Eric Barth of A Parallel Architecture describe their approach to design as an inextricably linked trinity of architecture, interiors, and landscape – all three of which they develop in parallel. Together with their team of talented architects and designers, they rely heavily on immersive 3-D design – which includes detailed modeling, virtual reality, and photorealistic renderings – in order to ensure a project's parameters are thoroughly understood, vetted, and conveyed before substantial resources are committed to building it.

Ryan and Eric established their award-winning studio in 2008 after more than 10 years of collaboration in Texas and California. Now, after more than 20 years of working together, their projects can be found all over the country. Throughout this tenure, their work has consistently embraced a "responsive modernism" – modernism driven less by stylistic factors and more by site-responsive problem-solving with solution-based design. This highly practical approach is filtered through an extensive process of refinement, emphasizing exquisite proportion and meticulous detailing. The very tangible satisfaction of turning an abstract concept into a physical space that you can walk through and interact with…this is the passion behind what drives the team at A Parallel. "Designing with our clients is a fun and rewarding process, but watching them joyously engage with their space for the first time is one of the great thrills of practicing architecture," says Ryan.

FACING PAGE: Meandering between towering sycamores and pecans along the shoreline, this Lake Austin residence's rough-hewn stone walls ground the building while providing privacy from the street.

TOP: A simple but exquisitely detailed palette of wood, stone, and steel give the home a warm and welcoming livability.

BOTTOM: The lakeside façade opens to nature through expansive glass and large sliding doors, expanding the functional living space of the home and blurring the line between indoors and outdoors. Photography by Casey Dunn.

"Outdoor spaces are seamlessly folded into the daily living experience." —Eric Barth

TOP: Inspired by the oasis-like shade—afforded by the site's dense tree coverage—the Canopy House employs an elevated roof structure to shelter the primary living spaces in the home—indoor and out. Above, a detached flex suite serves as pool cabana, guest quarters, or home office depending on the season and the homeowner's needs.

FACING PAGE: The home is organized around a central courtyard to maximize connectivity across the property while maintaining privacy from neighboring houses. Photography by Casey Dunn.

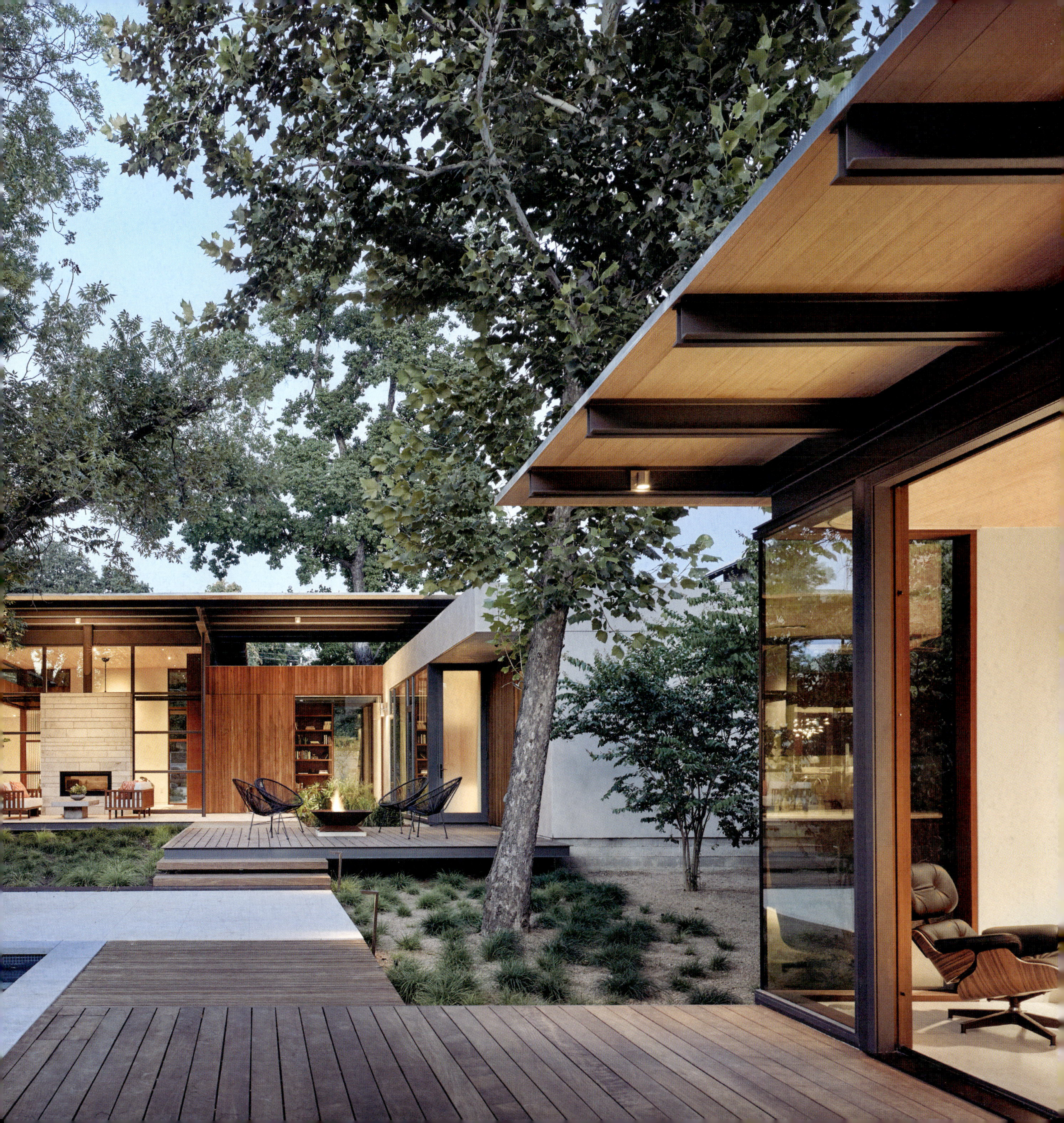

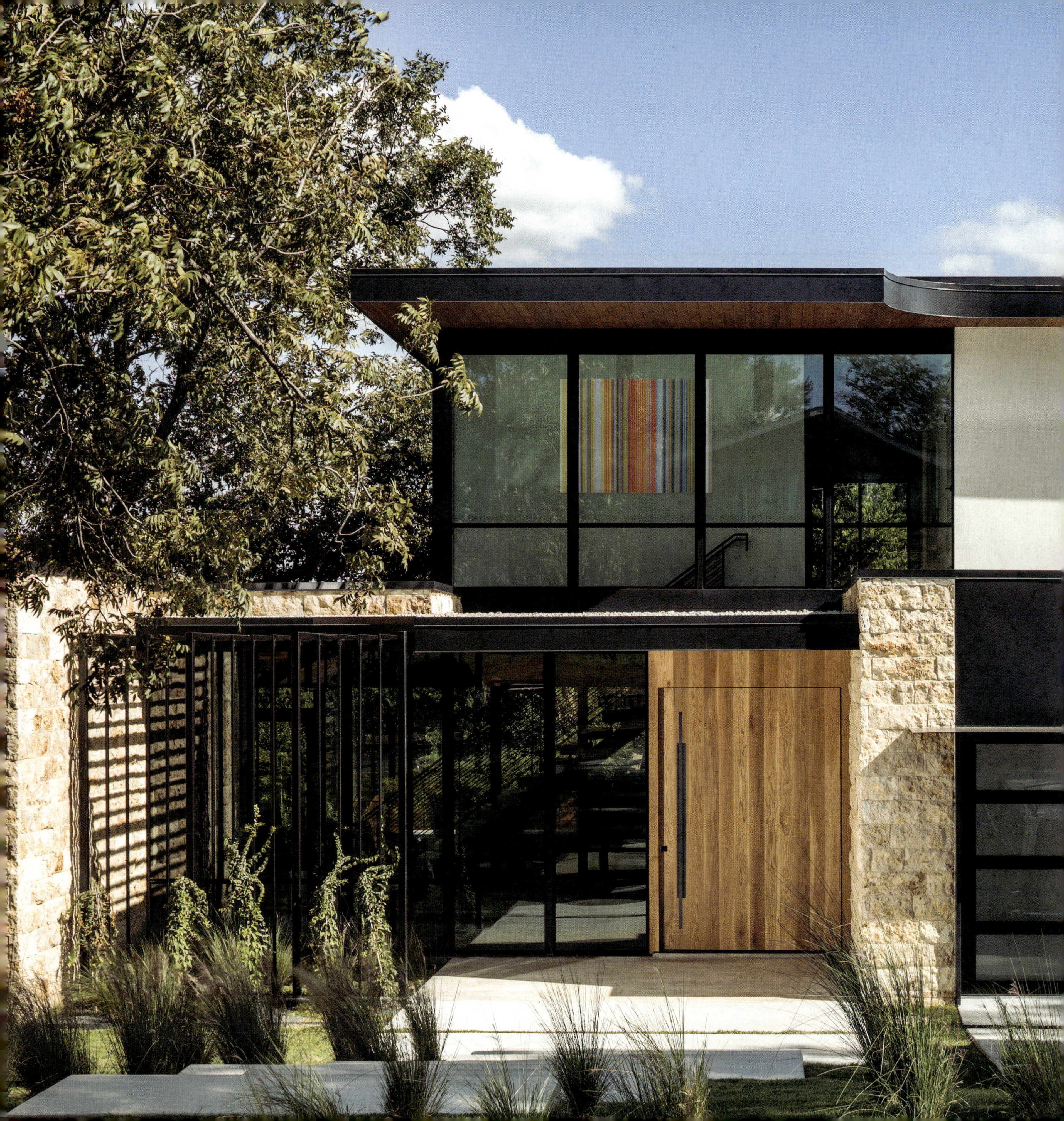

COXIST STUDIO
MEGAN LIN
FRANK LIN

Collaboration. Connection. Community. These are all words that illustrate the mission of coXist, a contemporary full-service architecture firm founded by husband-and-wife team, Frank and Megan Lin. Specializing in custom homes and boutique commercial spaces, they believe architecture is a series of moments that, when strung together, tell a story.

An essential part of their process is enhancing the connections between life and living – elevating how a person moves through his or her built environment. Through collaboration with their clients, team, contractors, and consultants, coXist strives to make client's lives easier by designing a livable space to call home; a place to make memories. The firm is also dedicated to designing for communities and generations to come, shaping the fabric of the future and creating spaces that coexist with their surroundings.

"Inspiration is found all around us in both the natural and the built environment if we just take the time to observe," says Frank. For coXist, the best design is one that reflects the lived experience with thoughtful human-inspired design, harmonious sense of place, and engagement of all five senses. It is these elements that distinguish timeless design from transitory trends.

FACING PAGE: This residence, built by F | I | A Homes, was designed as a grouping of small intimate stone pavilions, linked by glass portals to reflect the scale of the neighboring context. It embraces the contrast between the rugged earthiness of crystalized, rough-cut limestone and the smooth Venetian plaster of the upper level. Photography by Jake Holt.

"To understand light, there also must be shadow and to truly understand smooth, there must be rough. It is the balance of these elements that breathe life into a project." —Megan Lin

ABOVE LEFT: A flowing stair, concealed hidden closet doors, and a large wooden pivot door are one way to set the stage for a remarkable entrance.

ABOVE TOP RIGHT: Natural light floods the living and dining rooms; the two spaces flow together in the open floor plan with a fireplace serving as the focal point.

ABOVE BOTTOM RIGHT: The master bathroom uses smooth, natural limestone throughout to complement the exterior palette. A skylight above the shower bathes users in natural light.

FACING PAGE TOP: Contrasting the rough exterior, the kitchen uses natural but refined elements such as antique oak and honed concrete to add richness to the space.

FACING PAGE BOTTOM: The backyard showcases the seamless connection between outdoor and indoor while the curving second level responds to the tree and directs toward the downtown view. Photography by Jake Holt.

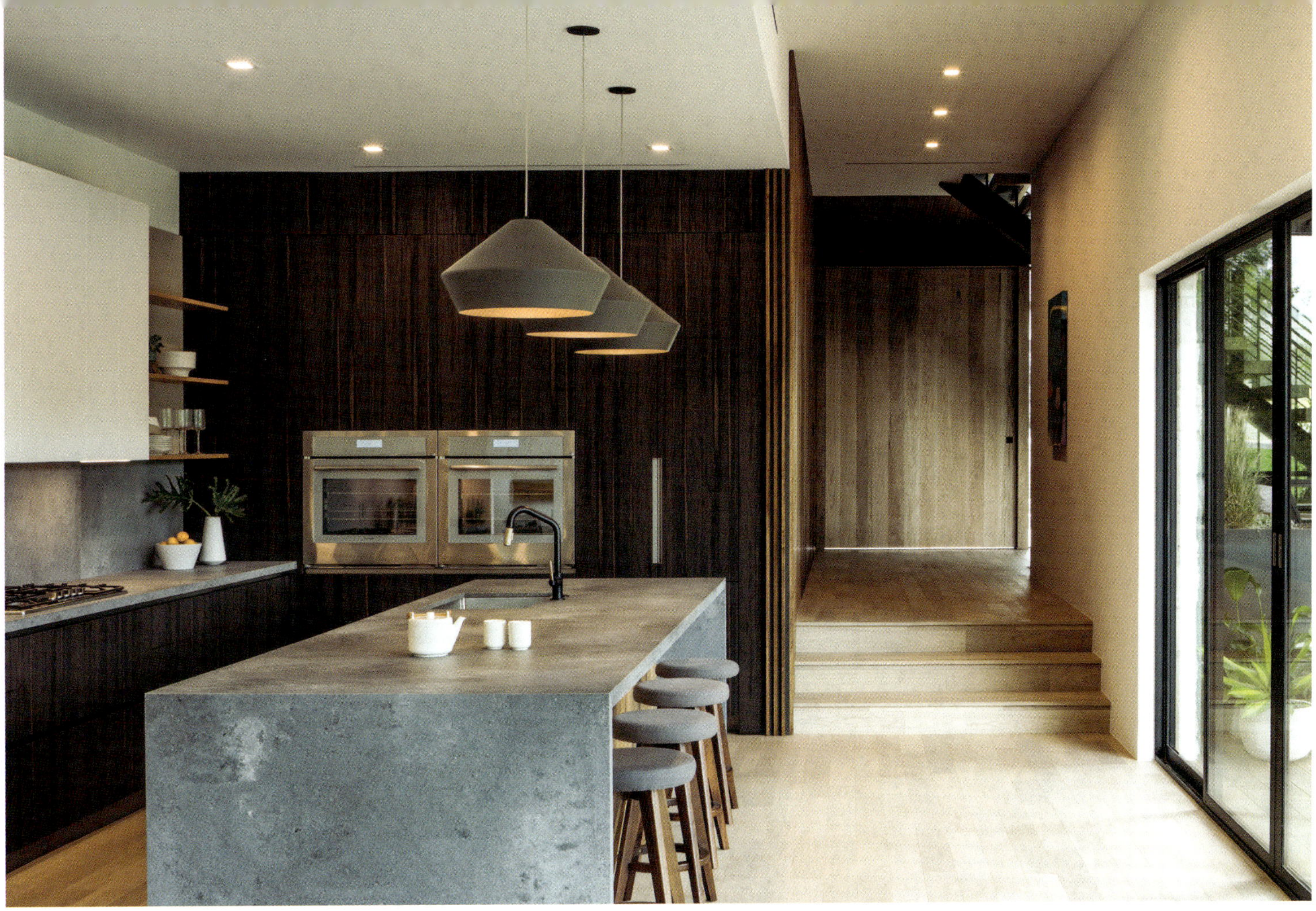

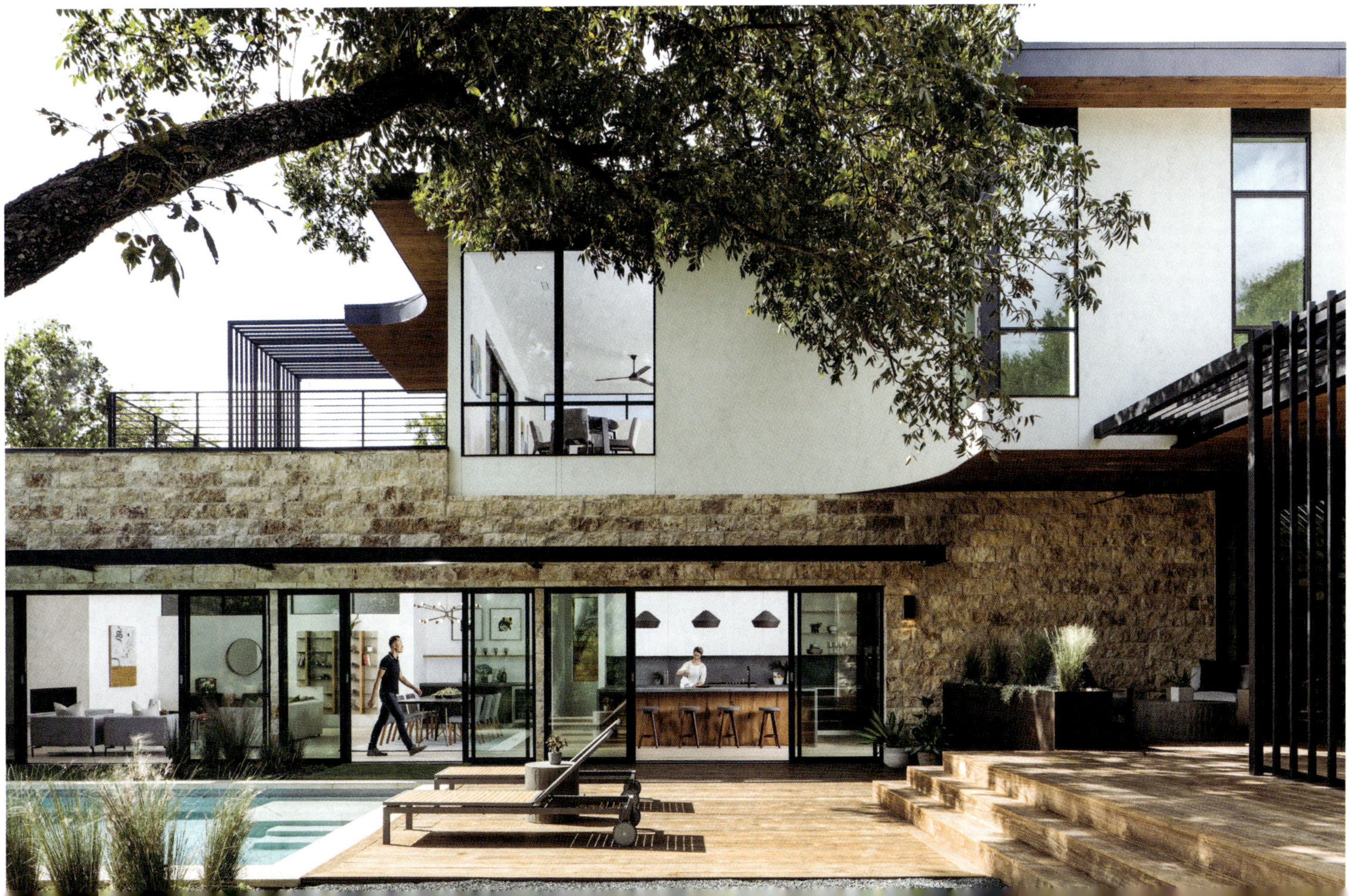

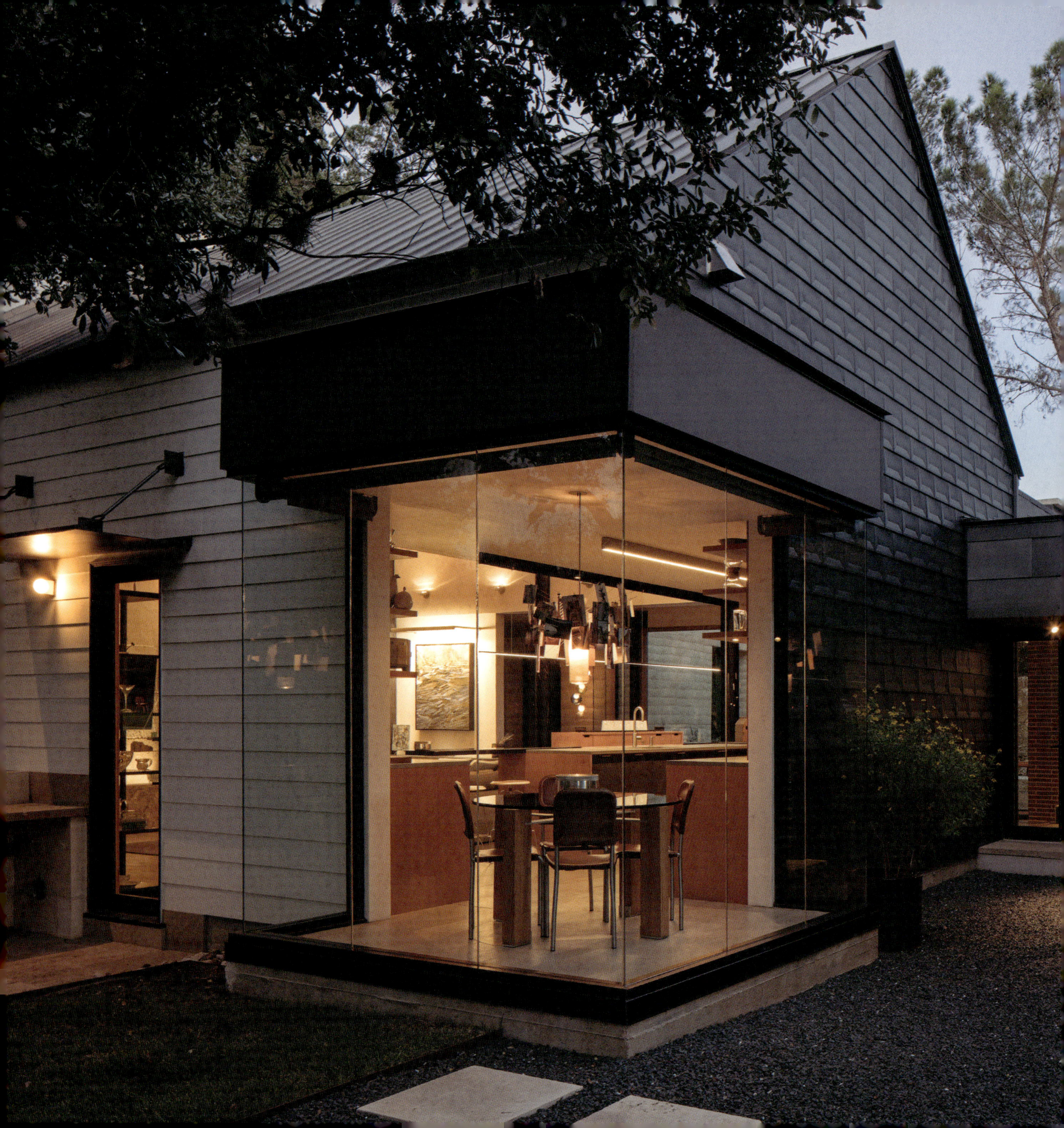

DARWIN HARRISON ARCHITECT

From a young age, Darwin Harrison knew he wanted to design homes – fueled by an early affinity for assembling LEGOs and drawing buildings, and a middle-school fascination with Frank Lloyd Wright and the stories behind the architect's projects. Now, he's doing just that at Darwin Harrison Design. As a one-person studio, he has the opportunity to be fully focused on each project in a truly one-on-one collaboration. The process is personal, and very special, with each client treated with the utmost respect. After all, Darwin sees the occupants of a house as the most important element of the design process. His goal is always twofold: to create a design that expressively weaves together diverse spaces and materials and, just as importantly, to build a meaningful relationship with clients that lasts beyond the completion of the project.

Growing up in West Texas has been a big underlying inspiration for Darwin. It's a challenging landscape with profound flatness and open skies that create a vast environment that is both intimidating and inspiring. "Things designed and built in that kind of environment have to be tough to survive, but also have a presence – staking a claim that they belong," he says. "The most simple, small structure on the plains can be seen as monumental and miniscule at the same time. So, even simple sheds inspire me for their clarity and simplicity." Ultimately, Darwin aspires to create something warmly modern and comfortable – something made of authentic, natural materials compiled in an honest fashion. It's a "what you see is what you get" attitude. He loves exploring evocative materials that delight and surprise, but that are always combined in a manner that is logical and appropriate.

FACING PAGE: House 5300 is a linear expression of the classic house shape interrupted by multiple courtyards. This view highlights the dining room, set up as a gallery space adjacent to the long hall and opening onto the courtyard. The glass cube is the breakfast room with kitchen and living room beyond. Photography by Paul Bardagjy.

"Our mission is to take the functional and make it poetic; to create a structure that ultimately stands on its own and illustrates the qualities possible when an intelligent, creative and meaningful approach is adopted during the design process." –Darwin Harrison

ABOVE: The rammed earth studio space and rough limestone blocks of the gable shape create a distinctive front façade. The solidity of the stone provides privacy and a strong material presence. The large windows in the rammed earth wall have tapered edges to enhance views from within the studio space.

FACING PAGE: A long gallery hall runs the length of the house making the circulation through the house a celebration; it's a pathway filled with art as well as expansive windows for views and natural light. Photography by Paul Bardagjy.

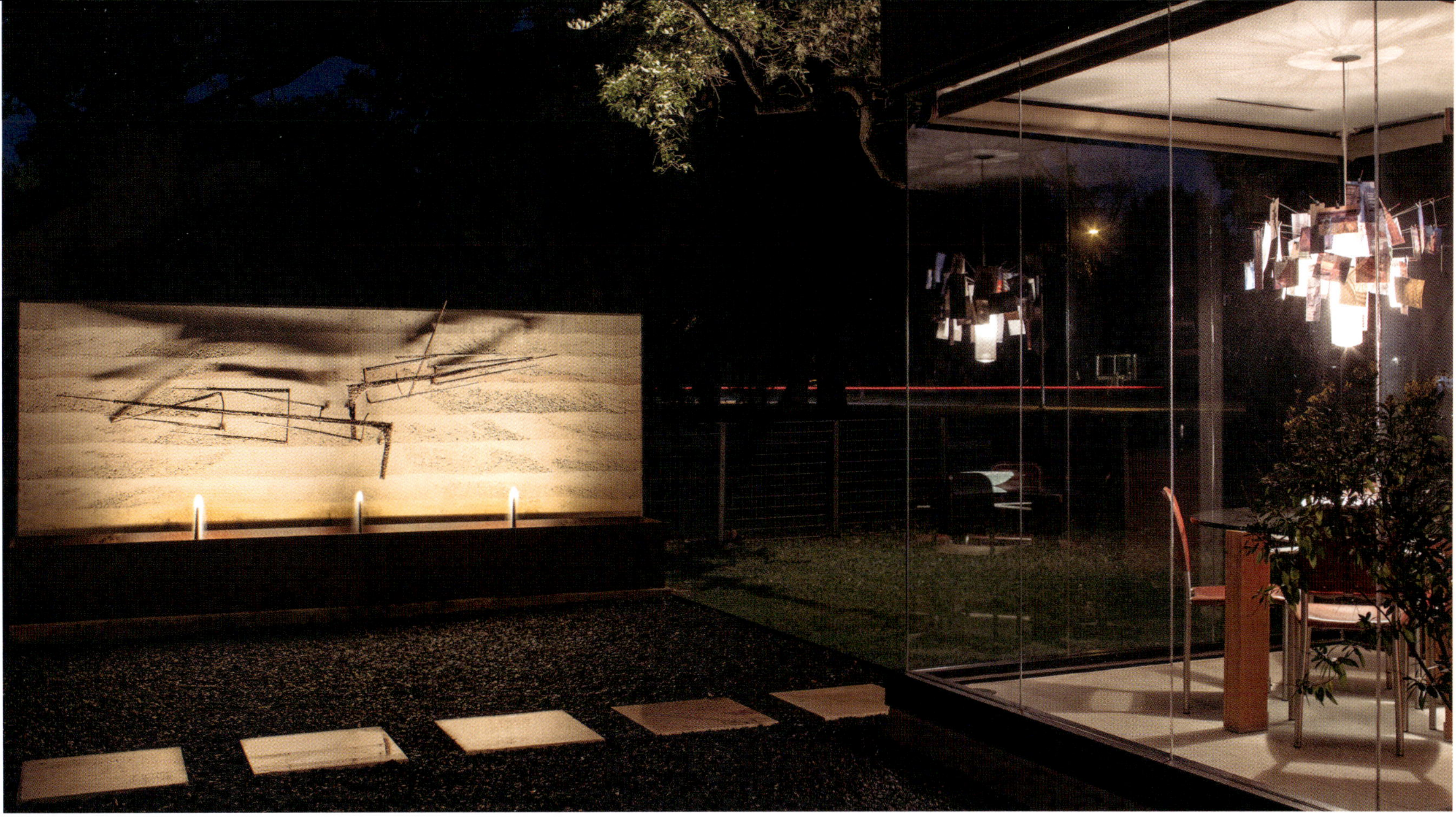

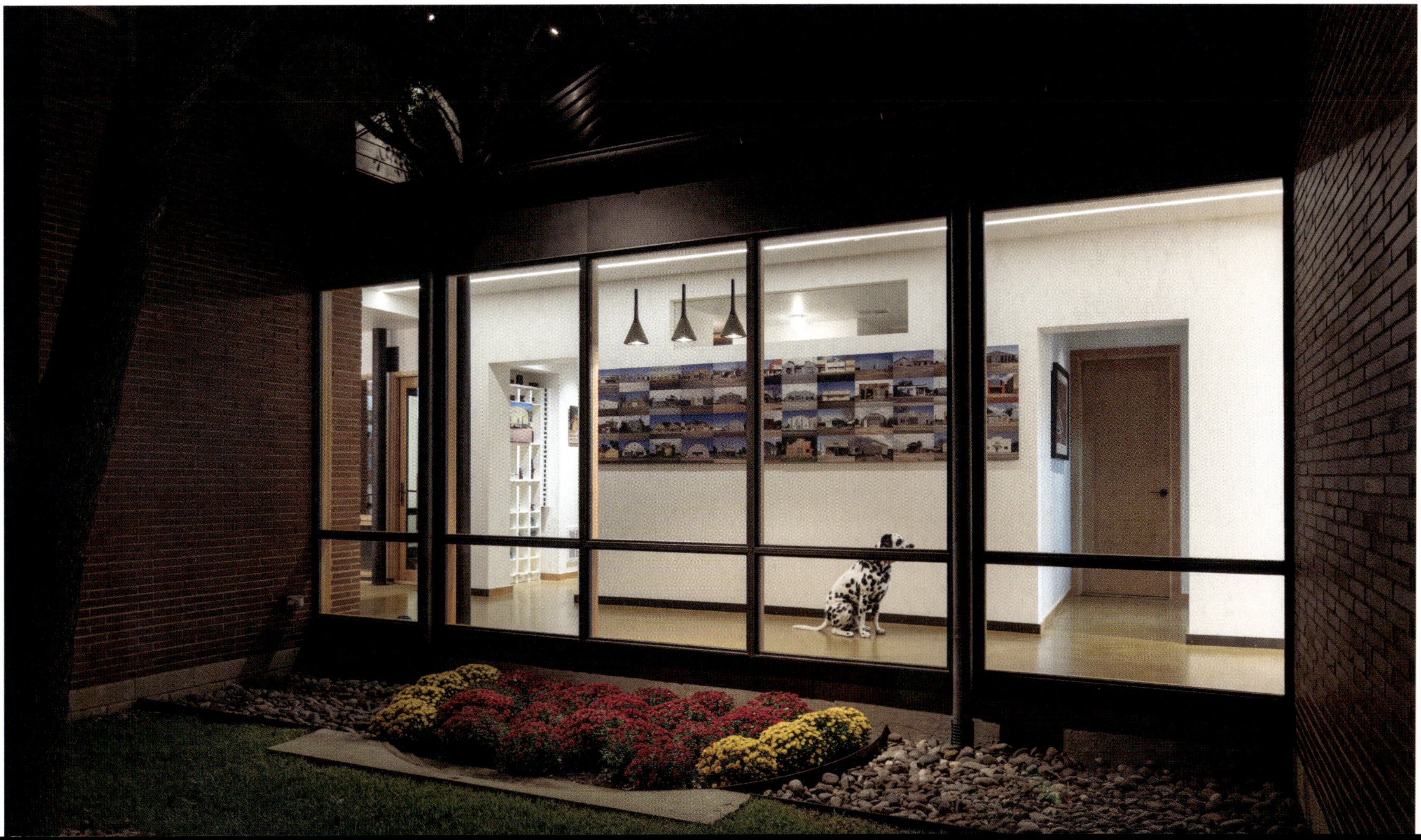

"The goal is always to design a home that the occupants don't want to leave." –Darwin Harrison

ABOVE: The living room is an interior expression of the gable shape with exposed steel and Douglas fir rafters. The stone wall is punctuated by portholes with glass blocks that merge with the raw steel shelves. The combination of solid wall and large windows allow both privacy and views to the majestic trees.

FACING PAGE TOP: The kitchen is open to the living room and features views to courtyards on both sides. The cabinets are Douglas fir with grey accents on a limestone tile floor.

FACING PAGE BOTTOM: The breakfast room is an extension of the kitchen, creating a space within a space where one can feel connected to the landscape beyond. Photography by Paul Bardagjy.

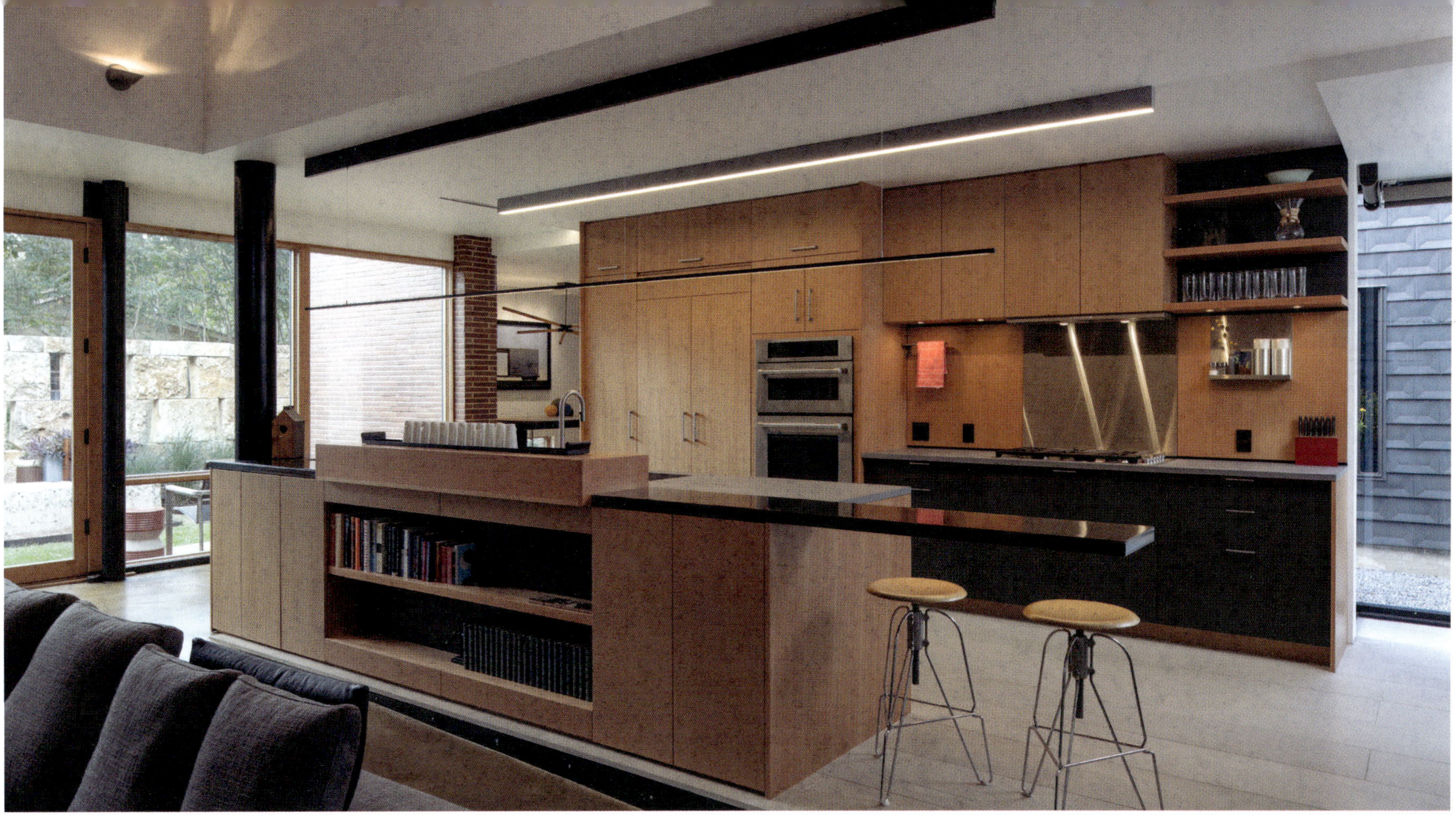

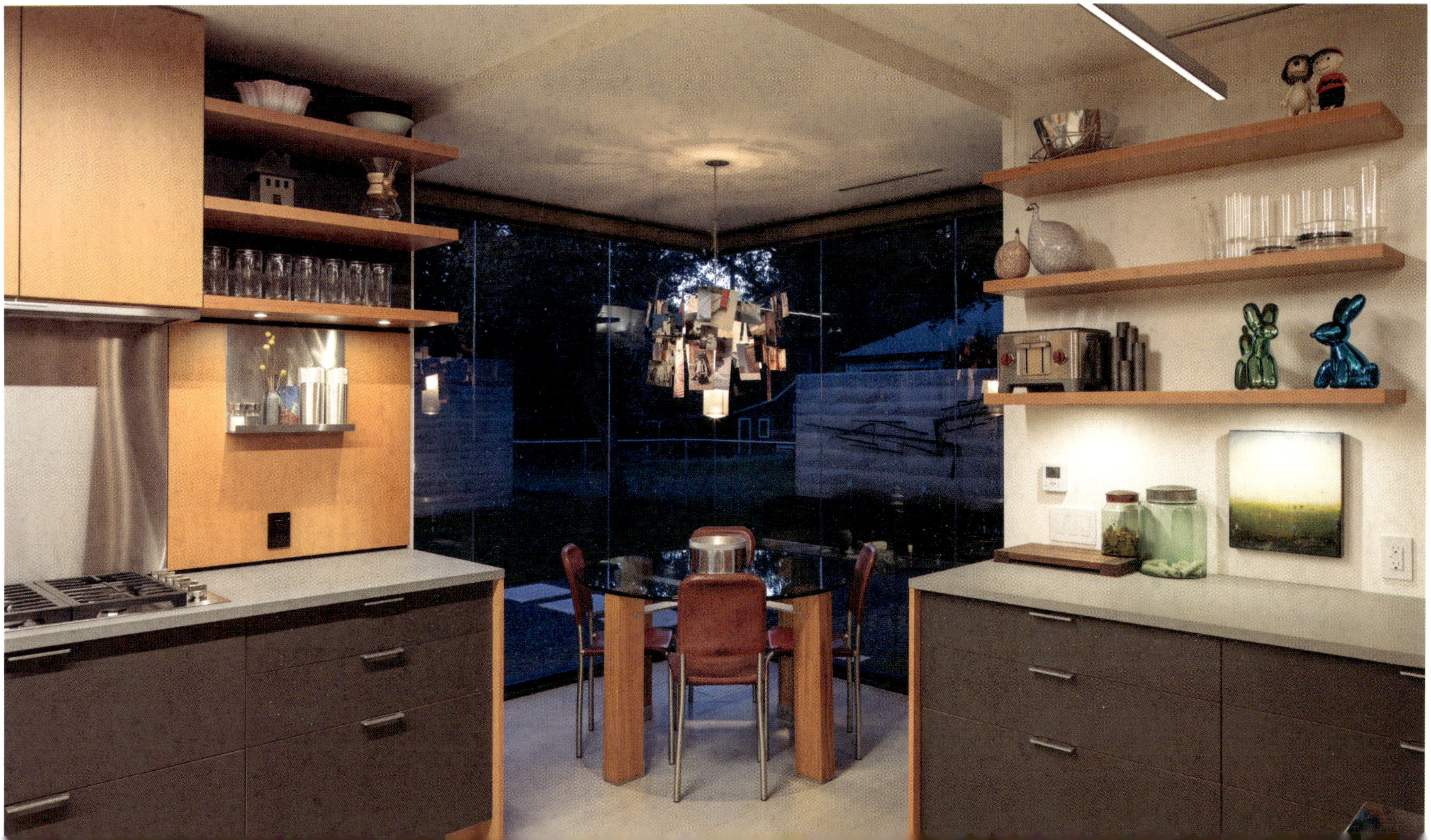

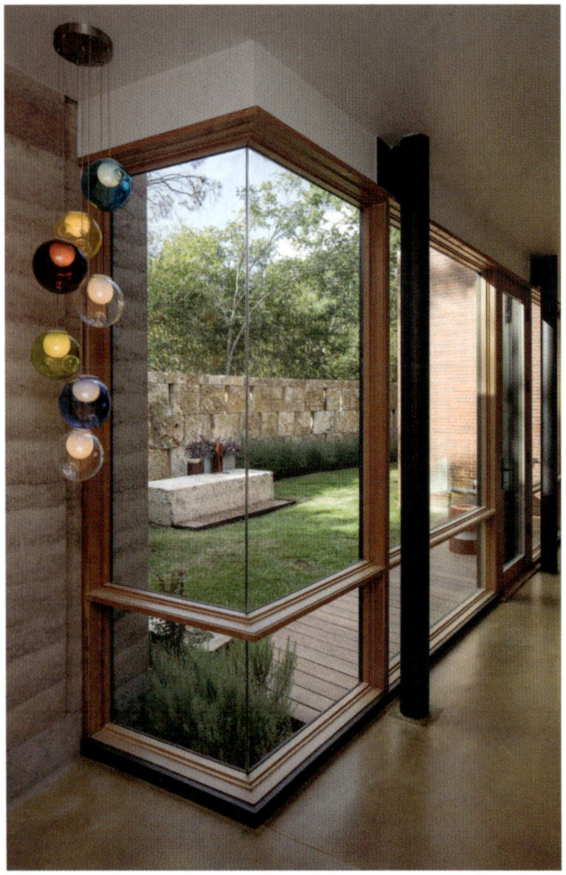
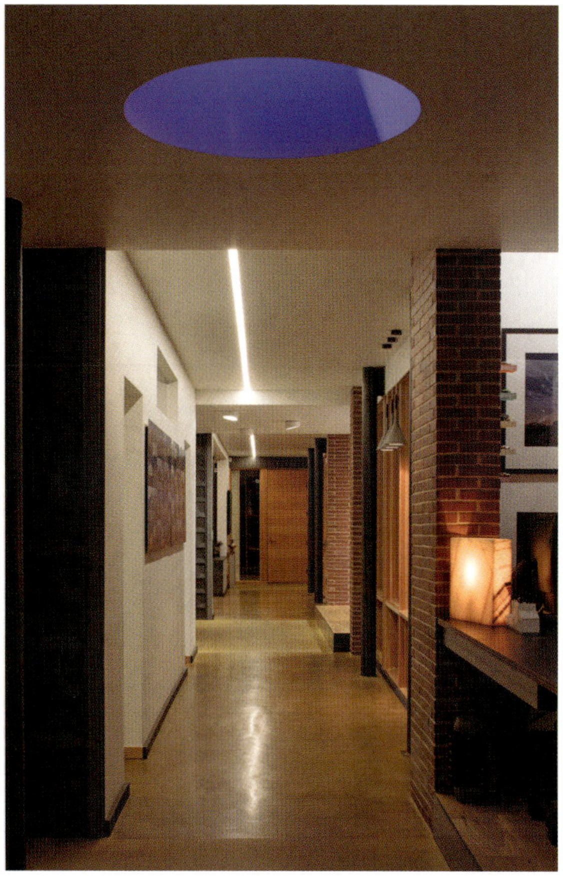
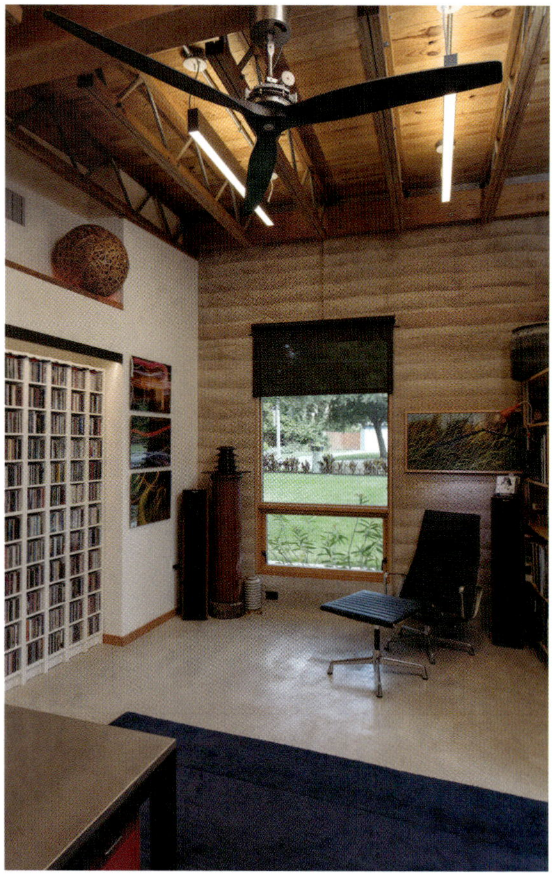
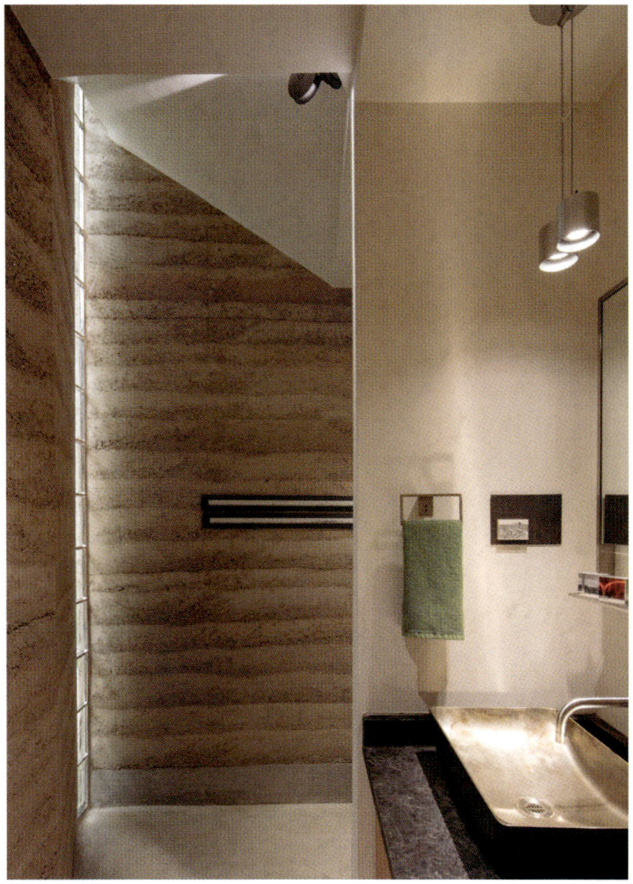
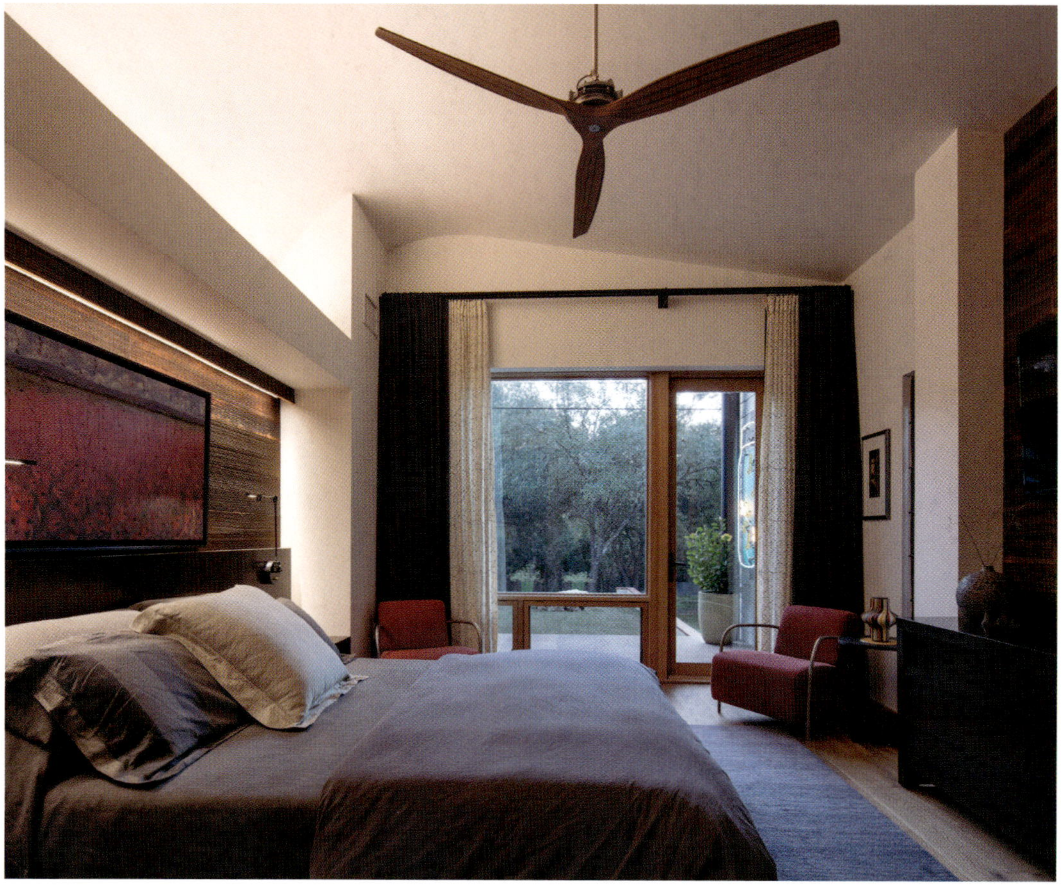

THIS PAGE TOP AND RIGHT: The back of the house has a covered patio allowing the gable shape to be expressed dramatically at the roof and side walls. The exterior of the studio shows the striations resulting from the rammed earth process.

FACING PAGE CLOCKWISE: The gallery hall extends from front door to back. The studio space interior has an industrial loft atmosphere with exposed joists and concrete floors along with the rammed earth walls. The master bedroom features an airfoil-inspired ceiling shape and views to the expanse of trees beyond. A dramatic, vertical section of thick glass bricks, accented with lighting, makes the powder room a small but dynamic space. Photography by Paul Bardagjy.

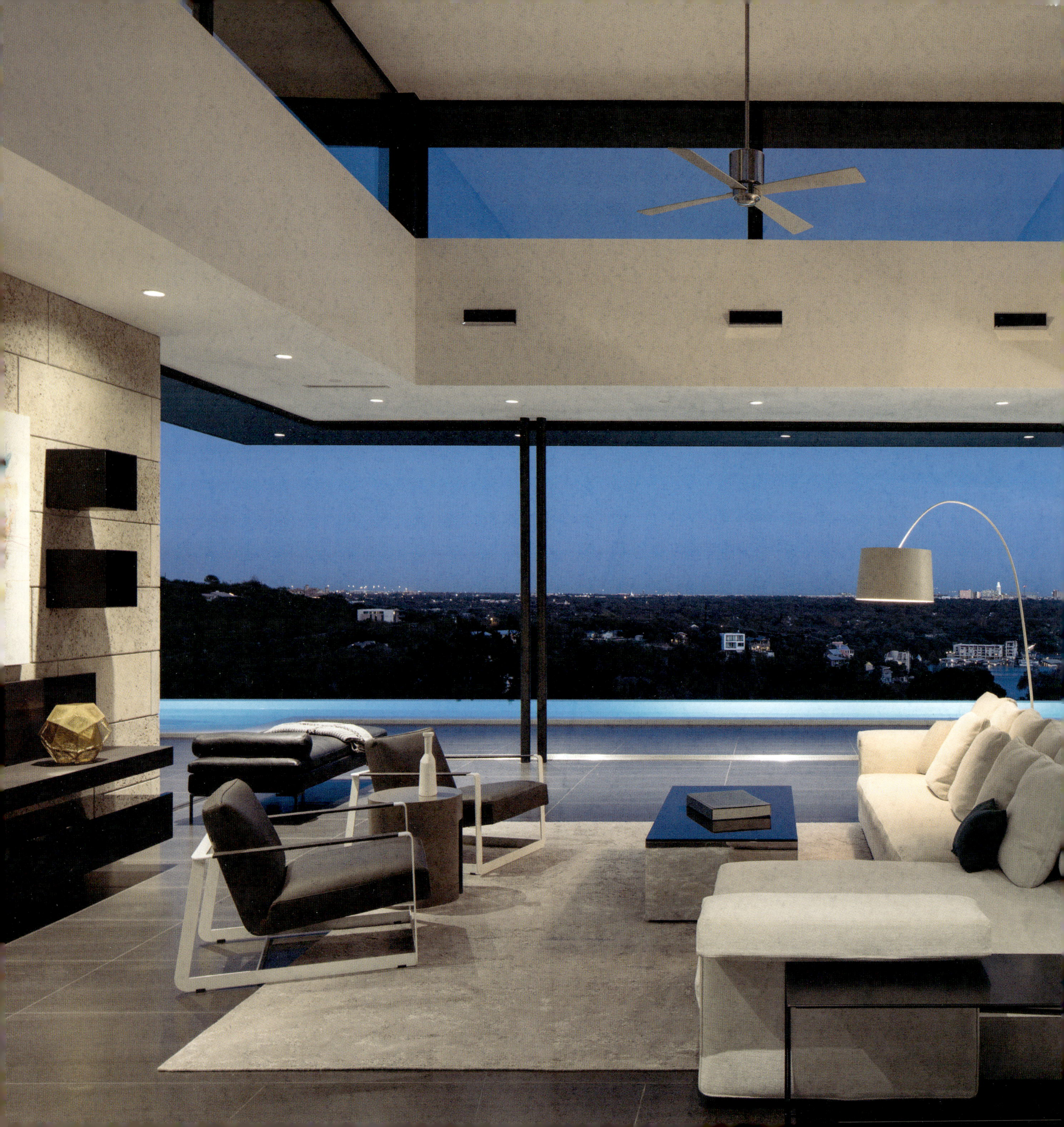

DICK CLARK + ASSOCIATES

Dick Clark + Associates is a full-service architecture and interior design firm based in Austin, Texas. Since 1979, we have been integral in Central Texas as a champion of good design and memorable spaces.

We approach our projects with a collaborative strategy as we identify the client's program and goals to guide the creative process. This allows us to design with freedom by using the breadth of architecture, not bound to a specific style. We focus on thoughtful, intentional design to create architecture that blurs the line between indoor and outdoor living. By pushing the envelope of contemporary architecture, our commercial and residential projects have continuously been part of the evolving creative vanguard of the city. Our designs contribute to every aspect of life in Austin and promote modern living in a transitional yet familiar way.

We believe in the ability of great design to create a sense of place, represent an individual's or organization's values, and enhance the lives of its inhabitants. We take our work seriously, but we balance high-quality, professional work with a welcoming, laid-back office environment where ideas flow and collaboration is constant. We pride ourselves in contributing landmark projects and inspirational spaces that encapsulate the unique quality and lifestyle of Austin."

FACING PAGE: The thoughtful openness of the plan makes the spaces both generous and functional throughout, and a single clerestory feature punctuates the continuous ceiling height over the living room. Extending interior materials out and bringing exterior materials in creates a polished and effortless flow from interior to exterior. Photography by Paul Bardagjy.

ABOVE AND FACING PAGE: A clean, restrained material palette provides a sophisticated backdrop to the captivating views, which are brought into the house at every opportunity through continuous full-height sliding glass doors across the back of the house. Photography by Paul Bardagjy.

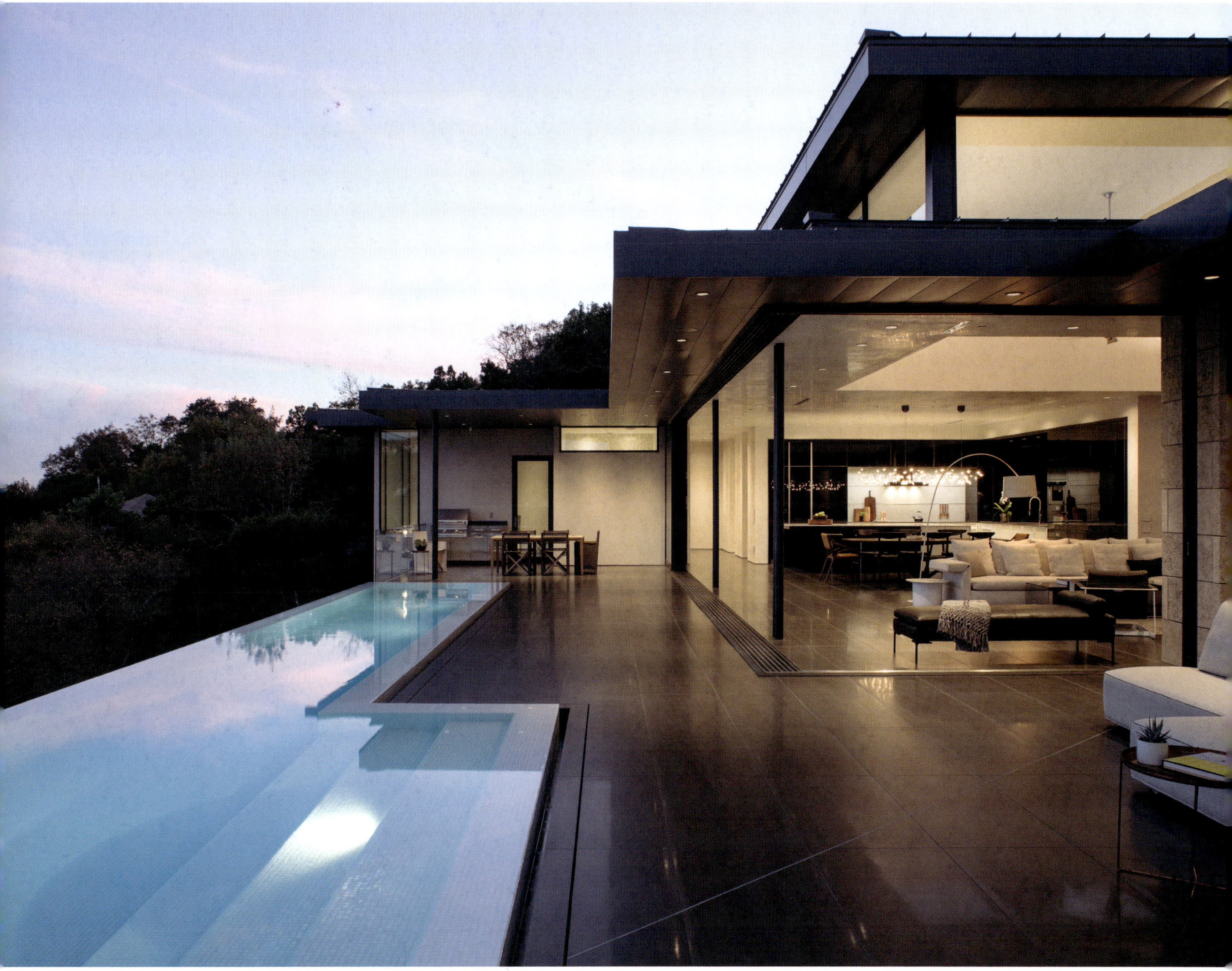

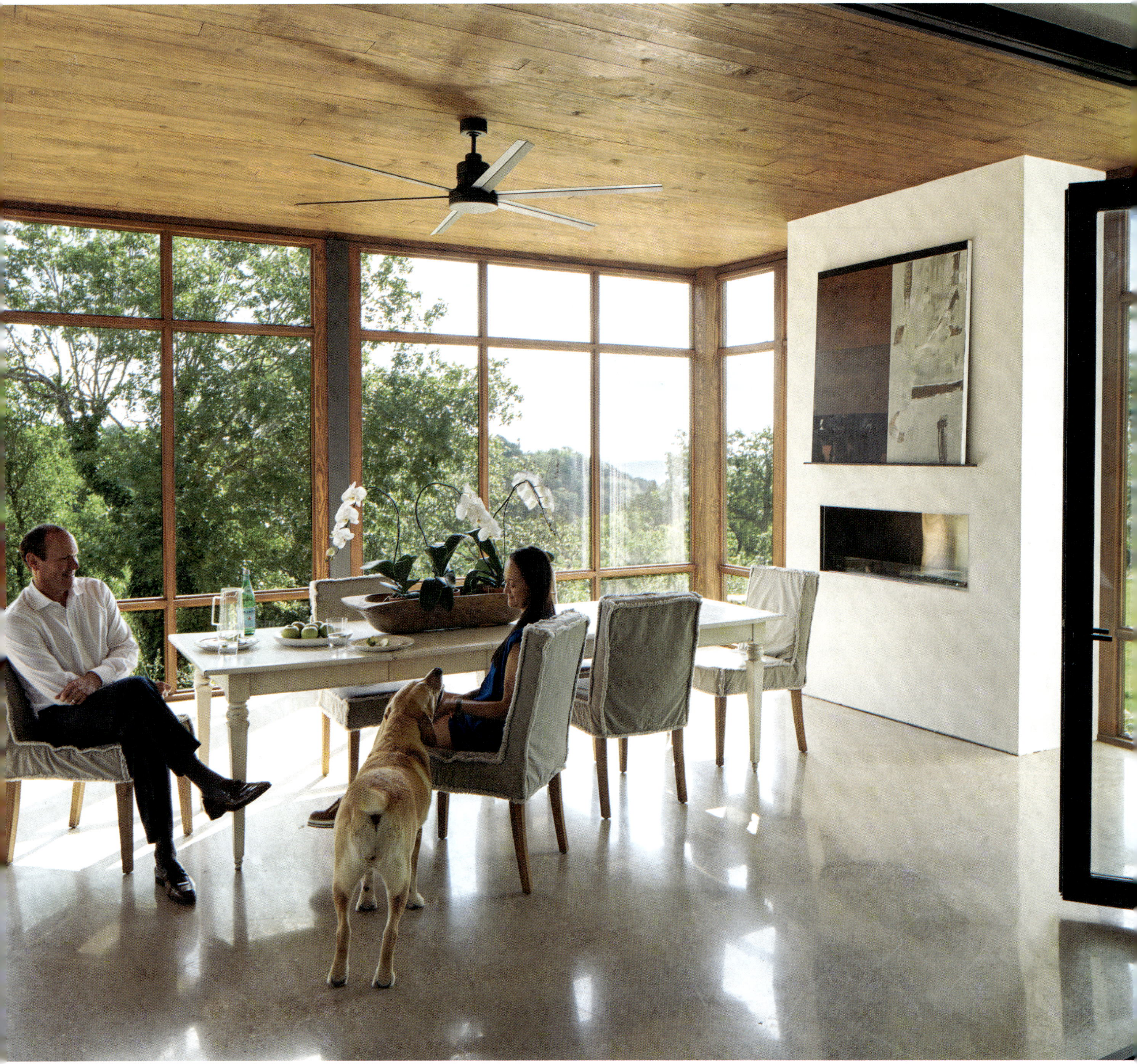

DK STUDIO
DIANNE KETT

DK Studio founder Dianne Kett's love of design began early on – she fondly remembers sketching houses from the time she was 8! Now, she's designing statement-making yet comfortable and efficient spaces that are reflective of her clients' unique lifestyles.

DK Studio's focus is on residential design architecture. But their passion – ever since the firm's launch in 2003 – is in creating spaces that are full of comfort and beauty for the people who experience them most.

The work of Dianne and her team of two female associates reflects an array of architectural styles because they cater to each and every client's artistic desires. And, that's how they prefer it; they love the challenge, as it would be far too uninspiring for them to envision the same thing again and again. But, no matter what the style, the elements they believe homeowners should never compromise on are windows.

This small and talented team also specializes in the planning and arrangement of rooms – so, if you want to achieve a lot in a little space (or any size of space!), they are your experts.

FACING PAGE: This Austin-area residence in West Lake Hills features a large screened porch with views toward north of downtown. An accordion door opens into the living room, facilitating an indoor-outdoor connection while the modern gas fireplace, embedded in the wall, is perfect for winter nights and ambience.

TOP: The front door is an extra-wide glass and steel door that allows for natural light to enter freely into the foyer.

BOTTOM: The dining area is bright and spacious; it's located just off the kitchen to face the new pool and captures views of the valley and rolling hills beyond.
Photography by Lars Frazer.

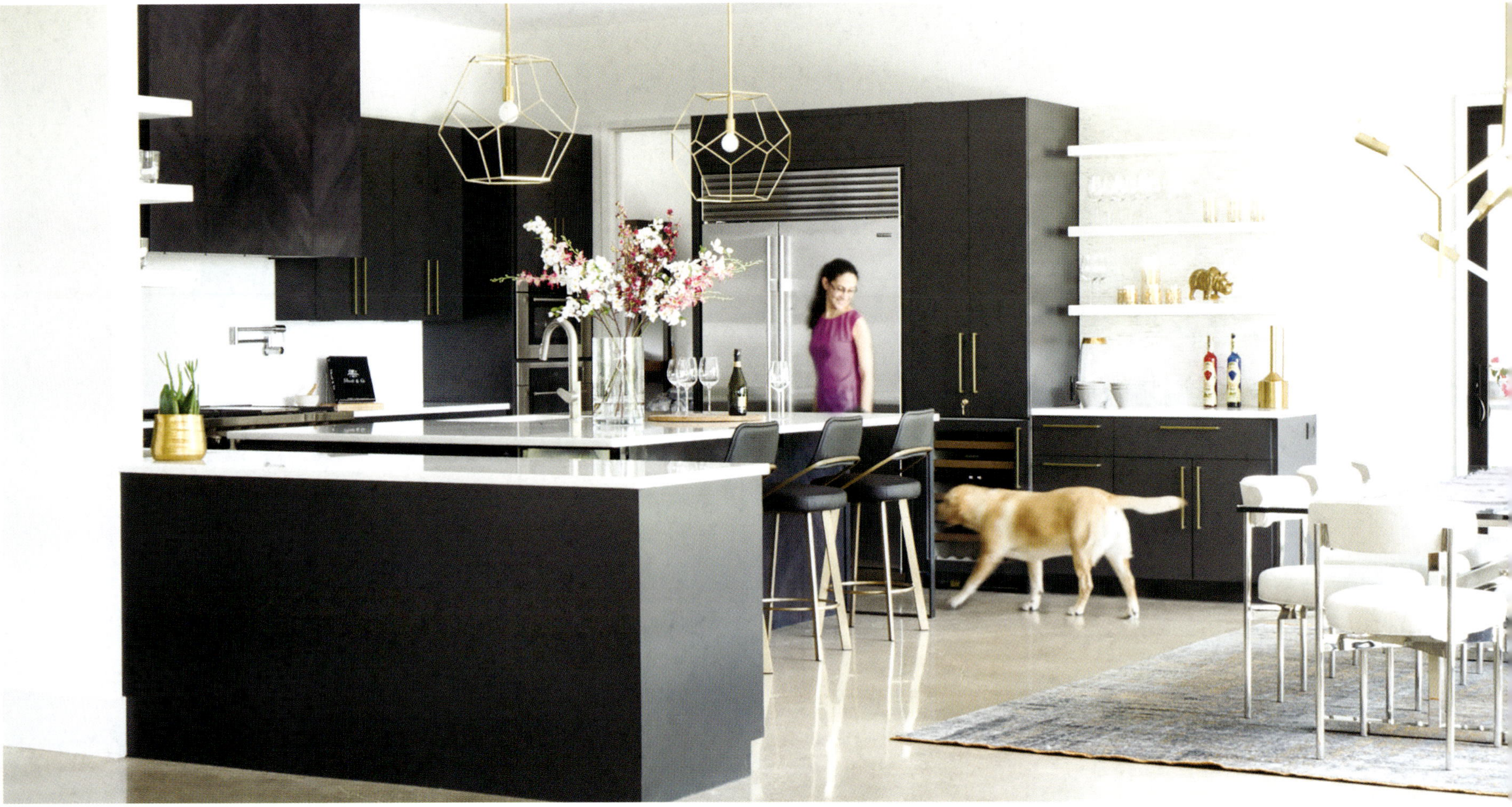

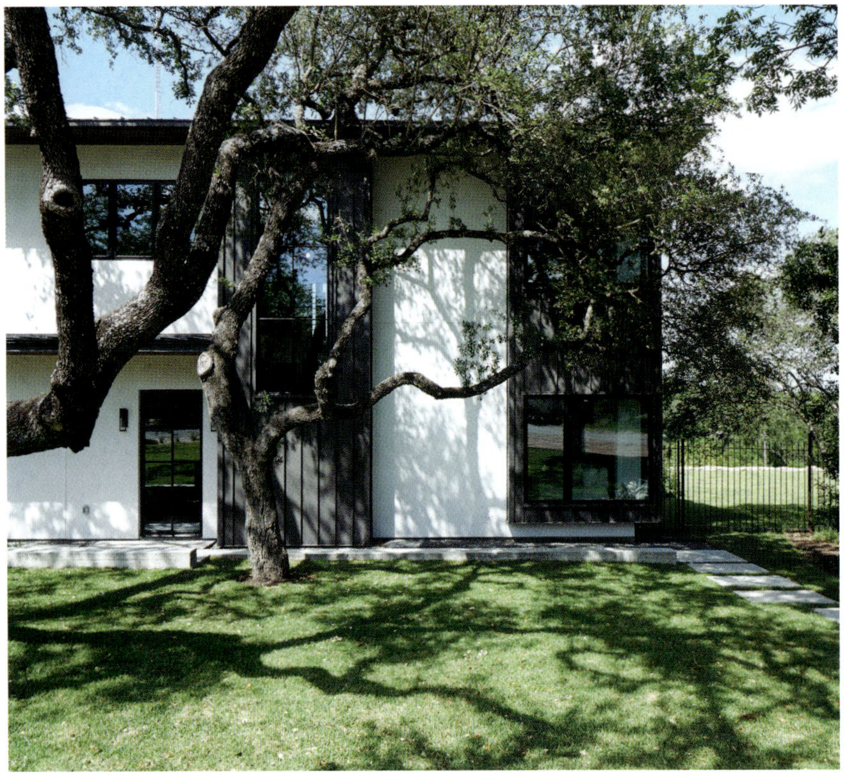

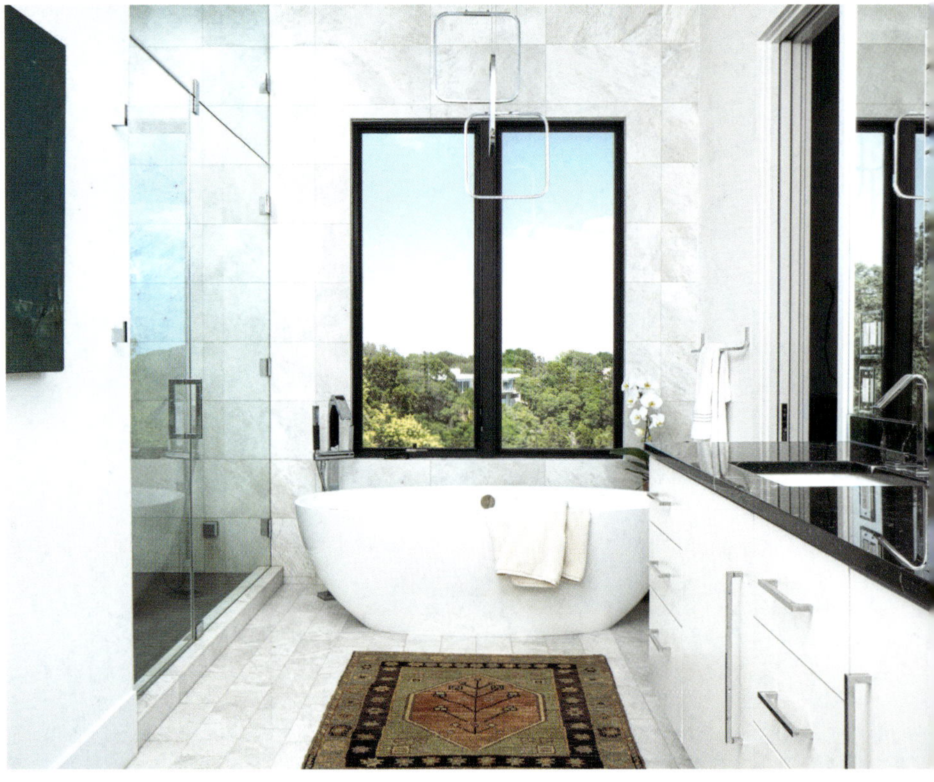

"An abundance of windows provides a really nice quality of light and also allows enjoyment of various surrounding views." –Dianne Kett

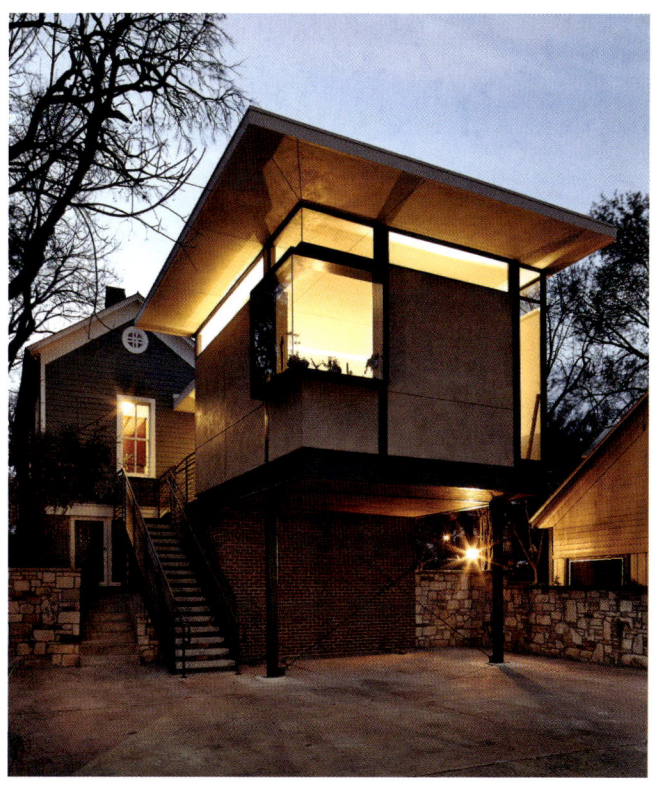

ABOVE AND RIGHT: This modern, office-space addition to a historic house in Austin was meant to be completely different than the original, more traditional home. The two structures are connected by a steel and glass hallway, echoing the white stucco and exposed steel of the new addition. Clerestory windows run along the perimeter to capture the best natural light while the cantilevered corner window provides sunny downtown views. Inside, built-in bookshelves and file drawers provide storage and a modern sectional frames a large, comfortable space for meetings.

FACING PAGE TOP: The kitchen area in the High Road house features black cabinets and a subtle herringbone pattern on the vent hood and island with accents of lacquered brass for a modern yet elegant atmosphere.

FACING BOTTOM LEFT: The exterior entrance from the ground floor brings you up into an immediately accessible glass-enclosed foyer. Views outward become ever more impressive as the ground below falls away and a palpable sense of suspension takes hold.

FACING BOTTOM RIGHT: The master bath includes a large walk-in steam shower with clerestory windows to view the sky and tree line while the tub sits under windows that look out to the valley and rolling hills beyond. Photography by Lars Frazer.

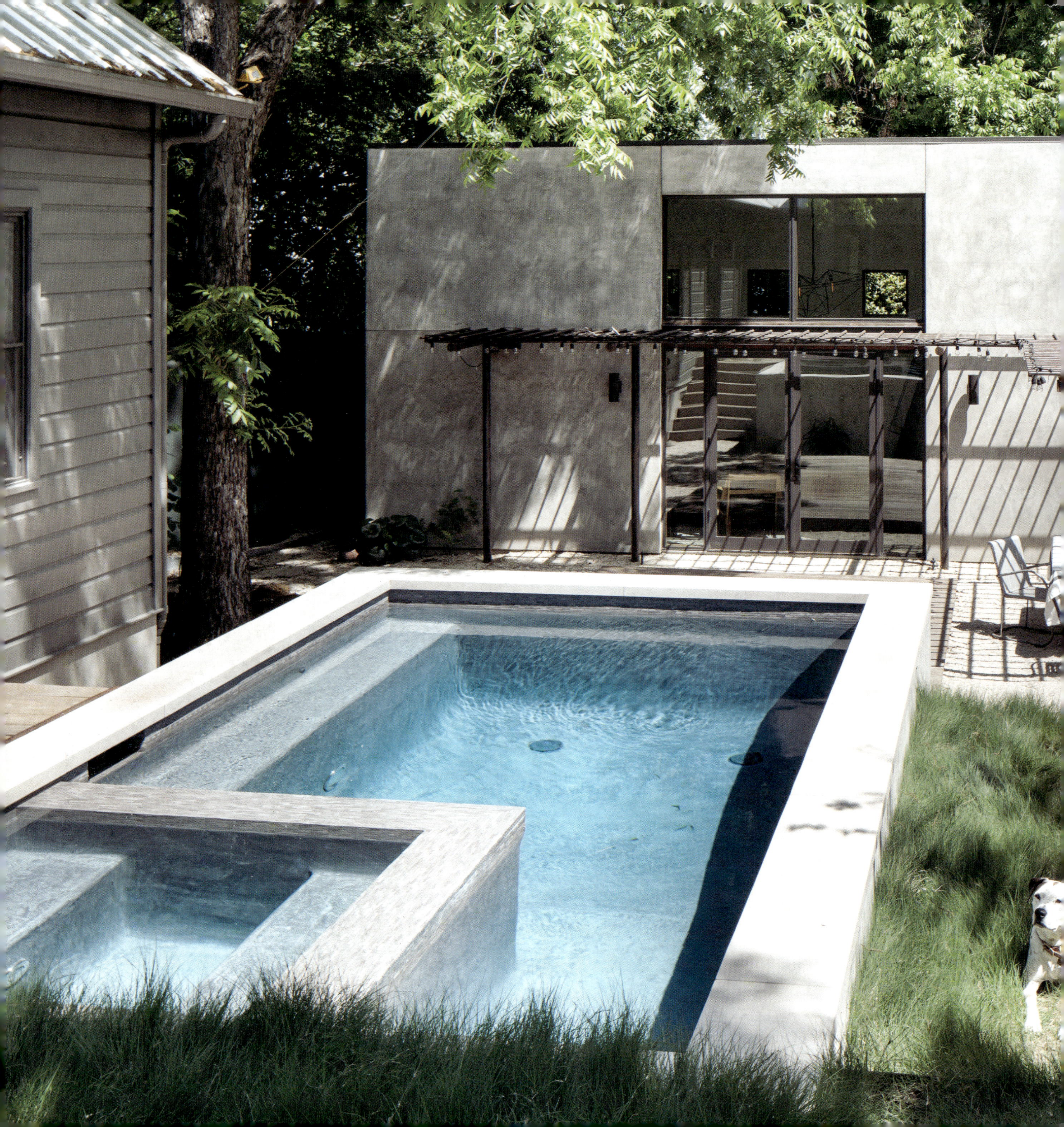

ELIZABETH BAIRD
ARCHITECTURE & DESIGN

Elizabeth Baird approaches her award-winning design studio with an ardent belief in the impact that good design can have on our everyday life.

"I love helping create custom spaces that respond to the particular way different clients live," she says, when asked what she enjoys most about her work. "Hearing feedback from past clients about how the projects I designed for them allow them to spend more time with their family, or more easily entertain their friends, or have a zen-like bedroom suite to retreat to after a long day makes me feel like I'm helping them improve their daily life, and that is very rewarding. I also love it when they say they rarely have to turn on a light during the day due to all the natural light in the space."

Elizabeth has loved the process of creating for as long as she can remember and welcomes the opportunity to design at all scales and across a range of styles. Her goal is to create spaces that respond to each site and client's personal tastes while also striving for thoughtful and fresh solutions. She leans towards clean, elegant spaces filled with warm and interesting materials and is always looking to forge a greater connection between the interior and exterior of a building.

Whether working on new construction or remodel/additions across both residential and commercial projects, Elizabeth and her team approach each new design challenge with excitement – along with the ultimate goal to provide personalized, thoughtful service and a better quality of life through strong design.

FACING PAGE: This project converted a previously nondescript sloped backyard into a beautiful outdoor living space with a new pool and new freestanding casita, providing additional space for living, entertaining, and guests. The clean aesthetic modernizes the entire feel of the site as well as the existing bungalow, which had previously been renovated.
Photography by Andrea Calo.

THIS PAGE: On the interior of the casita, there is a living space, a bar/kitchenette, a full bath, and a sleeping loft. Natural materials dominate the space — steel, wood, plaster, and stucco that bring the outside in for an overall effect of a warm light-filled, and tactile space.

FACING PAGE: A strong axis unites the existing house with the new pool and casita. The existing ground plane was raised so the pool view could be enjoyed from the house. The subsequent terraces create a series of outdoor rooms defined by grass, wood decking, concrete, stone, and steel. Photography by Andrea Calo.

"Reinforcing the site lines and the connections between interior and exterior creates a series of rich, layered spaces for an urban backyard oasis that feels much larger than it did previously." —Elizabeth Baird

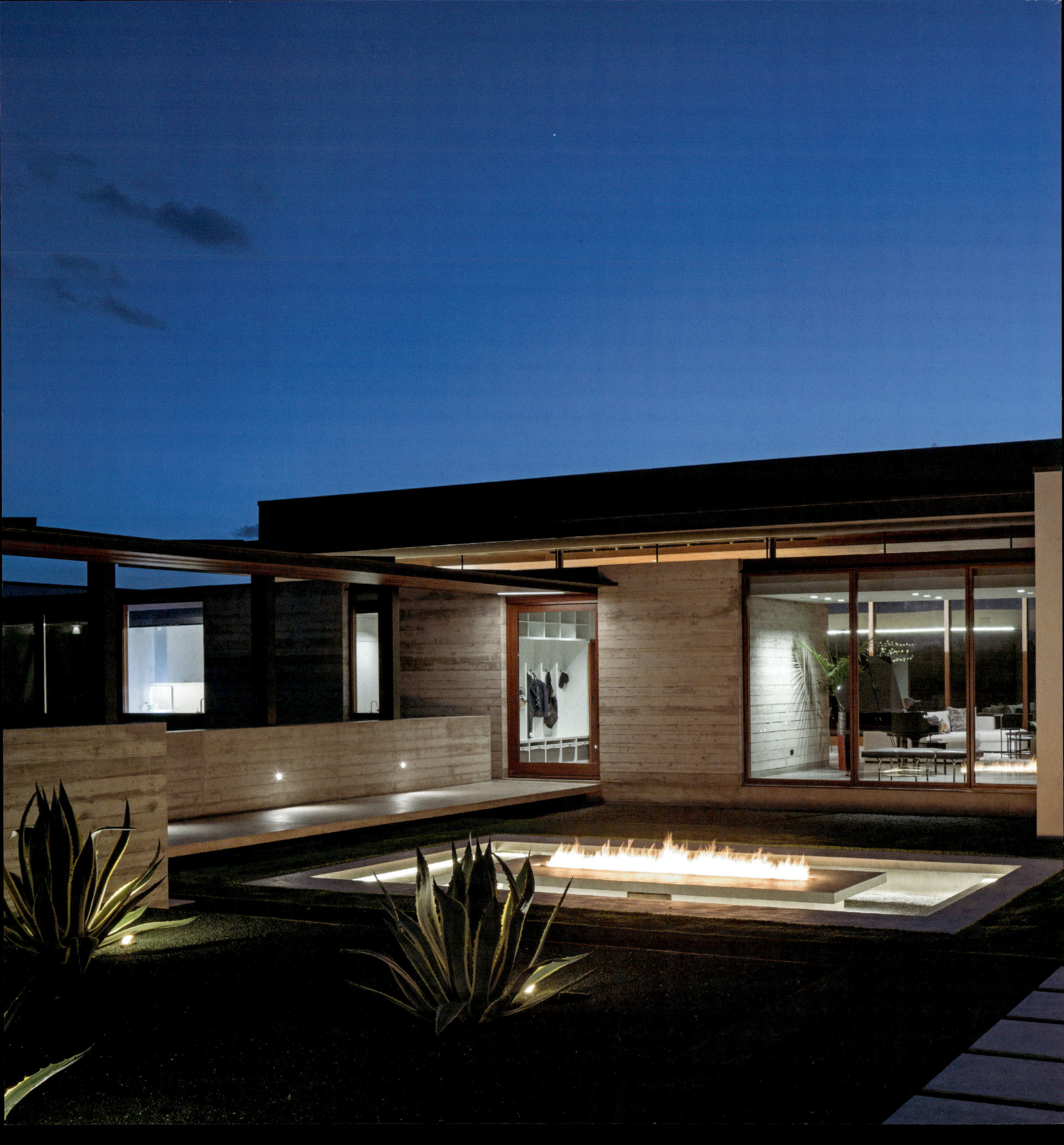

J   JAY CORDER
ARCHITECT

Jay Corder didn't really stumble into architecture. In fact, it was quite the contrary. There wasn't really a time when he didn't know that architecture was exactly what he wanted to do. As an only child, life spurred him to be imaginative from an early age. And his mother had a designer's eye, too, fostering his creativity and teaching him to see the beauty in even the smallest of things. Those formative experiences helped Jay develop a lens on the world that allowed for thinking big, seeing solutions first, and finding joy in the journey of the creative process.

Architecture is Jay's passion and a privilege; after all, he gets to help people bring their dreams to life. But, he also recognizes its inherent responsibility. A custom home is much more than a shelter. As the shell that protects a homeowner's most dear people and the treasures they've collected over time, it should be beautiful, well-designed, made of quality materials, and expertly crafted. It should be a place that adds to one's life experience – and the home's design and construction should reflect that.

So, it will be no surprise that Jay prioritizes a trustworthy partnership and personal connection with each and every one of his clients, ensuring that he understands their desires, dreams, and goals, both great and small.

Indeed, personal commitment is one of his and his team's cornerstones along with a modernist approach and aesthetic sensibility. For Jay, it's his life's work – personally and professionally – to bring vision to reality with efficiency, joy, and advocacy.

FACING PAGE: A sunken conversation pit with a fire element is the focal point of this house's public courtyard entry, which buffers the home from the street and drive court while allowing the adjacent living spaces to be visually connected. The breezeway beyond links the garage to the more private owner's entrance. Photography by Paul Bardagjy.

"Truly outstanding houses often begin with a single big idea, a must-have feature, or a pivotal architectural challenge."
—Jay Corder

LEFT: The zero-edge pool seamlessly connects to the outdoor living space and cabana beyond. Balconies off the main living areas and master suite overlook the pool.

BELOW: The house is sited to tuck into its sloped site and to be well below street level. This strategy belies the overall size of the residence and allows meaningful connection to views and the exterior. A simple, organic palette reflects this subdued approach.

FACING PAGE TOP: Large, motorized door panels pocket completely away at the main living level to bring in views, daylight, and breezes.

FACING PAGE BOTTOM LEFT: An exercise room on the lower level of the house overlooks a completely subterranean regulation half-court. The court's roof creates a flat lawn area for play and gathering while also concealing an otherwise unruly structure.

FACING PAGE BOTTOM RIGHT: The master bathroom was designed as a spa-like amenity. The tub offers breathtaking Hill Country views and the dual indoor-outdoor shower connects directly to the master terrace. Photography by Paul Bardagjy.

43

"The house is a study of the 'thin' spaces between interior and exterior and of a balance between elegance and utility."
—Jay Corder

RIGHT: The upper level of the house connects to the lower via a minimalist concrete stair tower lit by a slot window. Arrival on the lower level finds the owners in something of an amenity-rich, spa-like set of spaces including a billiards room, cabana, home gym, and swimming pool.
Photography by Tre Dunham.

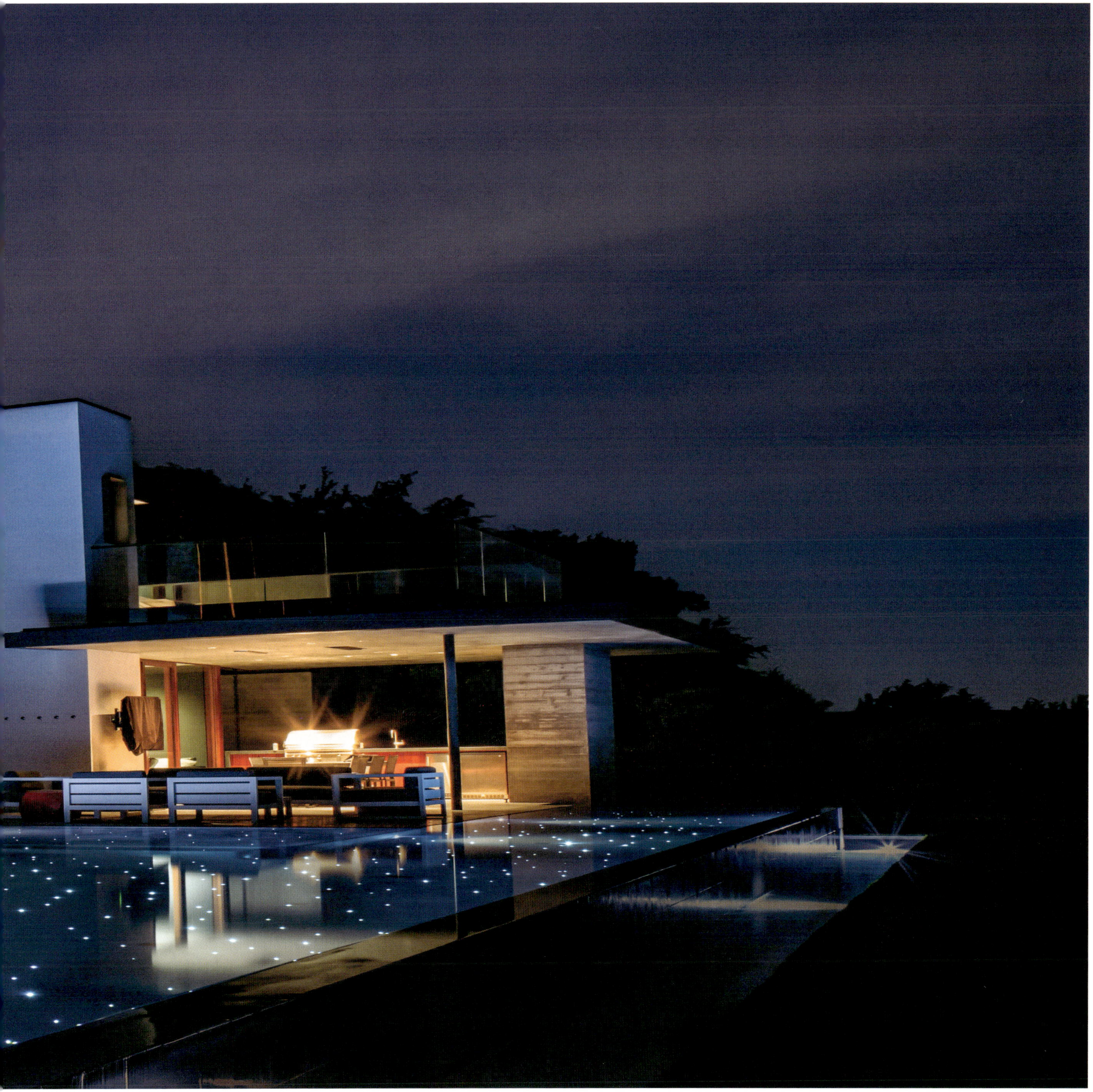

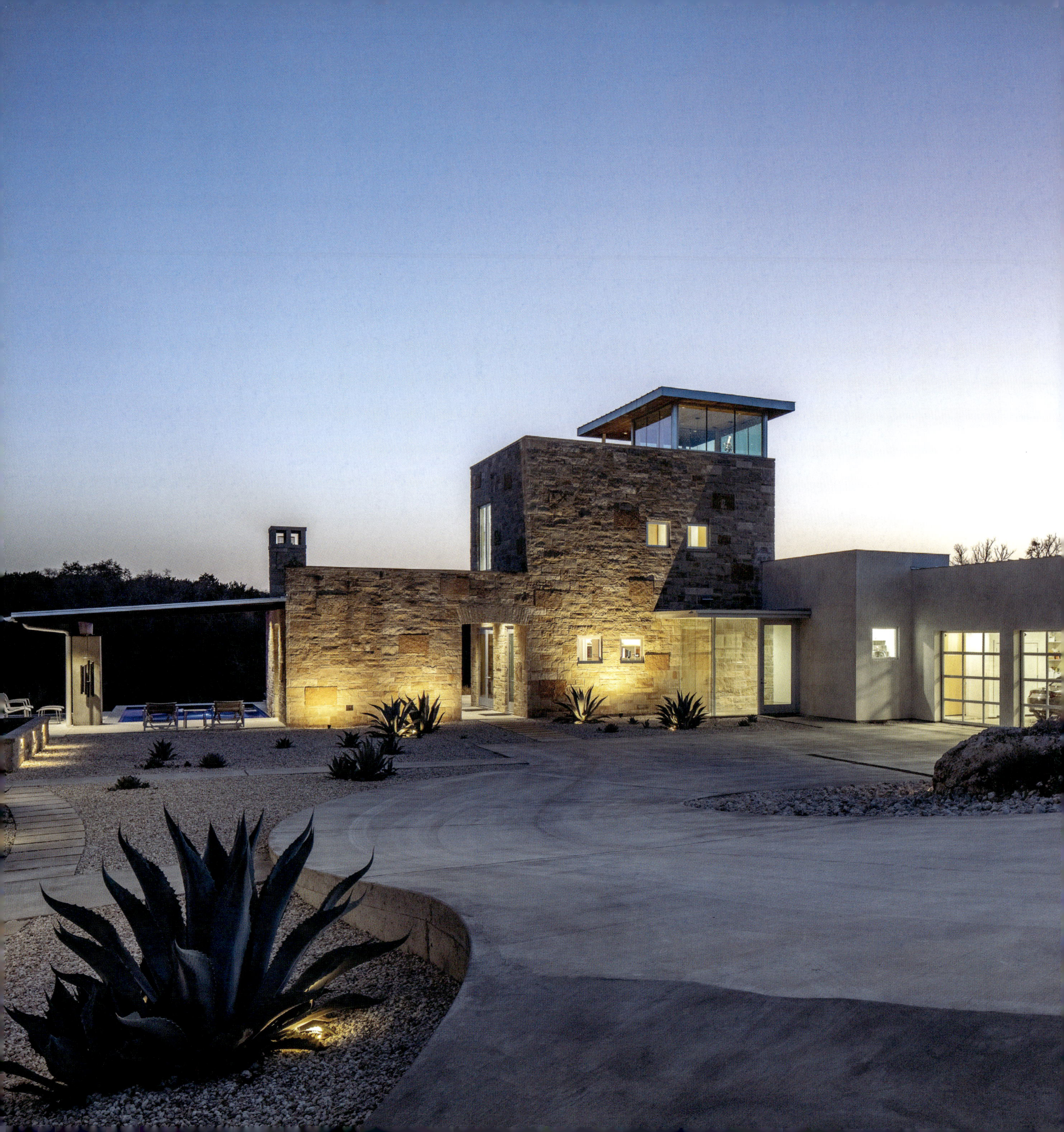

J JAY HARGRAVE ARCHITECT

Jay Hargrave has been designing and constructing buildings for residential, commercial, and hospitality clients since 1991. Growing up, he worked in the family business rigging and racing sailboats. The simple form of the sailboat hull – born out of the discipline of fluid dynamics, crew efficiency, and steel rigging – provided the seed that would grow into acumen for architecture.

Rational form, designing for human efficacy, detail and craft are intrinsic to realizing great design – and those are the values Jay prioritizes in every project, from tiny homes to tremendous estates, historical restorations to banks, and more.

Jay believes in modern, straightforward solutions that respond to the client's preferences, the site, and durability. His designs are timeless: simple and elegant, and executed with superior craftsmanship and sensible detailing.

FACING PAGE: Located on a ranch in north central Texas, this property overlooks Two Birds Canyon which has a spring-fed stream flowing into Leon River. The clients wanted a modern home that complemented the landscape and that would be durable and independent. All power is solar with battery backup, and water is provided by a 30,000-gallon rain collection system. The Main House is crafted in Texas limestone, with the Utility Building just out of frame to the left. Photography by Patrick Wong.

"The value of great design can only be realized when it is properly executed with craftsmanship." —Jay Hargrave

TOP LEFT: The view in the master bedroom looks out to a patio and its deep overhang. The horizontal fireplace in the wall provides modern warmth.

BOTTOM LEFT: The kitchen, with the dining room seen through the doorway to the right, features a custom 1,500-bottle wine storage cabinet opposite the exterior doors. The statement ceiling is structural steel and western cedar.

RIGHT: The dining room looks out to the covered outdoor kitchen with the wood-burning fireplace and pool beyond.

FACING PAGE TOP LEFT: The pool features a submerged spa and glass mosaic tiles.

FACING PAGE TOP RIGHT: The house unfolds as you approach the parking court below. From the crow's nest and roof deck, the views are unlimited.

FACING PAGE BOTTOM: The iconic shape of the Utility Building is intended to contrast with the modern design of the Main House. The Utility Building has two guest bedrooms along with a water treatment and distribution system and equipment storage. Photography by Patrick Wong.

49

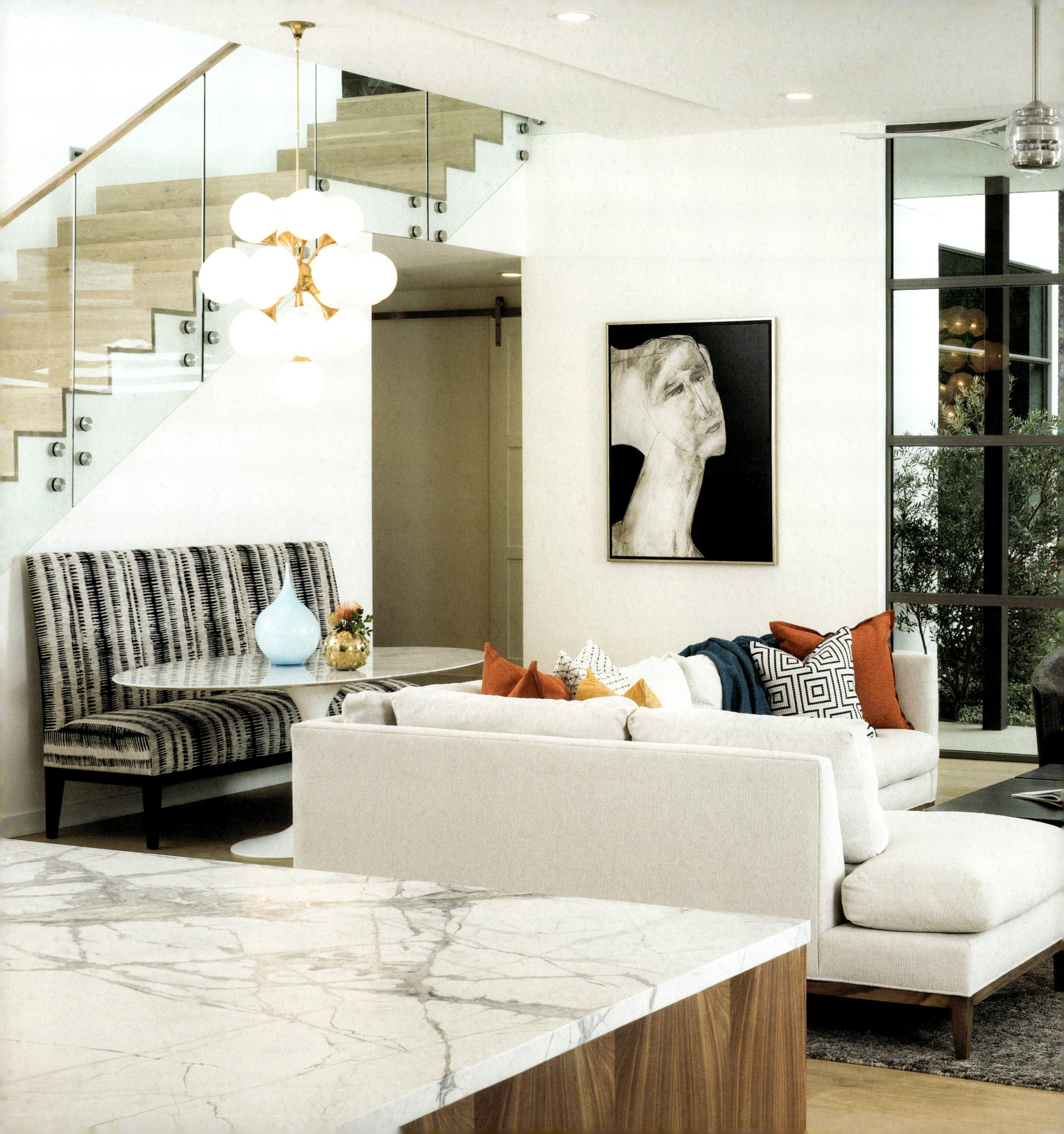

JEI DESIGN
JULIE EVANS

For Julie Evans, award-winning designer and founder of JEI Design, inspiration is ever-present – from travels near and far, history, art galleries, nature, and more, she mentally catalogs eye-catching concepts and ideas. And she harnesses all that inspiration into finding creative solutions that exceed her clients' expectations; that's what she finds most gratifying about her work.

Since 1983, JEI Design has been committed to creating exclusive and unique interiors, implementing the latest technology, innovative creativity, and in-depth industry knowledge. Indeed, the firm offers a complete range of services – from project planning, to collaborating with architects and builders on remodels and new construction, to finishing rooms with custom furnishings and special artwork – so that each space is meticulously tailored to their clients' lifestyles.

"Architects recommend us because we do not overpower their vision," Julie says. "Builders recommend us because we understand the building process and assist in making it as seamless as possible. Clients recommend us because we understand their needs and requirements – and we make their projects beautiful."

FACING PAGE: This family room is the anchoring point of gatherings. A neutral palette among the outdoor views provides a warm and welcoming space while allowing statement lighting and bold accents to add just the right amount of vibrancy. Photography by Jake Holt.

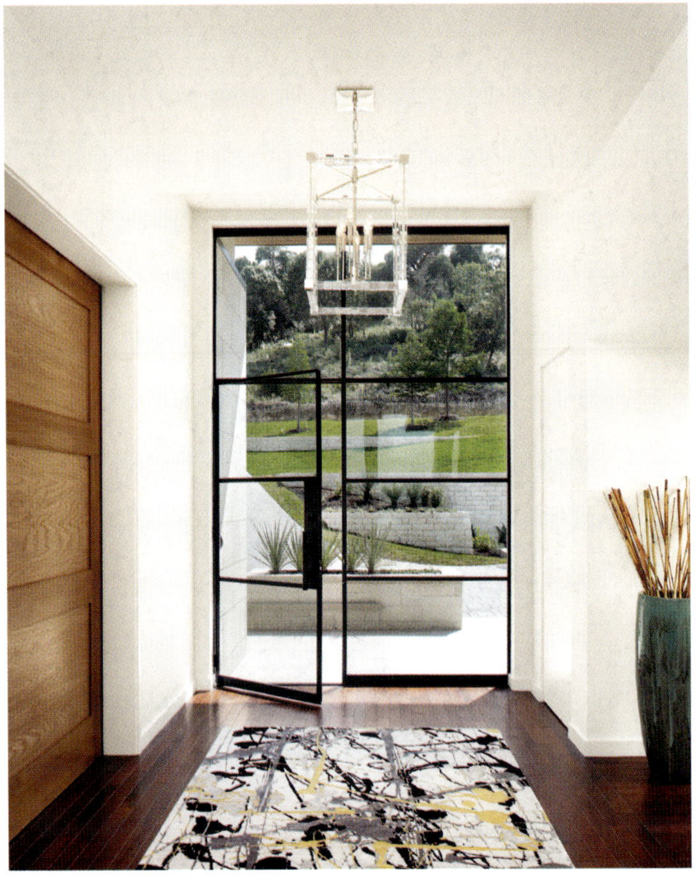
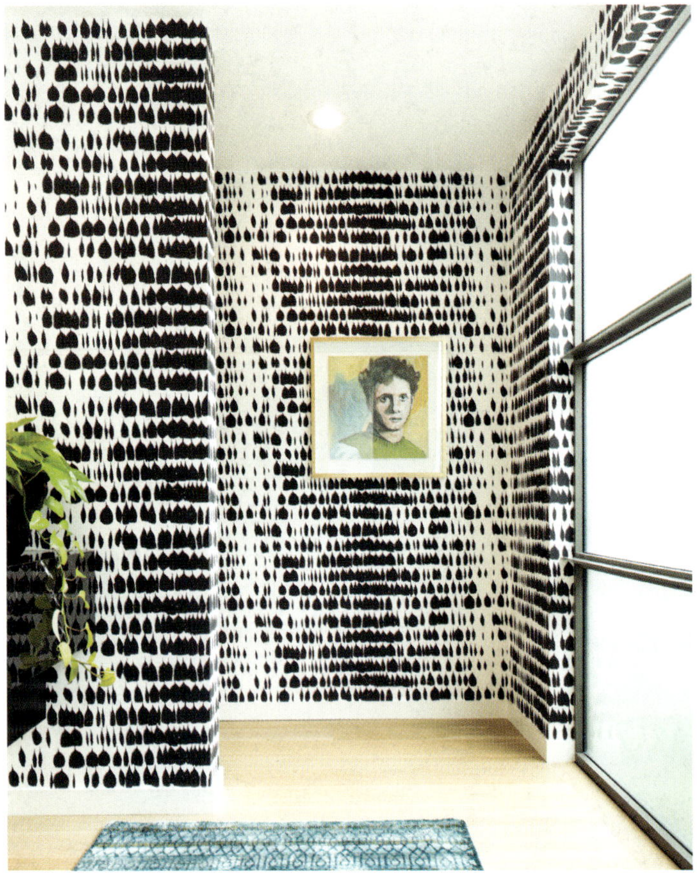
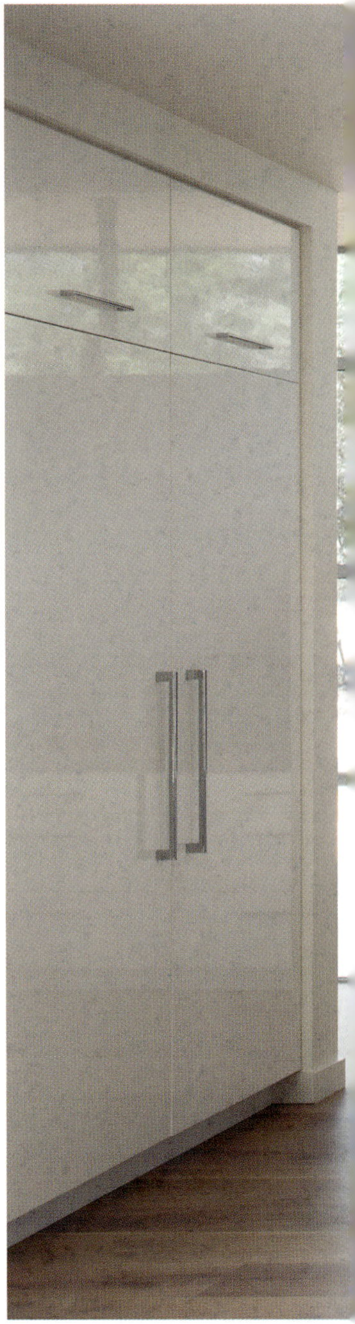
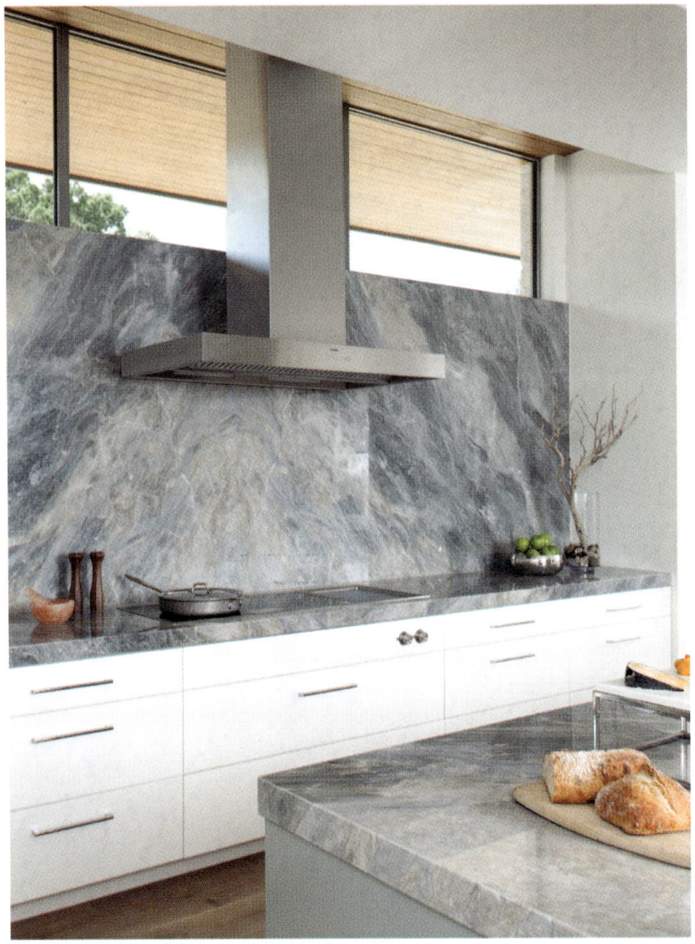
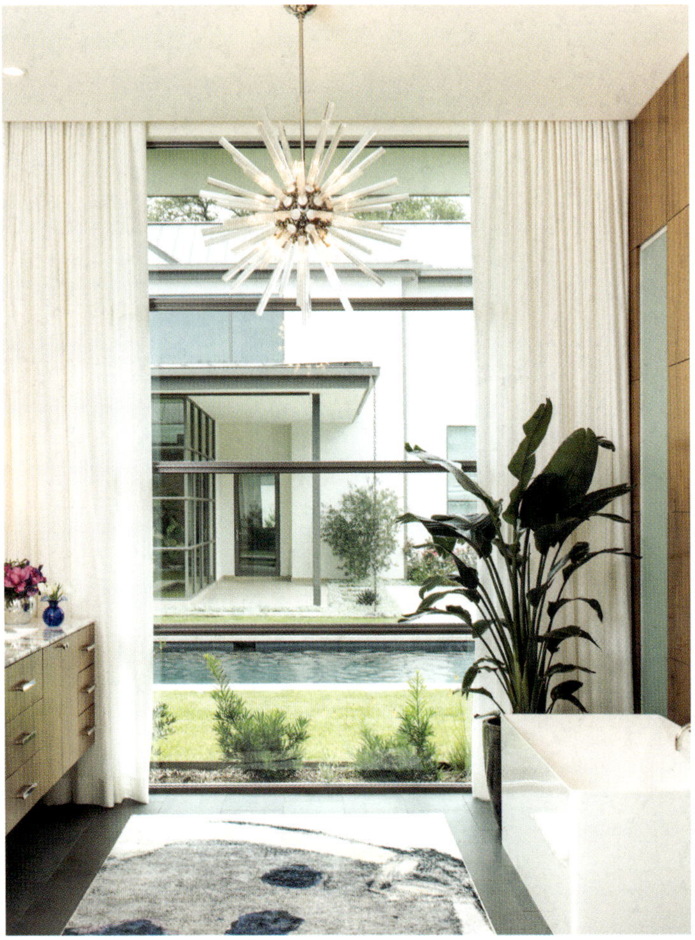

"I see a home as a piece of music with different movements, with continuity of style but different articulation in each space." —Julie Evans

ABOVE: We designed this contemporary kitchen to serve as the heart of family gatherings and social events, ensuring an inviting yet sophisticated aesthetic that is both stylish and practical. Chrome and leather bar stools along with the starburst, Sputnik-style light pendants add a splash of modernism to balance the natural, organic beauty of the Bardiglio marble on the countertops and backsplash. Photography by Ryann Ford.

FACING PAGE TOP LEFT: Grand entrances can be stunning in their simplicity. Photography by Casey Dunn.

FACING PAGE TOP RIGHT: The iconic Queen of Spain pattern, by Schumacher, dazzles the walls in this powder bath. Photography by Jake Holt.

FACING PAGE BOTTOM LEFT: Bardiglio marble was selected for the countertops and book-matched backsplash. The elegant cabinetry and functional layout provide the ultimate combination of style and practicality. Photography by Ryann Ford.

FACING PAGE BOTTOM RIGHT: Soft, diaphanous draperies enrobe this primary bath suite to create a luxurious and relaxing atmosphere. Photography by Jake Holt.

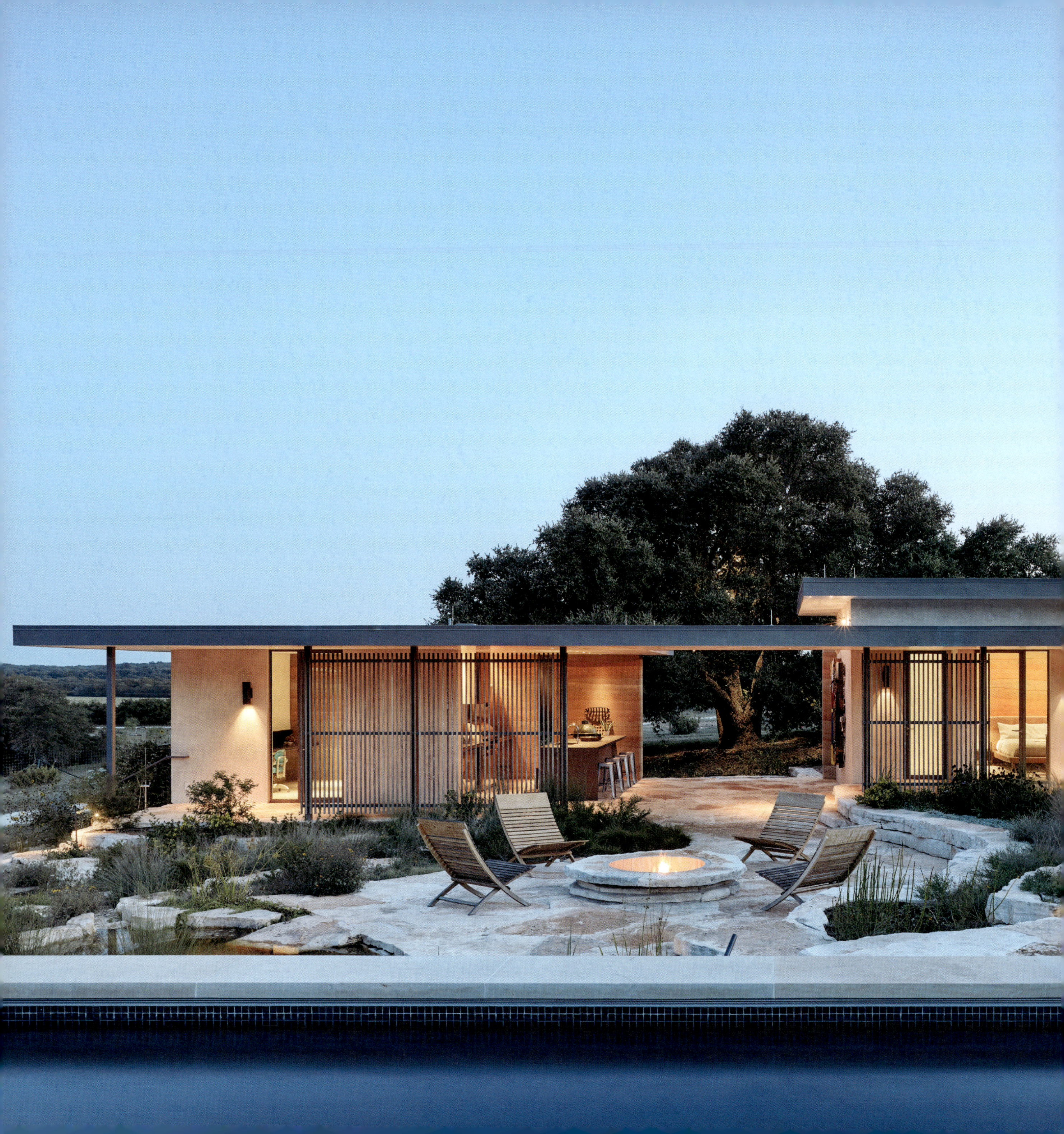

JOBE CORRAL ARCHITECTS

"Our design approach is rooted in the beauty of the site and the experience of place," says Camille Jobe of Jobe Corral Architects, a women-owned and operated firm that specializes in highly crafted residential structures. "Consideration of the individual moments and experiences of daily life is a theme that brings warmth and texture to our work," adds Ada Corral.

Jobe Corral has the unique capacity to work on many scales of design because they act as both full-service architecture firm and interiors studio. They find it most rewarding to conceptualize a property's master plan, create the narrative with their clients, and pull that thread all the way through the project – right down to the design of a chair at the dining table, the composition of found objects in a room, the fabric of the sofa, and every single other detail.

If you were to ask them to describe their style, the team would say they don't have one. For them, truly enduring spaces come from authenticity to the project conditions along with elegant, innovative resolutions. "You find the most important element of the home by listening and doing your very best to really understand your client," says Camille. Indeed, Jobe Corral prioritizes working with homeowners to create spaces that reflect their values and how they want to live in the world. It's the reason why each of their projects is so individualized – and so celebrated.

FACING PAGE: The ranch house guest wing opens up to create an outdoor kitchen and dining space. The limestone courtyard terraces with the landscape, forming a transition between the modern building forms and the more rustic natural land around them. Photography by Casey Dunn.

"We are artists and we are technicians. Spectacular buildings and spaces require that you not only live in both worlds, but understand that they are one."
—Camille Jobe

ABOVE LEFT: High wood ceilings give way to the more intimately scaled kitchen, giving the home a variety of types of spaces. Photography by Casey Dunn.

ABOVE RIGHT: The living room ceiling extends beyond the glass walls and over the lap pool. A steel trellis runs over the pool and along the length of the house offering protection from the strong Texas sun, while an opening in the roof allows a spot of direct light. Photography by Casey Dunn.

FACING PAGE TOP: The living room opens onto the courtyard to seamlessly bring the outside in. When the sliding glass doors are fully open, the pool deck becomes part of the living room itself. Photography by Casey Woods.

FACING PAGE BOTTOM LEFT: Rammed earth walls extend beyond the house to capture space for an outdoor shower off the primary bath. Photography by Casey Dunn.

FACING PAGE BOTTOM RIGHT: The earthen walls, leather bed, and custom steel bedside tables show the palette of materials used throughout the home. Photography by Casey Dunn.

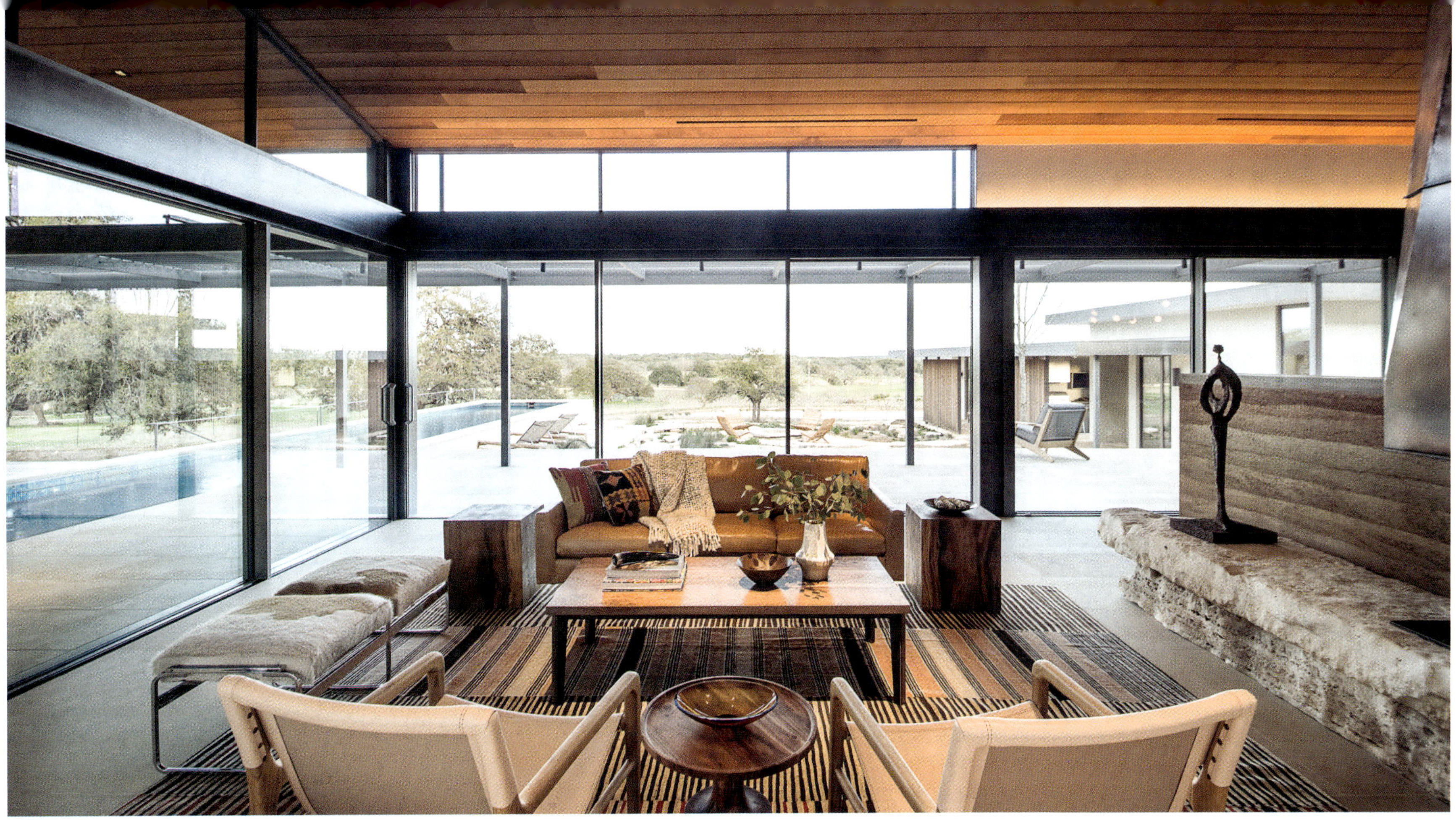

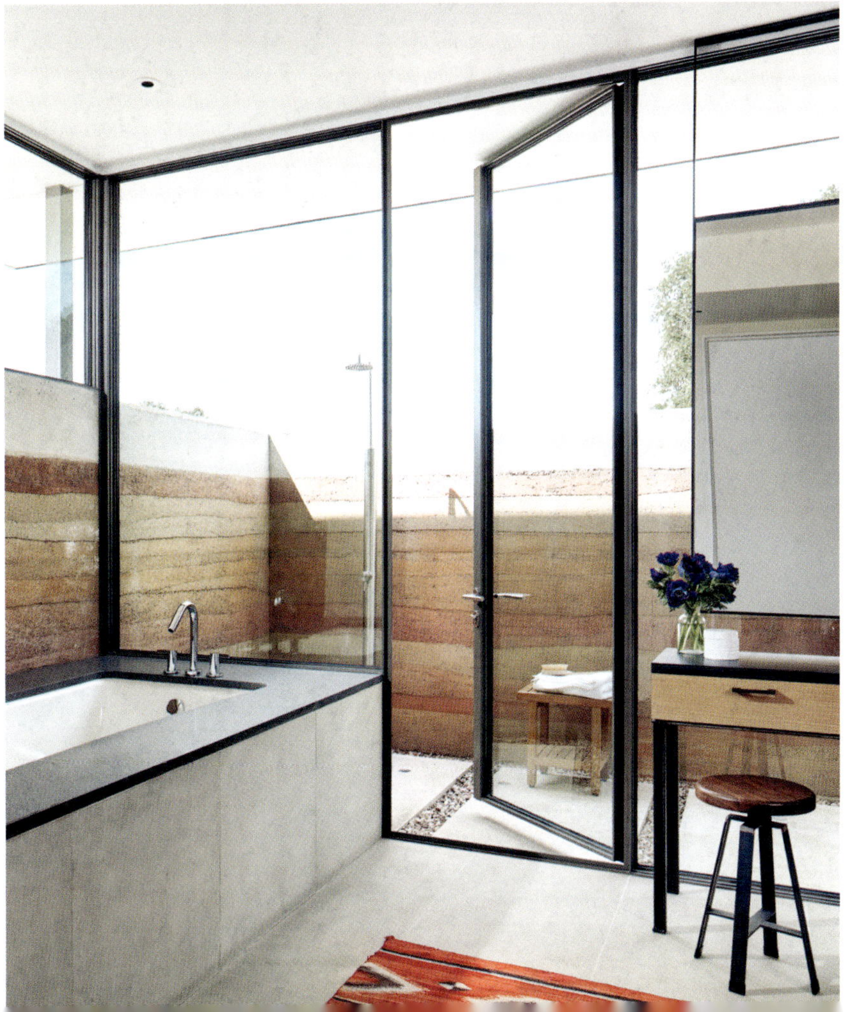

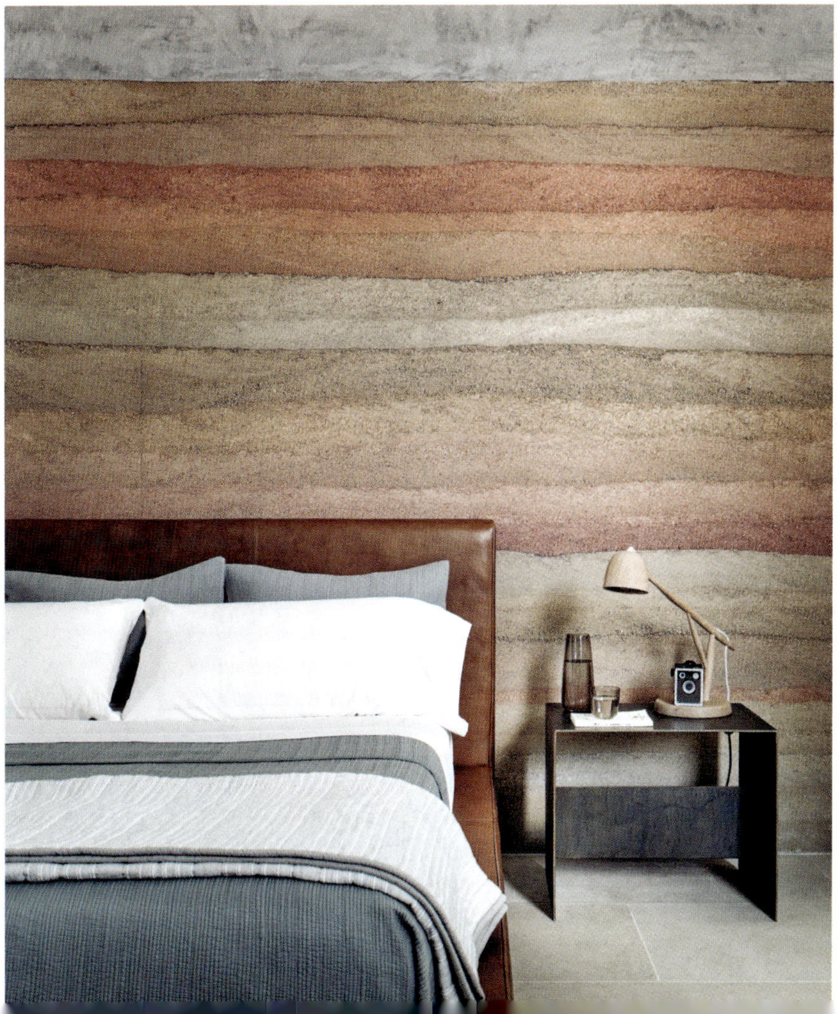

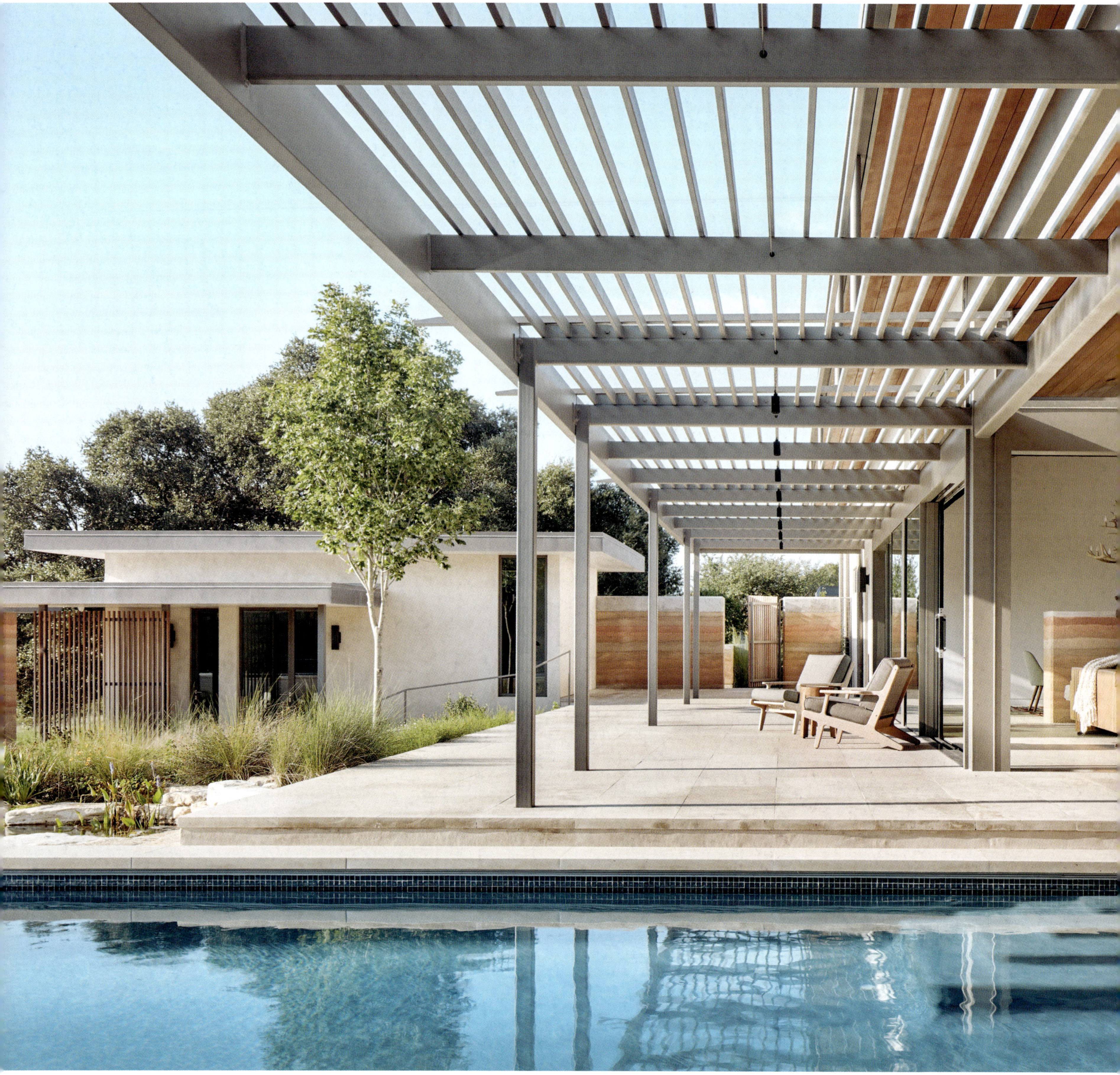

ABOVE: Rammed earth, copper, and limestone combine at the center of the home to create the hearth. The patinated metal is a perfect counter to the earthen walls.

LEFT: A series of screens and trellises provide respite from the sun while allowing views of the open landscape beyond. Photography by Casey Dunn.

"The individual moments and experiences of daily life inform our designs and bring warmth and texture to our projects." –Ada Corral

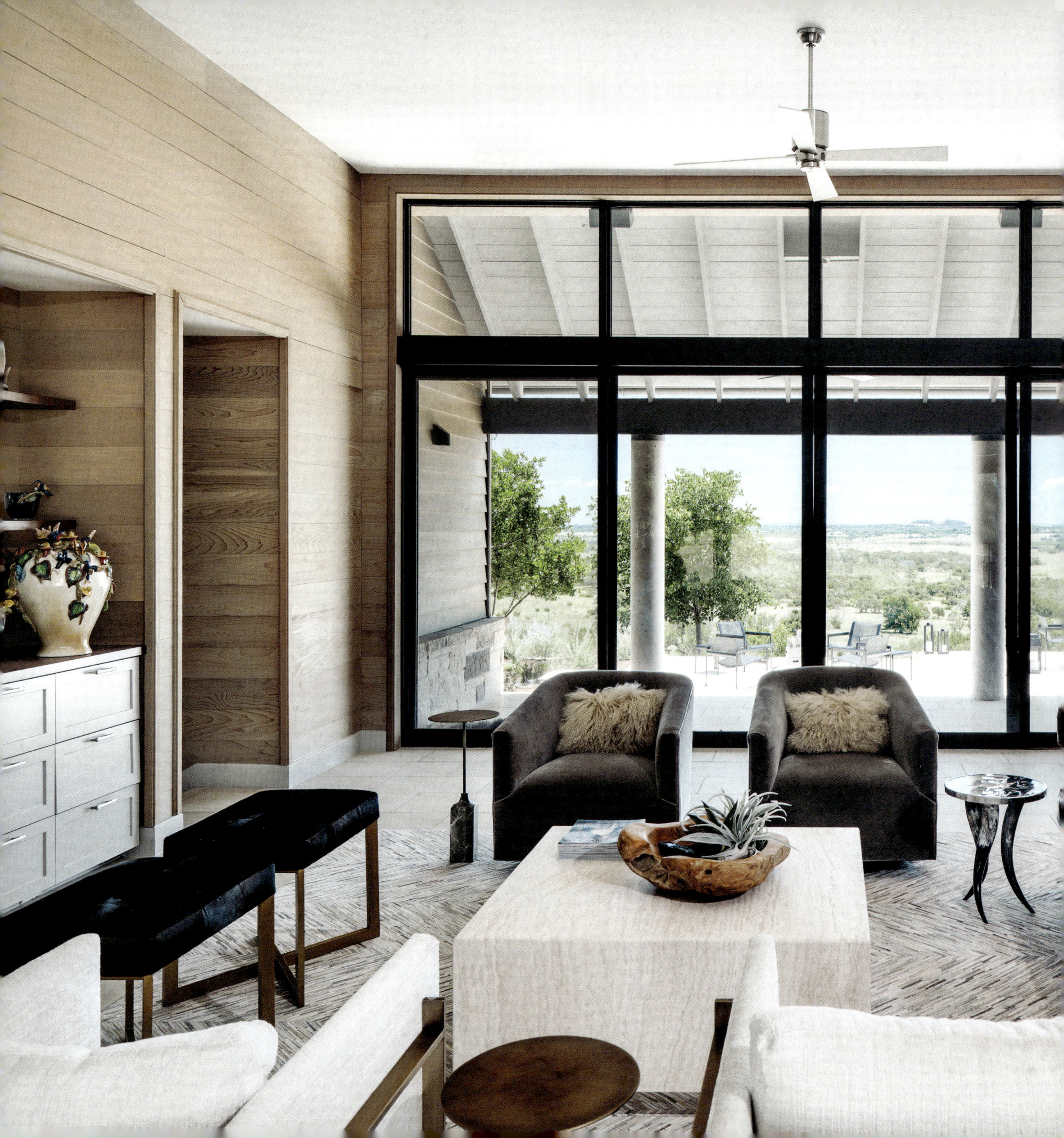

KASEY MCCARTY INTERIOR DESIGN

Kasey McCarty has focused her career on creating cultivated yet uncomplicated interiors that express and inspire the lives of those who inhabit them. She's constantly fascinated by the "bones" of a place, whether it's new construction or existing, residential or commercial. But, her ultimate goal is ensuring each space thoughtfully reflects the essence of her clients – how they live and how they want to live, both practically and aesthetically.

"Most people can describe exactly what they are looking for in their home, office, or restaurant but they just don't know how to get those ideas off the ground, " says Kasey. "My clients know how they want their space to feel and look – and we work together to make that happen. It's a visual translation." And, with more than 20 years of design, management, and construction experience (not to mention a stint in the Peace Corps in Bolivia upon graduation from university!), Kasey is an expert in this kind of full-scale translation and collaboration – a fusion of exterior architecture with the light, the location, the function, the personalities that move inside the space, and more. Her award-winning studio fosters an attention to detail and material investigation that sets them apart, working with each client – from concept through permitting, and right down to the pillows on the sectional.

FACING PAGE: At the Lampasas Ranch residence, rustic materials complement the home's modern finishes. The aged leather sofa paired with sleekly elegant side chairs is a perfect example of the eclectic combination. Natural, organic materials likewise align with the warmth of white cedar walls and abundance of natural light and mile-long views of Texas plains. Photography by Chase Daniel.

"I am old school and stick to the basics of balance, proportion, and contrast. When they are in harmony, it's a great day." —Kasey McCarty

ABOVE LEFT: The Harley Davidson pool table holds center stage in the home office of this bachelor-pad penthouse in the sky, originally designed for a generous entertainer with a kind soul and spirited energy. We resurfaced the piece to complement the eel-skin-pattern wallpaper.

ABOVE RIGHT: The poker room doubles as a guest bedroom with a console Murphy bed. The owner's boxing photo collection hangs over sleek, woven grasscloth.

FACING PAGE TOP: This penthouse features a complete west-facing 180-degree view of downtown Austin. Each room oozes with drama and a tongue-in-cheek nod to a den of iniquity – including the main living space.

FACING PAGE BOTTOM: The master bedroom features silk patterned wallpaper, a leather and chrome headboard, and provocative gold table lamps. The black back-painted glass wall reflects the northern view of Austin. Photography by Casey Woods.

63

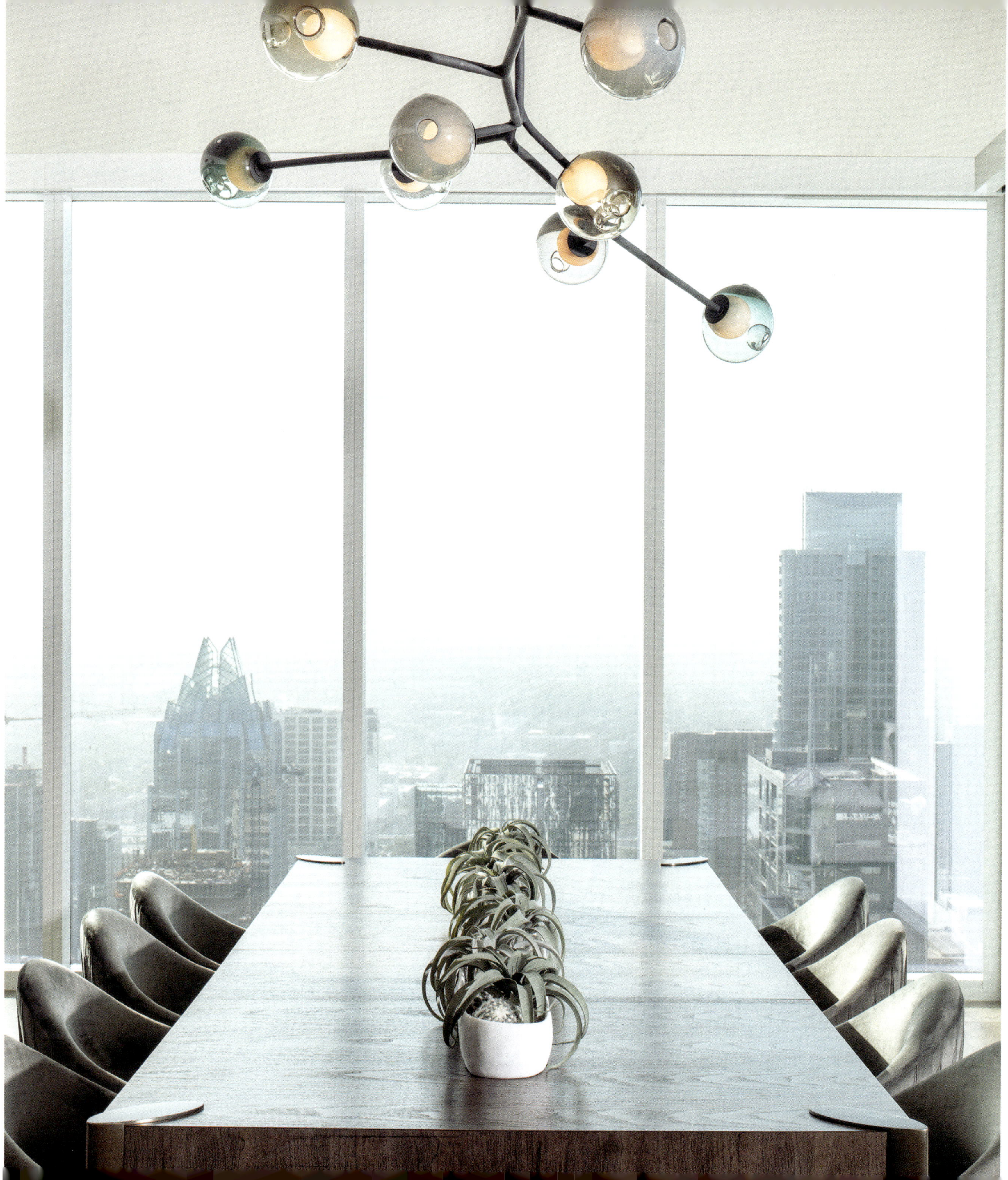

KELLE CONTINE INTERIOR DESIGN

Based in Austin, Texas, Kelle Contine Interior Design (KCID) isn't afraid to push limits to create unique and thoughtfully curated spaces through a detailed, full-service design approach. Their boutique firm specializes in residential and commercial interiors, encompassing a broad spectrum of project types. KCID collaborates with the finest architects, builders, developers and industry professionals to design memorable, luxury interiors both locally and across the country.

With an eye for impeccable design, KCID is recognized for a technically driven approach to the creative process and a positive perspective that is widely respected within the industry. Known for their comprehensive and holistic process, KCID believes collaboration across all disciplines is key and that every new project is an invitation to tell a one-of-a-kind story.

THIS PAGE AND FACING PAGE: Positioned in downtown Austin, this high-rise residence serves as a second home for our clients looking for an urban escape and was designed to be contemporary yet comfortable. Our firm focused on curating textural finishes and unique furniture that achieved our clients' desire for a relaxed sophistication. Natural light and extensive views play a significant role in the space, with floor-to-ceiling windows that show off the breathtaking Austin skyline from every angle. Key design features include the play on contrasted details in our dark and light kitchen, a flexible and luxurious living room arrangement, and surprise hints of color around each corner via art and accent walls. We worked to create a layered and calming experience by juxtaposing the architectural with the natural. All of these specific finishing touches, along with collaborative design and personal care, truly led to a quiet retreat amongst the clouds. Photography by Jake Holt.

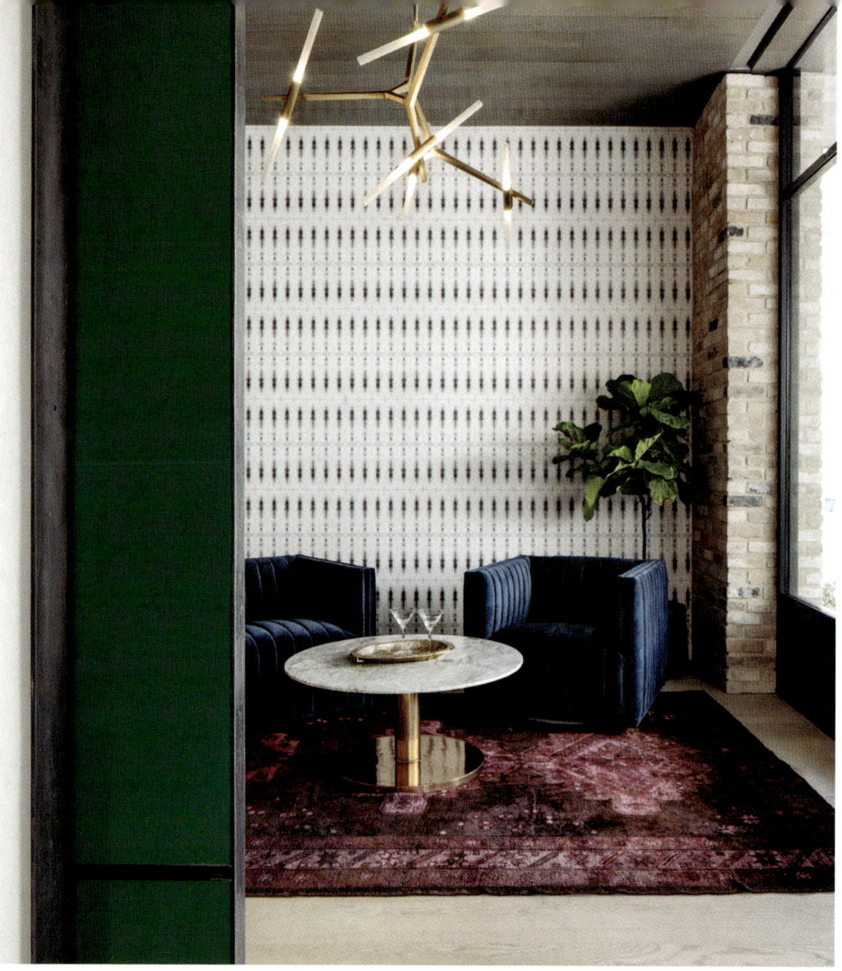
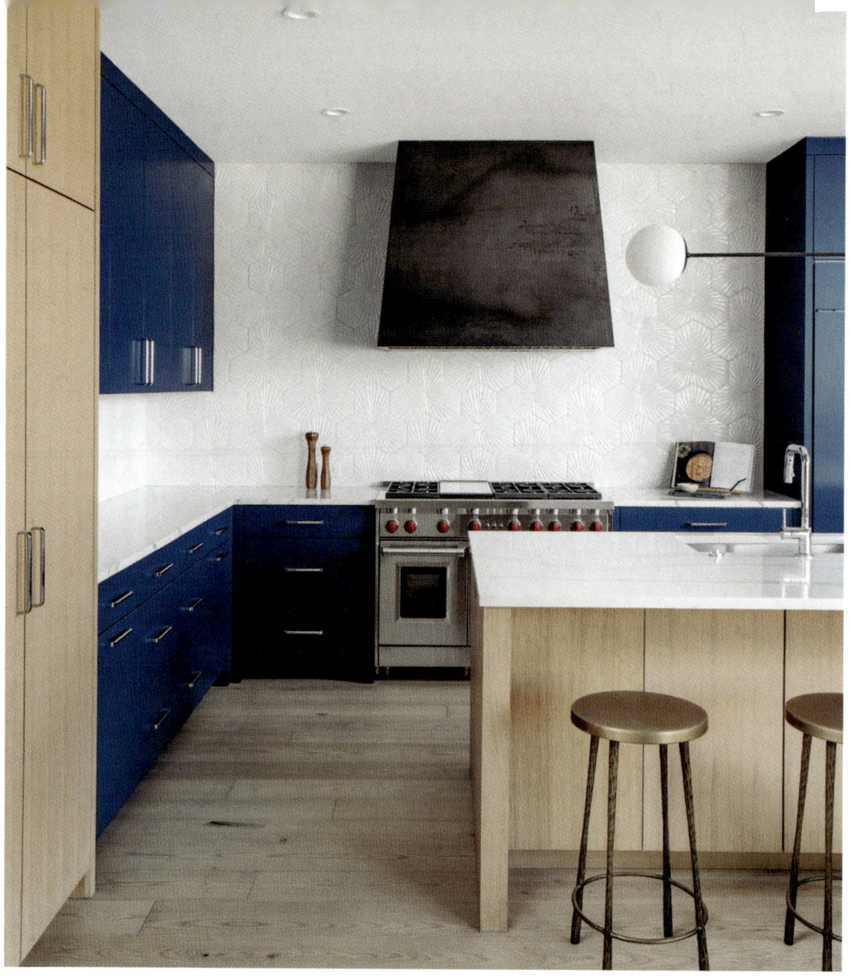
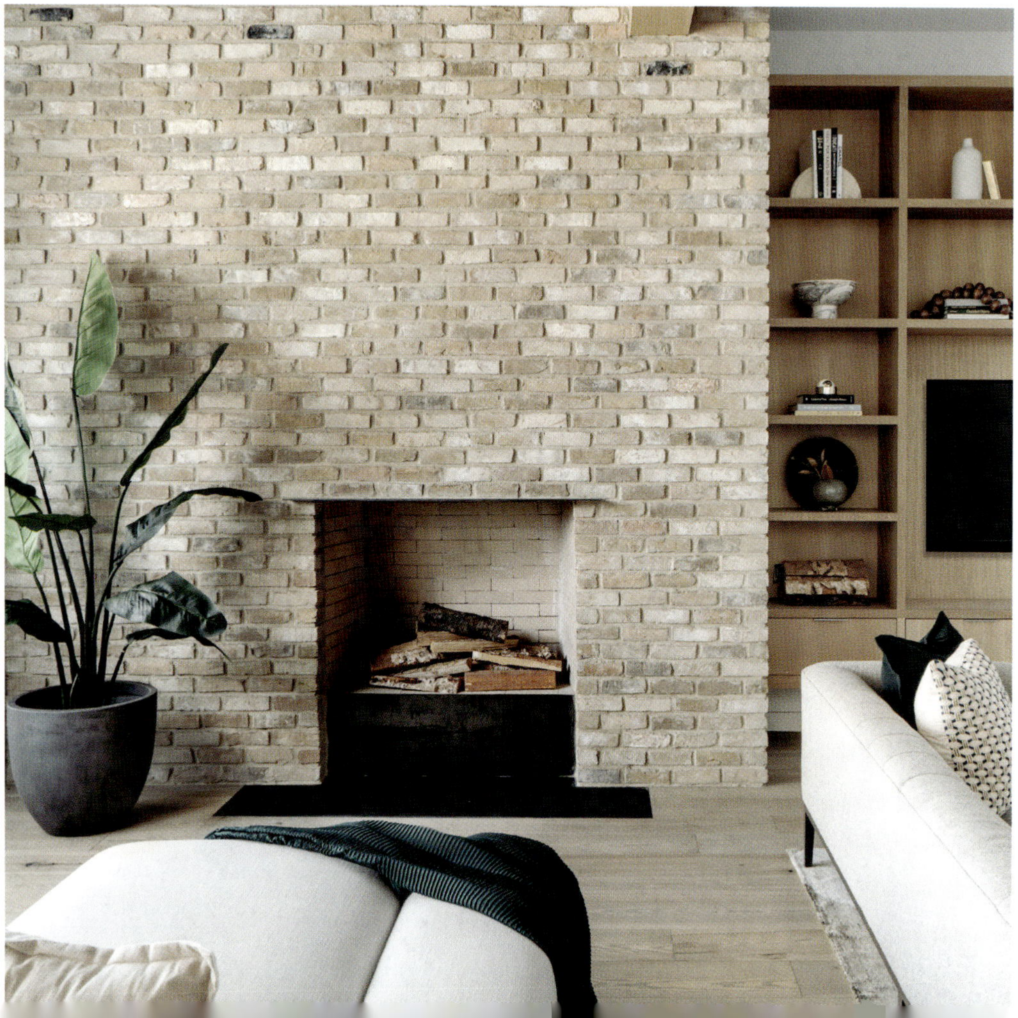
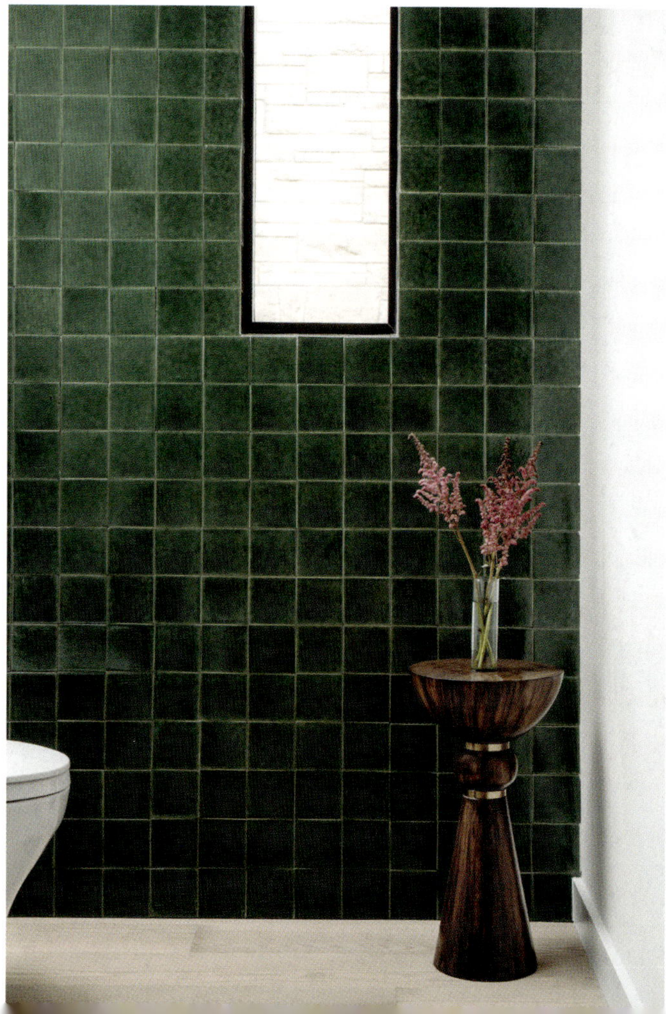

"A contemporary architectural approach in an otherwise traditional neighborhood, paired with an interior filled with unexpected moments of color and texture, create a stunning abode."

THIS PAGE AND FACING PAGE: Situated in the heart of one of the most architecturally dynamic neighborhoods in Austin – one that is rich in spirit and history – the Tarrytown Residence balances the concept of old and new, with a nod to modernity through a thoughtful marriage of materiality, color palette, and fixture selections. Rich, memorable jewel tones inspire the color scheme throughout, offsetting traditional antique brick and light ash wood flooring – all punctuated by satin brass and black trimmed fixtures for a contemporary infusion at key built-in elements. Incorporating furnishings into the space that offer clean lines with the right amount of softness allowed for an understated elegance that feels livable while honoring the goal of elevating tradition. Photography by Chase Daniel.

67

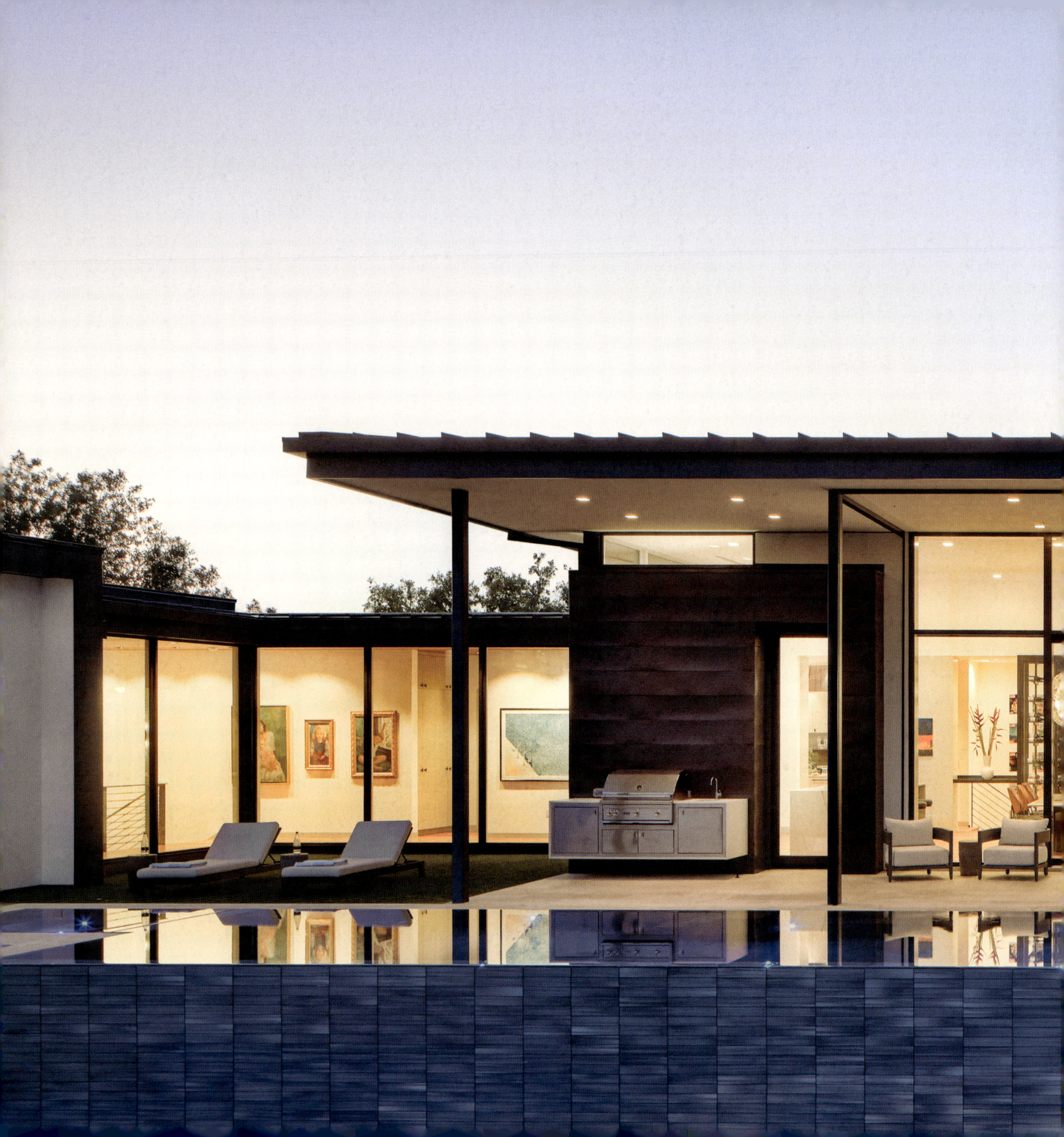

LARUE ARCHITECTS

Nationally recognized firm LaRue Architects has more than 500 private residences under its belt, each uniquely tailored to its owner and site. But just as beautiful as these properties are the relationships they've built alongside them.

Principal James LaRue and his close-knit team cultivate a family atmosphere that translates to their clients — many of whom have been ongoing for decades. Staying deliberately small lets the team cater to clients' needs with personal attention and hands-on problem solving. Indeed, the firm only completes a highly selective and limited number of projects each year in order to enjoy this close contact with clients. It wouldn't be out of the ordinary for LaRue and team to start a client meeting with lawn chairs and a cold beverage to experience the site at different times of the day, followed by a sketch on trace paper that continues the vision all the way through to a child's future wedding in the backyard.

They've perfected a "Hill Country Contemporary" vernacular that captures what people love most about living in the Austin area — from long views and big skies, to breezes through the treetops, glimpses of rolling hills, and frames of a vibrant cityscape. But, they also work just as comfortably outside of Austin to many cities across the U.S.

No matter the location, LaRue always strives for innovation married with timeless design that's not beholden to gimmicks or trends, continuing the firm's legacy of creating settings for an elegant and easy way of life.

FACING PAGE AND NEXT TWO PAGES: The panoramic views of downtown Austin's ever-changing skyline are central to this home. The great room's full-height glass is just one example of that, where sliding glass doors open to double the size of the living and dining spaces and truly blur the lines between interior and exterior. A glass gallery links the main living space to the master suite, which overlooks its own terrace lounge and features more spectacular views of the city. Photography by Casey Dunn.

"The unveiling of this transformative addition and remodel is fully experienced to the side of the home — from the front of the residence, there is just a hint of what is to unfold around the corner." —James LaRue

71

"This regional contemporary residence appears as if it has merged with the site in this beautiful, unpredictable park-like setting." —James LaRue

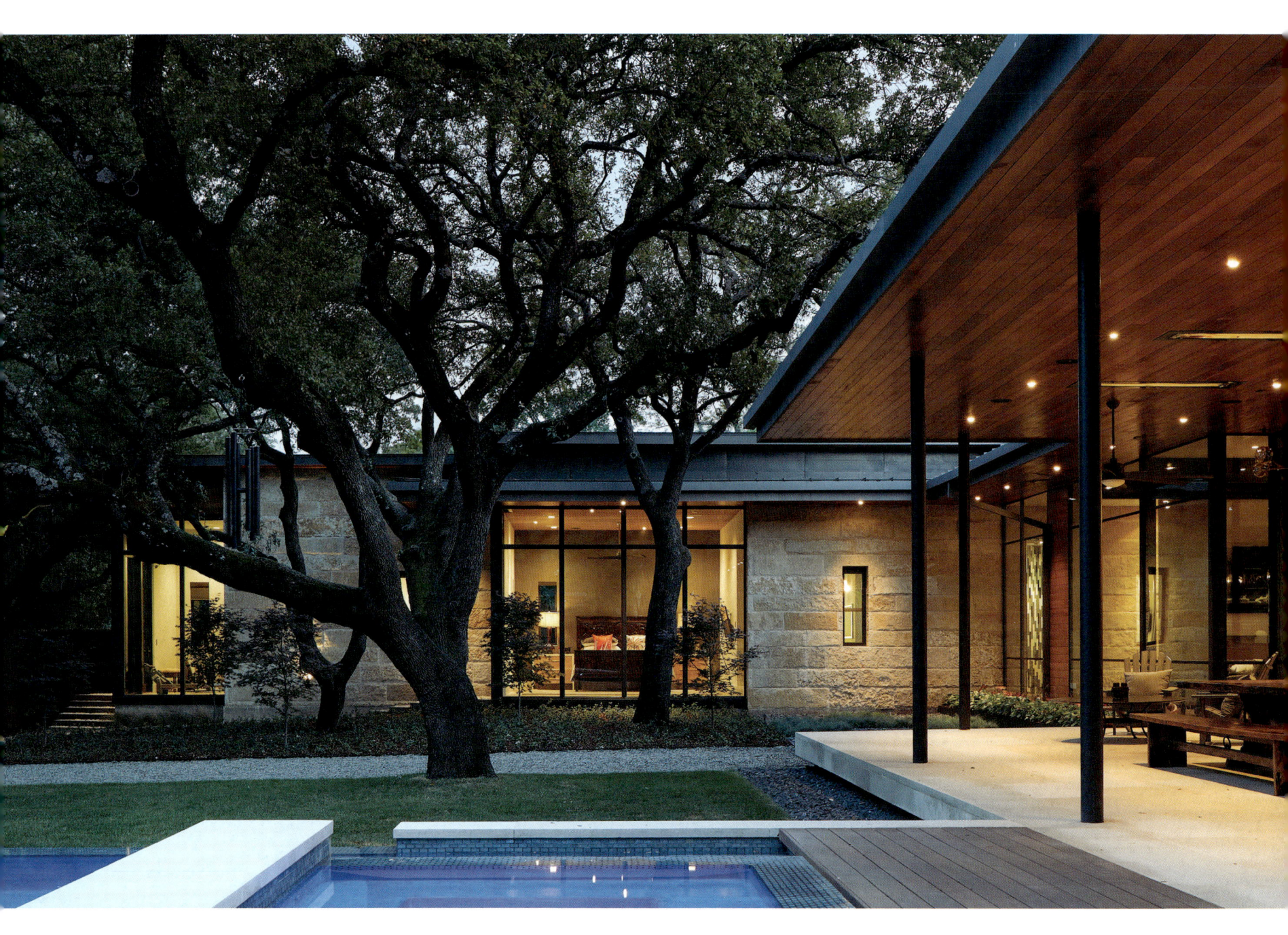

ABOVE AND FACING PAGE: Located on a prestigious street in Dallas, this innovative home replaced a prior house on this corner lot. Nestled within a canopy of mature oak trees, it offers an oasis from the city. The primary suite looks out to the pool; limestone walls and warm wood ceilings add to the organic setting. Photography by Dror Baldinger FAIA.

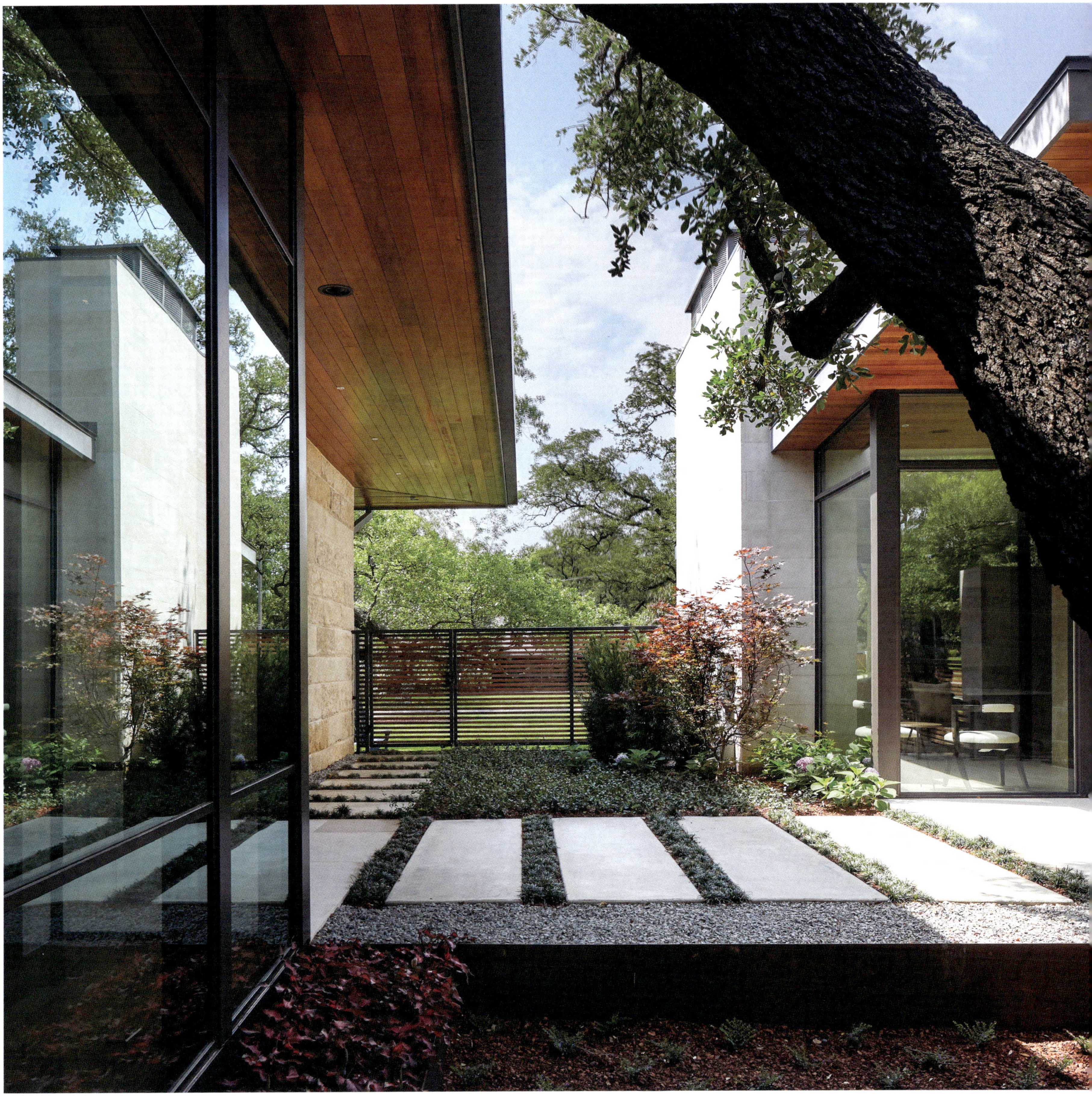

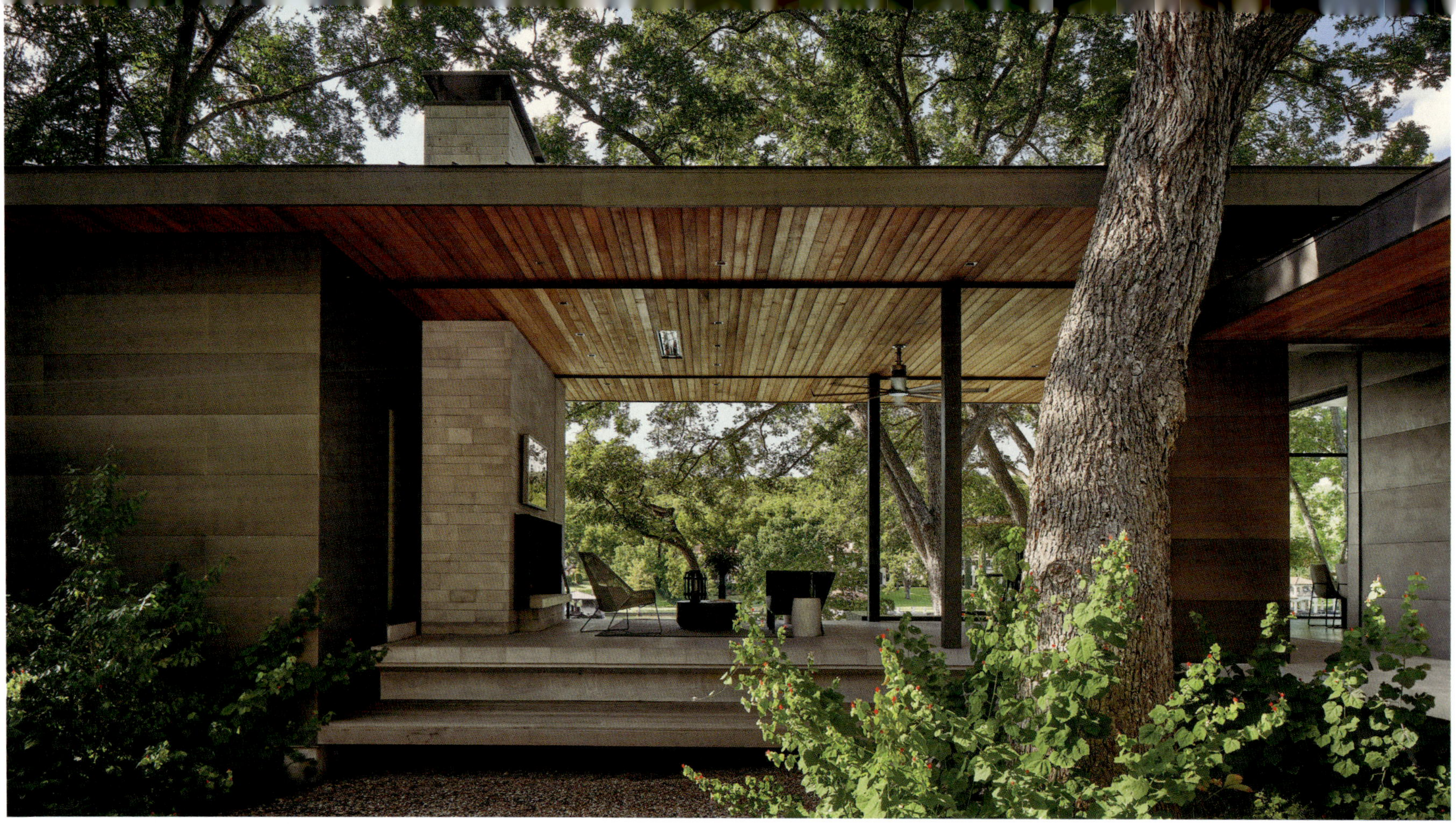

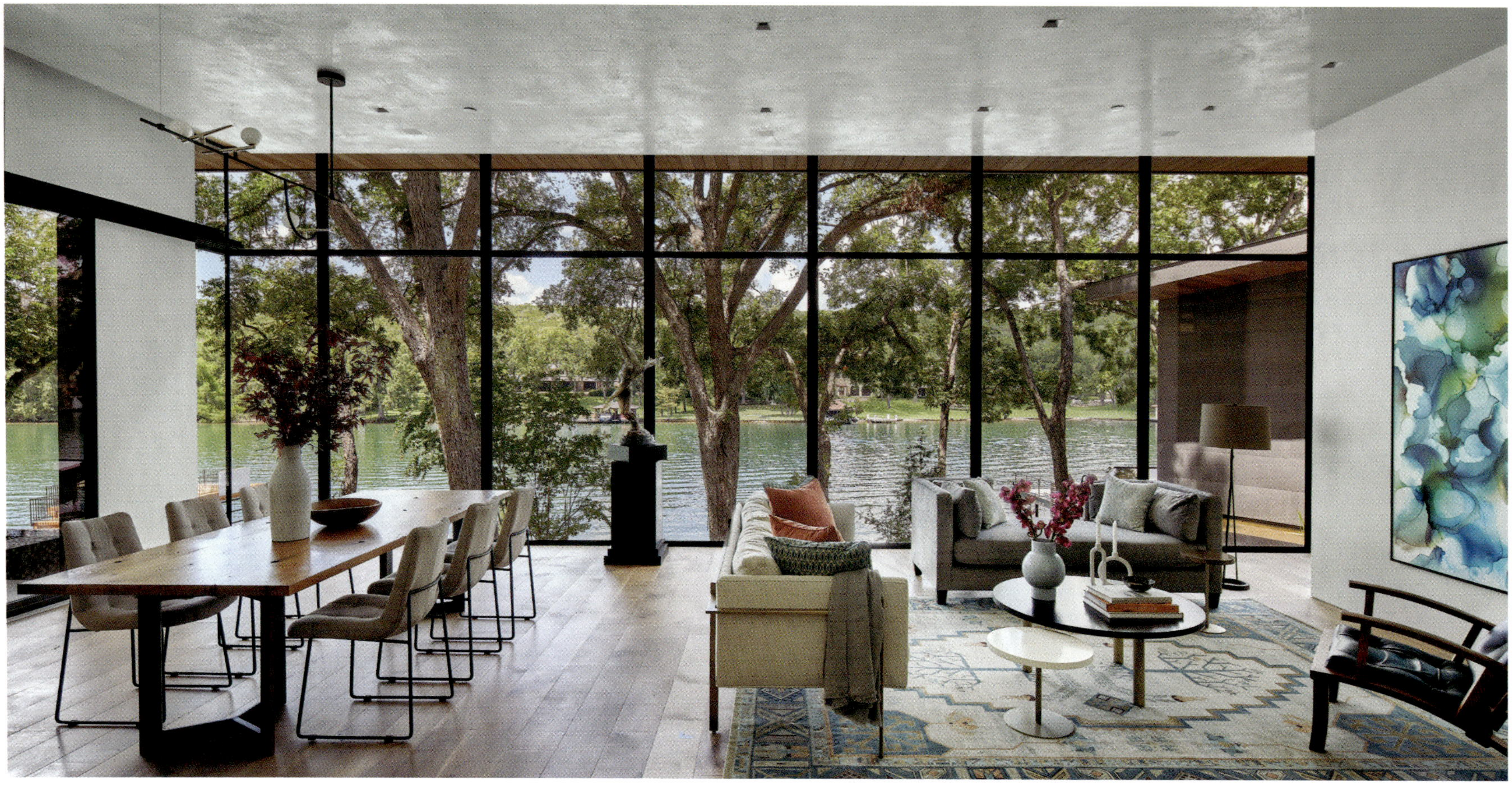

"The view out of the house is equally as stunning as the view of the house from the water." —James LaRue

ABOVE AND FACING PAGE: Located on a steeply sloped site above Lake Austin, this house has stunning views – and an outdoor living space that is just as much the heart of the home as its interior. The site-specific addition and remodel was designed in response to the two large oak trees on the property, with the structure tucking in between both. Vernacular limestone, metal wall panels, and warm wood respond to the region and the site. Photography by Dror Baldinger FAIA.

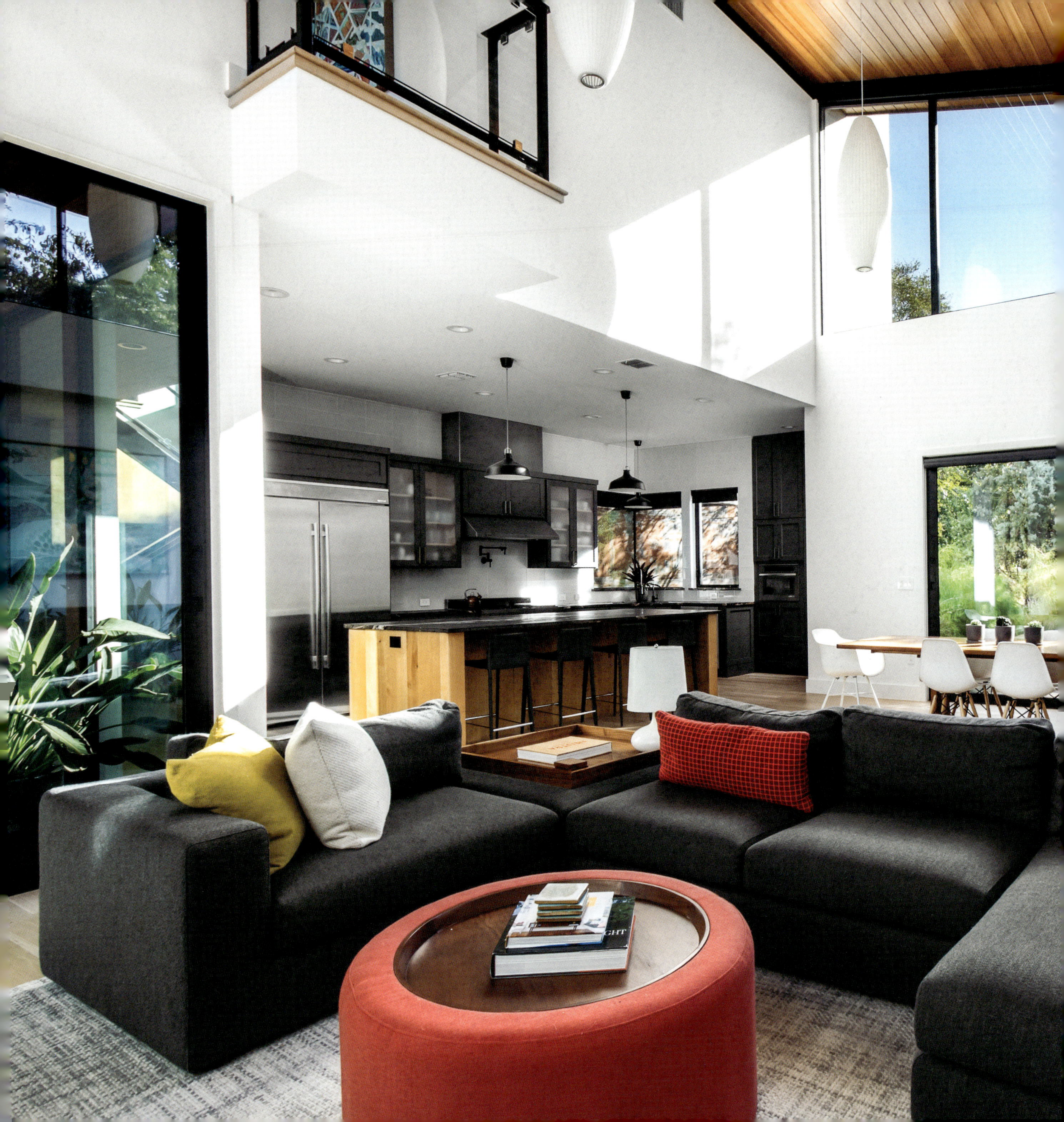

LEVESQUE & CO.

Levesque & Co. isn't just in the business of building high-quality homes, they build sanctuaries.

Nature, music, art, and more… these are the things that inspire Dominique Levesque and his team of skilled craftsmen and project managers to create thoughtful, sacred spaces to inhabit.

"It's our firm belief that, in this day and age, to offset the busyness and complexity of modern life, it's vital to create a true respite, a sanctuary that rejuvenates the mind, body and spirit," says Dominique. "Achieving an elevated space starts with thoughtful design that merges aspects of nature seamlessly into the interior while manifesting excellence in the construction phase by paying careful attention to detail, all of which is reflected in an exceptional final product."

Indeed, creating exceptional work is something they've been doing for more than 20 years, collaborating with architects, designers, and homeowners to build expertly crafted homes – ones that are carefully considered during each phase of the building process, all the way down to the landscape.

"We consider ourselves not just capable constructors, but also savvy artisans who can easily implement the architect's and designer's vision into a functional and beautiful reality," adds Dominique. "It's something that makes us just a little different from other builders."

FACING PAGE: This expansive and cozy interior highlights vertical-grain Douglas fir ceilings, which complement structural steel beams and extra-large Herman Miller cigar pendants. Generous amounts of light allow for the seamless blend of indoors and out, giving this home a sanctuary-like feel in the heart of the city. Photography by Brian Cole.

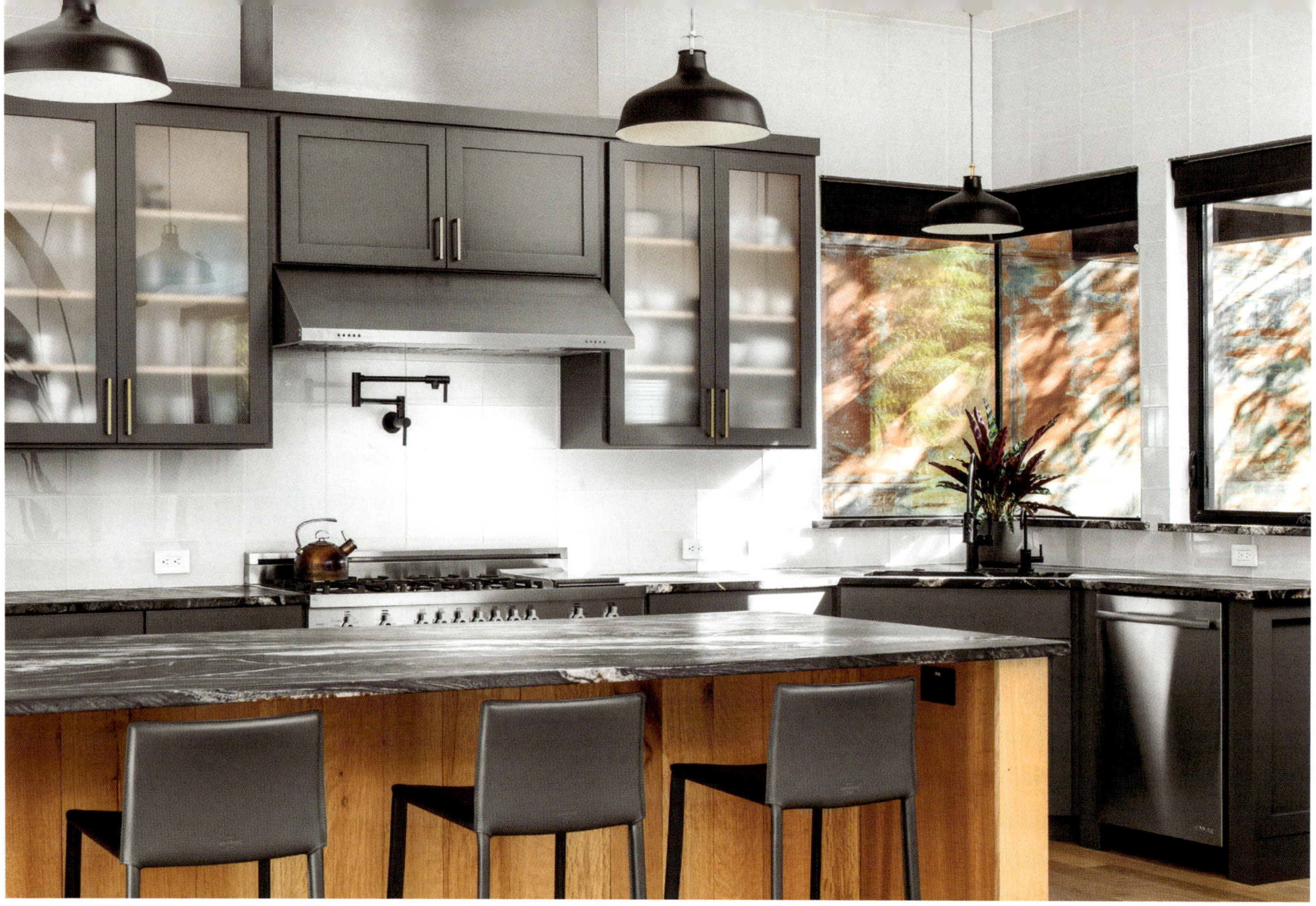

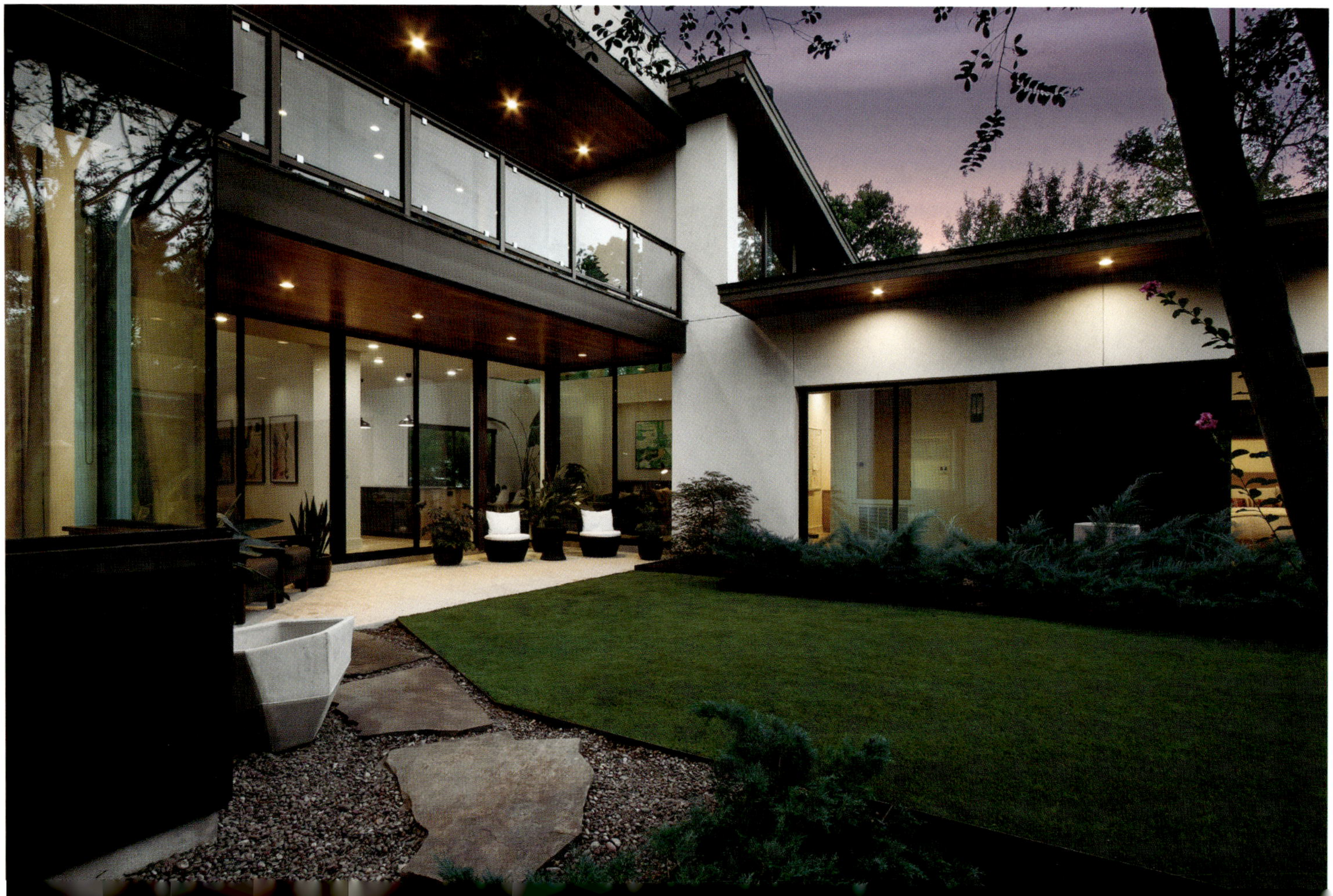

"Our desire is to make each project not just a home, but a sanctuary." —Dominique Levesque

THIS PAGE AND FACING PAGE: The unique use of steel plate, stucco, and glass behind the verdant landscape creates an unimposing yet bold modern structure. Photography by Brian Cole.

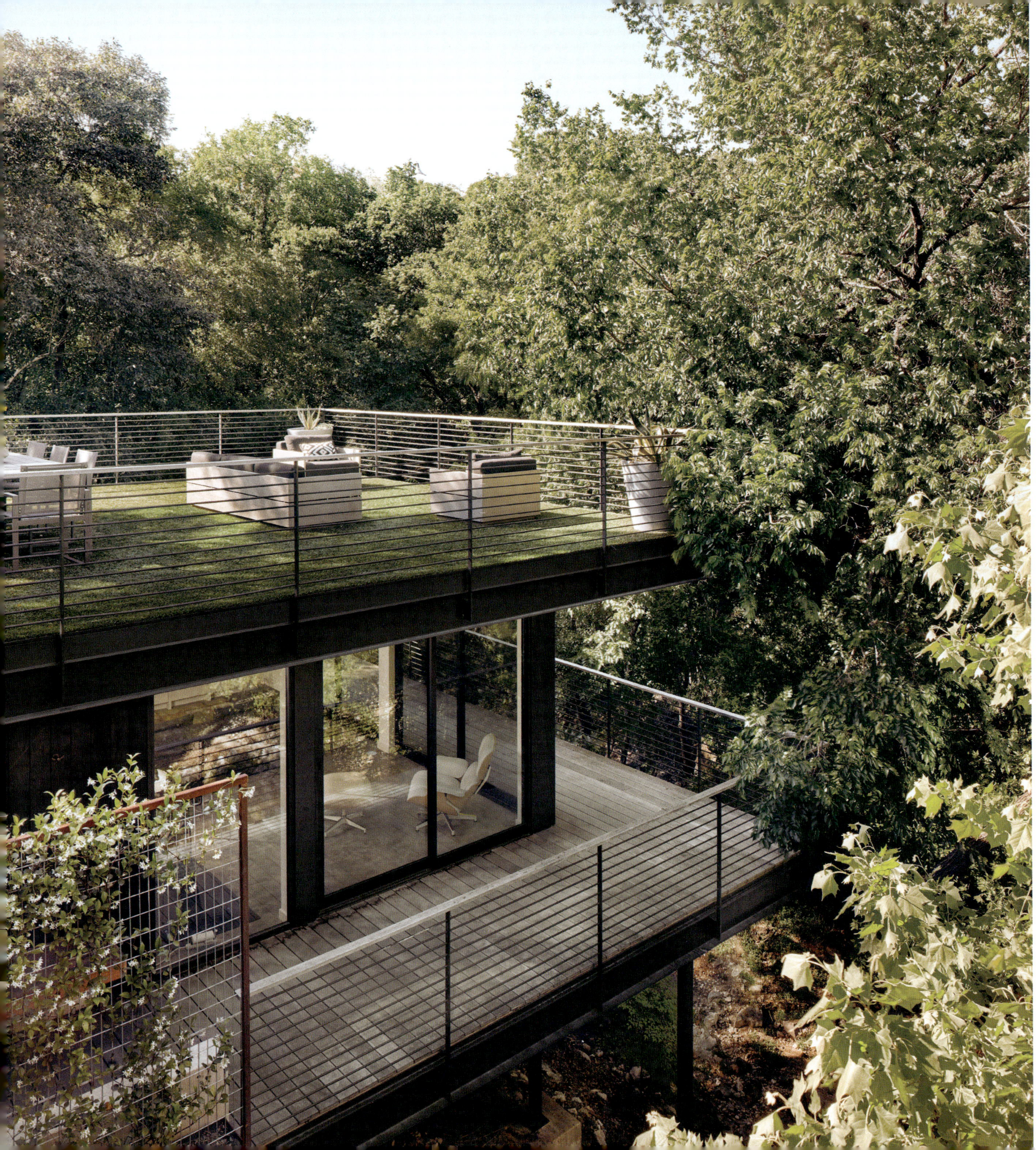

M

MATT GARCIA DESIGN

Started in 2011, Matt Garcia Design (MGD) is a boutique, residential design firm based in Austin, with an emerging national presence and clientele.

To experience an MGD-designed space is to be inspired by possibility – a timeless, modern design defined by thoughtful and meticulous attention to detail. Each project is an expression of the unique chemistry forged between client and designer. The firm's focus on client care and education elevates the process, leading to architecture full of energy, warmth, strength, tranquility, and rigor. Design solutions operate on multiple levels, from serving the practical needs of physical place and shelter to kindling more abstract expressions of personality and emotion.

As the firm has grown, it has developed a dedicated following of high-profile clients and collaborators, many of whom have become beloved friends and supporters as well as repeat patrons and design partners.

FACING PAGE: A beautiful, untouched site that was deemed "too steep" to build on – dropping 50 feet down to a dry creek full of wildlife and nature – became the home of the Stratford Creek residence. Large expanses of glass on the creek side give the homeowners a sense of floating above the creek from the living spaces and main bedroom.

TOP: The home was designed as two boxes: a two-story main living space for the homeowners and a separate, one-story guest house connected by a carport. Outdoor living areas offer additional space for entertaining – and enjoying the surrounding views.

MIDDLE: The main bedroom is flooded with natural light and treetop views.

BOTTOM: The really special quality about the home and site is that it feels like you are in the wild, yet you are only minutes away from downtown Austin and Zilker Park.
Photography by Casey Dunn.

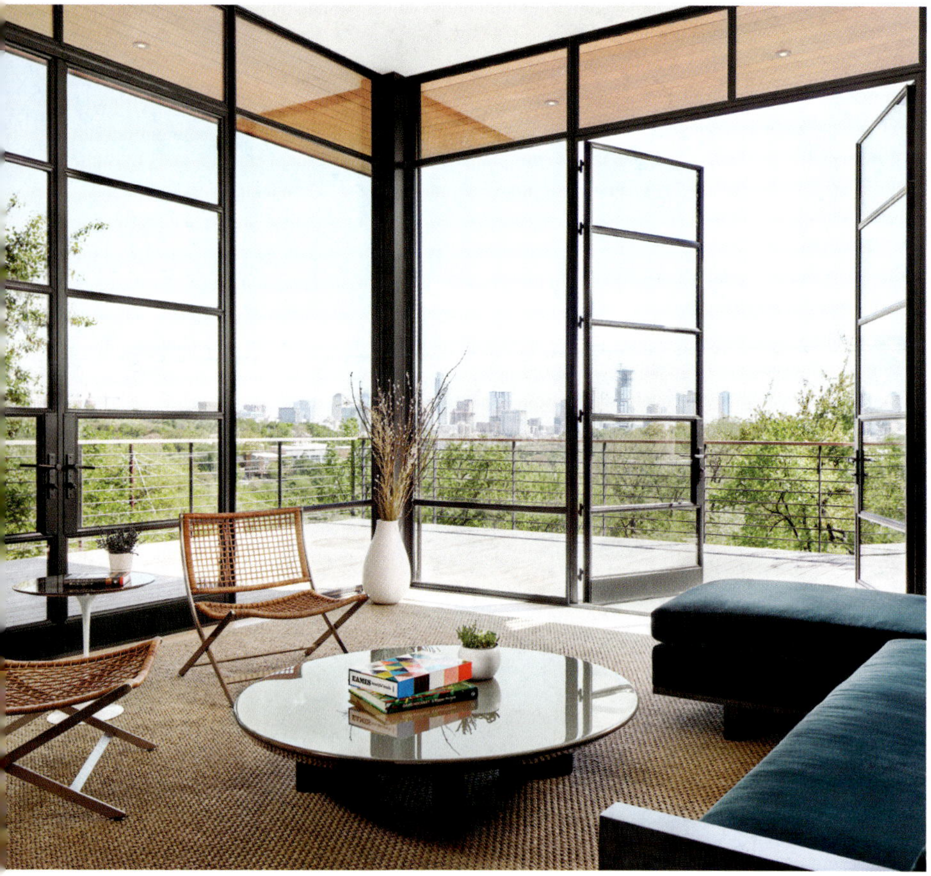

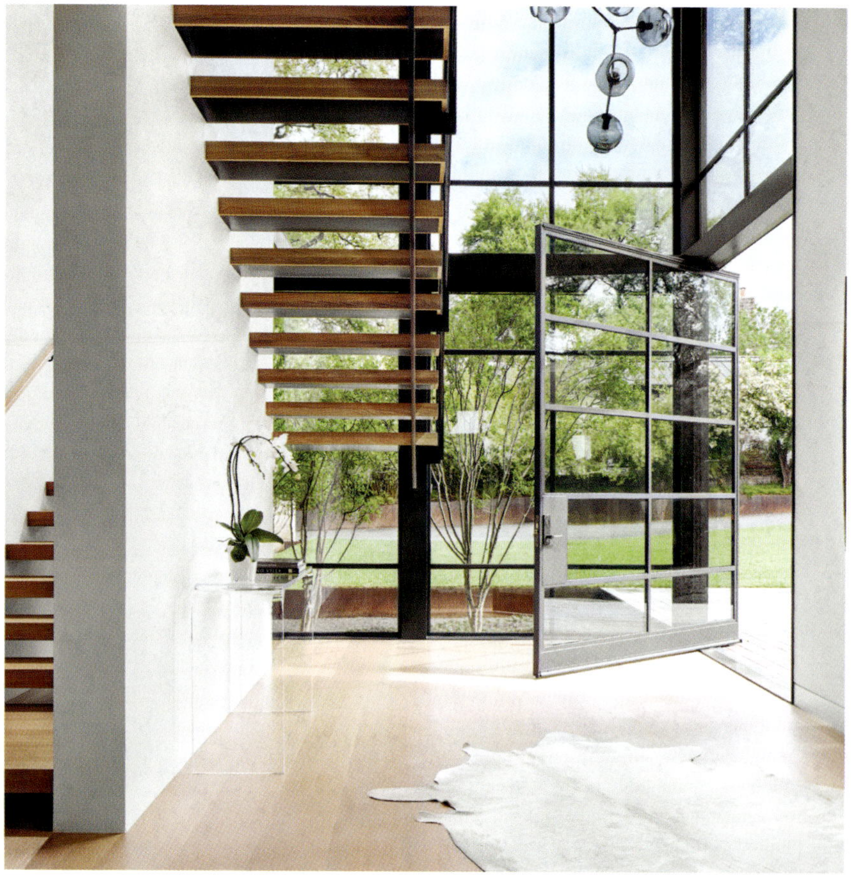

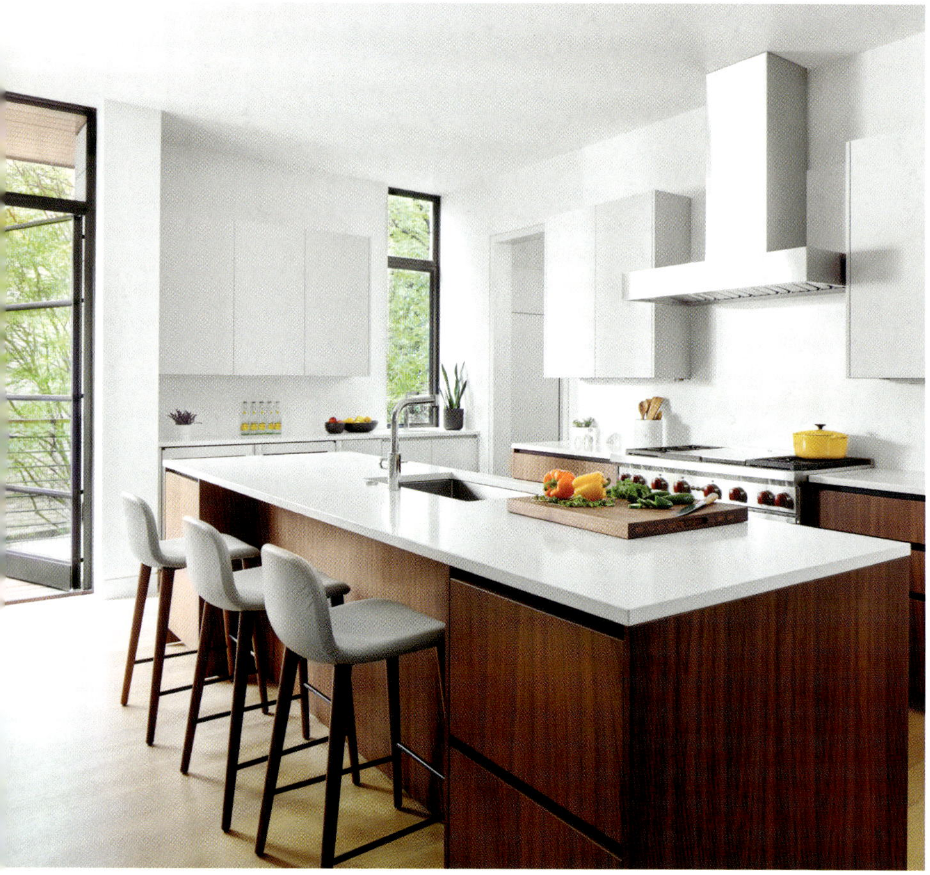

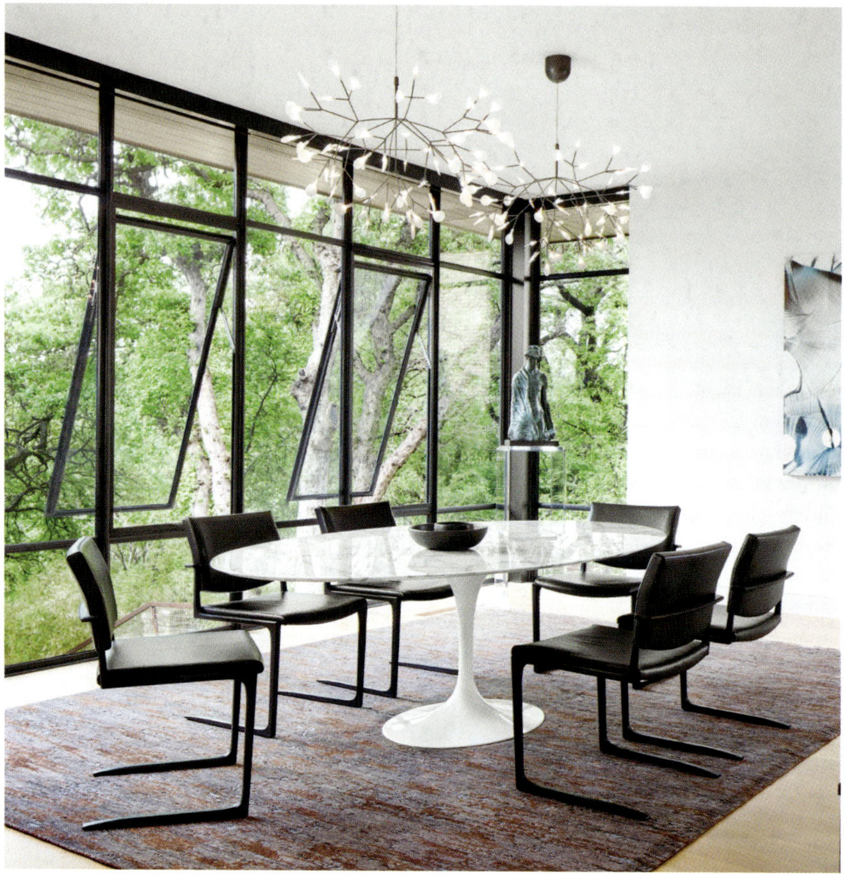

"Views reveal themselves slowly, as one makes way through the space culminating in a one-of-a-kind view from the casual sitting area at the far edge of the house where expansive windows connect interior to exterior." —Matt Garcia

ABOVE: A modern treehouse, the Pemberton Place residence is nestled between large heritage oak trees on a rare, one-acre lot in West Austin. A floating Ipe bridge leads to the front entry — a double-height glass box that contrasts with the cut limestone and western red cedar, offering a visual connector between the horizontal volumes.

FACING PAGE TOP LEFT: Floor-to-ceiling windows throughout offer unparalleled views of the ever-changing downtown Austin skyline.

FACING PAGE TOP RIGHT: The large steel and glass pivot door opens to an ornamental staircase of steel and white oak, which provides a glimpse of the minimal yet complex interior detailing.

FACING PAGE BOTTOM LEFT: The kitchen maintains a similar minimal aesthetic with rift-sawn white oak floors and cabinets paired with Venetian plaster walls.

FACING PAGE BOTTOM RIGHT: The wall of windows creates the experience of dining in the treetops. Photography by Casey Dunn.

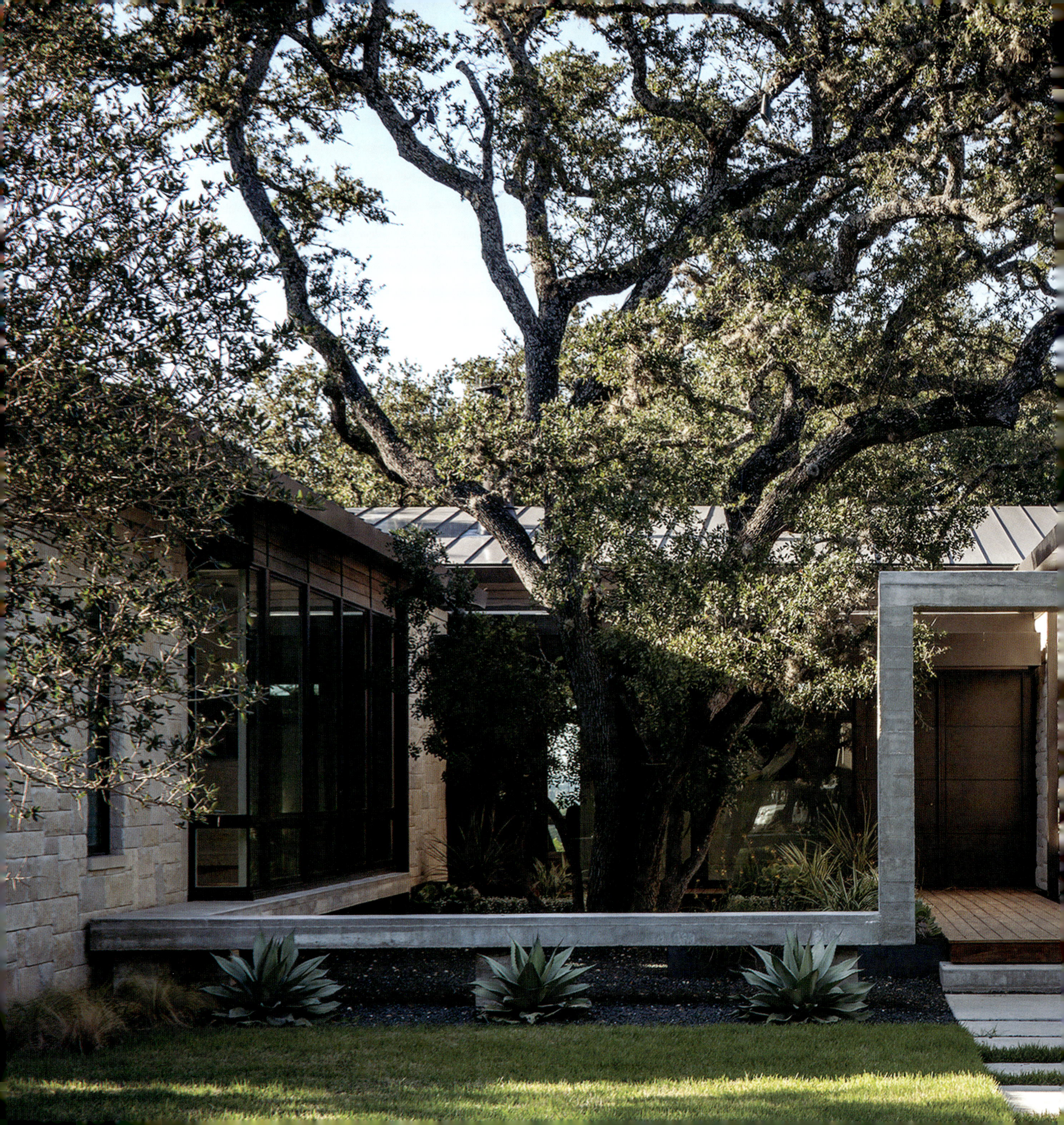

MCKINNEY YORK ARCHITECTS

Engage. Inspire. Belong. At McKinney York Architects, we believe the world is better when everyone feels connected to the people and places that surround them. Our Ridge Oak Residence transforms the flat-topped ridge it occupies into a choreographed sequence of spaces, each offering a curated experience of the art within and landscape without. Visitors pass through an entry portal formed by a ribbon of concrete which signals the transition into a zen-like courtyard. Here, the home embraces a massive heritage live oak, deferring to the spread of its canopy and sheltering a deep front porch. An elevated boardwalk bridges the portal and the porch, terminating at an opaque front door that directs guests' eyes to an adjacent gallery wall. These elements create a deceptively quiet architecture that shapes a dialogue between the structure and the landscape. Perched above Lake Austin with an expansive view of the Pennybacker Bridge and greenbelt beyond, the house is rooted to its place.

Inside, a vibrant collection of School of Paris paintings is the focal point of every space, from the living room, to gallery halls, to the kitchen. Gathered throughout the homeowners' marriage, the art collection engenders inspiration, visual pleasure, and fond memories for the homeowners. The scale, architectural detailing, and balanced natural light all contribute to highlighting the art, allowing it to animate the home. This home specifically belongs here and to these people.

FACING PAGE: Designed to thread through a stand of heritage live oaks, the Ridge Oak Residence genuflects to the trees. The roofs around the entry courtyard are angled to slip beneath the canopies, and the foundation cantilevers over critical root zones. At the entry, a floating concrete ribbon extends from the foundation to enclose the courtyard, folding and twisting to define an entry portal. Photography by Thomas McConnell.

"The scale, architectural detailing, and balanced natural light all contribute to highlighting the art, allowing it to animate the home". —Heather McKinney

ABOVE: The kitchen was designed to maximize wall space to host additional small artworks. An adjacent butler's pantry allows the owners to pare the kitchen down to the things they need on a daily basis while displaying and enjoying their paintings. Infrastructure is cleverly concealed behind custom slatted wood screens to minimize visual clutter and not distract from the art.

FACING PAGE TOP: The entry portal leads to an elevated boardwalk which begins the transition from landscape to structure. An opaque door blends into the surrounding façade and focuses the visitor's gaze on the adjacent gallery wall, where the owners' cherished art collection is introduced.

FACING PAGE BOTTOM: A subdued interior color palette provides a recessive backdrop for a vibrant collection of School of Paris paintings highlighted throughout the home. Gallery space is carefully juxtaposed with a generous use of glass to fill the home with balanced natural light and provide views of the trees and neighboring nature preserve.
Photography by Thomas McConnell.

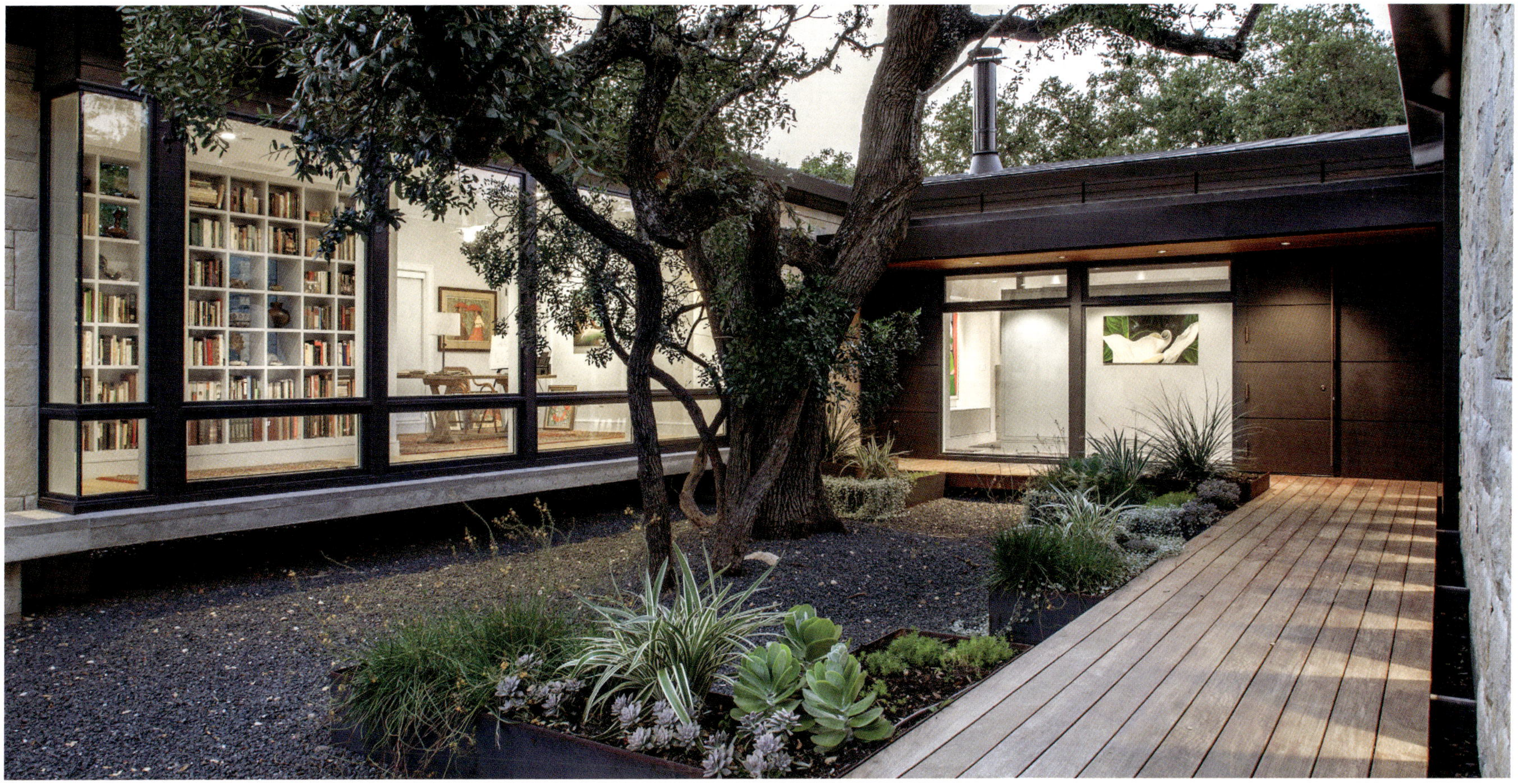

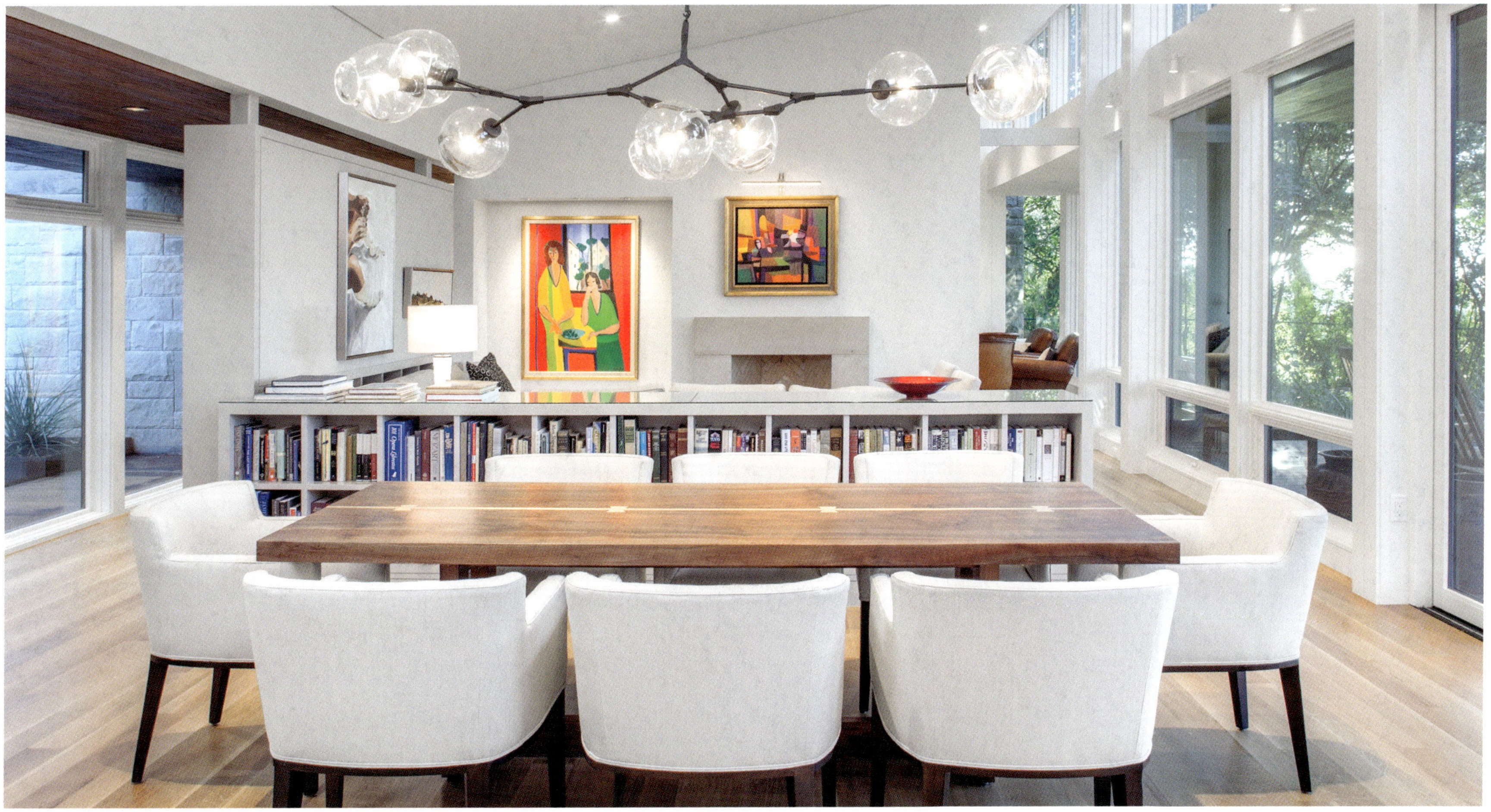

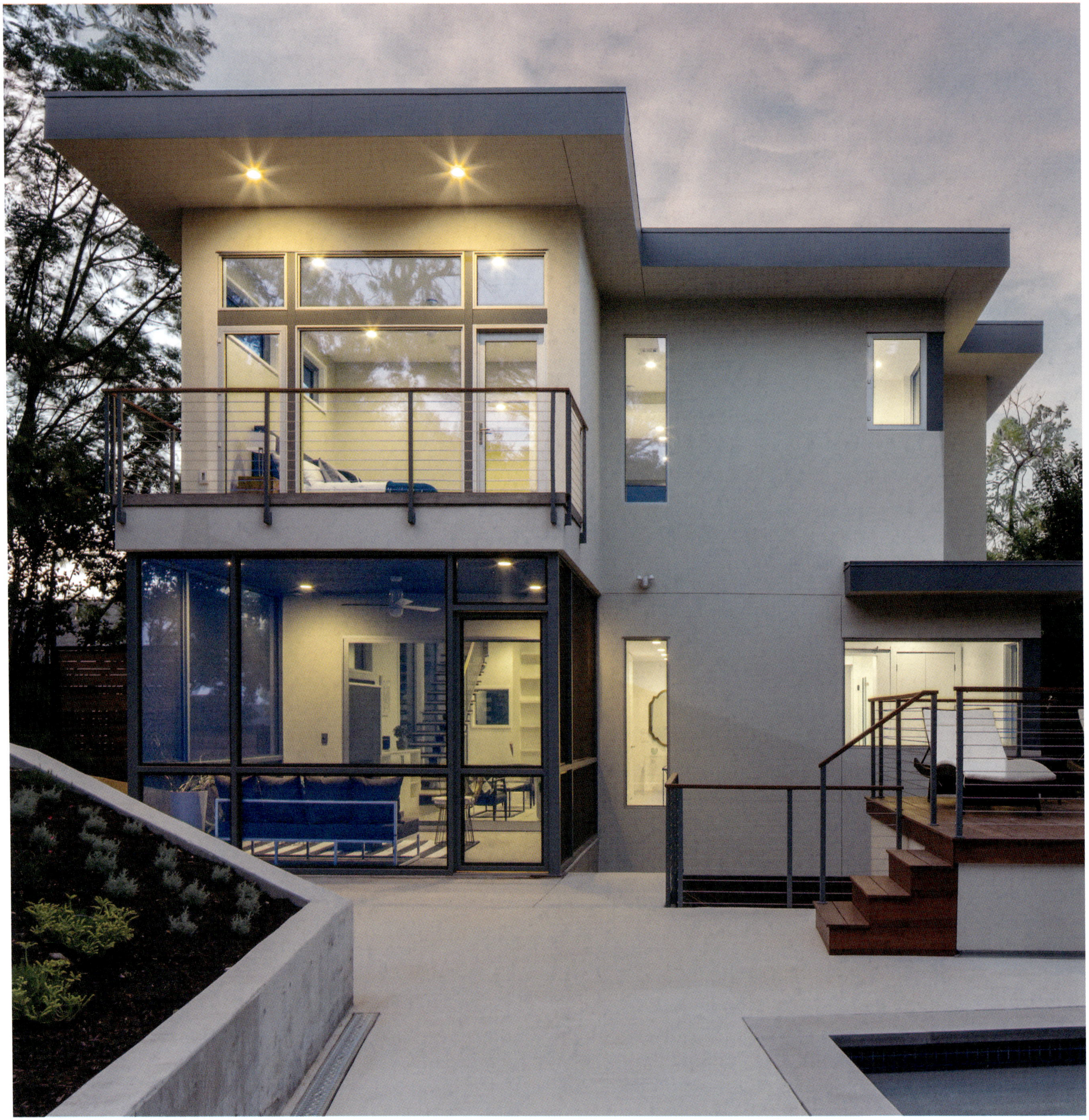

M MERZBAU DESIGN COLLECTIVE

Merzbau Design Collective principal J.C. Schmeil's strongest early memories are rooted in his experience of nature in the places he lived abroad, including Geneva, Stockholm, Abidjan, and Tokyo – or, more precisely, in how he perceived the intersection of nature and culture in those places. These perceptions defined his early understanding of architecture as active imagining, and he endeavors to create similar richness of experience in his own work.

A collaborative and iterative design process is central to the success of Merzbau's projects. They listen closely to clients' feelings about a space and anticipate how the homeowner might inhabit every room in different ways over time. This allows the team to tailor a design that welcomes active engagement and meets clients' needs while conforming to budget parameters.

By providing carefully considered views and access to the landscape, Merzbau also prioritizes the connection of a home to its site. Light, sound, and wind become materials in the creation of an architectural space. This sense of unity is of utmost importance to J.C. and his team because they believe thoughtfully considered design ultimately enhances our understanding of the world around us and allows us to experience harmony with our surroundings.

FACING PAGE AND TOP: The design of the Rutherford Residence addresses the dual nature of the site: intimate, lush, and steep toward the back; open and urban toward the front. The main bedroom suite, situated at the rear of the house, takes on a treehouse feel with a balcony overlooking the backyard and pool. Top photo by Brian Mihealsick. Facing page photo by Brian Cole.

BOTTOM: A steel-framed stair filters light from large windows on the west façade, rising toward the top floor living area and views facing Lady Bird Lake. Photography by Brian Cole.

"The simplicity and clarity of an architectural response evokes an awareness of one's environment."
—J.C. Schmeil, AIA

TOP AND FACING PAGE TOP: An 18-foot, multi-sliding patio door opens the living space to the pool and lounge, creating an urban oasis just a block from South Congress Avenue in the Bouldin Sisters Residence. Photography by Brian Mihealsick

LEFT: A restrained material palette and neutral tones accentuate the post-and-beam structure and help achieve a visually calm effect in the remodeled space of this Cat Mountain Residence. Photography by Leonid Furmansky

FACING PAGE BOTTOM: Reclaimed longleaf pine provides a warm complement to a steel and concrete screened porch, while layered views expand the space visually in the Kenwood Residence. Photography by Brian Mihealsick.

91

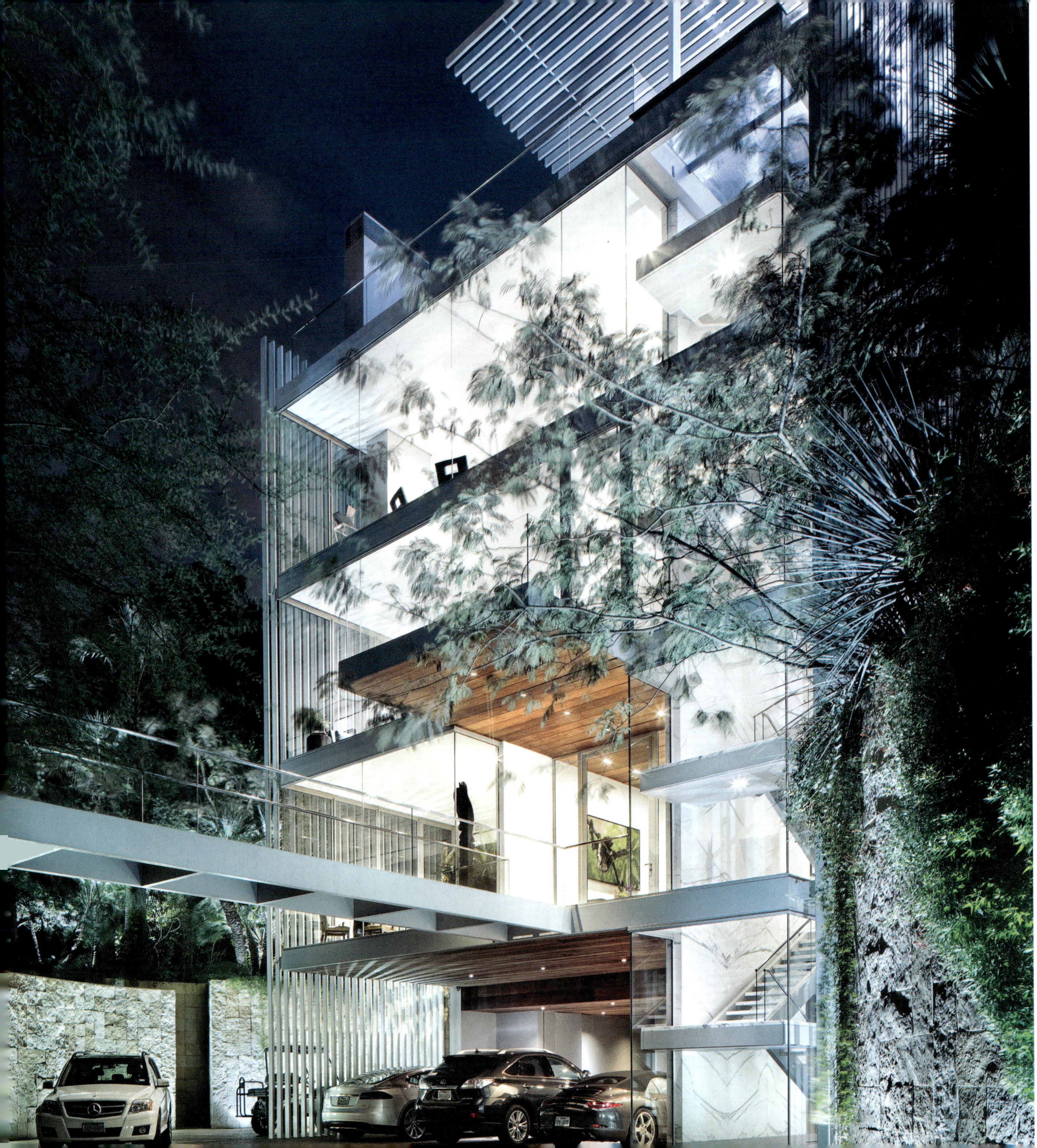

MIRÓ RIVERA
ARCHITECTS

Located on one of the few lots in Dallas elevated enough to enjoy a view of the downtown skyline, the five-story Vertical House rises dramatically above the treetops to capture views of the surrounding gardens and the skyline beyond. Characterized by clean lines, sheer glass walls, and sculptural sun shades, this sharply-detailed house offers an intriguing counterpoint to the tropical ambiance of its forest-like setting.

Starting at the lowest level, two 60-foot-tall exterior screen walls surge upward on both sides of the house, providing the home's primary structural support as well as offering shade and privacy to spaces within. The first floor of the residence—containing a carport and storage – is partially burrowed into the site and accessed via a spiraling driveway carved into the limestone bedrock. The main entrance to the house is located on the second floor (at natural grade), accessed via an exposed steel footbridge with glass handrails.

Balance, movement, proportion, rhythm: Design is artistry built for people's lives. The undeniably human element of architecture and design is a two-way street and only the best of the best master the balance of communication, collaboration, and creativity.

FACING PAGE: Moving vertically through the house from the entrance, every major space is immediately accessible from the glass-enclosed stairwell. Views outward become ever more impressive as the ground below falls away, and a palpable sense of suspension takes hold.

THIS PAGE TOP AND MIDDLE: Views are the focus of this home and all rooms point to the outdoors. The bathroom is a spa-inspired look with sublime marble walls and a rainhead shower. The bedroom will make you feel like you are in a treehouse as you overlook the island-style landscaped gardens.

BOTTOM: A detached pool house contains a gym and guest accommodations alongside a 65-foot lap pool. A tubular steel trellis echoes the design of the main house, in this case taking the form of a long, low-slung canopy. Photography by Paul Finkel.

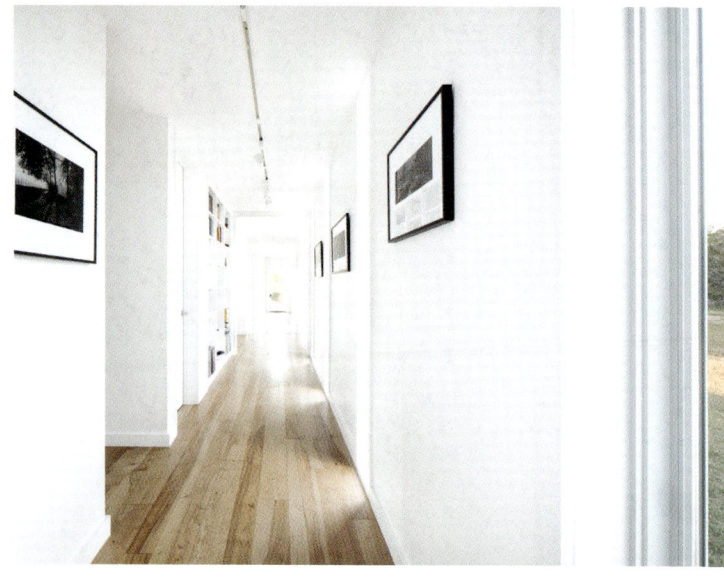

"It's a very complete project that spans all the aesthetic aspects of integration with the landscape, abstraction of the landscape, interpretation of rural architecture, and sustainability."
—AIA Design Awards Jury

TOP LEFT: Conceived as a prototype for a sustainable rural community, the Hill Country House serves as a beacon to show what could be: a self-sustaining home in a rural setting, virtually independent of municipal water and energy.

MIDDLE LEFT AND BOTTOM LEFT: The exterior of the home is defined by clean lines and a sculptural gable roof. The stark-white corrugated metal panel is broken at various intervals by warm cypress siding.

FACING PAGE TOP: Situated on a sweeping Texas Hill Country meadow, this private residence is defined by a series of jagged roof peaks inspired by the rise and fall of the surrounding hills. Lovingly referred to as "The Sanctuary" by its owners, an active retired couple, this modern take on the farmhouse vernacular is a place to bring people together and find spiritual renewal in a responsible, sustainable setting.

FACING PAGE BOTTOM: In every room, windows provide abundant natural light and frame views of the surrounding landscape. Throughout the interior, white walls and ceilings are offset by touches of limestone and soapstone, while pecan floors nod to the home's rustic locale. Photography by Paul Finkel.

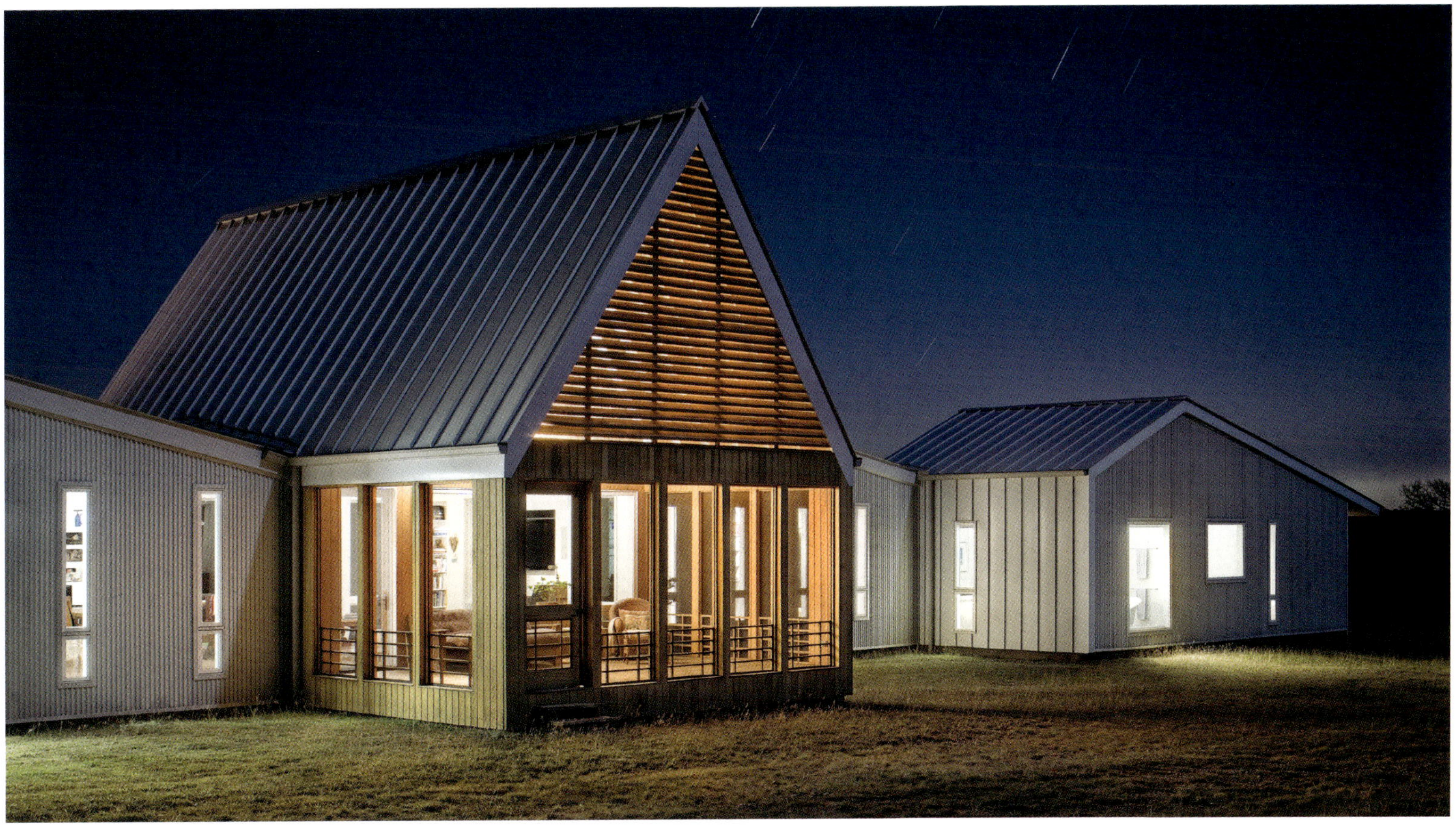

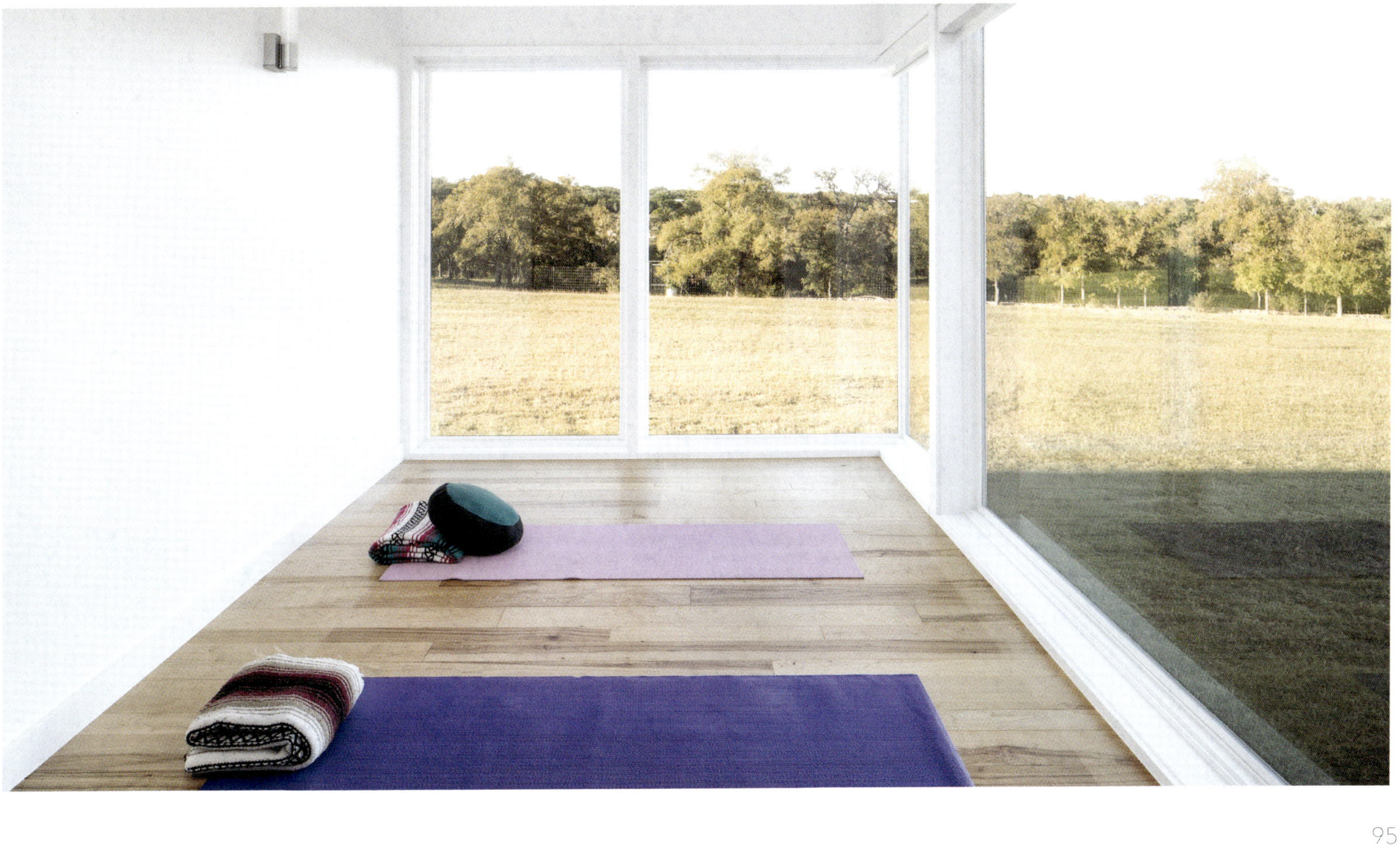

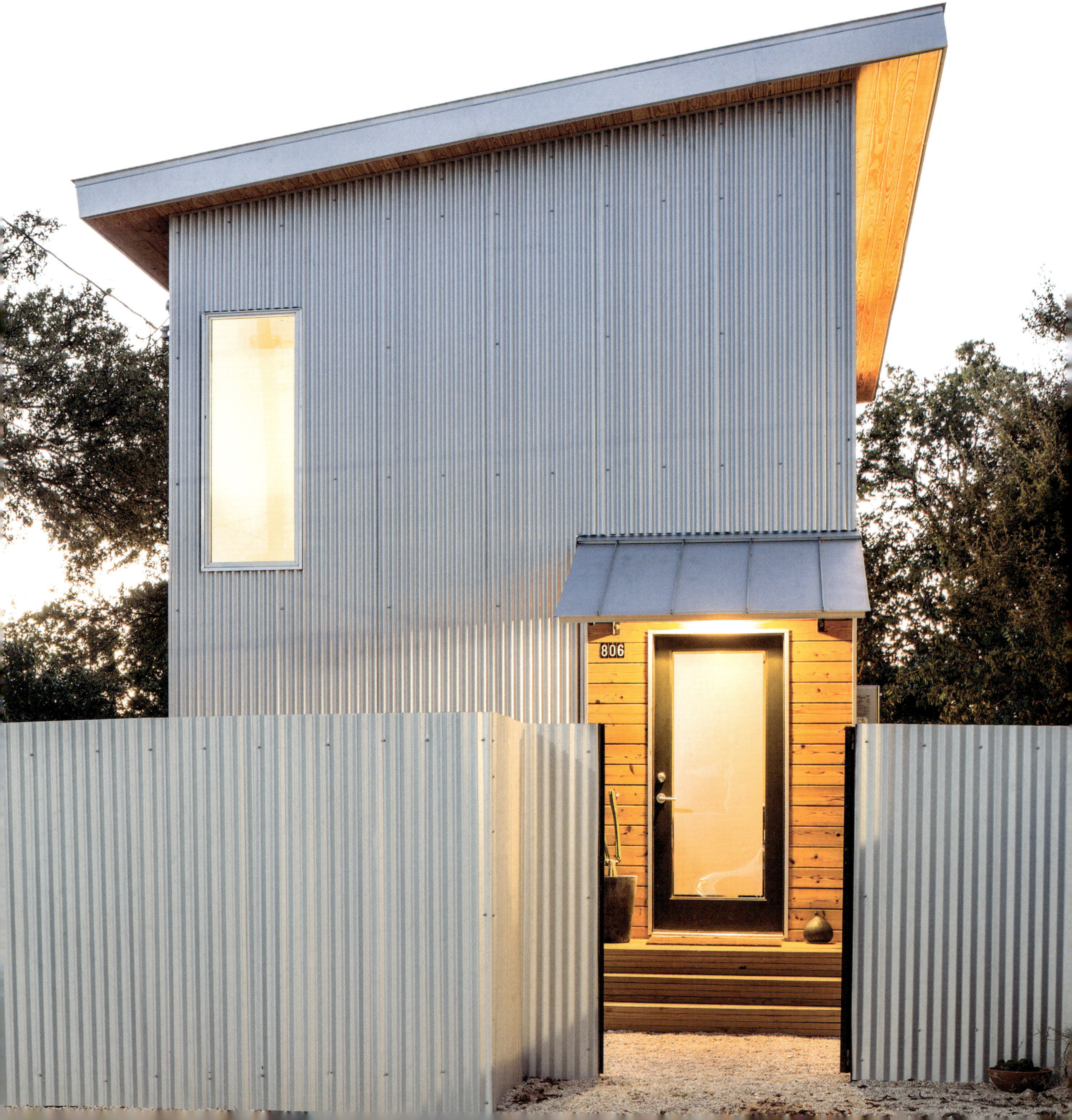
806

M MOONTOWER

The average home construction project often requires multiple, separate service providers — and homeowners are typically left juggling these critical relationships. It's a huge task that can easily become overwhelming for even the most experienced clients. It can also lead to unnecessary schedule delays, rising costs, and lots of personal stress.

That's where Moontower comes in. They believe there's a better way.

As a one-stop shop for architecture, construction, and interiors, they transform outdated homes, awkward structures, and raw land into beautiful, functional properties through an integrated, all-in-one approach.

That means they source or manage all required service providers, so the responsibility falls squarely on them which drastically simplifies the process, reduces stress, and eliminates redundant fees.

With Moontower, any renovation or new construction process is easily achievable. They're in the business of resetting any property to meet their clients' biggest dreams.

THIS PAGE AND FACING PAGE: A small, 1,100-square-foot home was the right solution for this client who wanted to create an East Austin abode on a tiny lot. By employing basic plywood, blackened steel, cedar and pine, and utilitarian lighting selections, Moontower created a space that embodies a minimal yet warm aesthetic. Every room is washed in natural light and all of the finishes are simple and durable. A limited palette of commonly used materials left room to create color and texture through art and objects. The back patio and a private entry courtyard allow for overflow areas when entertaining.
Photography by Jake Holt.

98

"By creating a modest addition and connecting the interior and exterior spaces, we extended the living area to create a comfortable home with room to grow." —Frank Farkash

THIS PAGE AND FACING PAGE: This artistic family of three loved their Highland mid-century home, but they knew it was too small and was also long overdue for repair. Their love for Marfa and passion for the Texas landscape inspired much of the aesthetic. Broad windows that match the height of the aluminum patio doors fill the new addition with light. The primary suite bathroom continues the aesthetic of the home. Photography by Melissa Preston.

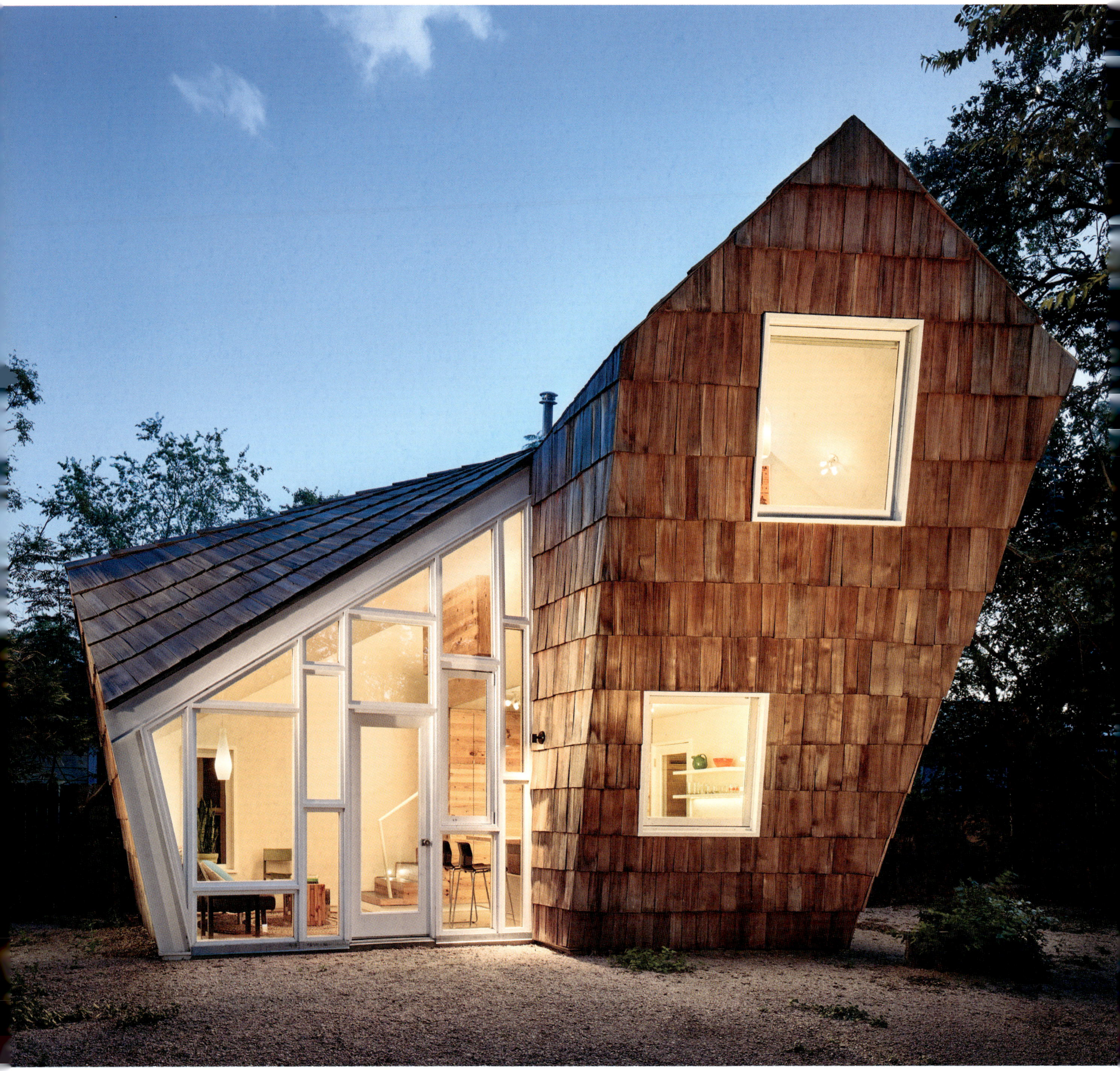

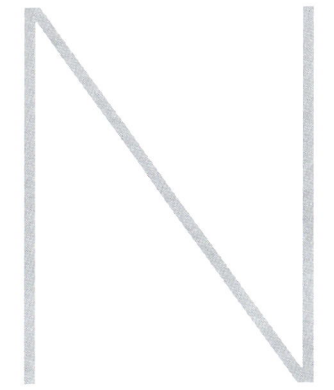

NICOLE BLAIR ARCHITECT

Austin native Nicole Blair established her award-winning architectural design firm, Studio 512, in 2004, rebranding as Nicole Blair Architect in 2019. For some of her more unique designs, like The Hive featured here, she also takes on the role of general contractor to build the project. Aaron Seward, editor of *Texas Architect*, said Nicole's projects "seek novel formal solutions to often mundane project types." With efficiency and the client's program in mind, Nicole carefully tailors the shape and detail of her buildings to succinctly solve all the issues at play. Nicole believes architects have a responsibility to minimize oversizing, avoid the use of new raw materials, and reduce energy consumption in their design solutions. Not only is this approach good for the environment, it also leads to pared-down, thoughtful, yet dynamic spaces crafted from local sources which enrich the overall experience. For a sole practitioner, collaboration is key – the relationships Nicole builds with clients, artisans, contractors, and subcontractors are directly reflected in the success of the end product. These relationships are as important to Nicole as the buildings themselves.

Nicole Blair's work has been published extensively – notably her 2015 project, The Hive, which was featured in *Architectural Record*. In 2019, the Texas Society of Architects named Studio 512 one of 10 Emerging Practices in Texas, and Nicole Blair was included in *Elle Decor's* A-list of Architecture as one of the 18 greatest living architects in the world alongside several Pritzker Prize winners.

THIS PAGE AND FACING PAGE: At 320 square feet, The Hive draws inspiration from Dutch and Japanese precedents that find creative solutions when faced with spatial constraints. To gain enough volume to fit a one-bedroom dwelling, walls tilt from the slab, evoking the shape of a beehive. Like a well-designed garment, a building performs best when tailored to the shape, movement, and environment of its inhabitants. Close examination of the actions performed in each space – sitting, sleeping, standing – informed the shape of The Hive. Kitchen walls lean out for increased counter space. Custom cabinet fronts and furnishings are made from reclaimed longleaf pine sheathing. Shou Sugi Ban flooring, stairs, desktop, and bedroom countertop material is produced locally. Cedar shake siding is repurposed roofing material from another house.
Exterior photography by Casey Dunn. Interior photography by Whit Preston.

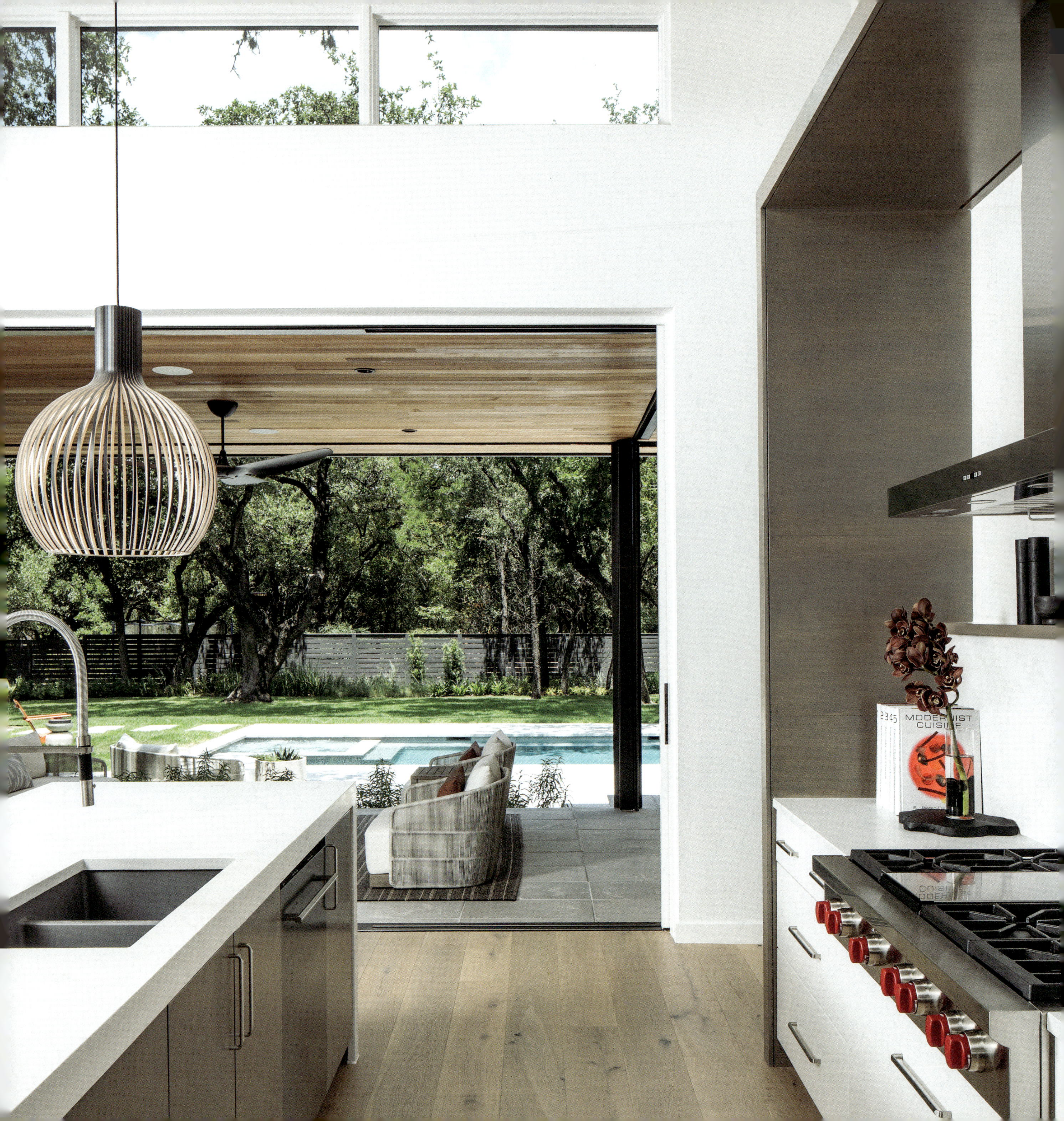

ROOST CUSTOM HOMES

If you ask ROOST's Dave Hernandez and Chad Watkins what they enjoy most about building livable, luxury homes, they'd tell you that it's the people. They appreciate the collaboration with talented architects, landscapers, and tradespeople; and they love working with clients to uniquely customize their homes for what's most important to them. "It's pretty fun to drive around Austin and see our portfolio standing strong and supporting happy, healthy lives," says Dave. Dave and Chad leverage decades of residential construction experience and detailed knowledge of code and building science to guide projects around the roadblocks and day-to-day issues that can derail budgets and timelines. After all, it's the "work behind the walls" that counts. "Trends and finishes come and go but a properly built structure will last many lifetimes," says Dave.

While they take their work and client needs very seriously, they are not self-serious. That means they approach problems as opportunities. They work with amazing partners and have fun with it – and homeowners enjoy the process every step of the way. They also consider their relationships with clients to be a partnership that extends long after the house is completed. When a massive snowstorm and power outage hit Texas in early 2021, ROOST was there to get clients back in a hot shower long before their neighbors – for houses they completed more than five years ago!

FACING PAGE: The kitchen is framed by a grain matched, white oak surround at the range top. The pocketing Weather Shield sliding door opens to an expansive rear patio featuring a vertical grain cedar soffit and recessed motorized screens. Clerestory windows allow for additional light to truly embrace indoor-outdoor living.

TOP: The varied material palette of the exterior enhances the linear nature of the architecture. The horizontal Corso brick, imported from Italy, and the vertical Shou Sugi Ban siding, produced locally at Delta Millworks, provide contrast. The steel fin wall and clear cedar soffit give the appearance that the roof over the entry is almost floating.

BOTTOM: An open dining plan brings the kitchen and living area together, while also remaining attuned to the outdoors. Furnishings and art are by Kelle Contine Interior Design.
Photography by Jake Holt.

"Trends and finishes come and go, but a properly built structure will last many lifetimes."
—Dave Hernandez

TOP: The ample eat-in kitchen is streamlined with perfect symmetry, as it flows effortlessly to the outdoors.

MIDDLE: Wraparound, blackout shades from Texas Sun and Shade are both functional and beautiful for this otherwise light-filled bedroom. The feature wall is a ceramic tile, designed to look like wood, for an organic approach to the walls.

BOTTOM: This backlit mirror, designed by Kelle Contine Interior Design, is a beautiful addition in the bathroom, which also features grain-matched white-oak cabinets with a waterfall detail that meets a deep tub recessed into the foundation.

FACING PAGE TOP AND BOTTOM RIGHT: Outdoor living is elevated even more with the covered porch along with a pool by Modern Design Build. The landscaping, designed by Lionheart Landscape Architects, enhances the natural feel of the property and embraces the many mature native Texas live oaks that initially drew the owners to the site.

FACING PAGE BOTTOM LEFT: The pool was designed to align views from multiple vantage points within the home. Photography by Jake Holt.

105

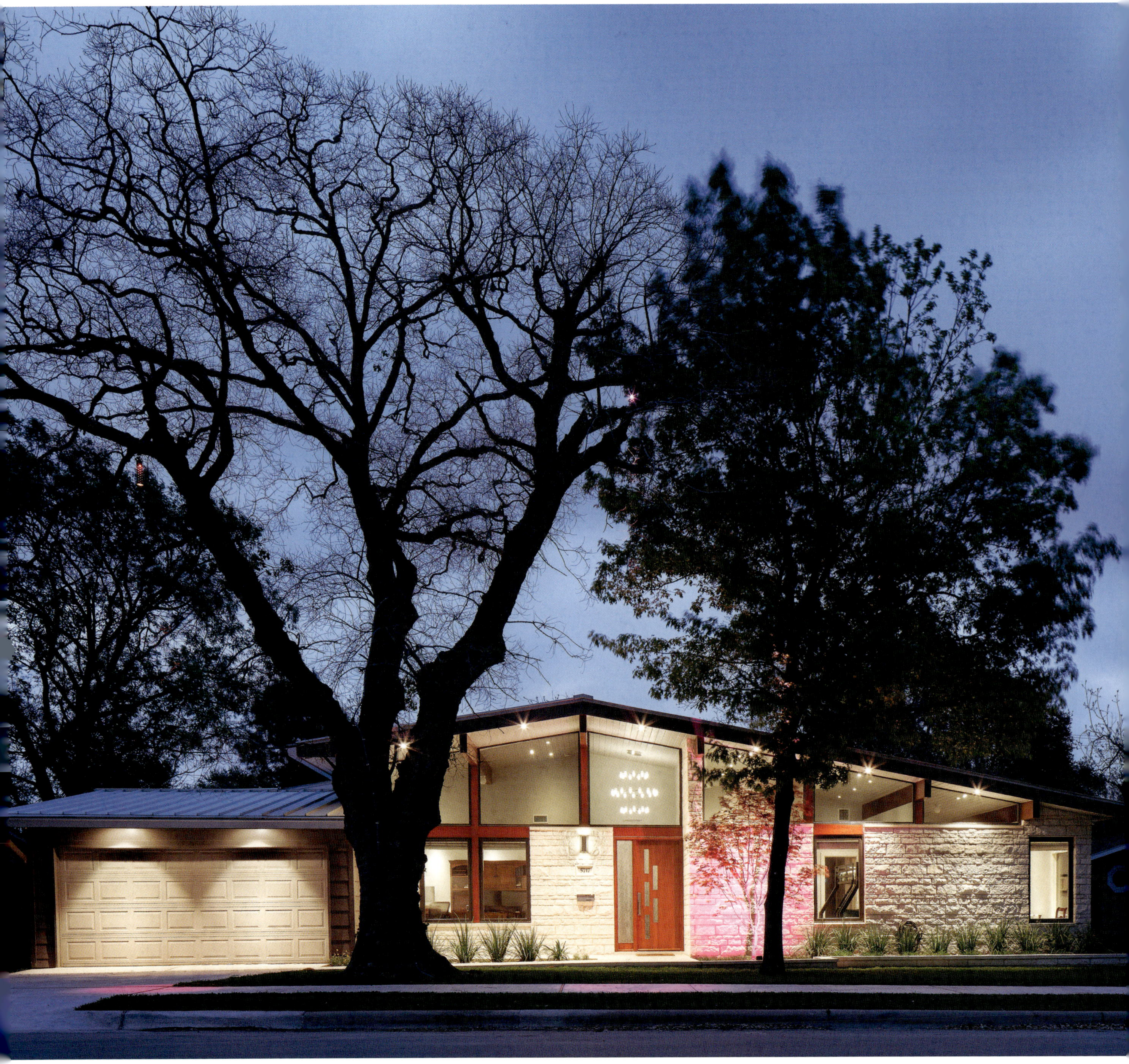

STUDIO STEINBOMER

Studio Steinbomer is a dedicated and talented team of design professionals led by Robert Steinbomer, AIA, Amy Bramwell, AIA, Jennifer Vrazel, AIA, and Jed Duhon, AIA, LEED AP. The team takes pride in their collaborative culture; it's what inspires them to develop strong client relationships. It's important to them that all clients are involved in each project in its entirety – from start to finish. Residential, commercial, historical, and institutional clients are all integral parts of this creative process.

Developing and nurturing client relationships is not only exhilarating for all parties involved, it also allows each partner to immerse themselves fully into their clients' vision and goals. While Studio Steinbomer gravitates towards a modern and contemporary style, the team has versatility that primarily focuses on their clients' aesthetic. The team also finds it imperative to take into consideration the context of each project, including the neighborhood and nature surrounding it. For 30 years and counting, Studio Steinbomer's ultimate commitment to quality, meaningful collaboration, and context-driven design continues to consistently produce artful, sensible, and value-conscious results.

FACING PAGE: The Allandale Midcentury Remodel was designed to be complementary in size, scale, and style to the neighborhood of mostly 1950s ranch houses.

TOP: The open concept kitchen and living room with light colors on the walls provide a brightly lit, ample space for family gatherings.

MIDDLE: The owner was recognized as a "Net-Zero Hero" by the City of Austin's Office of Sustainability. His dedication to sustainable systems in their home is exemplary.

BOTTOM: A metal roof with ample overhangs protect the interior, and tall, northeast-facing, high-efficiency windows allow for natural daylighting. Photography by Leonid Furmansky.

"The stone masonry carefully transitions between interior and exterior spaces, creating a cohesive language among the surrounding Texas Hill Country landscape and the home's modern architectural style."
—Ben Pruett

TOP: The Reimers Road Residence expresses modernity while remaining homey with its warm tones and balanced palette of materials.

BOTTOM LEFT AND RIGHT: The masonry walls became the anchors for the design, fulfilling the family's desire for the home to act as a threshold from the road to the openness of the Texas Hill Country.

FACING PAGE TOP: Sited at the edge of a bluff, this residence was designed to take full advantage of the fantastic northern views of the Texas Hill Country.

FACING PAGE BOTTOM: Cool concrete floors and white walls catch the sunlight that focuses the eye toward inviting colors, walnut fixtures, limestone accents, and vibrant green plants. Photography by Andrea Calo.

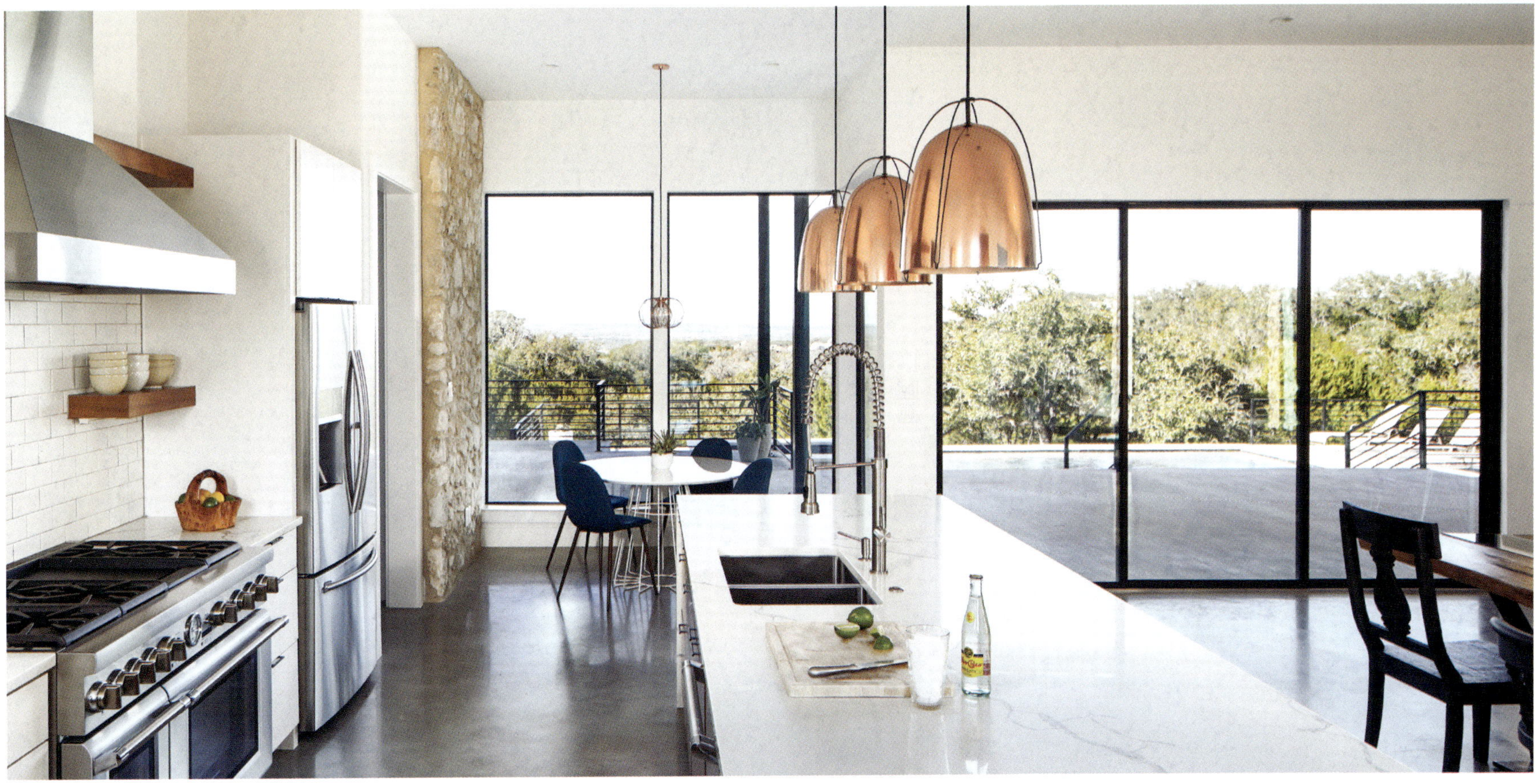

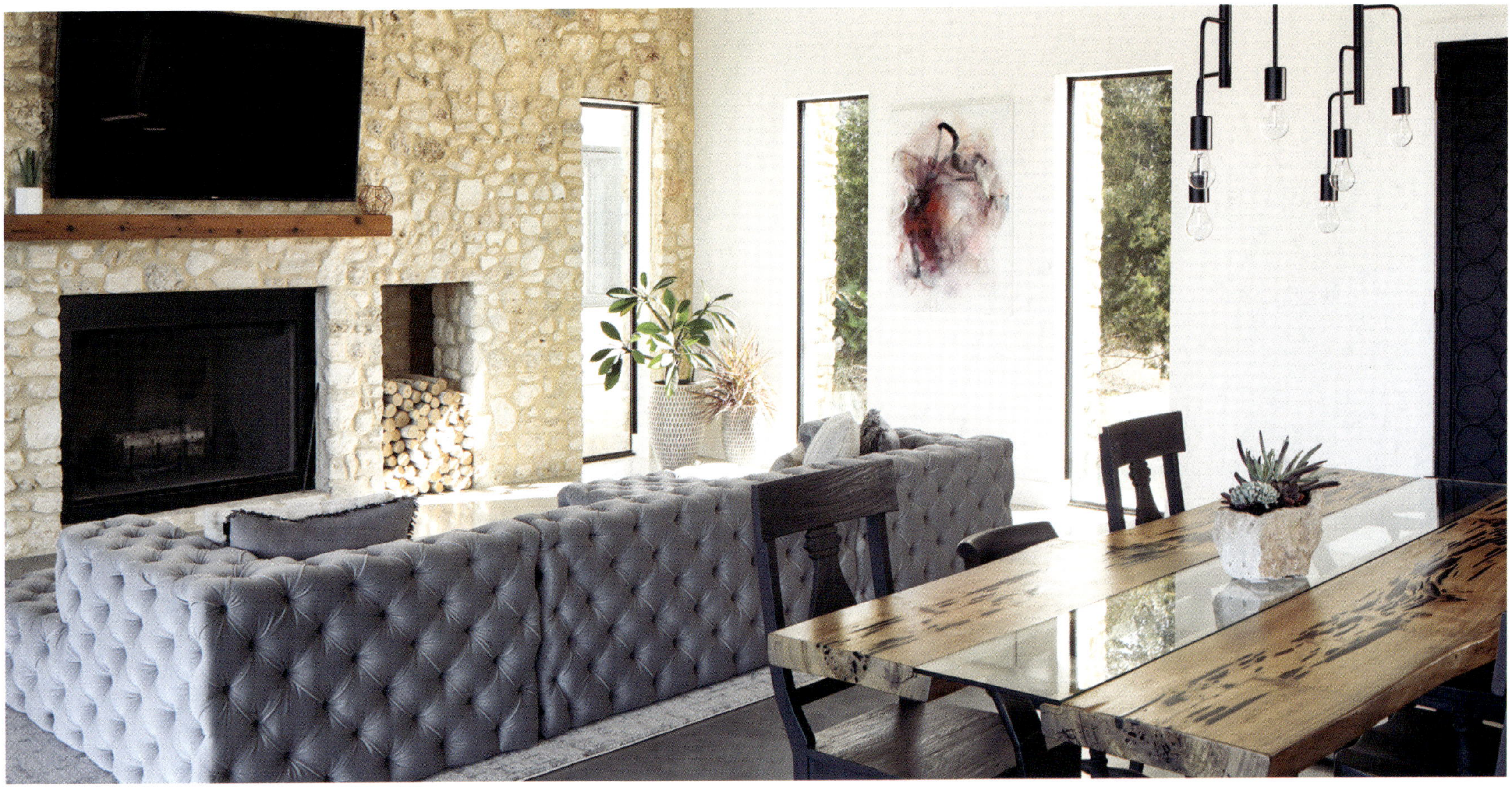

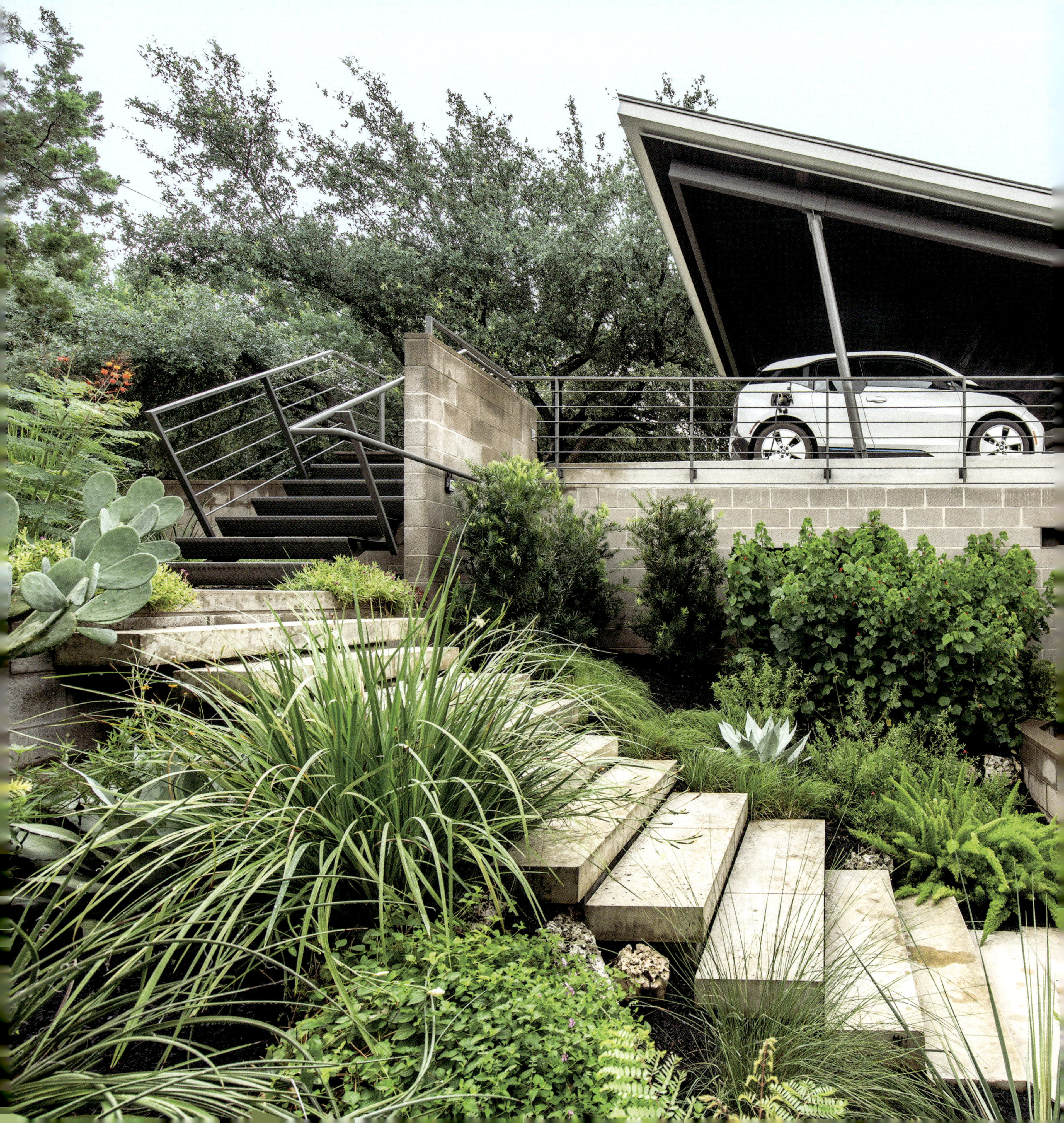

TOM HURT ARCHITECTURE

Having worked as a general contractor, framer, and carpenter early in his career, Tom Hurt, AIA, approaches design with a hands-on understanding of structure and construction. What that means for his award-winning architectural practice is that he and his team pursue, through design, uncommon beauty in common materials. It's one of the things they find most exciting across their full suite of services, from building design and master planning, to interior finish selection and exterior hard-scaping.

Tom Hurt Architecture's work, which encompasses residential, commercial, nonprofit, and multi-family buildings in Austin, San Francisco, and Germany, is known for its well-proportioned, dynamic forms and spaces as well as sensitive relationships to its site. The firm designs highly sustainable buildings – limiting building size by careful study of clients' needs and reusing and re-adapting buildings and building materials where possible. They've also developed exceptional daylighting expertise and the use of familiar, cost-appropriate building materials and construction techniques to create warm and unique projects.

"We pride ourselves on creating extraordinary experiences," says Tom. "Often a modern experience, a connected experience to light, the site and so many other things, can be achieved by just carefully arranging the same materials used in a more conventional house to create something really remarkable."

FACING PAGE: The narrow and steep wooded site offered opportunities to explore how the 2,200-square-foot Canyon Edge house sits on the hillside, responds to the natural environment, and how it is approached by vehicle. Photography by Adam Barbe.

"Part of the beauty of architecture is not unlike the fundamental beauty of art; it is a discovery of what is valuable and meaningful among the sensory overload and the abundance of the environment."
—Tom Hurt

TOP: The roof over the Canyon Edge carport welcomes the approaching driver, allowing the car to virtually enter the interior space and share the canyon view. The parked cars rest over the kitchen and are visible and present from the living area. Photography by Adam Barbe.

MIDDLE: The Canyon Edge living and exterior deck are at a level that floats beyond and over a natural ledge on the site, with the deck cantilevering into the canopy of the trees and creek valley below. Photography by Patrick Wong.

BOTTOM: Canyon Edge fits the eclectic, busy lifestyle of the client – a young family of four – who wanted an efficient house that carried a light ecological footprint. Photography by Adam Barbe.

FACING PAGE TOP LEFT: Westrock is an 1,100-square-foot structure that emerged from the existing low-slung home in Austin. In the lower levels of the addition, it carves itself into the center of the main house at the location of the original kitchen and living room. Photography by Ryan Farnau.

FACING PAGE TOP RIGHT: The white stucco tower of Westrock contrasts with the original, modest, low-slung 1950s residence. The tower is a stack of interlocking spaces: a sitting area, two offices, a reading room, a play loft, and two exterior observation decks. Photography by Ryan Farnau.

FACING PAGE BOTTOM: The Westrock project uses a network of exposed, stained, standard-lumber framing and digitally-fabricated plywood shapes – as work surfaces, benches, storage, shelves, and railings. The CNC-cut plywood was used to reduce cabinetry and carpentry costs and create built-in furniture on many of the walls to wring as much usable area out of the mostly small spaces. Photography by Shutterbug Studios.

113

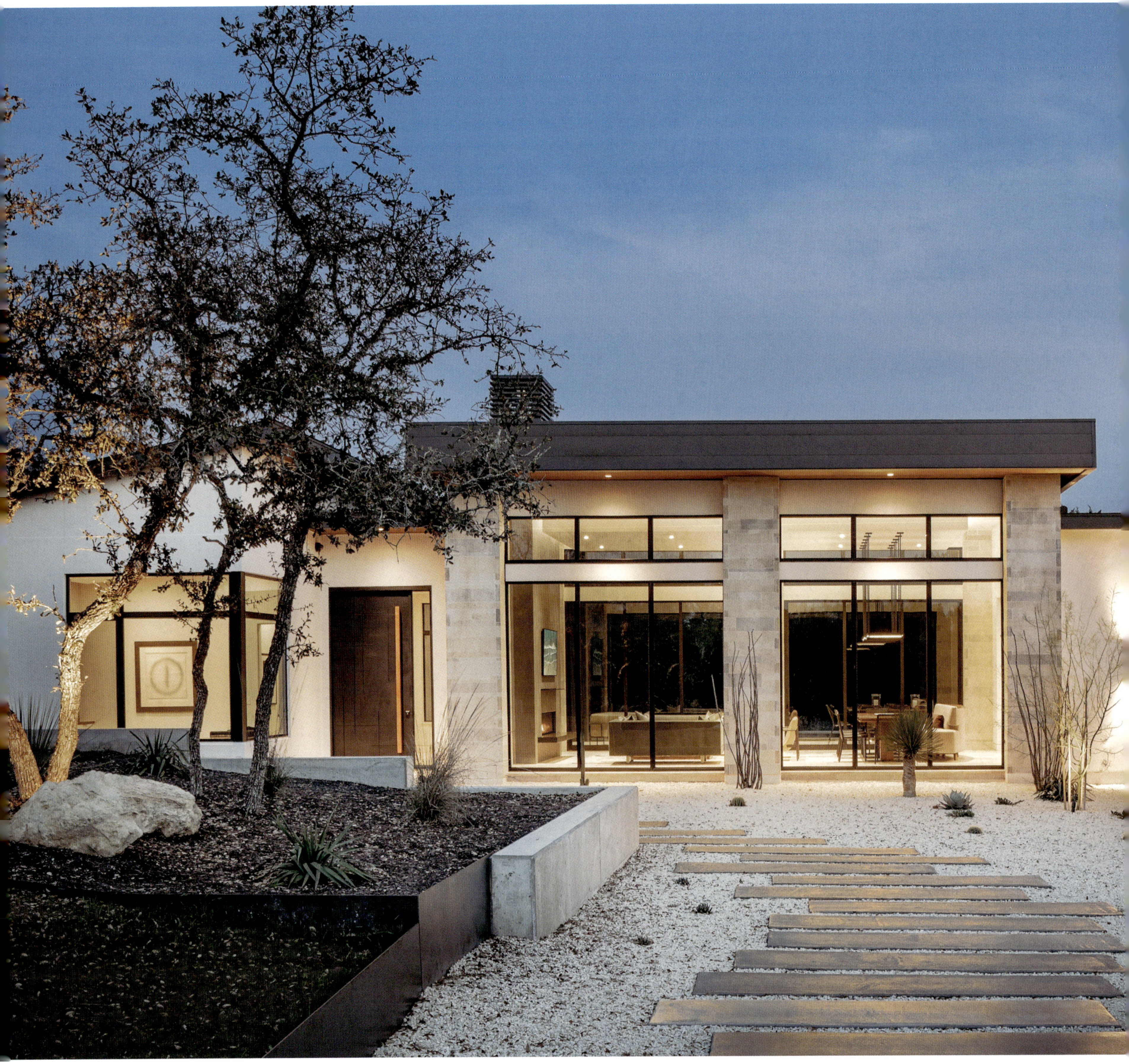

V VANGUARD STUDIO

The Hill Country is home for John Hathaway, principal architect and owner of architecture firm Vanguard Studio – and he will be the first to say that he gains much inspiration from his rustic, rural surroundings where timeless structures seamlessly integrate into the countryside. "I like for architecture in this area to have influences of this legacy of the past, whether through the simple clean forms or the warm patina of wood and stone," he says. "I always strive for the house to be a creation that is ultimately inspired by the site itself, complementing the existing beauty that's already there." It's that mindset – one that fuses the immutable qualities of the past with the progressive ideas of today – that has put Vanguard at the top with their 20-year history of award-winning designs.

The team specializes in luxury custom homes in the Central Texas area, prioritizing a meaningful connection with each and every client. After all, they know that it's this type of connection that really inspires a true custom home and influences the most important elements and goals of the home. Vanguard's innovative, personal, and efficient design process enables them to create within a wide range of styles and aesthetics while achieving superior results and surpassing client expectations. The team's combined years of experience studying architecture across the country and around the world – from California to Italy and back again – has contributed to their design dexterity. They innately understand the charm and characteristics of successful design and know what makes a home so special.

FACING PAGE: A combination of stone, steel, and glass creates the perfect modern yet tactile expression on this entry view. The home was built by Enve Builders, long-time collaborating partners with Vanguard Studio. Photography by Erin Holsonback.

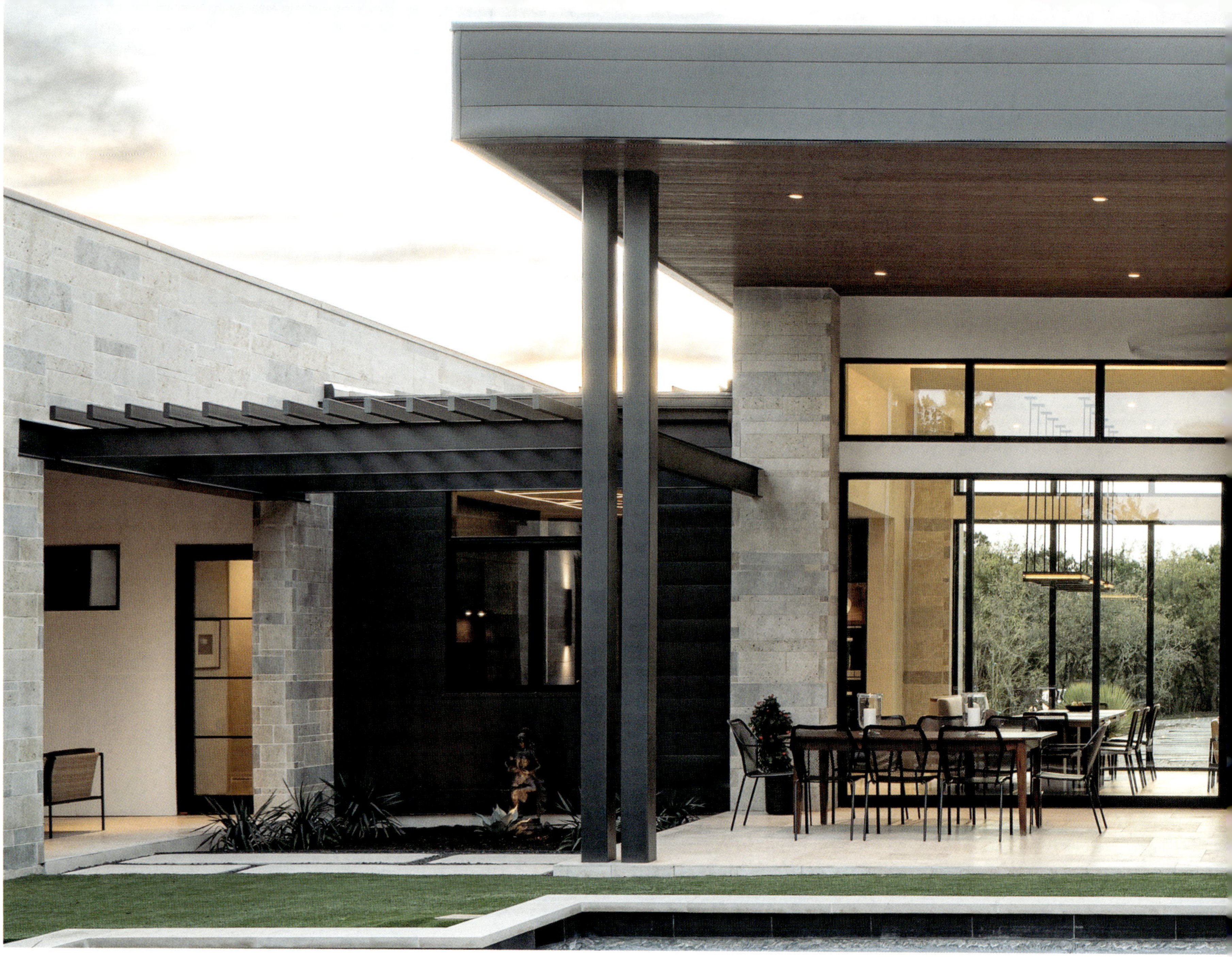

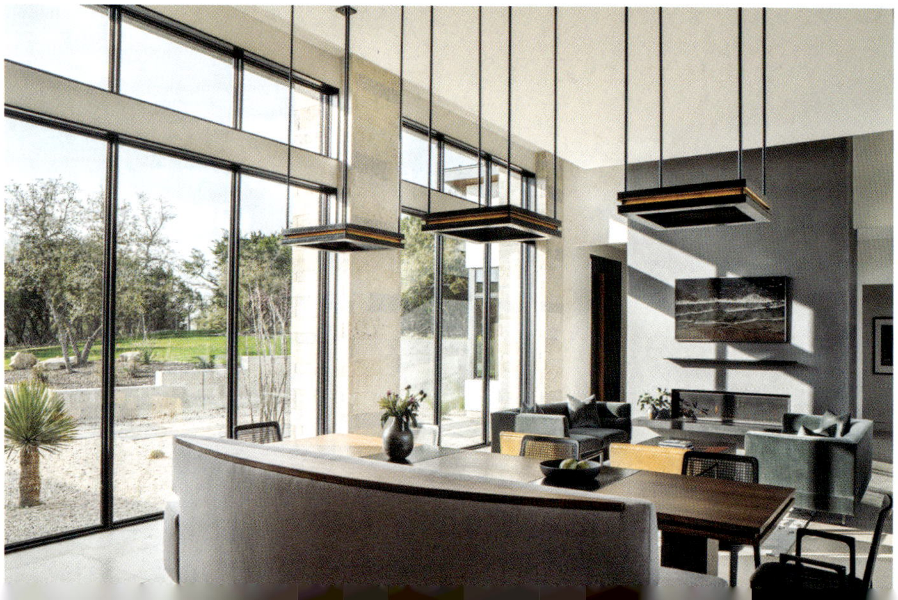

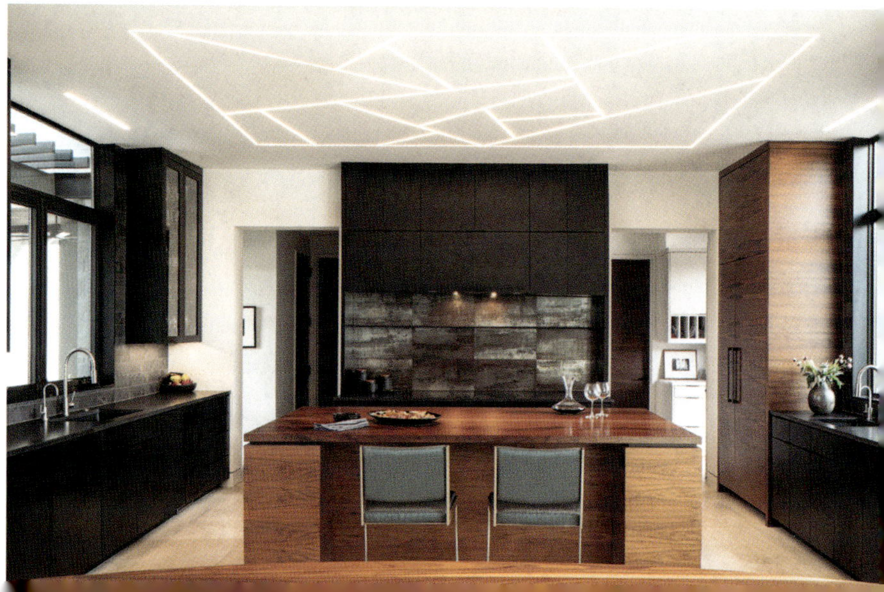

ABOVE: The floating roof plane defines the central living pavilion that anchors the house.

LEFT: This modern yet warm kitchen glows from its inlaid LED light troughs — a special custom touch.

FAR LEFT: This custom lighting fixture by Laura Burton Interiors helps define a more intimate dining space in the central light-lined living hall.

RIGHT: Metal siding, a steel trellis, and a smooth-cut stone exterior combine in beautiful harmony. Photography by Erin Holsonback.

"Architecture goes beyond the style of a home, and straight to the heart of creating spaces that connect the users to what brings them joy, while connecting them to the site in a meaningful way."
—John Hathaway

TOP: Flanking corner windows along with a steel and glass entry door create a free flow of the interior and exterior spaces.
Photography by Fine Focus Photography.

MIDDLE: A soaring, open kitchen still captures a sense of warmth and coziness through the use of soft materials and the custom light installation.

BOTTOM: This space is light, bright, rich, clean – everything a master bath should be!

FACING PAGE TOP: This Texas Hill Country home makes a magnificent impact by integrating Napa-style farmhouse elements.

FACING PAGE BOTTOM: Walls of glass in the back bring light and life into the heart of this home. Photography by Erin Holsonback.

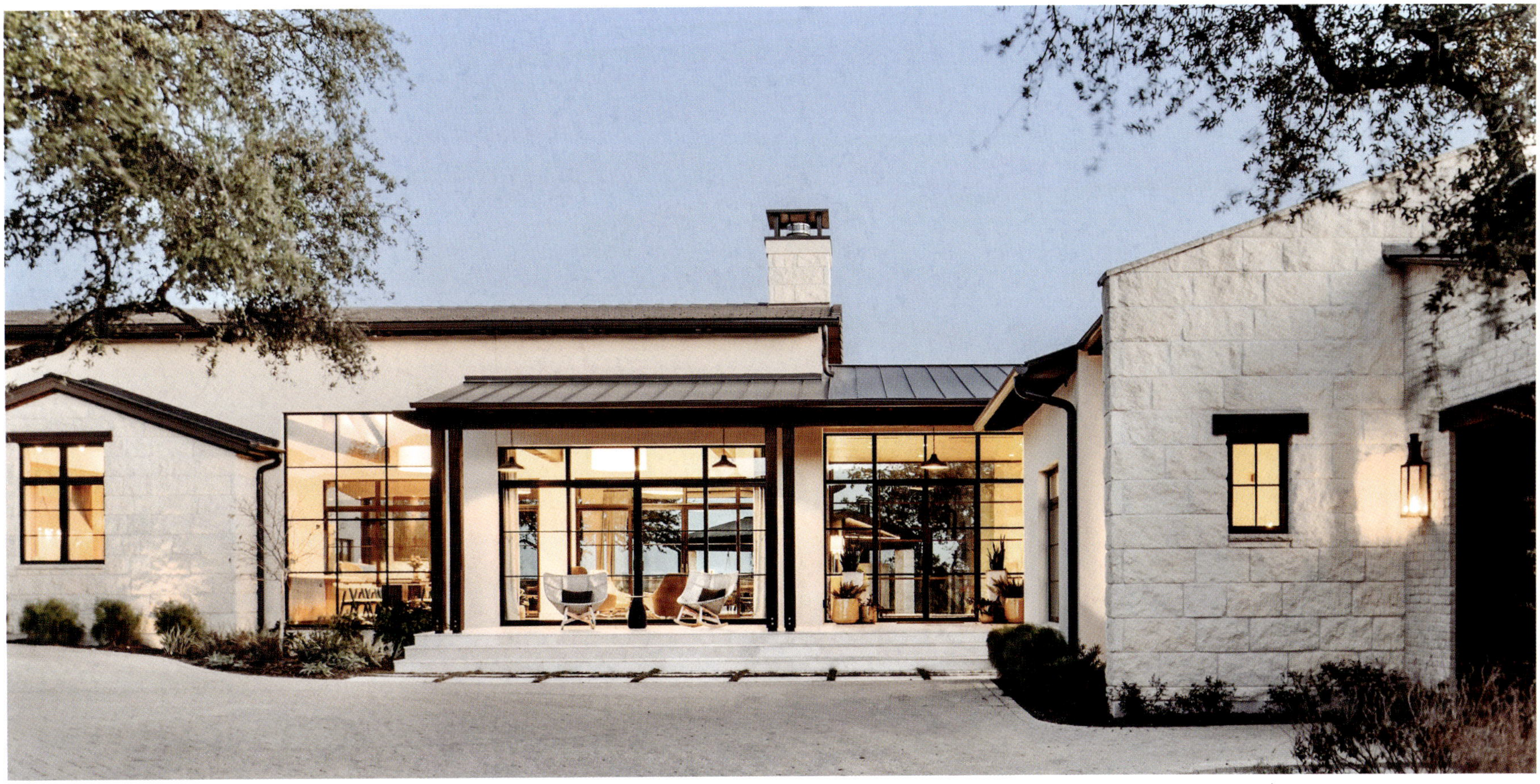

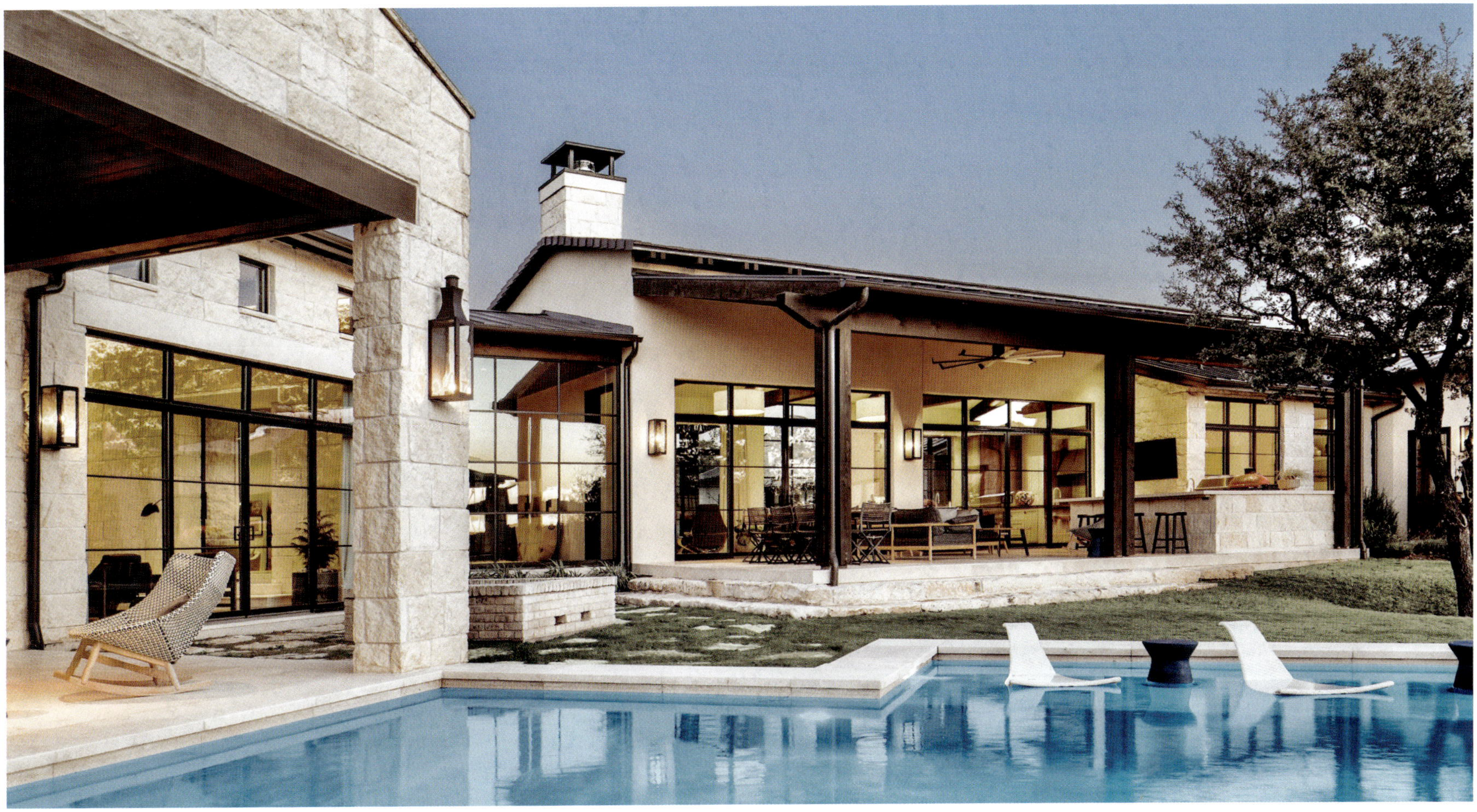

Built by SEBASTIAN CONSTRUCTION GROUP

Photography by Casey Dunn

DALLAS
FORT WORTH

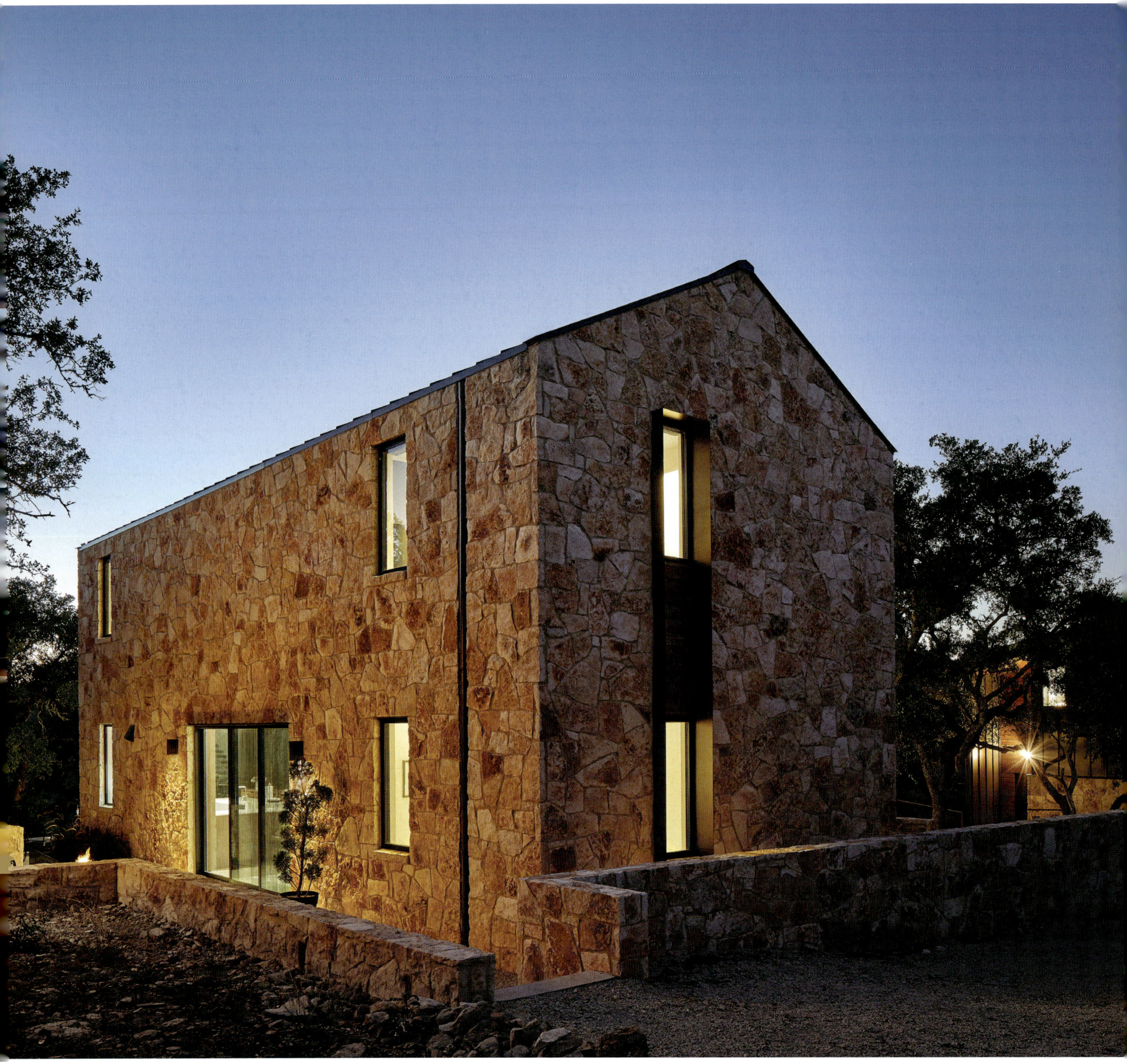

A GRUPPO ARCHITECTS

Shared ideas about architecture, design, and construction inspired longtime friends (and native Texans) Andrew Nance and Thad Reeves to form A Gruppo Architects in 2005, first as a traditional architectural design firm, and later, as a design-build firm focused on sustainable, modern residential and small commercial projects. From the start, they have cultivated a culture that emphasizes constant inquiry, a sense of exploration, and collaboration. Indeed, their name – A Gruppo, which is a subtle nod to fine architecture's roots in the Italian Renaissance – denotes not only a group of people, but also a group effort; one that hears critique and incubates ideas, draws on others' expertise, and explores innovative yet timeless design possibilities. "Being curious is really a prerequisite to being a good architect," says Thad.

Today, the team has dual offices, with Andrew in San Marcos and Thad in Dallas. That means they effectively work across many different areas of the state. It also means they've developed a distinctly modern Hill Country vernacular, influenced by Central Texas's unique mystique – and how its topography and landscape resonates with architecture. "Developing and recognizing some type of connection to the experience of these aspects of nature are very important in our work," says Andrew.

Naturally, the work of A Gruppo is also informed by their clients – they love it when clients bring their own ideas to the table, excited to create something new and unexpected. It all goes back to the tenet of collaboration where multiple inputs allows a design to be developed much further, yielding the best possible outcome.

FACING PAGE: Built of local Texas limestone, the residence embraces rustic charm and recalls the vernacular stone structures of the surrounding Hill Country in a modern way.

TOP: The native mott of oak trees was integrated into the courtyard. The glass structure connects to the stone boxes of the living spaces and bedroom.

MIDDLE: Natural light, views, and utility are balanced through thoughtful design of the master bath.

BOTTOM: The glass connector between the main structure and bedroom wing houses the dining room, taking advantage of the views to the Blanco River beyond. The limestone cladding continues inside, merging interior and exterior, to create a contemporary vibe mixed with Old World charm. Photography by Dror Baldinger FAIA.

124

"Staying in touch with natural light and access to nature is fundamental; it helps keep you grounded." -Thad Reeves

ABOVE: The living room opens to the cantilevered balcony – the backyard area – by virtue of the pocketing multi-slide doors. A roll-down screen covers the 16-foot opening, transforming the living room into a screened porch.

FACING PAGE TOP LEFT: The curving exterior masonry holds the line of the street. The glazed living areas provide transparency through the building, recalling the view to the trees that existed prior to construction.

FACING PAGE MIDDLE LEFT: The glazed area over the entry provides maximum transparency through the house. The cantilevered perch allows you to experience the volume of the space instead of observing from the edge.

FACING PAGE BOTTOM LEFT: The dining room floats between the glazed exterior walls. The divider wall provides an ideal place for art.

FACING PAGE TOP RIGHT AND FACING PAGE BOTTOM RIGHT: The palette of materials evokes a traditional warmth with the simplicity of modern design. The ground floor is bound by glazed walls at the front and back. The center partition provides separation between the main functions while still maintaining the feeling of openness. Photography by Charles Davis Smith FAIA.

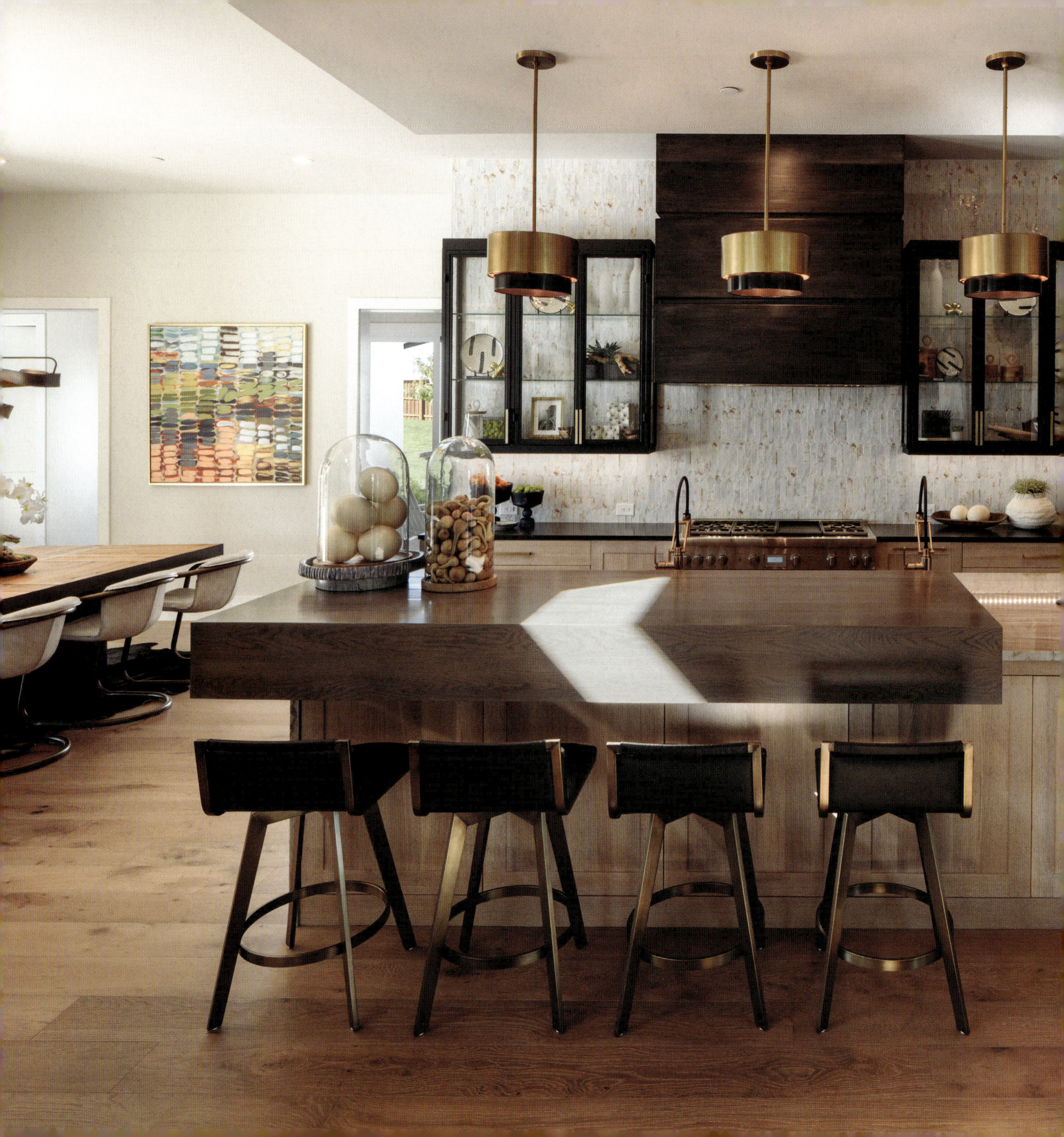

ELEMENTS OF DESIGN
TRACI DARDEN

Color, line, form, light, pattern, texture, and space. These are the seven basic elements of design and they are what inspire Traci Darden, owner and lead designer of Elements of Design. After all, she named her company after them! She's particularly attuned to space; for her, the importance lies not just in the overall layout of a home and within the boundaries of a room, but the function of it. "Creating a space that the client loves – not only because it is beautiful, but because it also just feels right to them and fits the client and their lifestyle - is what resonates most with me," she says.

As a full-service interior design firm, Elements of Design offers a wide variety of services — from hourly consultations to model-home merchandising to personalized service for full property renovations — to suit each client's unique needs and lifestyle.

Indeed, when asked what drives her design style, Traci will tell you that it's listening to the client and developing a plan that is livable and timeless. Her designs are touted as "thoughtful," as she puts her eyes to a project and comes at it from all angles, truly thinking of it from a lived-in perspective.

FACING PAGE: We integrated natural materials to convey warm elements, creating a modern Texas Hill Country aesthetic in this home. The kitchen affords every luxury in convenience and function as well as beauty. Glass-front, metal cabinets – sans backing – show off the gorgeous wall tile. The island is an innovative, modern rendition with multiple purposes; it sits cantilevered above the custom cabinets and waterfall quartzite counters below, visually blocking the sink from the living-room view. Pop-up electrical outlets in the island top also serve as wireless chargers; a functional addition that still maintains the integrity of the sleek design. Photography by Truitt Rogers.

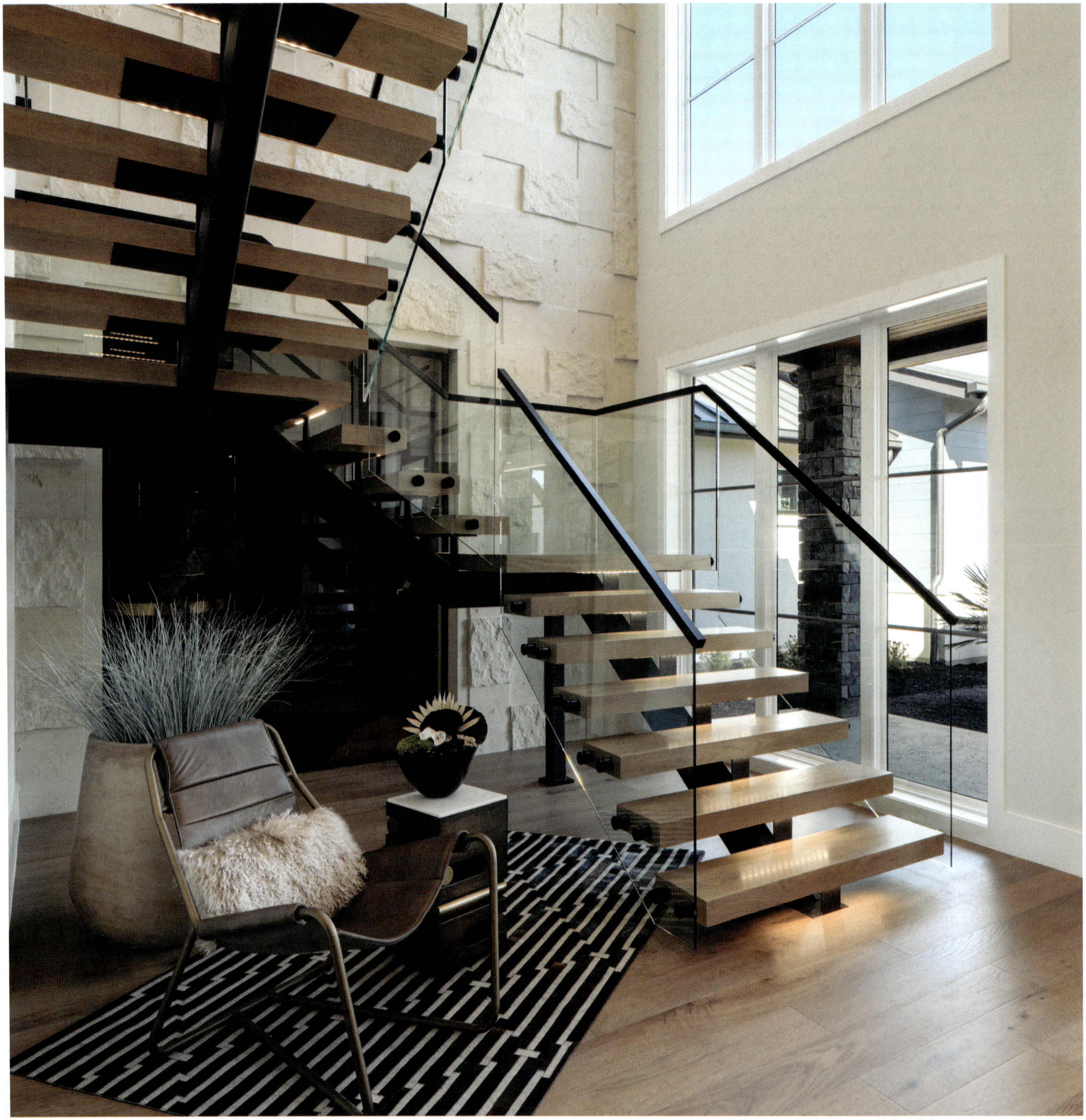

"Having the relationship with vendors that can see your vision and believe in your design really is crucial to the overall success of each project." —Traci Darden

ABOVE: A working kitchen is directly behind the main kitchen area, hidden behind a pocket door and offering abundant storage and functionality.

RIGHT: This contemporary office is located directly off the entry. We worked with the builder and architect to design a retractable glass system that fully opens the space to the living and entry. We also tucked away a pocket work station, complete with a built-in desk and filing storage, to keep clutter out of sight.

FACING PAGE: In the entryway, two levels of stairs float in front of a showstopping wall that we designed using a mixture of sizes and textures in stone.
Photography by Truitt Rogers.

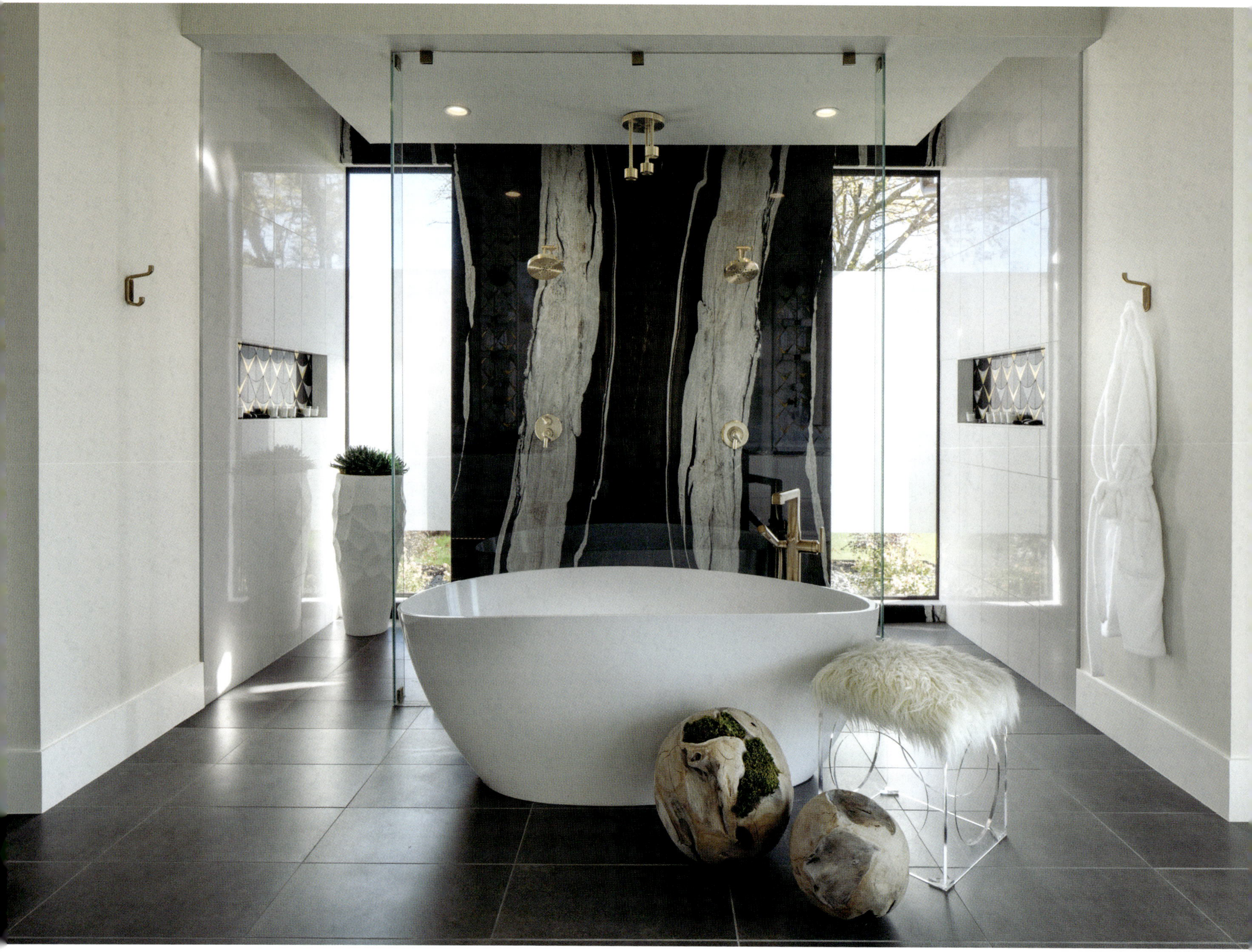

"One thing I love about my work is that it is never the same day to day or project to project. While I may be drawn personally to one style of design, I see the beauty in ALL design styles and finding the style that fits my client is my ultimate design style."
–Traci Darden

TOP: To highly contrast the light-finish wood floors, we used a lime paint in an "almost black" matte finish to completely drink up the reflections of the surrounding elements. Lacquered mirrors over the bed and contemporary pendants create a gallery effect.

MIDDLE: Floating vanity cabinets in a high-gloss painted finish contrast against the darker flooring in the master bath. A coffee bar between the master bedroom and bath offers a convenient caffeine fix.

BOTTOM: We designed a floor-to-ceiling fireplace in the great room, featuring layered wood trim finished in a dark stain to balance against the dark wood and metal tones of the kitchen.

FACING PAGE: We designed luxurious amenities in this master bath to melt away the most chaotic of days. The full wall of natural stone in the shower is entrancing. We also introduced natural light through full-length privacy windows. Oversized flooring continues in the shower to emphasize continuity. Photography by Truitt Rogers.

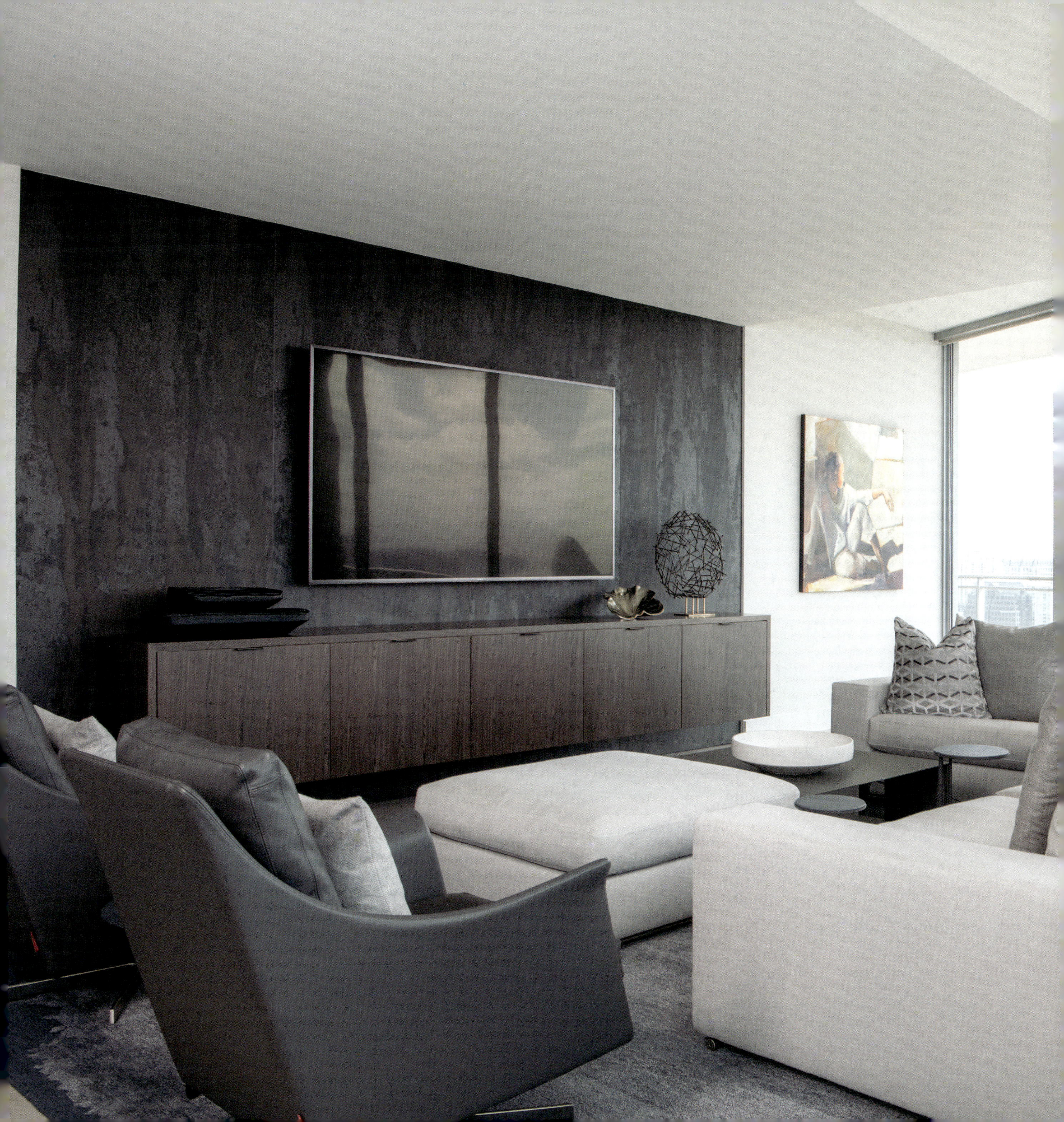

ERIC LAPOINTE ARCHITECT & SUSAN SMITH DESIGNS

Extraordinary design is the result of remarkable collaboration — and that's precisely what Eric LaPointe and Susan Smith bring to the table. Eric provides the structure, then Susan and her team come in with layers of art, textiles, and furnishings. Theirs is a natural chemistry that blends the architectural and design roles that are so essential in residential projects.

Although they've had the benefit of 10-plus years of experience working together, their collective goal has always been the same: to elevate modern style for a comfortable living environment with carefully curated, client-informed selections.

Eric and Susan are driven by inspiration, quality, and creativity yet they always remain mindful of functionality and rational constraints. With projects across the U.S., from Vero Beach, to Seaside, Kansas City, Vail, Lake Tahoe, Whitefish, and more, they also take much pride in the work they do in their own backyard, Dallas, Texas — especially when it involves making great homes for great families.

Indeed, that's what this featured project at the Azure, a luxury high-rise development, is all about.

FACING PAGE: There is no better example of our high-end product capabilities than this residence at the Azure. In addition to function and beauty, the design mandated utilizing a nearly 270-degree, uncompromised view of Dallas and its surrounds. The 5,400-square-foot unit features an open living space where comfort, cooking, dining, and bar all flow together. Photography by Michael Hunter.

"Extraordinary design is the result of remarkable collaboration." —Susan Smith

ABOVE: The clients provided a powerful, interactive opportunity to create a space tailored to their specifics, including the sleek, marble-clad kitchen.

FACING PAGE: There were few "bones" of the original unit that were not disrupted, including the incorporation of an adjoining one-bedroom apartment into the sweeping master suite which lacks absolutely nothing – from the completely custom-outfitted dressing room and closet to a sleek, spa-inspired master bath. Photography by Michael Hunter.

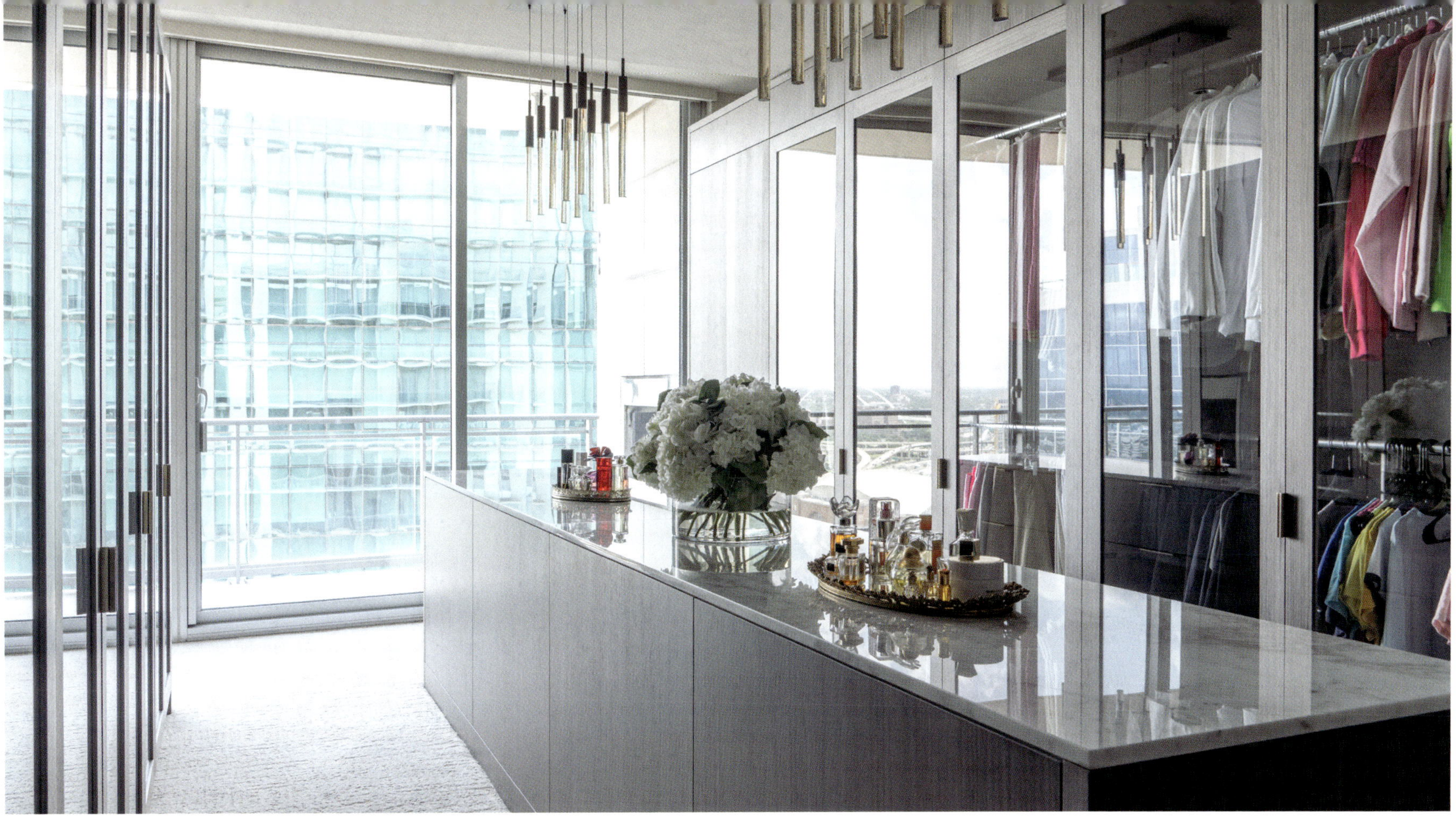

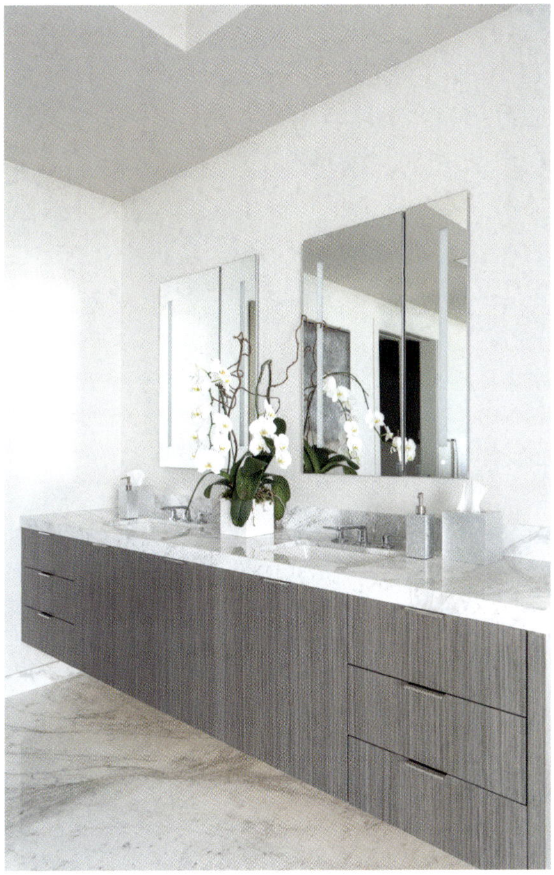

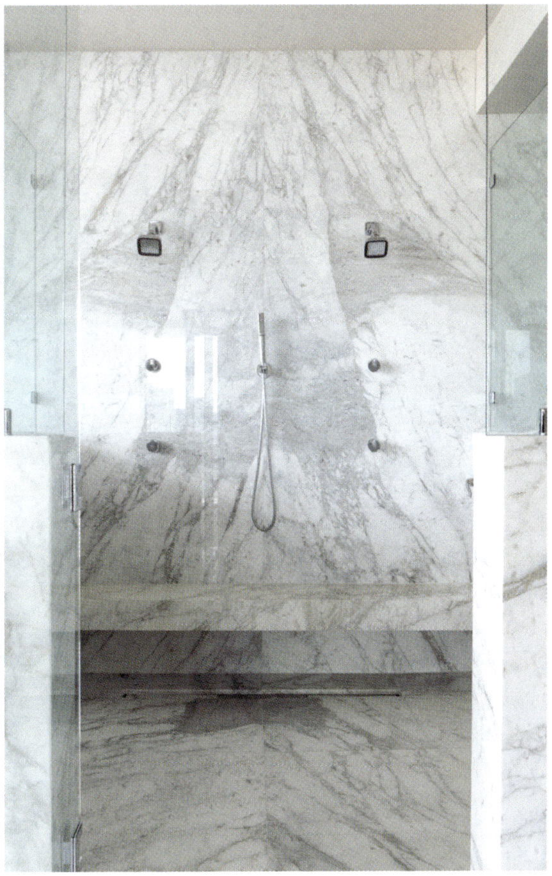

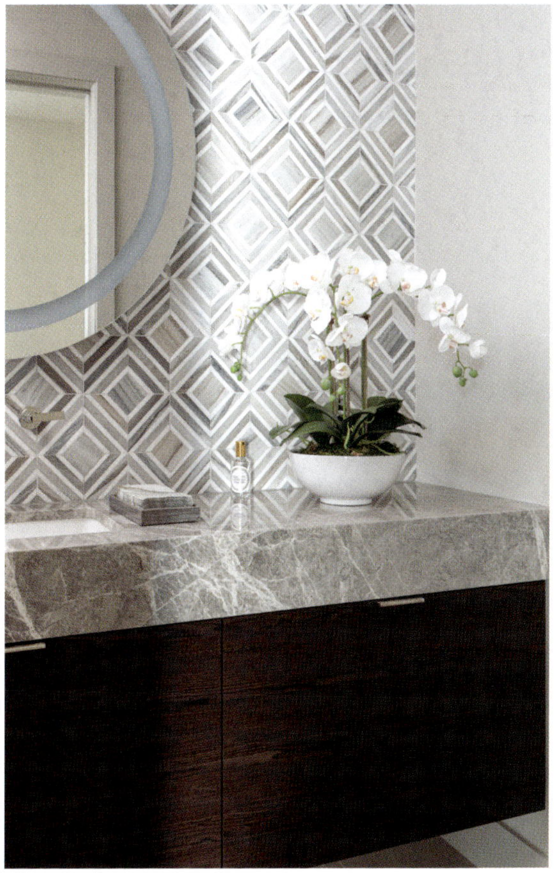

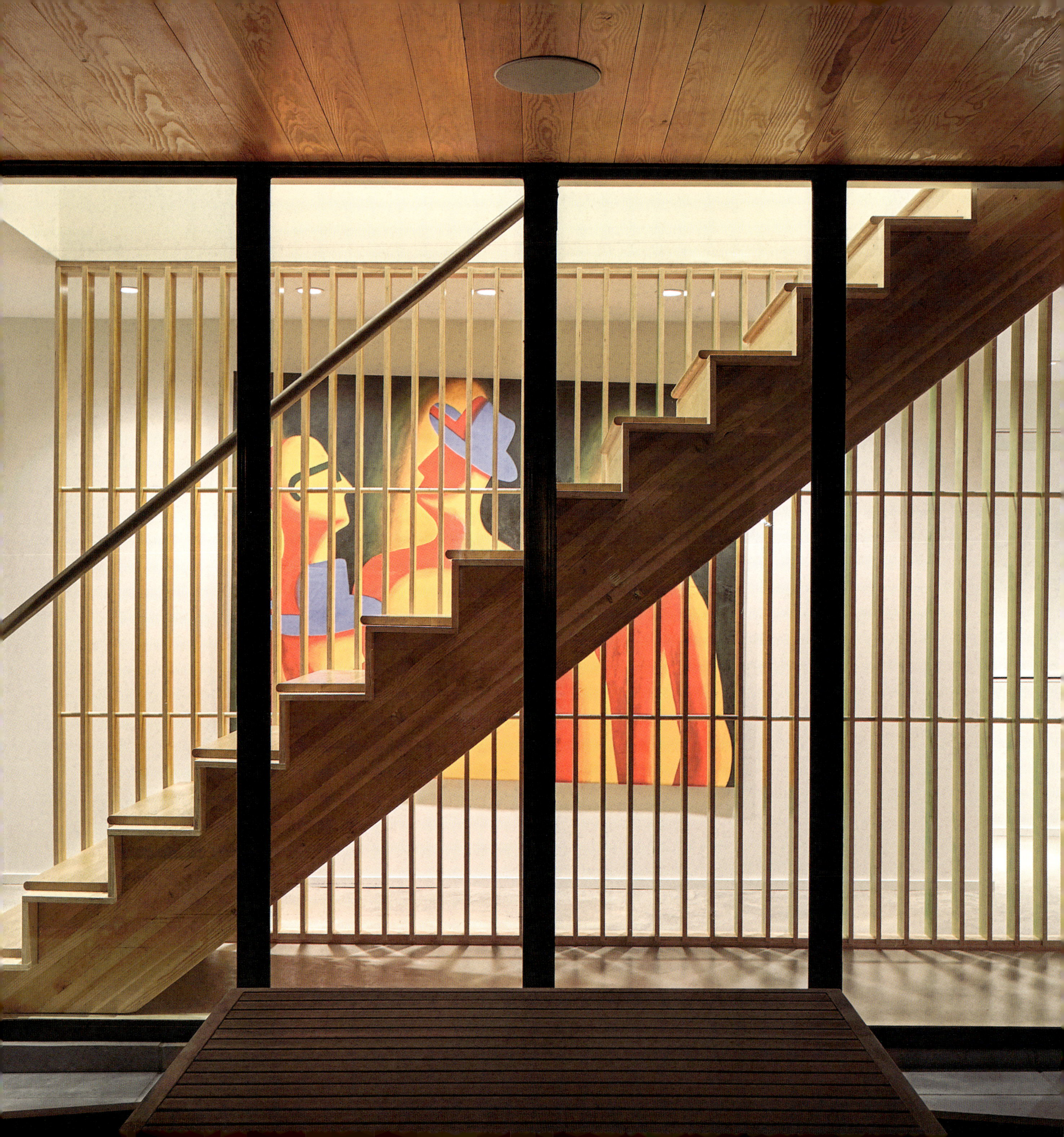

IBAÑEZ SHAW ARCHITECTURE

Gregory Ibañez, FAIA, and Bart Shaw, FAIA, co-founders of the Fort Worth-based boutique firm Ibañez Shaw Architecture, are guided by an optimistic and creative pragmatism and a belief that a bold, enlightened approach elevates the soul and enriches communities. No matter the project's type, scale, or location, the firm crafts distinctive, sustainable, and elegant designs that meet the needs of clients while responding to broader civic and social ambitions. Ibañez Shaw is committed to guiding clients through a transformative process through sustained principal involvement during the life of each project. They craft distinctive, sustainable, and elegant designs that not only meet the needs of their clients, but also respond to broader community and social ambitions. The firm's varied portfolio encompasses residential, retail, restaurant, commercial, and civic projects.

Casa Culebro is the home of Greg and his wife, Kathleen Culebro. The original portion of the home was constructed in 1932 and was in very poor condition when purchased. However, Greg felt strongly that the original portion should be preserved in order to respect the scale and history of the neighborhood. The resulting approach included a completely new interior, with 8-foot ceilings converted to light-filled vaulted spaces suited to the display of art, while the windows were replaced and the exterior stone was restored. A new addition was clad in plaster and weathering steel, complementing the original gables and Texas Millsap stone on the original façade.

FACING PAGE: The link between the original home and the addition is marked by a stair constructed from a wood beam and a plywood slat screen wall.

TOP: A steel and glass canopy was added to replace the original gabled entry, which was structurally unsound.

BOTTOM: The second floor is clad in weathering steel to harmonize with the original stone façade. Photography by Dror Baldinger FAIA.

"While the interior space flows seamlessly between the original and the addition, the exterior forms and materials reflect the contrast between modern and traditional architecture."
—Gregory Ibañez

TOP: The white, modern interior accommodates both modern art and Mexican antique furniture.

BOTTOM: The massing of the home reflects the older, single-story homes of the area and the new two-story projects that are replacing them.

FACING PAGE TOP LEFT: Aalto Web lounge chairs float behind a maple-screen media cabinet designed by the architect.

FACING PAGE TOP RIGHT: The stair screen wall features plywood slats with opposite faces stained in two different colors, creating a unique experience when entering or leaving the home.

FACING PAGE BOTTOM: Both old (stone and a gabled roof) and new (weathering steel with a flat roof) are clearly defined yet complementary in color and texture. Photography by Dror Baldinger FAIA.

139

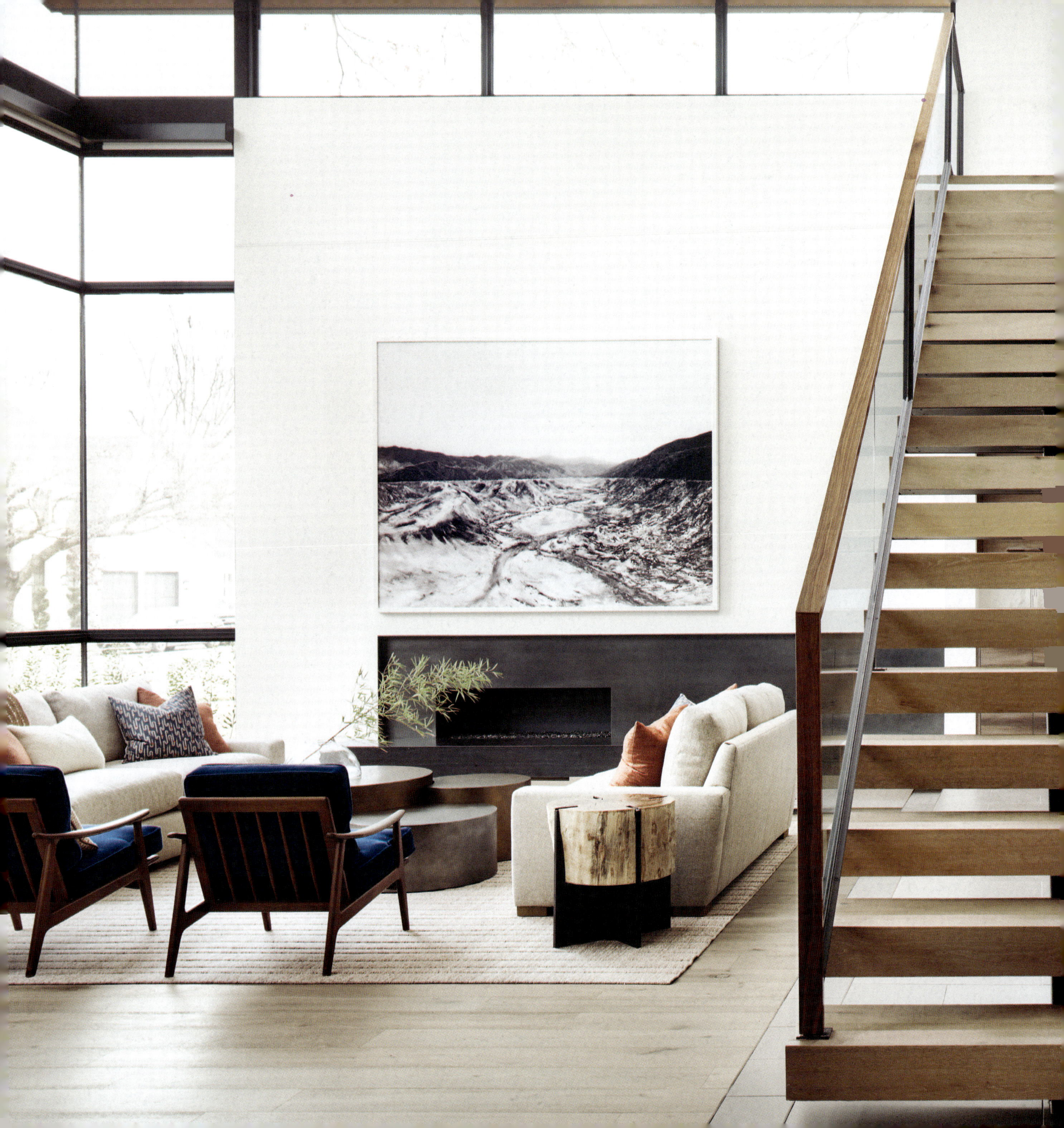

JEAN LIU DESIGN & CLINTON + COMPANY ARCHITECTS

"Great architecture harmonizes the connection between people, place, and structure. When a building artistically merges a family's living environment, with an authentic and gentle response to the land, you know you have something worth celebrating," says Will Clinton of Clinton + Company Architects. And, his words echo the full-service, multi-disciplinary architecture firm's approach to their work. They create residences and buildings that implement progressive design solutions tailored to serve each client's desires – all with a thoughtfully timeless and site-specific foundation at the core. After all, they believe the built environment should complement the natural.

The Clinton + Company team "lives architecture" in everything they do – it's a daily practice of paying attention to every detail and pushing for a new "best" every single day.

They also work with brilliant interior design firms – like Jean Liu Design – to bring the full vision to life. Jean Liu's team of design aficionados pride themselves on creating modern, edited, comfortable, and inspired spaces – and nothing makes them happier than helping clients translate their vision and lifestyle into a place they can call home.

Ultimately, it all serves what both Clinton + Company and Jean Liu Design consider to be the most important element of a home: how you feel when you're there.

FACING PAGE: The single stringer stair in the living room offers a very light appearance of structure, which takes you up to a library that is showered with natural northern light from a series of clerestory windows. The living room also sinks down to create a cozy, hunkered-in sitting environment amongst a grand space. Photography by Casey Dunn.

"When you feel great in a space – whether through balanced natural light, a cool breeze in the summer, or a warm, intimate ambiance in the evening – you know that you're experiencing an environment worth cherishing." –Will Clinton

ABOVE LEFT: Entering the residence, you are greeted by a western red cedar ceiling with textured limestone walls. The entry reduces the scale, creating a warm welcome as well as comfortable proportions for occupants.

ABOVE RIGHT: Looking south in the backyard, an oasis of green surrounds a sculpted lap pool. Photography by Casey Dunn.

FACING PAGE: The heritage red oak tree canopies over the front of the residence. Organizing the structure with a series of gabled forms reduces the overall massing of the program, weaving in exciting views of nature while paying respect to the scale of the neighborhood. Photography by Lisa Petrole.

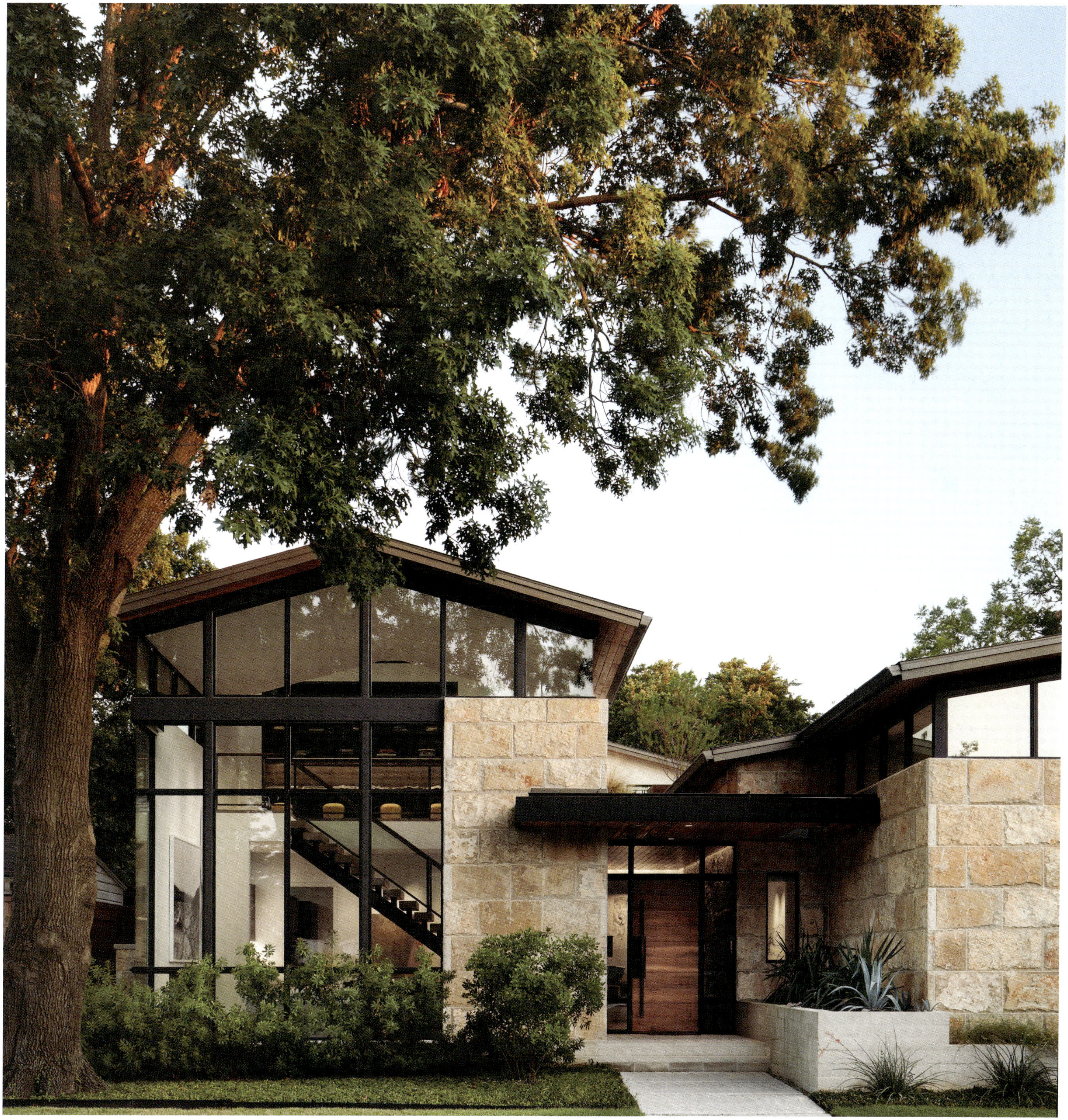

ABOVE: A ribbon window in the kitchen allows for beautiful natural light while providing privacy to neighboring residences. Photography by Casey Dunn.

FACING PAGE TOP LEFT: The stair strikes through the wet bar gathering space. Photography by Casey Dunn.

FACING PAGE TOP RIGHT: The wet bar incorporates the same ribbon window as the kitchen. Photography by Lisa Petrole.

FACING PAGE BOTTOM LEFT: The principal bedroom emboldens the naturalistic elements of the residence. The organically patterned wallpaper and walnut headboard with green velvet pillow create a casual, comfortable, natural environment. Photography by Casey Dunn.

FACING PAGE BOTTOM LEFT: Clerestory ribbon windows wrap around the principal bathroom, visually connecting to the big red oak tree. Photography by Casey Dunn.

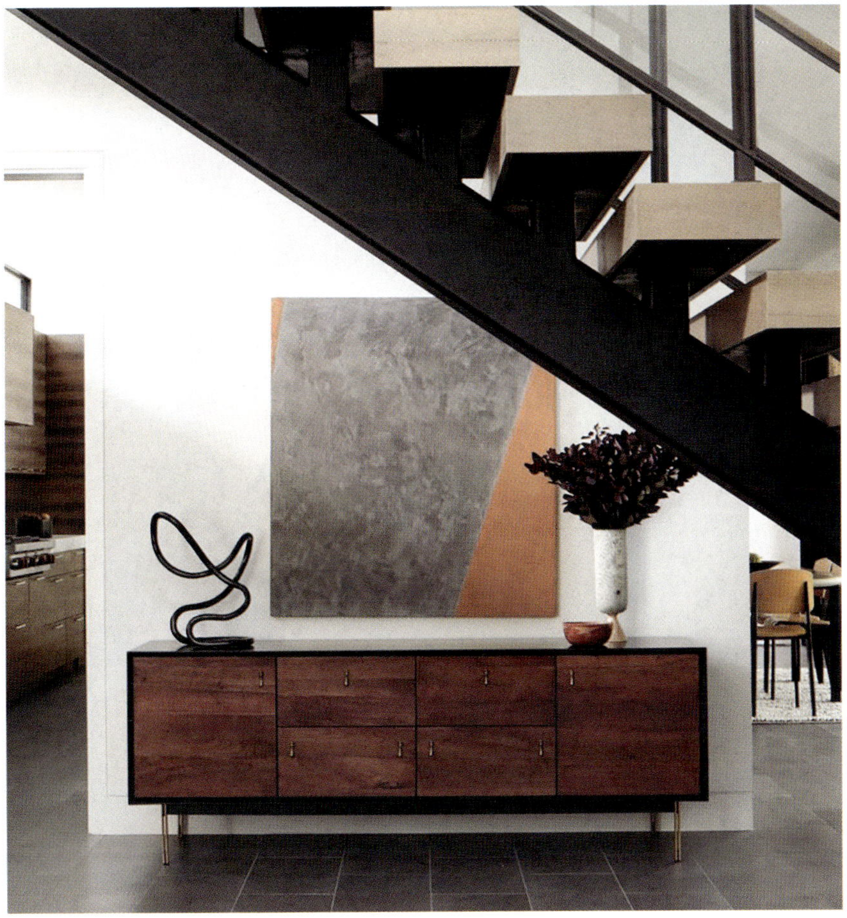
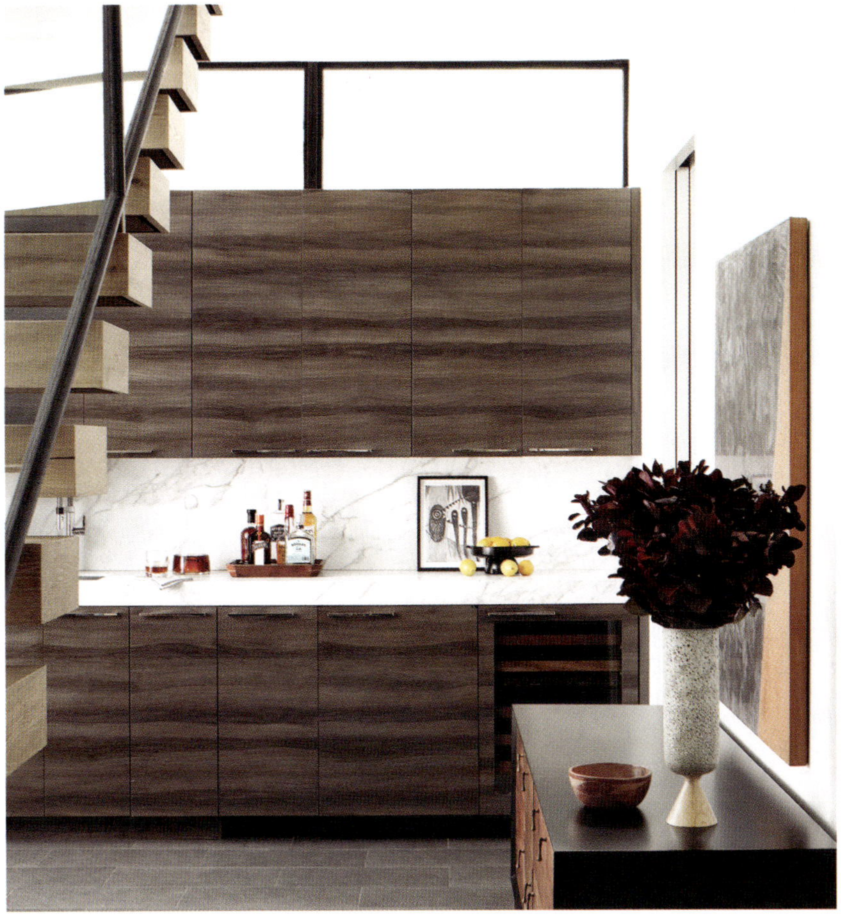
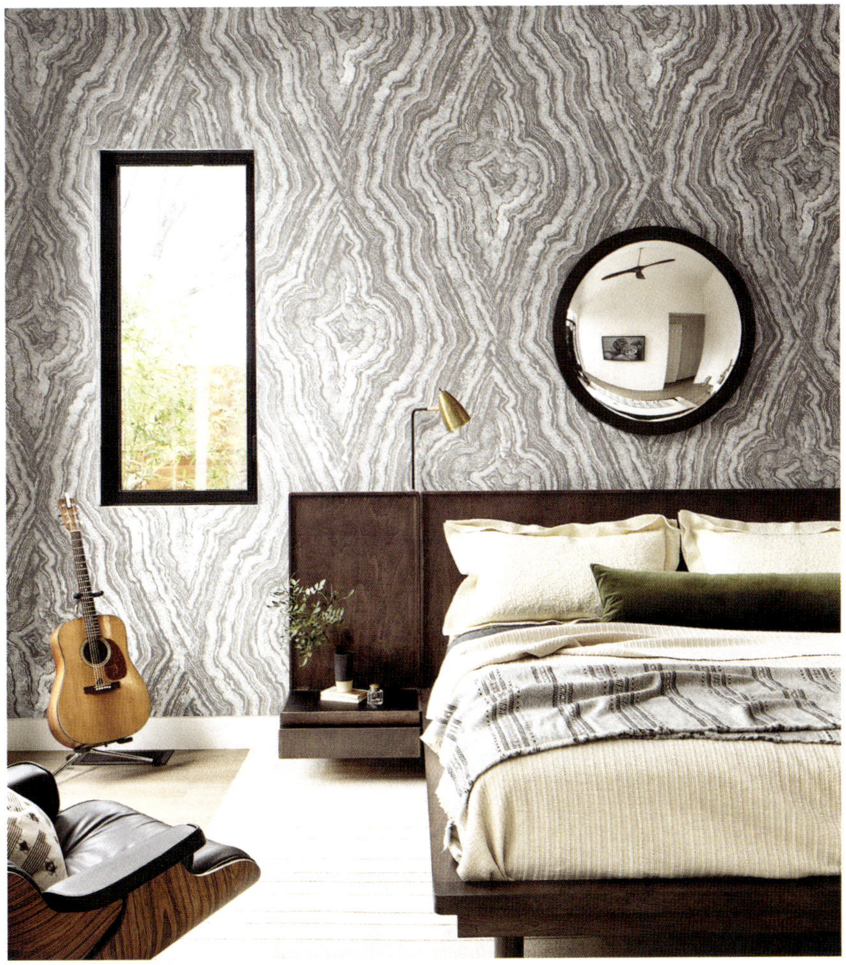
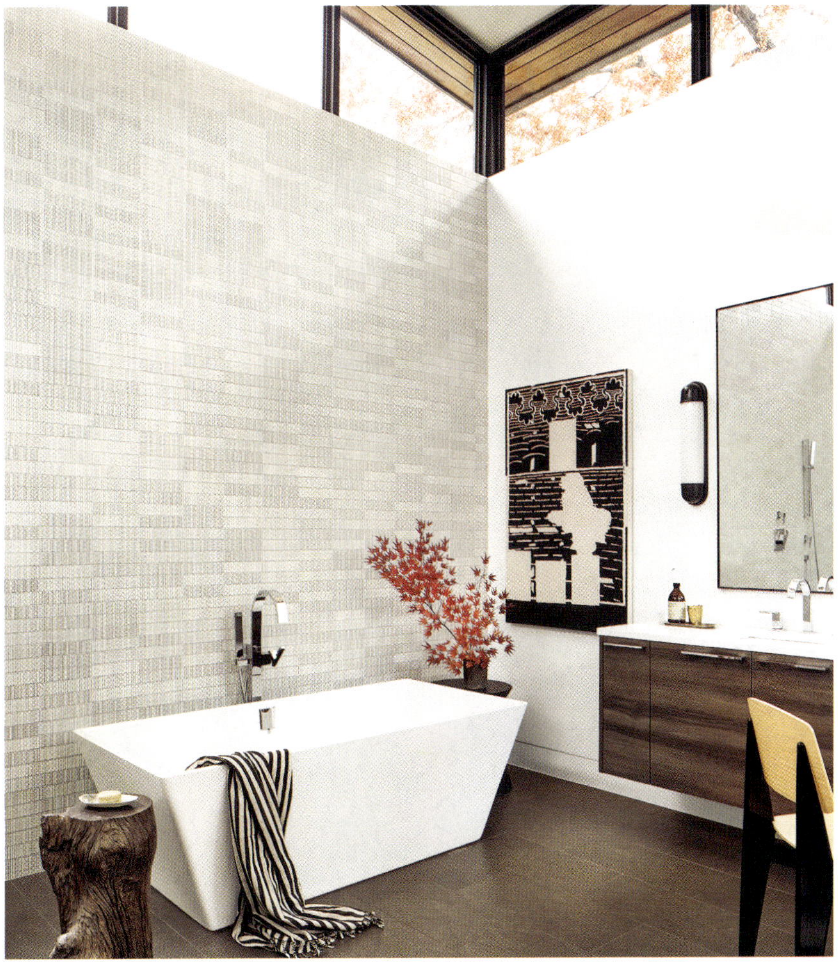

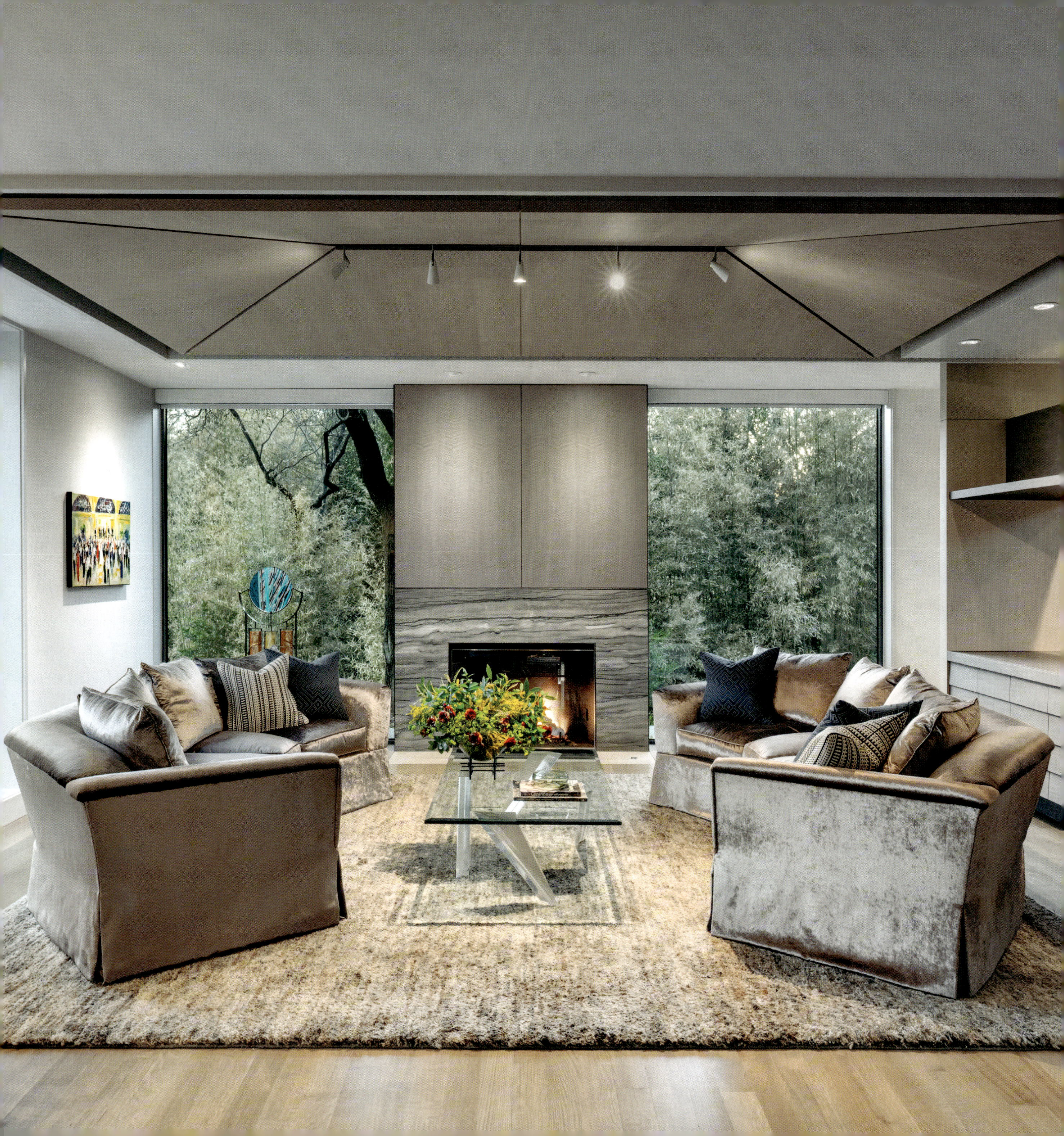

LINDA FRITSCHY
INTERIOR DESIGN

"We thrive on diversity, embrace challenges, and seek to define our clients' design goals in a way that supports their lifestyle," says Linda Fritschy of Linda Fritschy Interior Design. Her design firm has a single purpose: to provide client-inspired, understated interiors. Linda and her team work closely and collaboratively with clients to create interiors in styles ranging from modern to traditional. Each project is admired for a common thread – aesthetically balanced and skillfully edited interiors. Whether the project is new construction, a kitchen or bath remodel, or a refresh, her highly respected design philosophy is always thoughtfully applied.

FACING PAGE: Neutral color tones combine with a variety of textures in this formal living area making the room sing with perfect pairings. A shimmering velvet sofa sits on a plush jute shag rug. The fireplace is a honed sequoia slab topped with fine-grain silver oak. The clients' collection of art broadens the personality of this space, making it warm and inviting.

TOP: This highly functional kitchen offers creek views in three directions ensuring a beautiful and efficient space to eat and to cook. Dark wood details that travel around the room, along with a raised walnut bar top accent the serene monochromatic palette. Inspired by classic Murano glass vases, the lamps hanging over the island in harmonious organic colors create a welcoming feeling in the client's self-described "perfect home."

BOTTOM: Surrounded by warmth and nature, this breakfast area truly is the heart of the home – and one of the clients' favorite spaces. The open fireplace features repeated elements of exterior brick, hot rolled steel and concrete and can be enjoyed from the breakfast table, while cooking in the kitchen, or when watching TV in the den.
Photography by Charles Davis Smith FAIA.

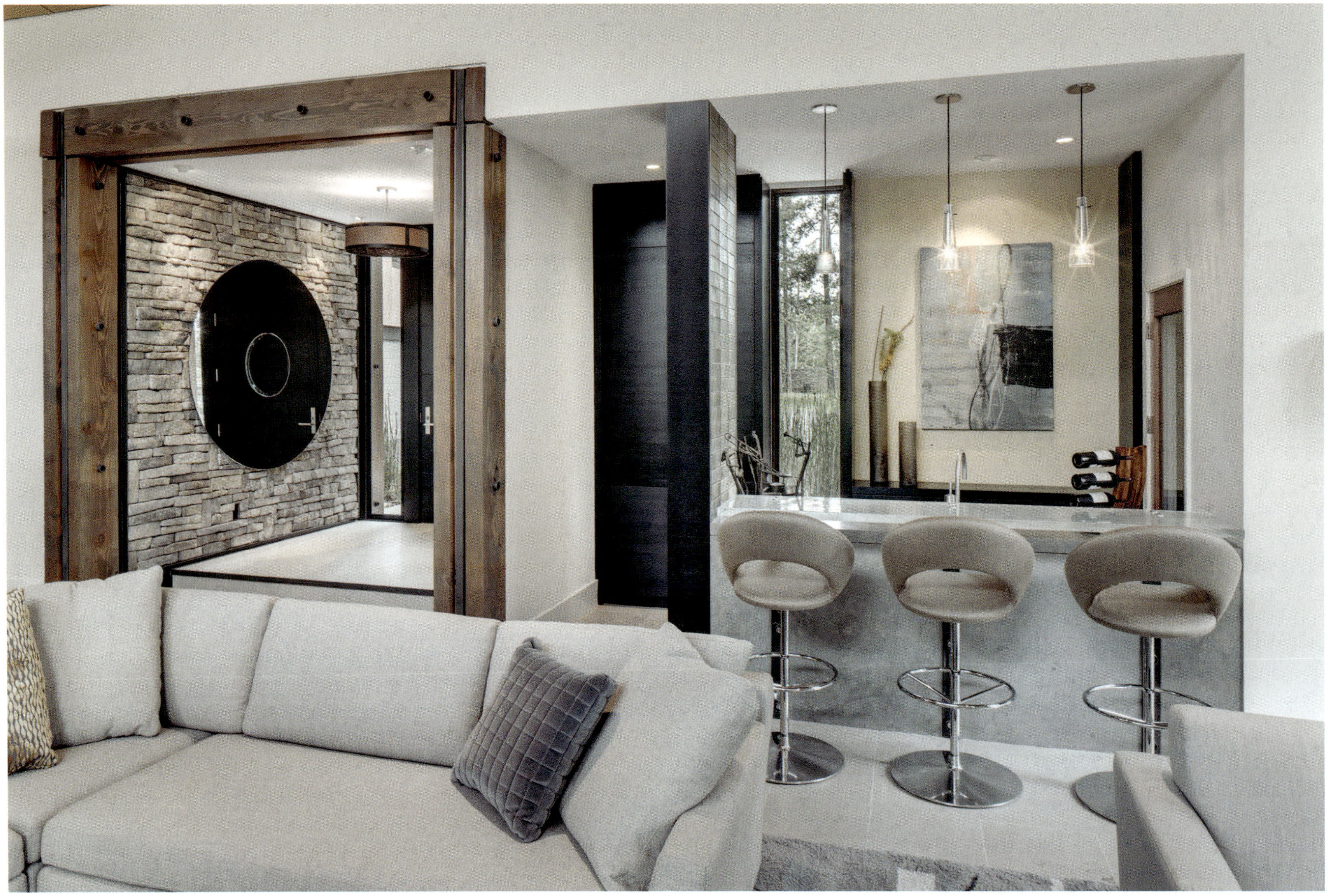

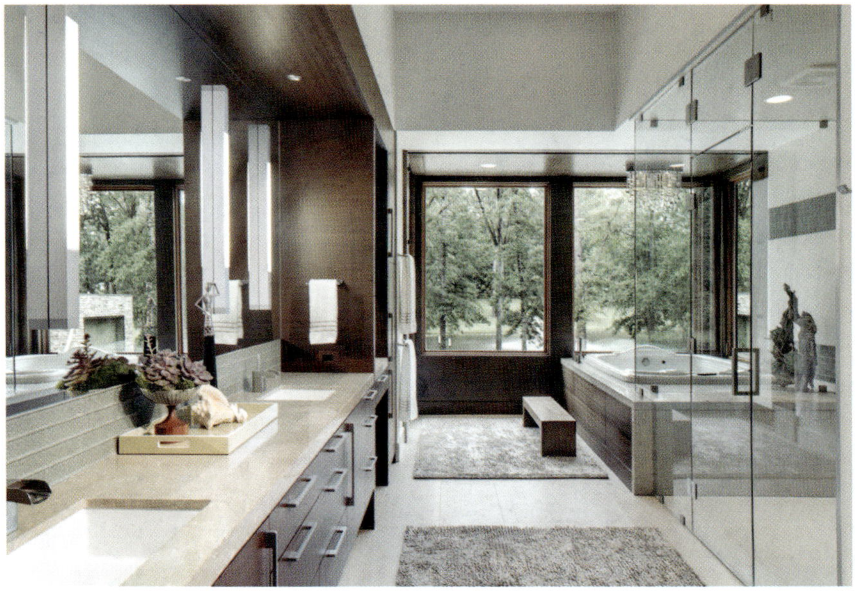

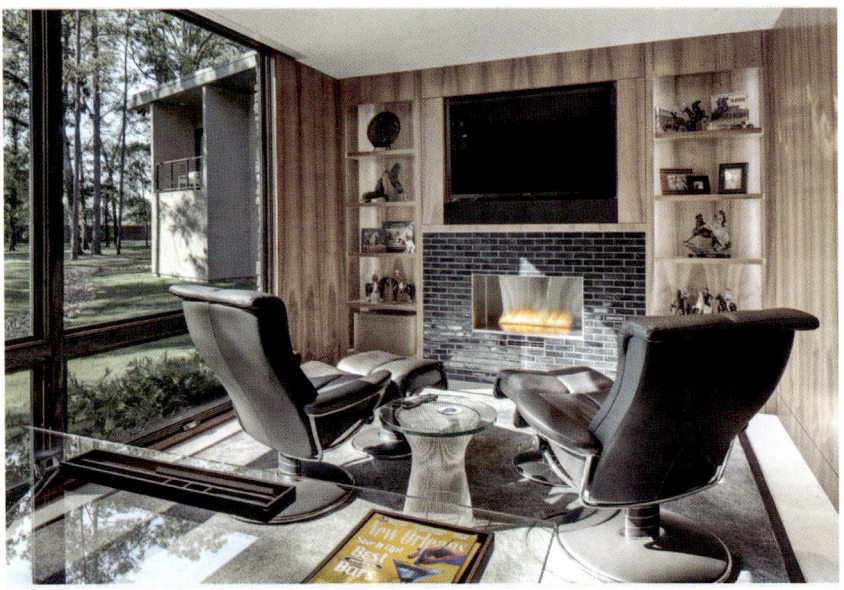

"A study in natural materials, this home showcases the union of wood, metal, stone, and glass to create a symphony of textures and elegance." —Linda Fritschy

ABOVE AND FACING PAGE TOP: Inspired by the purchase of the homeowners' dream land and their travels, this home is a peaceful sanctuary with a modern, edited approach. Expansive windows, stacked stone on the entry walls, and the extension of the travertine floors onto the patio all blur and expand the interiors. Purposefully arranged furniture provides the opportunity for entertaining, watching cherished football games, and observing the eagle that feeds on the stocked pond at sunset.

FACING PAGE BOTTOM LEFT: The handsomely masculine and highly personalized home office is a true retreat for the owner, where he can watch TV, catch up on work, or nap. Its understated beauty is achieved through golden koa wood on the walls along with ceramic and natural tile. Built-in shelves showcase western collectibles.

FACING PAGE BOTTOM RIGHT: Reminiscent of the owners' favored vacation properties, this spa-inspired master bath features clean lines, warm woods, and softly organic, neutral colors that resonate with the views outside. Photography by Charles Davis Smith FAIA.

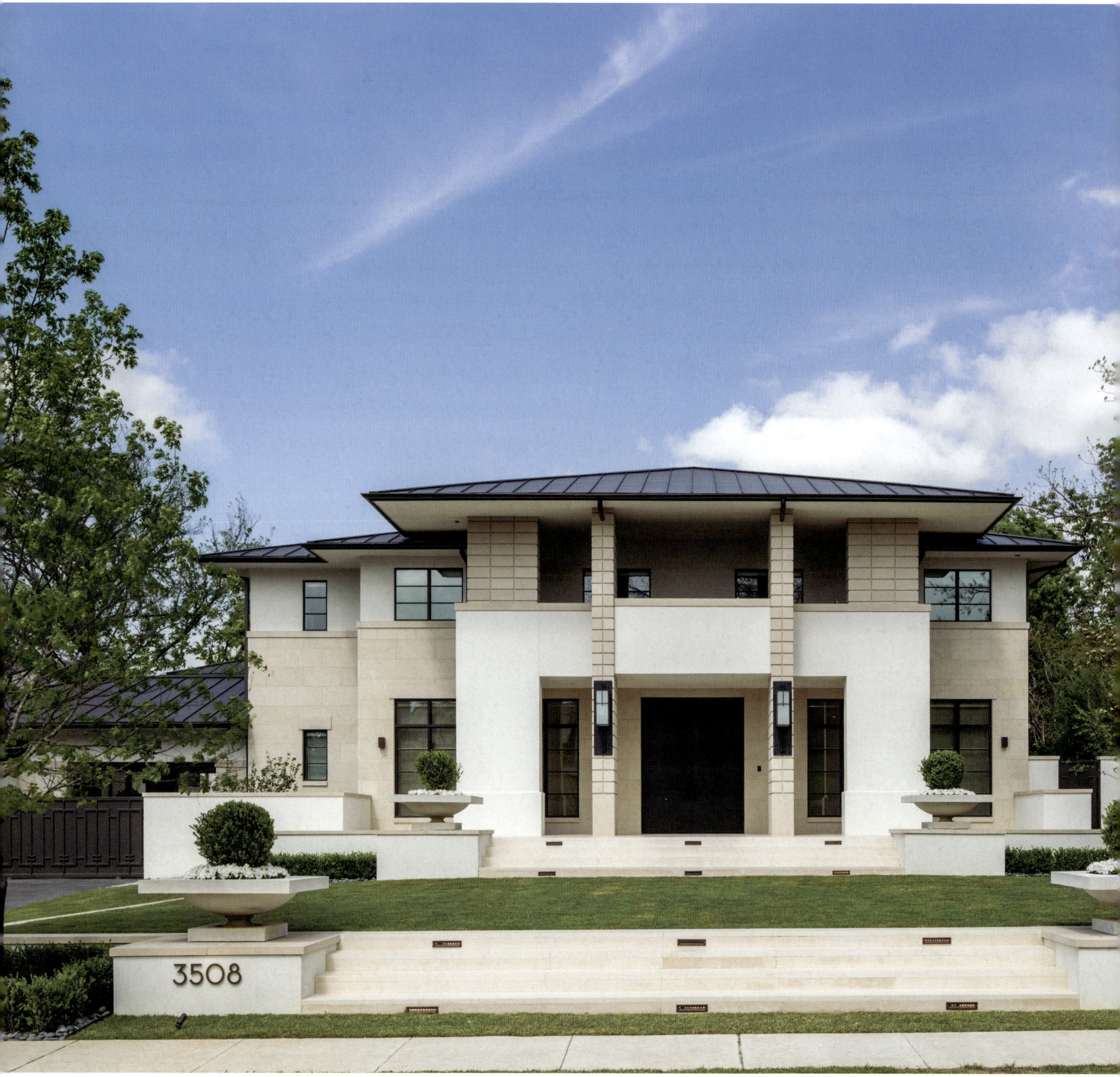
3508

L. LUMPKINS ARCHITECT

"My passion is helping every one of my clients put form to their definition of home," says Lloyd Lumpkins of L. Lumpkins Architect, Inc. "What inspires me most is seeing my clients' faces light up when they witness their dreams become a reality and when they encounter little surprises – like how the light falls in a space throughout the day – as they start to make these creations a home."

Born and raised in East Texas, Lloyd was influenced at an early age by the romantic revival styles of the early 1900s that are prevalent in the old neighborhoods of Tyler. He saw how classical forms and detailing combined with proper scale and proportions create an elegance and grace that enriched the neighborhoods. Extensive travels and work in Europe and Asia further gave him practical knowledge to pair with his talent for design.

Lloyd always hand-draws his initial ideas – many times in front of his clients in the initial design meetings. For him, there is a brain-hand-paper connection that he has never been able to replicate in any other ways and putting pen to paper is the best way to infuse emotion into a design. No matter the style, Lloyd designs houses to be homes that integrate the personalities of his clients and their families. Done right, he knows that the spaces he creates can become joyful places that elicit emotions and perfectly reflect who the clients are, with every room forming the foundation for lasting memories.

FACING PAGE: This Frank Lloyd Wright-inspired, modern prairie-style home looks forward as well as backward with its stately presence allowing it to fit in perfectly next to its historical neighbors. It is meticulously completed with luxury finishes and sophisticated details throughout.

TOP: The sculptural, cantilevered limestone staircase floats in front of the two-story glass wall and extends both up and down to the other levels of the home.

BOTTOM: The spacious kitchen is perfect for gatherings with seating options at the bar or the dining table. Photography by Reagan Jobe Photography.

"Homes that have a quiet, understated elegance excite me. They are more firmly rooted to their place and are undeniable in their presence without being ostentatious." —Lloyd Lumpkins

ABOVE: The pool becomes the focal point in the rear courtyard, flanked by the cabana and master bedroom.

FACING PAGE TOP: An 84-inch, three-sided, linear fireplace with its bronze metal overmantel is the focal point of the living room, punctuated by vivid blue furniture.

FACING PAGE BOTTOM: The upstairs balcony is an extension of the game room and provides beautiful views into the trees with its glass railings.
Built by Stephenson Custom Homes. Interior design by Sofia Joelsson Design. Photography by Reagan Jobe Photography.

153

"I love homes that delight the senses.
Our senses are where we anchor our memories –
sight, sound, touch, smells, and even taste." —Lloyd Lumpkins

ABOVE: As a modern Italian "abitazione" (dwelling), the inspiration for this home was the St. Regis Hotel in Rome, Italy.

FACING PAGE TOP: The magnificence of the main living area is extended to the rear portico when the floor-to-ceiling sliding doors are opened.

FACING PAGE BOTTOM LEFT: The bath, dressing area, and closet are combined in the guest suite to create an open and inviting space.

FACING PAGE BOTTOM RIGHT: The homeowners' suite bath is flooded with light from the floor-to-ceiling windows and white marble. Photography by Danny Piassick.

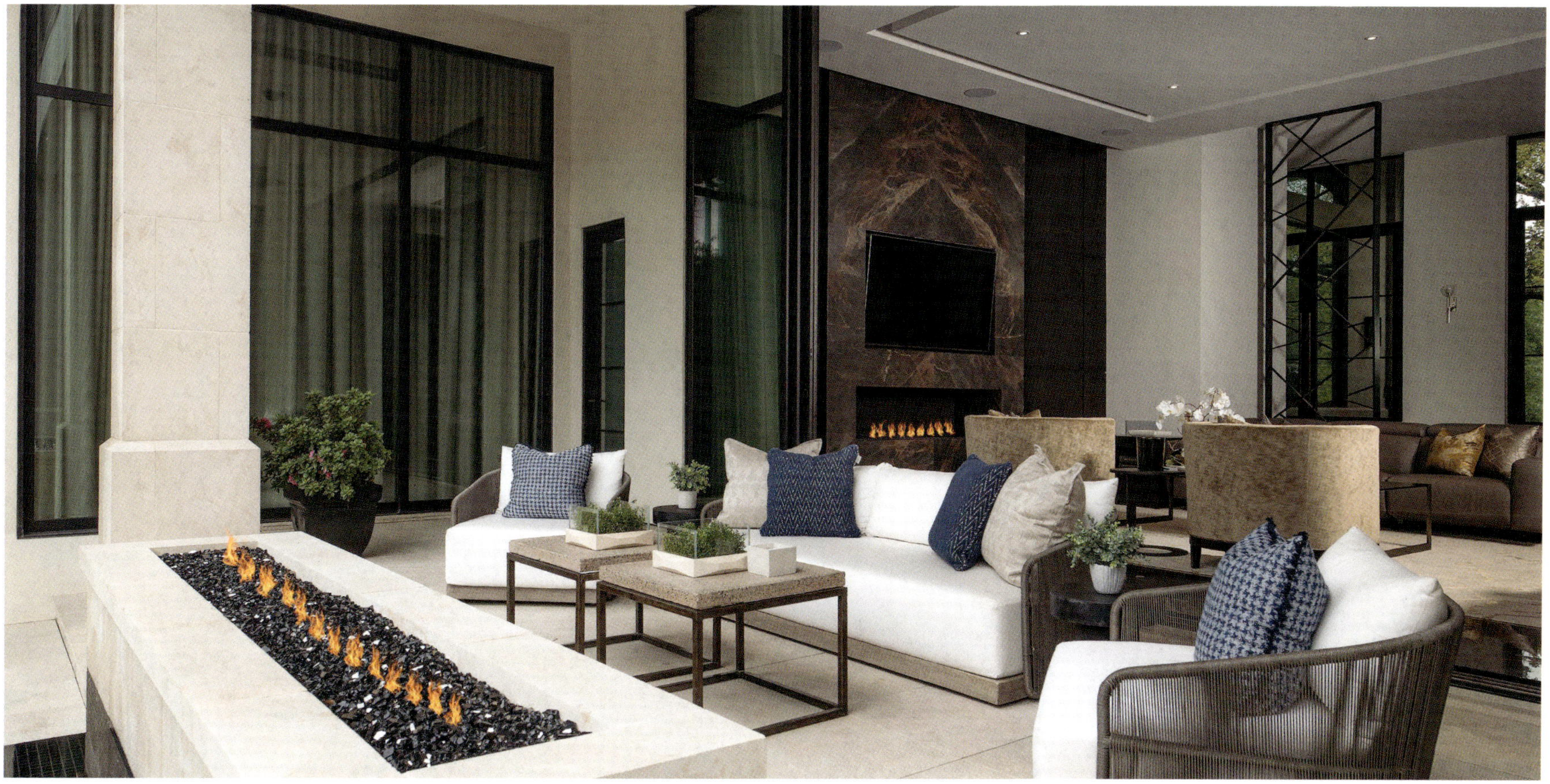

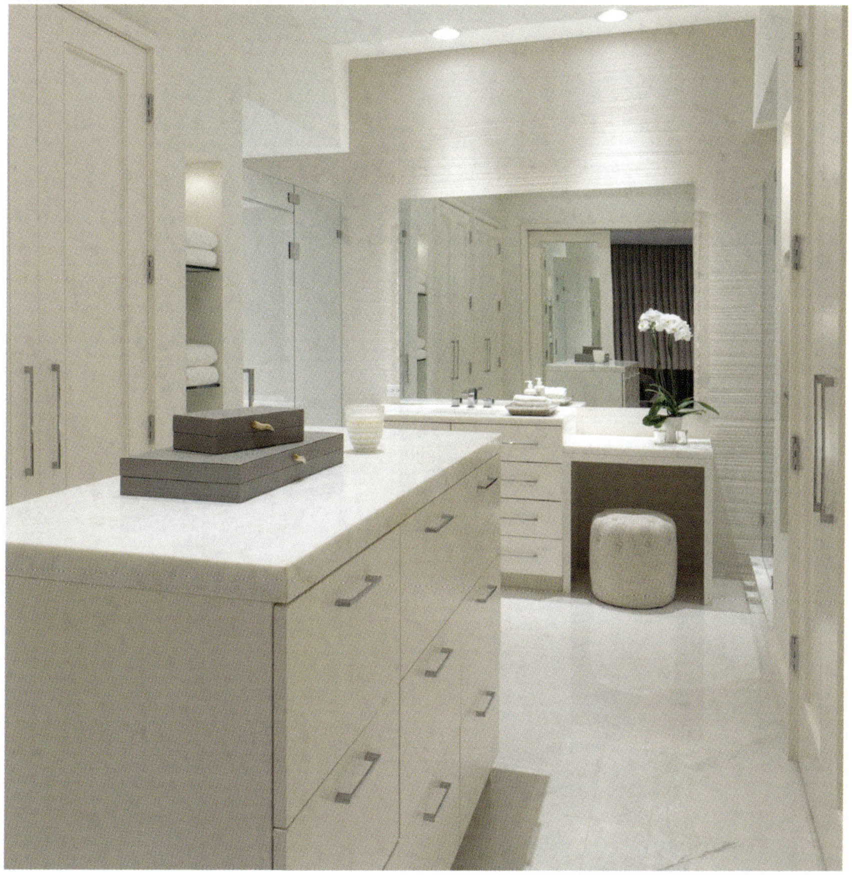

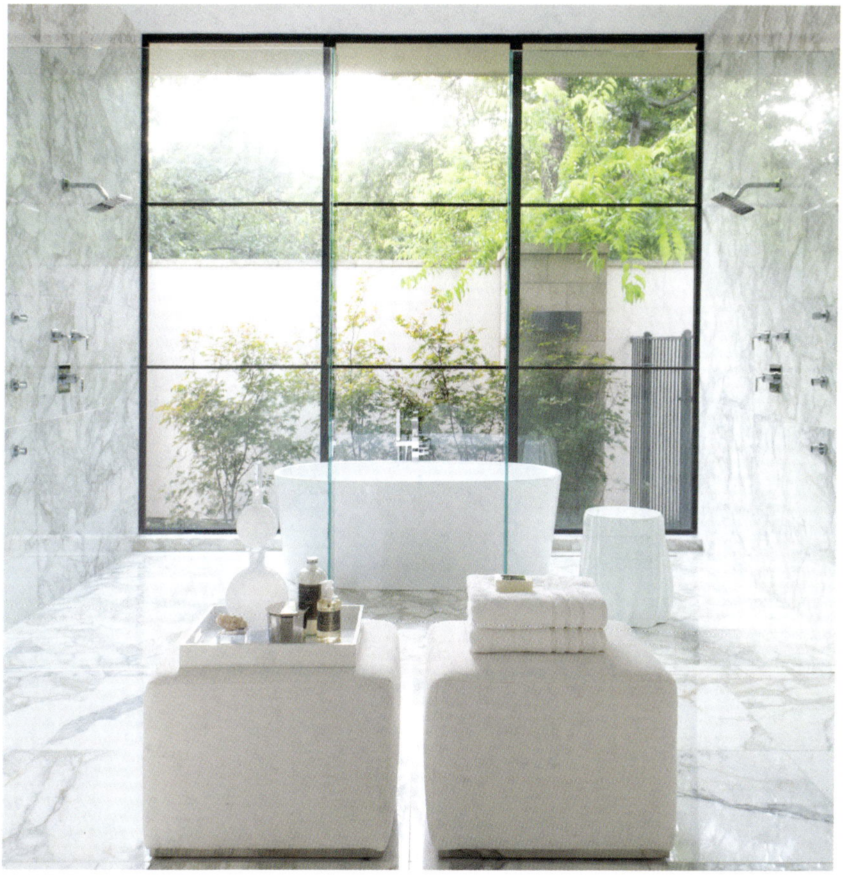

"My designs are developed from forms that are already in our subconscious memory. It helps bring warmth, comfort, and sense of belonging to the design – a sense of home." —Lloyd Lumpkins

ABOVE: The kitchen's polished lacquer cabinets and mirrored backsplash serve as an extension off the main living space.

FACING PAGE TOP LEFT: The back of the two-story formal living room is an undulating wall and open staircase.

FACING PAGE TOP RIGHT: This glass wine room is perfectly situated as an invitation to select a bottle upon entering the formal dining room.

FACING PAGE BOTTOM: The upstairs game room is open and spacious and offers views of the rear grounds as well as the entry portico on the first floor.
Built by Sharif Munir Custom Homes. Interior design by Rania Nassar. Photography by Danny Piassick.

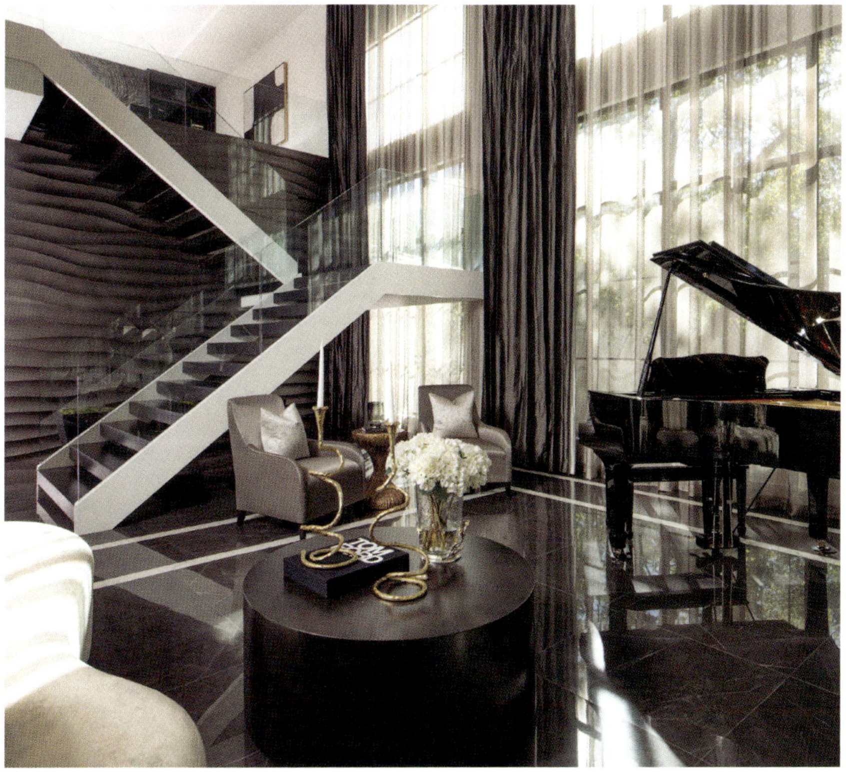

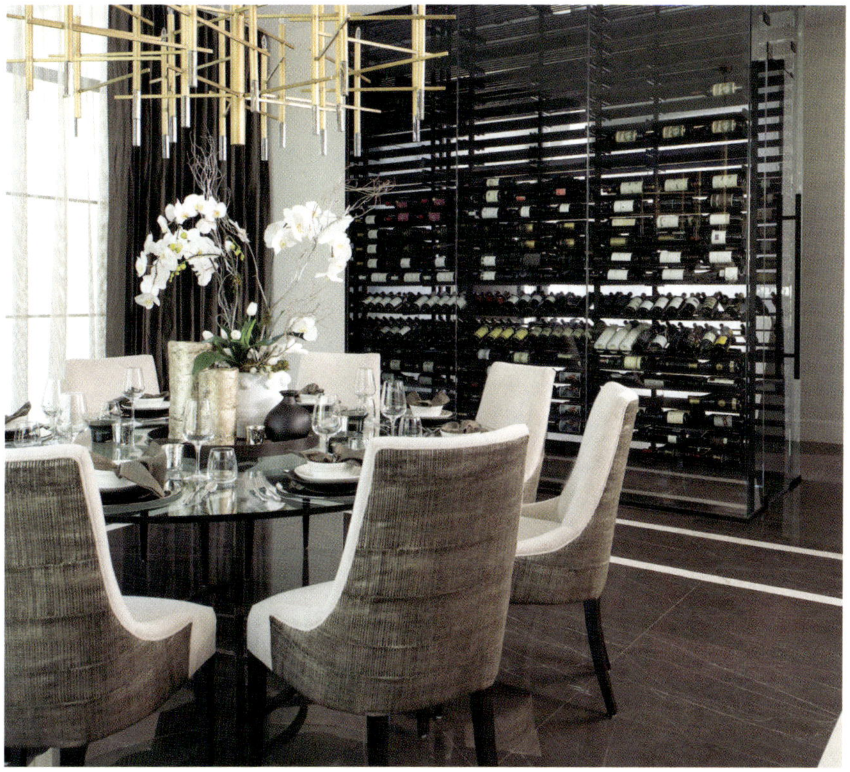

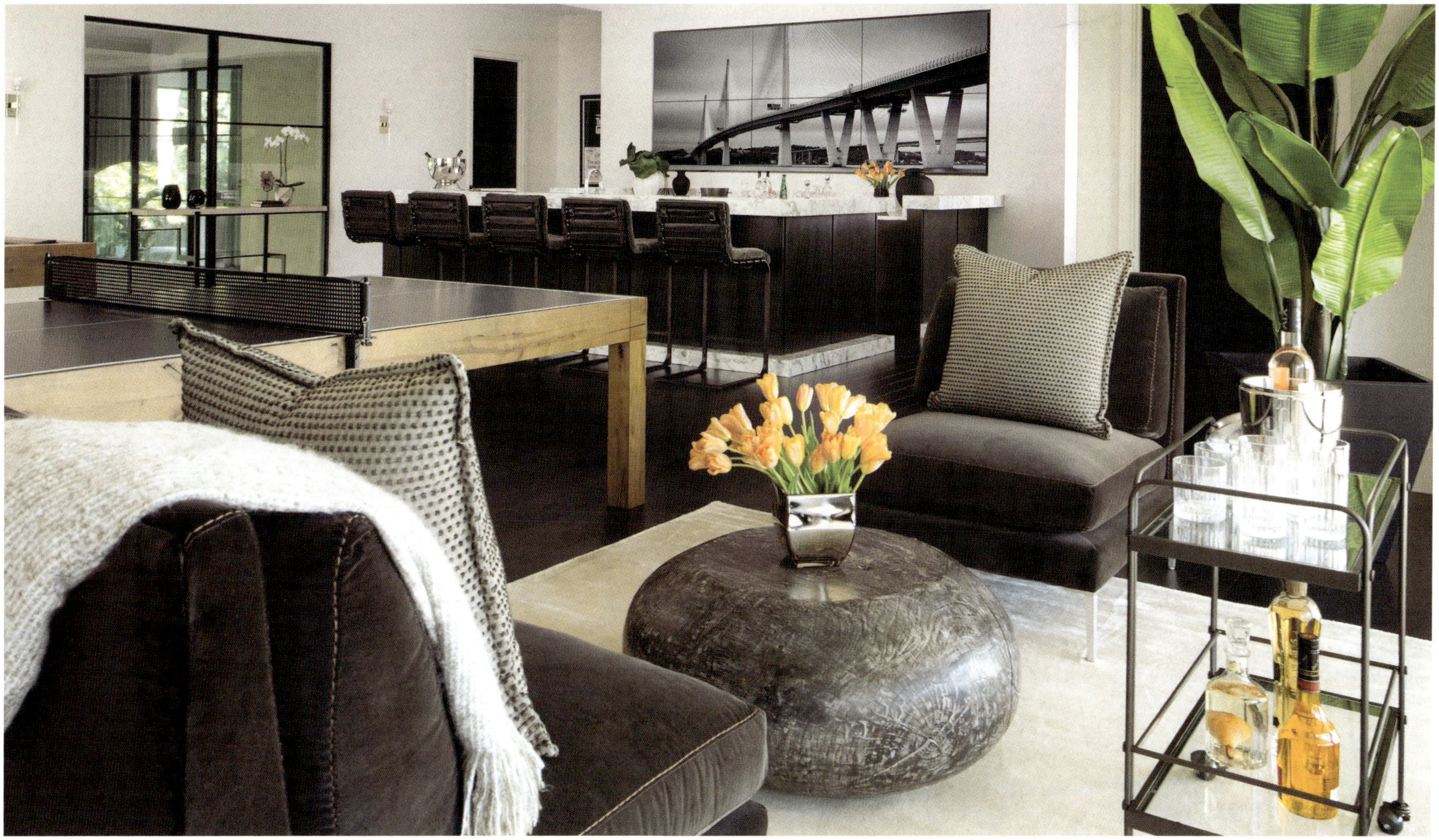

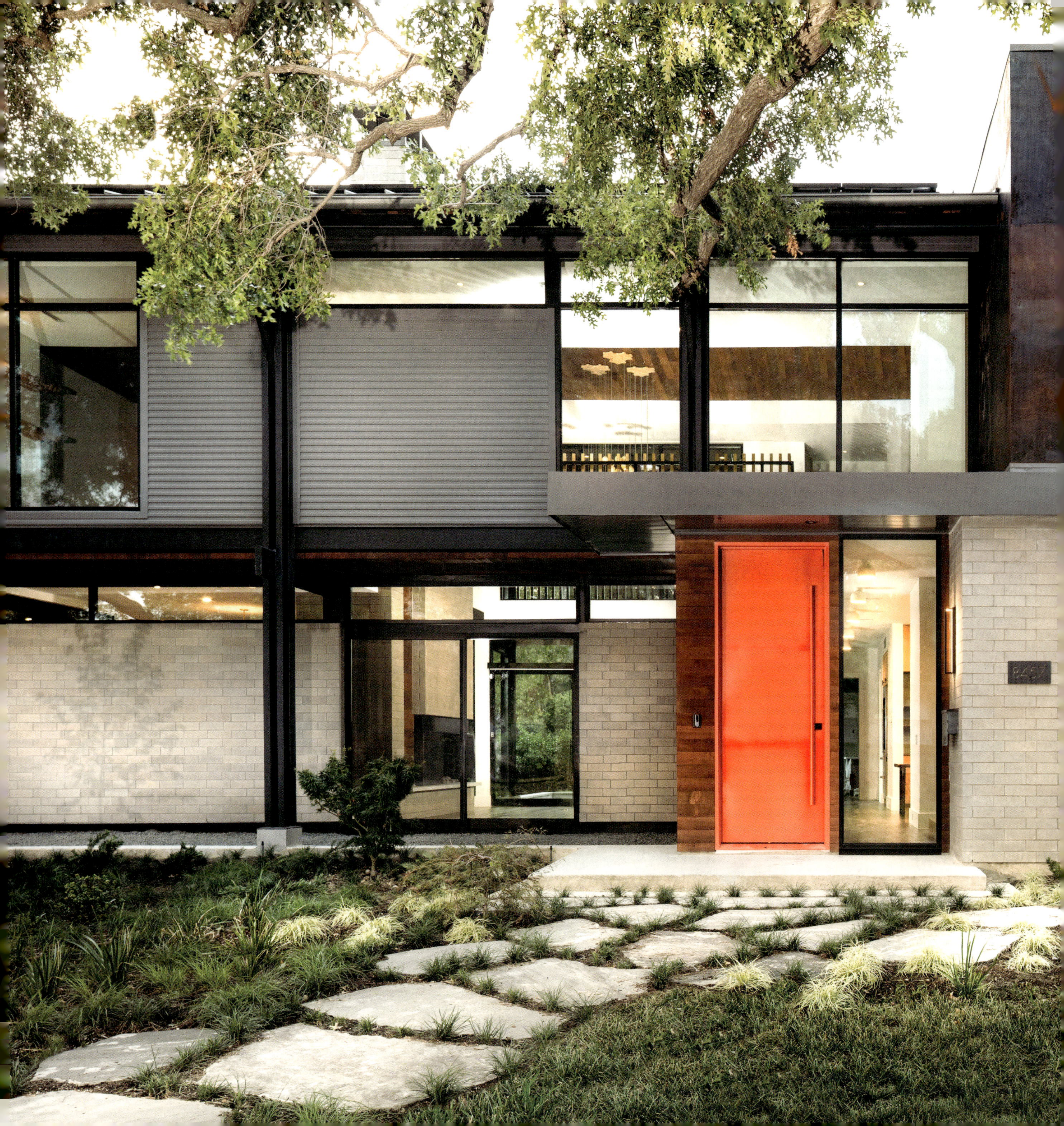

MAESTRI STUDIO

When Eddie Maestri, AIA, was five years old, his parents built a custom home – and, in his words, he was "obsessed" with the entire process. That obsession grew into a dream to be an architect, which he's fully living out at his namesake Maestri Studio, a boutique architecture and interior design firm that celebrates attention to detail and delivers a one-on-one level of service that fully prioritizes listening to and interpreting clients' needs, vision, and lifestyle.

Eddie's New Orleans roots, including the classical architecture of the historic Garden District, as well as his time spent studying in Italy, influence him to this day. No matter where his travels take him, from Kyoto to Stockholm, he finds great inspiration while soaking in the details of the architecture, interior design, and landscapes. "Our studio is made up of design-obsessed creatives who love to travel, enjoy art, and sketch, but our ultimate goal is to create a custom home – a complete vision, from architecture, to furniture, to art – that fits the personality and specific tastes of our clients," says Eddie. "Our team takes brilliant care to fulfill our clients' architecture and design aspirations – and everything is designed, curated, and carefully selected." To do the work, Maestri Studio leverages their diverse, versatile team of talents to expertly design any number of styles – from modern to classical – to create the perfect home for their clients. This variety of work constantly creates new, innovative design solutions – and they consider themselves to be problem-solvers who see challenges as the ultimate opportunity to move beyond the expected.

FACING PAGE: Inspired by a trip to Japan as well as childhood treehouse nostalgia, this 5,100-square-foot Dallas-area home with mid-century influences sits on a heavily treed, corner lot. The goal was to preserve every tree on site while inviting greenery inside through the wide expanses of glass. The homeowner wanted a bold, eccentric door – and this Golden Gate orange was just the right hue. Photography by Jenifer McNeil Baker.

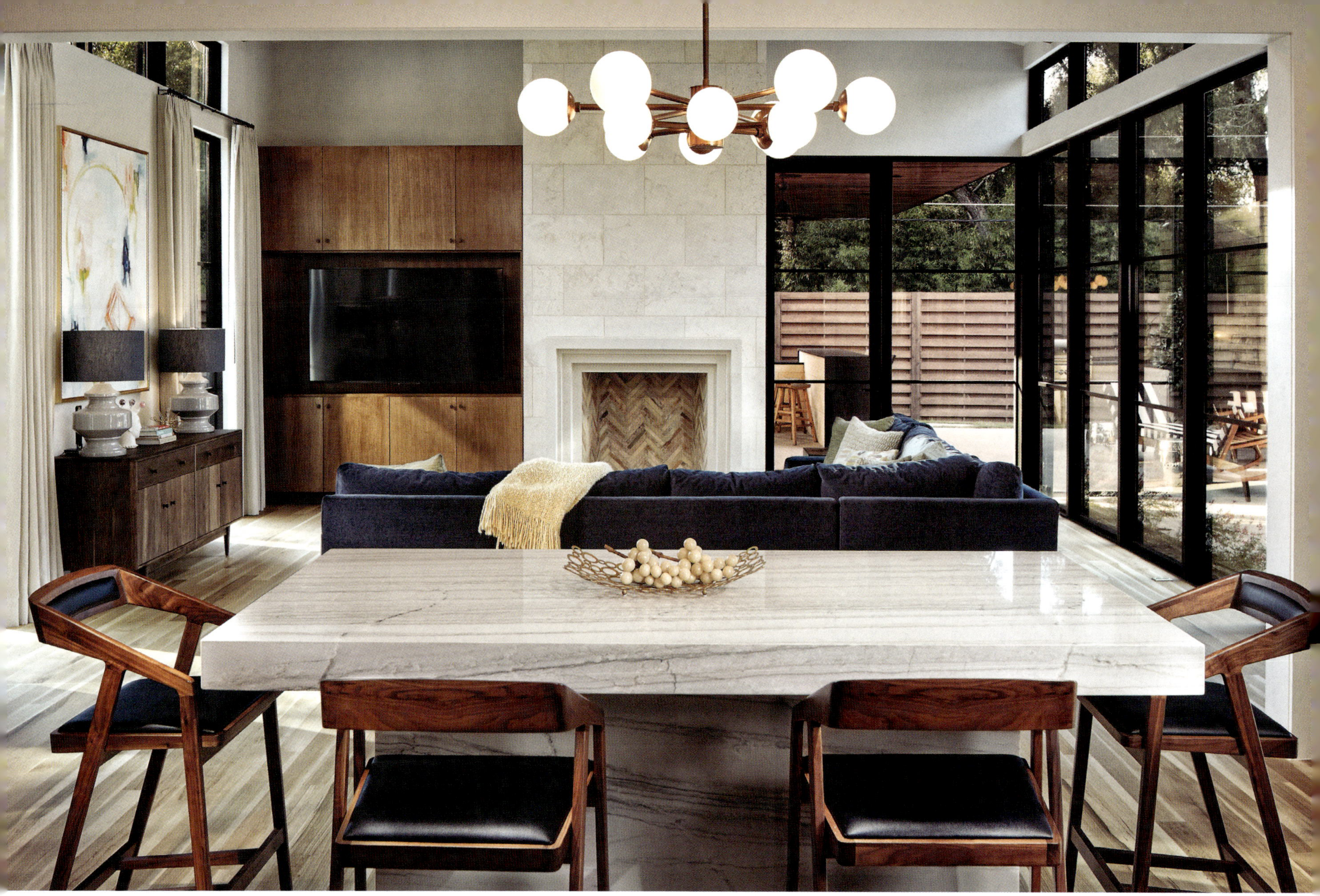
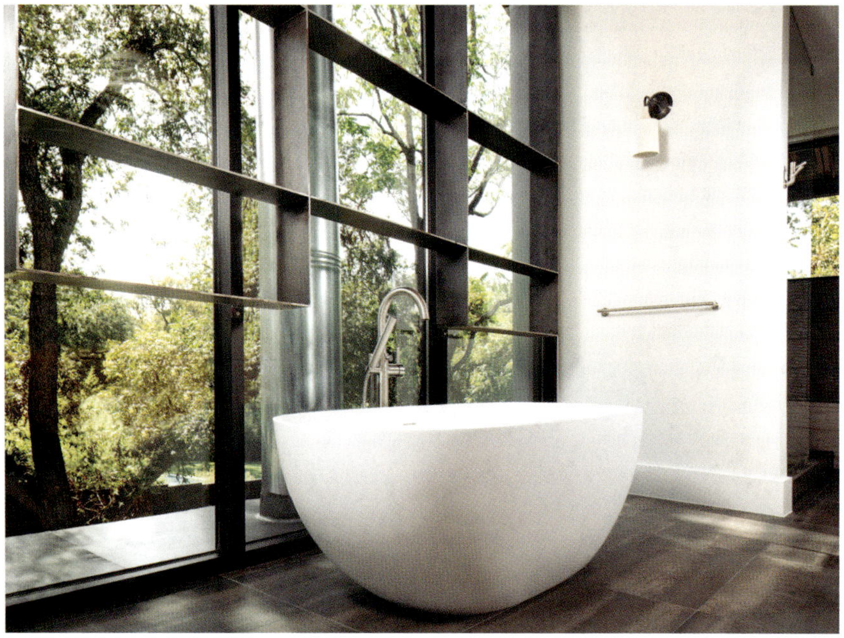
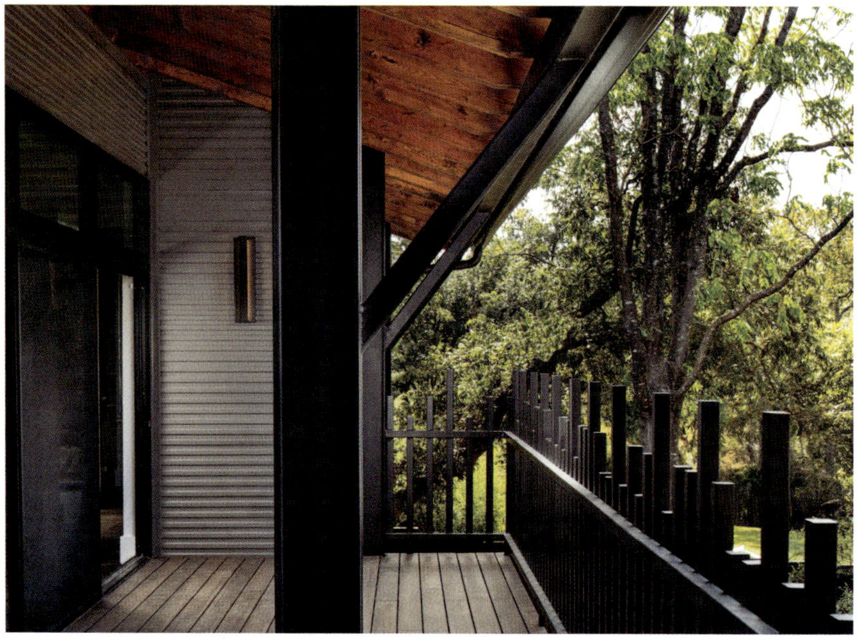

ABOVE LEFT: We custom-designed the console in this combined living and dining area, which also benefits from ample natural light via the clerestory windows. Photography by Aaron Dougherty.

ABOVE RIGHT: This light-filled, open gallery passageway shows a glimpse of how this house was built for entertaining. The doors to the front and back open out completely. The paneled wood ceiling and the interior structural steel columns – used here as a visual divide from the kitchen – are also continued through the exterior of the home, creating continuity. Photography by Jenifer McNeil Baker.

FACING PAGE TOP: This family room offers direct access to the outdoor pool and cabana. Inside, the custom, stone-wrapped table resonates with the custom fireplace, featuring an antique brick herringbone pattern. We also commissioned the abstract art piece for the side wall. Photography by Aaron Dougherty.

FACING PAGE BOTTOM LEFT: The master bath suite achieves a certain zen quality, overlooking the greenbelt. The flue outside tracks to the fireplace below; look closely, and you can see the steel hanging shelf system built around it. Photography by Jenifer McNeil Baker.

FACING PAGE BOTTOM RIGHT AND THIS PAGE BOTTOM RIGHT: At the back of the home, the glass box space on the first floor is the breakfast area, and upstairs is a full deck. The rust of the steel and wood accents provides warmth to the exterior palette. Photography by Jenifer McNeil Baker.

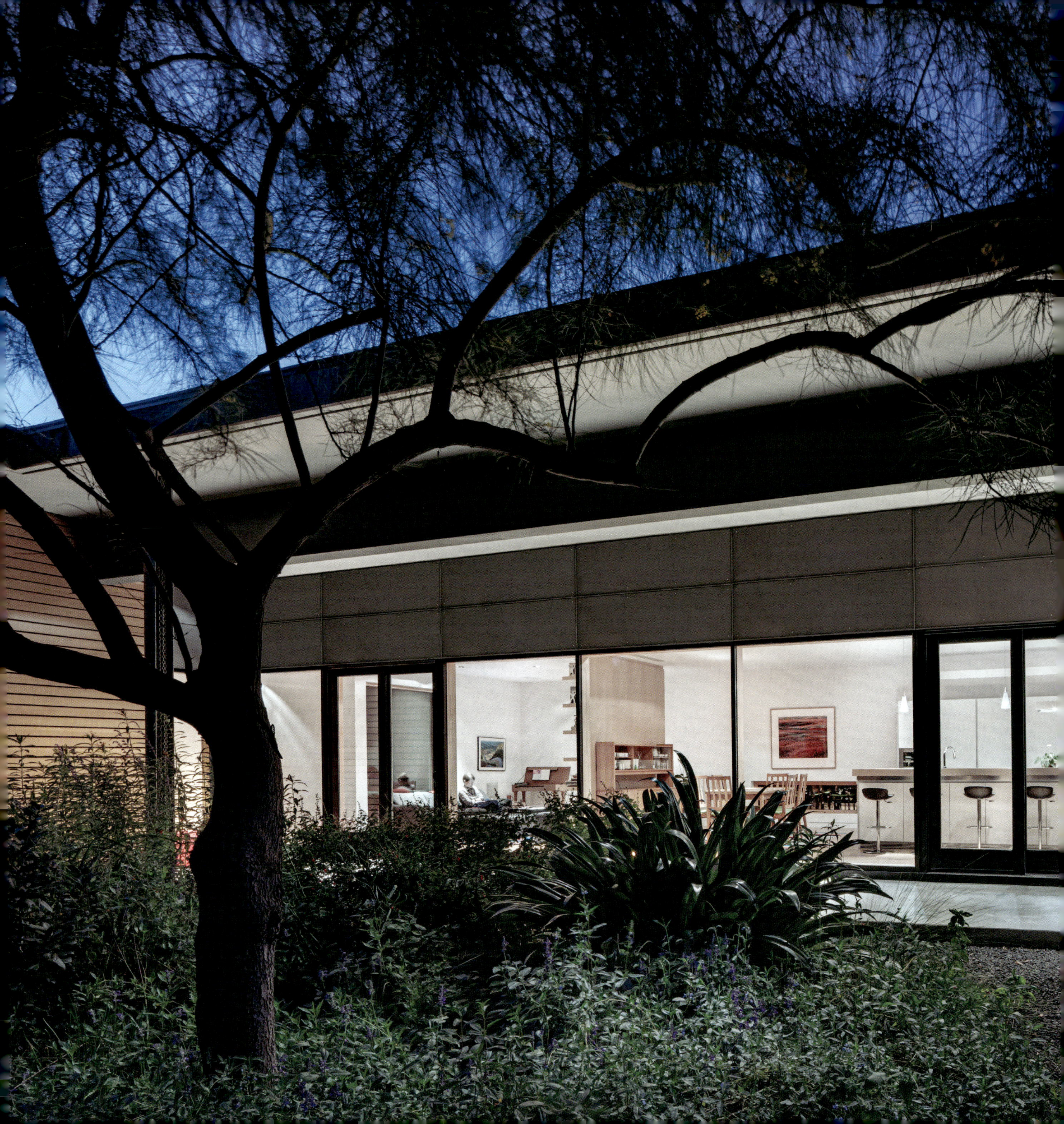

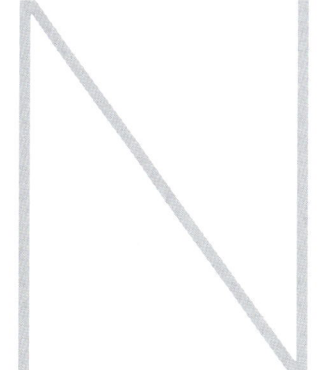

NORMAN WARD ARCHITECT & GEARHEART CONSTRUCTION

Completion of the Moretti house and landscape is only the beginning. The house has a narrative – initial ideas filled with creativity that soon became realized for all to know. Once past the green entry gate, courtyards, a glass bridge, and private garden are revealed.

Two courtyards serve as "Containers for Daylight." Sunlight moves about the courtyards, filling the interiors with changing ambient light until the day draws to an end. Morning begins a new day and sunlight once again fills the rooms. As an invitation for nature to be a part of this narrative, the south garden is open to the sky, filled with shadow and light and attracting butterflies, small birds, bees, and geckos. The south porch and window wall places the garden and the interiors on full display. The deep porch canopy contributes to the soft light within the house, while the garden is filled with a play of shadows and light throughout the year.

Courtyards, porches, and even breezeways have been a large part of the architect's work. Celebrating the sun's light and shadows is an ongoing pursuit. The contractor's conversations with homeowners Peter and Johanna Moretti along with the architect bridged his understanding of the design approach and quality of construction goals before beginning construction. This dialogue continued throughout the entire process, making a collaborative journey of imagination and thoughts of construction.

FACING PAGE: The south porch and garden.

NEXT PAGE LEFT: Moretti's studio is placed in the south garden. A walkway enclosed on two sides with glass serves as a bridge, linking the studio with the main house.

NEXT PAGE RIGHT: Two cubic courtyards are inserted within the house. Sunlight is constantly in motion within these courtyards. In the morning, light falls on walls facing east; by midday, light has moved across the ground, and by afternoon, light is moving up walls facing west. Sunlight connects day to night and season to season. The south porch and window wall links the garden and house. Photography by Charles Smith FAIA.

"I have found joy living in my house. My eyes are constantly drawn to nature just beyond my windows. I am connected to the natural world, from season to season."
—Johanna Moretti

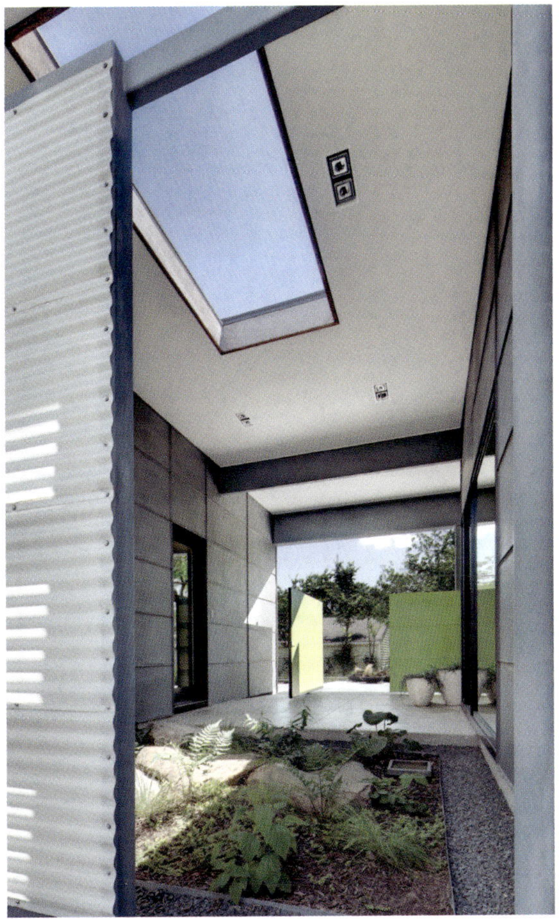
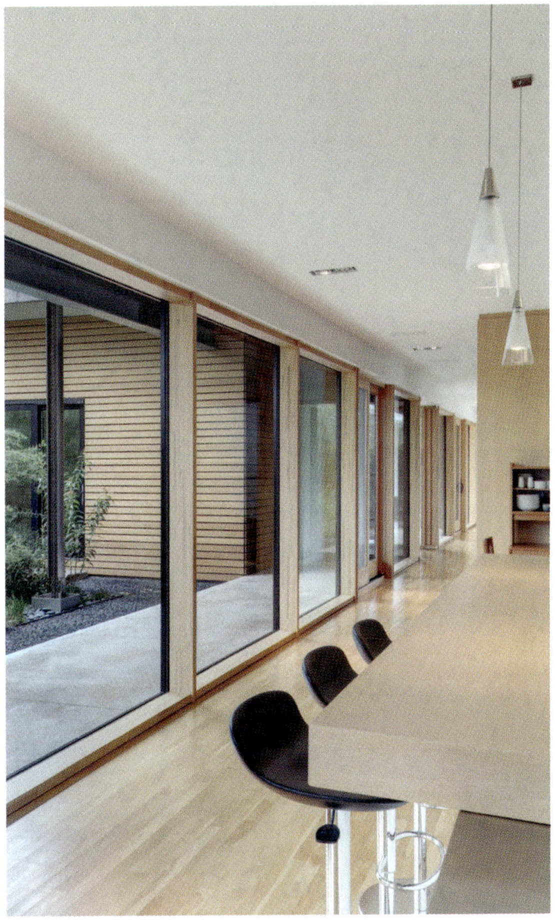
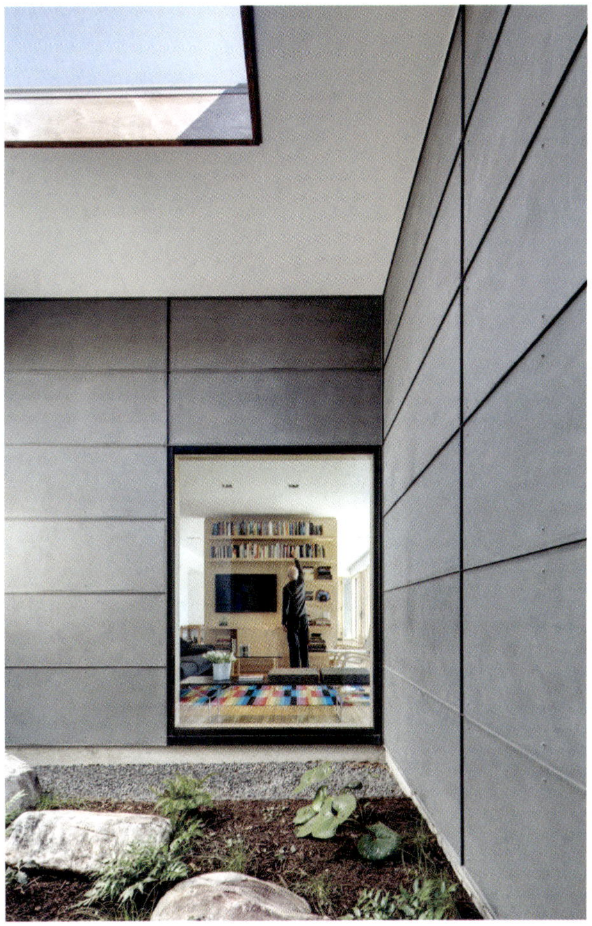
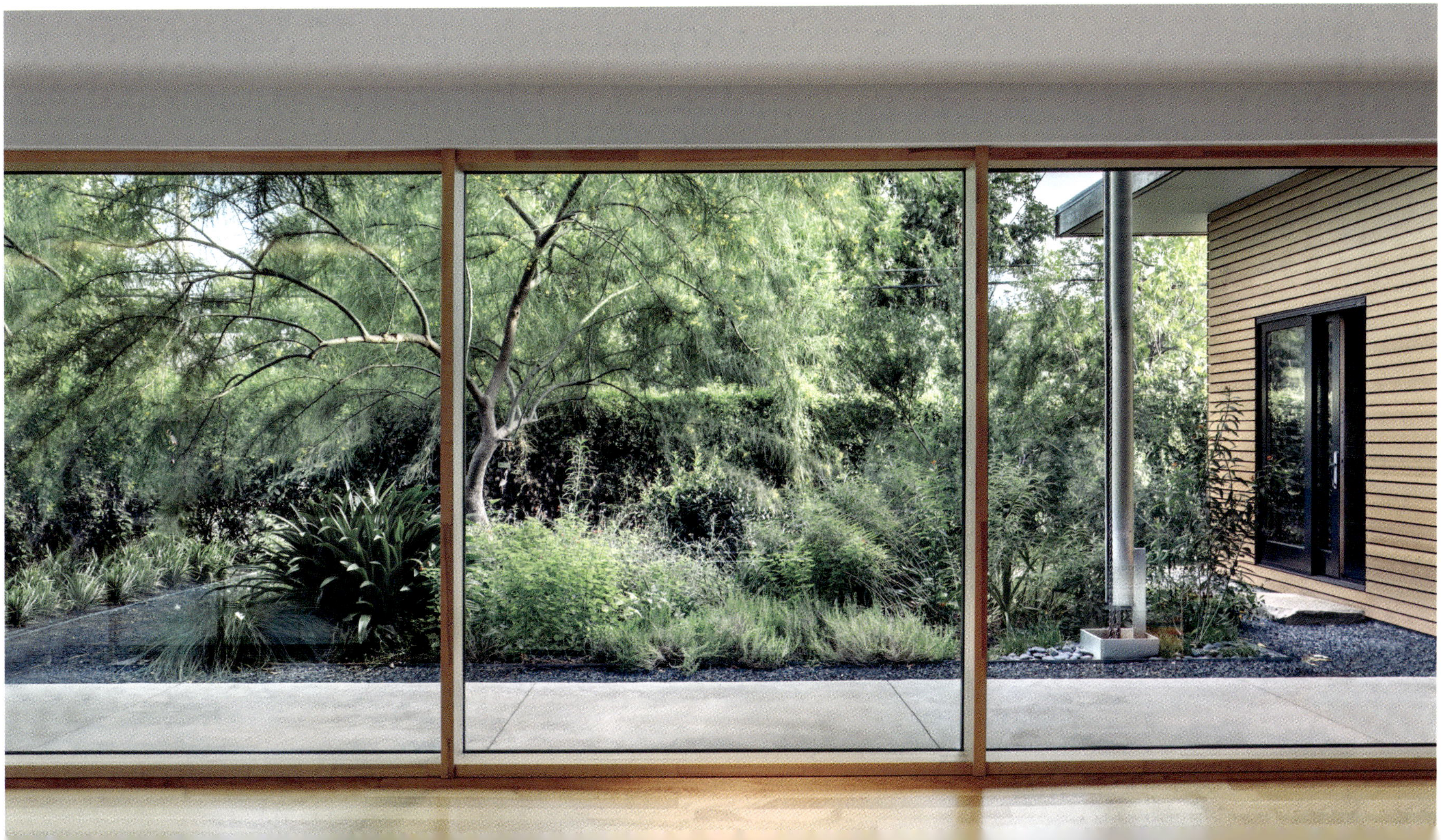

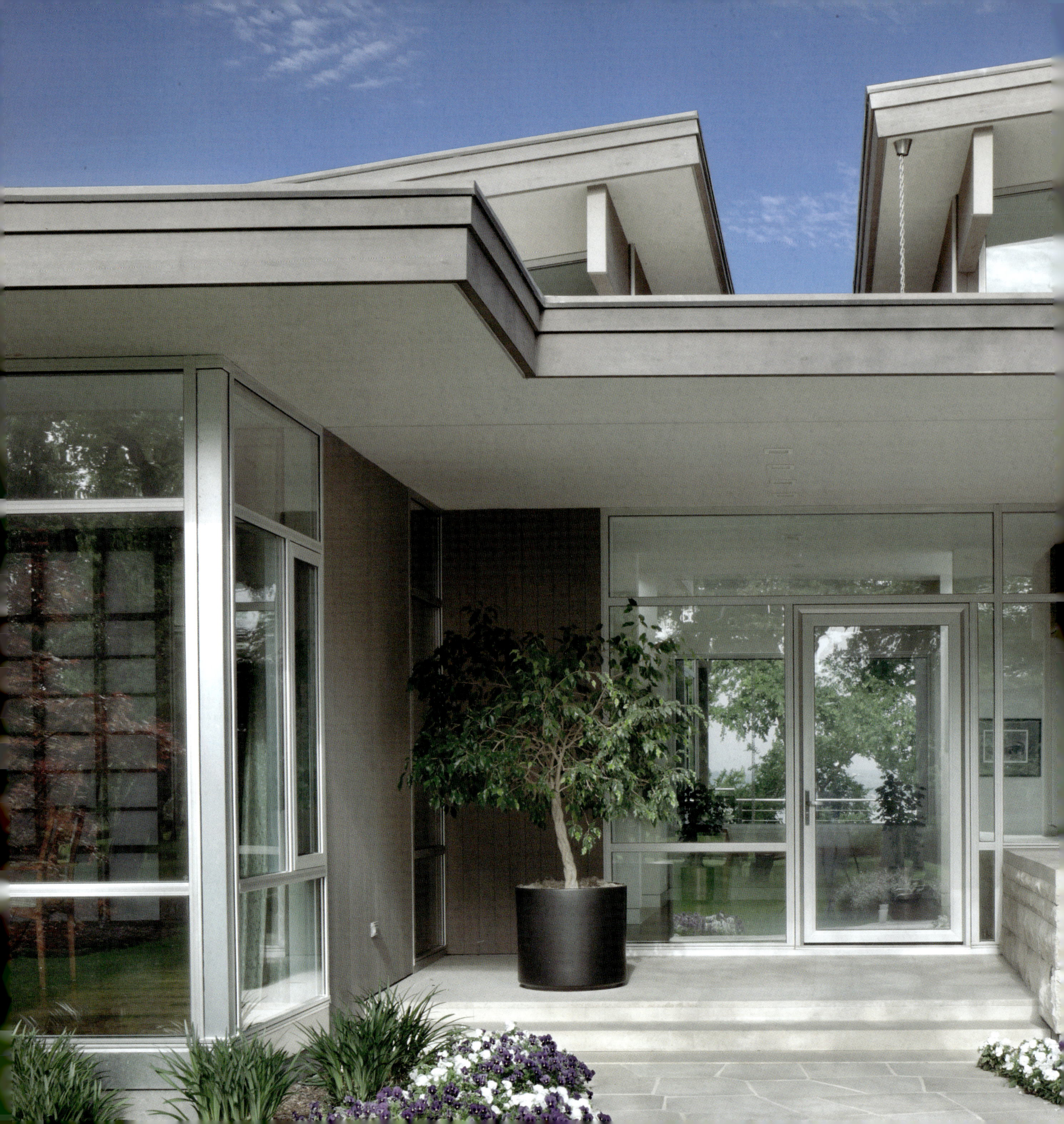

"All the natural light coming into the house is wonderful. Along with the sunrise and sunset views, we enjoy the changing light and shadows throughout the house. Love the modern, simple design Norman made for us. Incredible!"
—Betsy Schaffer

FACING PAGE: The house for Rick and Betsy Schaffer is positioned on a plateau's edge overlooking Eagle Mountain Lake. A variety of native hardwood trees form a canopy of filtered sunlight and shadow on the plateau.

A fully glazed entry is recessed under its own porch canopy. The porch is an interplay of arriving and a viewing of a western horizon beyond.

Lifting the roof canopy above the living areas invites morning sunlight and shadows to fill the rooms. The wall above the hallway is fully glazed between glulam beams with views towards the eastern sky.

Arising from profound clarity of thought and a deep joy of making, the architect's houses are a celebration of craft, creation, art, and life.

Building began with preserving an idea in tandem with the nature of the plateau. A well-defined construction path, under the tree canopy, leads to the construction site. Native hardwood trees and the natural state of the plateau were protected. This was the beginning of construction.

The joy of making is also a story of the contractor. A celebration of craft is clearly delineated for all to see. Photography by Charles Smith FAIA.

ABOVE: Lifting the roof canopy fills the room with morning sunlight and shadow.

FACING PAGE TOP LEFT: Screens with thick translucent paper refracts and diffuses sunlight. The screens can slide open or close for privacy without completely blocking light and sound.

FACING PAGE TOP RIGHT: Multiple levels of daylight travel along the hallway. The dining room screens are refracting and diffusing light, daylight is glowing softly above the hallway ceiling, and light and shadow within the courtyard are in constant motion.

FACING PAGE BOTTOM: The Schaffer House is an assembly of clearly defined volumes, under simple roof forms. Photography by Charles Smith FAIA.

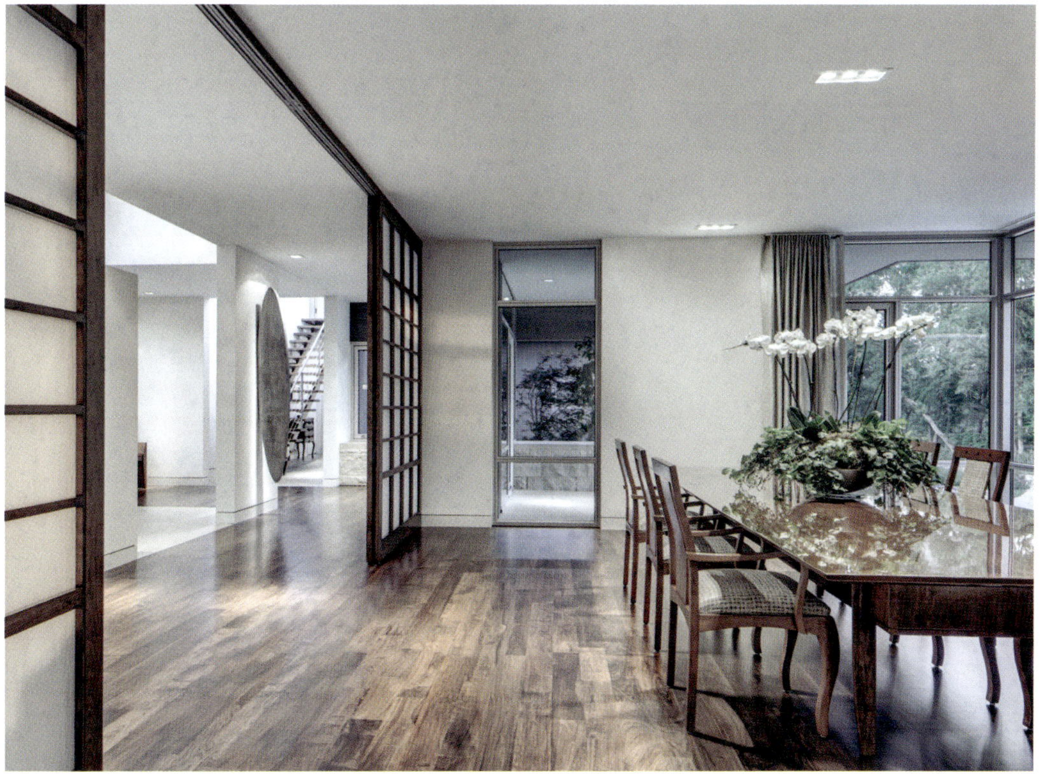

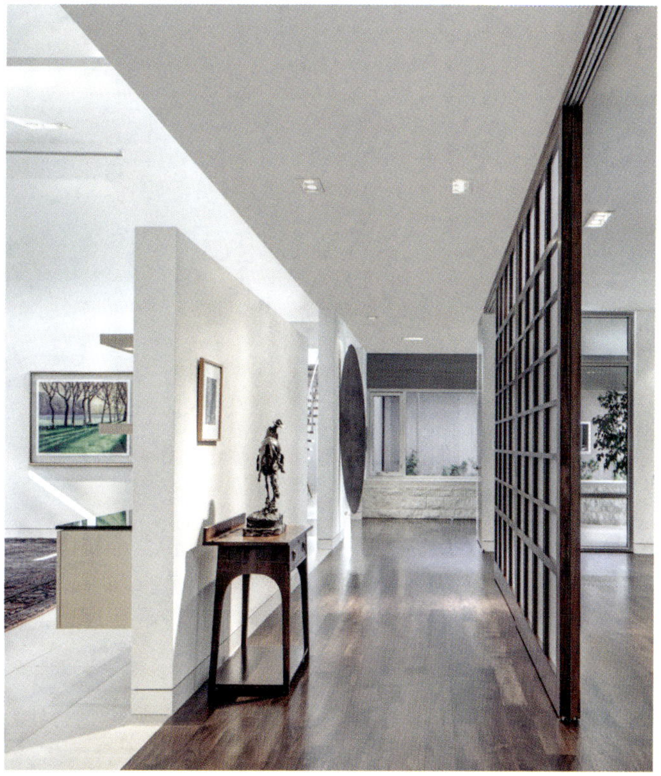

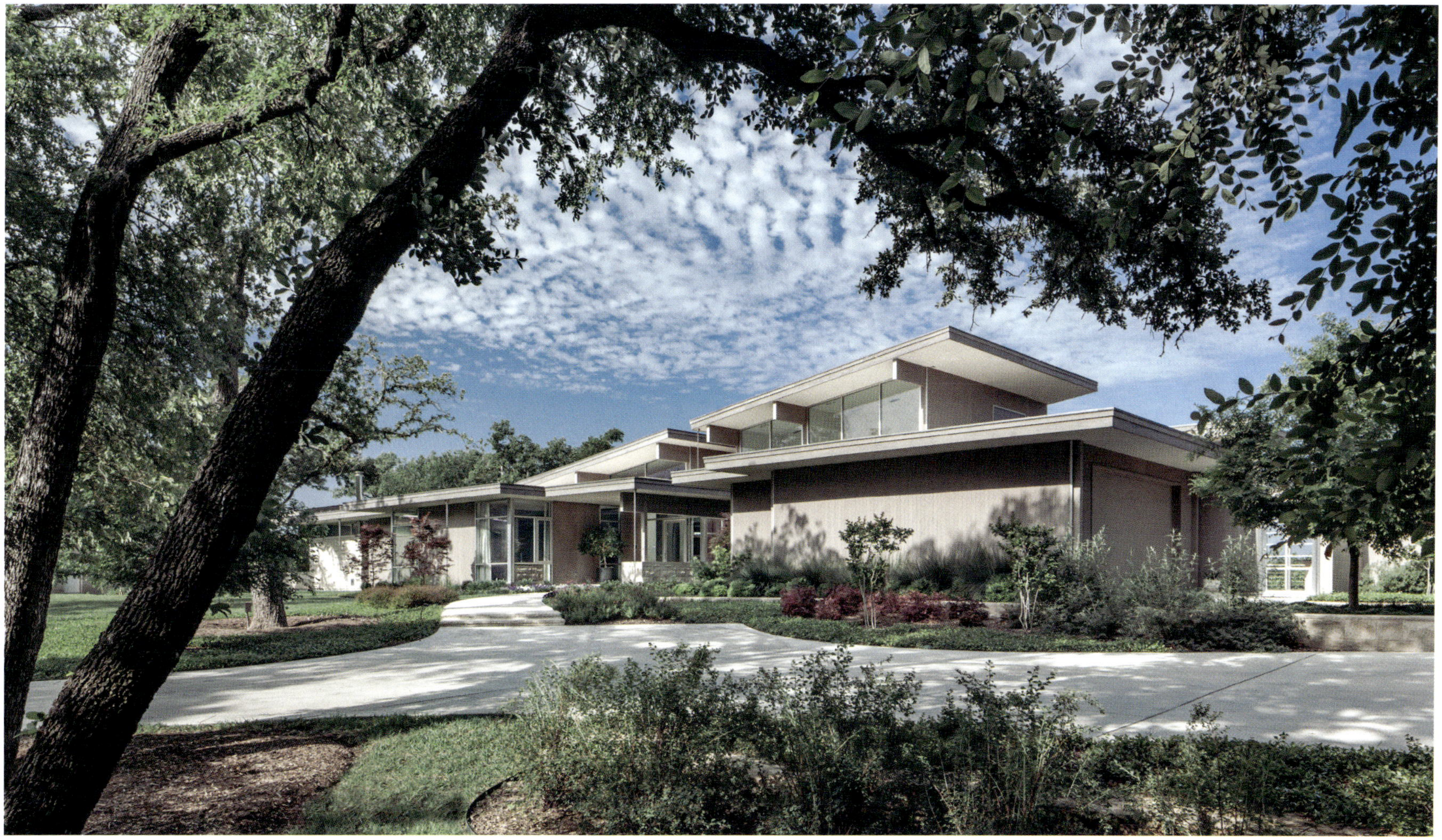

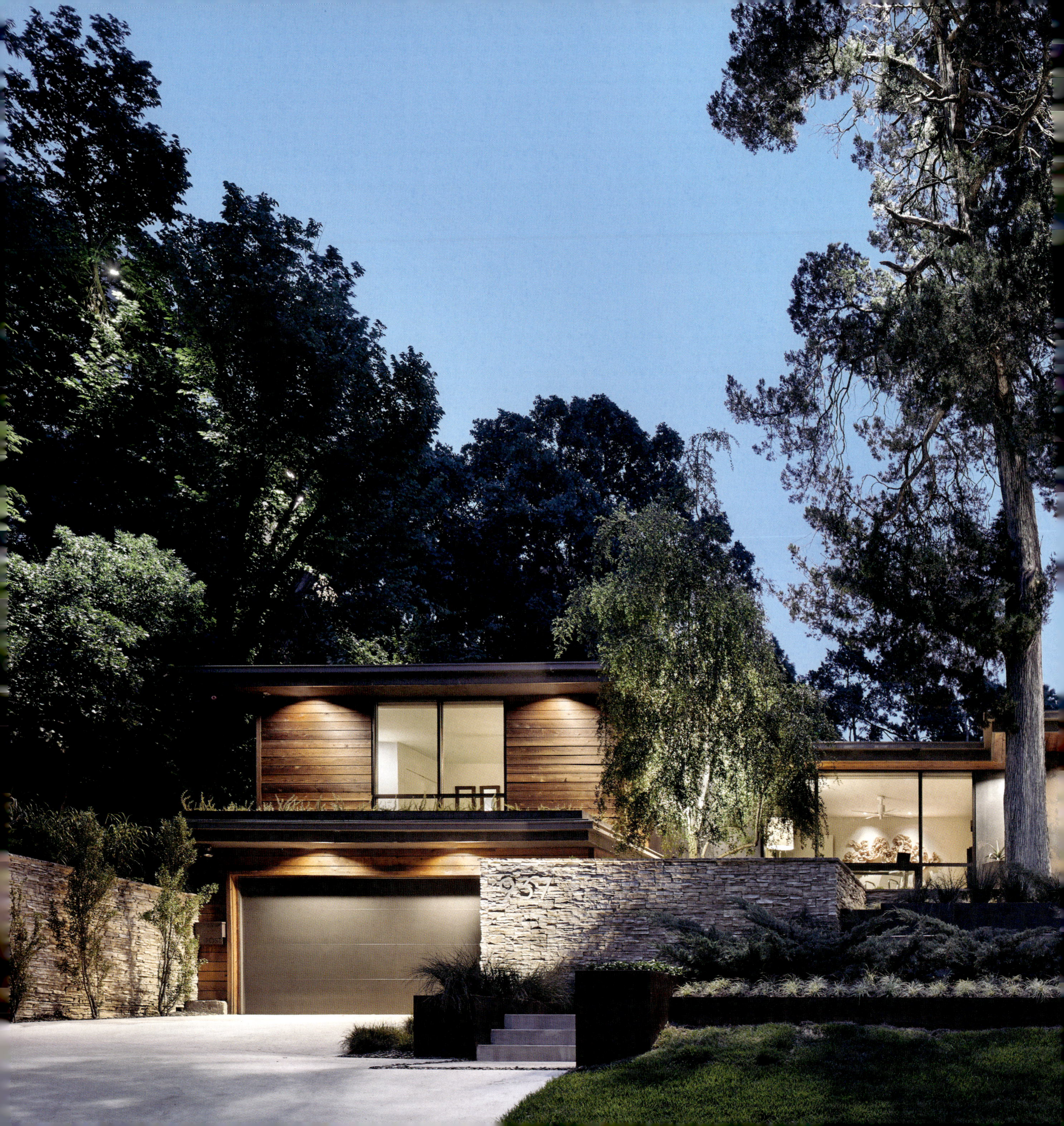
937

R

RGD+B

Connection. That's how Rene Gracia, founding partner and creative visionary behind RGD+B, describes his compelling style of work. He believes that architecture has the power to unify – and that design can lift us above the turmoil of daily life and connect us all to something greater than ourselves. At the same time, there is inspiring grounding from spaces and materials that maintain a strong connection to their natural surroundings.

For as long as Rene can remember, he's been fascinated by modern design and architecture – and the emotional response it elicits. "As the world around us swirls with obligations and distractions, it is all the more important that the space we inhabit provide us the comfort we need to dwell in serenity," Rene says.

At RGD+B, they spend their time and energy to create that space, whether it be a ground-up private residential project or an extensive reconstruction. Their spaces elevate the spirit and inspire a more mindful lifestyle. They consider themselves successful when their clients feel supported to lead more healthful, meaningful, and vibrant lives.

FACING PAGE: With the house perched 25 feet above street level, layered spaces and planes on the horizonal and vertical establish a human scale. Visitors are greeted by the sound of water as they approach the house, which flows from a shallow reflecting pool nestled below a glass jewel box. The floating bench halfway up the walk offers a place to stop and take in a view of the wooded environment. Photography by Benjamin Benschneider.

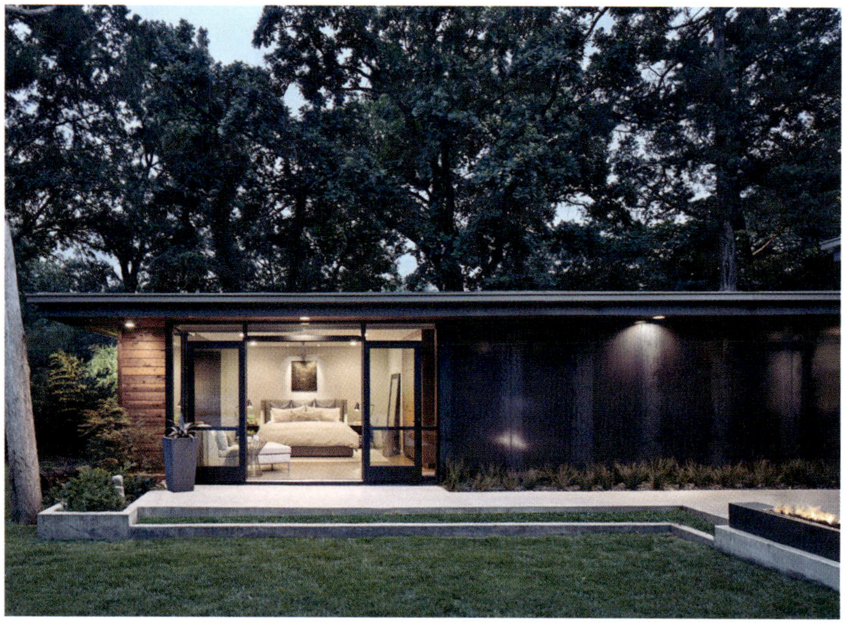
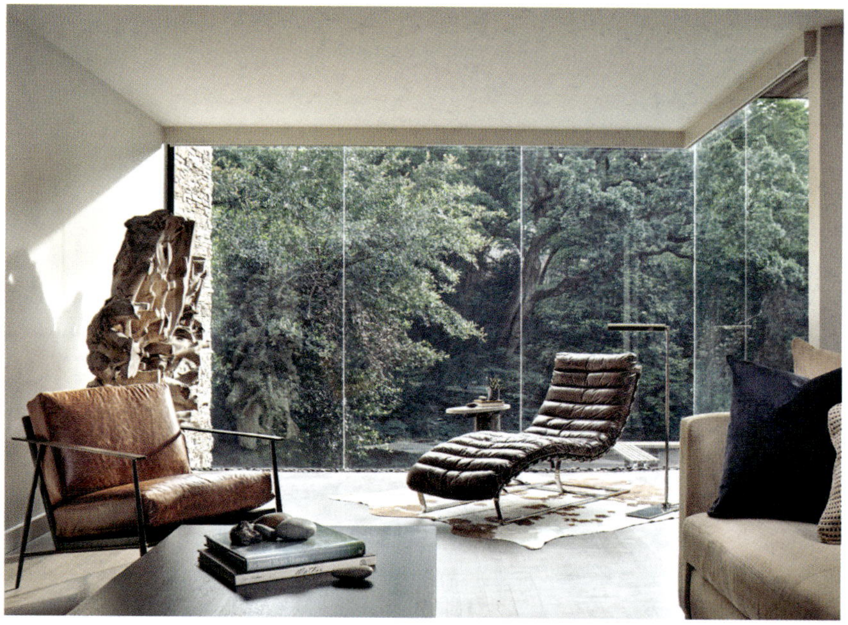
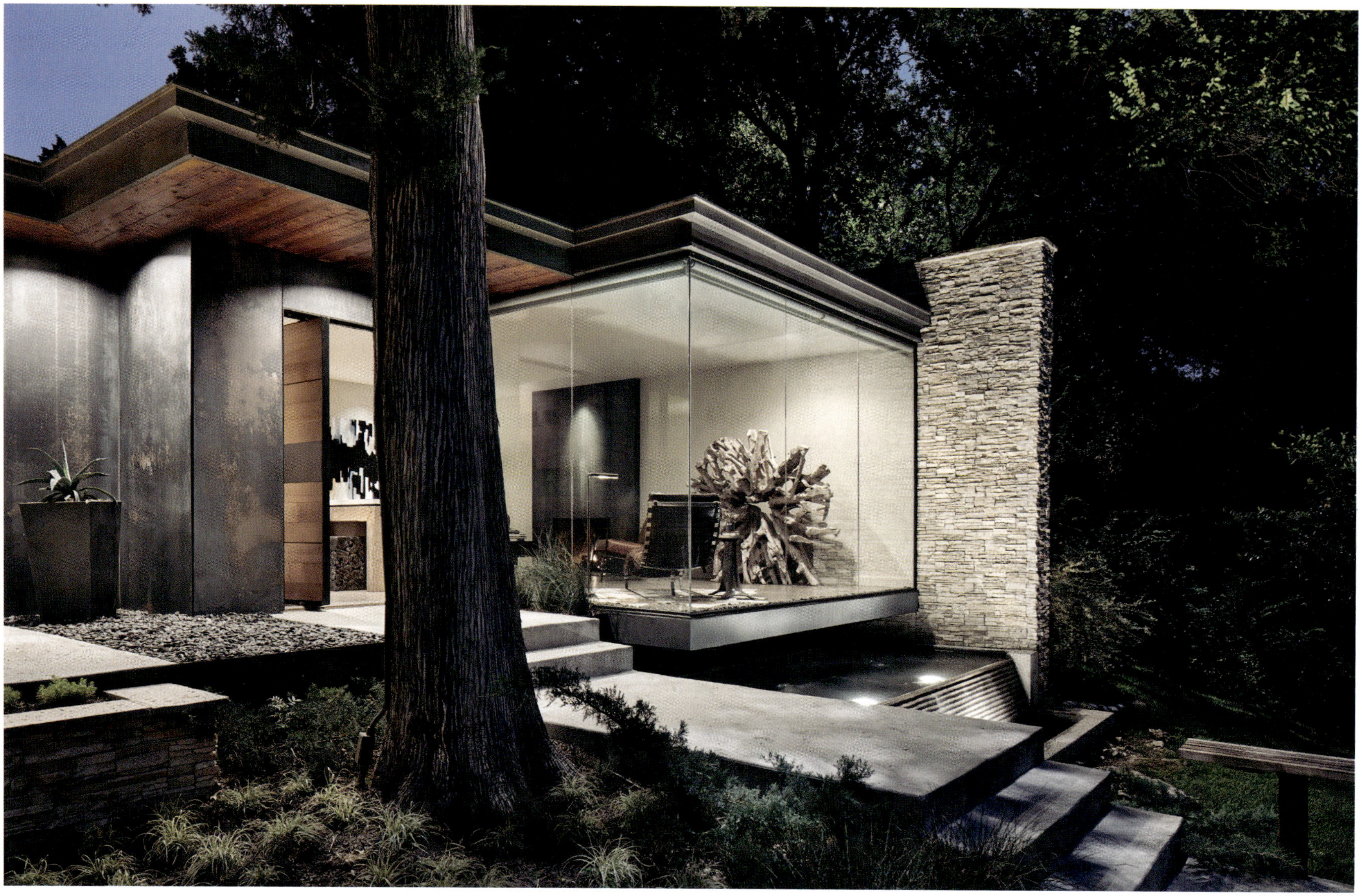

ABOVE: The site and house together collaborate to create a lush rear yard. A wall of glass enhances both the exterior and interior experience, allowing for consistent views of the wooded surroundings and terraced landscape.

FACING PAGE TOP LEFT: As the rear glass transitions to steel, the reflective quality of each begins to connect and reflect the natural surroundings.

FACING PAGE TOP RIGHT: Natural views form the focus of this home. The glass jewel box set above the reflecting pool gives the sensation of floating in a treehouse of glass with Mexican beach pebble providing a textural layer against the transparency of the glass to the nature beyond.

FACING PAGE BOTTOM: Spaces within the home transform with the light throughout the day. The reflecting pool creates an interplay with materials and space. In the evening, the reflection of water dances on the ceiling and blurs the line between interior and exterior. Photography by Benjamin Benschneider.

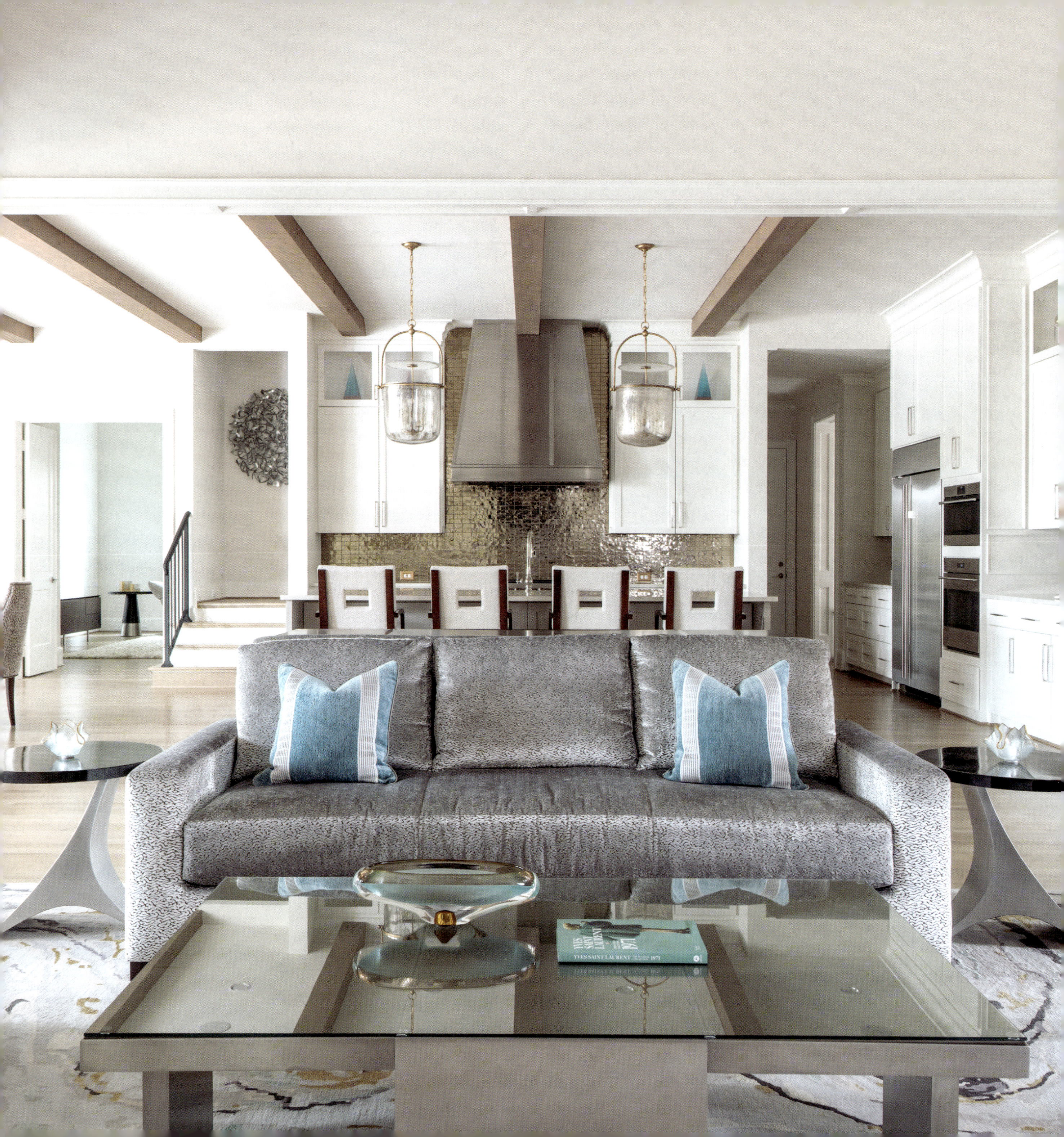
YVES SAINT LAURENT 1971

RICHARD TRIMBLE & ASSOCIATES

At Richard Trimble & Associates, relationships count. They know a positive rapport with their clients is key to a successful design – and they prioritize their clients' hopes and dreams before anything else. By establishing common goals early on, the firm ensures that the results they deliver are the results their clients expect.

The team has the necessary experience and flexibility to guide clients through every step of the project – from design and planning to implementation and maintenance. Whether it's a new home or the remodeling of an existing one – or even redecorating a corporate office – the professional interior designers at Richard Trimble & Associates assist with every facet of the project.

Those projects are wide and varied, including private residences throughout the United States, the Caribbean, and Europe. Whatever the vision, the eye of the experienced interior design team at Richard Trimble & Associates can bring it to life.

FACING PAGE: We had previously designed a large traditional home and corporate offices for this client, so a relationship was already in place when they decided to downsize into a new, modern home. The goal was to create a comfortable, functional space – with no formal rooms. The open-concept living plan features a sitting area around a fireplace with views to the dining area and kitchen and also into a den and TV area.

TOP RIGHT: The den was designed to be a comfortable space to relax and watch TV. An unusual grouping of sculptures form a unique cocktail table in front of the custom sectional. The luxurious area rug is a contemporary interpretation of a shag carpet.

BOTTOM RIGHT: The dining area features a whimsical, black-and-white photo of a giraffe. The stainless-steel contemporary piece in the stair landing is part of a special collection of art. Photography by Michael Hunter.

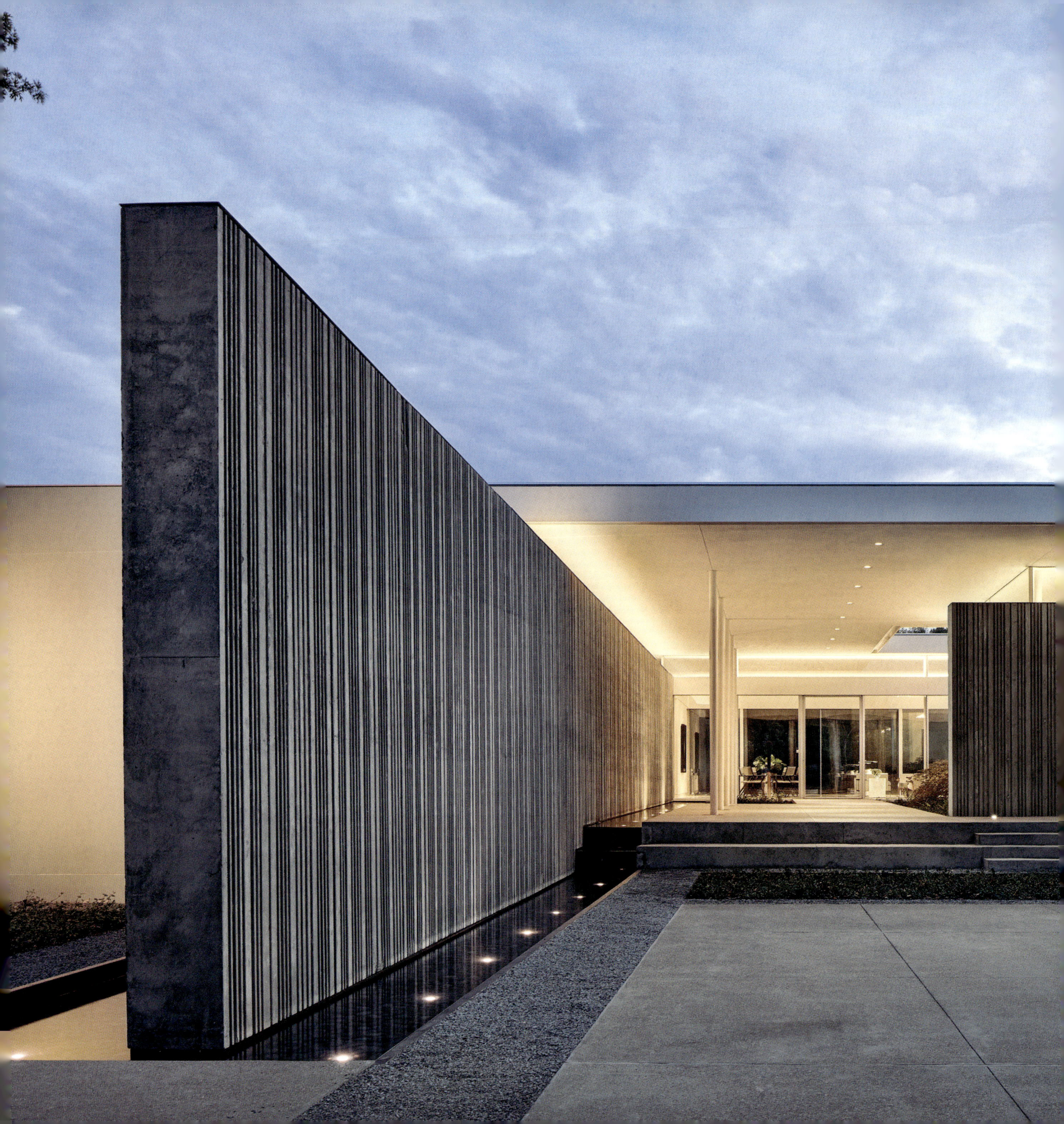

SEBASTIAN CONSTRUCTION GROUP

Founded in 1948 by self-trained architect, George Sebastian, Sebastian Construction Group has been under the leadership of John Sebastian, an architect himself, since 1992. Constructing meaningful architecture has been the driving passion behind the work of the firm for many decades, and it is this company core value that has guided it through its growth over the years. John's continued commitment to executing the architect's design intent is seen at every level of the firm, as he provides the highest level of quality that is without equal in this market.

In the early years, George Sebastian built his reputation on a pursuit of perfection and the very finest craftmanship. As the size and complexity of the company's projects grew, John recognized the need to modify delivery systems to maintain the focus on quality while simultaneously improving control over cost and schedule. This significant shift led to the intentional recruitment of talented people from the commercial construction sector whose updated systems and processes made Sebastian better suited for large-scale estate projects.

Over the past seven decades, Sebastian has evolved into a unique hybrid construction group that has found success in integrating the best aspects of the old craftsman builder with the capabilities of the larger, more sophisticated commercial builder. It is this strong foundation that allows the company to support what John and his team love most of all – bringing the very best architecture to life.

FACING PAGE: The entrance to this 10,000-square-foot home is illuminated specifically to emphasize the reflecting pool wrapping the architectural concrete wall.
Photography by Casey Dunn.

"The most exciting part of this project is the fact that the architect's design is a prototype — it has never been built before. It has around 400 linear feet of custom architectural concrete walls that will never be replicated."
—Ben Davis,
Sebastian project superintendent

TOP: At the back end of the home, the spine wall juts out into the infinity swimming pool, which reflects the framework of the home.

BOTTOM: Interior designer Magni Kalman created the perfect balance of modern design and comfort in the home's main living space.

FACING PAGE TOP LEFT: The Panoramah! window and door system allows natural light to fill the dining area and provides guests with a view of the outdoor covered terrace.

FACING PAGE TOP RIGHT: The master bath showcases an incredible stand-alone bathtub serving as a statement feature of the room.

FACING PAGE BOTTOM: An open-air central courtyard features a rain-catching and planted impluvium surrounded by floor-to-ceiling panels of glass that integrate the indoors with the outdoors. Photography by Casey Dunn.

179

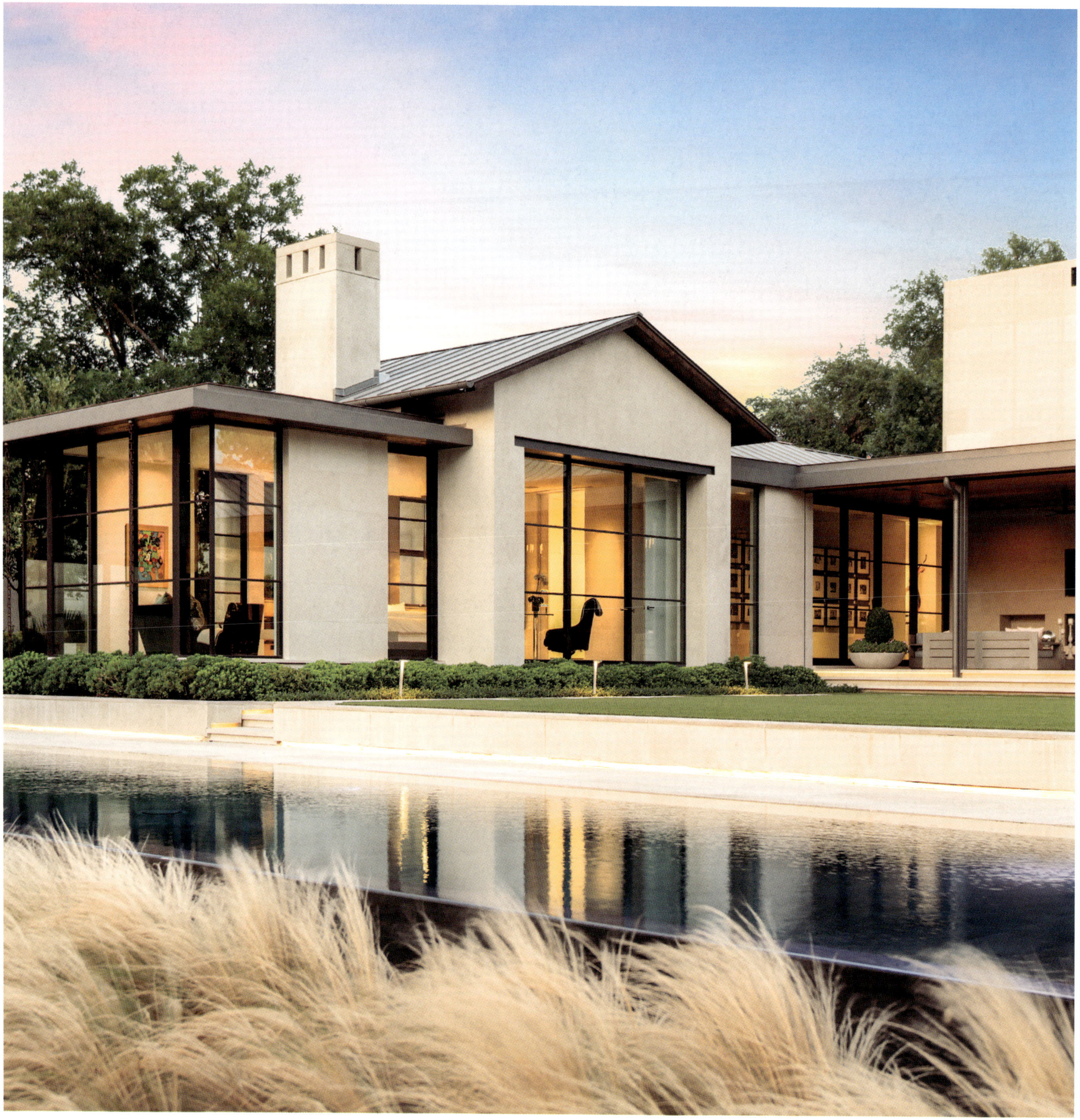

ABOVE: The dark walnut paneled ceiling warms the bright living space of this home, as the steel-framed window and door units allow an influx of natural light.

FACING PAGE: The negative-edge pool is amplified by Mesa Design's landscape design work, which includes a highly manicured lawn panel surrounded by low plantings. Photography by Nathan Schroder Photography.

ABOVE LEFT: The exterior of the home is comprised of both Texas Lueders Limestone and stucco, which is complemented beautifully by the metal "paint grip" roof.

ABOVE RIGHT: Porcelain floors – with the appearance of highly polished concrete – are used throughout the entertainment areas of the house, dramatically reflecting all types of light.

FACING PAGE: A quiet reflecting pool greets you as you enter the house, which boldly reflects the modern architecture and art within the home. Photography by Nathan Schroder Photography.

"Neutral selections for furnishings and interior materials allow the artwork to shine beneath a carefully designed interior lighting system." —SHM architect

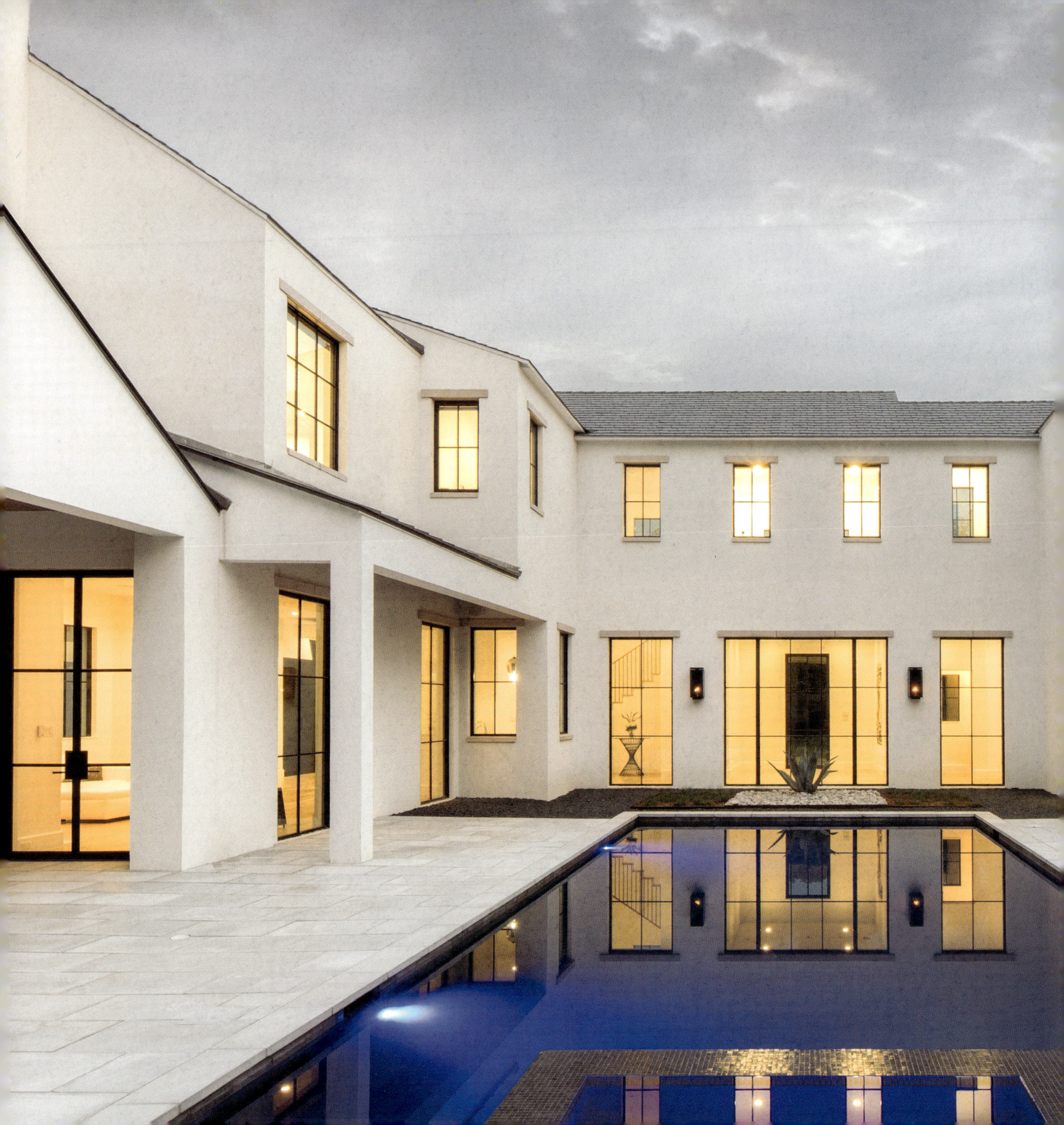

STARR CONSTRUCTION

Gary Starr's longtime fascination with architecture – and homes, specifically – had him driving around his Colleyville, Texas neighborhood as a teen, just to look at houses and walk new construction sites. Now, he does that daily – except the houses and the sites are his own, so to speak. Starr Construction's philosophy is to not just build beautiful homes for their clients, but also to foster ongoing relationships. Their goal is for each client to be as happy with the whole experience as they are with the finished product: their new home.

Gary has built his team much the same way as he builds homes – carefully and with intent. From the solid foundation of construction expertise to the final critical element of homeowner relationships, Starr Construction is passionate about detail and excellence – both in their product and in their people.

A hands-on approach also sets Gary apart; he visits job sites weekly, if not daily, and stays involved in the process from start to finish. His ultimate passion is to take every structure to the next level with new and innovative building techniques that exceed his clients' dreams.

FACING PAGE: Oversized windows and custom steel doors flood the interior of this home with natural light and give way to beautiful views of the backyard oasis from almost every room of the house. Photography by Costa Christ Media.

"Building the highest quality home is just the beginning. Creating lasting relationships with our clients is the heart of our business." —Gary Starr

ABOVE LEFT: Floor-to-ceiling custom-mulled windows illuminate the interior of this home, bringing the warmth of sunlight into the foyer. Clean lines, Lueders limestone, and select white-oak wood floors lead to the formal dining room at the end of the grand hall.

ABOVE RIGHT: The elegant floating marble vanity, with integrated sink and mirror-mounted sconces, creates a contemporary look and feel in this guest bath. Brass fixtures echo the lining of the light casings.

FACING PAGE TOP: The timelessness of this black-and-white kitchen is achieved by the oversized white marble waterfall island and backsplash, married with the ebony-stained red-oak contemporary cabinetry. The use of chamfered doors and drawers eliminates the need for cabinet hardware, maintaining a clean uninterrupted line.

FACING PAGE BOTTOM: Upon entry to this home, you're greeted with a wall of Kolbe windows that provide an uninterrupted view of the large pool in the backyard retreat. Photography by Costa Christ Media.

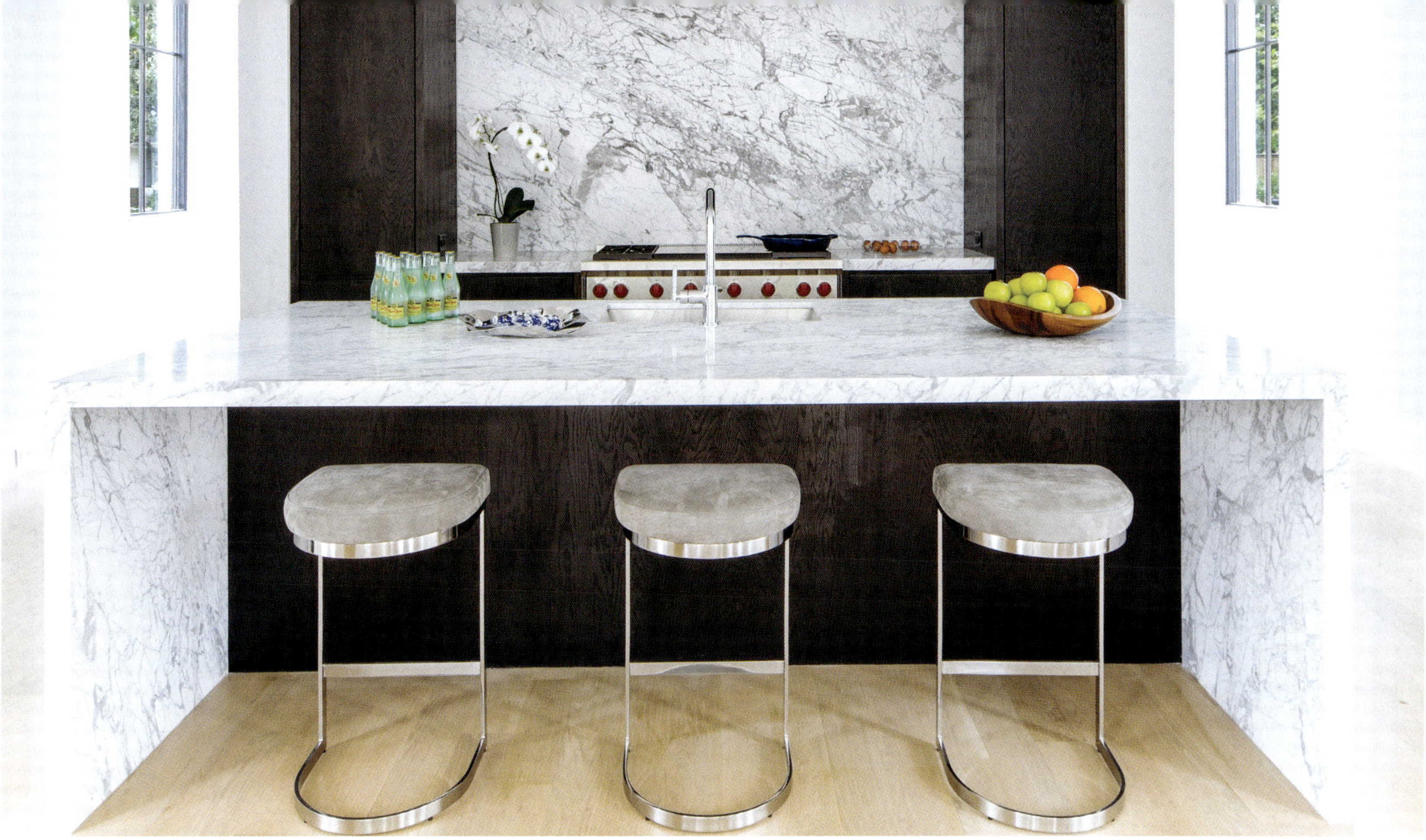

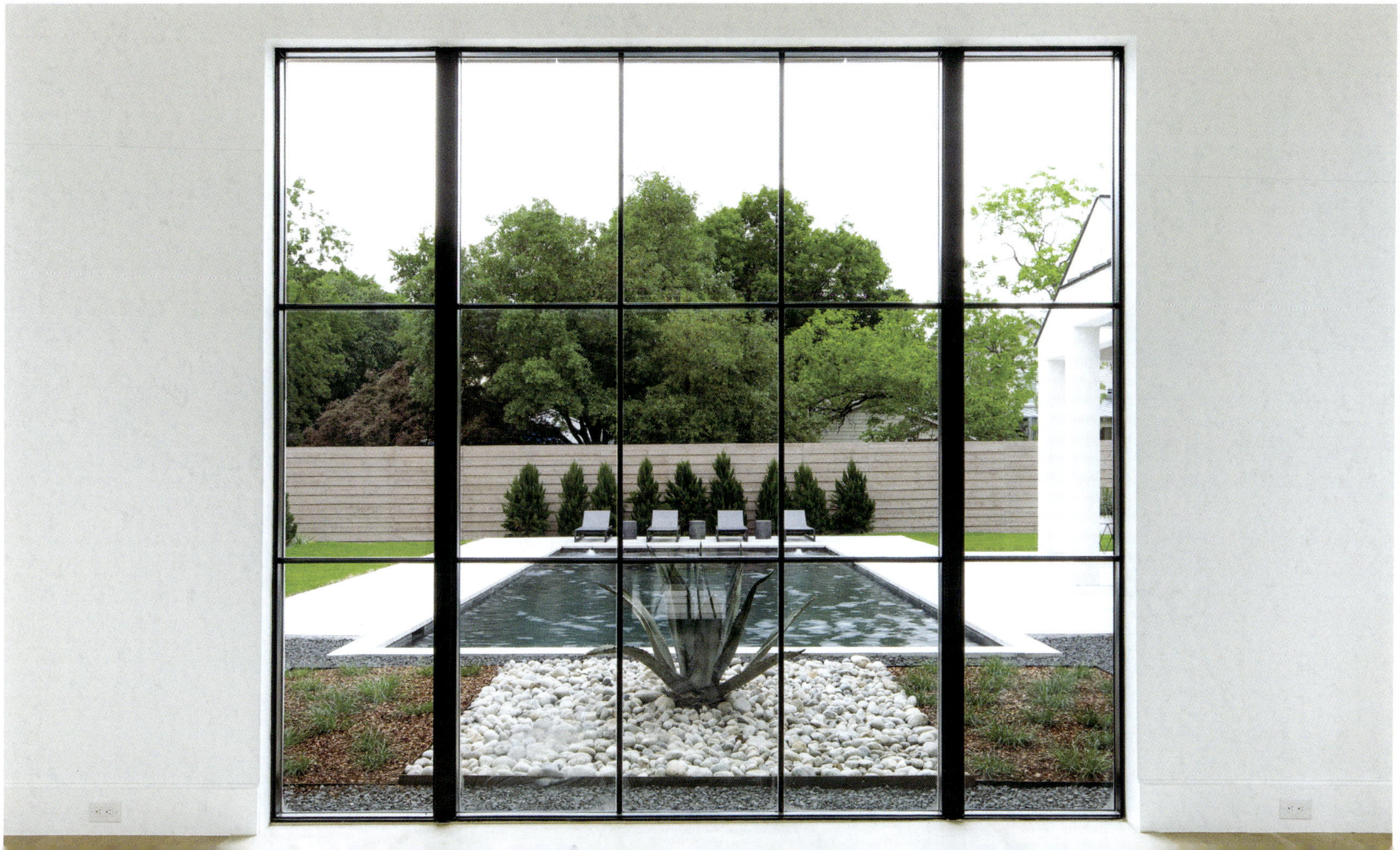

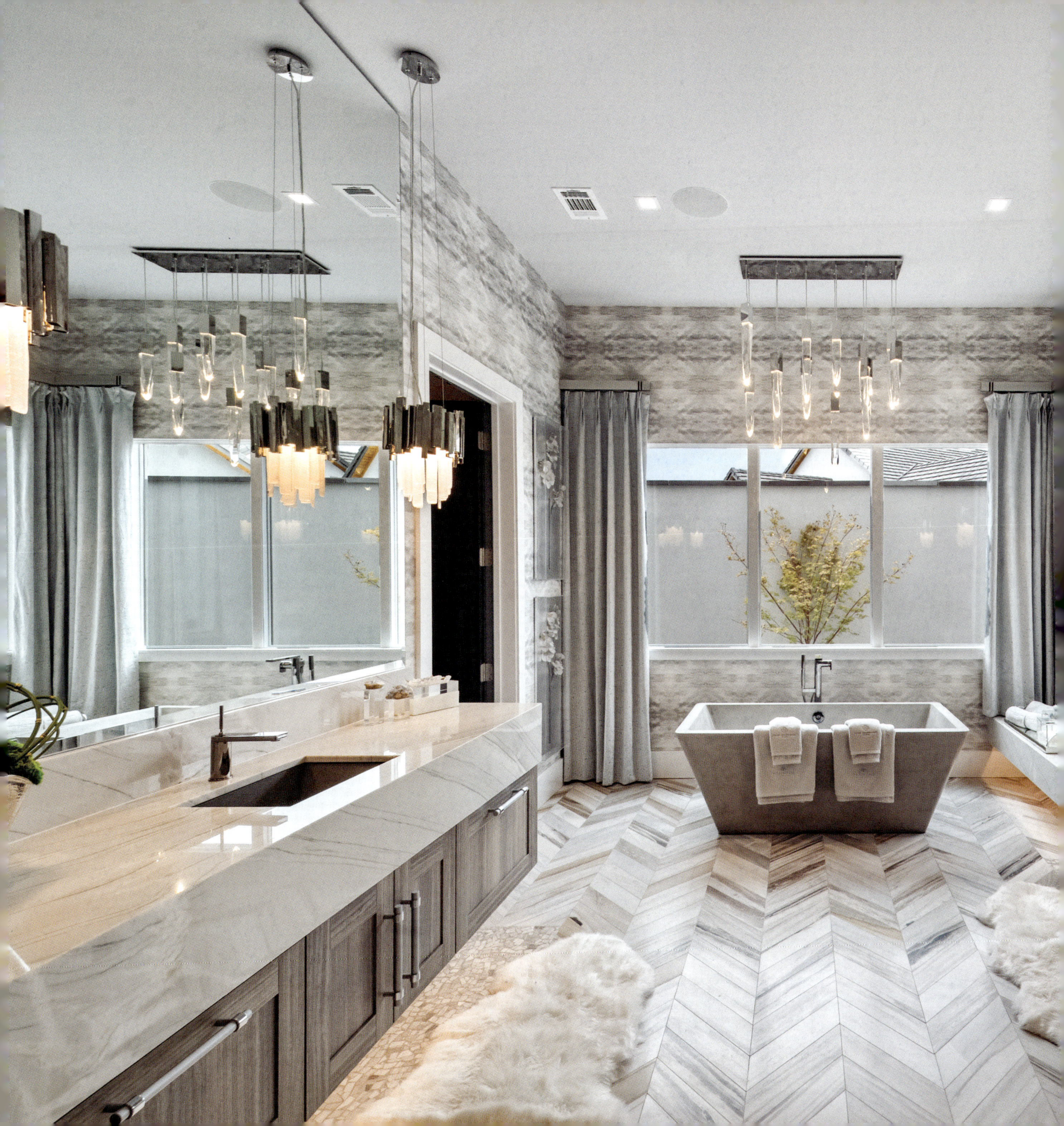

SUSAN SEMMELMANN INTERIORS

"Life isn't about what you get, it's about what you give, and I want to give what I have to you," says Susan Semmelmann of Susan Semmelmann Interiors. Her motto is "the spirit of living is in the giving," and her gift is designing beautiful, one-of-a-kind spaces for others. It is something she has been doing for more than 23 years, and she's passionate about the inspiration that comes from making the most out of every square inch of a home for her clients.

Susan has always said that a home is where we find life – and she takes that seriously when it comes to creating happy, fulfilling rooms that are tailored and personalized to every client's unique lifestyle and how they want to feel in the spaces they occupy.

Interestingly, when she sets out to design a space, she always starts with fabrics first. Fabrics tell a story – and when she and her team find the perfect fabric to reflect a client's style, taste, and personality, she has found that the rest falls into place to create the perfect outcome!

FACING PAGE: Taking influences from a luxurious hotel in New York City, the WillowTree home shows off glossy, resort-style details that extend to the master bath. The sophisticated gray palette mixed with dark wood, soft rugs, and statement lighting creates modern warmth. Photography by Realty Pro Shots.

"This home brings nature to the design element of every room. Everyone relates to nature in a positive way." —Susan Semmelmann

ABOVE LEFT AND RIGHT: Dark natural woods are repeated throughout, including the staircase and the study, which features distressed, black hardwood planks on the ceiling. Monochromatic photography elevates the impact of this rustic-contemporary home's organic influences.

FACING PAGE: Like the master bath, the WillowTree kitchen is sleekly stunning in radiant grays with floor-to-ceiling custom cabinetry that is both beautiful and functional. The colossal island is a central place for family and friends to gather. Photography by Realty Pro Shots.

ABOVE: The two-story fireplace is the focal point of the living room, right alongside the built-in bookcase shelves. Lush fabrics soften the high contrast of the black accents while sliding doors offer a casual extension of the space to the outdoor entertaining area.

FACING PAGE TOP: The open-concept kitchen is the heart of the home.

FACING PAGE MIDDLE: The bedroom exudes peaceful serenity with its neutral palette of taupe, gray, and cream. Patterned carpets, luxe textures, and silver and mirrored accessories ensure the space is far from one-note.

FACING PAGE BOTTOM: The breakfast area offers a more intimate, cozy space for casual dining. Photography by Realty Pro Shots.

193

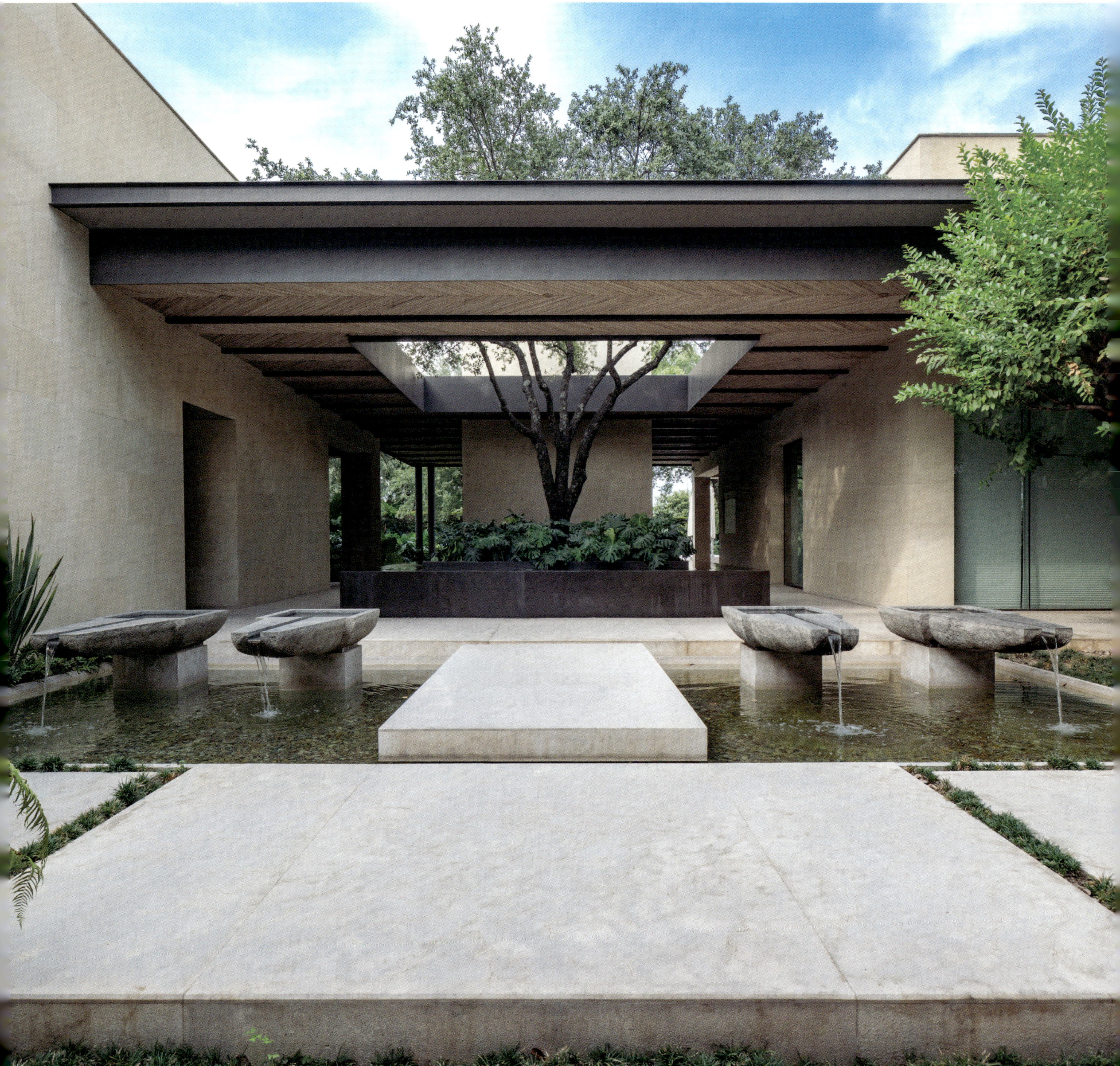

TEN PLUS THREE
GONZALO BUENO
MAURICIO LOBEIRA
VICTORIA RUBIES

A collective desire to reinvent is what guides Ten Plus Three founders and partners Gonzalo Bueno, Mauricio Lobeira, and Victoria Rubies. They not only aspire to exceed the expectations of their clients, but to do so with an inspired and functional approach that celebrates the client's aesthetic, raises their quality of life, and broadens their imagination for beauty and harmony. This is what characterizes success for them.

The firm is internationally recognized and has a reputation for award-winning work that is defined by diverse, timeless elegance merged with modern-classic sensibility. Their designs are distinguished by a daring combination of dissimilar elements in materials, structures, styles, and objects — always distinctly curated through a highly attuned process. The end result? An original and seductive mixture. They're not designers known for repetition in their work.

Whether it's a residential project, a commercial project, or something else entirely, they strive for the transformation of a space in accordance with the characteristics of the environment. They are characterized by their experience and passion and they always work to deliver a thrilling creative journey for each of their clients.

THIS PAGE AND FACING PAGE: Casa Nilo was created from the beginning with two ideas in mind: to be able to entertain and to hold a very important art collection. The house can open and close into smaller or larger spaces, allowing from 10 to 100 people with grace and coziness. The main entrance offers a big welcome — hinting at the scale and grandness, but also providing a sense of relaxation with the garden, water features, and the limestone façade's natural textures. The home is serene in its colors with a monochromatic palette that allows the art to be the focal point while giving it a unique and sophisticated feel filled with culture. Photography by Travis Petty.

TOP AND BOTTOM: Floor-to-ceiling walnut wood panels add to the warm, earth tones used to design this high-rise residence, where a Bosco Sodi art piece rests above an early 19th-century Japanese console in the foyer. The open floor plan for the living, kitchen, and dining room creates a spacious area that accommodates a large Promemoria table with custom-designed chairs and rug using Perennials fabrics.

FACING PAGE TOP AND BOTTOM: This intimate entertainment lounge was the result of a significant makeover for an outdated space that the homeowners dreamed of transforming into the ultimate destination for hosting and entertaining. The goal was to brighten the space by adding metallic-white silk Phillip Jeffries wallpaper throughout and maximize the light from the many windows in this lounge. The open floor plan welcomes the mix of two different seating areas that are perfect for hosting a variety of events, with many bespoke pieces.
Photography by Stephen Karlisch.

"A black-and-white color palette and brass accents give off a sexy ambiance."
—Gonzalo Bueno

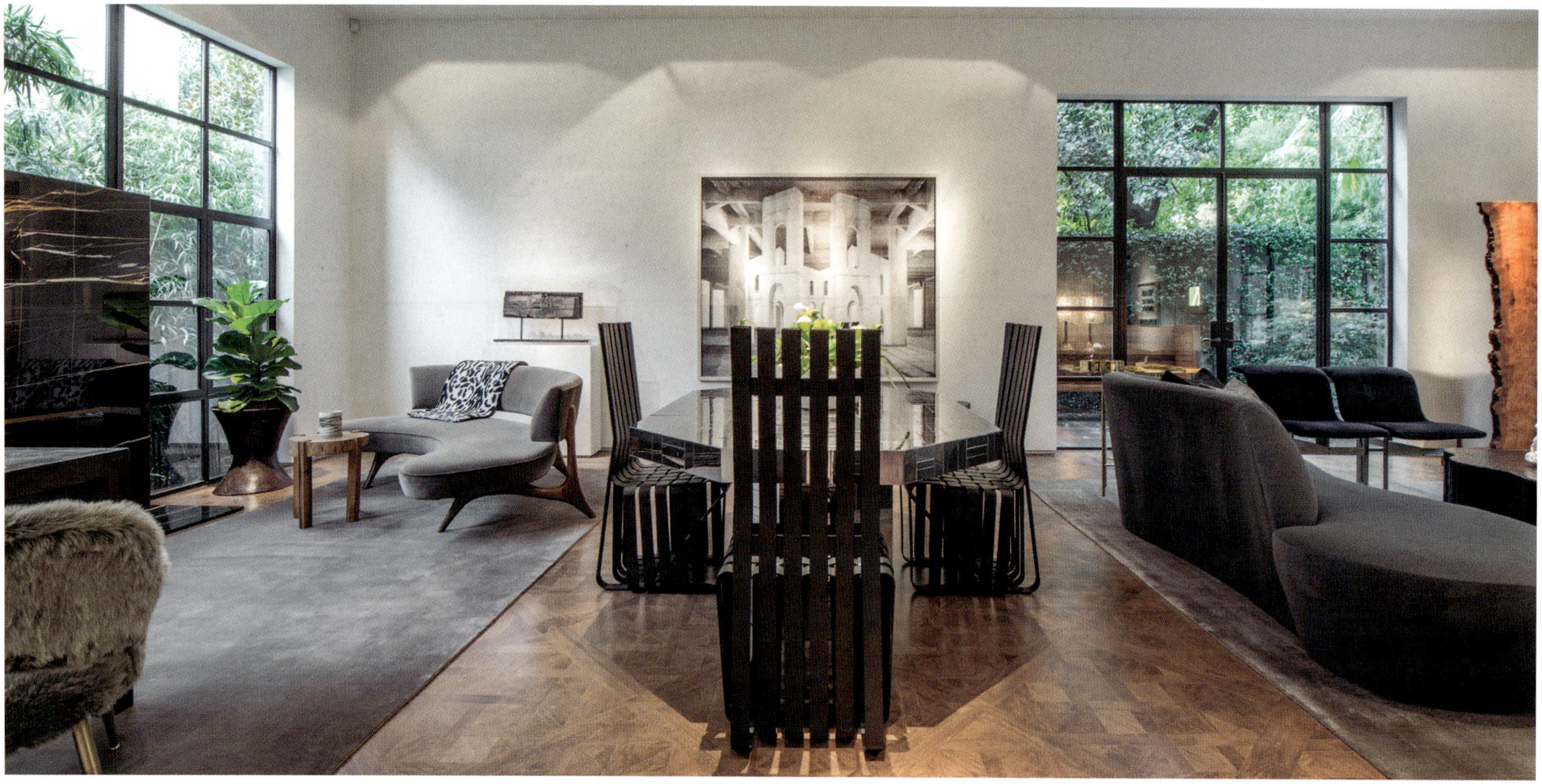

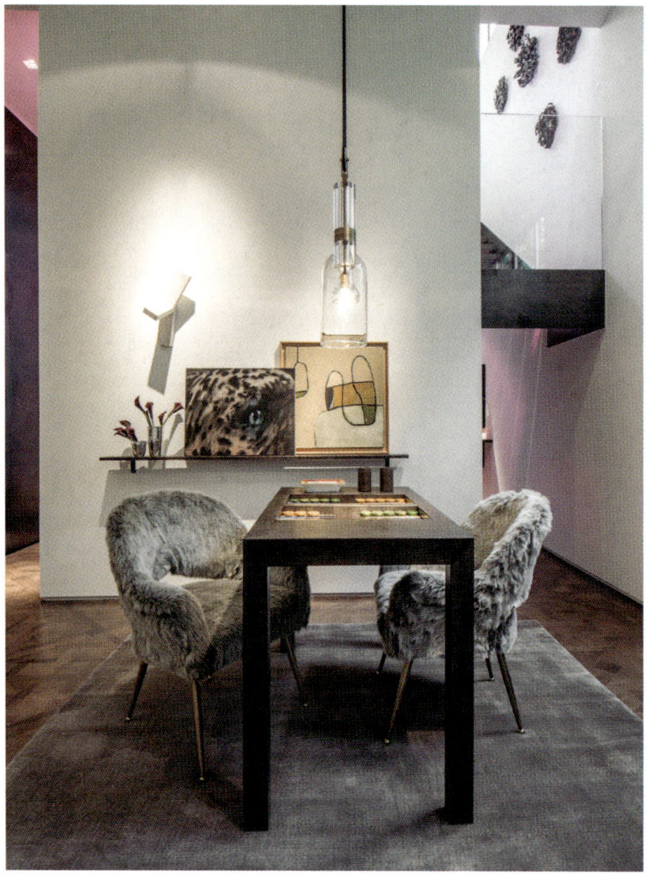

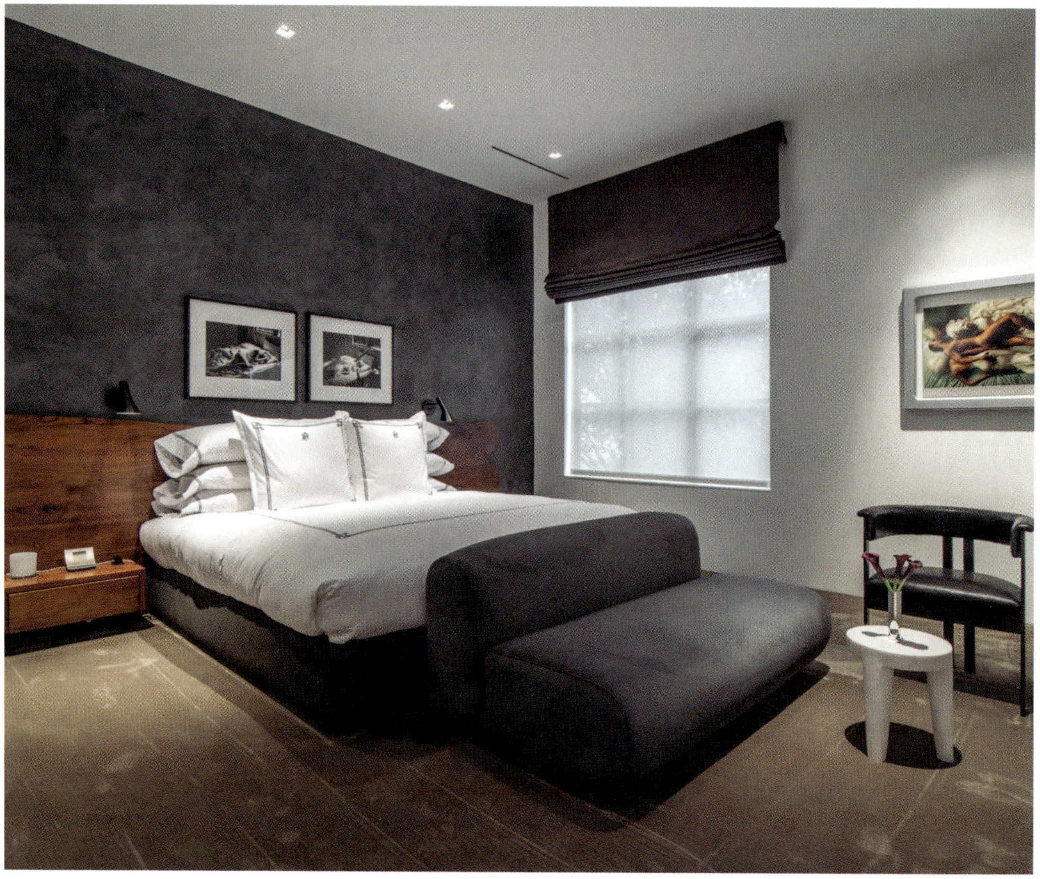

TOP AND BOTTOM: Beautiful, honest, and pure are some of the thematic elements that define the open-concept design in this spectacular home. A modern architectural design permitted the ability to tell a multilayered story of comfort while integrating forward-thinking design and fine art. The living room features a piece by figurative painter Francis Beacon, Promemoria's Chelsea chairs, and a Christian Liaigre sofa behind a Hudson table. Photography on this page by Nick Johnson.

FACING PAGE TOP: The color palette was intentionally kept neutral and earthy to enhance the art. High-backed, vintage Frank Gehry chairs play off the Paul Evans Cityscape Dining Table, placed in the center of the room to provide a more sculptural statement. Vladimir Kagan sofas in both seating spaces create cohesive harmony.

FACING PAGE BOTTOM LEFT: A vintage backgammon table and chairs offers additional layers of personality.

FACING PAGE BOTTOM RIGHT: Charcoal-gray Venetian plaster walls create a sexy bedroom with a one-piece Claro walnut slab bed from Hudson. Photography on facing page by Lisa Petrole.

"Elegance and timeless sophistication best describe this project. The muted grandness that flows throughout the house forces the eye to look around as soon as you enter the home." —Mauricio Lobeira

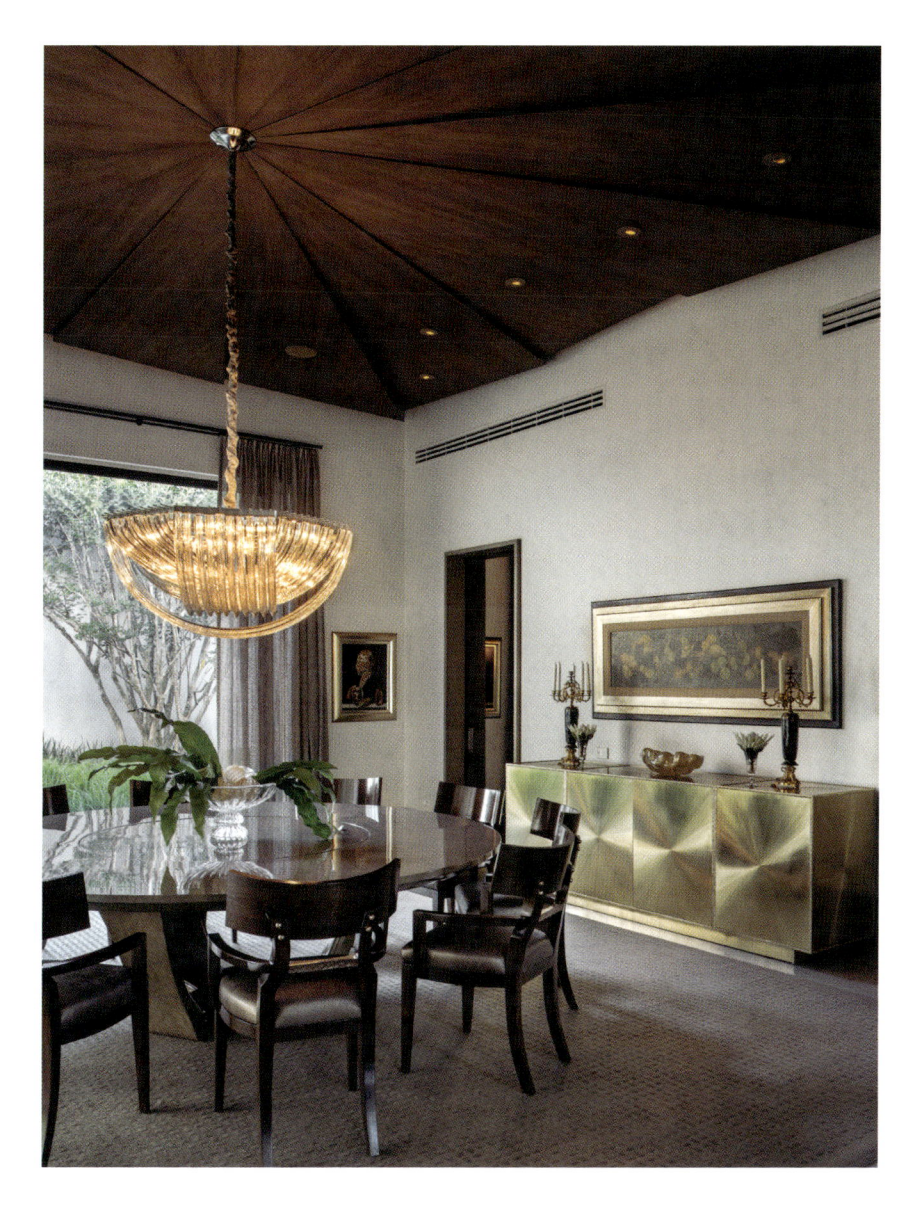

ABOVE LEFT: The elegant dining room exudes coziness from a fine wood ceiling design, centering the eye to the grand Venini chandelier. It's all balanced by an outstanding credenza by Sylvan SF and Jean de Merry chairs.

ABOVE RIGHT: The grandness of the living room, with its extraordinary ceiling height, is accentuated by soft, long draperies by Perennial Fabrics. The natural light is a focal point of the space, changing the atmosphere as the day passes.

FACING PAGE: The floor design is so subtle yet so strong. The main door is a piece of art, representing Mexican craftsmanship at its best and designed by Ten Plus Three to suit this extraordinary home. Photography by Mike Kelley.

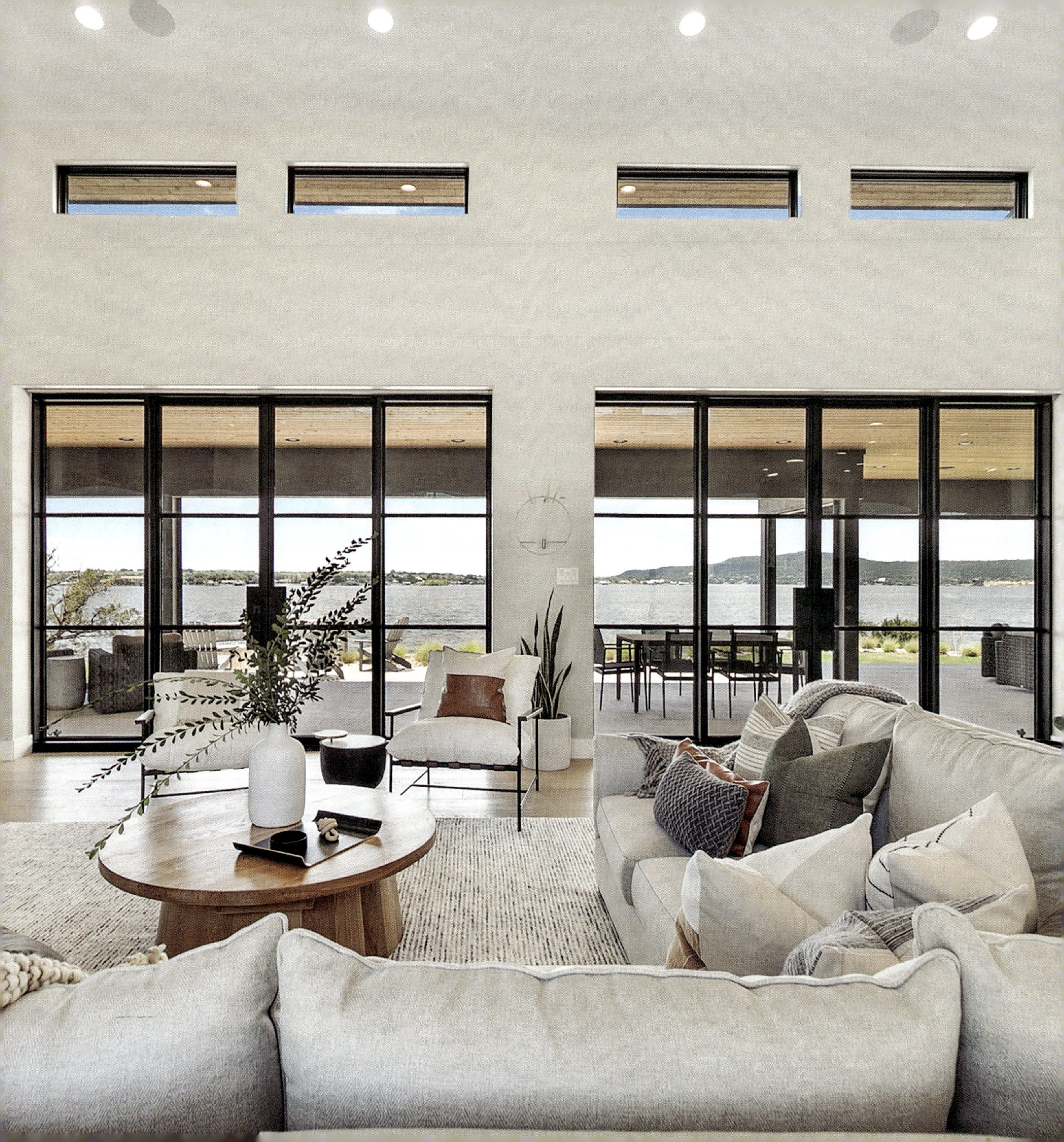

URBANOLOGY DESIGNS

"Our approach to the home is very design-forward," says Ginger Curtis, founder of Urbanology Designs which offers both full-service interior design and walk-through consultations. "We look past the here and now to what is ahead. We believe in creative thinking to lead the design process – to give us those one-of-a-kind moments." Together with her amazing team of hardworking and wildly talented women, she creates comfortably beautiful, functional spaces that are a breath of fresh air and a deviation from the norm – and ones that may even break some rules, too.

A California girl at heart, Ginger's had a love for beauty and design since she was a child. She credits camping trips to Big Sur and Yosemite as well as time spent in her grandparents' Carmel Valley backyard for her wild and deep love of all things organic and unrefined. It's one of the single biggest impacts in her design today. Growing up, she likewise watched her mom make their house a home – even in the most tumultuous times. Having a place of refuge meant everything to her, and that's what she strives to create for each and every one of her clients.

FACING PAGE: Inspiring and dramatic lake views can be absorbed from the comfort of a large, relaxed-modern sofa sectional. Neutral fabric colors and a bevy of perfectly arranged pillows beckon one and all to curl up and take it in without distraction.

TOP: A flawless flow of warm, desert colors complements white oak floors, neutral fabrics, and leather accents in this open floor plan, where modern fixtures and clean design merge with the right layering of Australian Outback vibes.

MIDDLE: We designed this dining room with a singular focus: immersive views of the lake. The expansive, neutral wood tone table is cozied up with 10 comfortably upholstered, Parsons chairs. Hanging from a suspended platform with built-in lighting, the sleek light fixture was selected for its ability to melt away into the views.

BOTTOM: Massive lake-view windows do the heavy lifting in this luxurious, corner bedroom. Beautiful white linens, pops of natural color, and a simple design aesthetic create a sacred aura for rest and renewal. Photography by Norman & Young Photography.

Designed by LAKE | FLATO & ROTTET STUDIO

Photography by Casey Dunn

HOUSTON

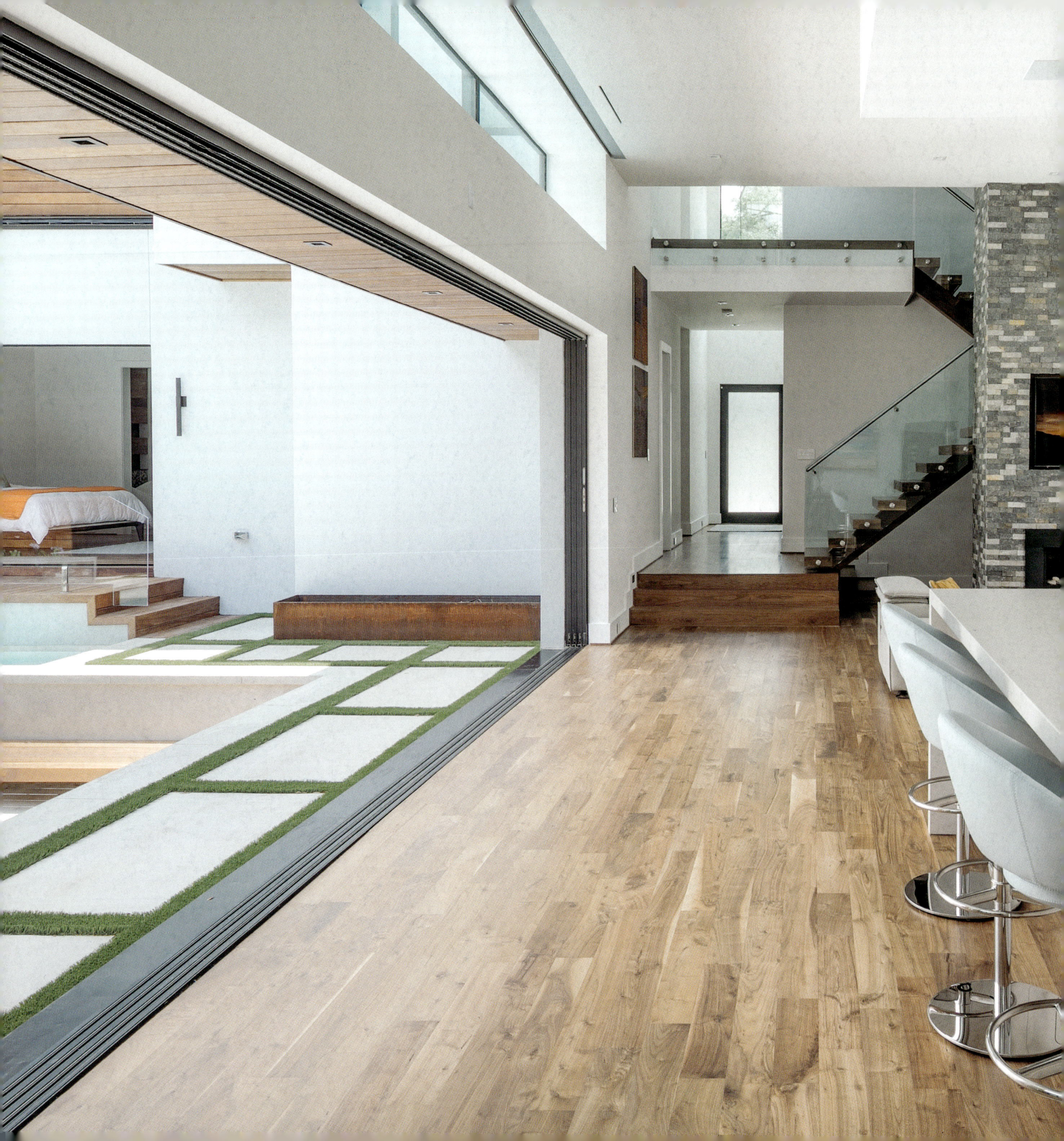

2 2SCALE ARCHITECTS
GREG SWEDBERG

"Flow is important to me. I see life as a fluid dance, so naturally I enjoy learning about how my clients move through space, interact with each other, and how they hope the unique aspects of their lives may be improved by the new homes we create," says Greg Swedberg, AIA, founder of 2Scale Architects. That sense of curiosity has been with Greg since the third grade when he knew he wanted to be an architect. It started with drawing a poster in school, then he "designed" his dream home at age 8 – and he never looked back.

Creating homes is a responsibility he doesn't take lightly, knowing his projects will shape the lives of homeowners for 10, 20, or 30-plus years. So, it will come as no surprise that he characterizes his "style" of work as compassionate and collaborative, combined with an attempt to create beautiful, timeless architecture. All the while, he coaches his clients through the varied aspects of his work in an effort to truly be a teammate on their journey.

Being a firm of only two architects – with Jesus Aponte's invaluable point of view joining 2Scale in 2014 – they have a distinct advantage to deliver a personalized approach as they answer unknown challenges and solve complex problems with elegant, thoughtful responses.

FACING PAGE: The homeowners were inspired by the arid, contemporary designs of western Australia. When a home opens to the land in this way, the yard becomes a room that's interconnected to the interior spaces. Bedrooms, kitchen, and living spaces all enjoy the layering of light from multiple sides, further blurring the definition of being enclosed. Photography by Benjamin Hill.

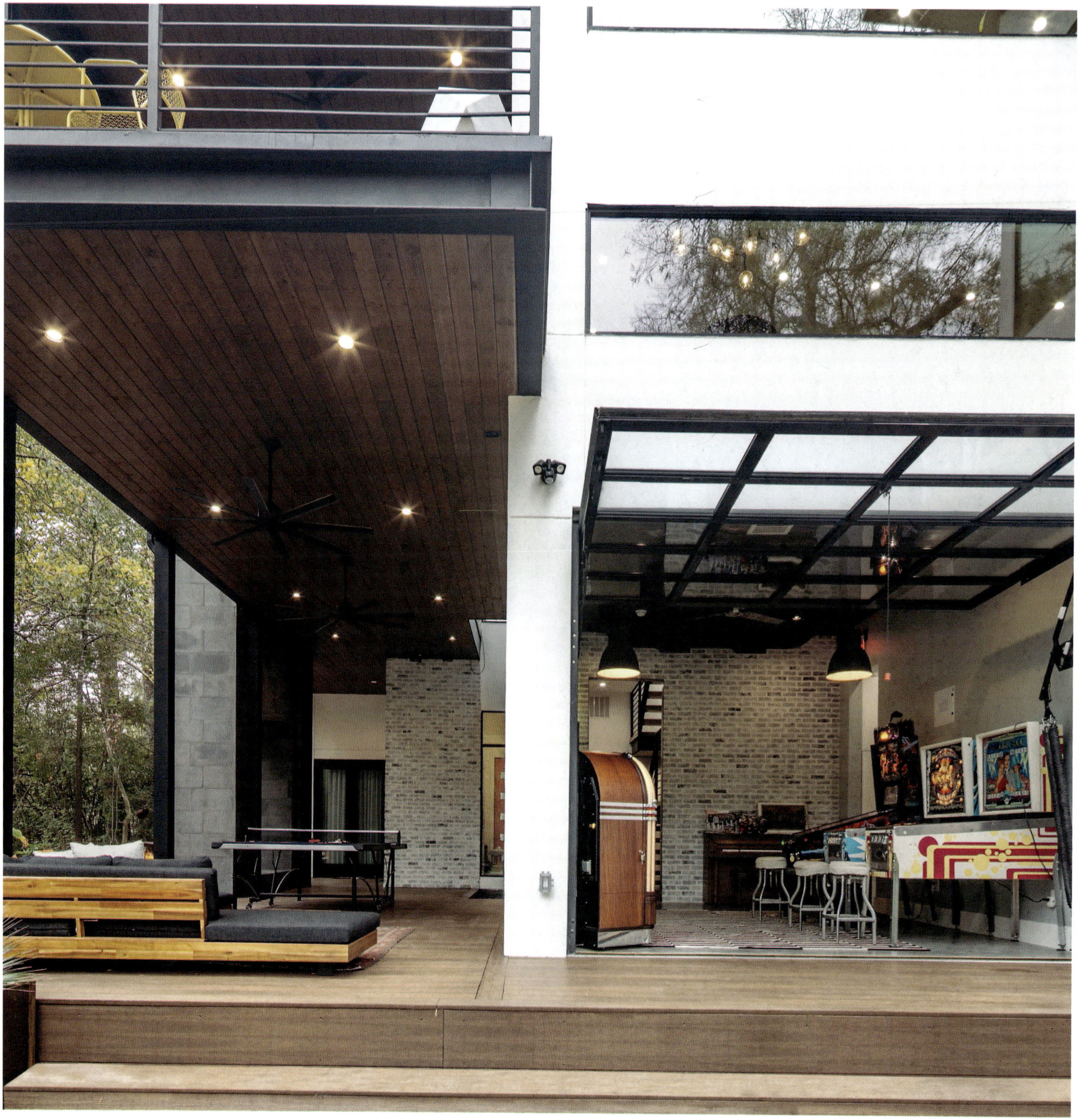

ABOVE: The choice to put the living, dining, sleeping, and entertaining spaces on the second level of this home came early in the process. We captured views up and down the tree-lined golf course in a space the homeowners often refer to as the "treehouse."

RIGHT: While understandably different, the home's shape intentionally nods to the neighborhood's '80s contemporary homes. The exterior roofs and materials delineate different uses within the home. Varied exterior textures continue into the interior spaces, further reinforcing the contrast between light and heavy, private and public parts of the home.

FACING PAGE: Space for an outdoor ping-pong table tucked into the forest, with views to the golf course and retro game room, make the atypical ground floor of this home a real treat. The cantilevered balcony further responds to the home's unique site, by bringing the living spaces close to the trees. Photography by Benjamin Hill.

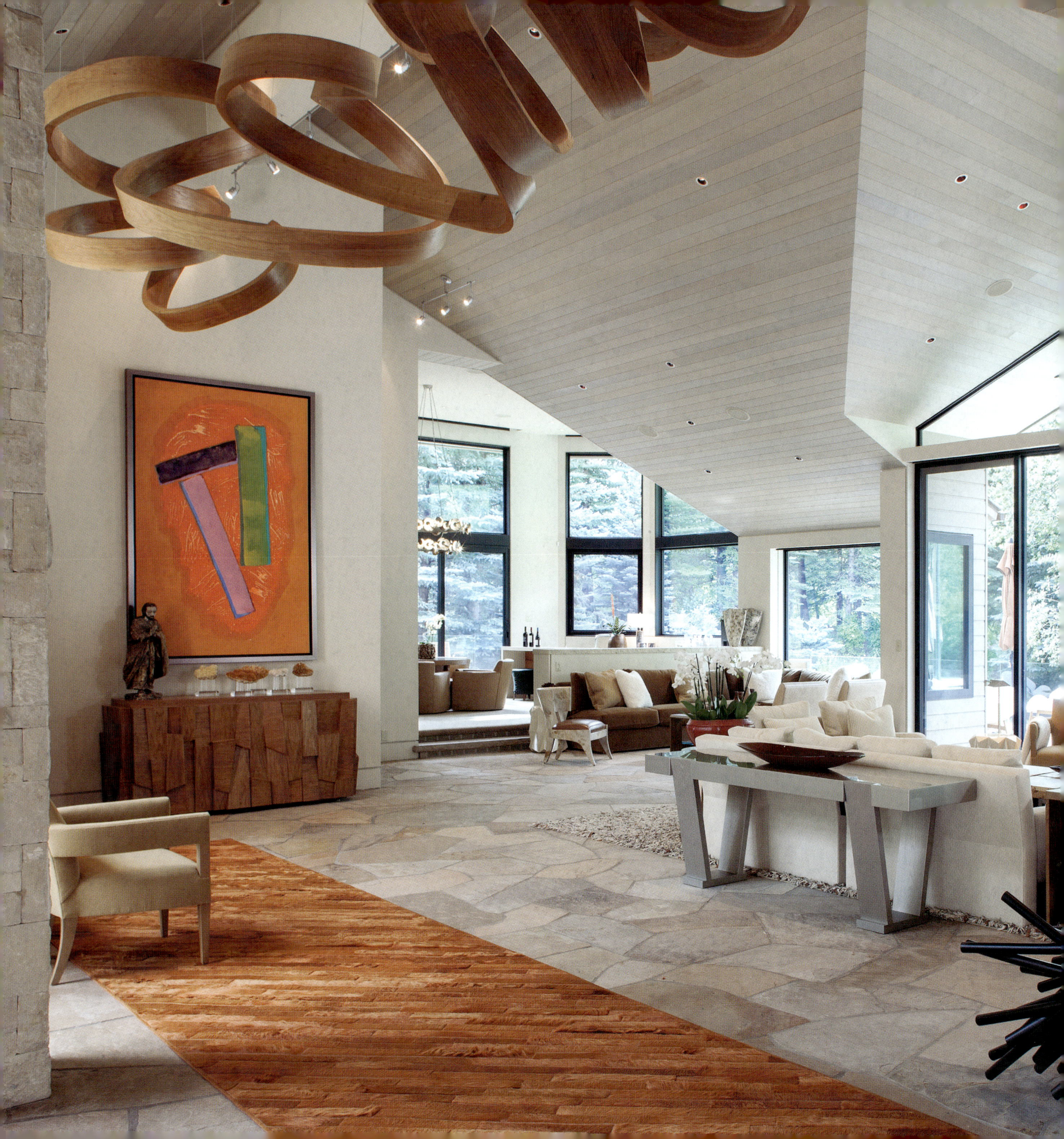

BORDELON DESIGN ASSOCIATES

Bordelon Design Associates' mission is to create comfortable, uplifting, and memorable experiences for their clients. This is something the founder, Maria Bordelon, ASID, holds to the highest degree of importance – and it's what she finds most rewarding about her work. To that end, she personally designs and directs conceptual schemes and styling for each and every project along with architectural details that are coordinated with distinctive furnishings. It's all part of the interior design firm's commitment to excellence across their residential, hospitality, commercial, multi-family, and retirement community projects.

Nature, soft contemporary styles, and architectural materials, as well as clients' aesthetics, offer endless inspiration for Maria. But, above all else, she places the utmost priority in creating spaces that are "livable."

FACING PAGE: The entry reflects exterior views of lush foliage surrounding a private pond. Throughout the residence, all sight lines expose the beautiful landscapes.
Photography by James Ray Spahn.

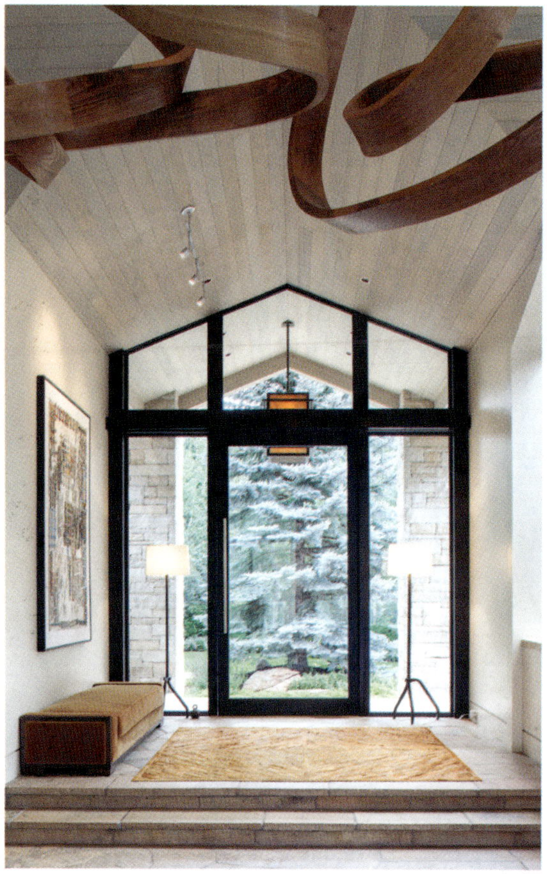

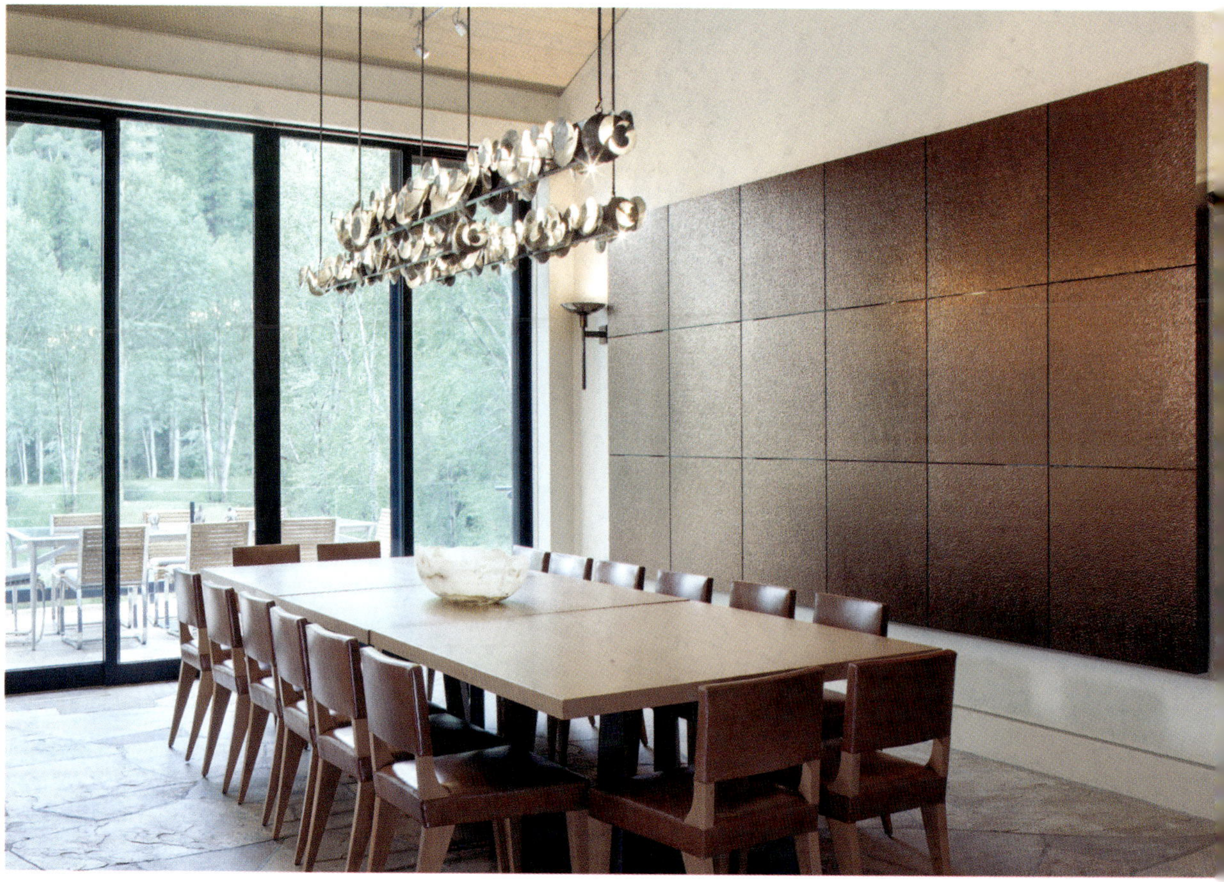

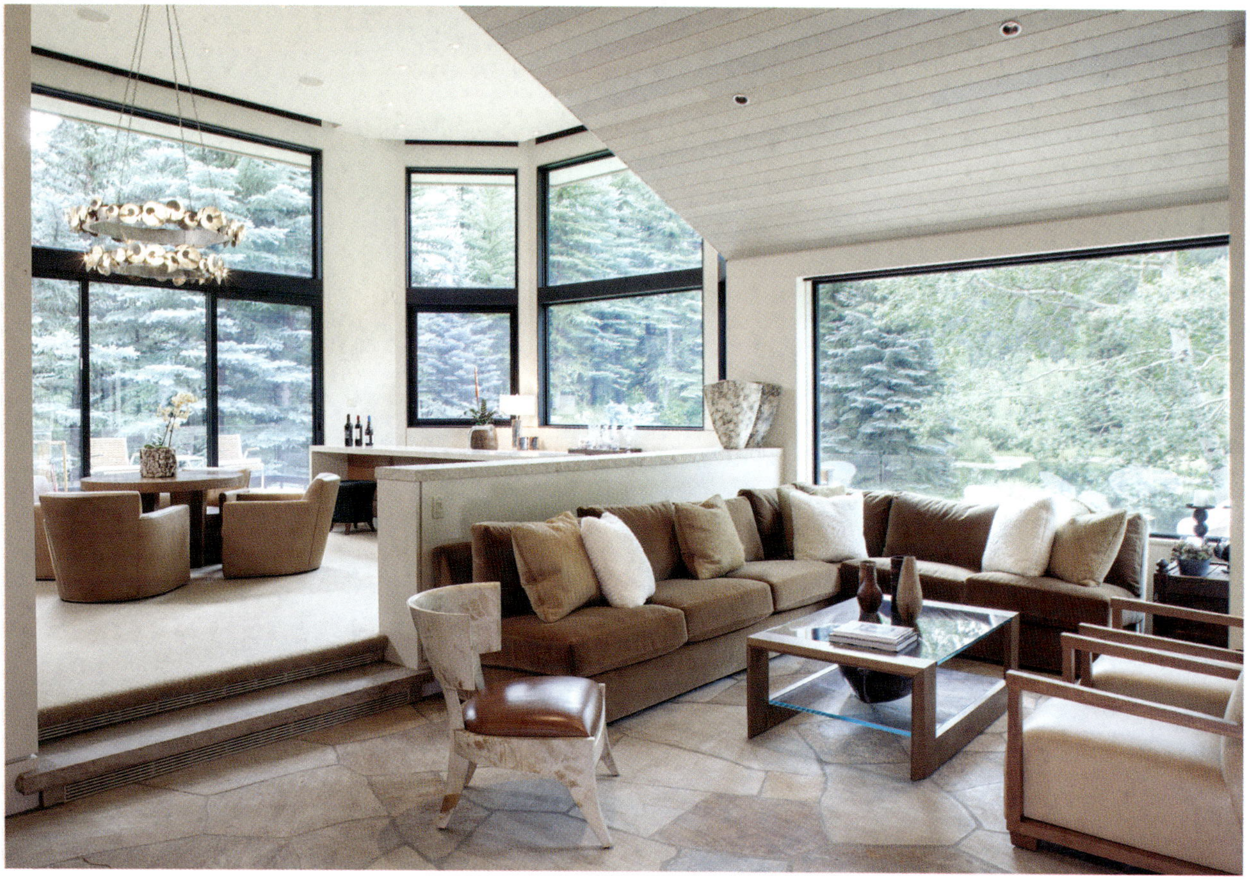

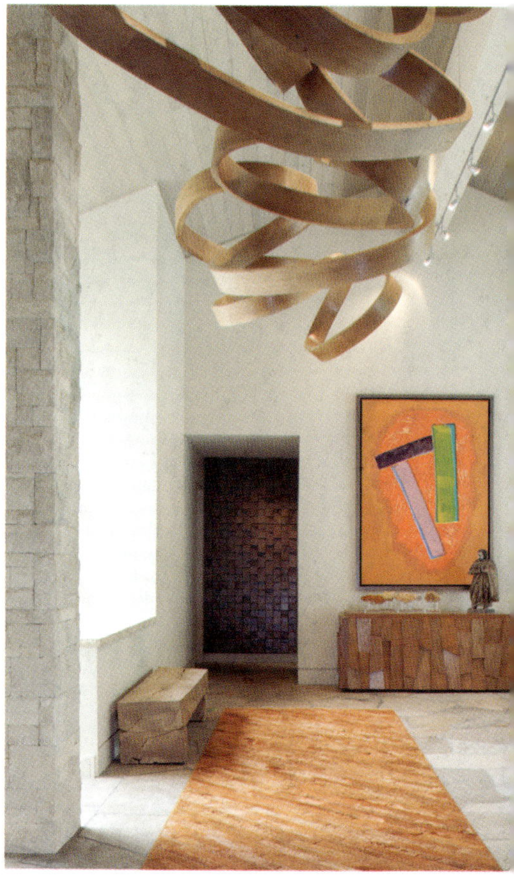

ABOVE LEFT: The dramatic entry to the master suite is framed in wood walls and rich wood doors with leather inset. The eye-catching chandelier is a mix of brushed chrome and royal purple art glass.

ABOVE TOP RIGHT AND BOTTOM RIGHT: The master bedroom is treated as a secluded, private space. Tactile, soft, and inviting textiles were emphasized with a fur throw, fabric wall, and wall of draperies likewise producing a serene and relaxed feeling. The master bath is a completely bespoke area. The sink area provides side lighting for shadow-less grooming.

FACING PAGE TOP LEFT AND RIGHT: The glass entry area is the first view of the color scheme that permeates the living spaces – neutrals with bright orange accents. The dining area is part of the expansive, open living room and emphasizes wood tones with a copper wall to punctuate the panoramic views from the large windows.

FACING PAGE BOTTOM LEFT AND RIGHT: The entire living space is appointed with elegant and comfortable furnishings and bold art. Photography by James Ray Spahn.

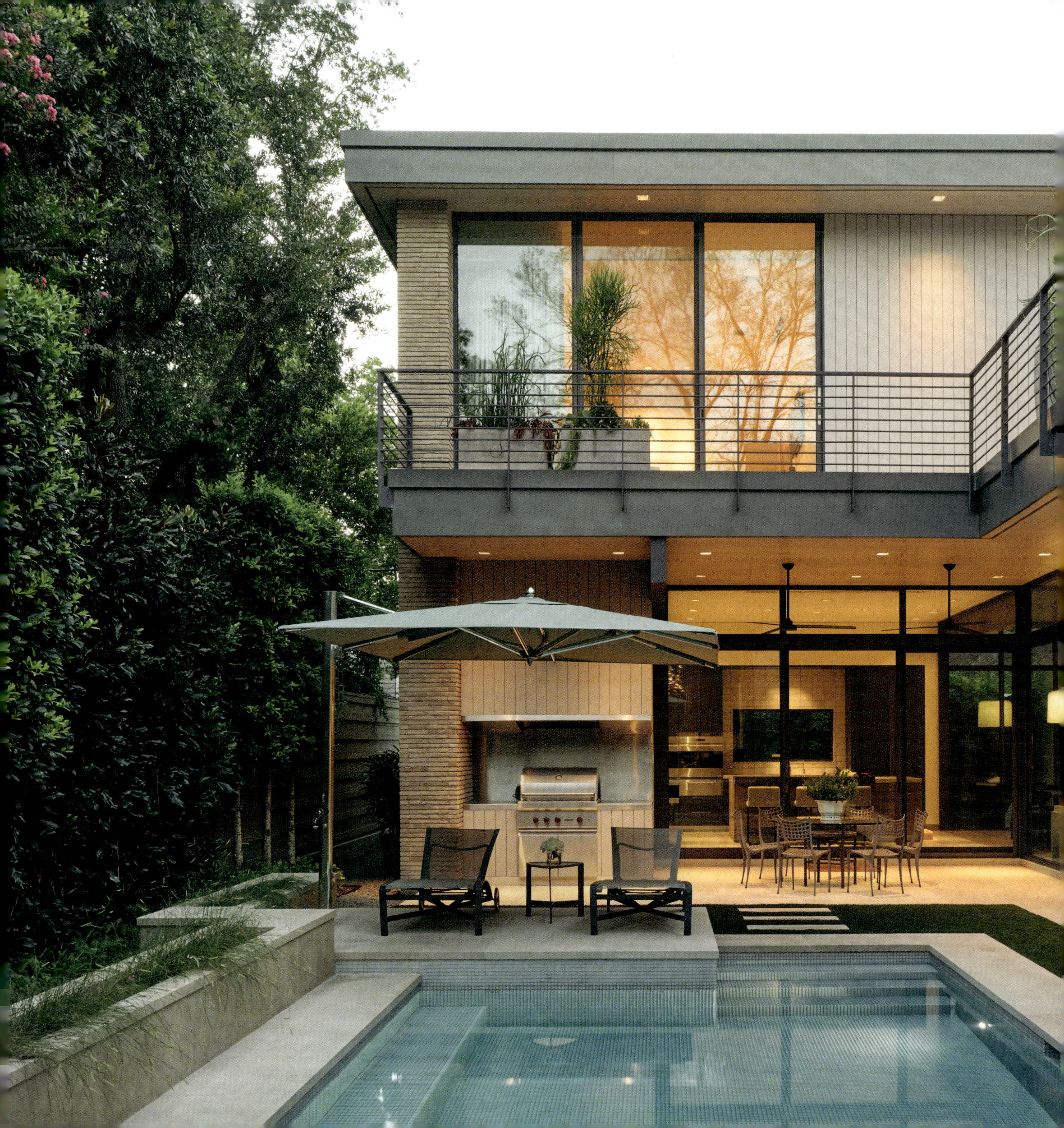

DILLON KYLE ARCHITECTS

"Our fresh, contemporary designs are based on a keen understanding of architectural heritage and location, combined with a forward-thinking vision for the future," says Dillon Kyle of Dillon Kyle Architects.

Their designs are also based on an adept understanding of their clients. The talented team takes each one of their clients on a journey of discovery, exploration, and meaningful collaboration, drawing them into the creative conversation.

While each of their designs is wildly different to meet the unique needs of their clients, their projects are always architecturally sophisticated, spatially rich, and thoughtfully executed.

"We're fluent in the language of space, light, and proportion," says Dillon. "Balancing progressive ideas with restraint and elegance, we design houses and buildings that fit into their neighborhoods, from one-of-a-kind residences, to cultural and educational facilities, commercial buildings, and beyond."

FACING PAGE: Overlooked by the second-floor terrace, the courtyard of this Houston residence – a collaboration between Dillon Kyle Architects, Thomsen Company, and Ann Wolf Interior Decoration – is accessible to both levels of the house, offering generous natural light and ventilation. Photography by Chris Luker Photography.

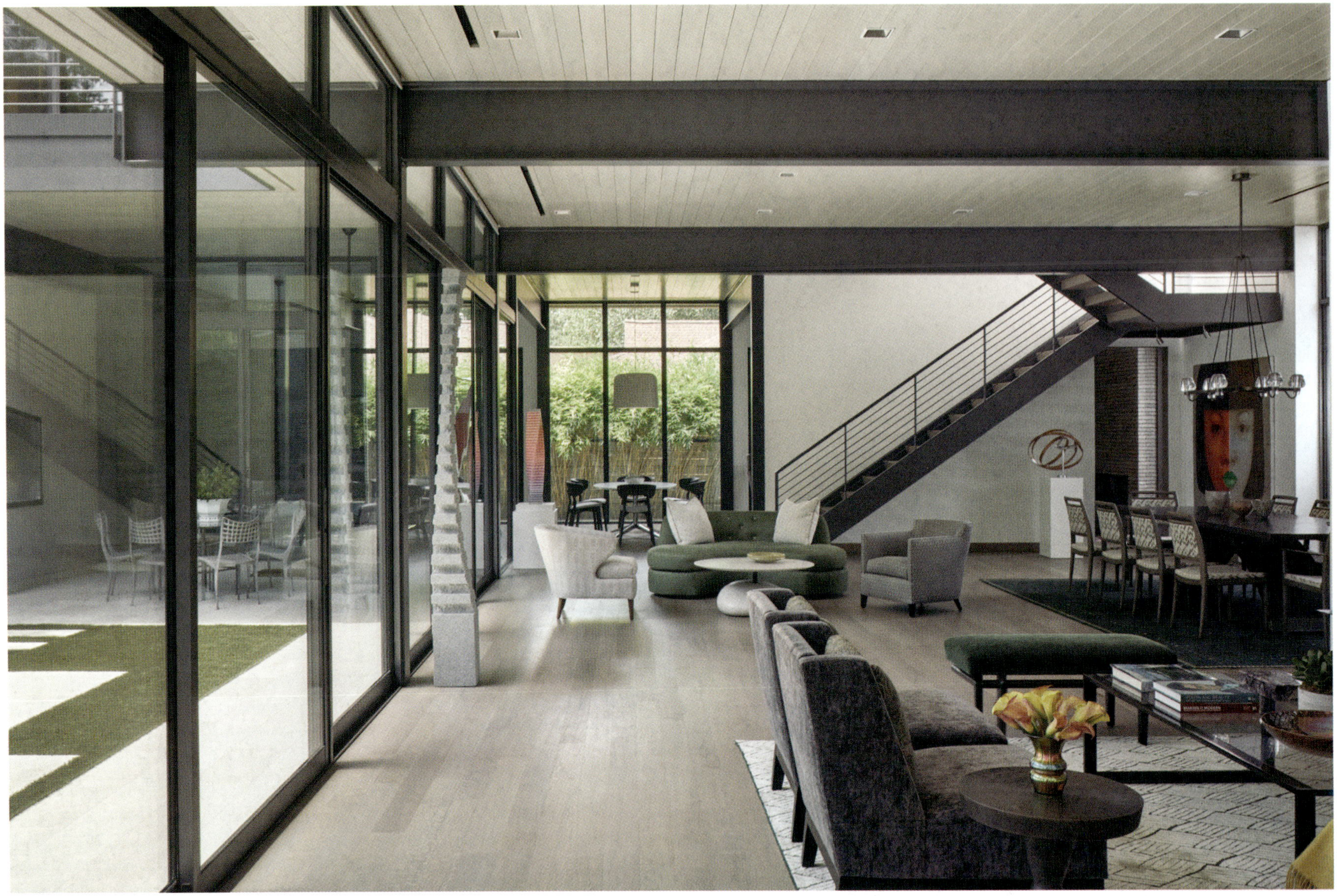

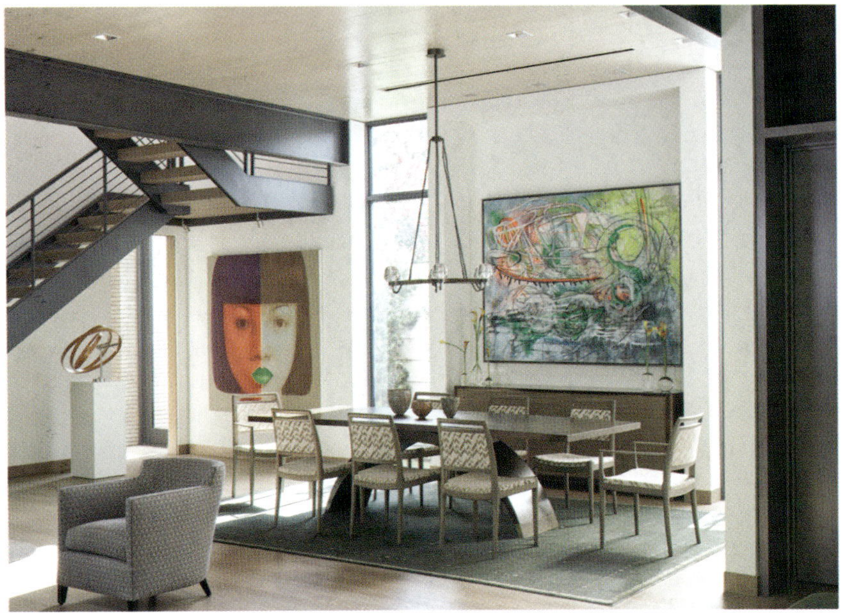

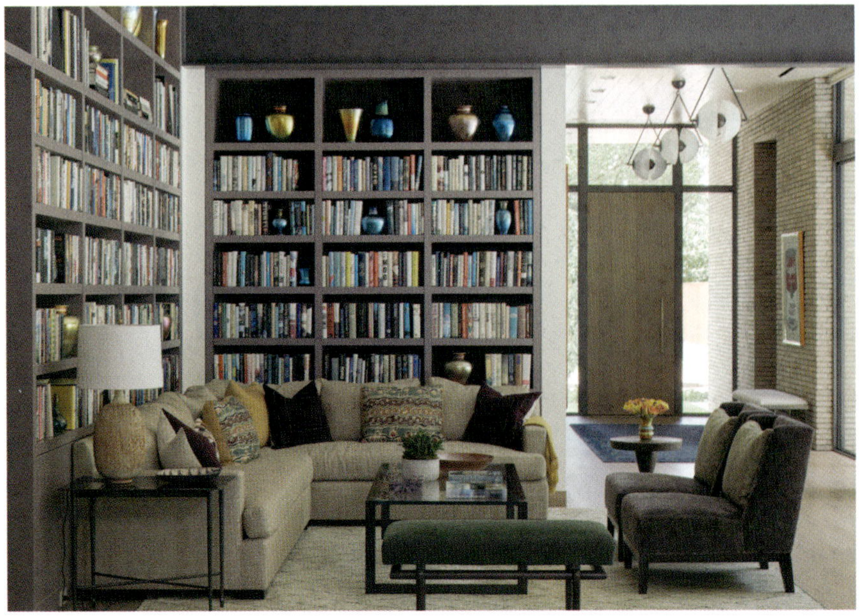

"We're fluent in the language of space,
light, and proportion." —Dillon Kyle

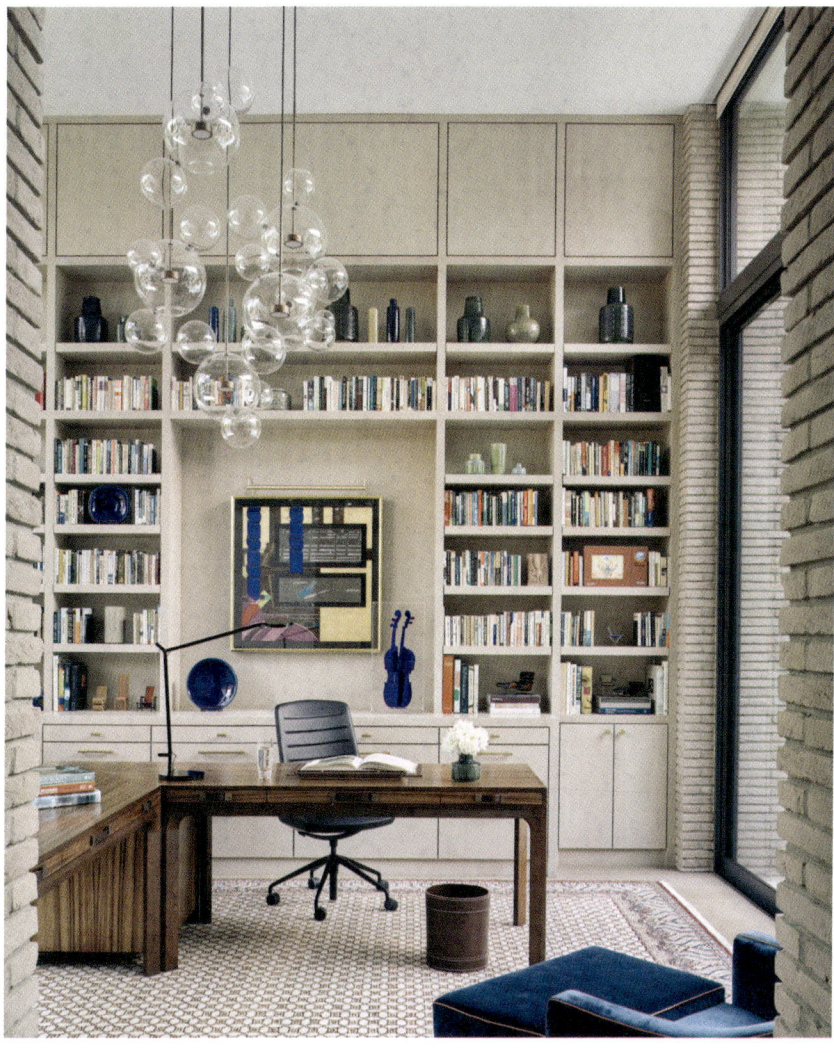

ABOVE LEFT: The kitchen emphasizes the home's minimal, clean-lined aesthetic.

ABOVE RIGHT: A shared office for two, with a custom desk and built-in bookshelves, benefits from an elevated view of both the front and back yards.

FACING PAGE TOP: The open plan of the first floor flows out to the courtyard, encouraging circulation between the interior and exterior spaces.

FACING PAGE BOTTOM LEFT: The open living and dining areas allow for flexible use of the space, casual entertaining, and varied viewpoints of the owners' contemporary art collection.

FACING PAGE BOTTOM RIGHT: A library sitting area with built-in bookshelves anchors the entry and provides a comfortable space for reading or relaxation.
Photography by Chris Luker Photography.

"Our fresh, contemporary designs are based on a keen understanding of architectural heritage combined with forward-thinking vision."
—Dillon Kyle

TOP: Another Houston residence, a collaboration between Dillon Kyle Architects, Thomsen Company, and Chapman Design, was inspired by the modern houses of Palm Springs. The entry is set into a curved brick façade and sheltered by a large carport.

MIDDLE: Organized in a flared U-shaped plan, the central pool courtyard is framed by public and private wings of the first floor.

BOTTOM: The serene primary bedroom enjoys a private porch and walks out directly to the pool courtyard.

FACING PAGE TOP: Generous natural light from oversized transom and clerestory windows brightens the streamlined kitchen.

FACING PAGE BOTTOM: A cozy library with built-in bookshelves and a banquette provides a comfortable retreat and privacy for the primary bedroom suite beyond. Photography by Peter Molick Photography.

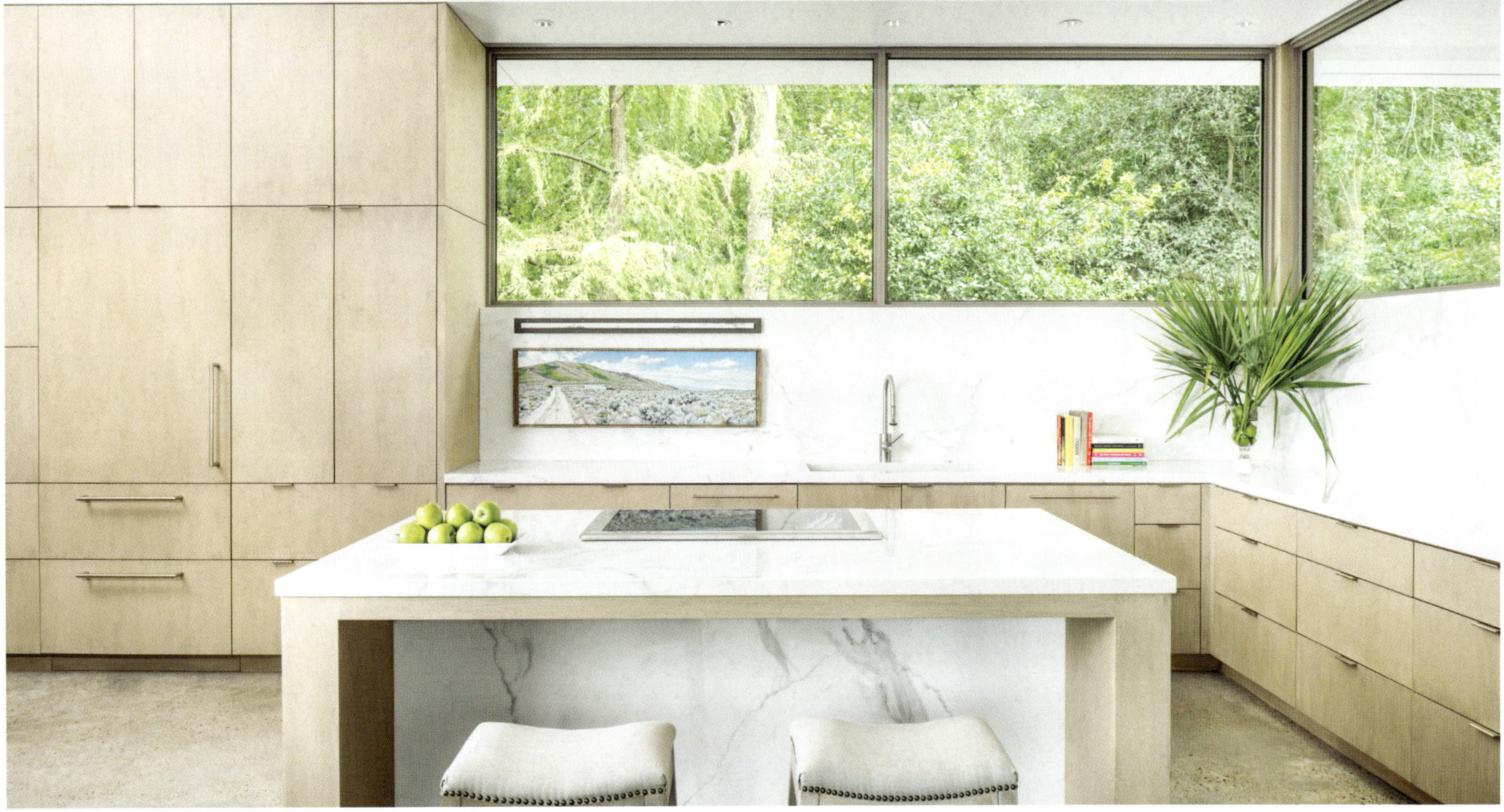

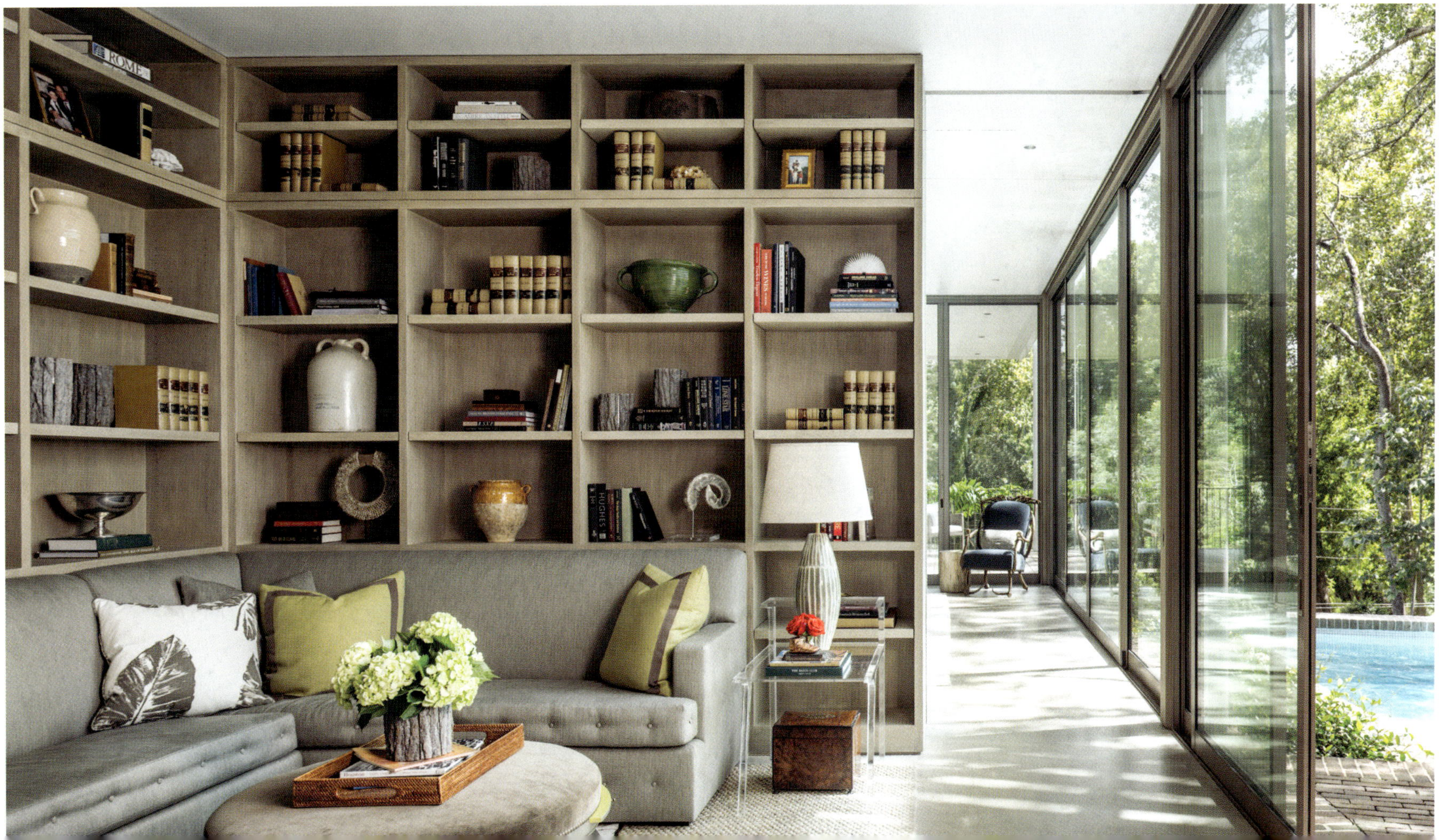
ROME

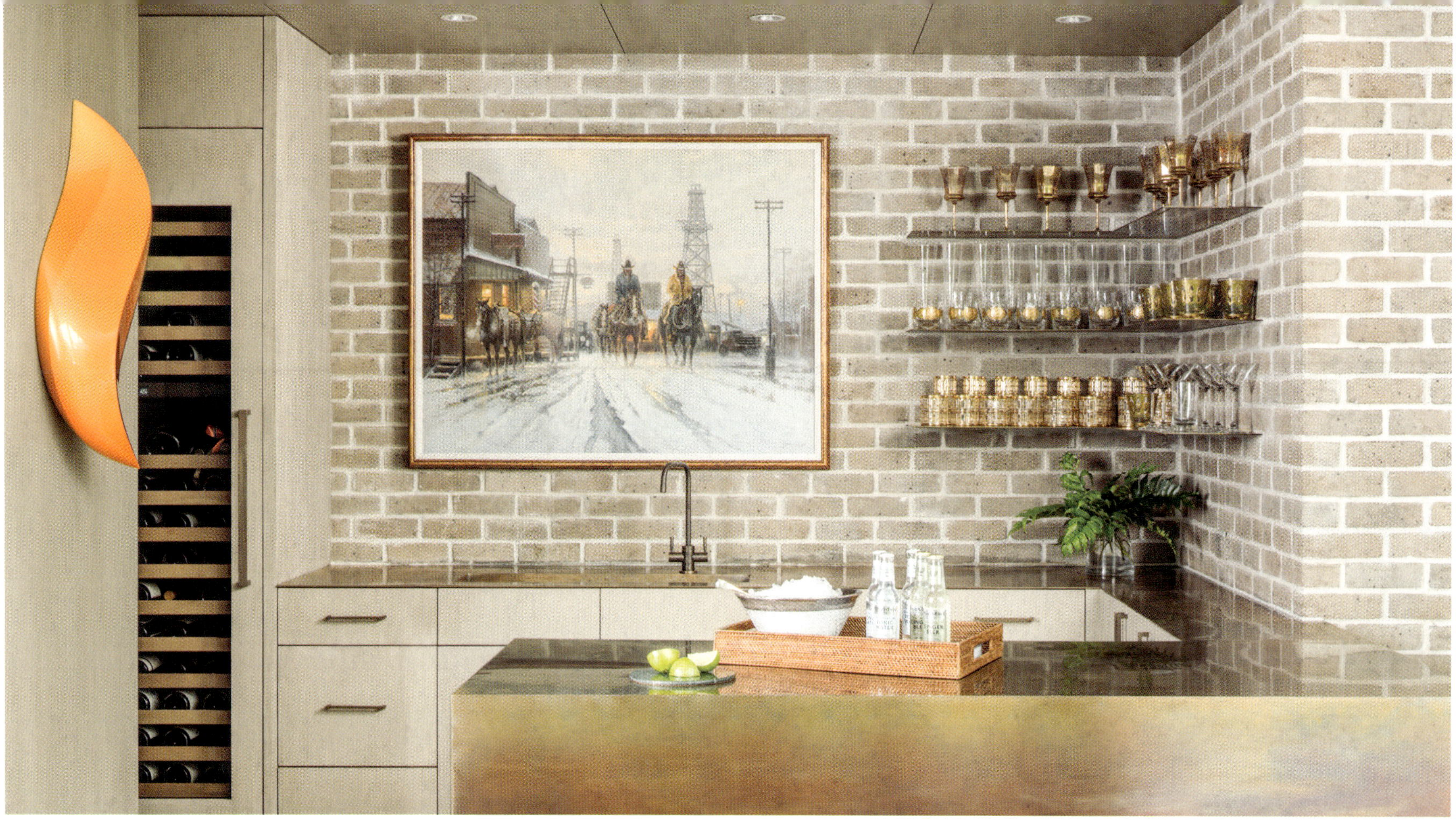

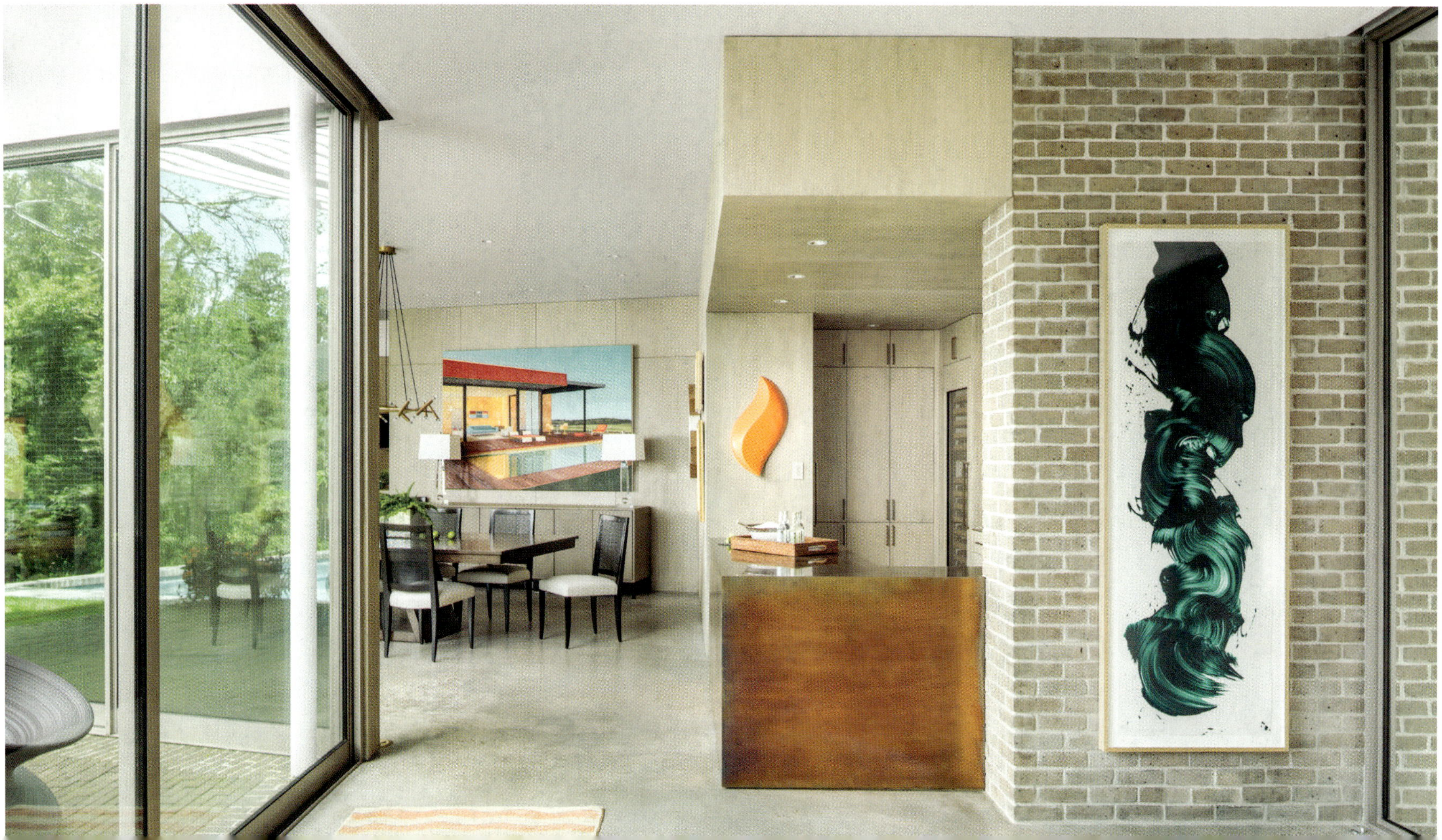

"It's about balancing progressive ideas with restraint and elegance." —Dillon Kyle

ABOVE: The living room flows out to a covered terrace with a view of the bayou beyond, underscoring the connection between the interiors and the outdoors.

FACING PAGE TOP: Custom corner shelves and a bronze counter create a clean-lined, welcoming bar.

FACING PAGE BOTTOM: White oak paneling and polished concrete floors create a neutral backdrop for the dining room. Photography by Peter Molick Photography.

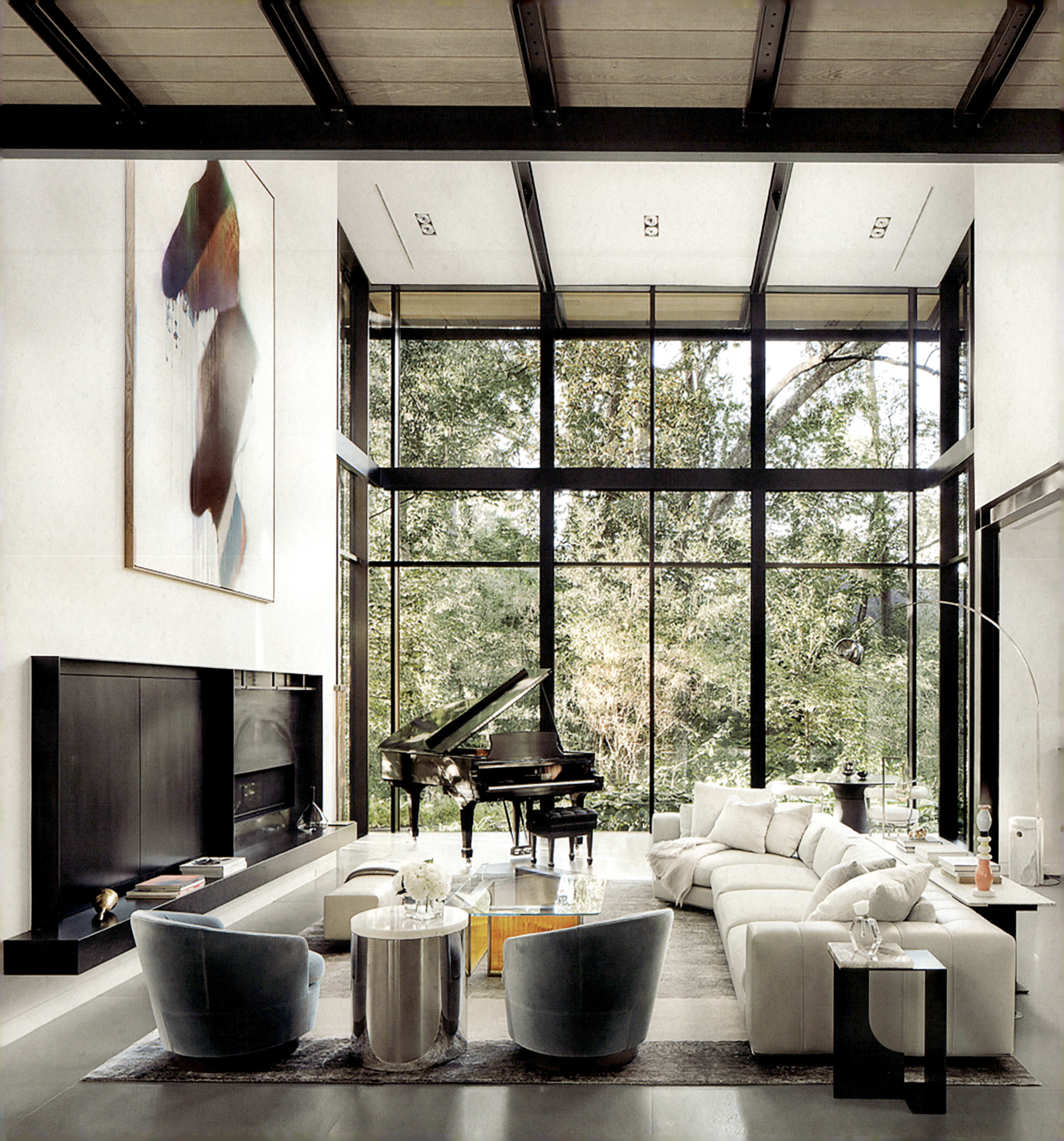

ROTTET STUDIO

An international leader in the architecture and interior design industry, Rottet Studio delivers stunning, functional, and timeless spaces that promote a better way of life through the built environment. They are known as innovators, not followers.

Rottet stays ahead of the design curve by setting trends through the application of vast knowledge and experience, continuously striving to deliver environments that not only satisfy clients' needs but achieve a level of success beyond even their wildest expectations.

Rottet's principals have worked together for more than 35 years offering a broad range of services, including building architecture; interior architecture and design; site planning and landscaping; product design; graphic design; branding; and art curation — and they have best-in-class design professionals in Houston, Los Angeles, and New York.

With an extensive, international portfolio of corporate, hospitality, residential, and maritime projects for leading companies and brands, the WBE-certified firm is recognized as one of the finest design practices in the world with more than 65 million square feet of built design and a vast array of award-winning projects and product designs.

FACING PAGE: The minimal interiors of this modern home in Houston with architecture by Lake | Flato, draw attention to the massive double-height window wall and allow a connection to the outdoors while offering a cozy place to relax or entertain. Taking cues from the natural surrounds, Rottet Studio curated an elegant setting with tables and consoles of their own design, softly curved lounge seating, and important artists' lyrical pieces.
Photography by Casey Dunn.

"The interiors are minimal at heart and true to the architectural spirit of the home. Sightlines were an integral part of the design from the beginning and each room has a distinctive point of view to the landscape in order to provide a peaceful indoor-outdoor connection."

ABOVE LEFT: The voluminous living room is the heart of the home and the place to relax by the fireplace, entertain throughout the night, or to be inspired by artists such as Katharina Grosse, Damien Hirst, and Anish Kapoor which subtly blend with the home.

ABOVE RIGHT: The entry foyer is bright and open, blurring the lines between nature and the interiors through illusions such as a floating wall and floor-to-ceiling windows while a Cleve Gray painting, deep in lyrical nature, adds a soft movement as if bringing in the breeze.

FACING PAGE TOP LEFT AND RIGHT: The dining room is nestled behind a transparent wood slat wall away from the kitchen and living room to provide a quiet, intimate environment that is also open to the natural flow of the home when entertaining. Beneath the floating staircase lives a Jo Hovell sculpture; it's transparent material form complements the interior design of the home.

FACING PAGE BOTTOM LEFT AND RIGHT: The master bedroom suite in this custom home is a theatrical experience as soft morning light slowly seeps in to showcase the museum-quality art and furniture collection. Featured here are works by Joe Mancuso, Troy Stanley, and Rottet Collection. Photography by Casey Dunn.

225

"This Memorial residence was conceived as a contemporary rendition of an old-world Mediterranean estate. The design concept alludes to a centuries-old estate consisting of two stone structures that were eventually connected by a metal and glass annex then 'wrapped' in a new contemporary plaster façade while crumbled limestone courtyard walls, crushed granite pathways, and reclaimed wood beams from the south of France allude to the home's fairy-tale history."

TOP: Structured lines and a mixed use of smooth and raw limestone introduce the theme of this Mediterranean-meets-Modernist home in Houston.

BOTTOM: The peaceful interior courtyard behind the natural limestone wall is a true escape featuring a stone bench under the shade of an olive tree and a reflecting pool, which is home to koi fish beneath the lily pads.

FACING PAGE TOP: A pair of Richard Serra etchings rests on the living room's limestone mantle; the fireplace surround is carved marble with Michelangelo stone. Rottet Collection end tables flank the sofa.

FACING PAGE BOTTOM LEFT: In the living room, a Sol LeWitt gouache hangs over Roberto Lazzeroni's Chambre Close chair.

FACING PAGE BOTTOM RIGHT: The dramatic chef's kitchen is framed by centuries-old reclaimed wood beams from a church in the French countryside and features top-of-the line appliances including a Le Cornue stove. Photography by Eric Laignel.

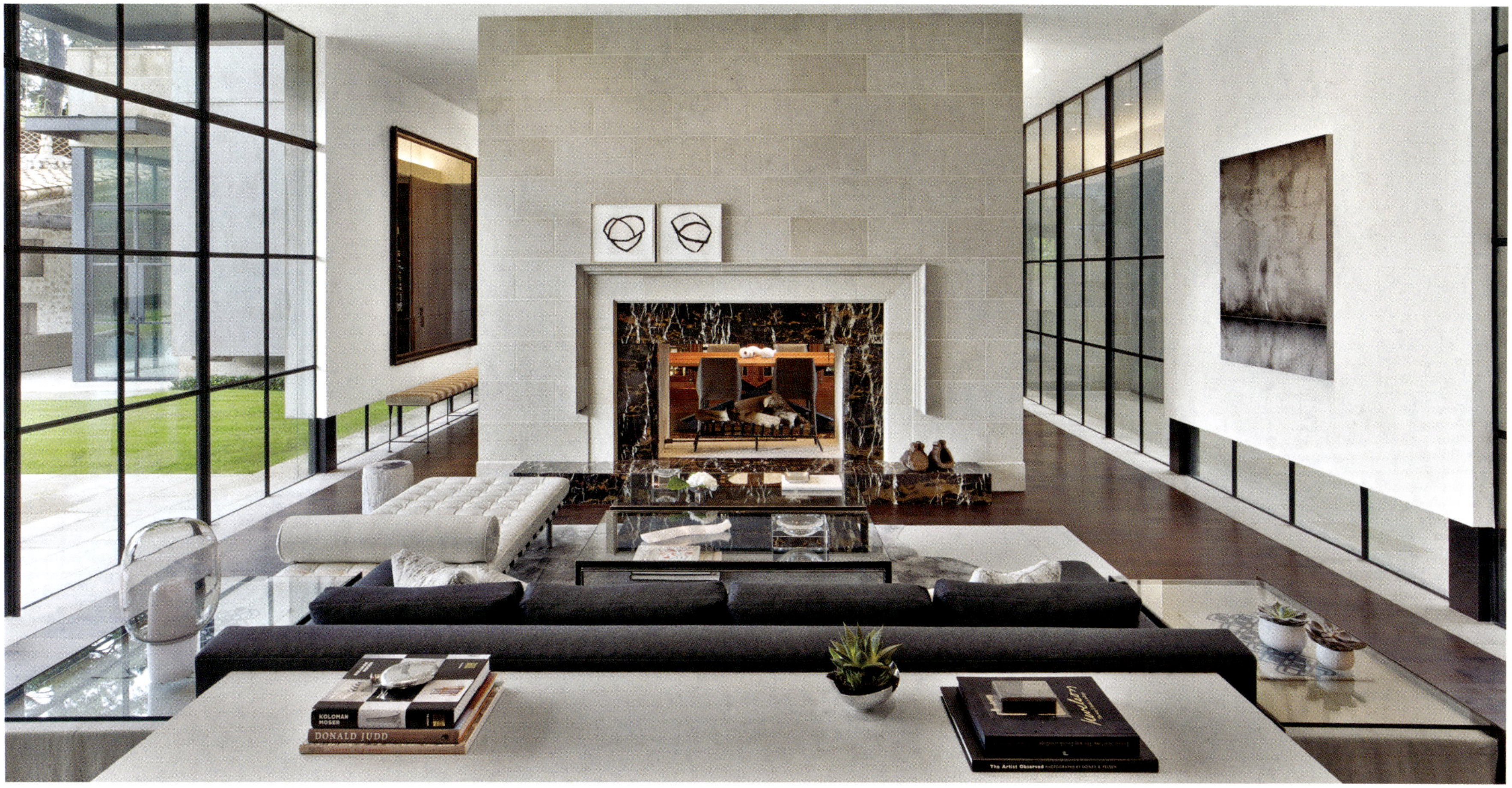
KOLOMAN MOSER
DONALD JUDD
The Artist Observed

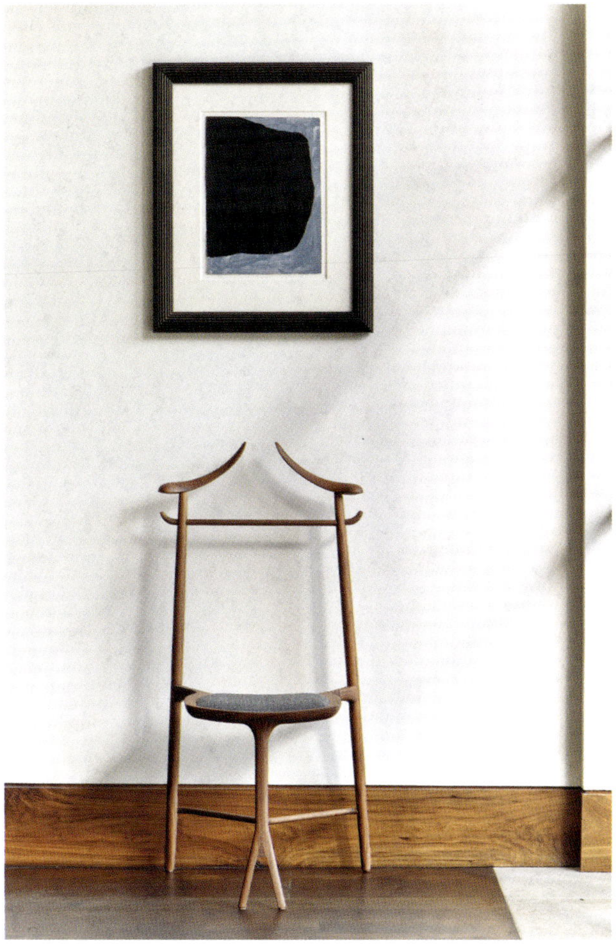

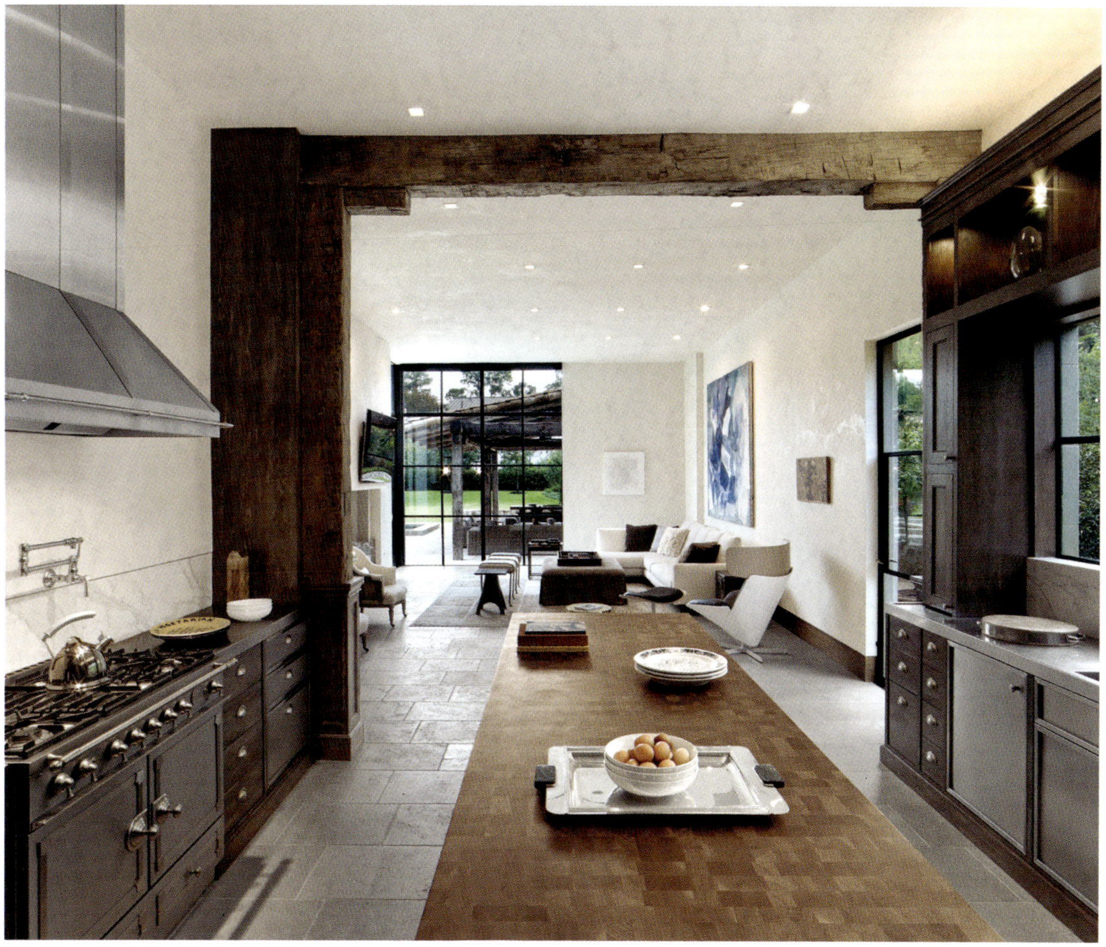

Designed by CRAIG MCMAHON ARCHITECTS

Photography by Dror Baldinger FAIA

SAN ANTONIO

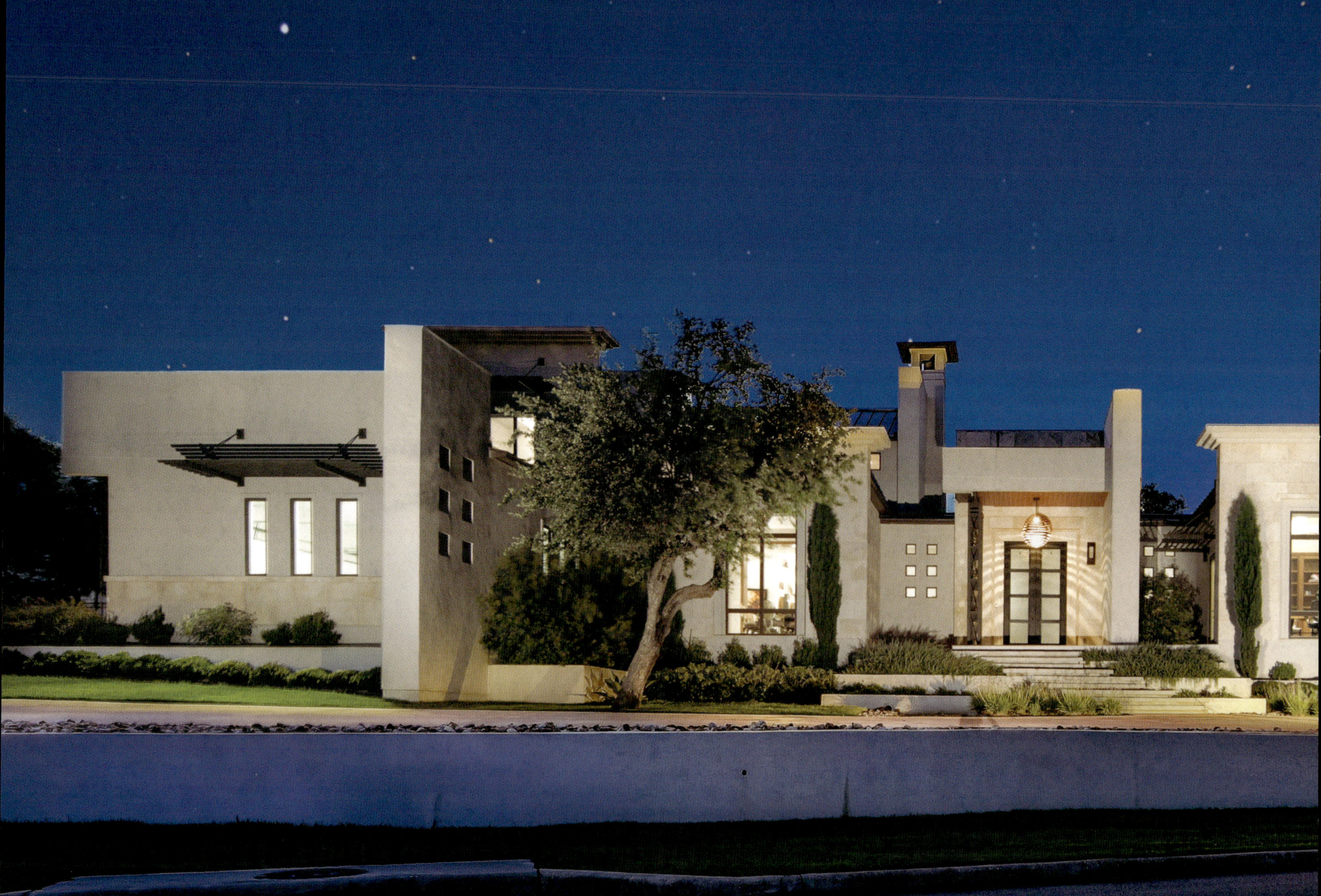

A-DESIGN
BY GUSTAVO ARREDONDO

Gustavo Arredondo's life's work — and passion — is designing dream homes that embody every part of a homeowner's lifestyle. He is recognized for the sophistication in the designs he creates, fostering luxurious living that reflects a broad range of styles — from classic Italian to warm Tuscan, traditional French Country, rustic Texan, transitional, contemporary, and more.

Gustavo's world travels and multicultural clients inspire him to think creatively and to enthusiastically bring a fresh approach to the table for every home design he tackles. Technology comes into play, as well, since his clients are able to see their distinct vision come to life on a screen — right down to the landscaping.

Always committed to quality and elegance with an unmistakable love for his art, Gustavo has paved the way for creating incomparable design solutions and exquisite homes that captivate all who see them.

FACING PAGE: This sprawling, contemporary stunner offers a dynamic shell for the equally sleek interiors outfitted by A-Design. A flat, parapet wall, mixed-siding exteriors of stone and stucco, and geometric windows contribute to the statement-making quality of the home.
Photography by Shutterbug Studios.

"Lifestyles are perfected by creatively crafted design."
—Gustavo Arredondo

TOP: The formal dining area is simple yet luxurious, exuding warmth through wood as well as cool elegance with the recessed ceiling, textured walls, and contemporary lighting.

MIDDLE: The master bath's white-on-white aesthetic is bright, light-filled, and beautiful — with light woods offering organic warmth and crystal lighting that echoes the circular recessed ceiling.

BOTTOM: Glass-front cabinets, a white backsplash, and stainless steel appliances alongside a huge central island create an even more open feel for the kitchen while making it the perfect place for gathering.

FACING PAGE TOP: With the dining area fully opening to the resort-style patio outside, there are truly no boundaries between indoor and outdoor living.

FACING PAGE BOTTOM: The wood trusses in the open-concept living room introduce a sense of rustic sophistication while monochromatic walls and furnishings allow for lush textures, bold art, and the metal two-story fireplace to pop most effectively. Photography by Shutterbug Studios.

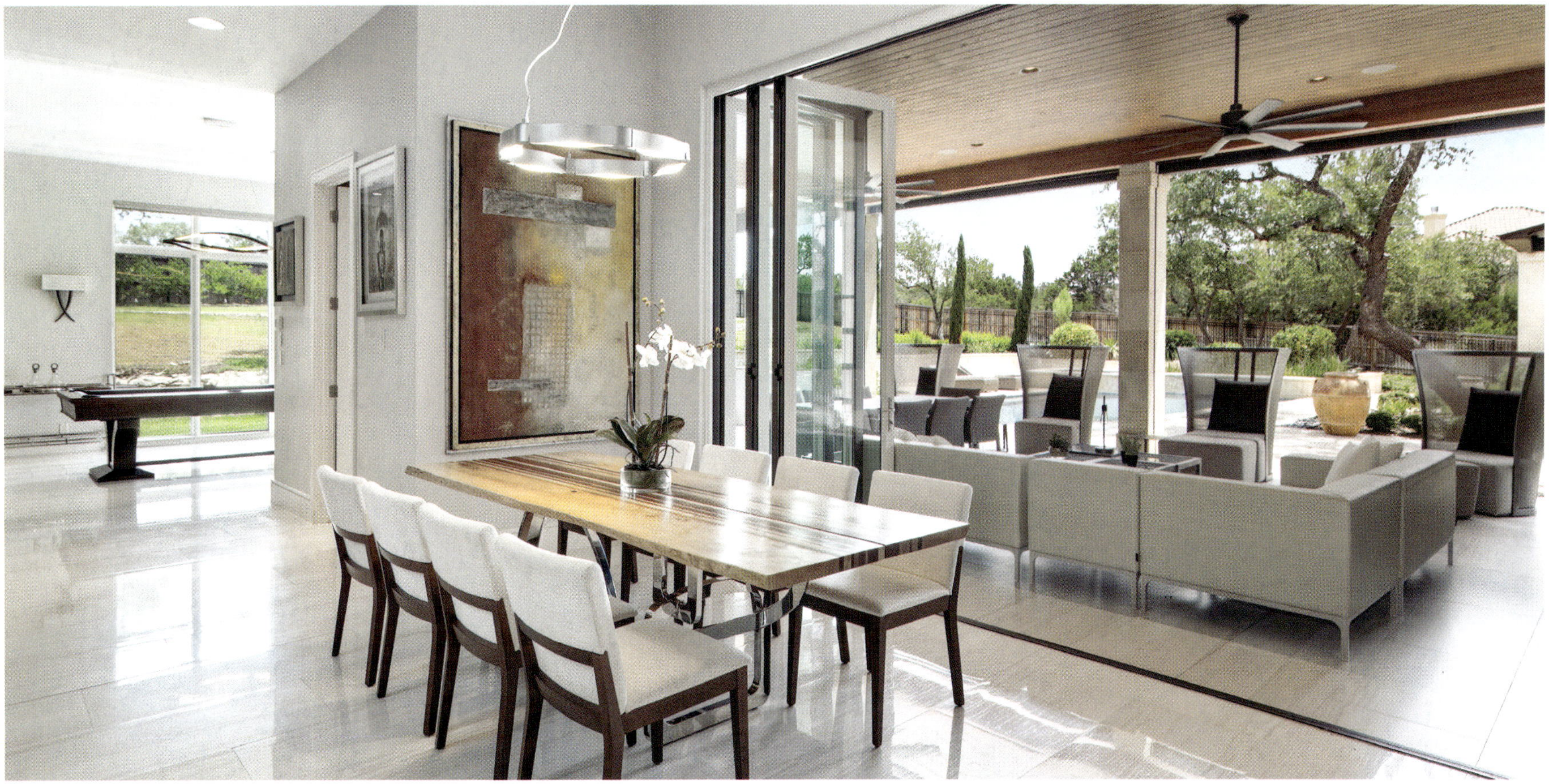

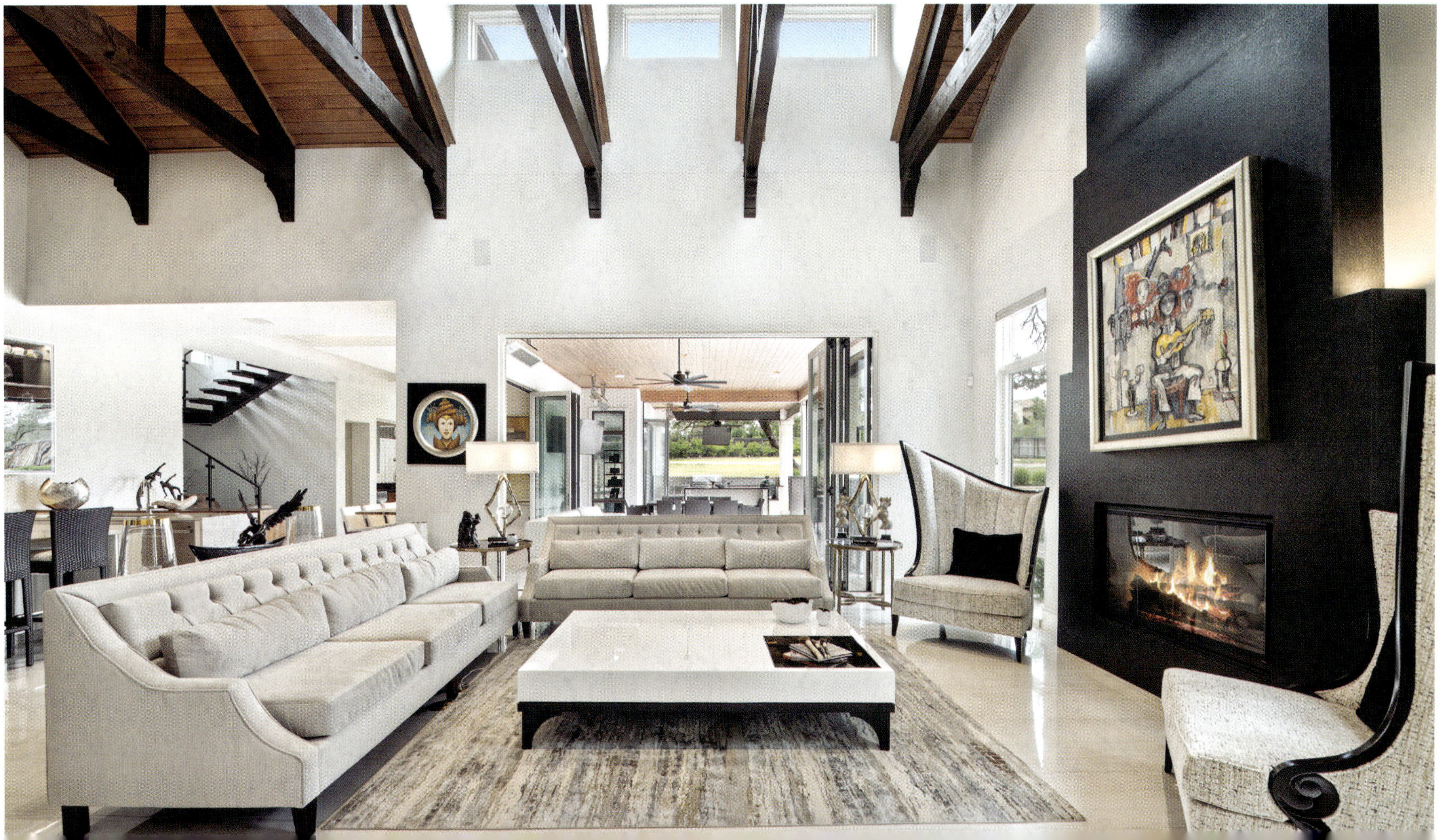

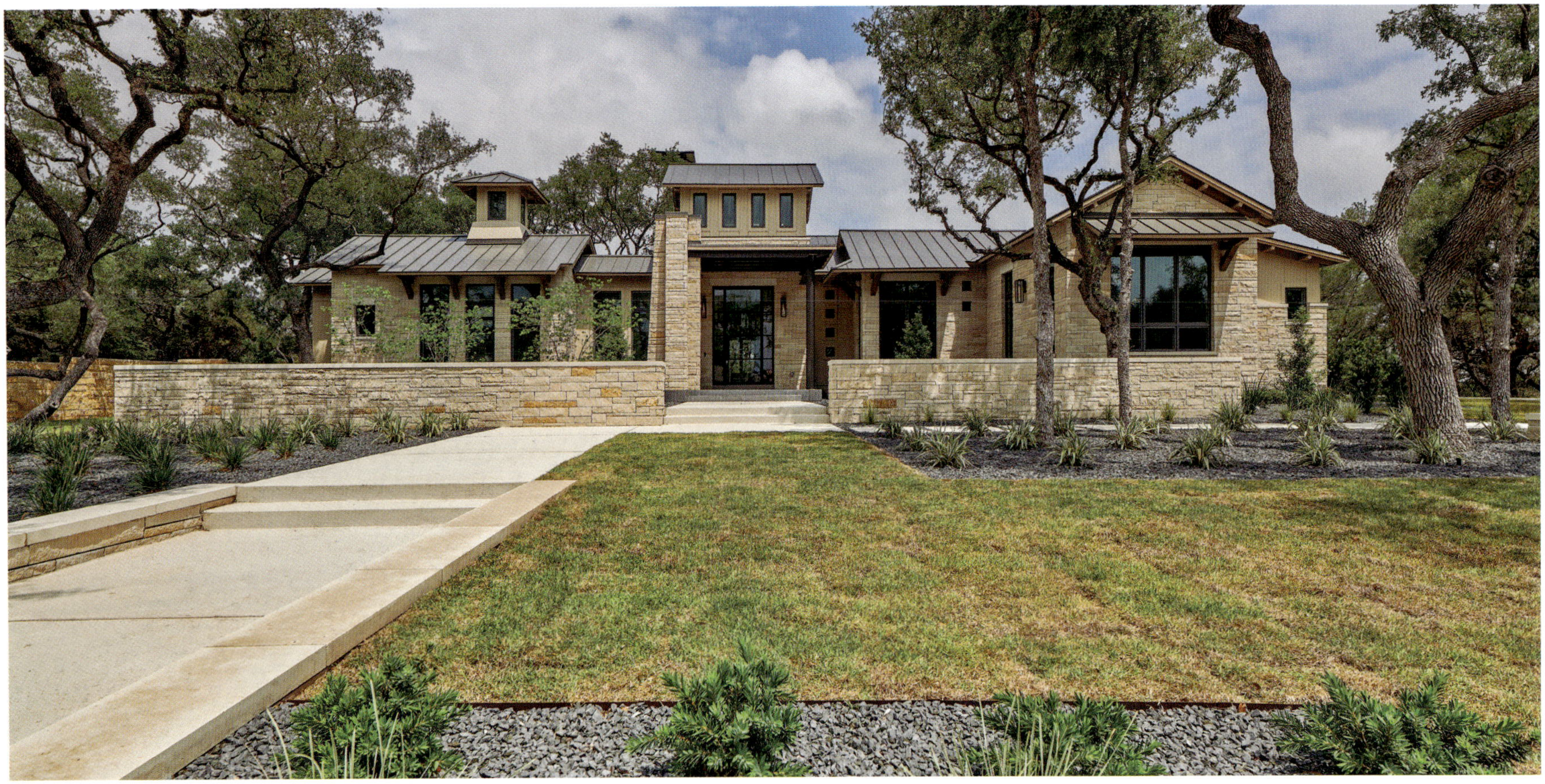

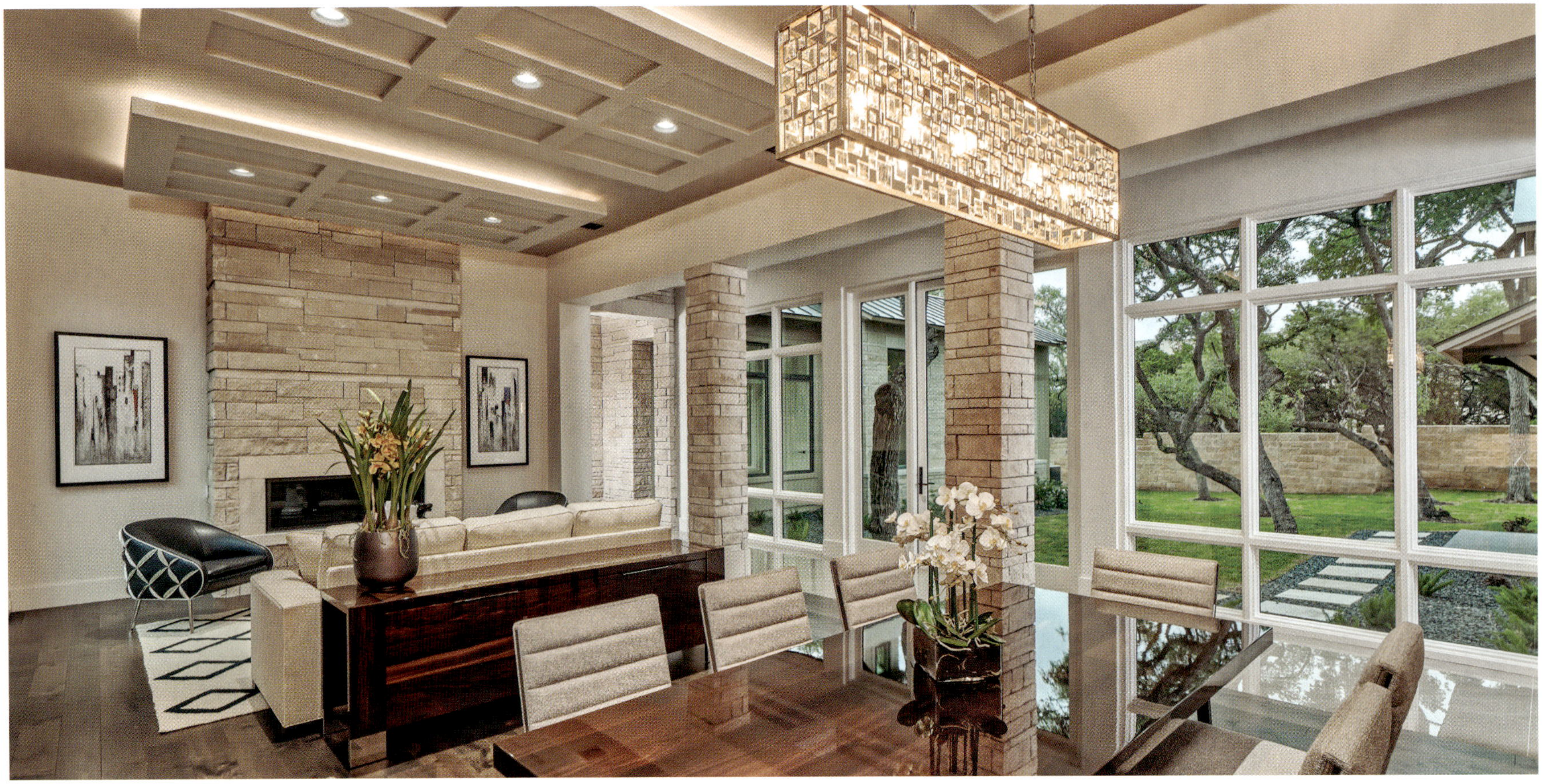

"When combining styles - the old and the new, the vintage and contemporary - there is a sweet spot. You have to marry it all up just right so the unexpected feels collected." —Gustavo Arredondo

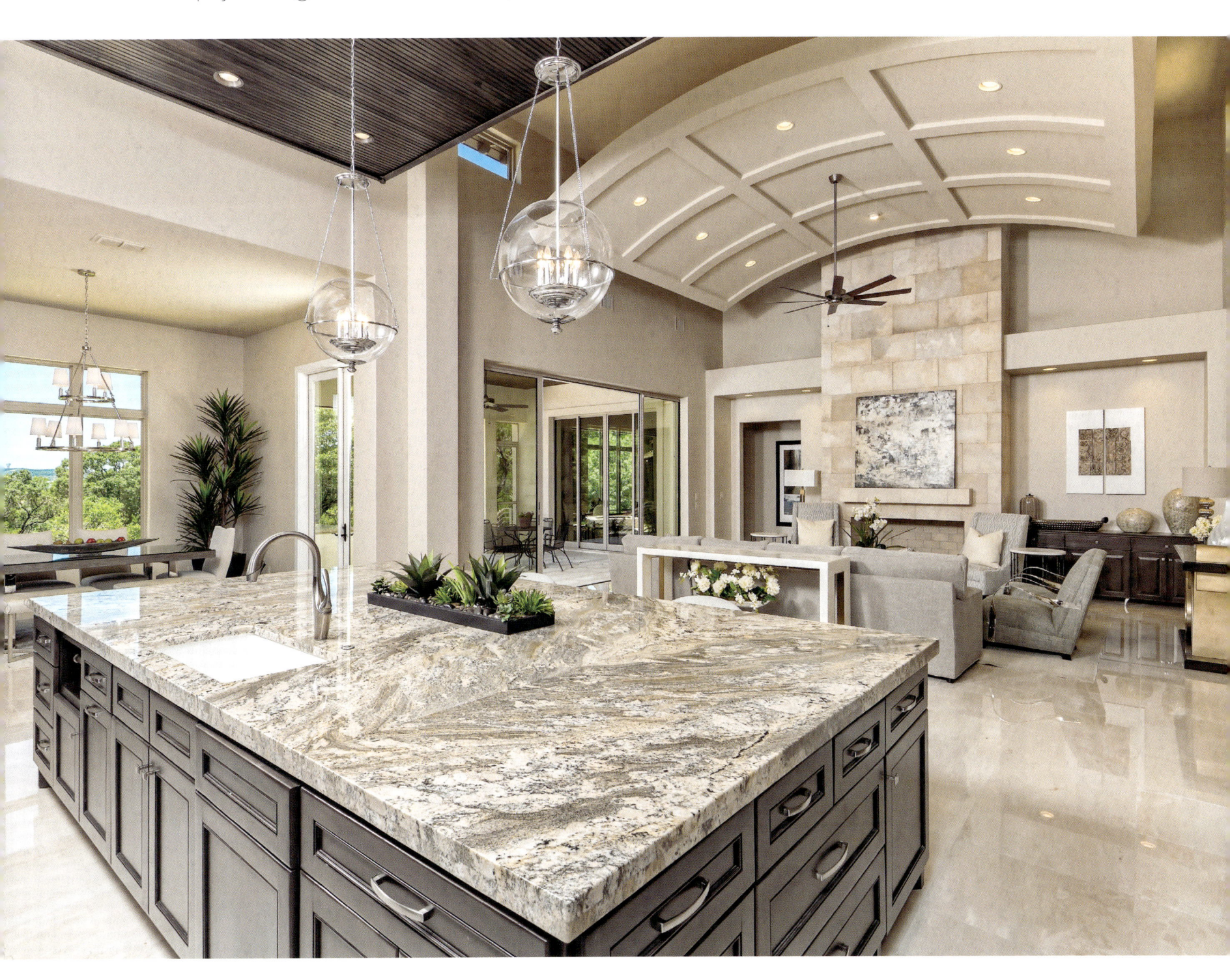

ABOVE: This open-concept kitchen, living, and dining area relies on a neutral color palette for quiet sophistication that allows for details like glass-orb light fixtures, dark wood ceilings, and an arched, suspended ceiling to take center stage. Photography courtesy of A-Design by Gustavo Arredondo.

FACING PAGE: Elevating Hill Country modern style, this home radiates with natural warmth punctuated by streamlined furnishings and contemporary lighting. Photography by Jason Roberts.

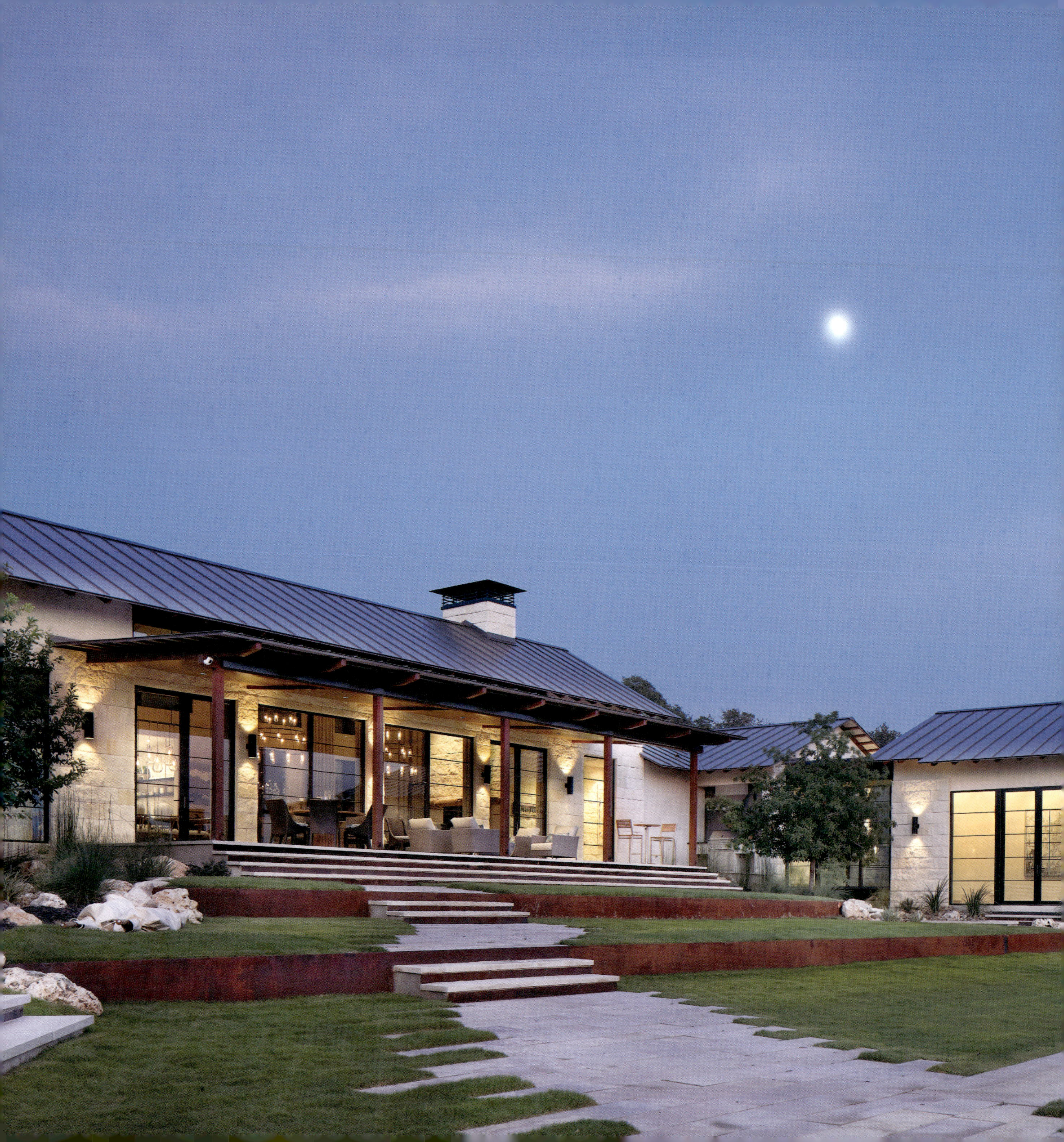

CRAIG MCMAHON ARCHITECTS

After spending 20 years working for large firms across the country where he designed large-scale commercial projects, Craig McMahon found himself leaning toward the artistry and hands-on experience of owning a small firm that focused on the creative aspect of design and construction. He enjoys the process of creating and crafting an environment where his clients grow, laugh, dream, learn, and live – as does his team who closely collaborate on each project. The mission at Craig McMahon Architects is to think holistically about a project from the ground up – to the very last detail. They're passionate about developing ideas into livable reality and improving their clients' quality of life through artfully crafted spaces and unique environments.

Their spirit of collaboration extends not only to clients, but also to local artisans, craftspeople, subcontractors, and others working on each house. Craig and his team know the importance of bringing everyone together early in the design process – and they value all input. While Craig McMahon Architects' projects are diverse and varied, what unites them all is a prioritization of year-round, outdoor live-and-work environments. For example, the firm creates private courtyards by framing the yard with the house, garage, and other structures; they bring exterior materials inside; and they fill rooms with natural light. They also value the art of traditional building methods, mixing them with innovative techniques, applications, and technology for timeless, beautiful, and functional results.

FACING PAGE: Located in Cordillera Ranch, the Greystone Point modern ranch home sits just above a small canyon on 10 acres with unobstructed views to the west. The linear, natural limestone on the exterior walls, along with the smooth-troweled stucco, pewter-colored metal siding, and stained wood eaves, are inspired by German construction influences of the previous era. Interior design by Kathleen DiPaolo. Construction by Johnny Canavan Custom Homes. Photography by Dror Baldinger FAIA.

THIS PAGE AND FACING PAGE: From the onset, a transparent connection to the outdoors was embraced in the design of the Greystone Point home. The site-driven floor plan locates the main living spaces at a higher point on the property and then the bedroom wings gently step down the sloping hillside. Ten-foot floor-to-ceiling glass doors and windows blend the inside and outside. A bridge leads to the three-sided, glass-enclosed and cantilevered master wing, which includes a library, bedroom, and bathroom. Photography by Dror Baldinger FAIA.

239

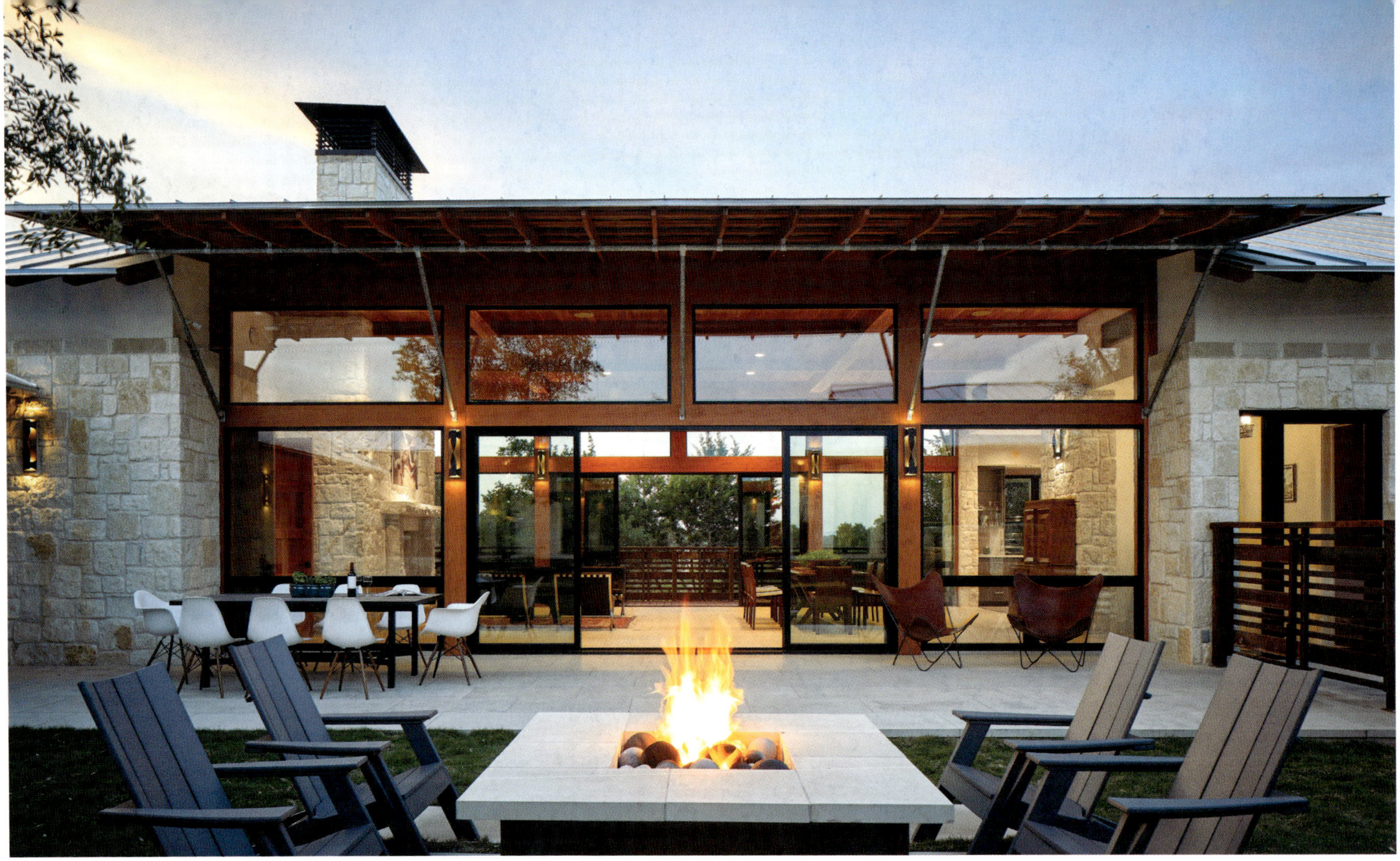

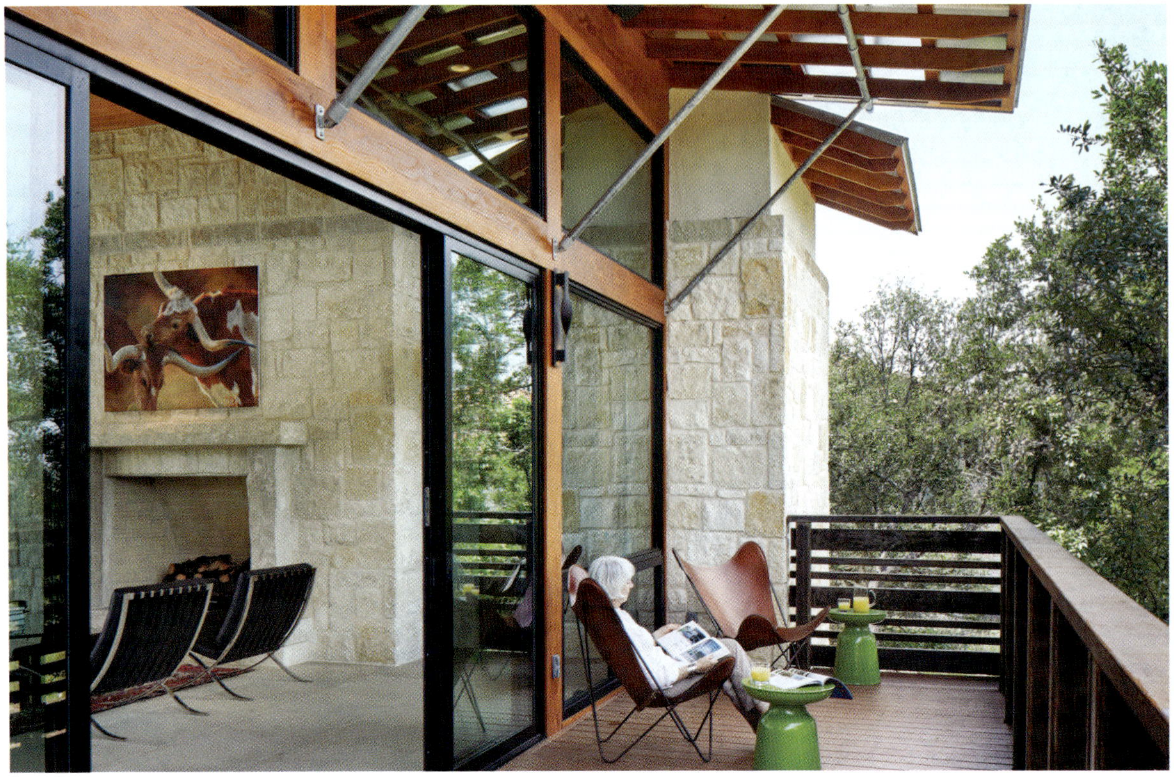

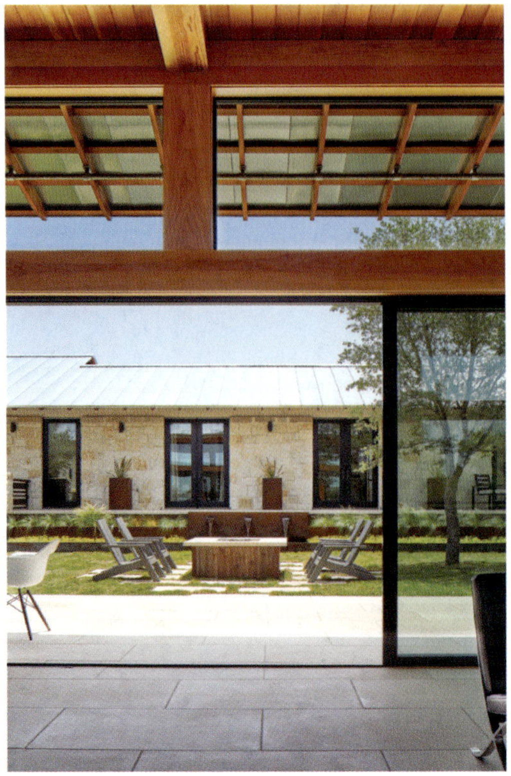

"The indoor-outdoor courtyard acts as a private sanctuary in the center of the home." —Craig McMahon AIA

ABOVE AND FACING PAGE BOTTOM LEFT AND RIGHT: When relocating from the East Coast, the owners of this 3,600-square-foot Augusta home wanted a Texas ranch-inspired property to establish a "central retreat" for extended family. Cordillera Ranch, just outside of Boerne in the Hill Country, fit the bill – with its unique connection to local experiences, including fly fishing, equestrian, golf, tennis, and swimming amenities. The residence was designed as two different zones: a main home connected to a guest house that's attached to the garage. The two zones surround a central courtyard.

FACING PAGE TOP: The main design feature of the home is the uniquely placed living area – an all-glass, single-wide room that extends the spirit of the indoor-outdoor courtyard and opens directly to the cantilevered deck, offering dramatic views to the golf course. Interior design by David Collum. Construction by Johnny Canavan Custom Homes. Photography by Dror Baldinger FAIA.

"We worked with the homeowners to create a fun, inviting, and truly livable space that fully engaged the history of the area while being uniquely modern." —Craig McMahon

ABOVE AND FACING PAGE: Piebald Ranch was designed as a ranch retreat in southern Texas with ample indoor and outdoor spaces for relaxing and entertaining. The six-bedroom, five-bath ranch home allows for both the homeowners and visitors to have their own private setting or engage in a larger party setting while enjoying the firepit and pool. Interior design by Aimee Escamilla-Studio E. Construction by Johnny Canavan Custom Homes. Photography by Craig McMahon AIA.

243

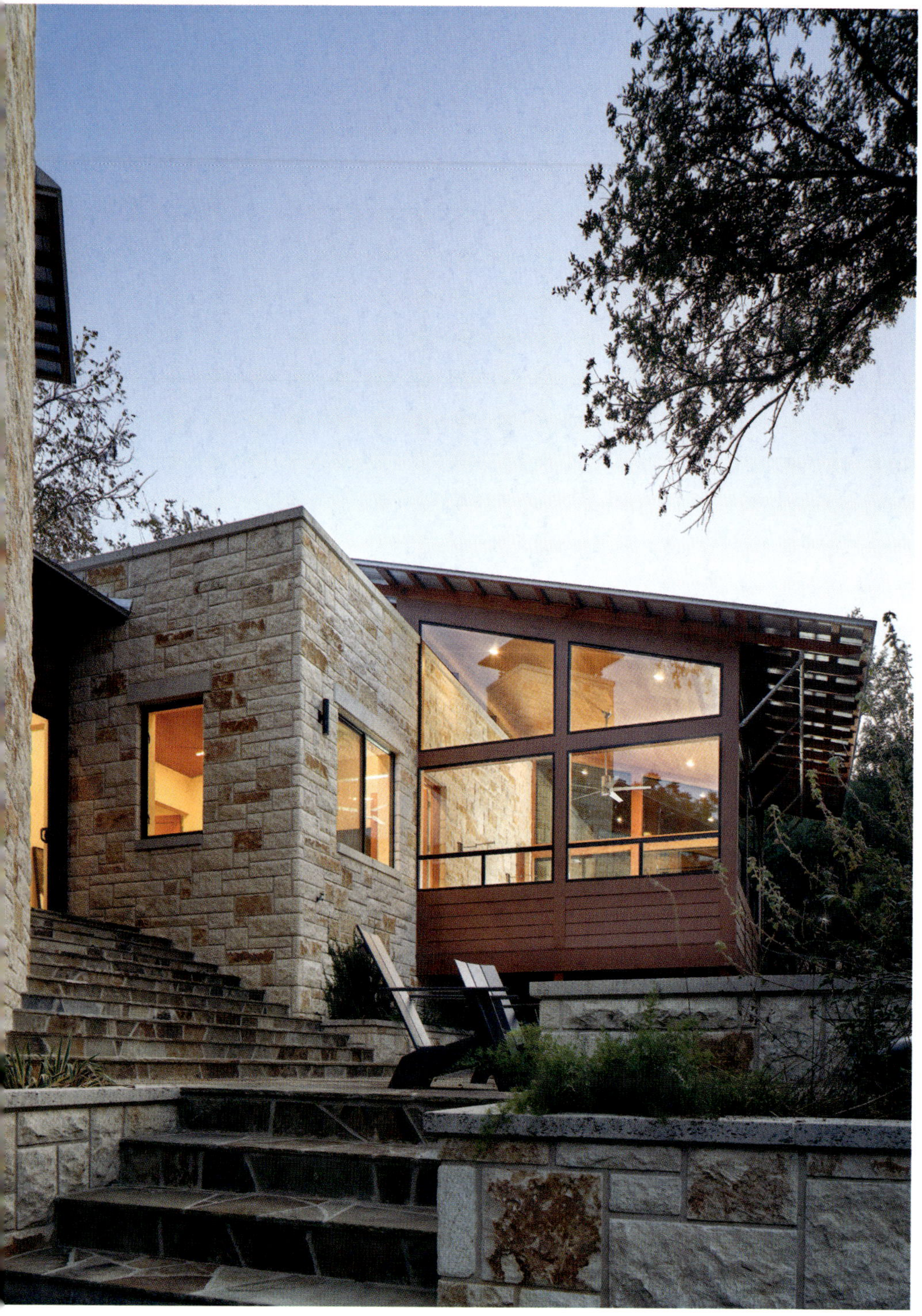

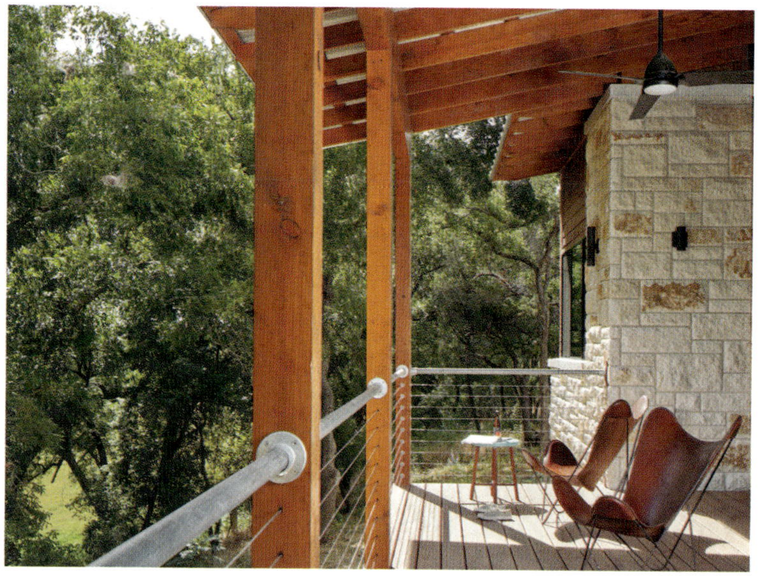

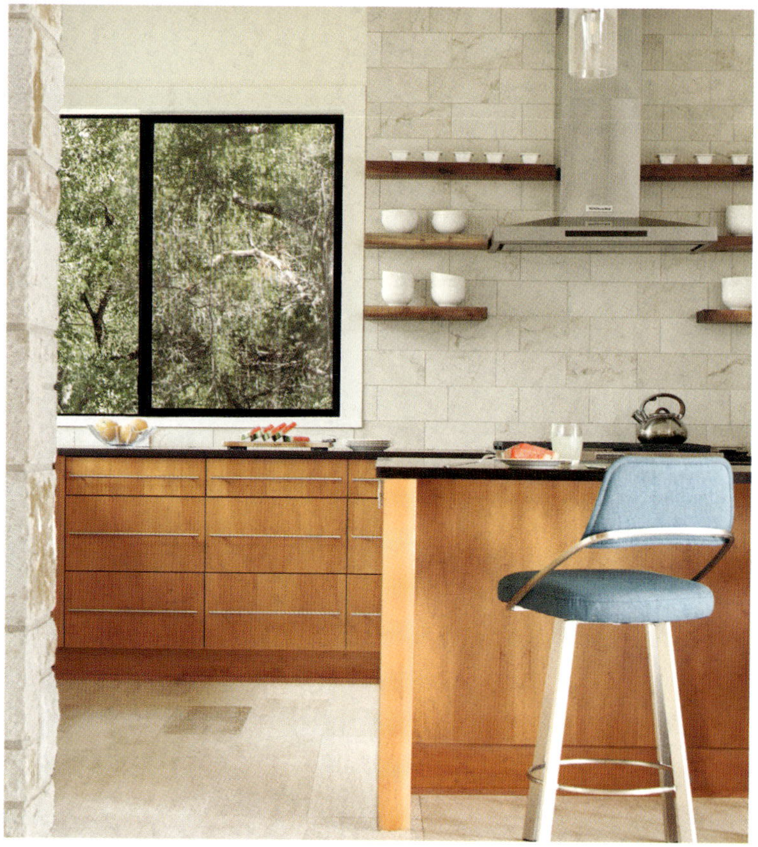

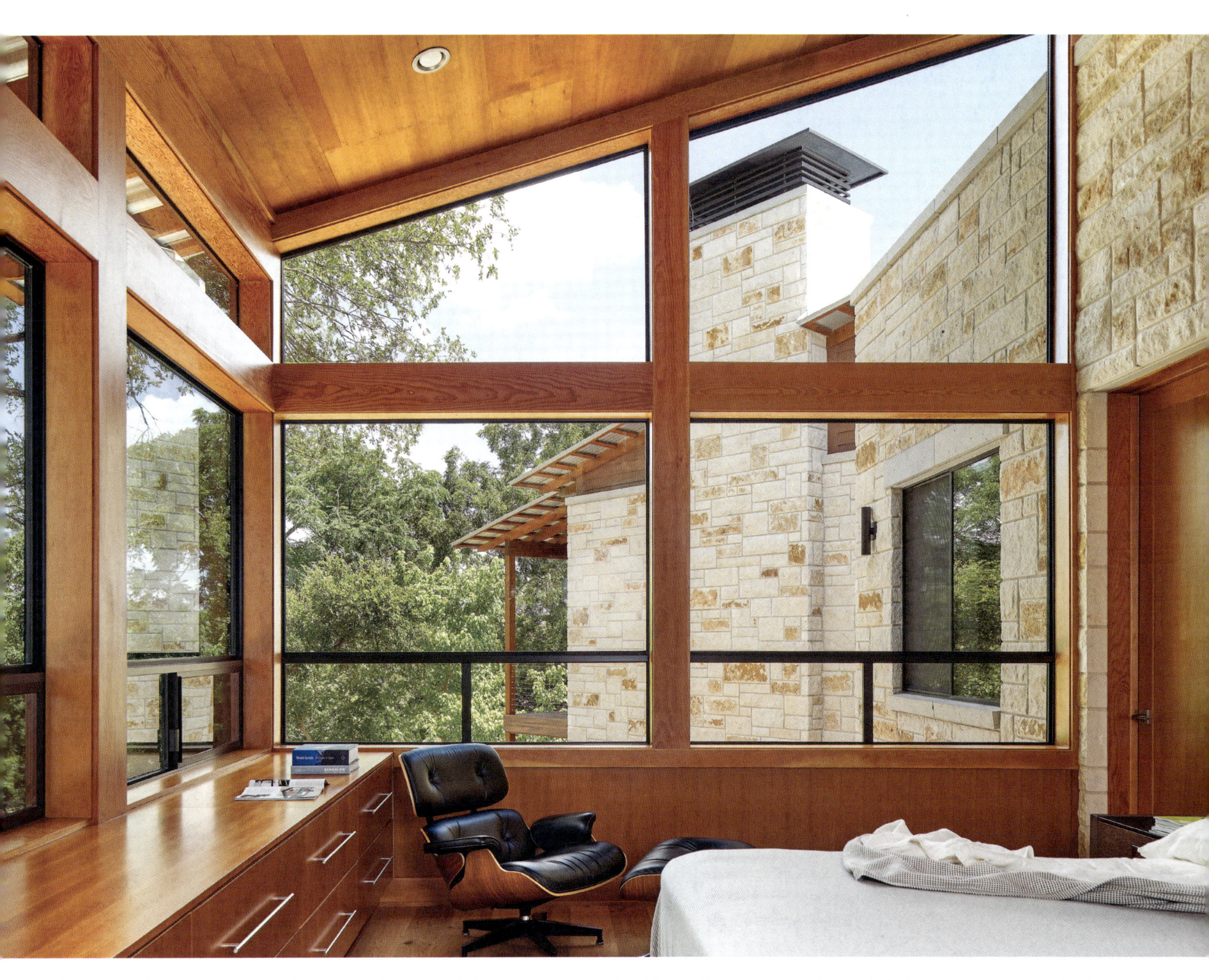

THIS PAGE AND FACING PAGE: Located on five acres of land along the Lampasas River, just outside of Belton, this new residence celebrates the "spirit of camping on the land." Tucked into the site via a hidden ranch road, the home sits above a rocky limestone bluff overlooking the fields and river below. Exteriors crafted of Hill Country limestone and paneled siding complement the surroundings, while dual porches on each side of the central living areas as well as large expanses of glass windows and doors embrace the view. So, too, does the master wing, which unfolds to an all-glass master bedroom perched in the tree line. Construction by MF Construction. Photography by Dror Baldinger FAIA.

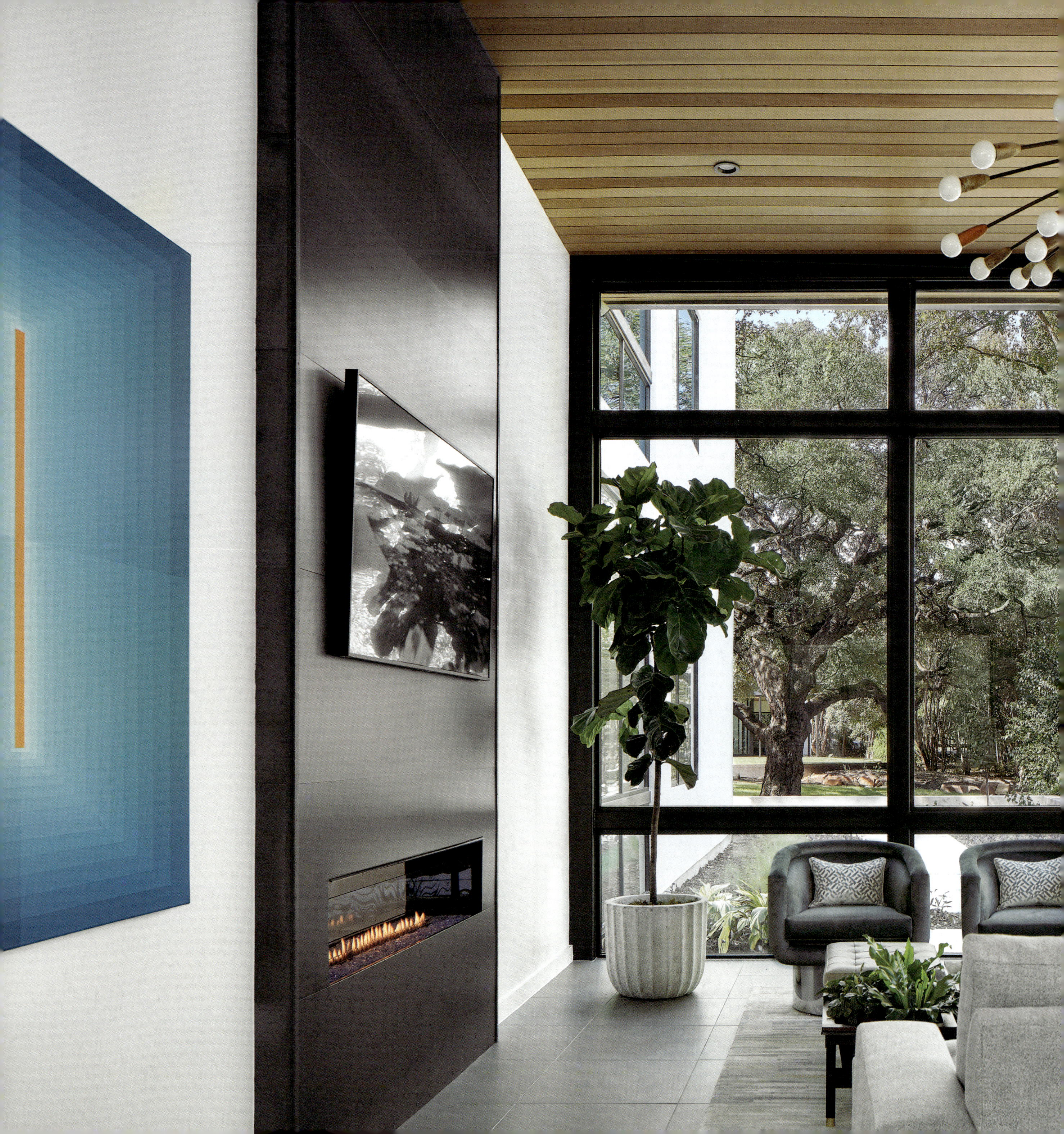

ELIZABETH HAYNES ARCHITECT

"I enjoy the process of creating and crafting an environment where my clients grow, laugh, dream, learn, and live," says Elizabeth Haynes. She and her team closely collaborate on each project and that spirit of collaboration extends to clients as well as local artisans, craftspeople, subcontractors and others working on the house. They bring everyone together early in the design process and value all input.

That's because the ultimate mission at Elizabeth Haynes Architect is to think holistically about the project from the beginning to the last detail. They are passionate about improving their clients' quality of life by delivering artfully crafted projects and unique living environments — and they enjoy developing ideas into livable reality.

You'll often find their work celebrating the continuity between indoors and outdoors. They bring exterior materials inside — stone, wood, steel — and fill rooms with daylight. And, all of their projects allow clients to enjoy year-round outdoor living and working environments. They also value the art of traditional building methods by mixing them with innovative techniques, applications, and technology.

FACING PAGE: Surrounded by two acres of warm woods, this hidden oasis of a residence in the Northwood area of Alamo Heights is enveloped by lush trees and creates visual connections to the organic setting from almost every interior space, including this living area. The large expanses of glass invite the majestic oaks inside — where the statement lighting mimics tree branches. Photography by Dror Baldinger FAIA.

ABOVE: The master suite takes advantage of the striking spillway that winds through the property. The bedroom is perched just over the spillway, which transforms into a dancing creek bed during times of rain.

FACING PAGE RIGHT: The master bathroom likewise maximizes the view through the suspended vanity and minimal mirrors.

FACING PAGE TOP AND BOTTOM LEFT: The kitchen and dining area offer the same minimally beautiful ode to organic tones and natural light. Photography by Dror Baldinger FAIA.

"I enjoy the process of creating and crafting an environment where my clients grow, laugh, dream, learn, and live." —Elizabeth Haynes

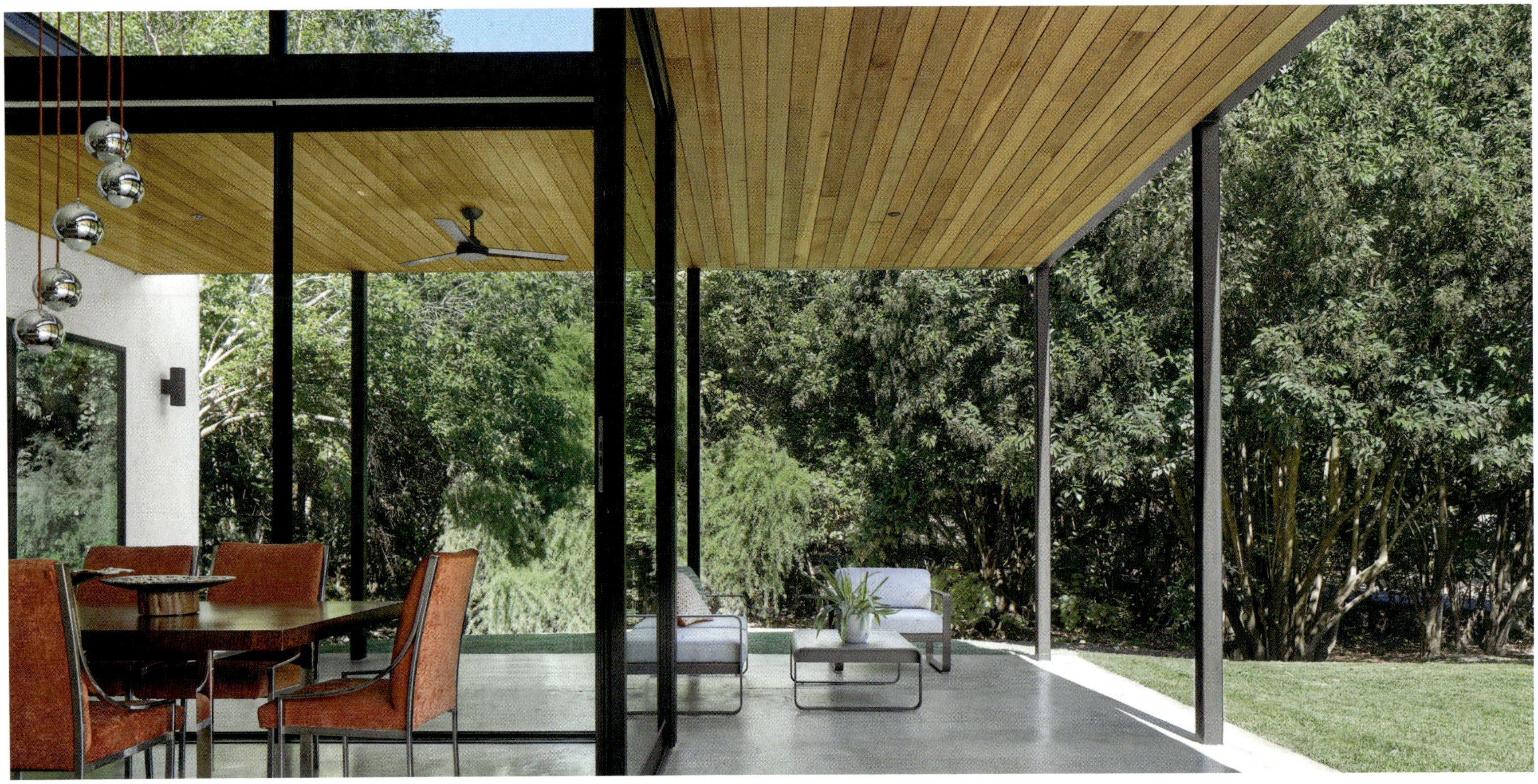

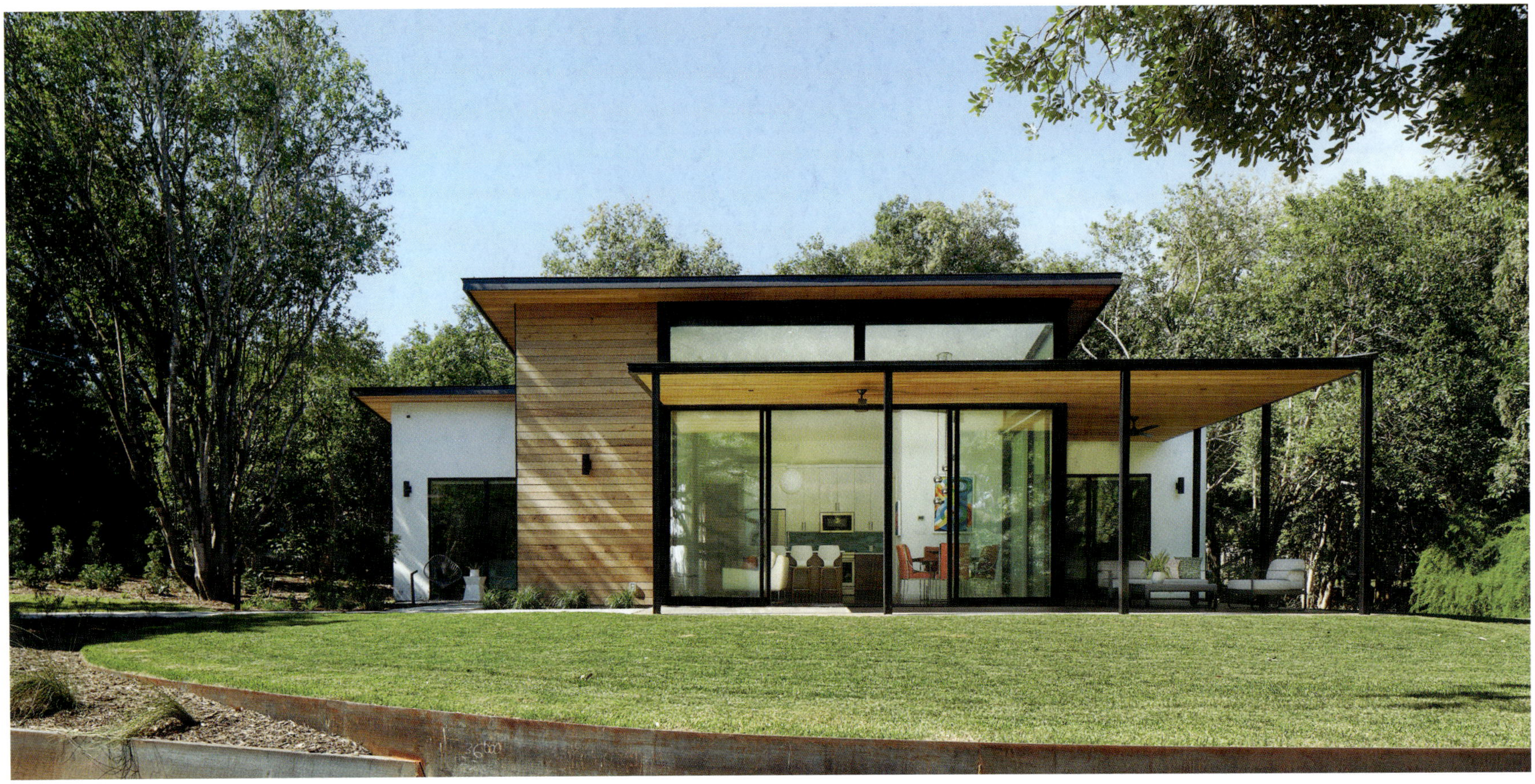

ABOVE: The architect envisioned the tree as the center axis around which the two structures, a main house and a casita, would revolve.

FACING PAGE TOP: The owners were experienced when it came to construction projects, partnering beautifully with the architect and builder to bring their bold indoor-outdoor vision to life.

FACING PAGE BOTTOM: Glass cubes, straight lines, and stucco lend the structure its contemporary quality while cedar and steel accents recall rural South Texas structures. Photography by Dror Baldinger FAIA.

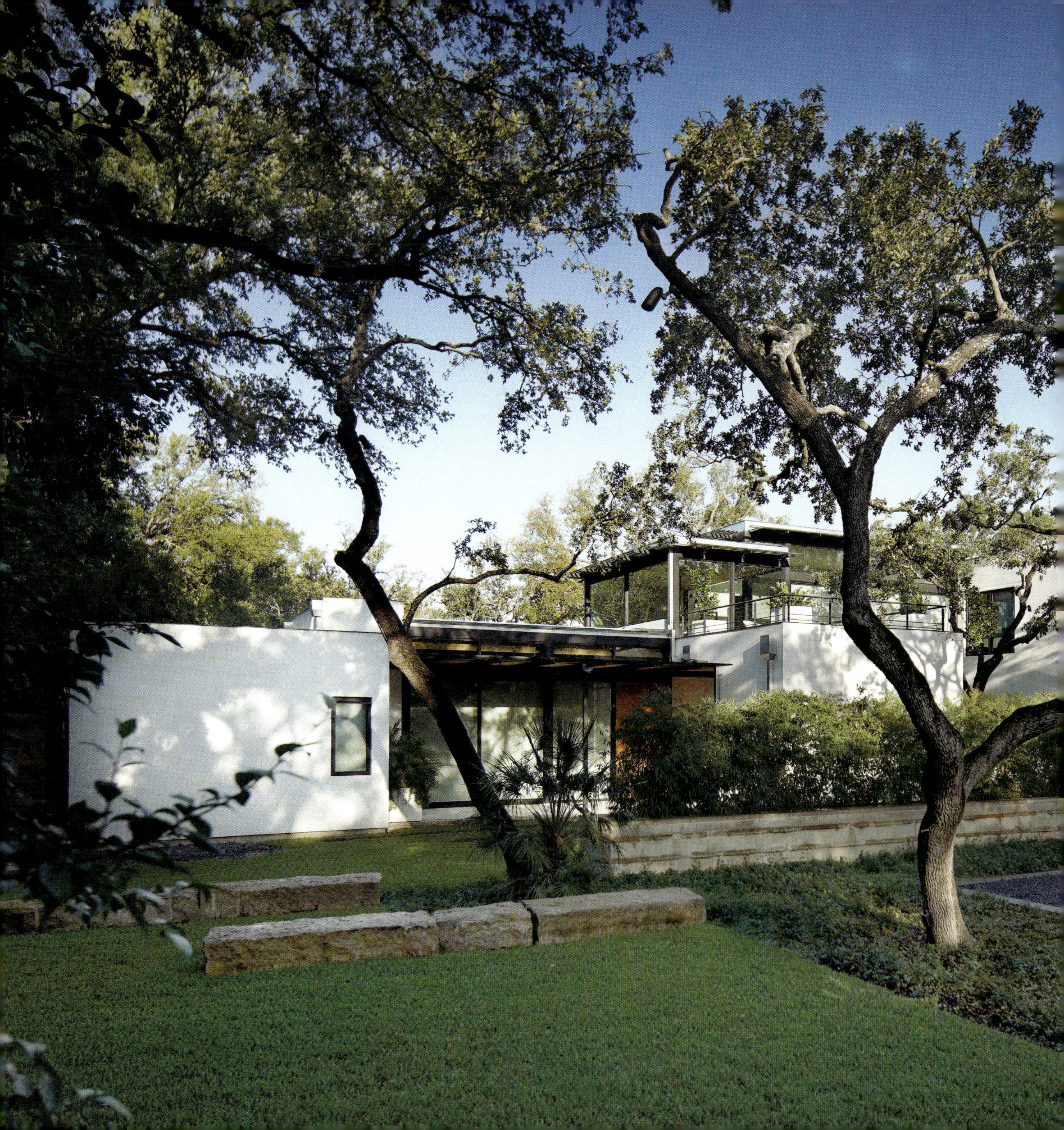

JOHN GRABLE ARCHITECTS

A passion for the human experience – the stories of people's lives and the role architecture plays in them – is a driving force behind John Grable's award-winning designs. So, too, is his love and respect for the land, which comes with a keen understanding of how buildings can gently coexist with nature.

So, you could easily say that John's architecture ultimately celebrates life. By connecting to history and expressing a deep love of craft and material, his work articulates purity and simplicity, and elevates the relationship between man and nature.

It is with this same empathetic and enthusiastic attention that he listens to the dreams and aspirations of each of his clients, bringing them into the design process to create a synergy of creativity, comradery, and growth between client, architect and trades alike. Through this intentional collaboration, John and his team push solutions to the next level of fine art – solutions driven by craftsmanship, a nearly lost art from prior generations.

John acknowledges that architecture is a team sport and emphasizes that clients should never sacrifice the quality of people who are a part of the process – one can never cover all the bases without a uniform body of thought, creativity, and talent. This philosophy is evidenced by his team, which he refers to as "his favorite project" and represents the next generation of talented architects who will continue a legacy of thoughtfully crafted and timeless solutions.

FACING PAGE: This residence's white stucco boxes, bounded by mill blocks, recall the adjacent quarry and define the front elevation – a composition that lies within the boundaries of heritage live oak trees. The stucco walls become an everchanging canvas for shadow and light throughout the seasons – the gifts from Mother Nature. One is reminded of time, yet the spaces are timeless throughout the day. Photography by John Grable Architects.

ABOVE: The living room's double-height space – inspired by light and space artist James Turrell – captures dynamic, natural light throughout the day and solidifies the connection with the sky, the interior, and the land.

FACING PAGE TOP LEFT: A custom water feature, carved from one of the mill blocks, provides a serene backdrop of trickling water that echoes within the courtyard where a mott of heritage live oak reside.

FACING PAGE TOP RIGHT: A custom fireplace, crafted with cuttings of the landscaping stones, is centrally located to tie the interior gathering spaces together. It provides a visual connection to the stone placed throughout the site.

FACING PAGE BOTTOM: A deep porch offers generous space and shade for outdoor living while sliding glass doors effortlessly bring the interior and exterior together. Photography by John Grable Architects.

255

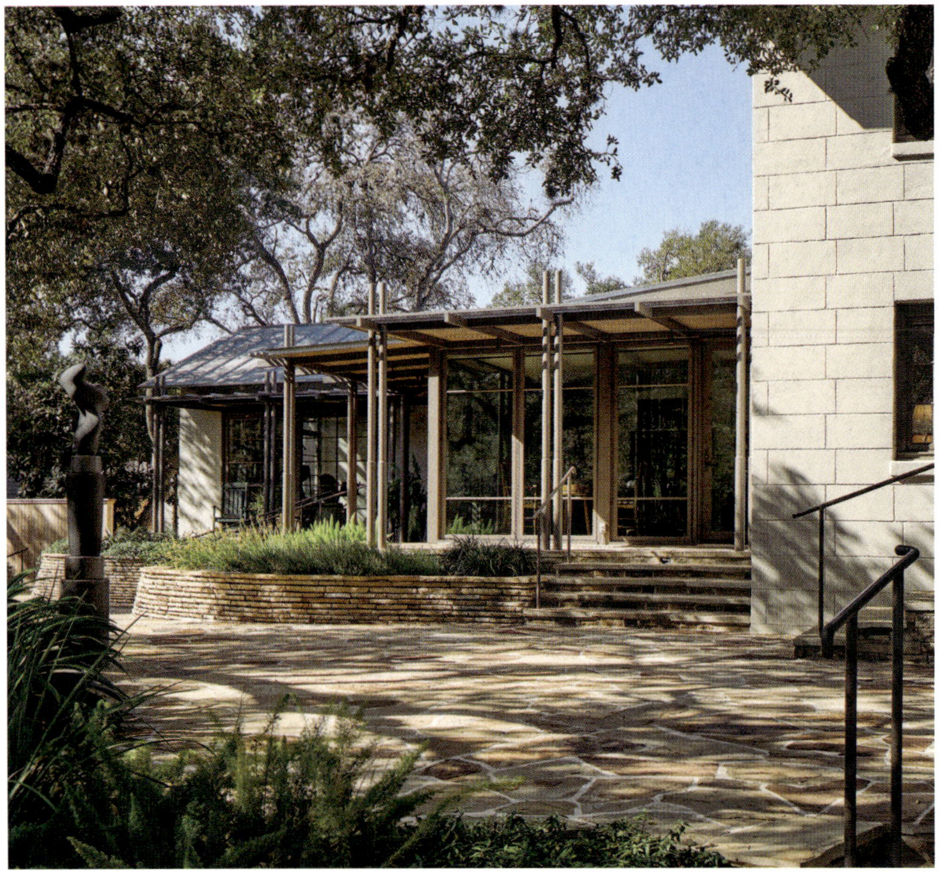

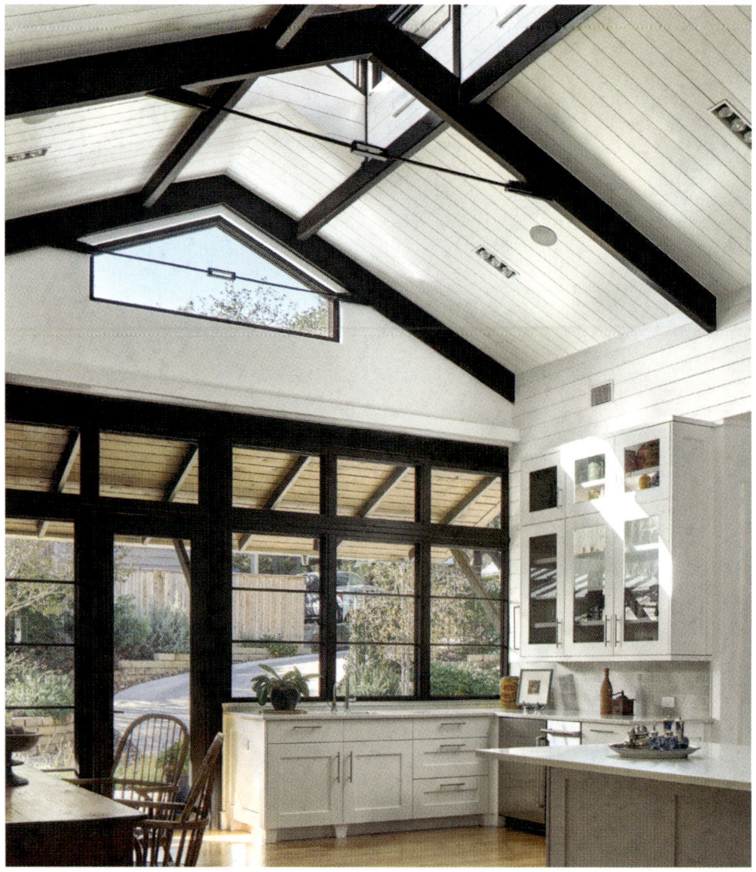

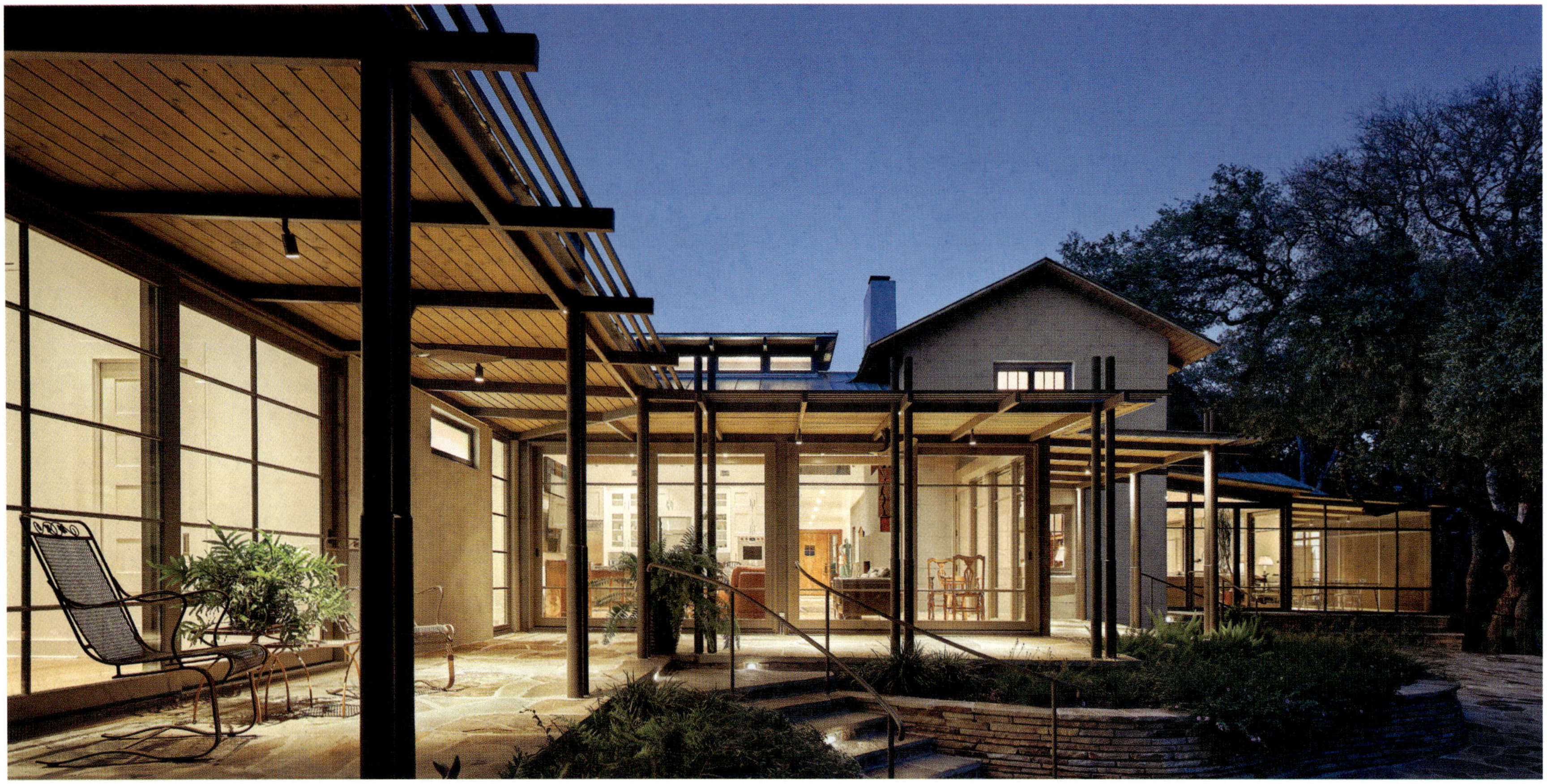

"By connecting to history and expressing a deep appreciation for craft and material, we can articulate purity and simplicity and exalt the relationship between man and nature."
—John Grable FAIA

TOP: The bronze, wire-screen porch of this historic 1930 German homestead is a transparent element that ignites the natural light into a warm glow while immersing one into the beauty of the verdant, landscaped courtyard that features a sculpture by Danville Chadbourne. Painting by Danville Chadbourne.

MIDDLE: The original one-room-wide, two-story structure was preserved to maintain the heart and soul of the home, providing a reminder of the many family memories lived there. The ceiling of the original structure is painted "sky-blue" in reference to historic Texas porches. Paintings by Mary Ann Hollingshead.

BOTTOM: The new kitchen provides generous space for family gatherings that starts at the 18-foot island and spills onto Texas longleaf pine furniture. The exposed gable structure and cupola recall the original Texas vernacular by revealing the exterior of the original homestead while animating the space with a warm, natural light. Sculpture by Danville Chadbourne and painting by Reginald Rowe.

FACING PAGE TOP LEFT: Sited along a dry creek bed that has become the community's favorite walking trail, the porches act as welcoming gesture to the neighborhood. Sculpture by Danville Chadbourne.

FACING PAGE TOP RIGHT: Built around the original homestead, the new construction delicately embraces the structure with stepping forms of glass façades, providing a positive-negative connection of the old and new.

FACING PAGE BOTTOM: Deep overhangs provide protection from the harsh Texas sun while framing views to the landscape and providing warmth via western red cedar. Photography by Dror Baldinger FAIA.

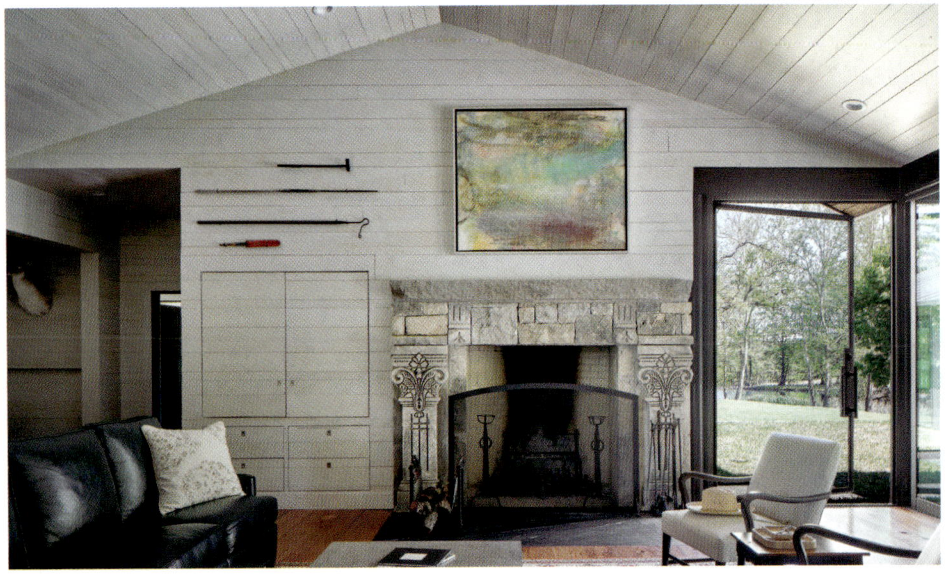
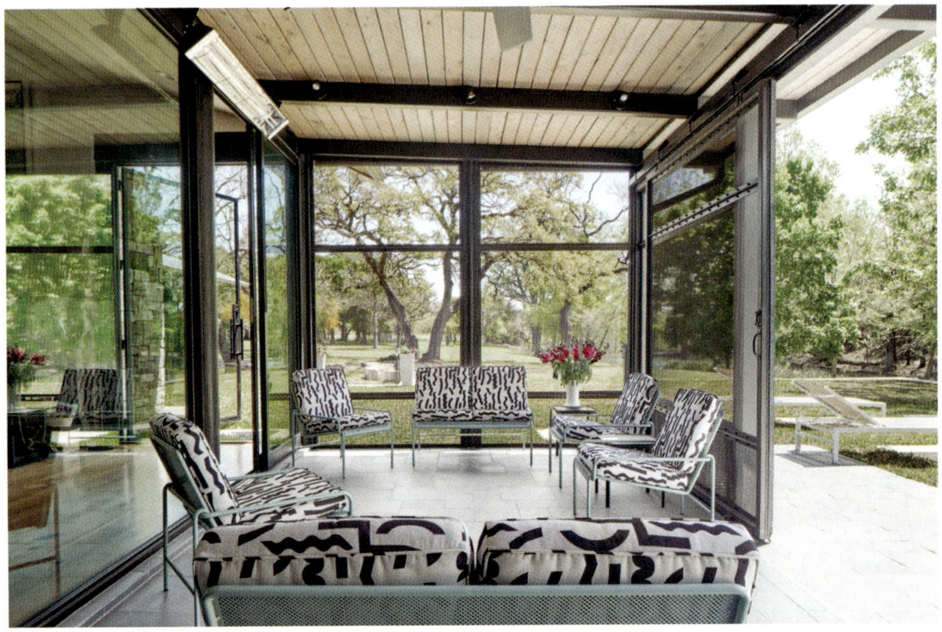
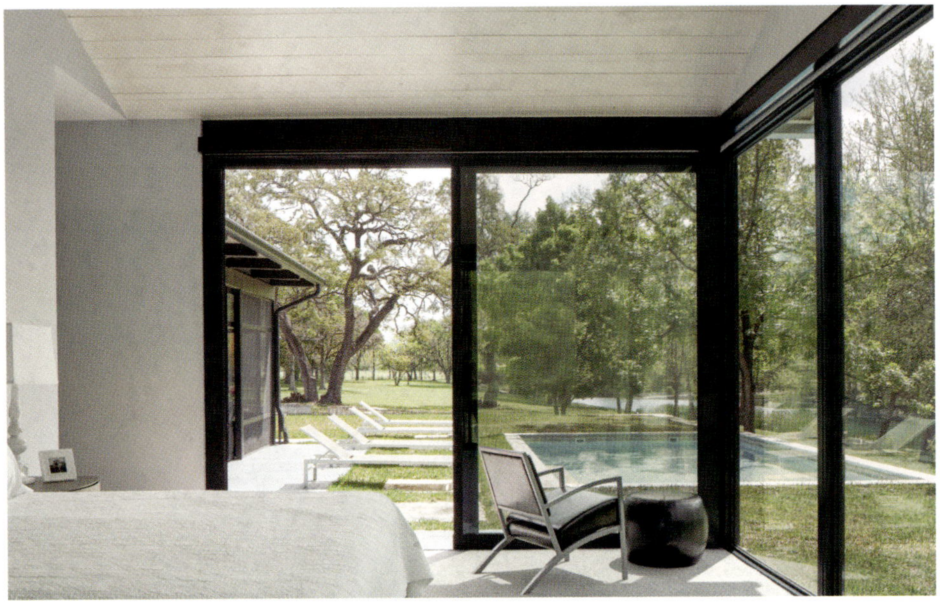
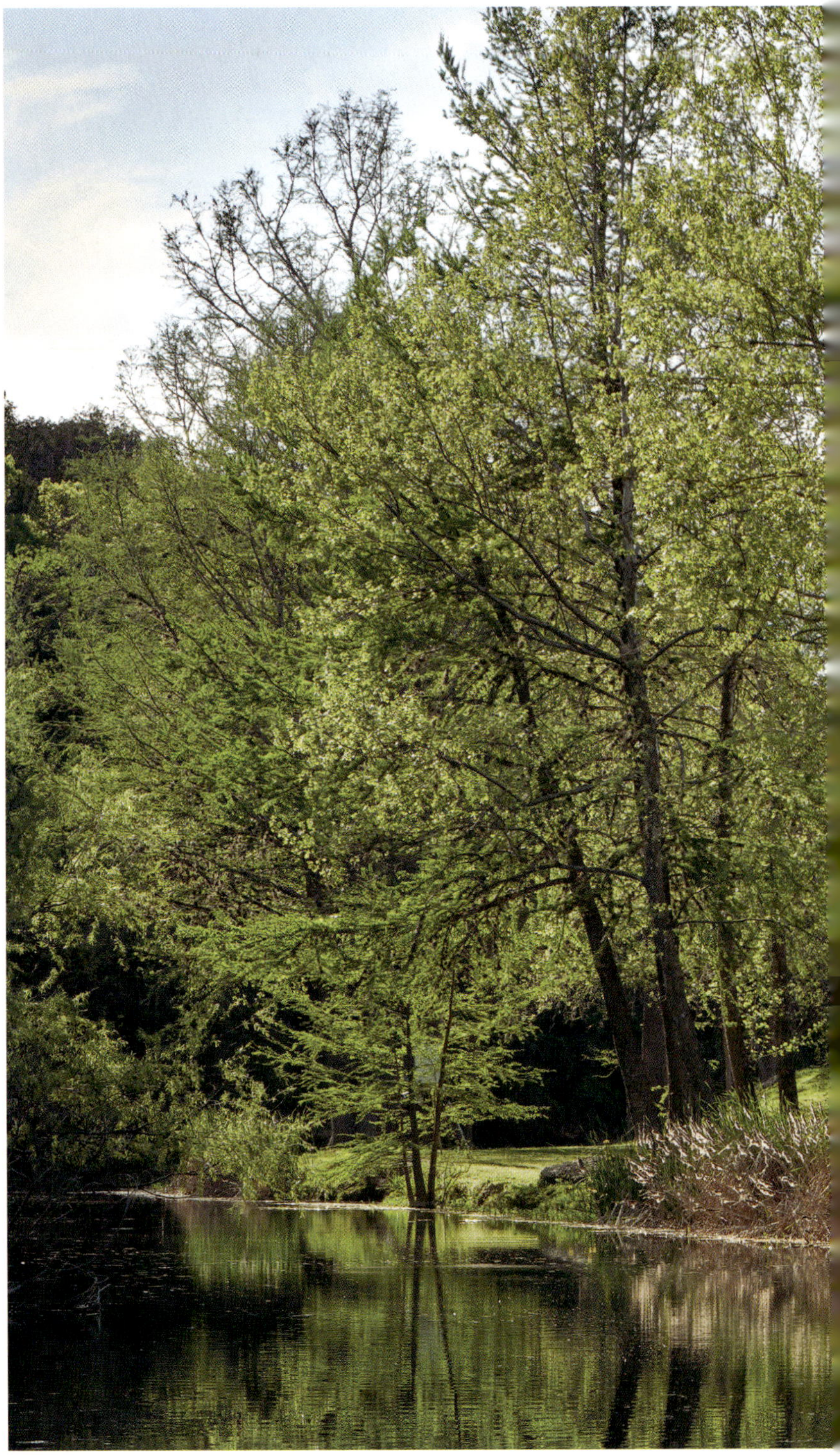

ABOVE: This project embraces the memories and knowledge base of the homeowners who grew up in the country. Through their experiences and travel, they have returned to the roots of their youth, creating a timelessly modern composition of a classic country home.

FACING PAGE TOP: Virgin-timber pine boards on the floor, harvested from an old cotton gin, reflect a warm glow and stand in contrast to the new whitewash shiplap walls that are adjacent to the relocated homestead fireplace – an homage to the original settlers.

FACING PAGE MIDDLE: A custom screen porch affords a gradual transition from the indoors to the outdoors while capturing the breeze and maintaining a vibrant connection to the site. Simple, time-honored building practices, such as deep overhangs and space heaters, offer comfort throughout the year.

FACING PAGE BOTTOM: The primary bedroom is surrounded by glass on three walls overlooking the pool and nearby creek and canyon, providing a sense of immersion into the landscape and harnessing the quiet echoes of the river canyon. Photography by Leonid Furmansky.

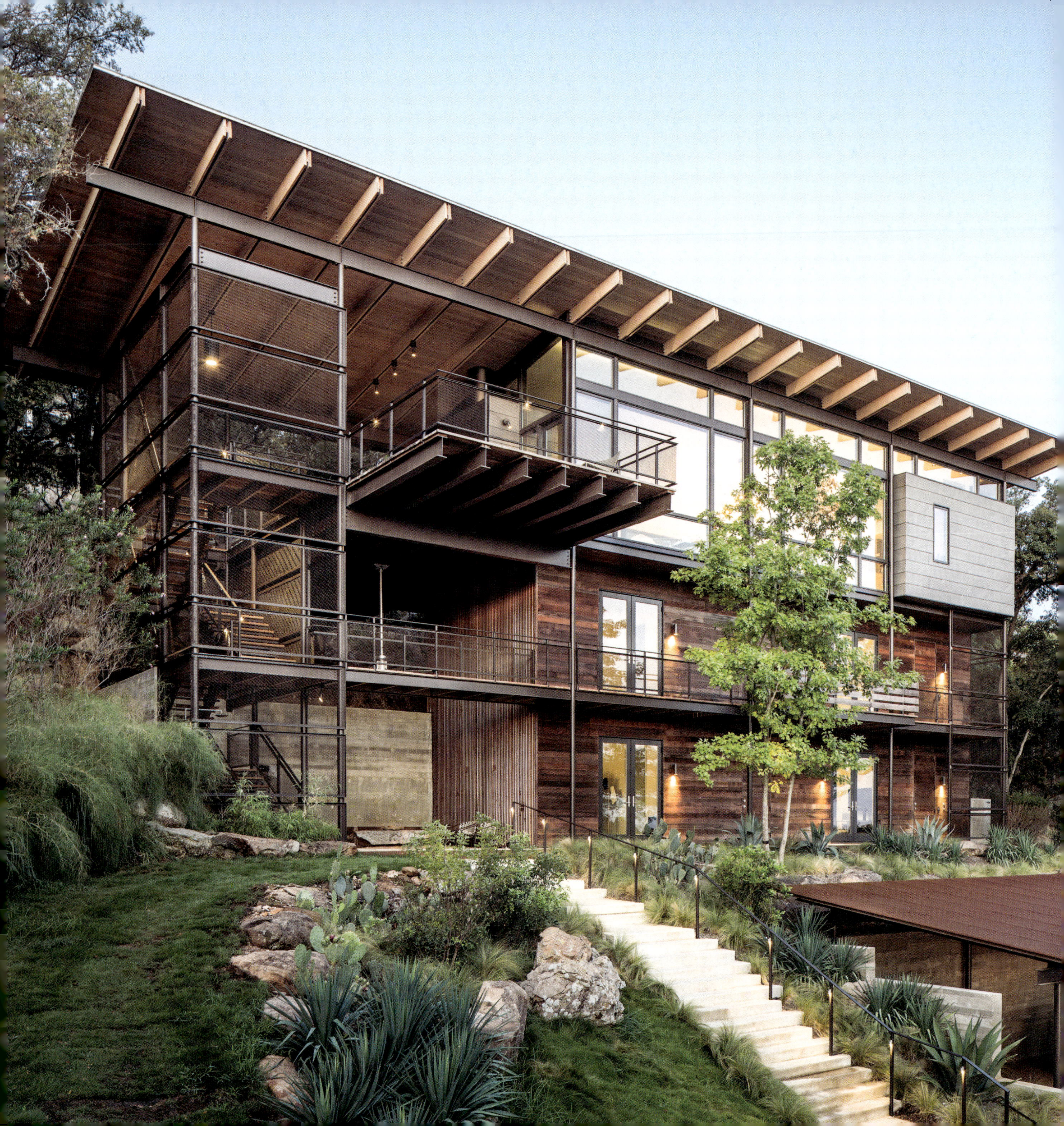

LAKE | FLATO ARCHITECTS

The design professionals at Lake | Flato Architects respond to every project, whether rural or urban, traditional or contemporary, with one purpose: to make the home intrinsically rise up from its place, acknowledging the geographic, historical, and cultural context surrounding it. They believe that the details of the design will then naturally lead to healthy, enjoyable, and sustainable residences. As the specifics of the home emerge during the design process, various topics are addressed to help inform the final design, such as the intended use of the rooms, technologies that enhance practicality, and regional materials that link home to its surroundings.

Lake | Flato's collaborative studio environment certainly facilitates this concept as each person's passions and talents are utilized in many capacities. Inspired by both old and new architecture, the team expresses beauty not by a particular style or era, but rather by buildings that are responsive to the environment and inherently timeless.

FACING PAGE: In response to the site's steeply rising topography, a vertically structured house quickly became the design direction for the firm's Blue Lake Retreat. The three-story residence dramatically culminates at the top floor, floating just above the tree line to provide a nearly 180-degree view of the lake beyond. Photography by Andrew Pogue.

THIS PAGE: Thoughtfully framed views highlight the site's aqua/terra connection of the lake beyond and rugged hillside behind, while operable windows and doors invite prevailing breezes through the home for natural ventilation. Photography by Ryann Ford.

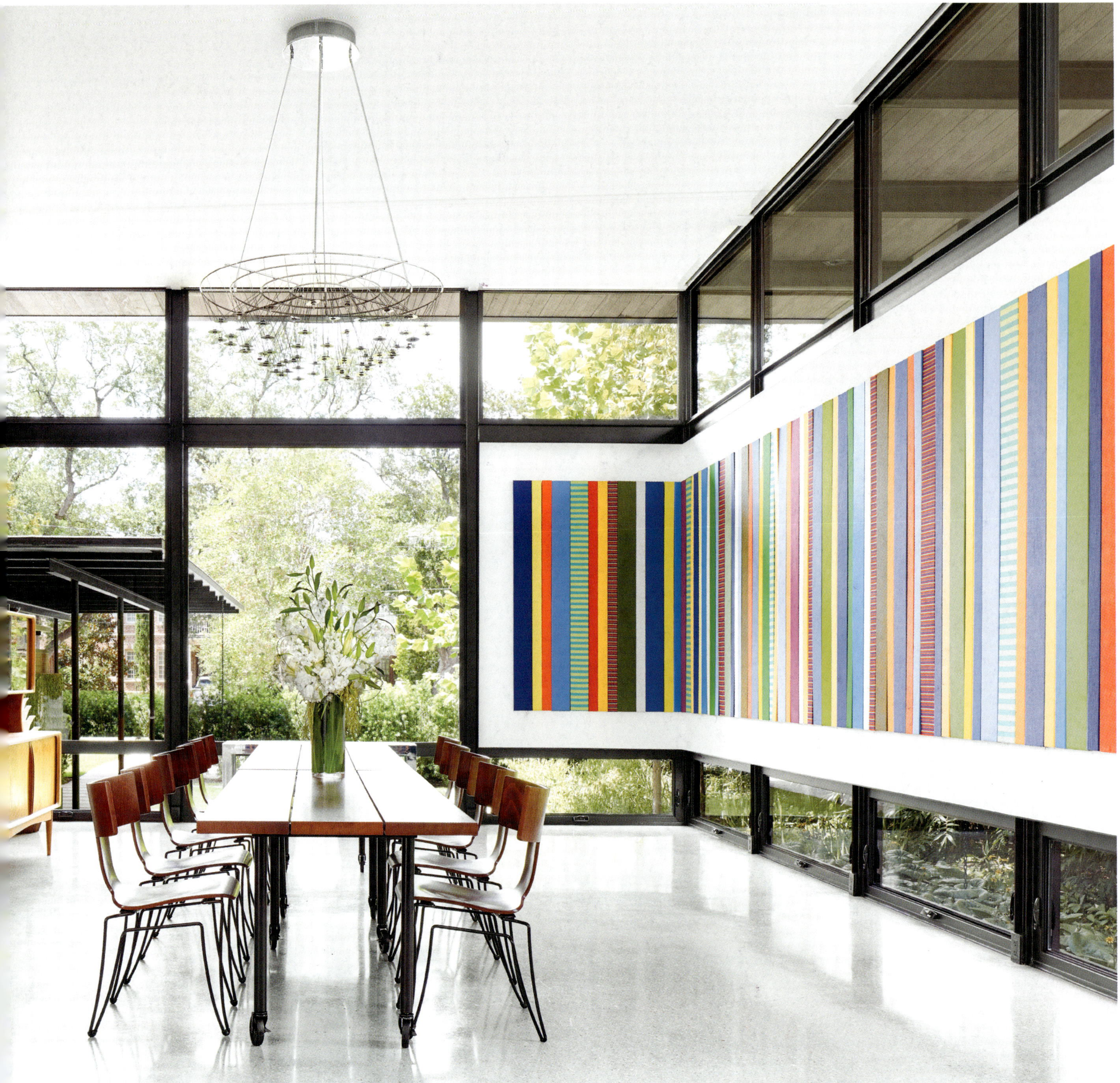

FACING PAGE AND ABOVE: Bellaire Residence sits on a narrow lot within a densely occupied, urban neighborhood. Inspired by modular design, the client sought a modern home in which to gather both indoors and out. Careful configuration activates the site through thoughtful arrangement of various rooms around a series of landscaped courtyards and terraces. A Lake | Flato Architects + Natalye Appel + Associates collaboration. Photography by Casey Dunn.

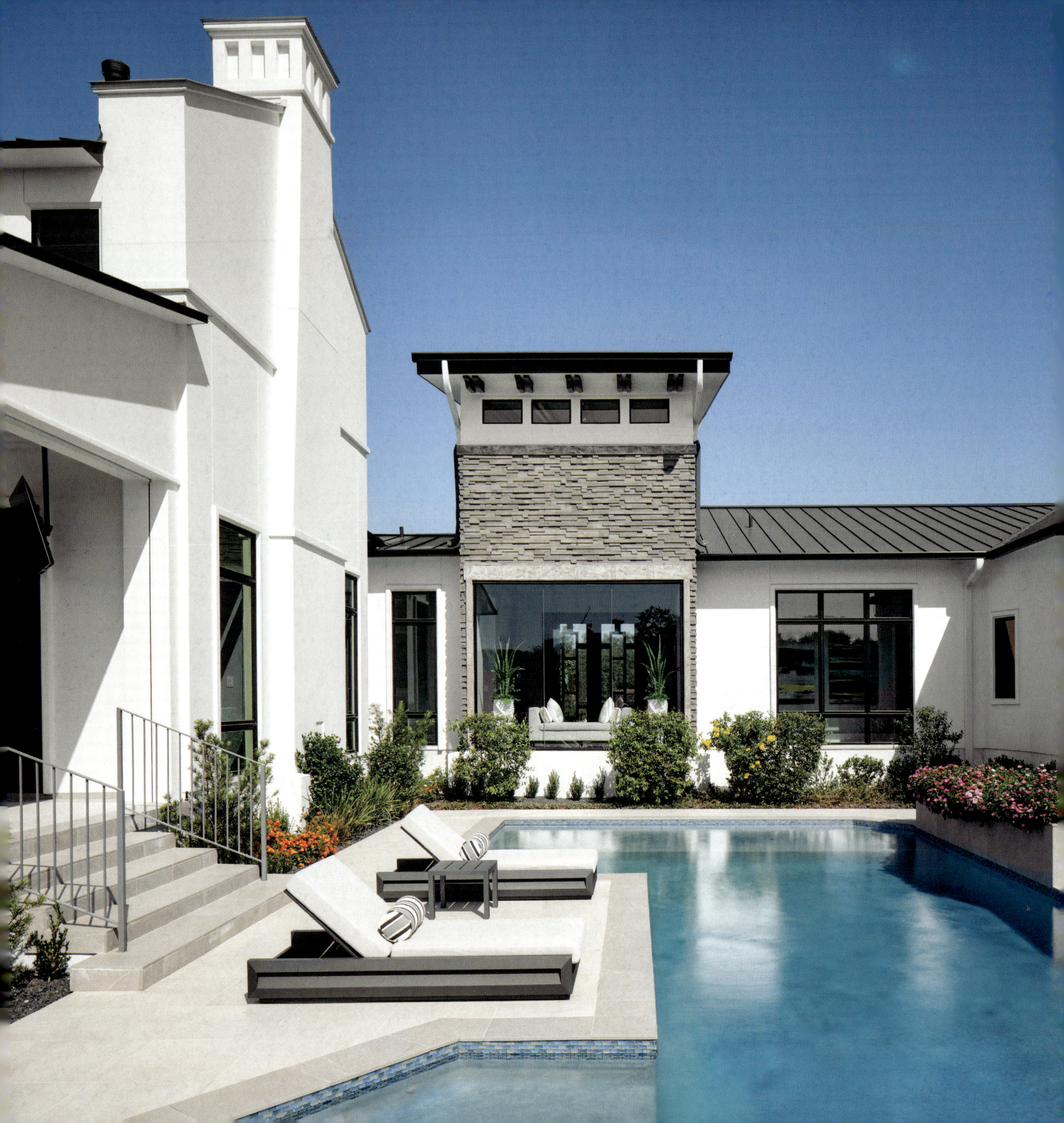

LORI CALDWELL DESIGNS

For interior designer Lori Caldwell, spaces shouldn't reflect any one specific time or style. Timelessness inevitably results from keen design choices and personalized selections of things like furniture, art, and lighting. At her namesake firm, Lori and her team hone in on the design hopes and dreams of her clients – and the functional elements that enhance their lives, both aesthetically and functionally. The Lori Caldwell team knows the finished product not only has to be beautiful, but it also has to work; it's an art form that must be as practical as it is eye-catching. Although it's no easy task, Lori has perfected this delicate balance.

Sophisticated, simple, elegant, and functional – these are just a few of the words that are used to describe the work of Lori Caldwell Designs. From new construction to remodels, space planning to interior and exterior selections, nothing is out of their realm. They collaborate with builders and architects to perfect the details of a space – including flooring materials, cabinetry, paint colors, countertops, and much more. They also assist with any purchasing needs that may arise – a benefit that gives homeowners access to trade prices and pieces they won't find anywhere else.

FACING PAGE: Outdoor spaces are just as important as interior spaces in this home designed by architect Gustavo Arredondo and built by Roberto Kenigstein. It is really important to keep the outdoor and indoor areas cohesive, especially when the outdoor areas are directly visible. Photography by Matthew Niemann Photography.

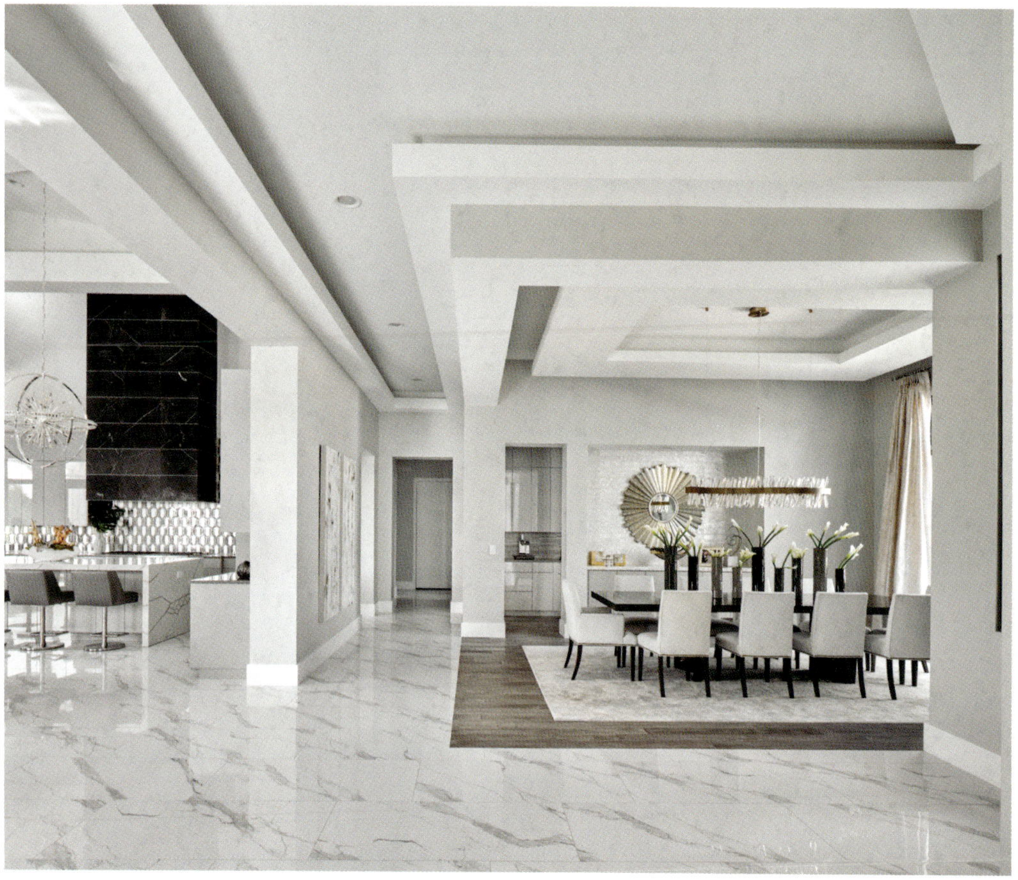
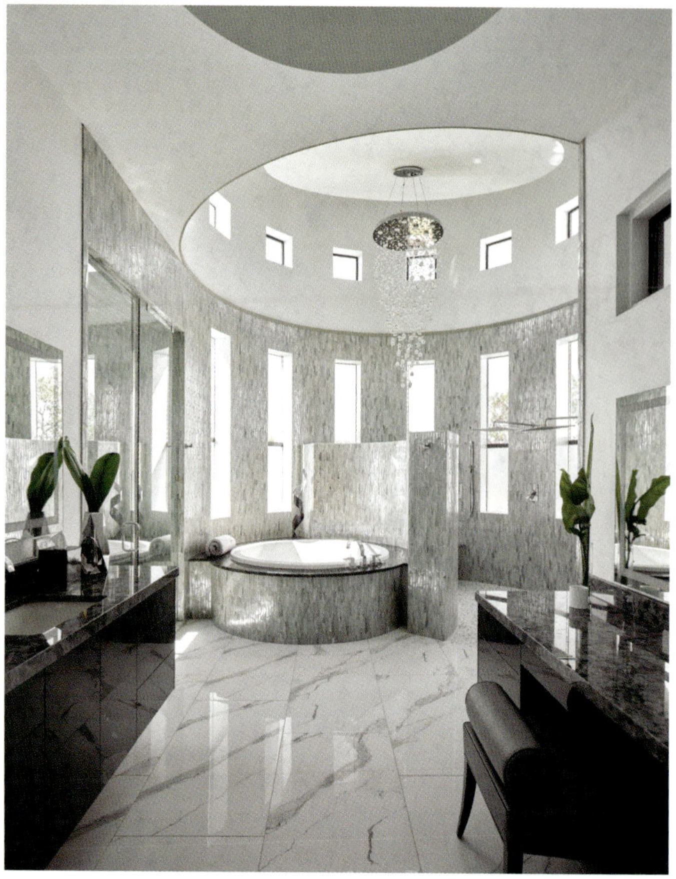
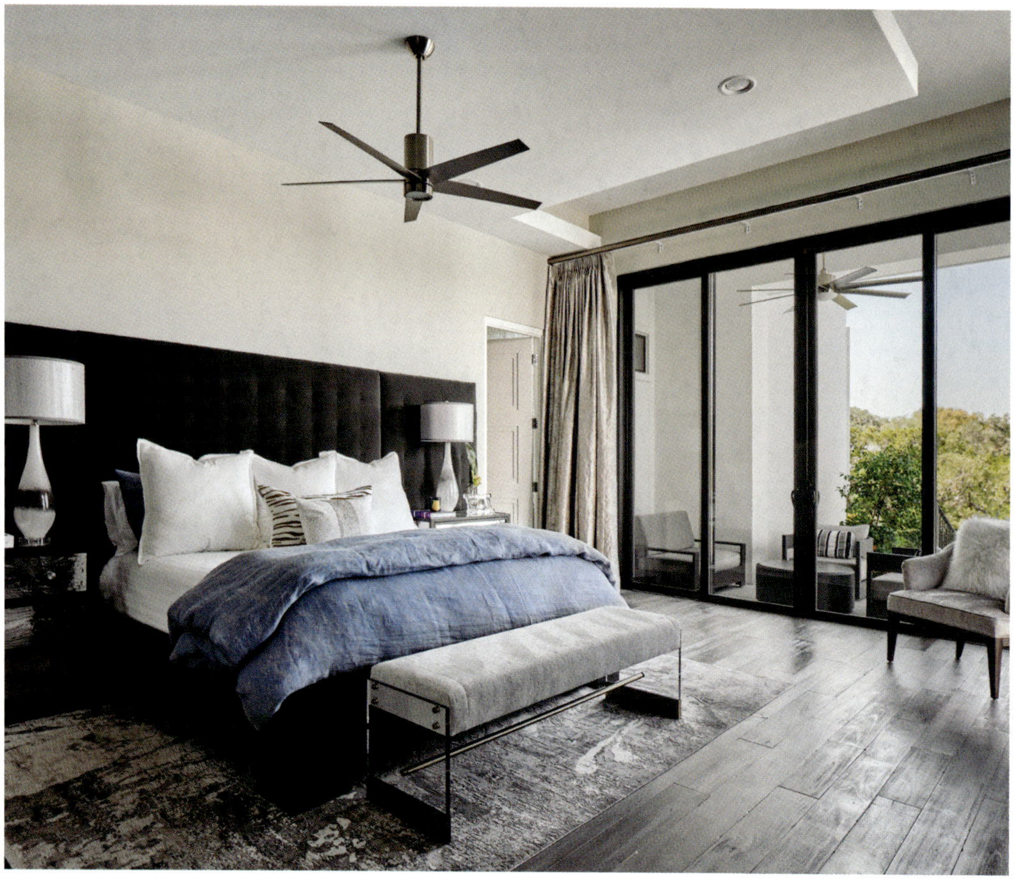
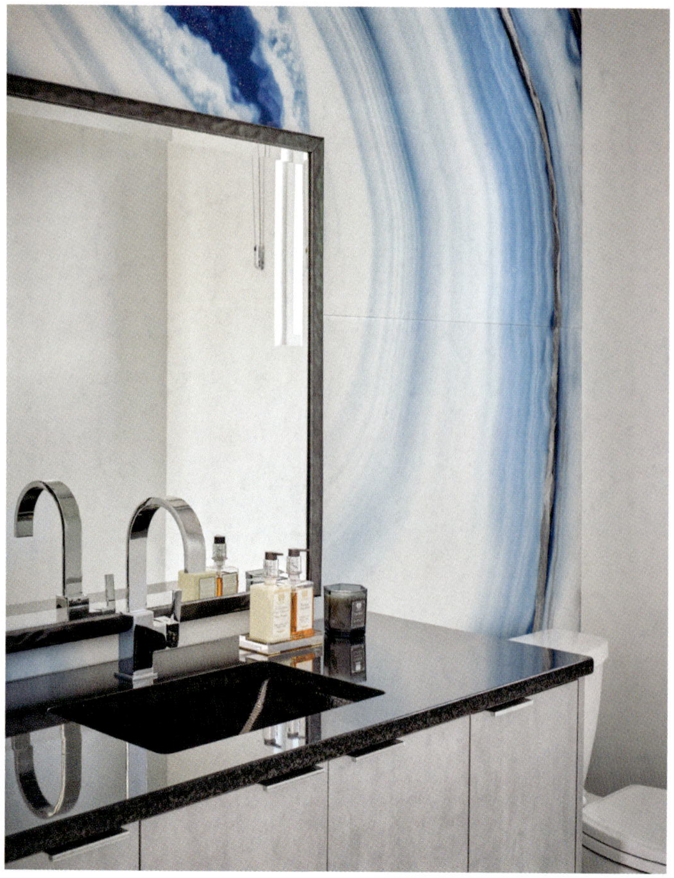

"There are no rules in design." —Lori Caldwell

ABOVE AND FACING PAGE TOP LEFT: The client wanted a space where she could entertain and it was important to have a beautiful and elegant – but also comfortable – space to cook and dine with friends.

FACING PAGE TOP RIGHT: This stunning master bath is a reflection of the clients' big, gorgeous personality.

FACING PAGE BOTTOM LEFT: We always want our spaces to feel like a home – and that's the case with this master bedroom.

FACING PAGE BOTTOM RIGHT: This pool bath is a reflection of the selections made for the swimming pool. Bringing the gorgeous turquoise blue from the exterior into the home, we stepped out of the box with this room to have a little fun. Photography by Matthew Niemann Photography.

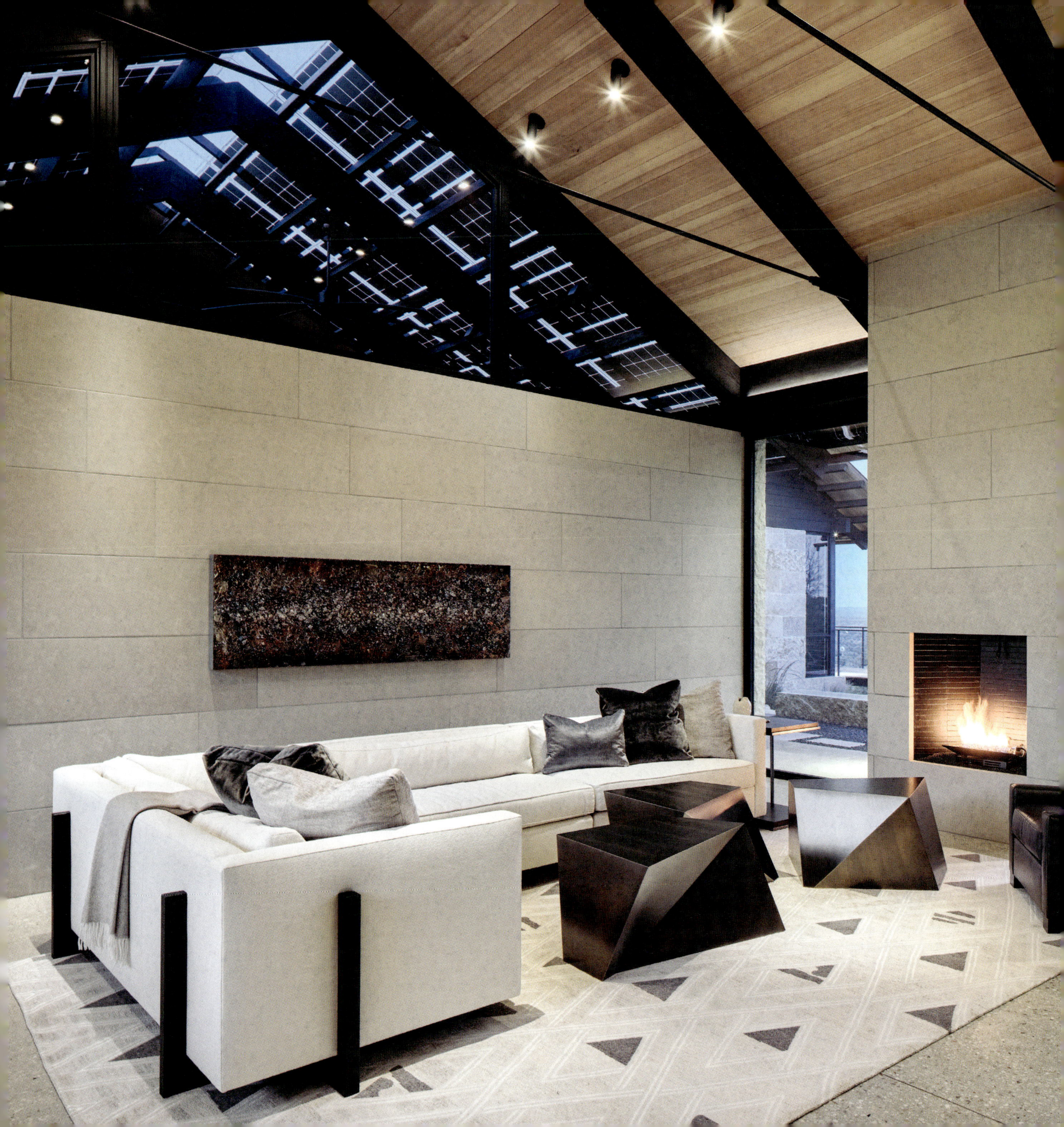

NR INTERIORS
NICOLE ROBERTS WINMILL

Growing up in a historic Victorian home with beautiful craftsmanship and special details is what sparked Nicole Roberts Winmill's interest in creating captivating spaces.

Today, as principal interior designer and founder of NR Interiors, she creates contemporary homes with special custom details that are personalized just for her clients. Her studio is invested in the complete design of a home; they manage the specifications and interior design details needed for the highest quality construction or remodel. And they continue in similar form by providing everything from fine custom furnishings and window coverings, to curating art and accessories, to overseeing all the finish selections necessary to bring the envisioned space to life – down to the finest of details. After all, it is all in the details for Nicole and her team to ensure the complete design brings joy and functions optimally to elevate the client's quality of life.

An example of that is this featured project, where the soul of the home is anchored in both the hilltop setting and the modern architecture by Lake | Flato that frames the magnificent Hill Country views. In fully furnishing this modern-organic residence, NR Interiors designed custom pieces that complemented the architecture and created a comfortable environment to reflect the colors and textures of the views.

FACING PAGE: Counterbalancing the sleek finishes of the architecture, highly textural furnishings, lush fabrics and a natural-dyed hand-knotted rug offer a welcomed and imperfect organic quality. Photography by Matthew Niemann.

TOP LEFT: The primary suite's custom furnishings, bedding, drapery, and artwork were designed to complement the modern architecture while offering an elegant, serene environment for peaceful reflection.

TOP RIGHT: Soft accents of sage and silvered blues were incorporated to echo the colors of the magnificent, long view. Special effort was spent designing custom drapery that integrated into the architecture and operated easily to open wide the prized view.

BOTTOM LEFT: Mirrors are suspended in front of the primary bath's expansive window that bathes the room in natural light to highlight the freestanding quartzite slab tub wall.

BOTTOM RIGHT: The office is a uniquely narrow space that doubles as a TV room, so designing a versatile modular sofa at the center allows the homeowners to move the back to view the TV or the opposite wall of windows.

FACING PAGE TOP LEFT: The breakfast nook provides a cozy place for meals, watching the wildlife, and reading a book.

FACING PAGE TOP RIGHT: The custom bronze and wood asymmetrical cocktail tables are the sculptural focal point to an otherwise strictly linear space.

FACING BOTTOM: The primary bedroom appears to float as it cantilevers on the corner of the home with expansive windows to capture the view. Photography by Matthew Niemann.

"To add balance to today's modern homes, I incorporate unique, natural materials and layer with rich textures to create a warm environment for clients to comfortably enjoy."
—Nicole Roberts Winmill

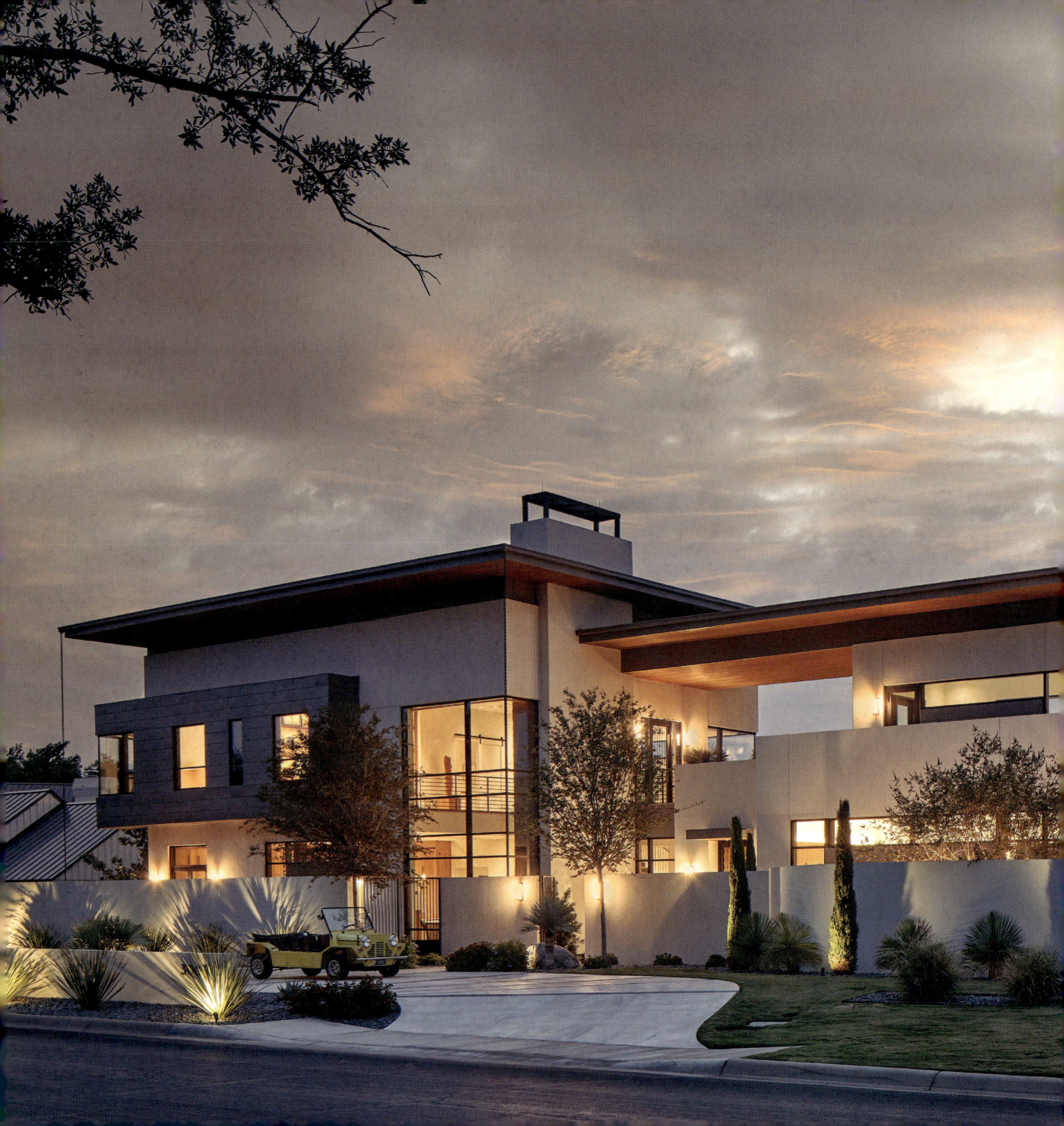

OVERLAND PARTNERS

A passion for art — and how it integrates into architecture — is what drives the dynamic creative energy of Tim Blonkvist, FAIA, founding partner of Overland. He also happens to be a painter and sculptor in his own right and credits the intersections of those disciplines as the place where ideas come to life. Tim and the creative team of diverse talents at Overland thoughtfully integrate art, technology, and craft to create highly sustainable designs in places worthy of affection across Texas and throughout the world. Knowing that architecture has transformative power and is a dialogue between the invisible and the visible, Overland seeks to unlock the embedded potential of each project, place, and client.

Tim and the Overland residential team approach every home as an adventure to join clients in bringing their dreams to life through understanding what is yet to be discovered and translating visions into deeply inspirational outcomes. Overland believes that the destiny of each project is unique. They remove assumptions and limitations and they take away defaults, refusing to play small or listen for outcomes they have heard before. With a notable spirit of collaboration, Tim and the Overland team bring a strong set of values and a timeless design philosophy that's tailored to each client and that shapes their relationships and their work.

FACING PAGE: A retreat and gathering place for welcoming family and friends, the Midland Residence is also a foundation for fostering new beginnings. Situated on a unique piece of property in the heart of a small community in Midland and viewable from all sides, the home balances presence with comfort and privacy. Overland's Tim Blonkvist, FAIA, who is a Midland native and knows the site well, worked closely with the client to envision the home as a beautiful, sculptural piece of architecture. Reflective of her interest in sustainability, the home not only meets the everyday functional needs of the client but is an inspirational 3-D manifestation of architecture in the 21st century. Photography by Dror Baldinger FAIA.

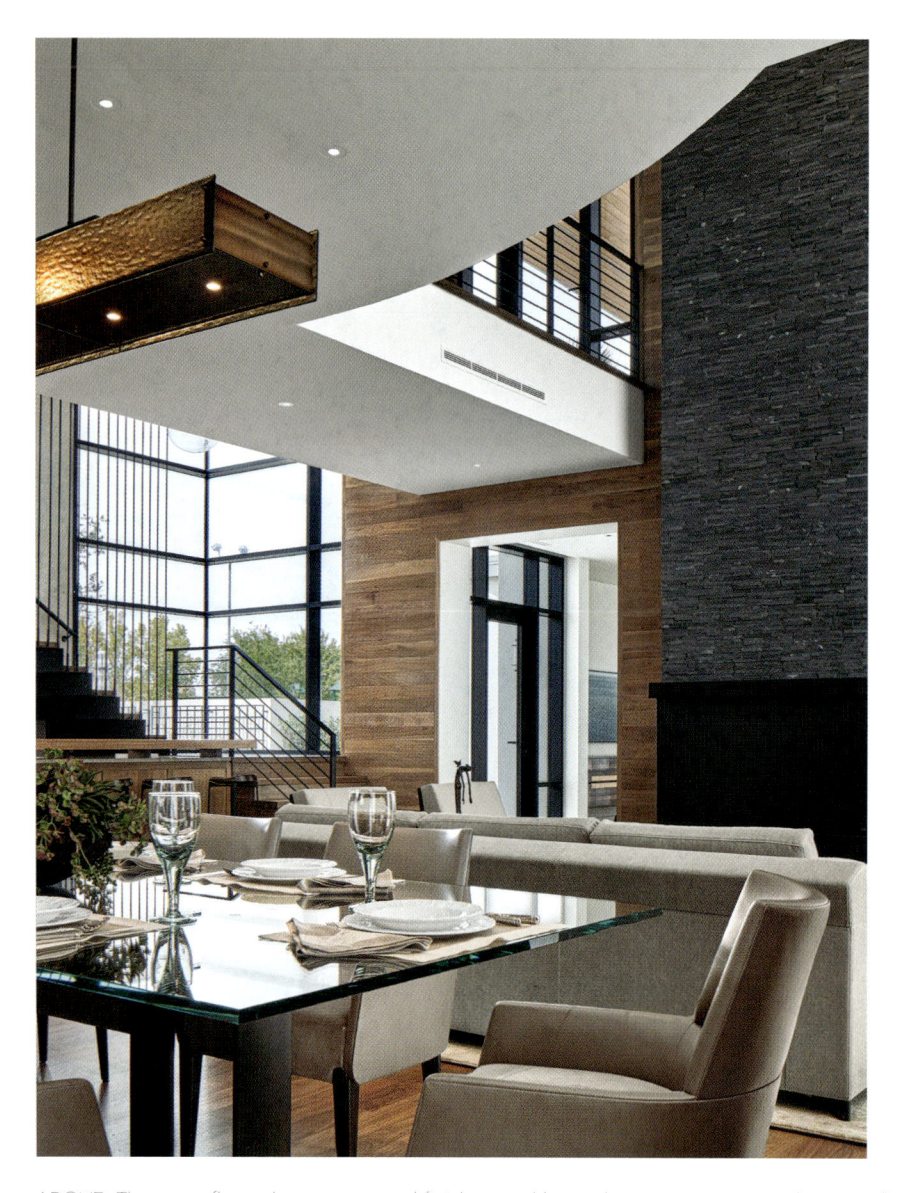

ABOVE: The open floor plan, warm wood finishes, and layered textures create a welcoming, flexible space for intimate gatherings and larger groups in the dining area. The juxtaposition of curvilinear forms with cubist elements of design softens the expression and experience of connection between the home's volume. Elements of art are integrated throughout.

FACING PAGE TOP: The kitchen is the heart of the home with views to the outside.

FACING PAGE BOTTOM: Architect Tim Blonkvist, FAIA, designed the grand front door, which was inspired by Lynn Ford and hand-carved by Gene Hausmann. The detailed, geometric pattern welcomes guests into the foyer where art and sculpture accent the modern décor. Photography by Dror Baldinger FAIA.

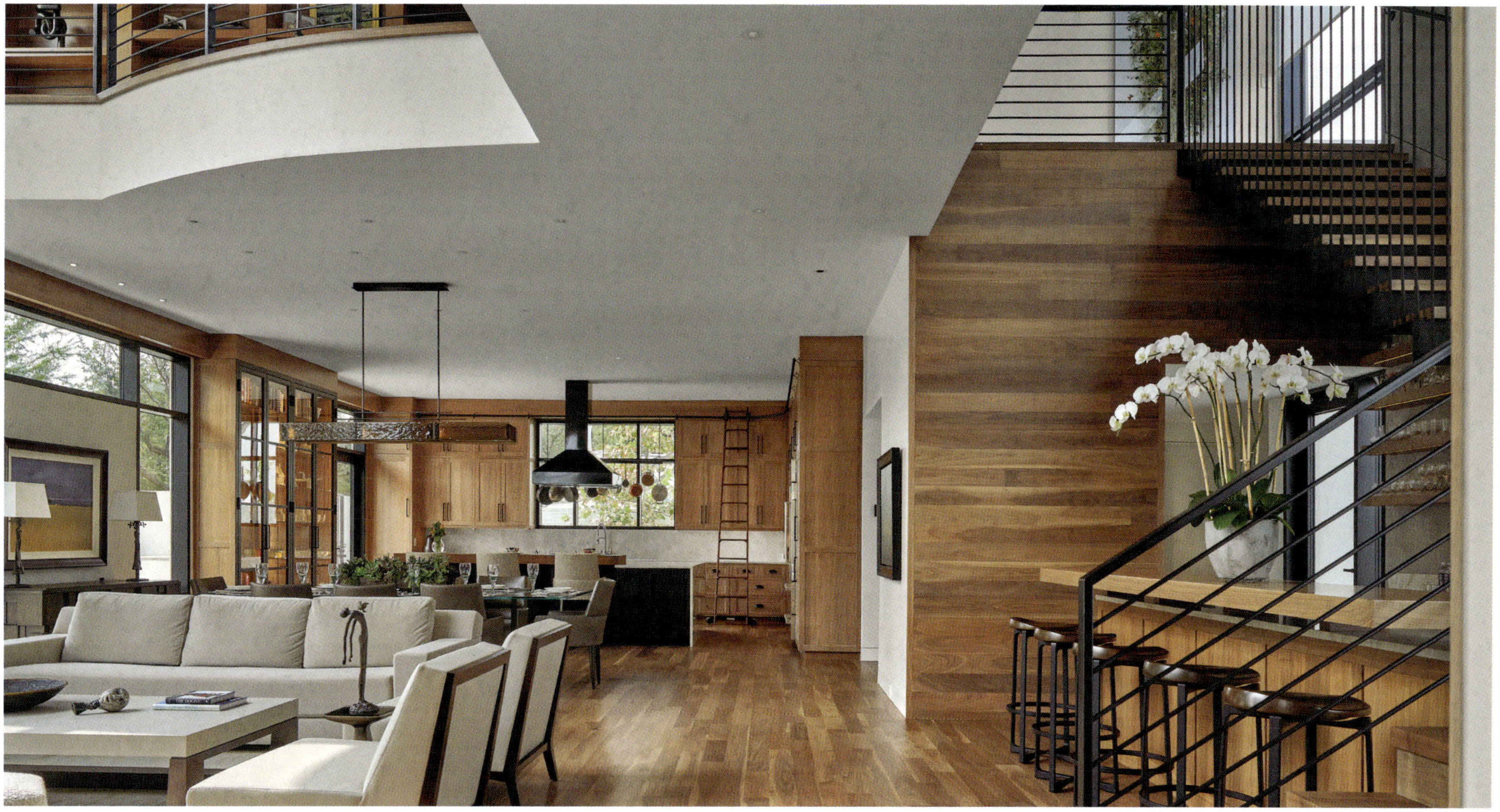

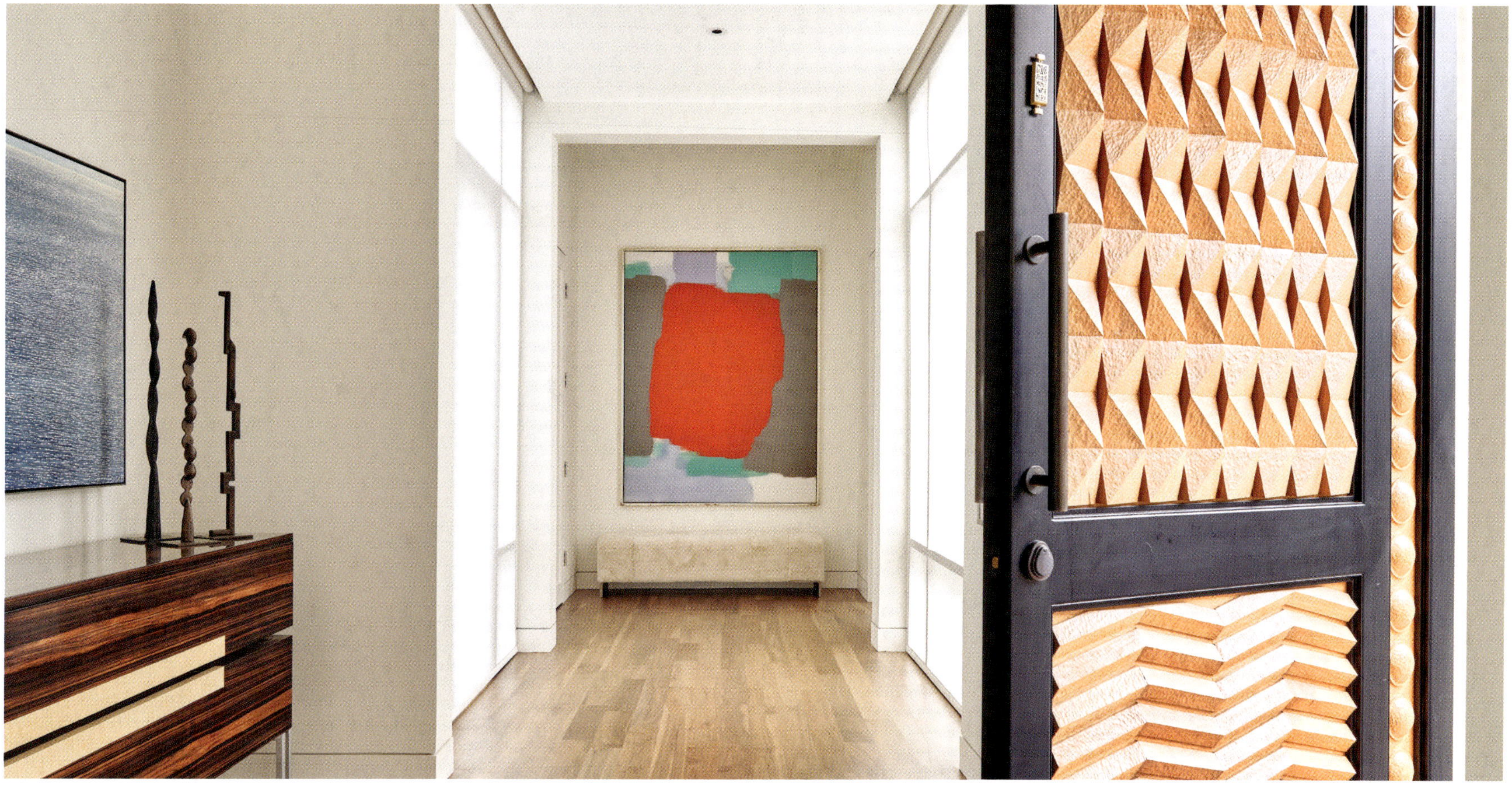

THIS PAGE: A haven for respite and relaxation, the master suite strikes a balance between privacy and nature. The calming palette and natural materials also integrate curved forms inspired by Le Corbusier. The dressing room features custom millwork, upholstery, and lighting.

FACING PAGE: The interplay between the outdoor and indoor spaces of the home are centered around an interior courtyard and pool. A walkway to the home spa on the second floor overlooks the pool and provides 360-degree views while connecting the two wings of the home. Photography by Dror Baldinger FAIA.

"This home is a testimony to the strong character of the client and commitment to bringing her dream to fruition." —Tim Blonkvist

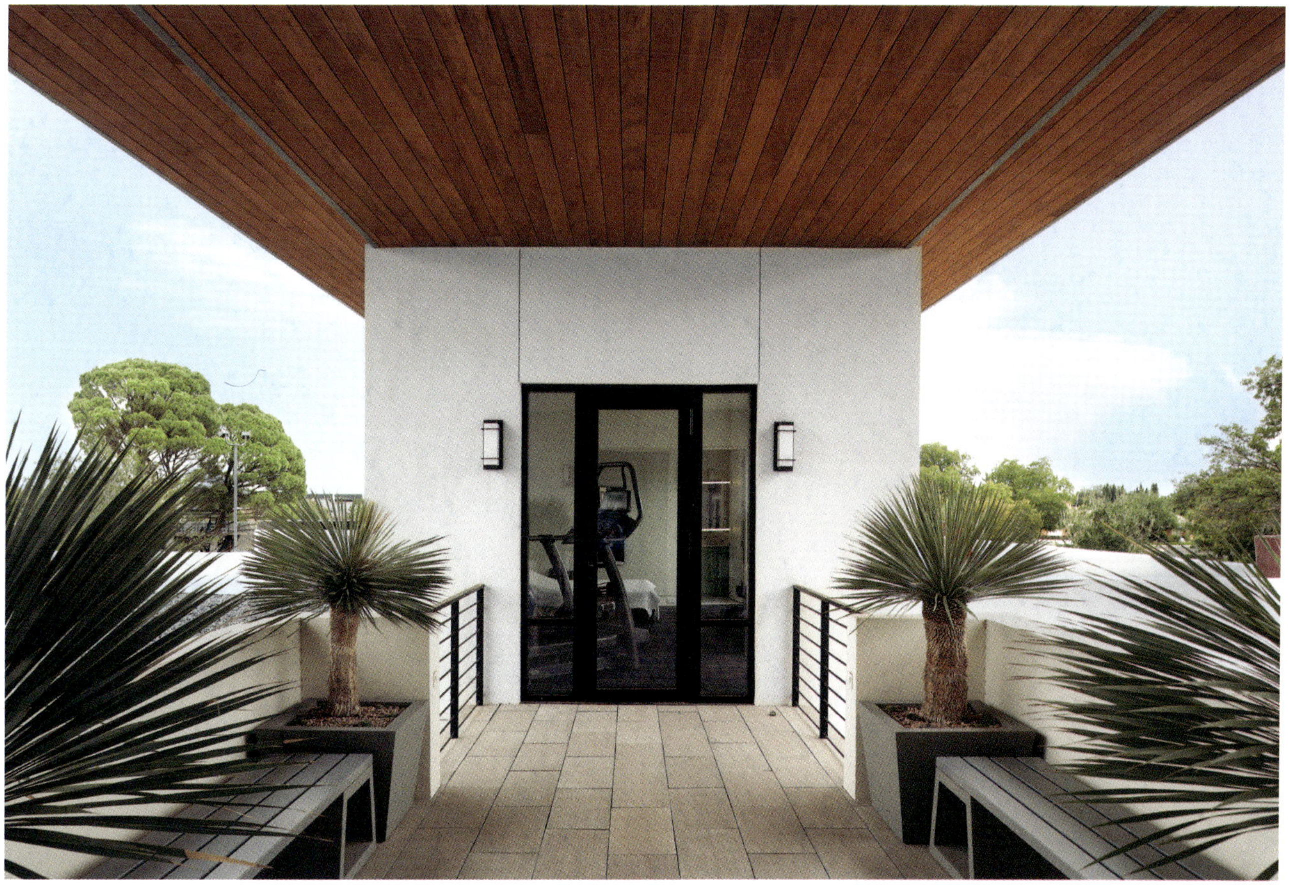

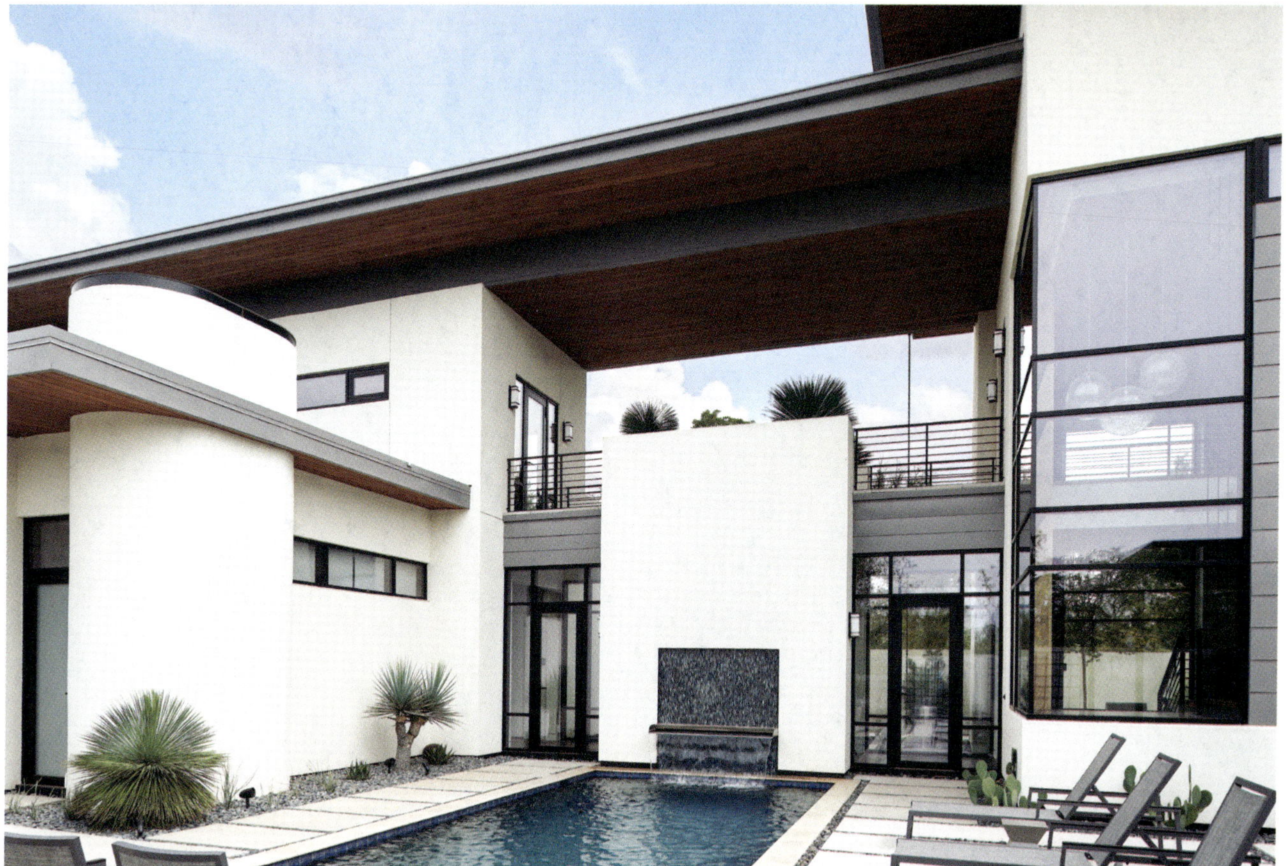

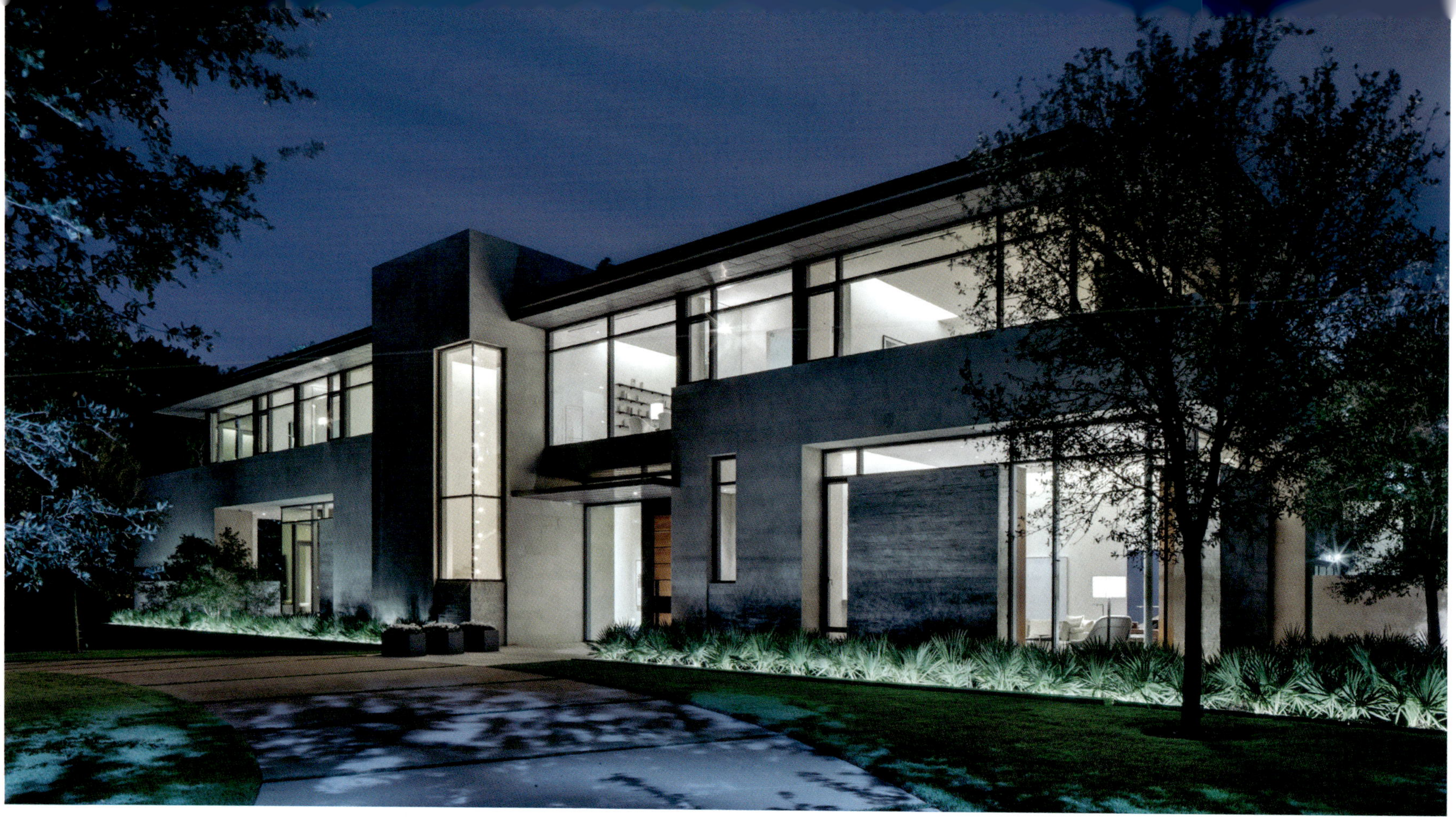
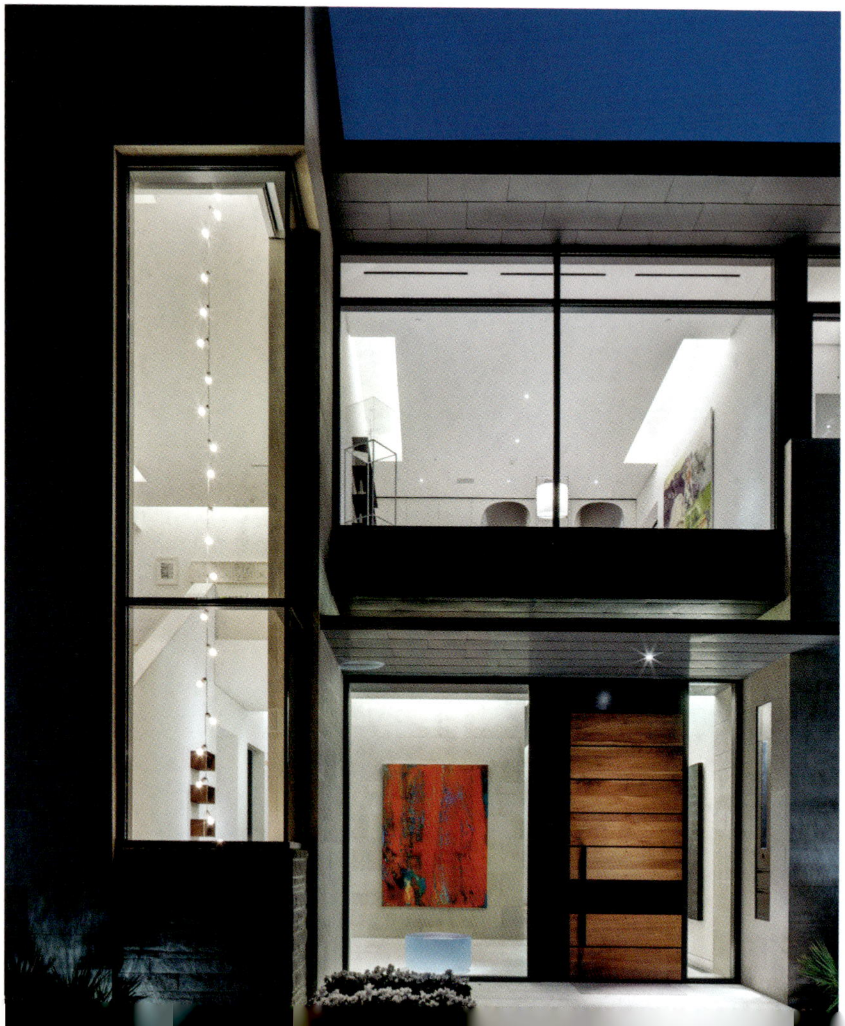
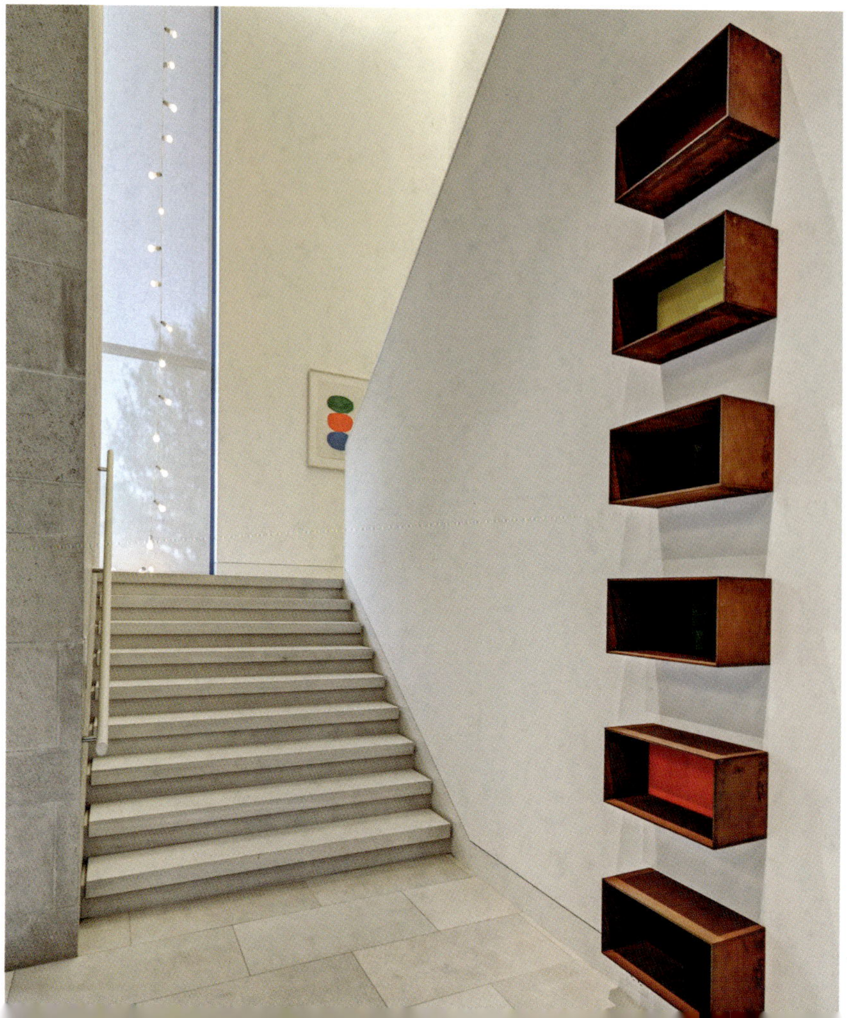

THIS PAGE AND FACING PAGE: This Dallas home is carefully arranged to envelop and preserve the natural landscape, which includes many heritage oaks and culminates in a glass-walled master suite that bridges a tributary creek and yields exceptional views. The presence of the creek bluff engenders a sense of uncultivated wilderness that is unique within the suburban context, effectively creating an oasis in the city. With more than 100 masterworks of modern art, the clients desired a home that would not only complement their collection but also allow them to experience art in their daily lives and share it with the community. Photography by Charles Davis Smith FAIA.

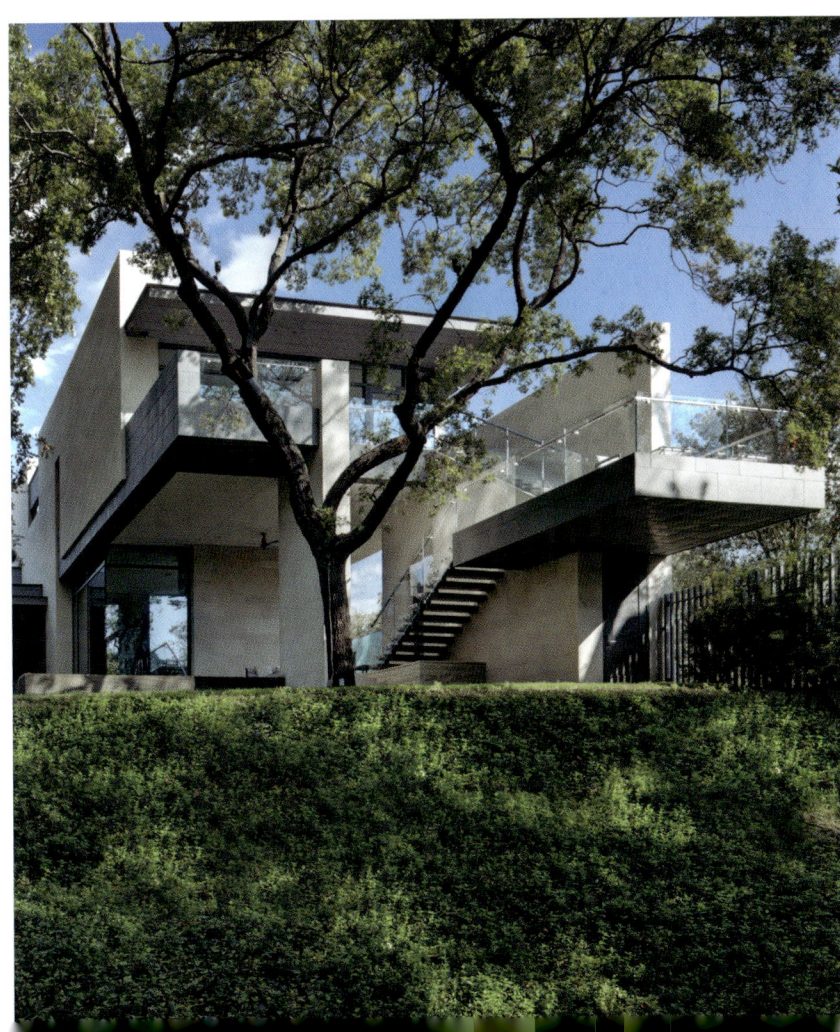

THIS PAGE: This recreational pavilion, adjacent to the main home on Horseshoe Bay, features materials that were selected to match the existing structure with glass walls overlooking the lake and operable 16-foot sliding glass doors connecting to the pool terrace and north lawn.
Photography by Leonid Furmansky.

FACING PAGE: The large, angular wall and roof of this lake house extend out to protect the outdoor living area from the western sun, focusing an expansive view of the lake to the north. Photography by Dror Baldinger FAIA.

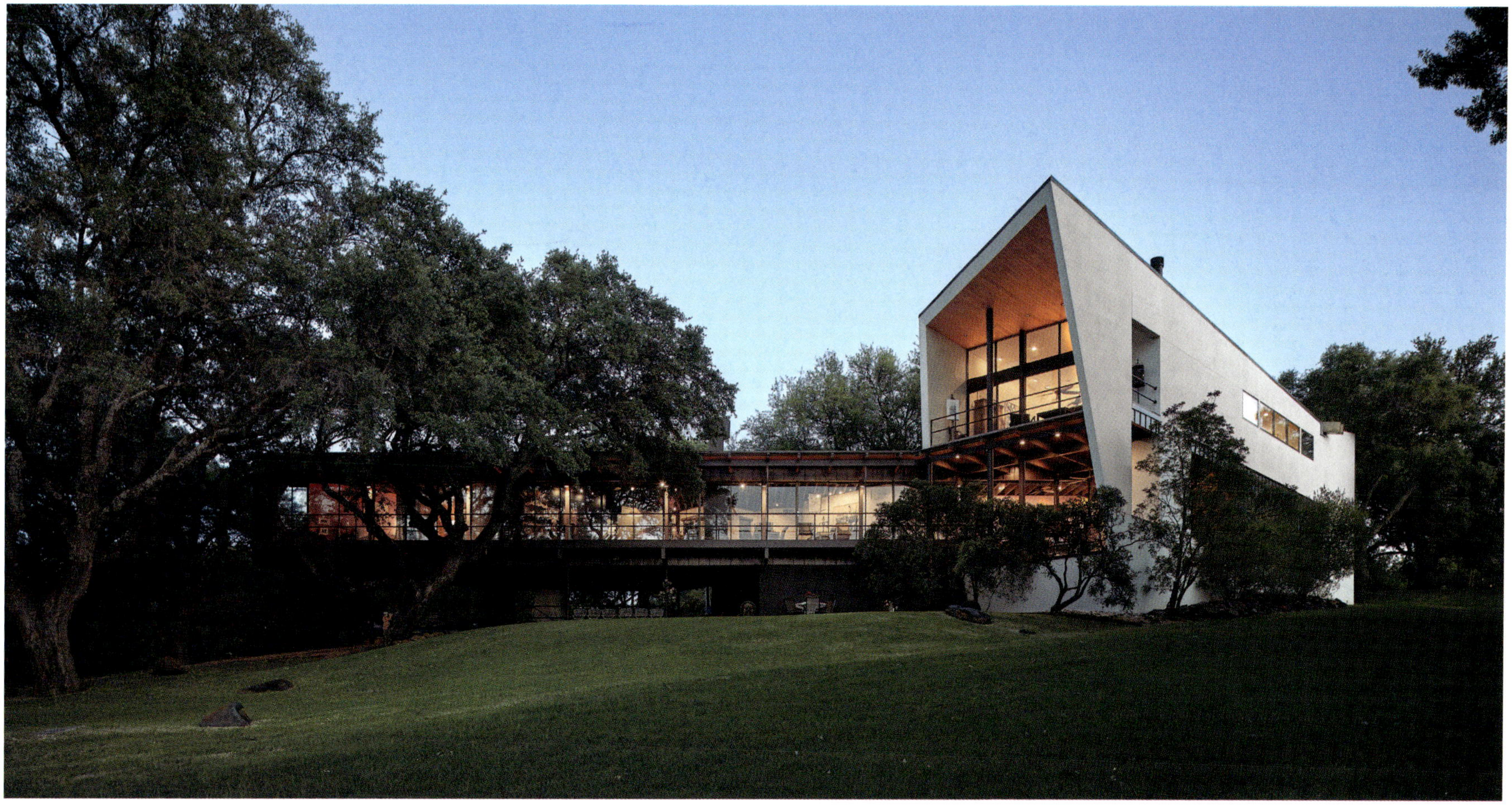

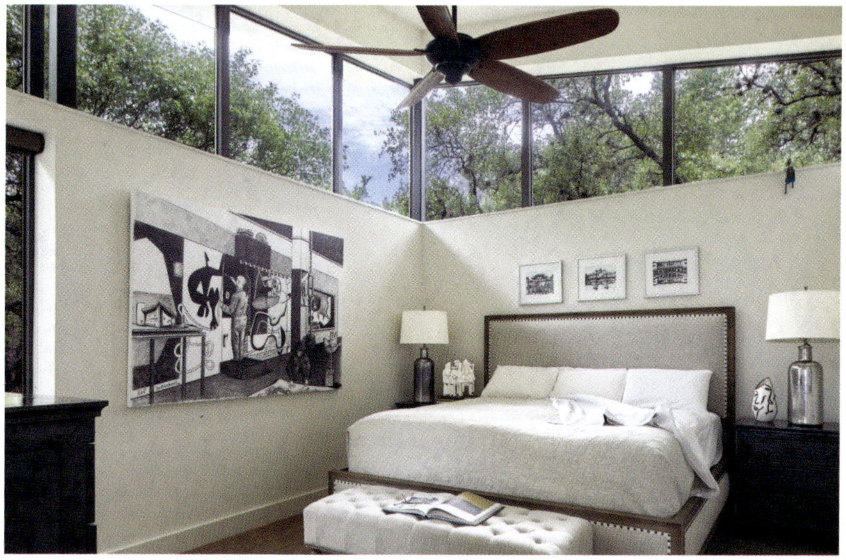

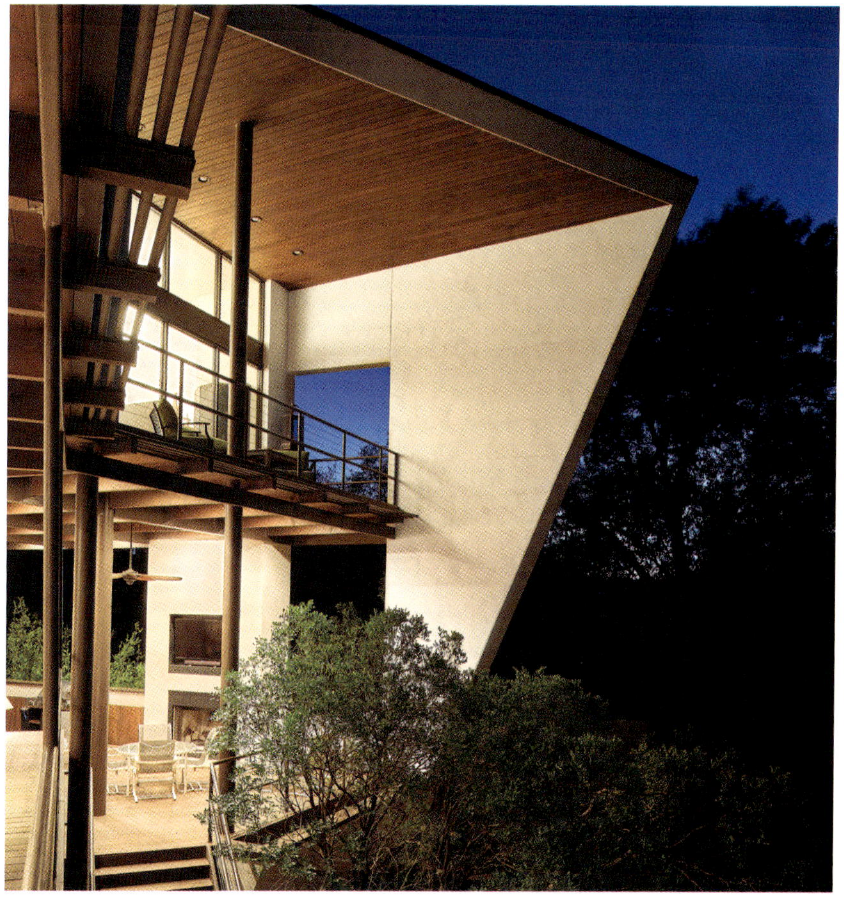

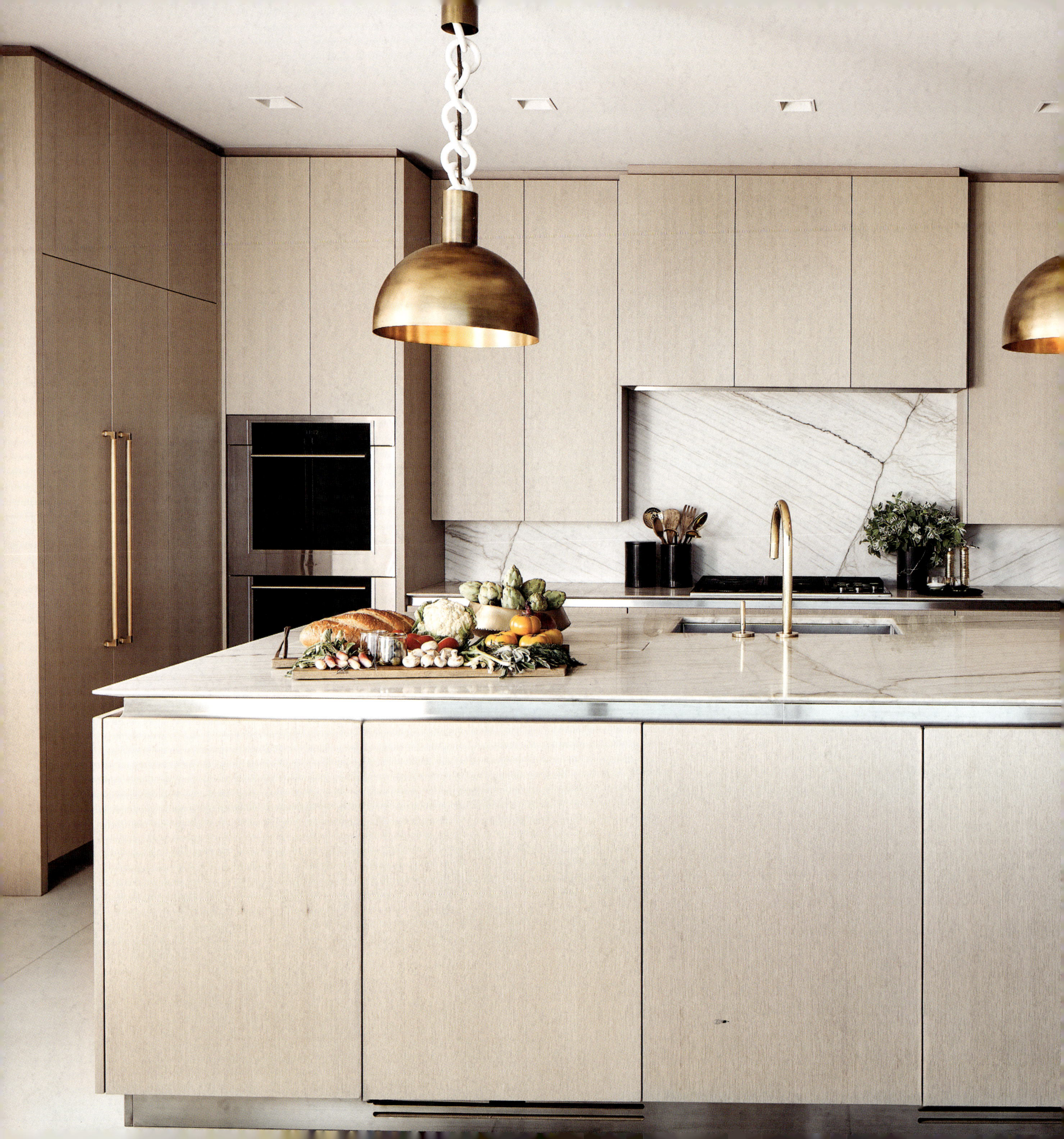

P

PALMER TODD

When it comes to the state-of-the-art luxury tile and custom cabinetry, Palmer Todd stands out and has become synonymous with brilliant design and unparalleled craftsmanship not to mention architectural and installation expertise. The company was founded in 1995 on three basic concepts – creativity, collaboration, and community – and they live by those tenets every single day.

The result? Twenty-six years' worth of superlative beauty in kitchens, bathrooms, closets, and specialty projects such as pools, staircases, commercial areas, and more – all designed with the highest quality standards and an obsession for creating the most exquisite spaces. The designers on staff have several decades of combined experience and know that every detail counts when innovatively weaving together functionality with beauty.

With a commitment to timelessness, no matter the style, the Palmer Todd team is always thinking about the way their homeowners move through a room, experience an area, use a particular space – and they're passionate about ensuring that it's both purposefully and stunningly well-designed.

FACING PAGE: Clean lines and balance define this modern city kitchen with a large center island, Downsview cabinetry, and brass features throughout. Bespoke details combined with innovative technology create a space that is both elegant and functional.
Photography by Stephen Karlisch.

"We are obsessed with the highest quality standards and with creating the most exquisite spaces." —Lynley Bravo

ABOVE LEFT: Natural light from the adjacent cityscape fills every corner of this bright bathroom. Poise and reflection are paramount to the atmosphere of this elegant space. Photography by Stephen Karlisch.

ABOVE RIGHT: This contemporary powder bathroom is complete with an eye-catching vanity, full-length mirrors to let light in, and natural stone. Photography by Matthew Niemann

FACING PAGE TOP LEFT: Bold splashes of color and movement were key to creating this electrifying powder bath. The homeowner desired a space that was both eclectic and fun — and this design delivered in full. Photography by Stephen Karlisch.

FACING PAGE TOP RIGHT: A palette of soft neutrals used in this kitchen captures the light and invites you in. Pops of rich blue and purple jewel tones add beautiful finishing touches to the elegant, polished atmosphere that is both welcoming and stylish. Photography by Stephen Karlisch.

FACING PAGE BOTTOM LEFT: This modern city kitchen is both cutting-edge and inviting. With custom light fixtures made in Italy, a large center island for preparing food, and streamlined storage space, this kitchen acts as the heart of the home. Photography by Matthew Niemann.

FACING PAGE BOTTOM RIGHT: Beautifully detailed closets never fail to add a dose of luxury to a home. This elegant space showcases the clothing and accessories within rather than simply storing them, accounting for every detail to create the ultimate dressing room complete with the most luxurious touches. Photography by Matthew Niemann.

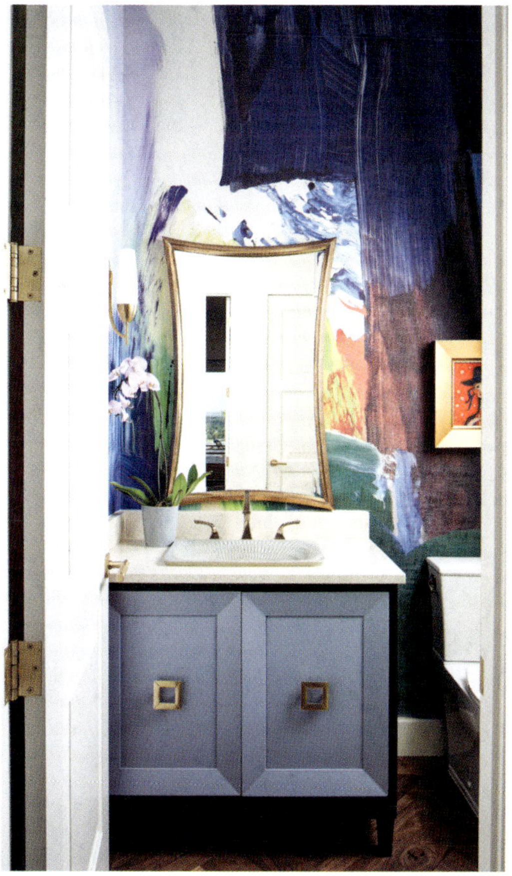

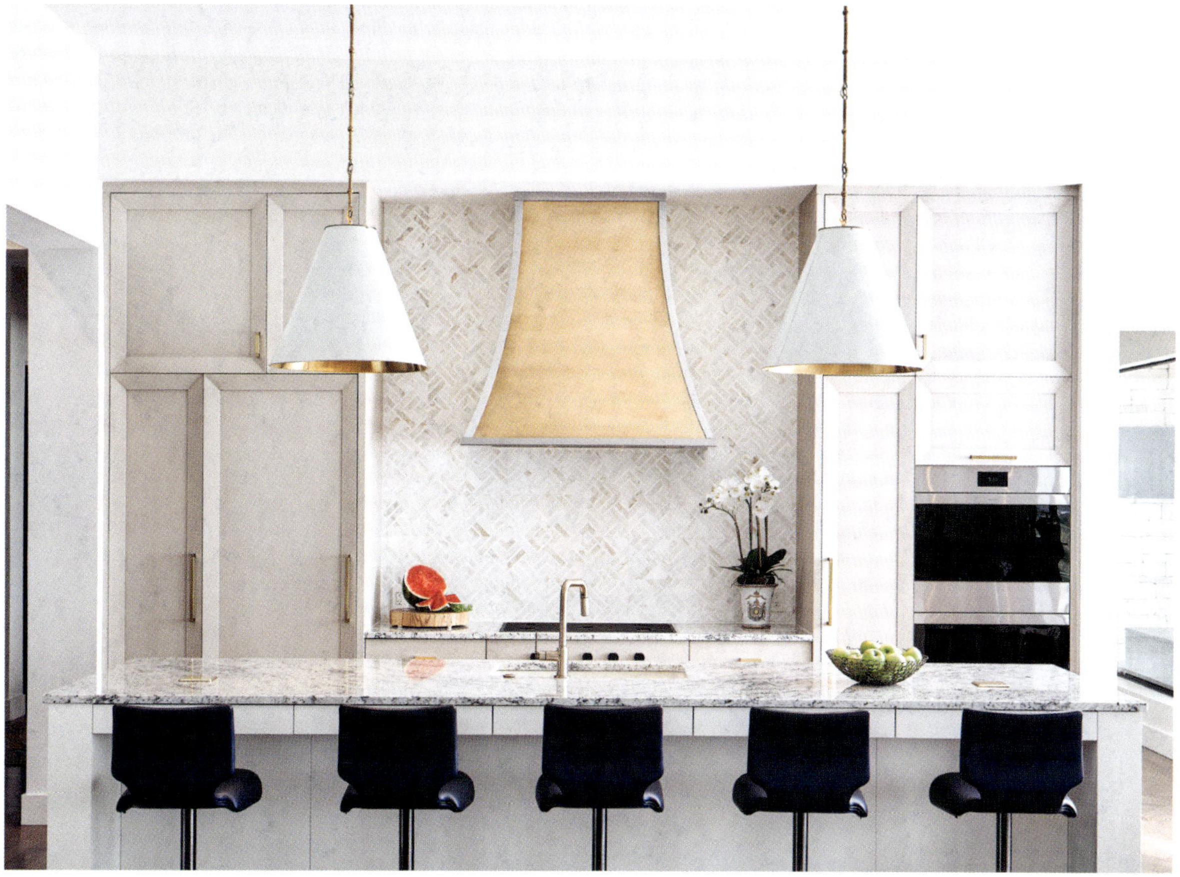

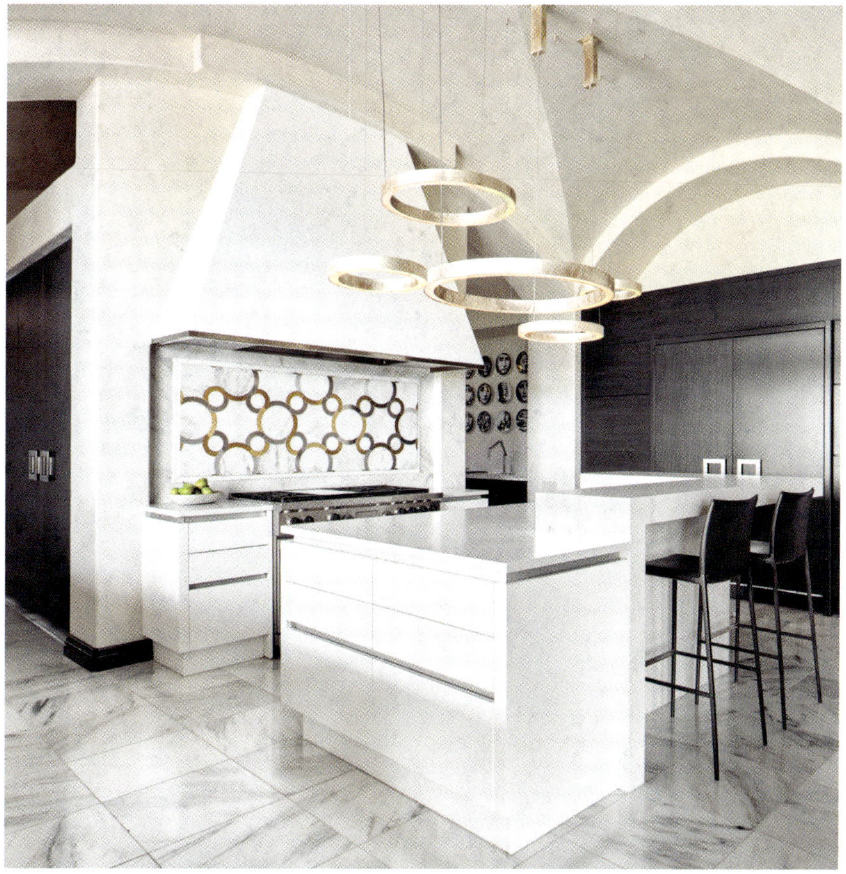

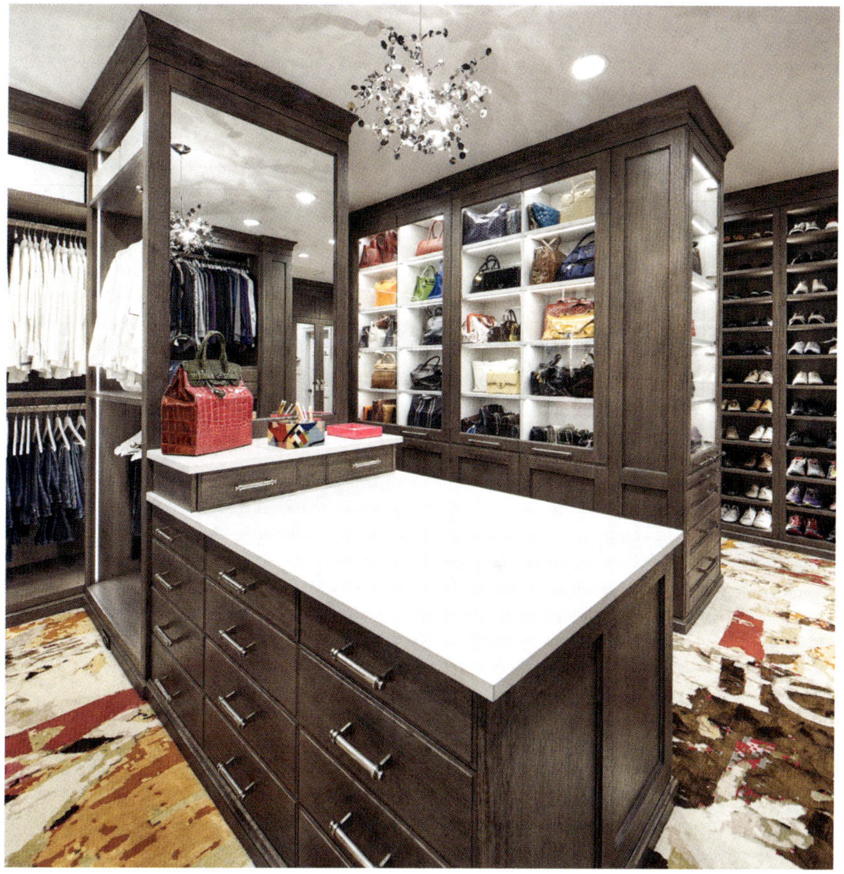

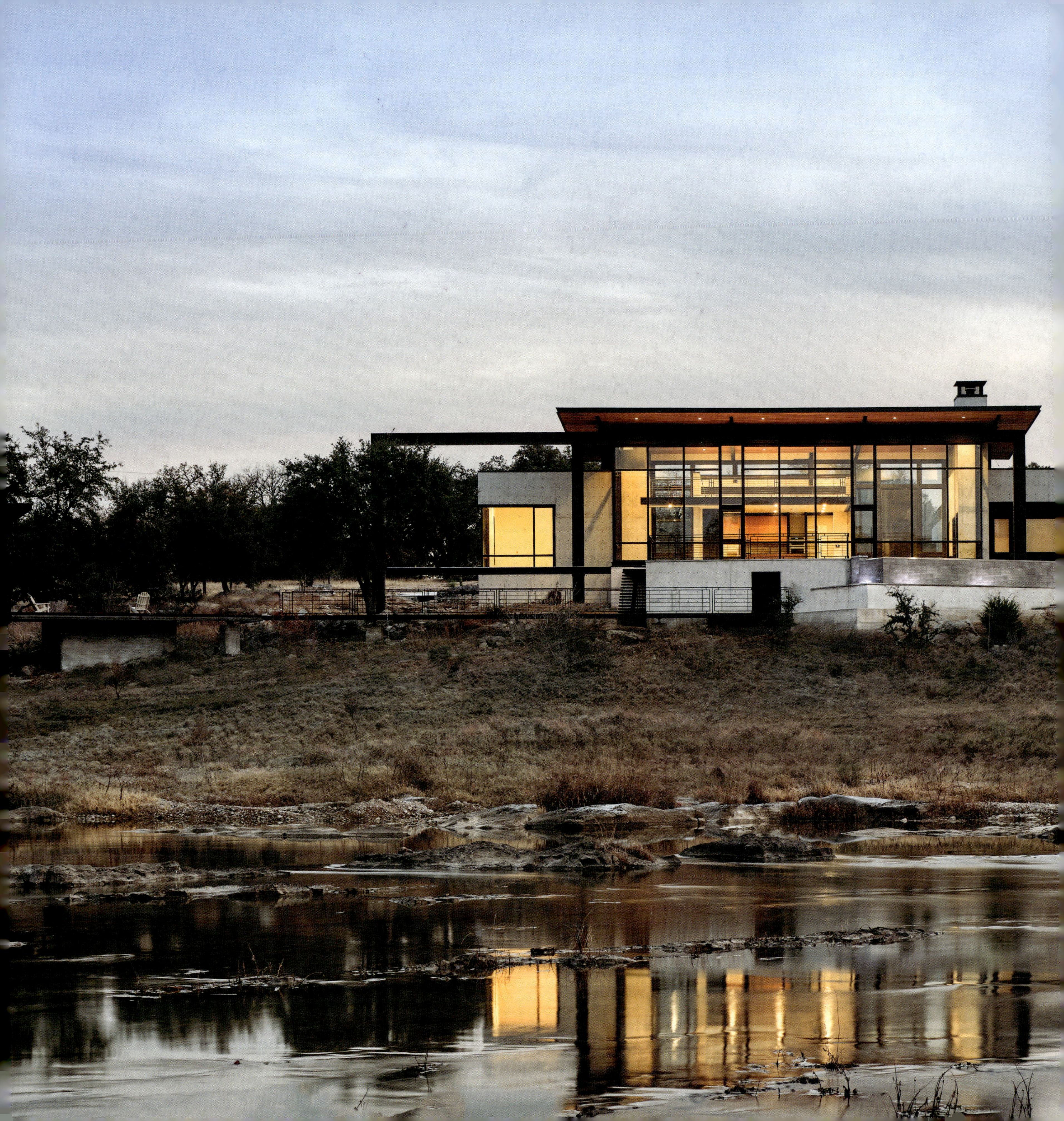

T.A.D.A.

Total Art Design & Architecture (TADA) is a progressive design practice based in downtown New Braunfels, specializing in high-end residential and commercial design, fabrication, and construction and led by architects Brett Davidson, AIA and Patrick Winn, AIA.

TADA's multi-disciplinary team gives the practice a unique ability to not only dream of extraordinary works alongside their clients, but also help bring these ideas to life with their own hands. Senior project manager Lucas Mackey leads TADA's fabrication and construction management efforts alongside senior fabricator Chris Pomrenke.

Highlighted here is one of TADA's first design-build projects, a 3,000-square-foot residence in Johnson City. Designed as a single gesture of concrete rising from the dolomite rock formations of the Texas Hill Country, this home opens itself to the Pedernales River and beautiful cascading sunsets with a 40-foot wide and 18-foot-tall sliding steel and glass window wall that nests into the exterior flying steel frame. This project is a product of TADA working closely with an amazing team of designers, consultants, contractors, and specialists, including: structural engineering by Leap Structures (Austin); interior design by Purveyor Design (Austin); concrete specialty by Modern Builders (Wimberley); cabinetry and countertops by Alpha Millworks (San Antonio); specialty woods by U.S. Lumber Brokers (Austin); landscape by Land-Flo (Fredericksburg); and steel fabrication and construction by TADA's in-house TADA-Build.

FACING PAGE: This Johnson City residence overlooks the Pedernales River.
Photography by Matthew Niemann.

ABOVE LEFT: One long bar of cast-in-place architectural concrete anchors the house into the bluff with a sunrise bedroom on the east and a sunset bedroom on the west.

ABOVE TOP RIGHT: The motor-court side of the house is designed to guide guests to the focal point of the front entry and slowly reveal the experience of the river and cliffs beyond through the layers of solid vertical concrete plains.

ABOVE BOTTOM RIGHT: The structure of the home extends to a "flying" steel frame that receives the rolling steel and glass wall.

FACING PAGE: The north-facing steel and glass window wall slides outboard of the home to open the kitchen, dining, and living areas to the patio and pool, overlooking the Pedernales River below. Photography by Matthew Niemann.

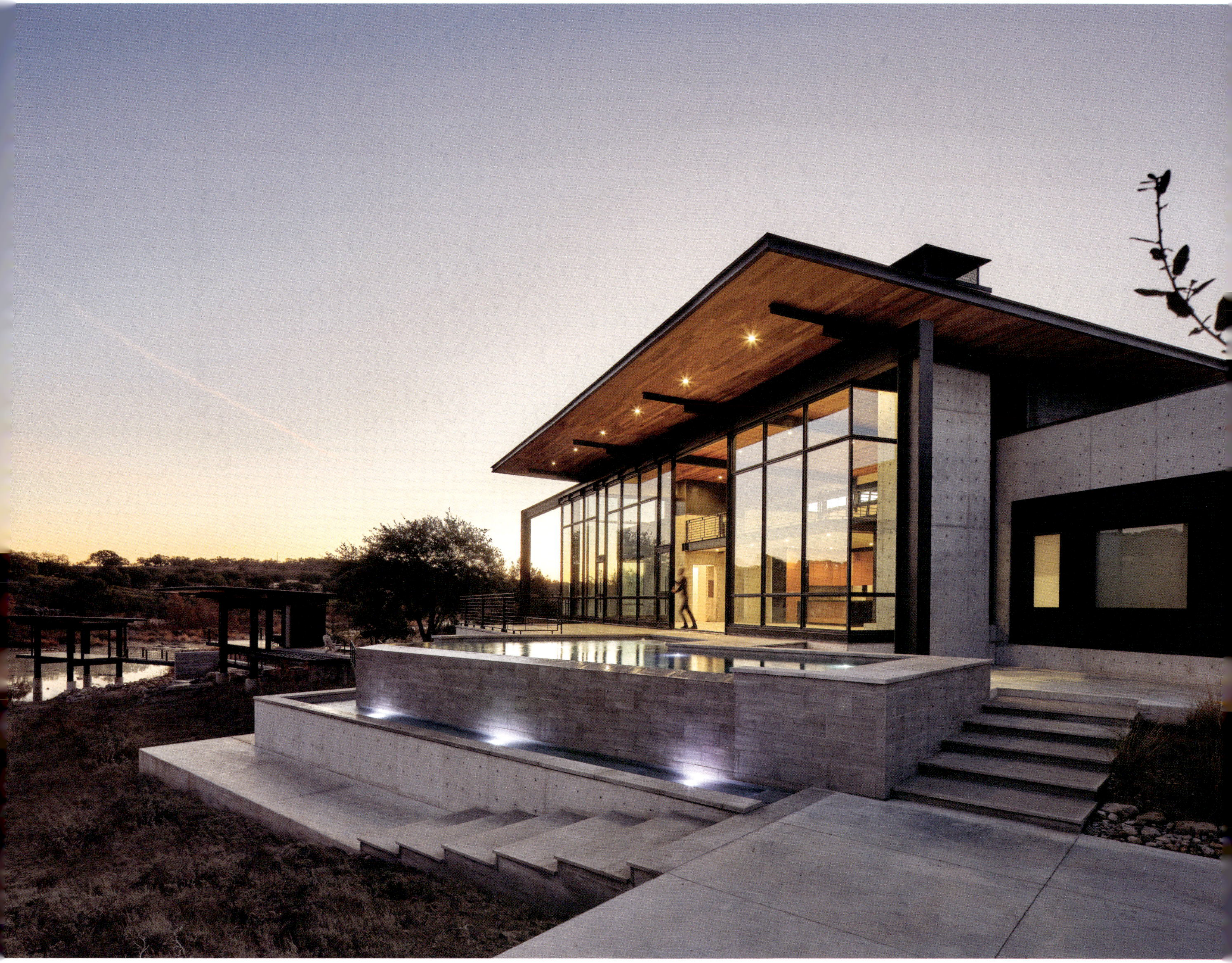

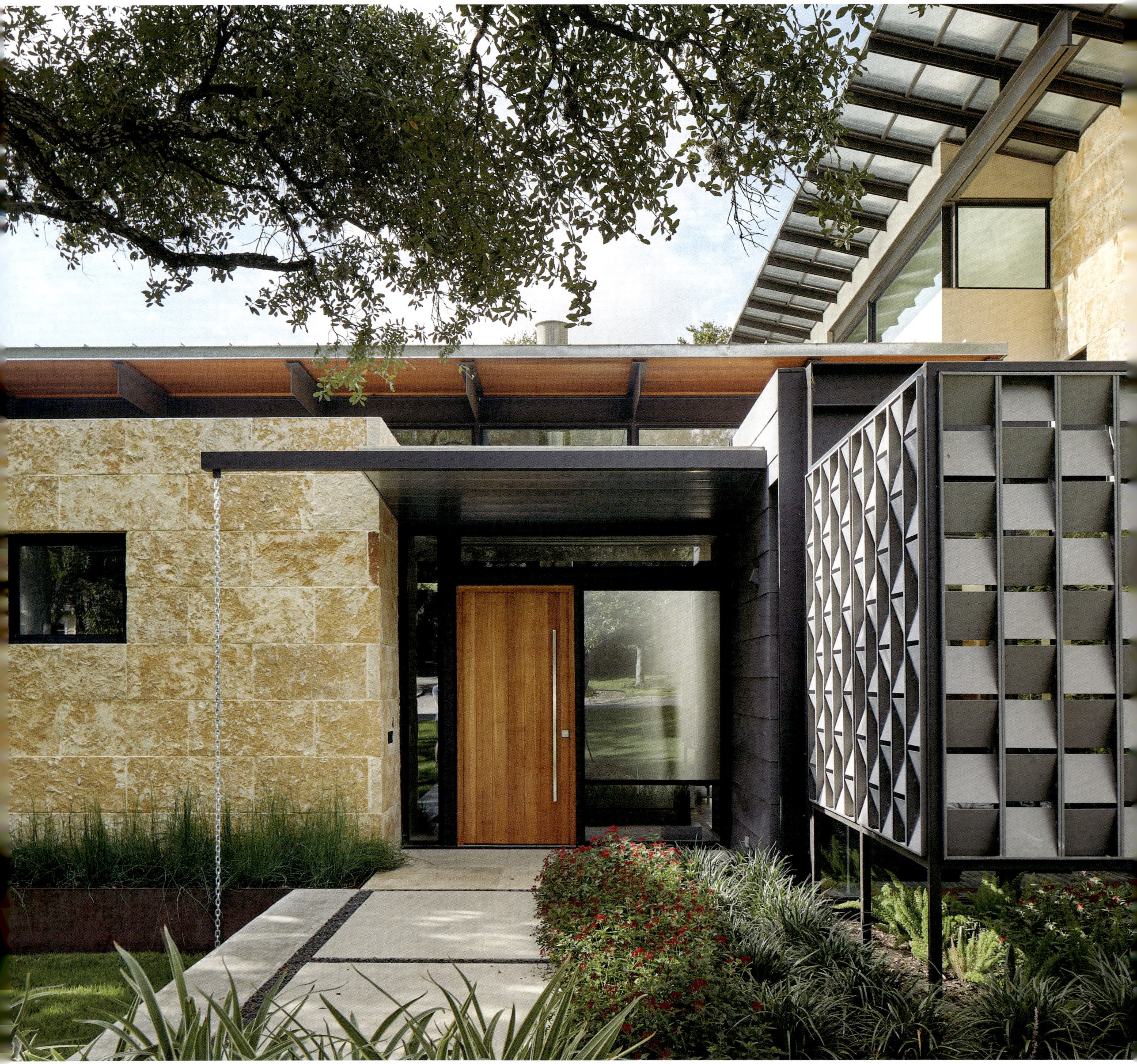

TOBIN SMITH ARCHITECT

"We believe architecture is the ultimate act of commitment to a place – both as a response to and embodiment of a unique set of conditions, says Tobin Smith, principal of Tobin Smith Architect, an award-winning practice founded in 2007. "We compose heightened and memorable sensory experiences through the organization of space and deployment of materials."

A combination of climate, culture, and context informs their work from the initial broad-brush planning to the resolution of the tiniest details, culminating in a cohesive solution. Each project begins with their client's objectives and is developed with a focus on functionality, efficiency, and pragmatism in addition to poetic notions. "Clarity in the final design is achieved through a process of refining and honing until all that is left is absolute and eloquent," Tobin adds. "Completed structures represent the culmination of many desires; above all, we strive to collaborate with our clients to create places of truth, meaning, and inspiration." His firm's portfolio is broad, encompassing rural and urban as well as residential and commercial endeavors. Their projects have been featured in local, state, and national publications and have received recognition for design excellence.

FACING PAGE: Honimoon House incorporates taut lines, deliberate rhythms, and composed geometries that create a chorus of architectural precision immediately evident upon arrival.

TOP: The living room's north-facing clerestory windows provide a glimpse of the front yard's oak canopy and allow diffused light into this gathering space.

BOTTOM: The main bedroom projects from the primary volume of the home and hovers in the rear oak canopy adjacent to the elevated pool. Photography by Dror Baldinger FAIA.

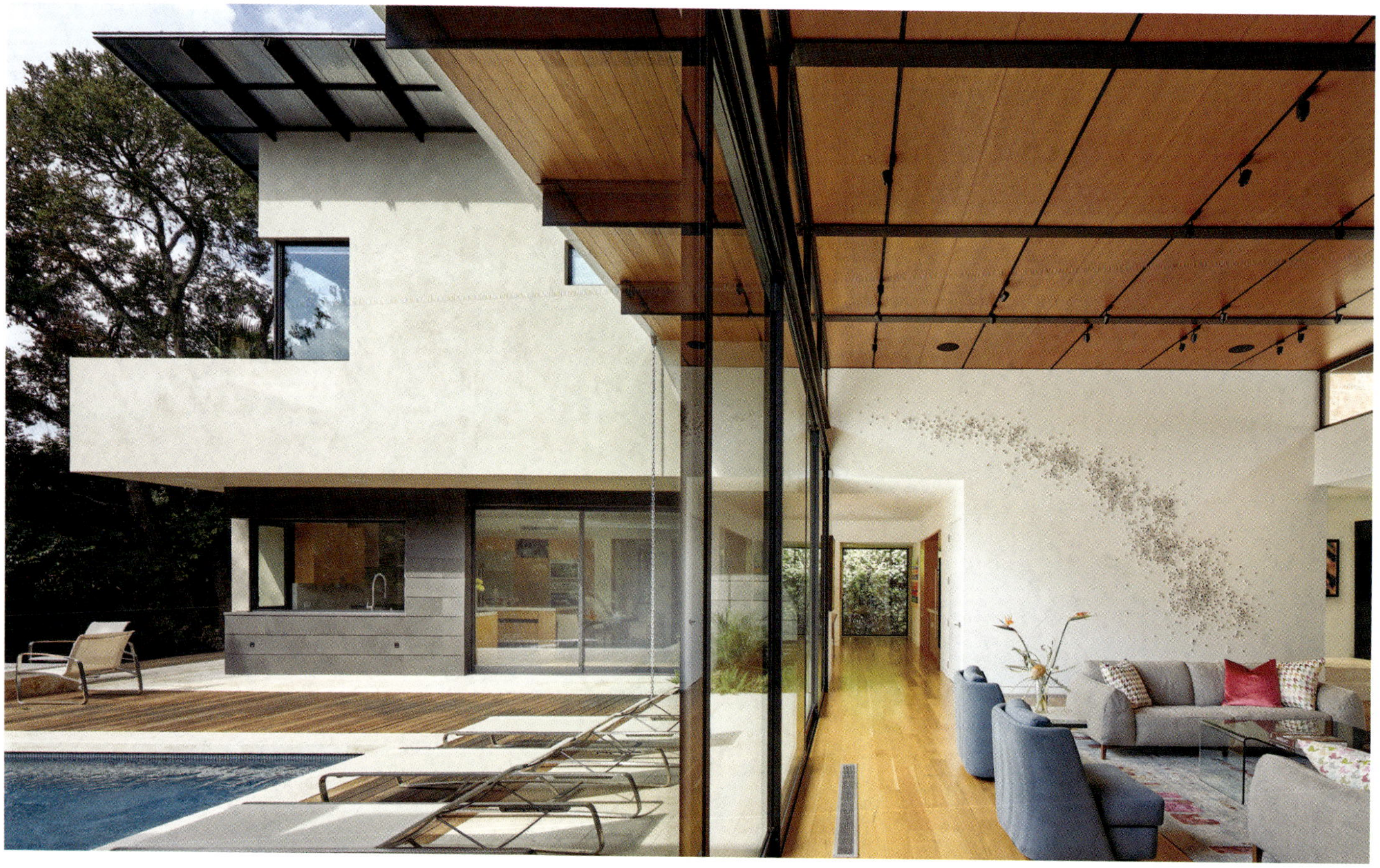

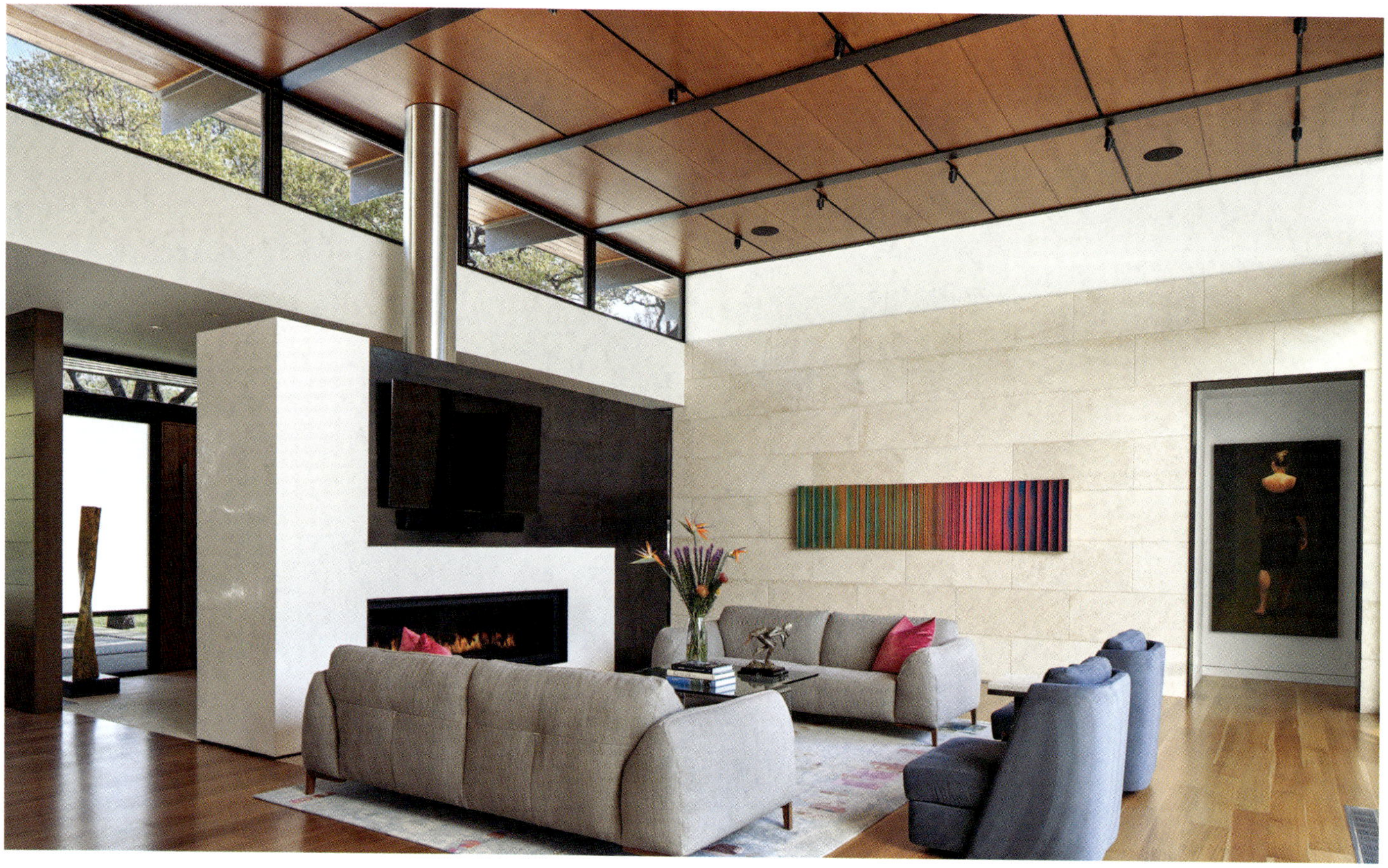

"The presence of varying intimate and expansive experiences in a home accommodates the numerous rituals, events, and emotions of daily life."
—Tobin Smith

TOP: The eroded corner of the main bedroom opens this space to the pool court where water, trees, and sky captivate the senses.

MIDDLE: This floating volume of interlocking polished plaster and blackened steel displays art objects, guides circulation, and integrates fire and media.

BOTTOM: Art is set in dialogue with the outdoors in the dining space – a realm open to the living room.

FACING PAGE TOP: Material continuity and expansive openings blur the line between interior and exterior in the central realm of the home.

FACING PAGE BOTTOM: Fire and water activate the outdoor space between the structure's asymmetrical wings. The wall-to-wall glass of the living room connects indoor and outdoor experiences. Photography by Dror Baldinger FAIA.

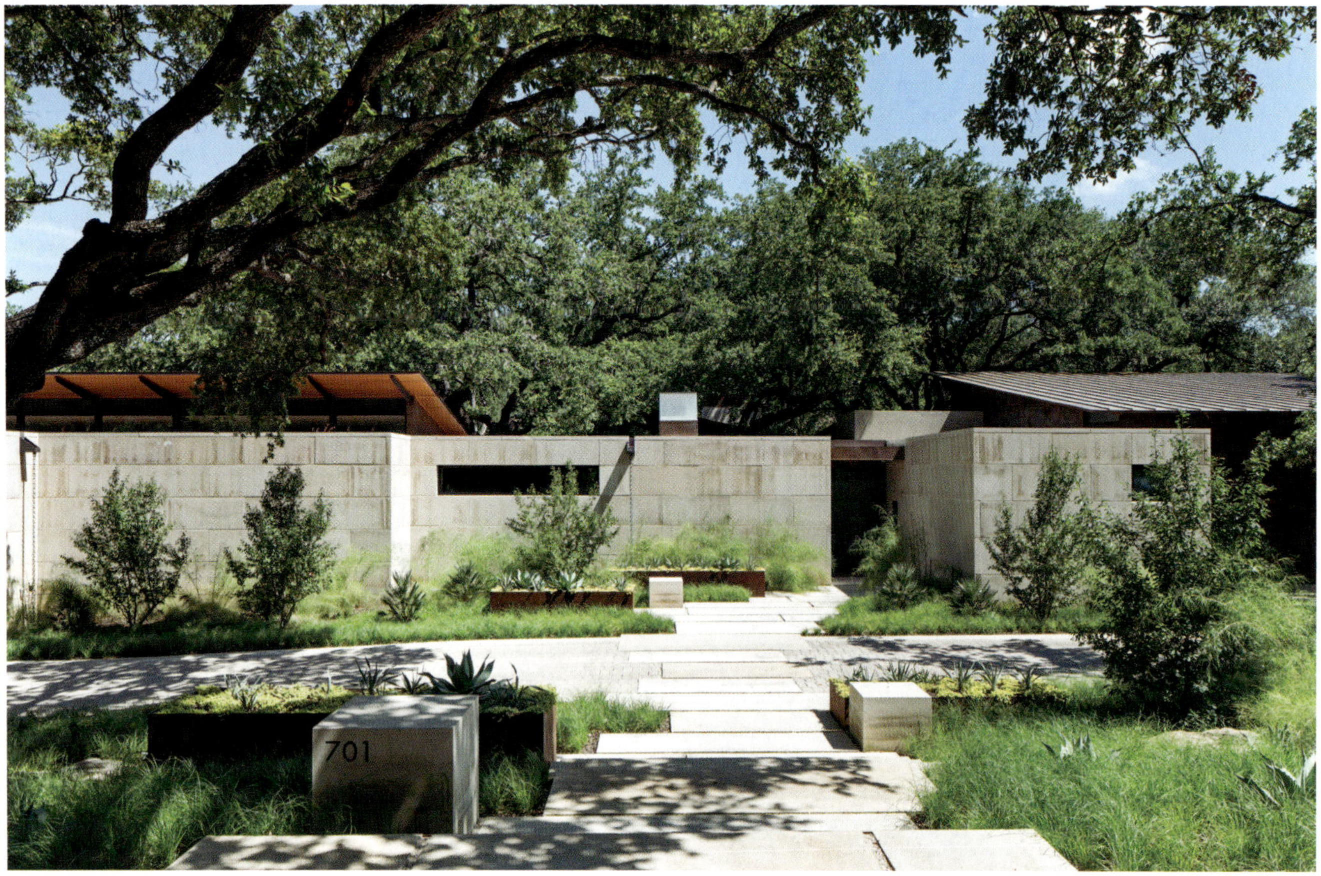
701

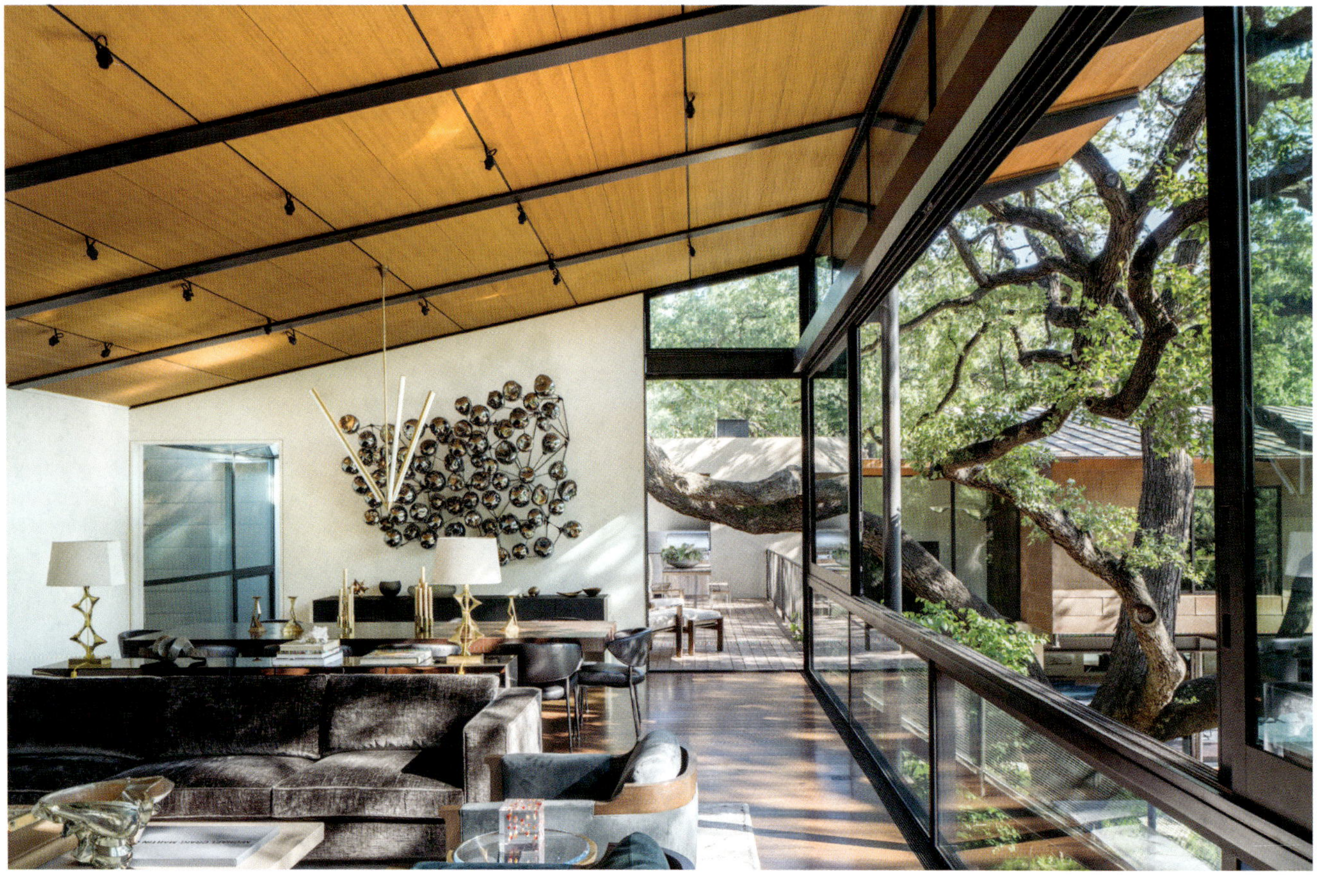

"Carefully curated art, both inside and out, adds a layer of intensity to the experience of site and structure." —Tobin Smith

ABOVE LEFT: At Ravine Retreat, an architectural moment composed of exquisite materials frames organic sculpture and ephemeral landscape, celebrating both.

ABOVE RIGHT: The living and dining space – a bridge straddling the ravine – was conceived so that the site's most dynamic conditions could be experienced and appreciated with the most intensity.

FACING PAGE TOP: A meandering path leads to a shadowy gap in the front stone wall – a portal of mystery and suspense.

FACING PAGE BOTTOM: The 36-foot operable glass wall converts the living and dining room into a tree house when weather permits. Photography by Mark Menjivar.

"Our work radiates emotion and awakens the senses in celebration of the unique aspects of each particular site."
—Tobin Smith

TOP: The main bedroom, a manmade nest in the tree canopy, cantilevers like the branches around it over the south bank of the ravine below.

MIDDLE: Wrapped in travertine, the spa-like main bath is a realm of serenity and relaxation.

BOTTOM: A spacious island, capped with soapstone, accommodates food preparation and casual dining under the levitating presence of a cloud-like form.

FACING PAGE TOP: Stacking glass panels open the game room to the pool deck, connecting these informal entertaining areas.

FACING PAGE BOTTOM: Hovering forms cradle the central heritage oak and overlook the zero-edge pool and adjacent ravine. Photography by Mark Menjivar.

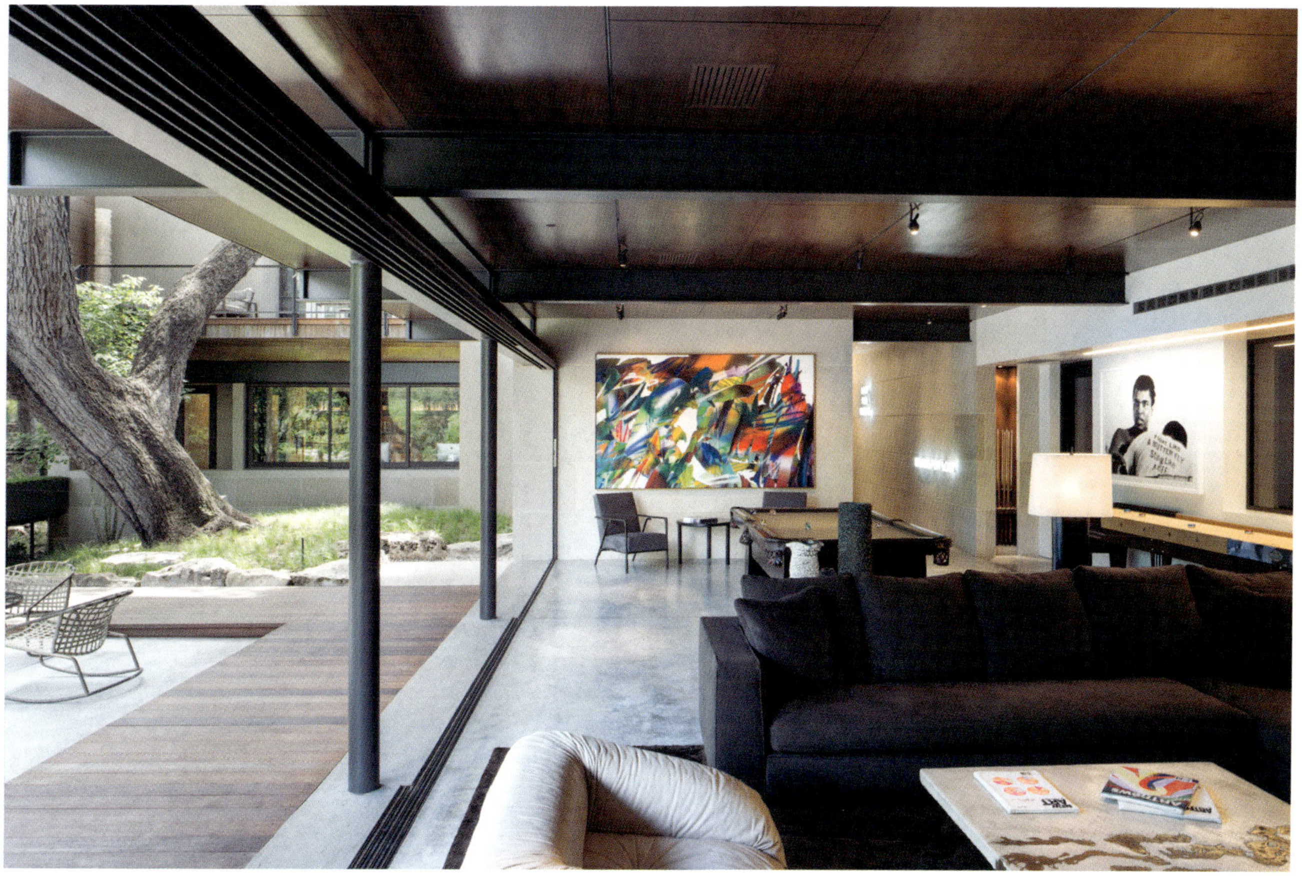

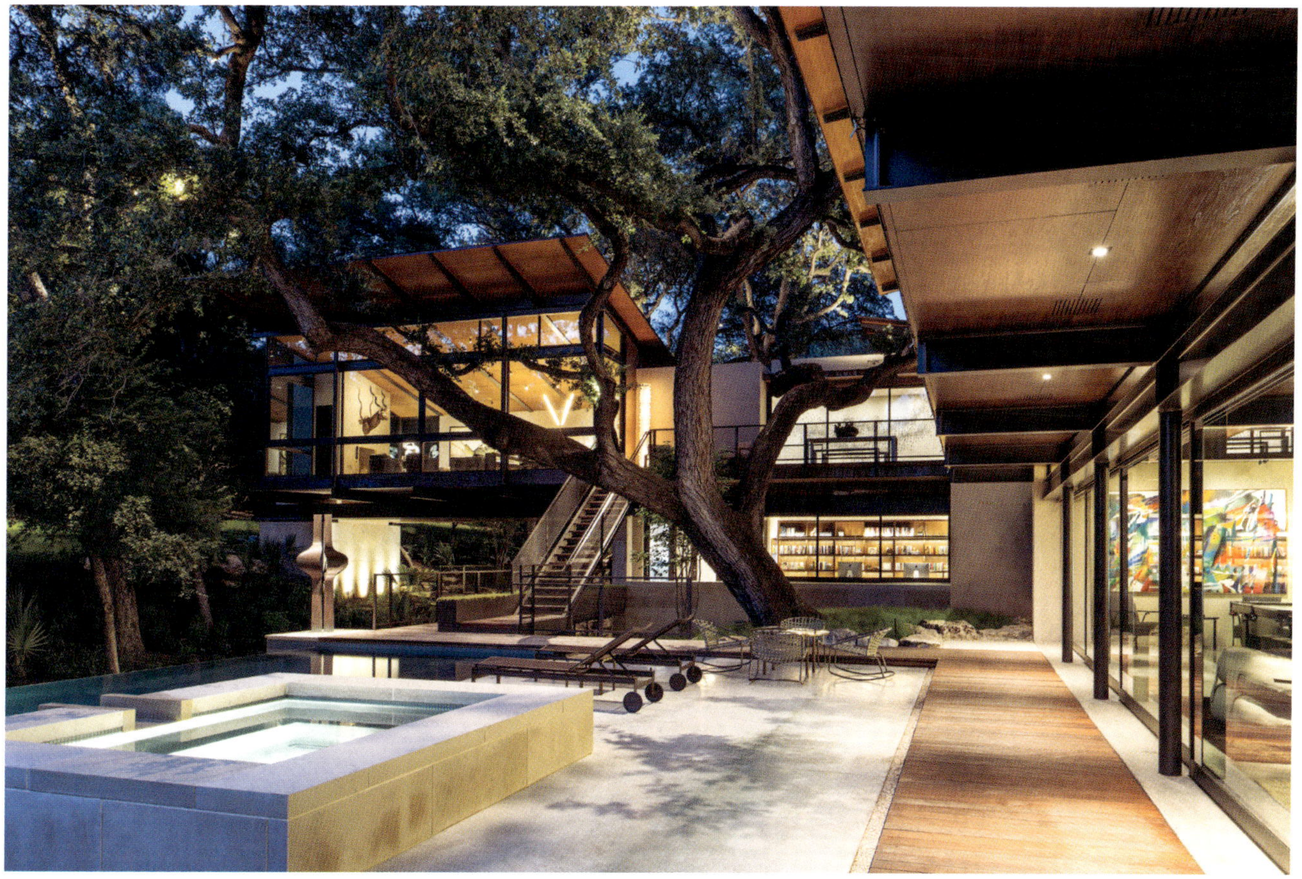

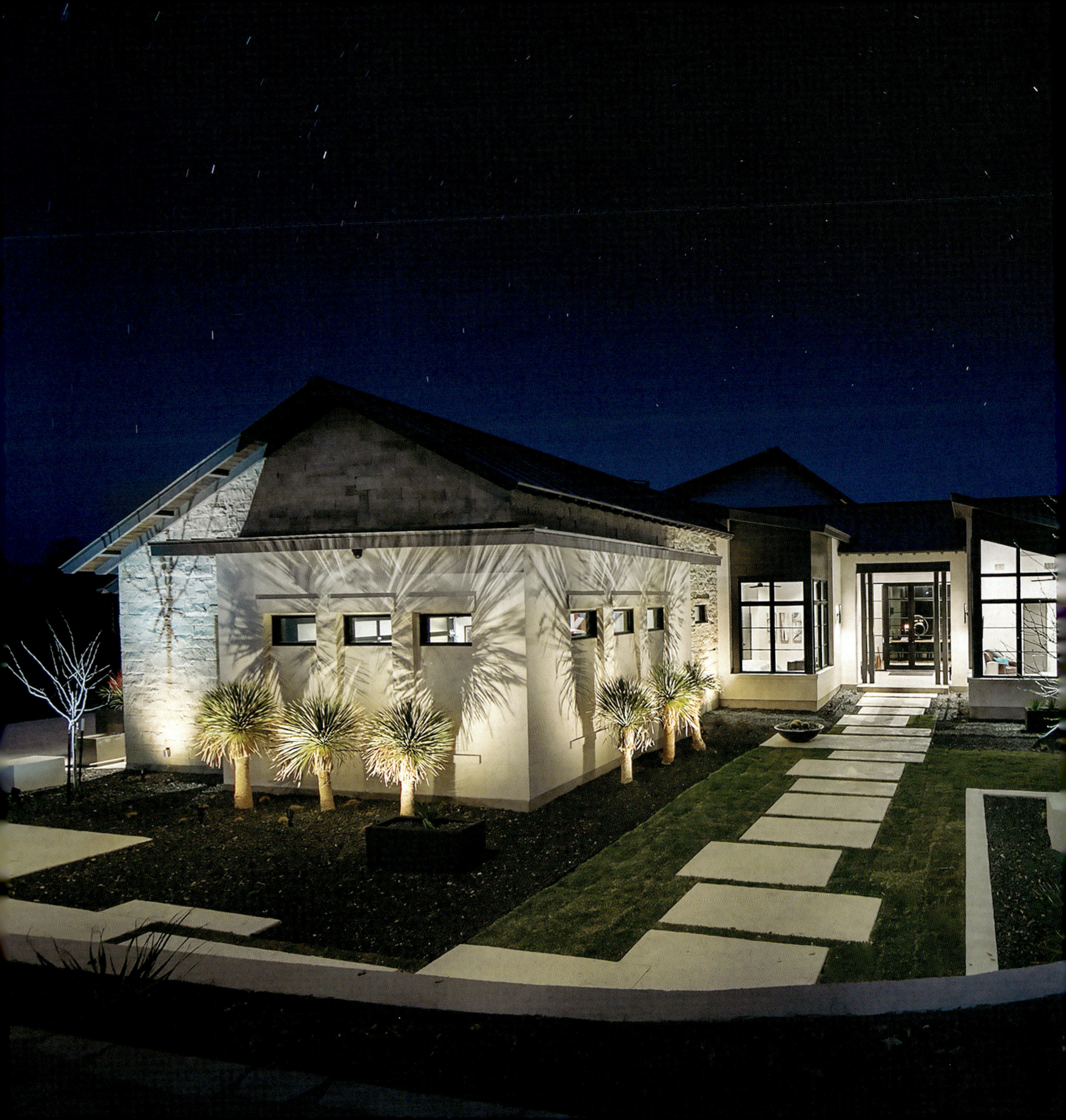

TODD GLOWKA BUILDER

Todd Glowka Builder's tagline is: We build dreams, one home at time. And, it's a fitting one, considering Todd and his team are not only driven to produce the most exceptional, highest quality homes on the market, but also ones that stand out for their unique and aesthetically pleasing characteristics.

As an award-winning luxury custom home builder in the Texas Hill Country, Todd Glowka Builder works across a range of locations and landscapes. But, they also specialize in estate lots, private ranches, golf course communities, and exclusive subdivisions.

Todd's hands-on, "old-school" approach to homebuilding underscores constant communication and collaboration between client and builder – from concept to completion. And his team of professional architects, structural engineers, designers, interior decorators, title companies, and mortgage companies all ensure the experience is a pleasant process for their clients, every step of the way.

Todd also limits the number of homes they build, allowing him to maintain an extreme level of quality in each and every home. Their goal is not to be the biggest – just the very best – at what they do.

FACING PAGE: This one-of-a-kind, 7,129-square-foot golf course estate is situated on one of the most acclaimed golf holes in Texas – hole #16 of the famed Jack Nicklaus Signature golf course in Cordillera Ranch. Native Texas Hill Country limestone was used throughout the exteriors in conjunction with a light, hand-troweled stucco and vertically applied steel siding to unify the indoor and outdoor design. Photography by Lauren Keller - LRES Marketing.

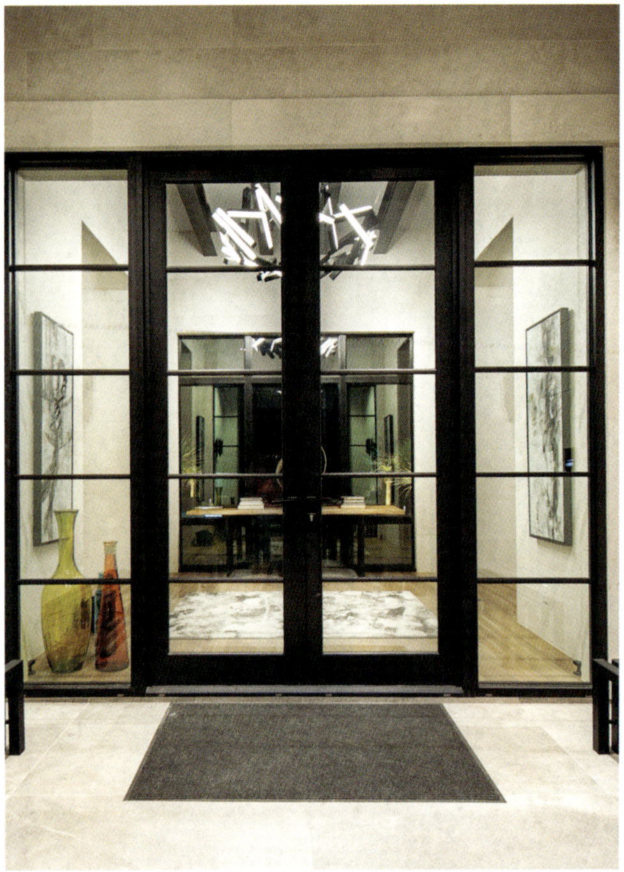
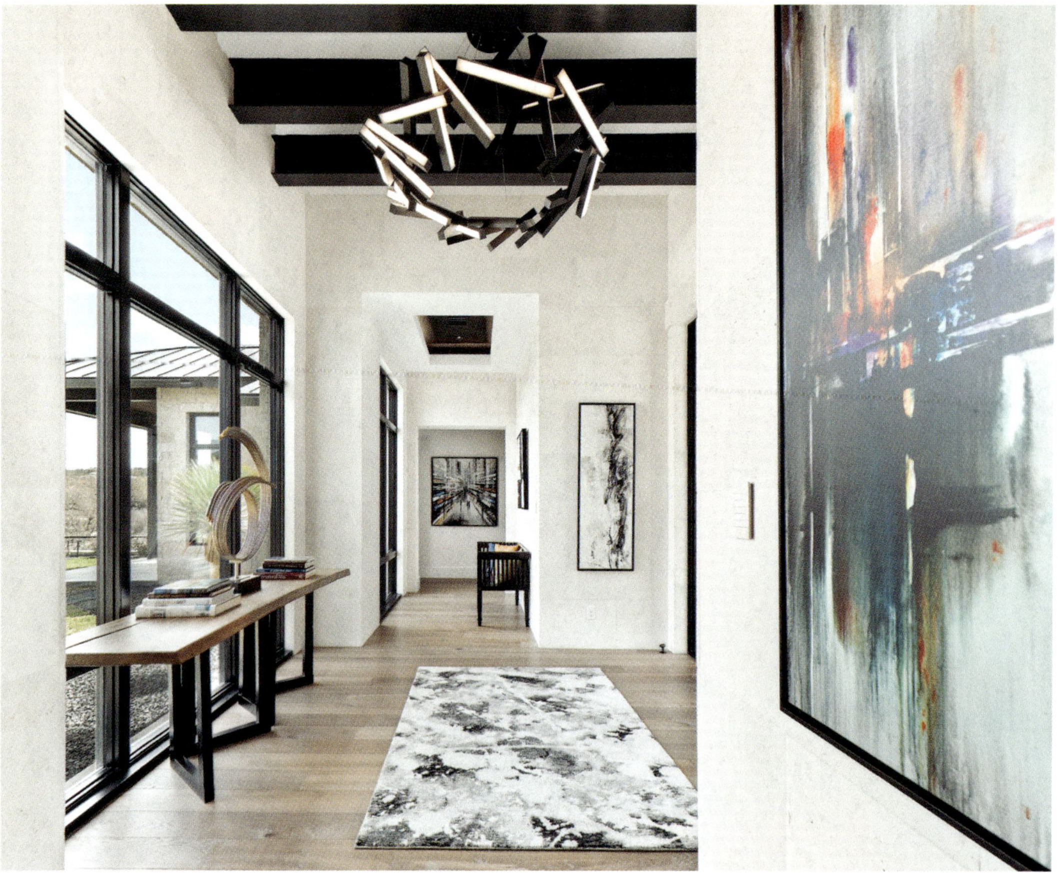
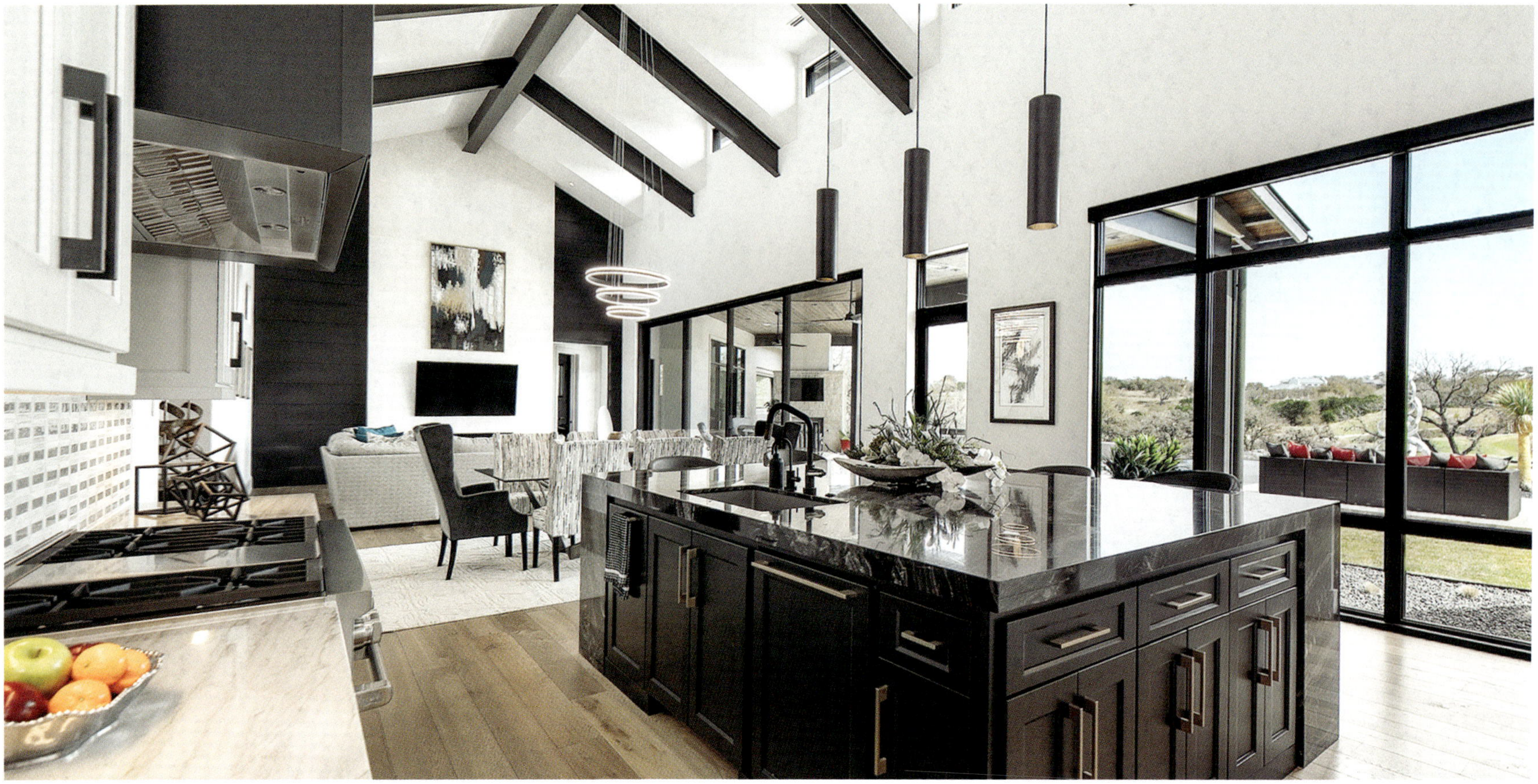

THIS PAGE AND FACING PAGE: Designed by renowned architect Gustavo Arredondo, the modern custom home features an exposed, structural steel layout accompanied by custom "black matte" Windsor wood-clad windows and La Cantina sliders. Smooth walls, sleek appointments, and other modern touches complement the interiors throughout. The great room was imagined in a clerestory style with exposed steel I-beams and it directly overlooks an outdoor terrace, complete with a resort-style pool. The master bedroom suite has its own private terrace, too, with the master bath likewise taking advantage of the views via sliding mirrors that reveal a large window.
Photography by Lauren Keller - LRES Marketing.

"High-quality materials equal long-lasting homes and happy clients."
—Todd Glowka

THIS PAGE AND FACING PAGE: Set amidst the gorgeous scenery of the Texas Hill Country, this 5,881-square-foot contemporary masterpiece is nestled on 13.3 acres in Cordillera Ranch. Throughout the interiors of the single-story home, the rustic warmth of wood, stone, and massive ceiling timbers mingle with sleek, modern lines to magnificent effect. Outdoors, a fully equipped kitchen overlooks an exquisitely designed custom pool with exterior landscaping that creates the ideal Hill Country aesthetic. Photography by Lauren Keller - LRES Marketing.

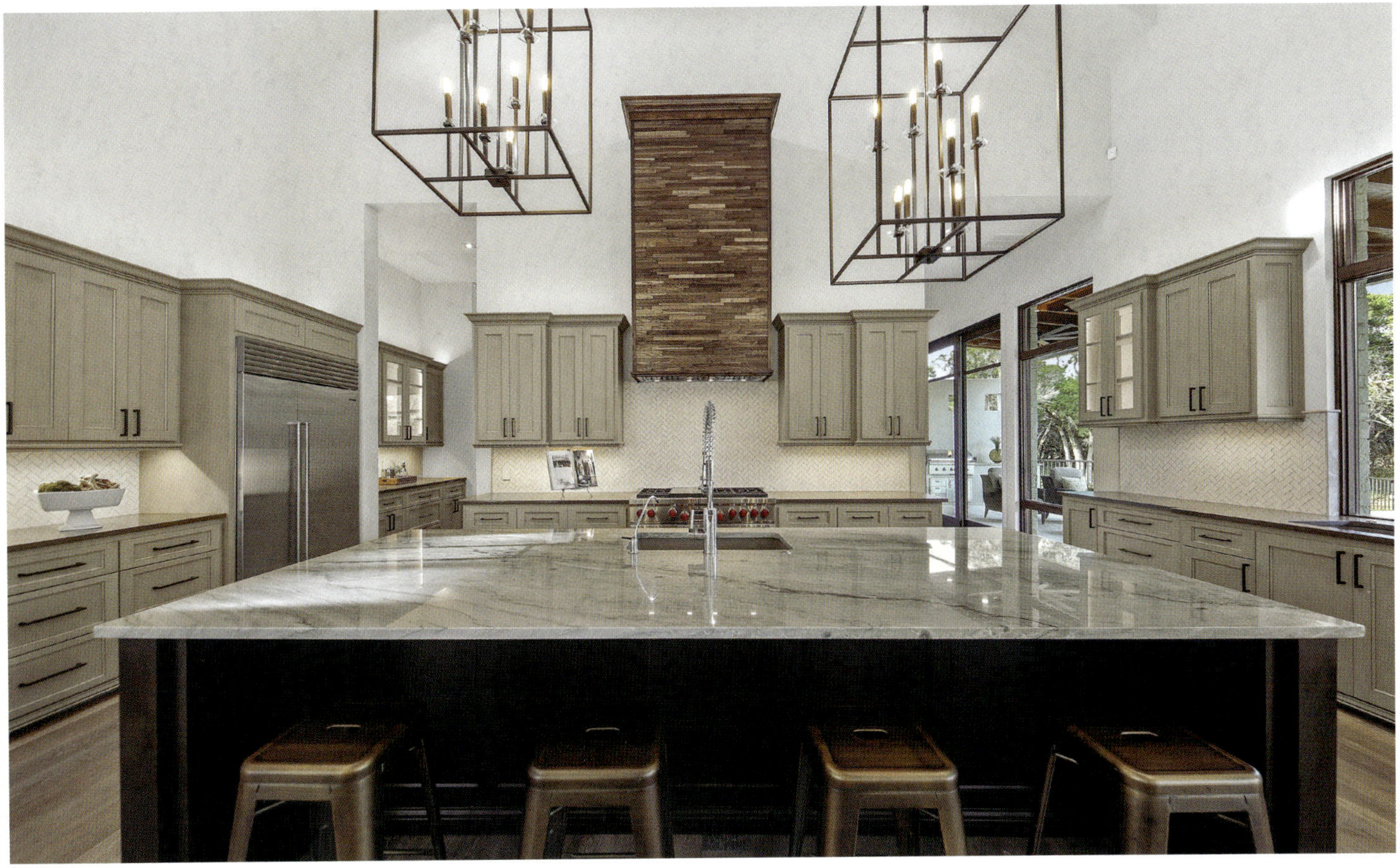

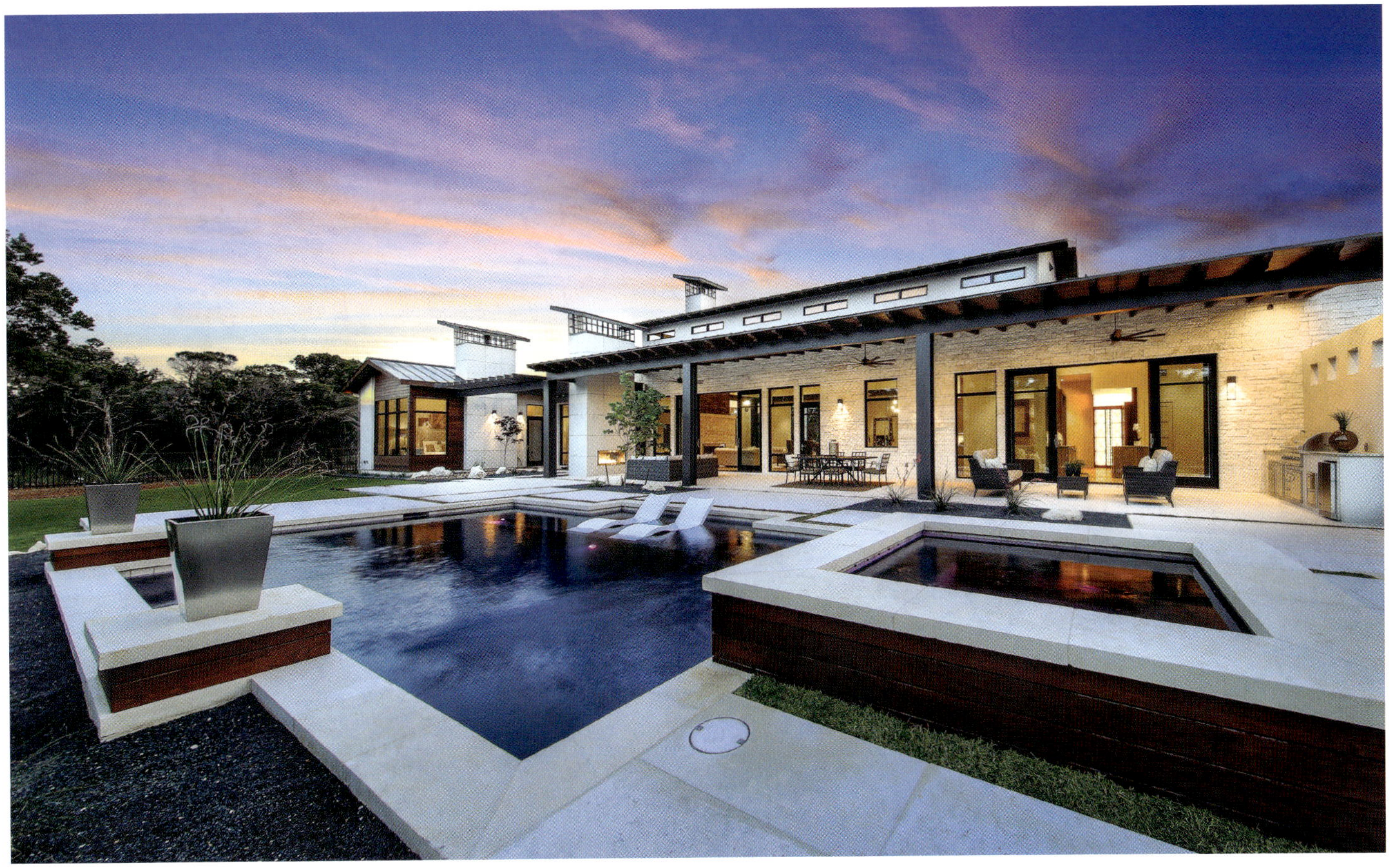

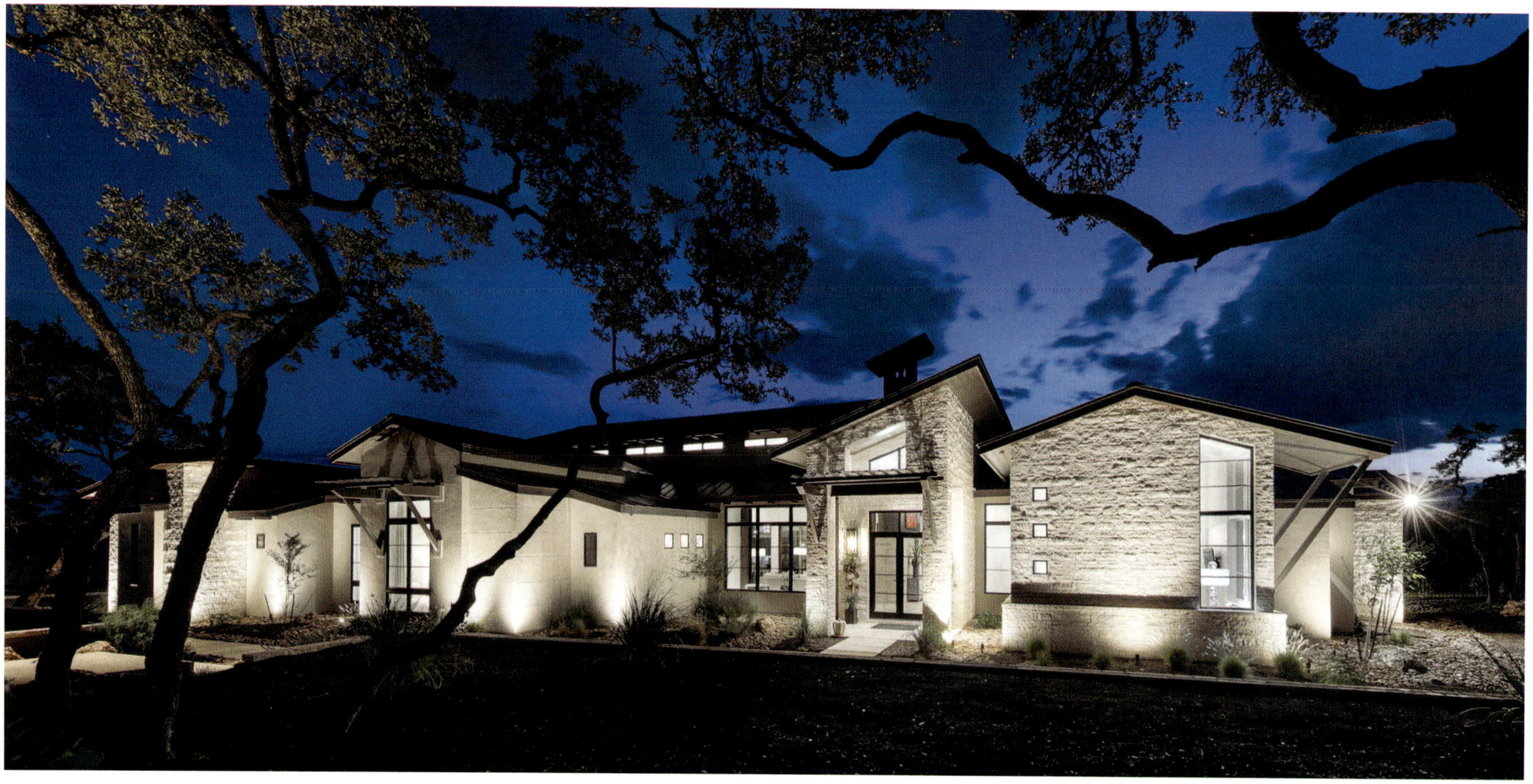

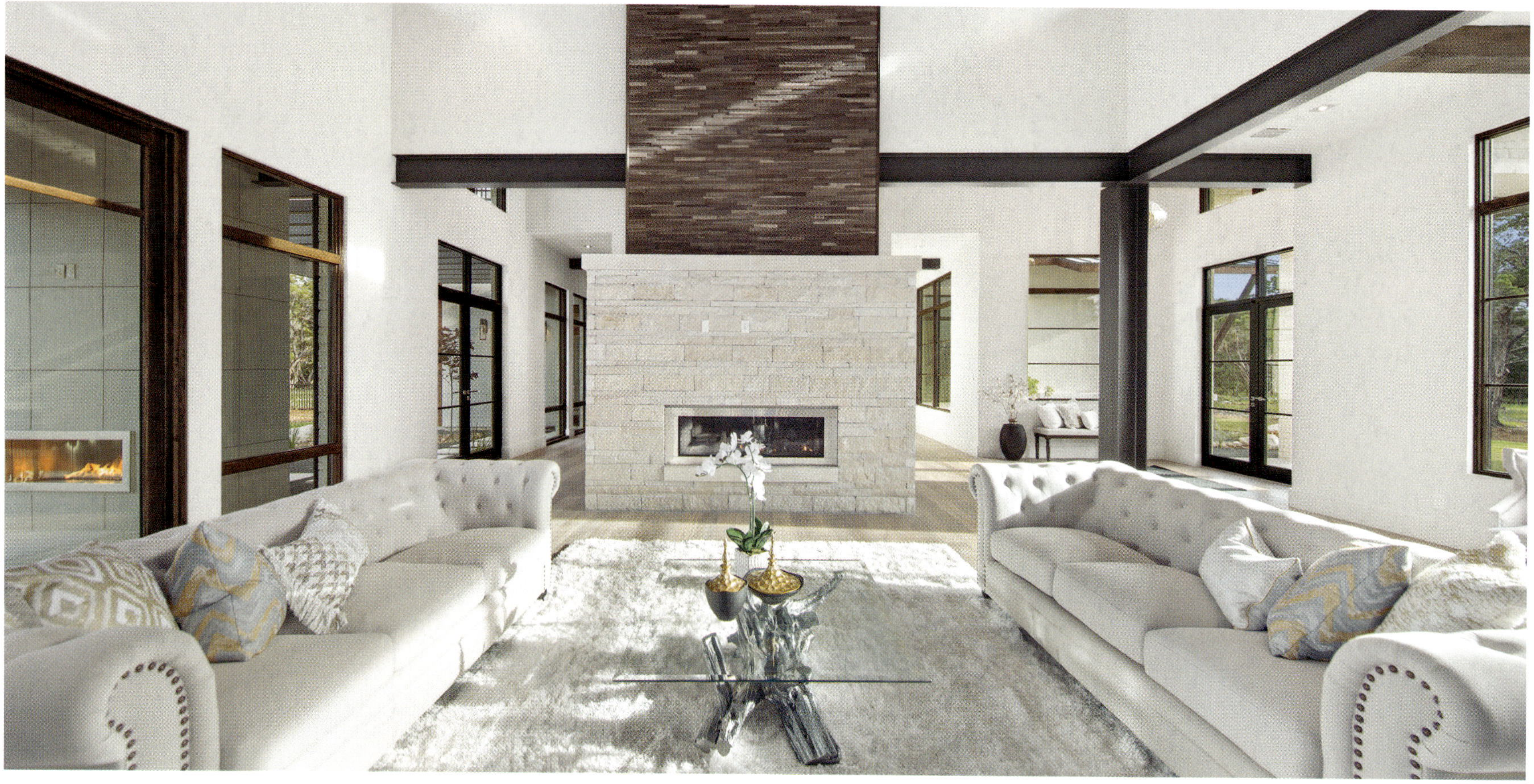

THIS PAGE AND FACING PAGE: This transitional, 4,539-square-foot home is located just outside of Boerne in Stone Creek Ranch. Clean, contemporary lines mix with traditional Texas Hill Country finishes to make this home truly unique. The open-concept kitchen, dining, and living spaces have soaring 23-foot ceilings, which are highlighted by large sheetrock beams. Features include two linear-style contemporary fireplaces, wood and aluminum windows, and bespoke finishes throughout. Photography by Lauren Keller - LRES Marketing.

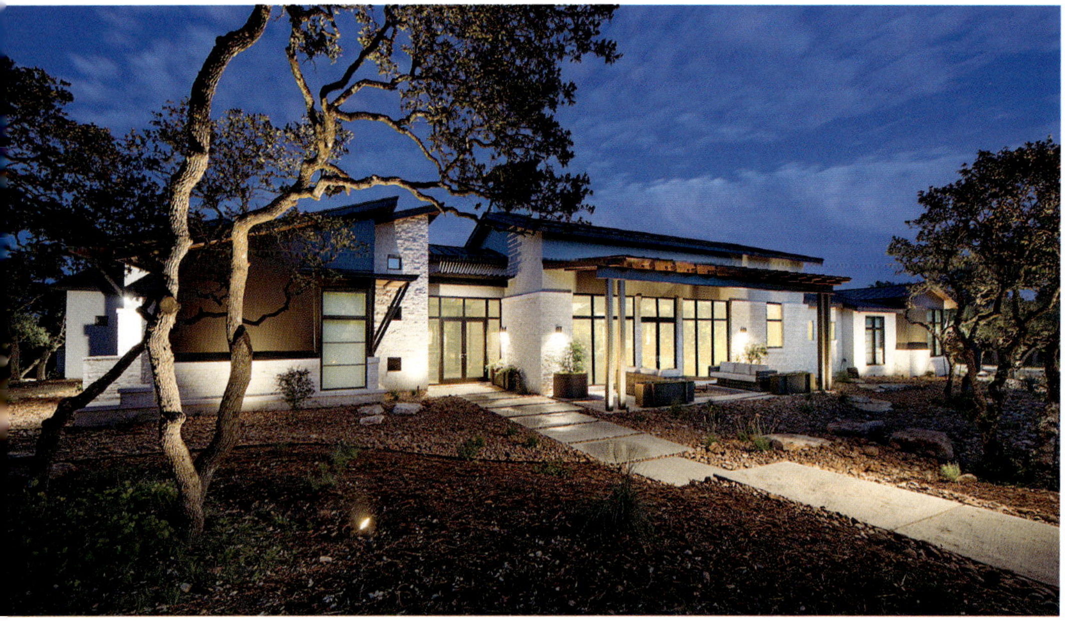

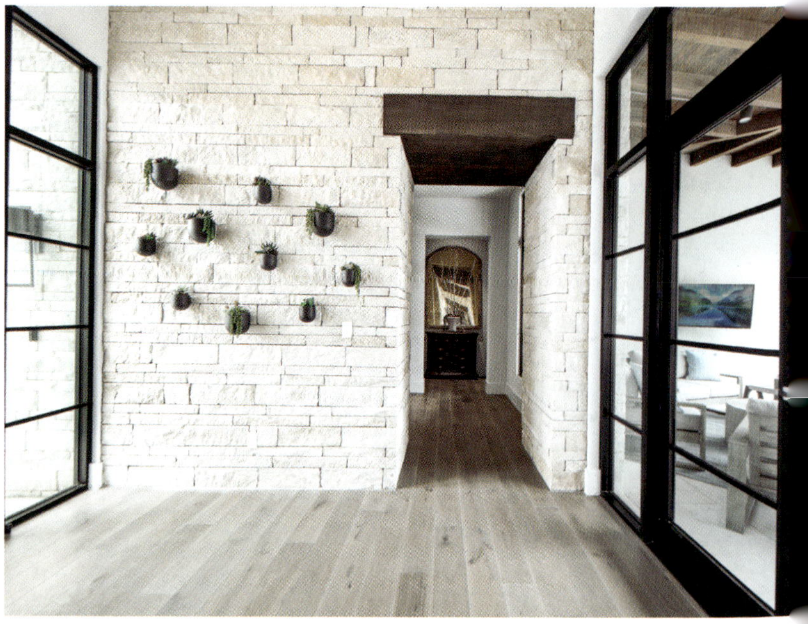

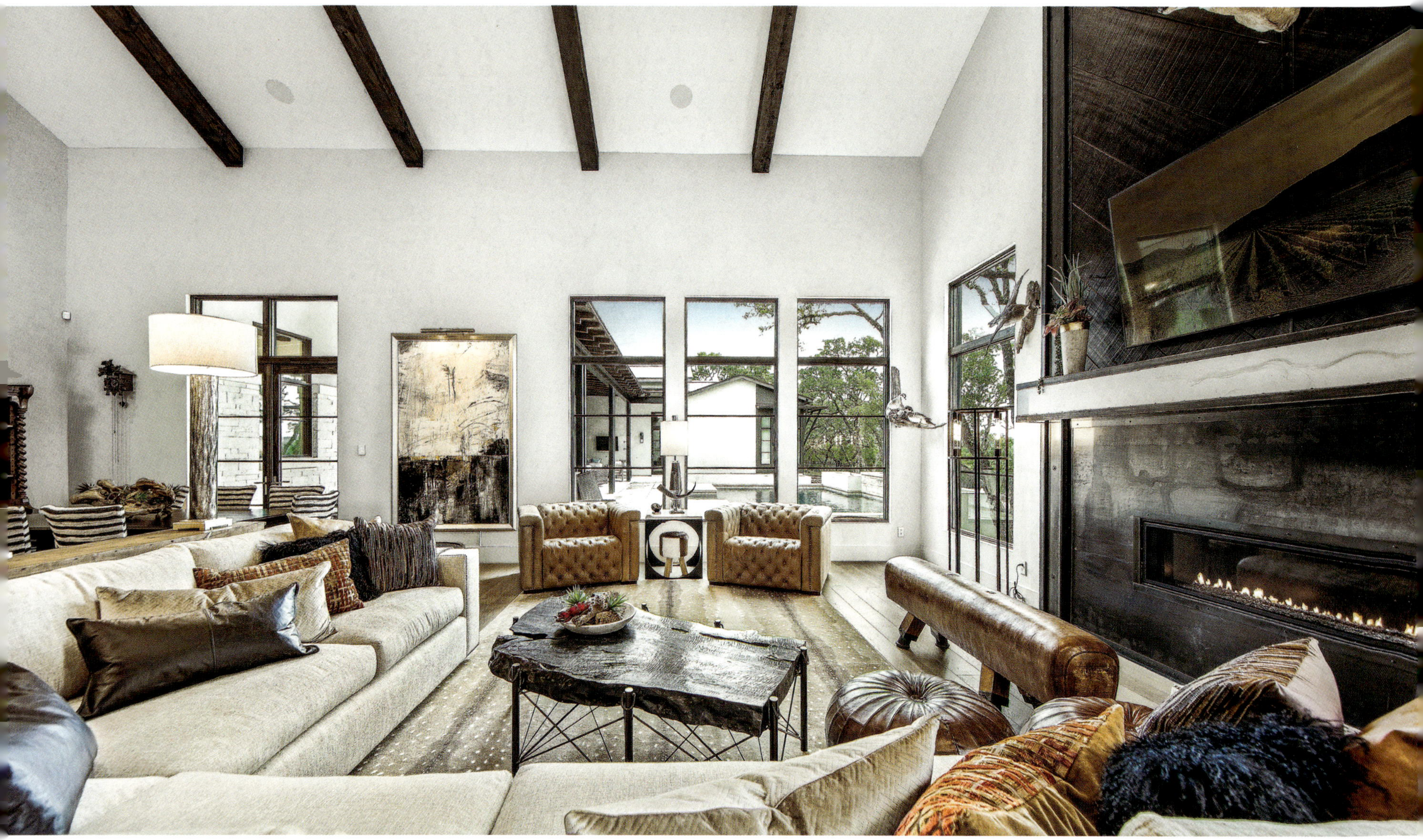

THIS PAGE AND FACING PAGE: Keeping with today's design trends, the Monteola Estates residence features the eclectic combination of modern lines blended with the Texas Hill Country architectural style - all sitting on 5.3 park-like acres. Steel siding, stone, stucco, large banks of glass, wood floors, and timbered ceiling treatments are mixed with clean, modern porcelain tiles and barn doors. Features include four bedrooms, two living areas, a wine room, outdoor kitchen, linear-style swimming pool, three-car garage, one-car porte-cochère, and matching barn. Photography by Lauren Keller - LRES Marketing.

Designed by RHOTENBERRY WELLEN ARCHITECTS

Photography by Paul Hester, Hester + Hardaway

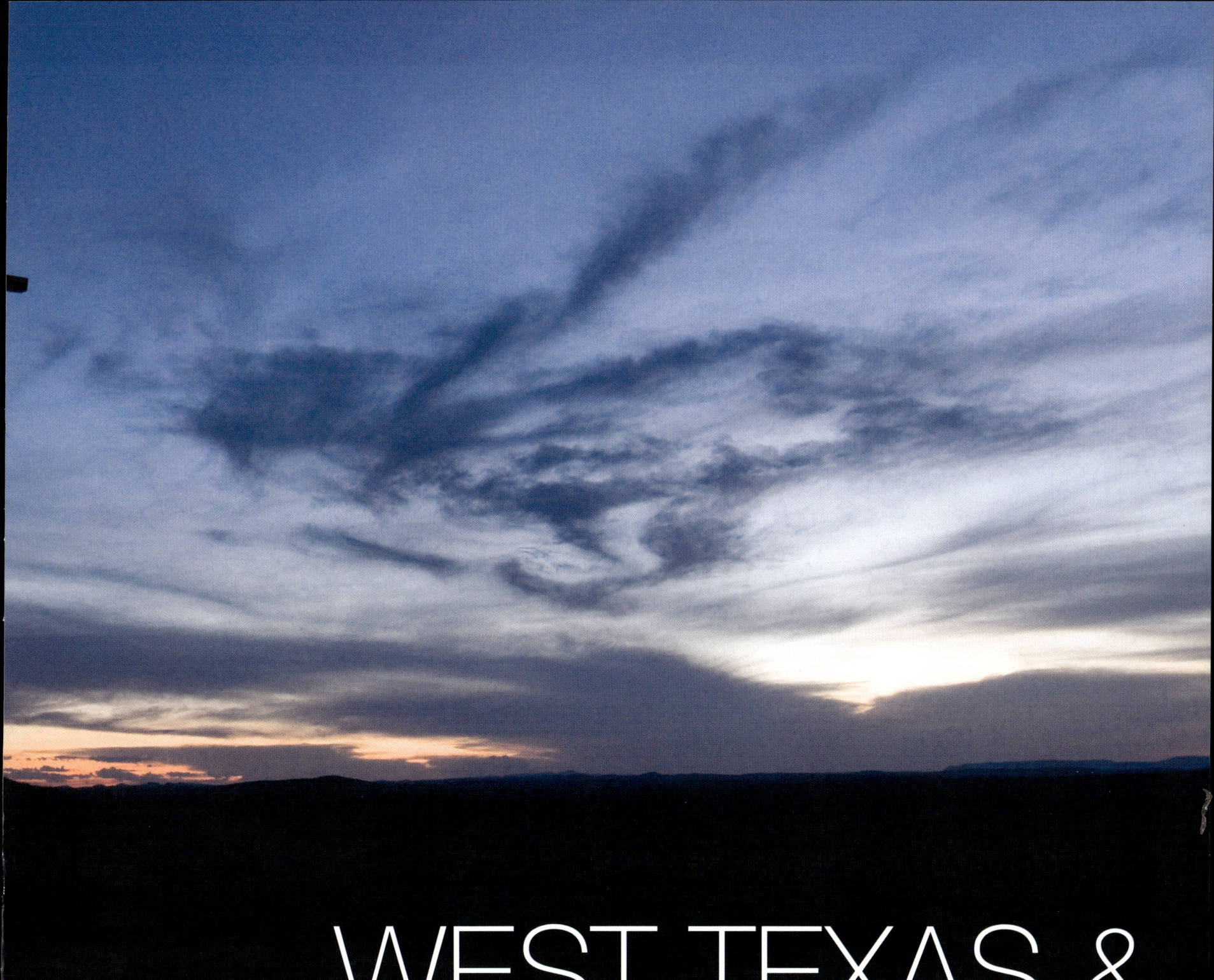

WEST TEXAS & THE HILL COUNTRY

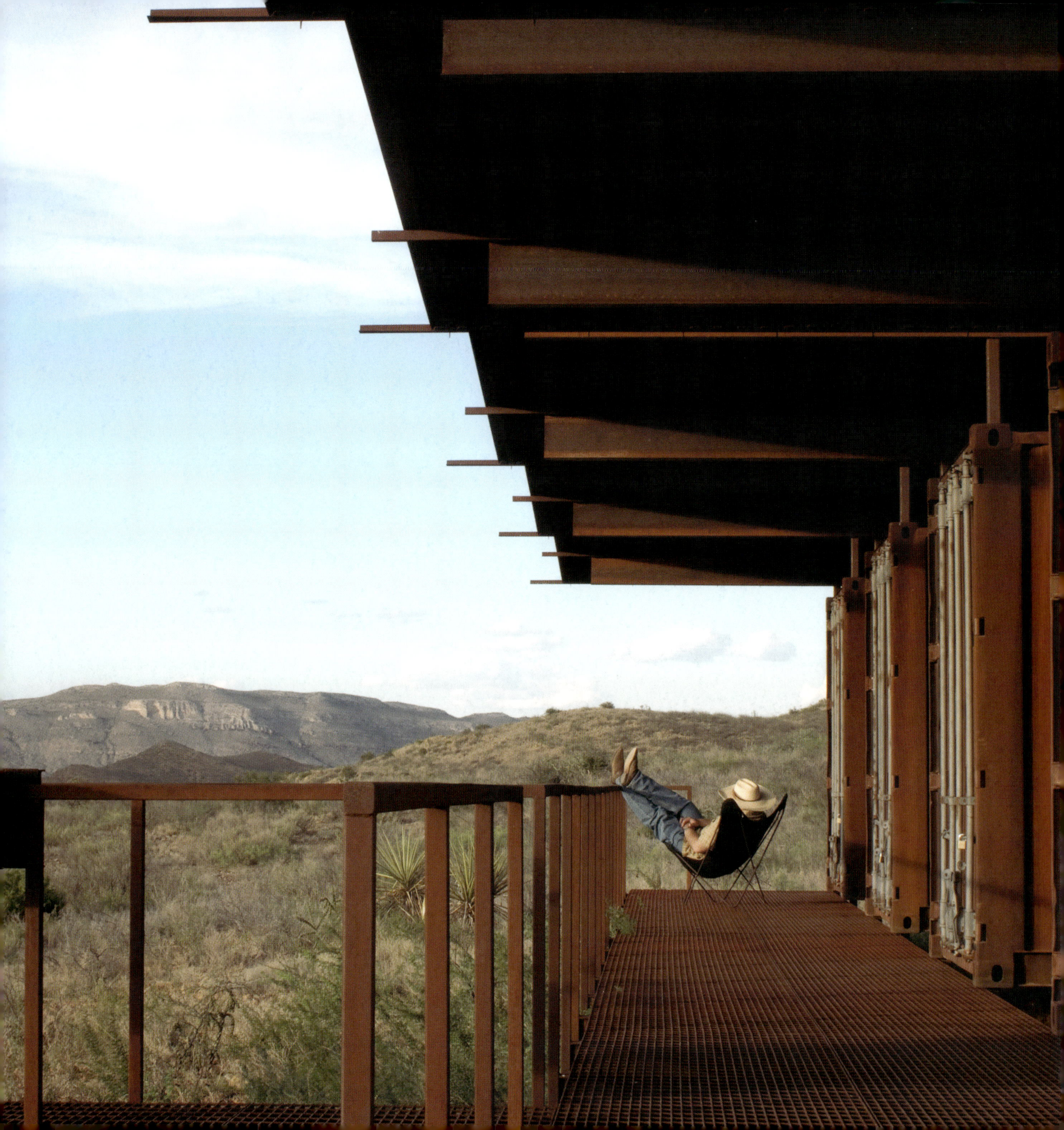

RHOTENBERRY WELLEN ARCHITECTS

When it comes to the influences behind Rhotenberry Wellen Architects' impressive designs, the firm looks to history and nature to inform their work. They are inspired by the traditions of their Modernist forebears in architecture as well as the humble structures that define the regional vernacular. Their designs also prioritize a rational response to climate and context along with fluid integration into the surrounding landscape.

The award-winning firm was originally formed in 1988 when Jim Rhotenberry and Mark Wellen merged their practices — and they have since brought in TJ McClure, Andy Chandler, and Cale Lancaster as partners.

Collectively, they believe in elegant executions with details brought about by a desire for legibility and collaboration with dedicated craftsmen. They search for moments of clarity and delight that engage the occupant, thereby elevating the human spirit. Most importantly, they strive to provide a framework to enhance the lives of their clients.

FACING PAGE: The weathering steel construction, comprised primarily of five shipping containers joined by bar-grate decks, blends effortlessly into the landscape with structures that float above grade, lightly touching the earth and allowing for the occupant's protection from spiny plants and hostile wildlife.

TOP: The large sliding doors, used in this Cinco Camp property, open the units to expansive views of the vast, mountainous landscape of far West Texas while providing a means of ventilation.

BOTTOM: Ample, overhanging roofs float above each unit to provide protection from the intense desert sun. Photography by Paul Hester, Hester + Hardaway.

"Over the years, our firm has renovated and expanded numerous architecturally significant houses designed by respected architects of the past. We strive to find solutions sensitive to and respectful of the original design intent while satisfying the client's desire for a current lifestyle." —Mark Wellen

TOP LEFT: A skylit platform provides a cozy area of solitude while defining a pleasing termination of the view from the entry.

TOP RIGHT: The original exposed post-and-beam structure and window frames were reconditioned and complemented by a new, unfinished metal roof and siding.

BOTTOM LEFT: The large sliding door units integrate interior and exterior living spaces.

FACING PAGE TOP: The original carport space was reappropriated to expand the kitchen and dining space. All public areas open through new glazing systems to the central courtyard.

FACING PAGE BOTTOM: A new cabana and pool were added to complete the outdoor living space, providing a focus for the large backyard.
Photography by Paul Hester, Hester + Hardaway.

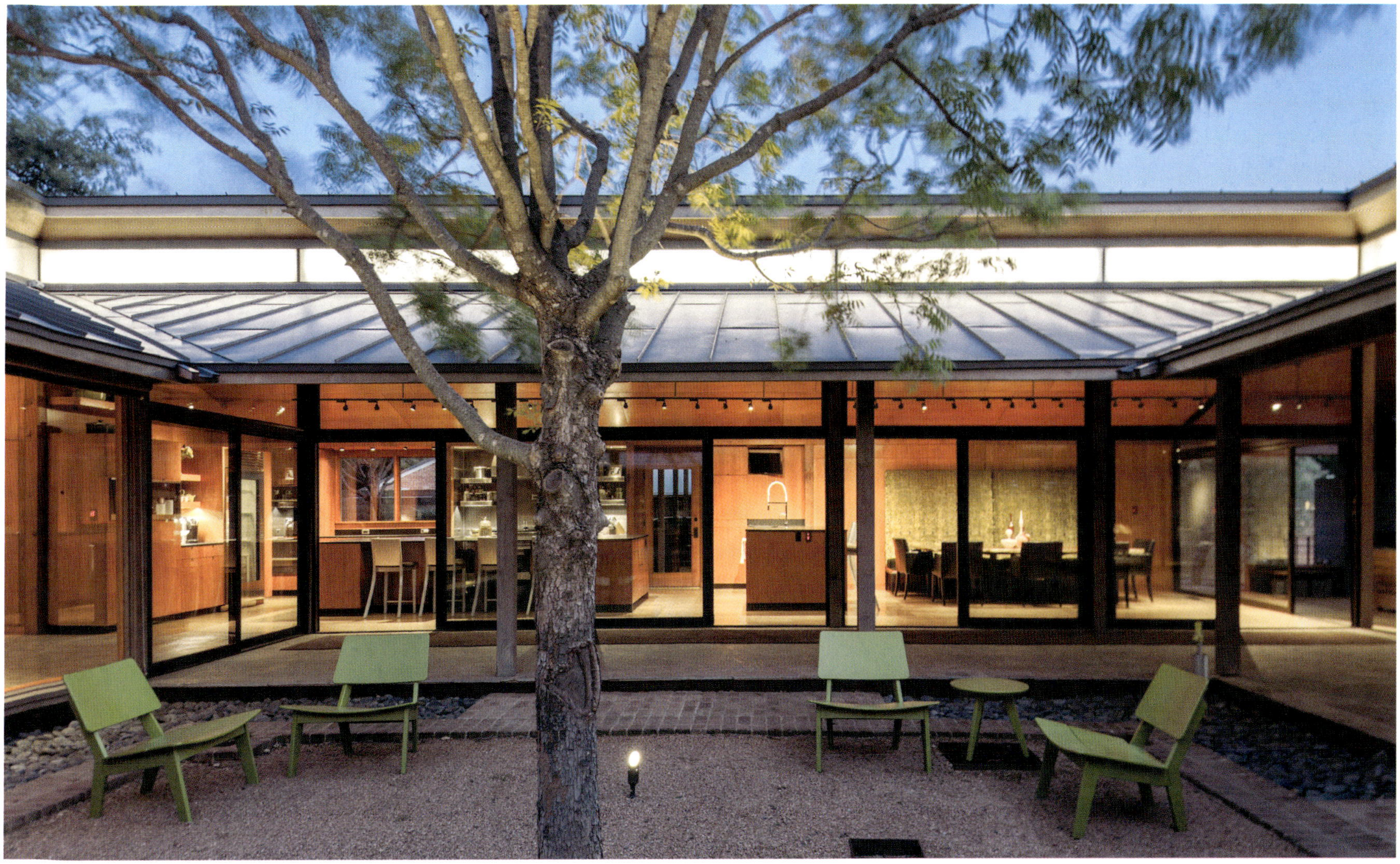

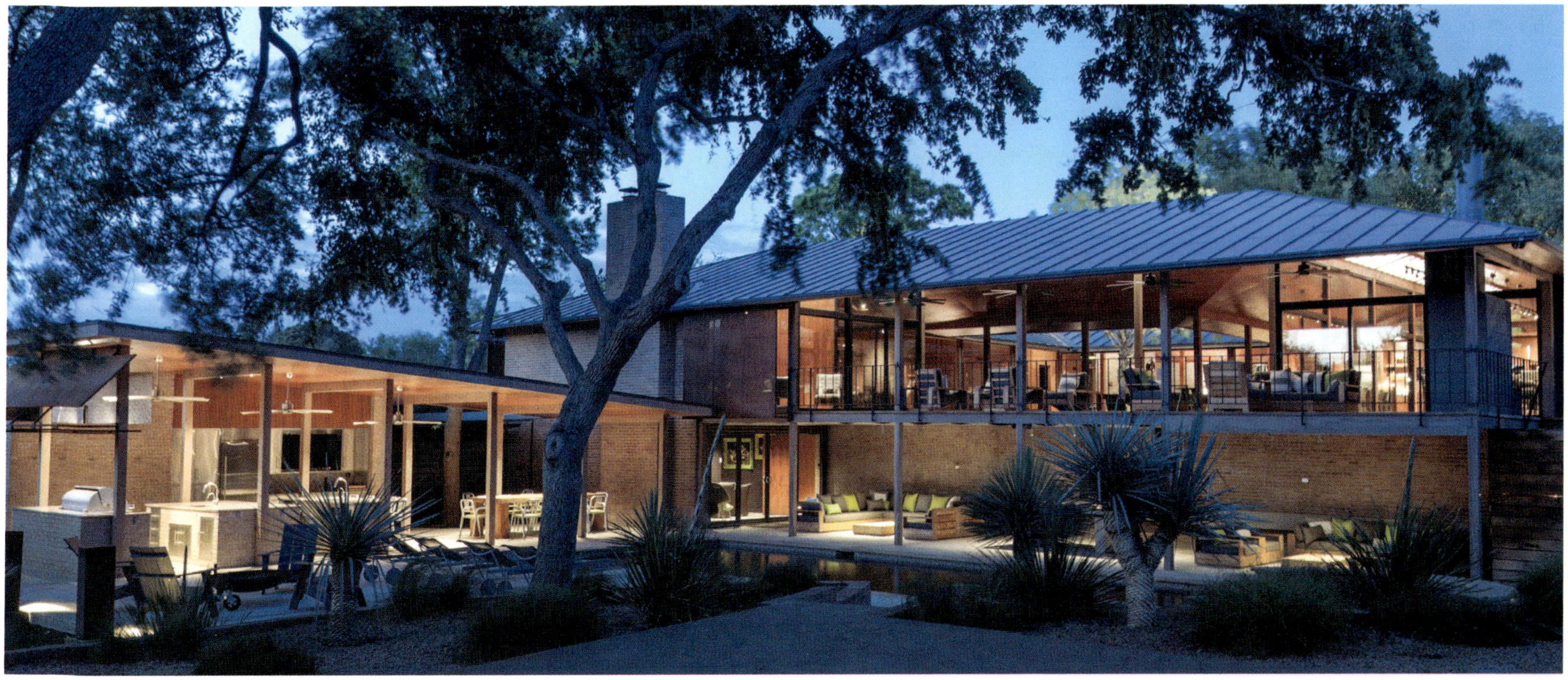

"Dietert Ranch is the product of an ongoing pursuit to interpret time-honored, historic building forms through the lens of contemporary agri-industrial building types." –Mark Wellen

ABOVE LEFT: The broad canopy of the roof provides numerous well-protected outdoor spaces, both at the ground level and at the second-level balconies.

ABOVE TOP RIGHT: The dog trot serves as the entryway while referencing a timeless Hill Country precedent.

ABOVE BOTTOM RIGHT: Interiors are finished with vertical-grain Douglas fir paneling, accented by hand-crafted steel shelves, door and window casings, and custom hardware.

FACING PAGE TOP: The house sits completely disconnected from a sheltering shed roof with the entire structure resting on a plinth that's nestled between trees on the landscape.

FACING PAGE BOTTOM LEFT: The exterior material palette is comprised of galvanized steel structural elements, concrete, and perforated weathering steel screens.

FACING PAGE BOTTOM RIGHT: The pool serves as a collector for rainwater and provides the soothing sounds of running water. Photography by Paul Hester, Hester + Hardaway.

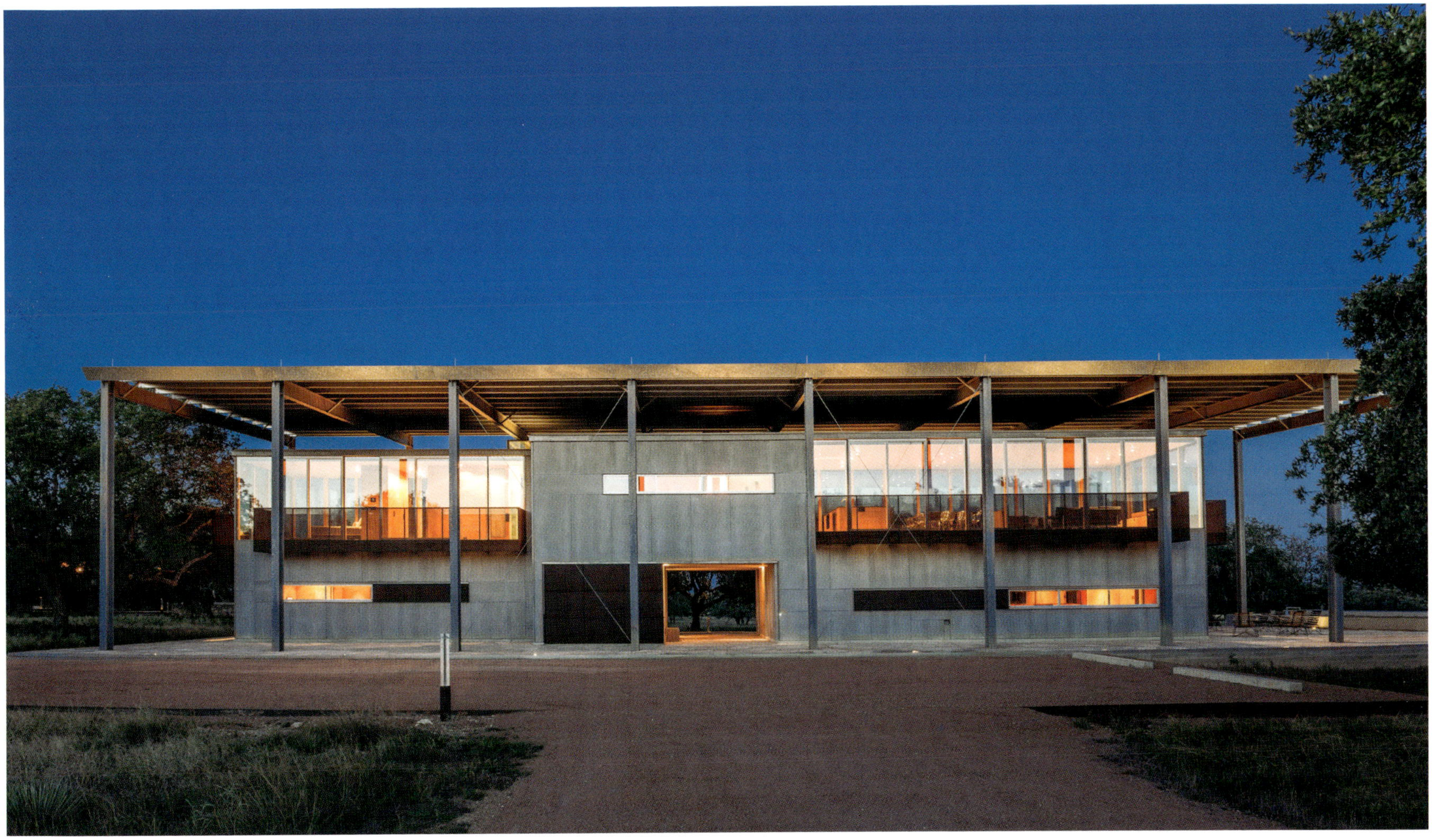

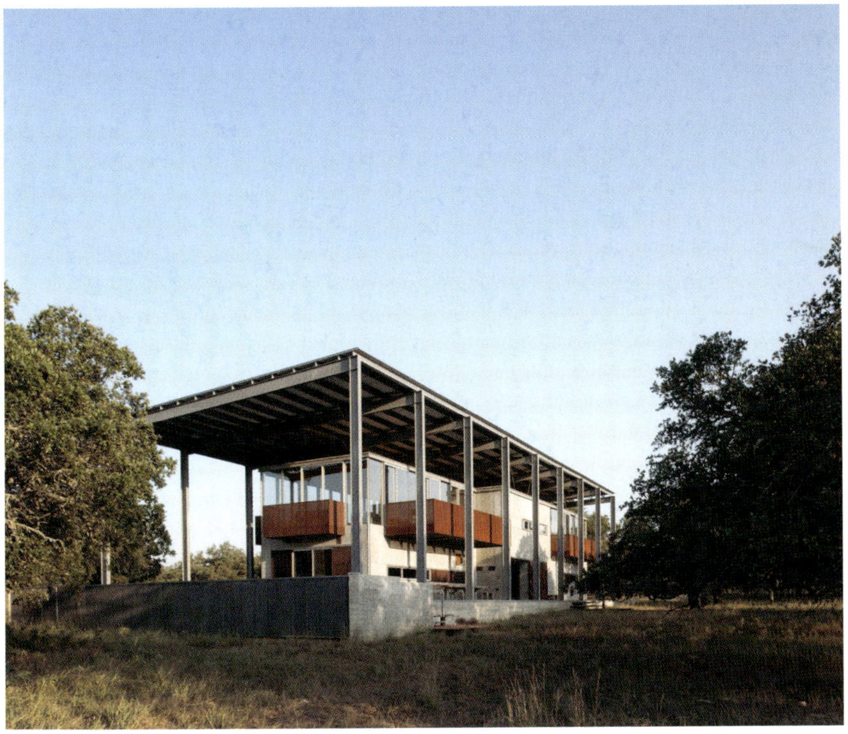

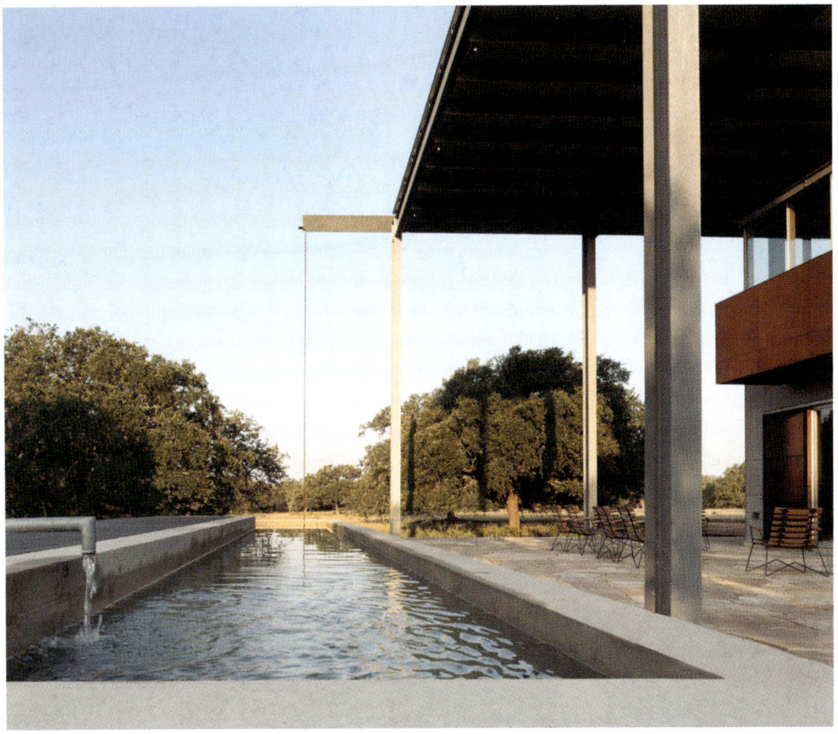

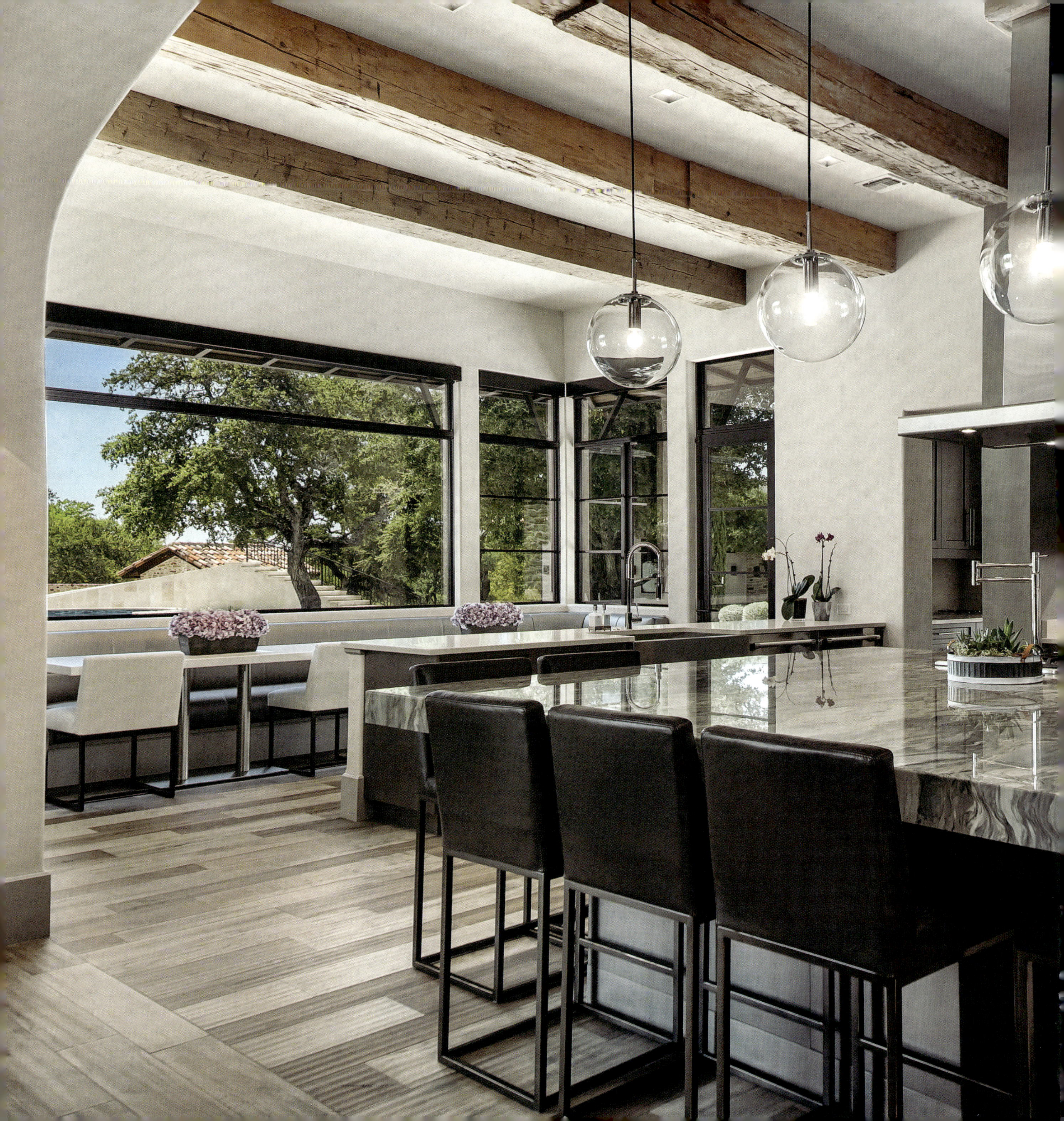

KELLY HALLMAN DESIGN

Although Kelly Hallman of Kelly Hallman Design spent 11 years in the brokerage industry, she has always had an eye for design. So, she turned her long-time passion for color, textiles, and spatial visualization into a thriving professional interior design career — and she never looked back.

However, it's actually her experience in the business world that elevates her creative work even more. That's because her corporate know-how ensures a smooth, streamlined process — and a careful respect for budgeting and scope for each of her clients, who she works with collaboratively.

Whether it's decorating, building, or remodeling, Kelly has the unique ability to see the potential of a space and translate it through hand-sketched floor plans and storyboards before bringing the vision to life.

Her work is most often characterized as a mix of timeless interiors and modern simplicity although she readily creates within a variety of other styles, as well. For her, the most important element of a home is the synergy between how it looks and feels and the personality of the homeowner.

FACING PAGE: Fusion quartzite slabs were bookended for this extra-large kitchen island, which plays off the nearby fabric on the custom built banquette.

TOP: The textured tile alcove and barrel ceiling are highlighted by crystal light fixtures while framing the view to the outdoor pool.

MIDDLE: We used American clay for the walls and ceilings throughout the house. It creates a great backdrop for the subtle colors in one of the home offices.

BOTTOM: The handmade wall and shower tile features a vertical basketweave pattern.
Photography by Jeremiah Dearinger.

TOP: We designed a custom metal barn door to disguise access to a closet where the firewood for the fireplace is stored in the main living area.

BOTTOM LEFT: Leathered Venus quartzite countertops and the Tabarka tile backsplash add a timeworn feel.

BOTTOM RIGHT: This custom-designed floating vanity includes a notched section to serve as a makeup area.

FACING PAGE TOP: For this project, we worked with the homeowners to bring to life their design vision. This Tangerine River crystal tile in the foreground was selected by the client to be the most outstanding feature in the master bathroom.

FACING PAGE BOTTOM: The kitchen was one area where careful consideration was given for the homeowners' art collection. Eames molded plastic stools were acquired for the island to supplement existing pieces they owned in this room. Photography by Jeremiah Dearinger.

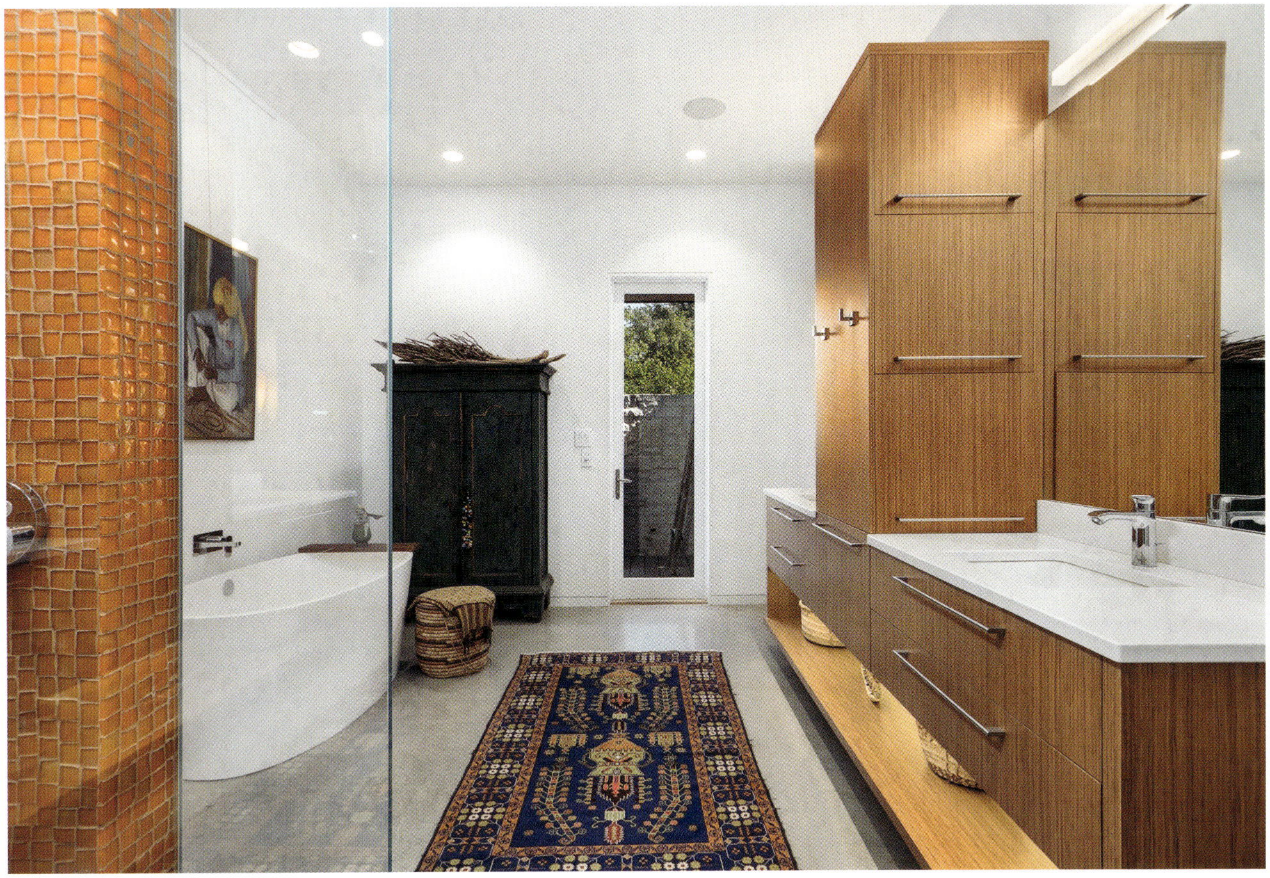

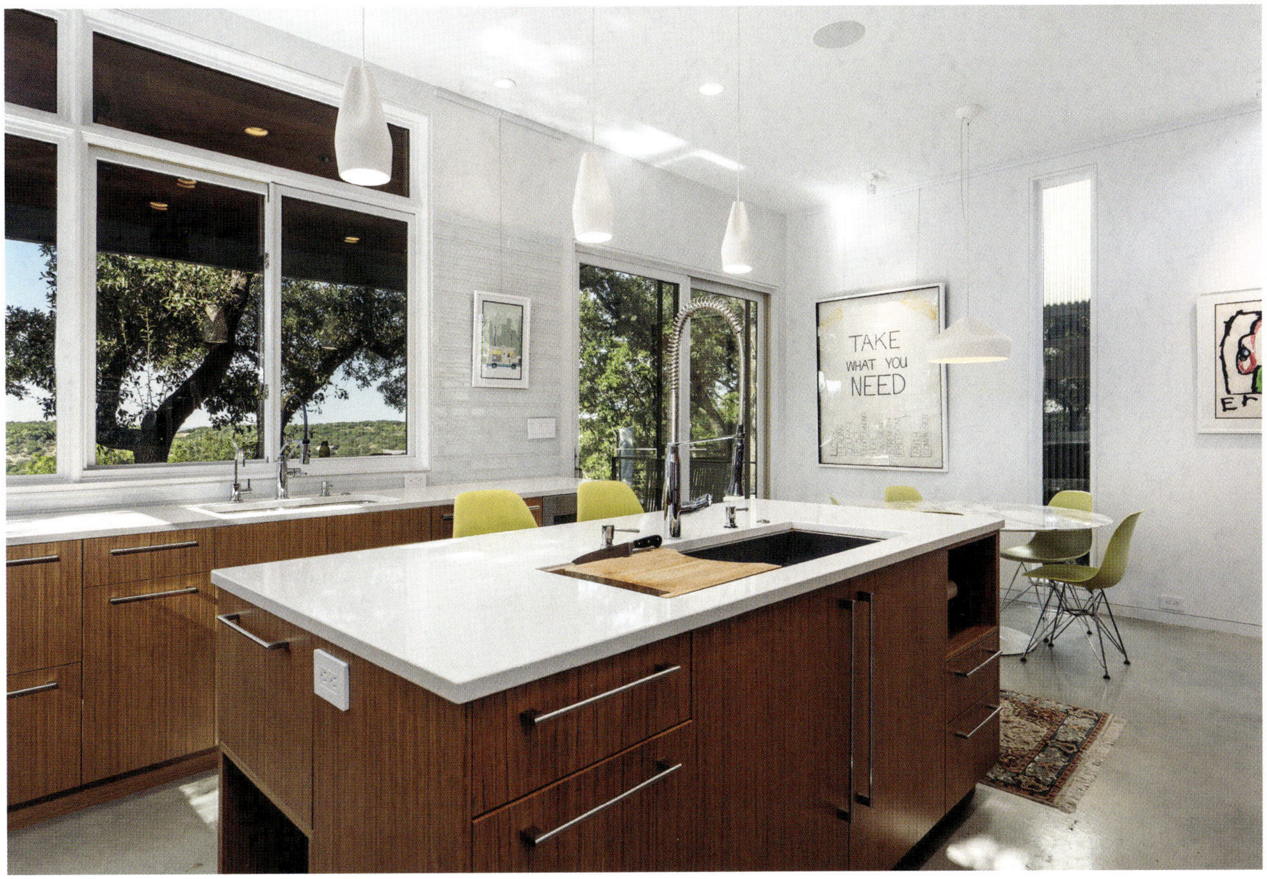
TAKE
WHAT YOU
NEED

"The most important element of a home is the synergy between how it looks and feels and the personality of the homeowner." -Kelly Hallman

ABOVE: This family country house was originally built in 1913 and the current owners are the third generation to have now made it their own. The living room is the only room that didn't have its footprint altered on this down-to-the-studs renovation.

FACING PAGE TOP: The refrigerated glass-front wine storage was the client's idea, to make use of the space under the stairs near the dining room.

FACING PAGE BOTTOM LEFT: The handmade Pratt + Larson filigree ceramic tile above the stove offsets all the angular elements in the kitchen.

FACING PAGE BOTTOM RIGHT: Originally a bedroom, the space now serves as the master bath with the centerpiece being the freestanding tub. Photography by Jeremiah Dearinger.

321

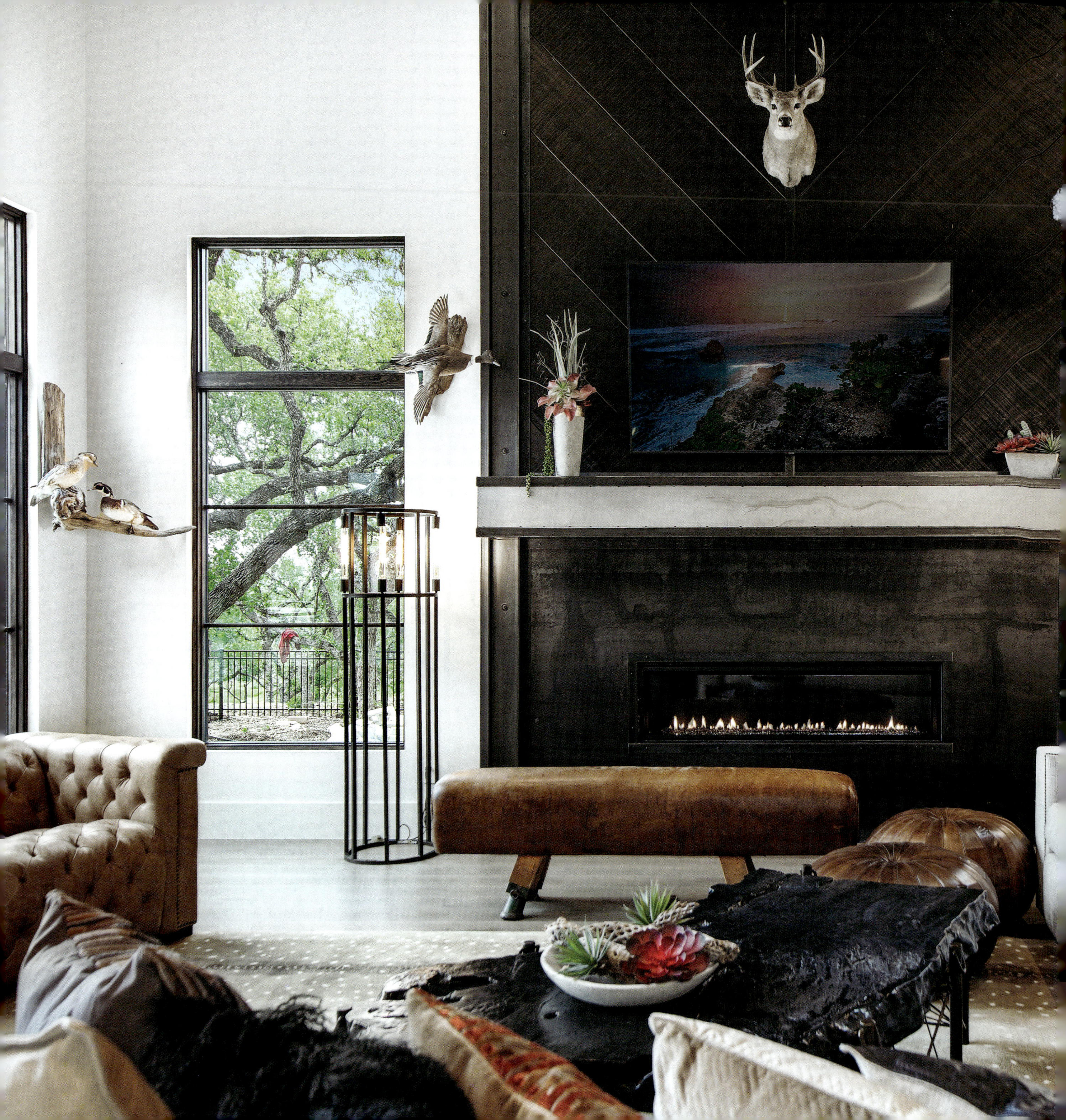

B
BORNE DESIGNS
JESSICA CLAIBORNE-BADE

Borne Designs' owner Jessica Claiborne-Bade grew up playing with colors and putting fabric and patterns together. Her mother was a designer with an eclectic eye and it influenced Jessica's own aesthetic. "I learned very early on that a beautiful space doesn't have to perfectly match or have symmetry," she says. She loves mixing clean, contemporary aesthetic with a rustic vibe and old history with new materials, pairing the seemingly disparate styles together in perfect harmony to create a more lived-in, seasoned feel. And, it's what she does every day at her relationship-based boutique firm. She and her team have succeeded in creating a niche market because not only is Jessica an interior designer, she has built and managed high-end multimillion dollar homes which has given her steadfast knowledge across every aspect of the construction and project management process.

Borne Designs' work is streamlined and highly personalized for their clients, and they shepherd them every step of the way – from coming up with a vision of the ideal home to collaborating and working in tandem with architect, builder, tradespeople, vendors, and artisans to guarantee an impeccable outcome. They ultimately love giving their clients the gift of a home they've always dreamed of.

FACING PAGE: We provided the design coordination and construction management for this beautiful Hill Country ranch home built by Todd Glowka. Integrating a rustic vibe into the clean, contemporary look gives a nod to the home's outdoor surroundings, with the taxidermy literally bringing the outside in – with a whimsical spirit.
Photography by Lauren Keller - LRES Marketing.

324

"The kitchen is not only the heart of a home where families come together and share their day, but it seems to be the place that they interact with each other the most."
—Jessica Claiborne-Bade

RIGHT: Bunk beds never had it so good as these custom, built-ins that offer a fun alternative for guest quarters, too.

BOTTOM: From the kitchen, there's a natural flow into the dining area that's perfect for entertaining along with the living area — all of which directly open to the outdoors. It's one big, inviting, warm, and welcoming space.

FACING PAGE TOP: We usually start the design process in the kitchen and this farmhouse-style design was no different, setting the tone for the rest of the home. Antique, reclaimed timbers and flooring run throughout the kitchen and beyond, offering a woodsy counterpoint to the antique Pegasus marble countertops, painted shiplap, and modern, geometric Walker Zanger backsplash.

FACING PAGE BOTTOM LEFT: The reclaimed wood floors in the master bedroom are a natural progression to the private deck overlooking the scenic Hill Country.

FACING PAGE BOTTOM RIGHT: Symmetry is implemented here to impactful effect, with the patterned tile and dual mirrors and sconces juxtaposed with a rustic wood vanity.
Photography by Lauren Keller - LRES Marketing.

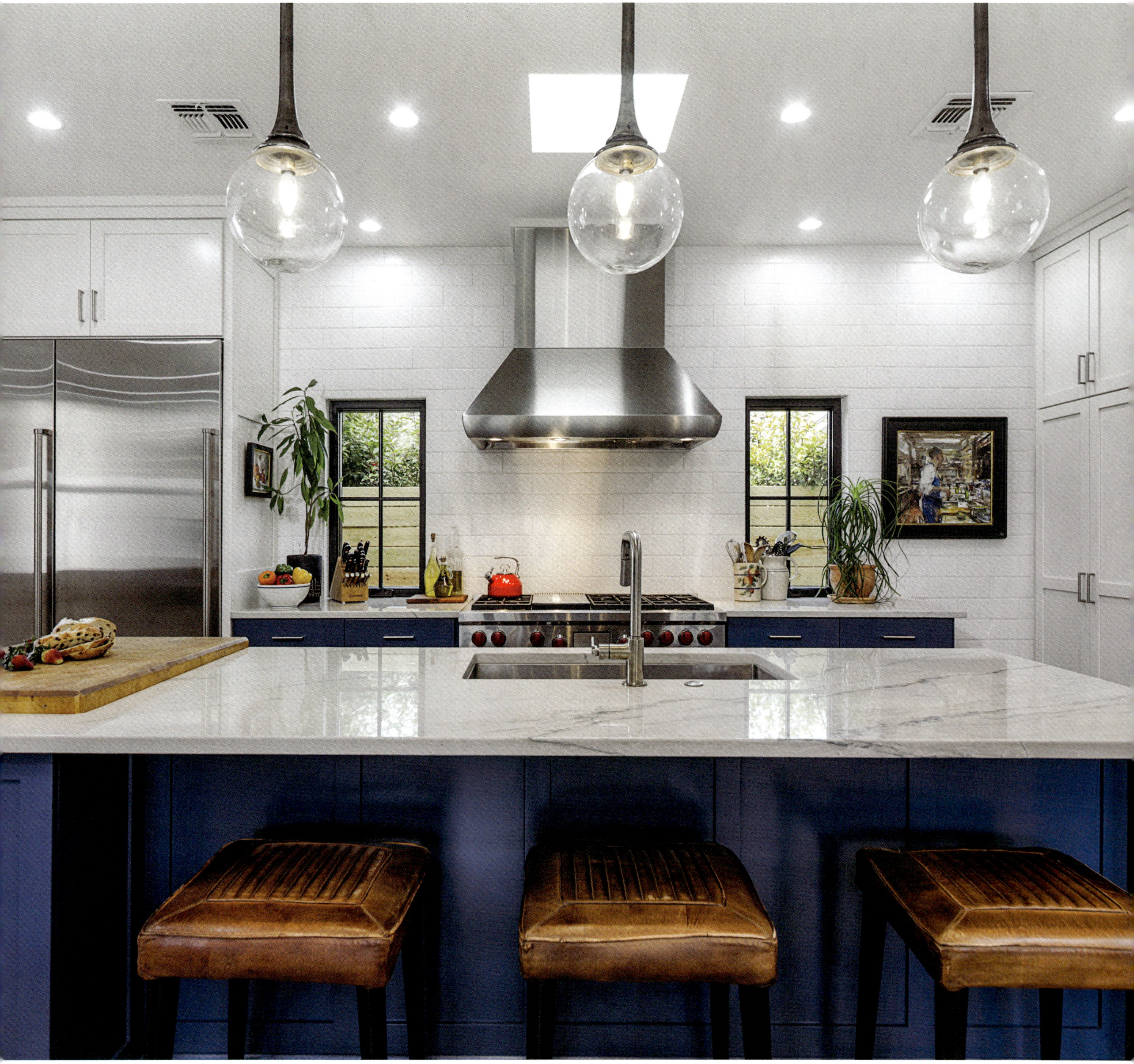

LAUGHLIN HOMES + RESTORATION

Relationships are important to Richard Laughlin. He treats his staff and trade partners with respect and has retained the region's top talent. A third-generation and locally grown builder, Richard was voted "Man of the Year" by his hometown Chamber of Commerce. The team is involved with a number of charitable organizations, emphasizing a spirit of community pride.

Everyone who works with Laughlin Homes + Restoration appreciates their work ethic, perfectionist nature, and policy of open communication. They let homeowners know that there will be "opportunities" along the way – it's all part of the creative process – and that they love nothing more than coming up with creative solutions that push the project to the next level.

Since 1984, the design-build team at Laughlin Homes + Restoration has been enhancing the beauty of the Texas Hill Country with handcrafted custom homes and historically detailed restoration projects.

Laughlin has also been awarded several Best in American Living Awards by the National Association of Home Builders and was named the Remodeler of the Year and Custom Builder of the Year by the Texas Association of Builders. He also received the 2019 Remodeling Entrepreneur of The Year Award by The Fred Case.

THIS PAGE AND FACING PAGE: The Laughlin design-build team beautifully transformed this 1950s-era maze of small rooms and tight hallways into an inviting, spacious home with a serene environment suitable for entertaining – all the while respecting the scale of the original structure and the aesthetics of the surrounding historic neighborhood. In the kitchen, an antique maple butcher block – a family heirloom – was integrated into custom cabinetry, which was styled to be functional and efficient. The kitchen seamlessly combines with the living space, offering an ideal setting for smaller gatherings, while a 600-square-foot covered patio and outdoor kitchen provide the perfect place for year-round entertaining. Photography by Jeremiah Dearinger.

"The estate was crafted with detail, as a home first — a combination of private living spaces and entertainment areas for family and friends to enjoy while also incorporating winery offices." – Richard Laughlin

ABOVE AND FACING PAGE: Expansive glass, antique timber, elegant chandeliers, and natural stone blend seamlessly against the American Clay wall finish in this exquisite 16,000-square-foot property. This chateau provides the owners with a sophisticated home that meets their desire for a combination of private living spaces, six bedroom suites, office space for conducting winery business, and multiple entertainment areas. Furniture-grade cabinetry and locally crafted mahogany doors combined with granite, marble, iron, and stone are functional, timeless elements of design. Salvaged beams and shiplap materials add warmth to the modern tone of the home while the aluminum-framed windows flood rooms with natural light. Distinctive amenities, including the lazy-river pool with lanai and six fireplaces, create an intimate, resort-like feel. Photography by Adam Hahn with Wingman Imagery.

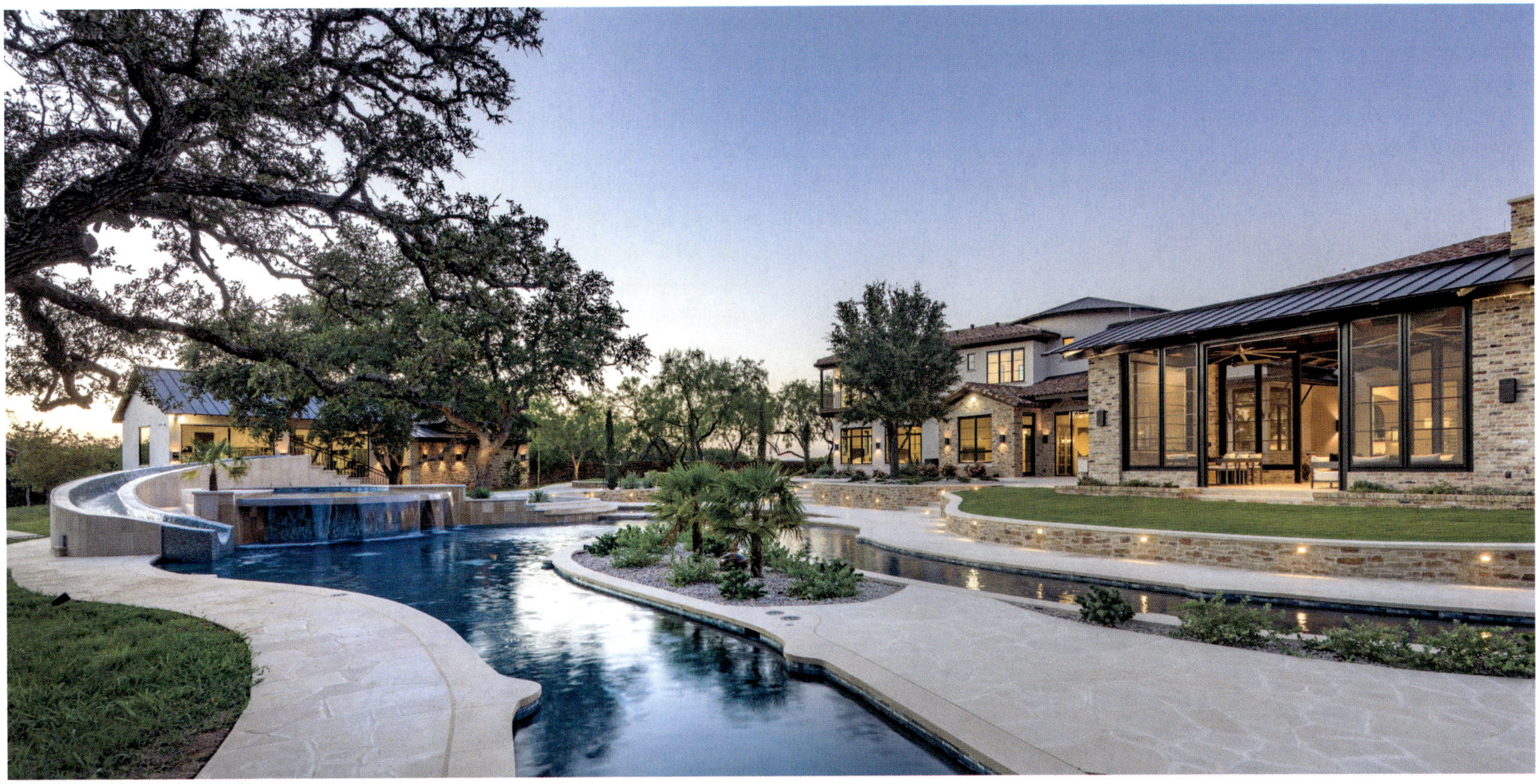

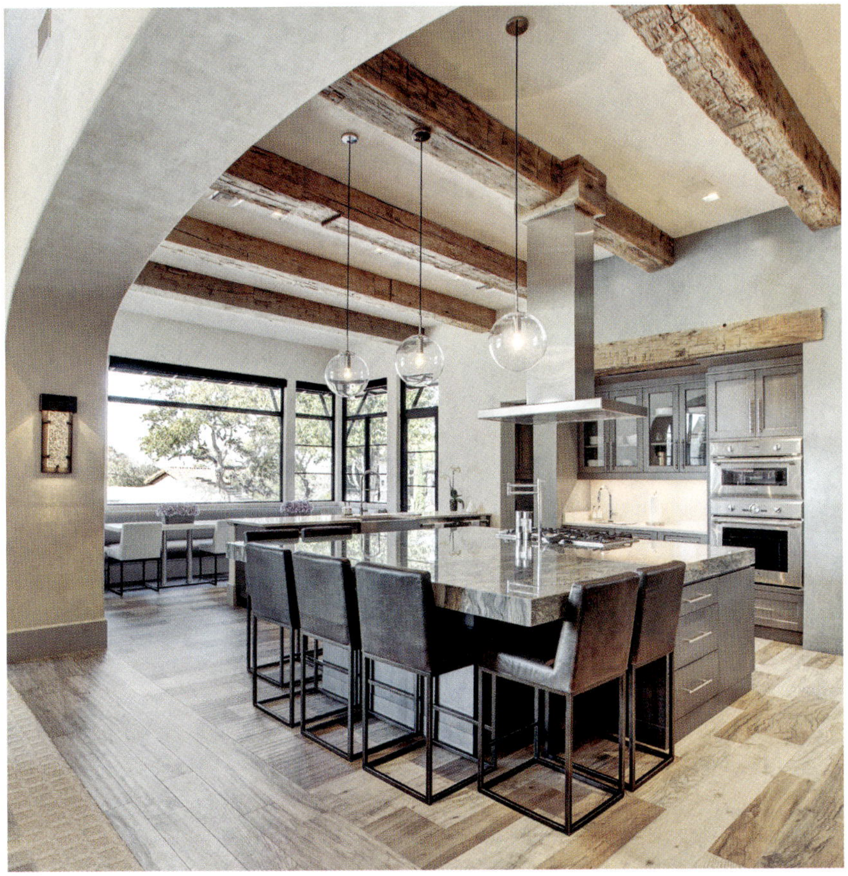

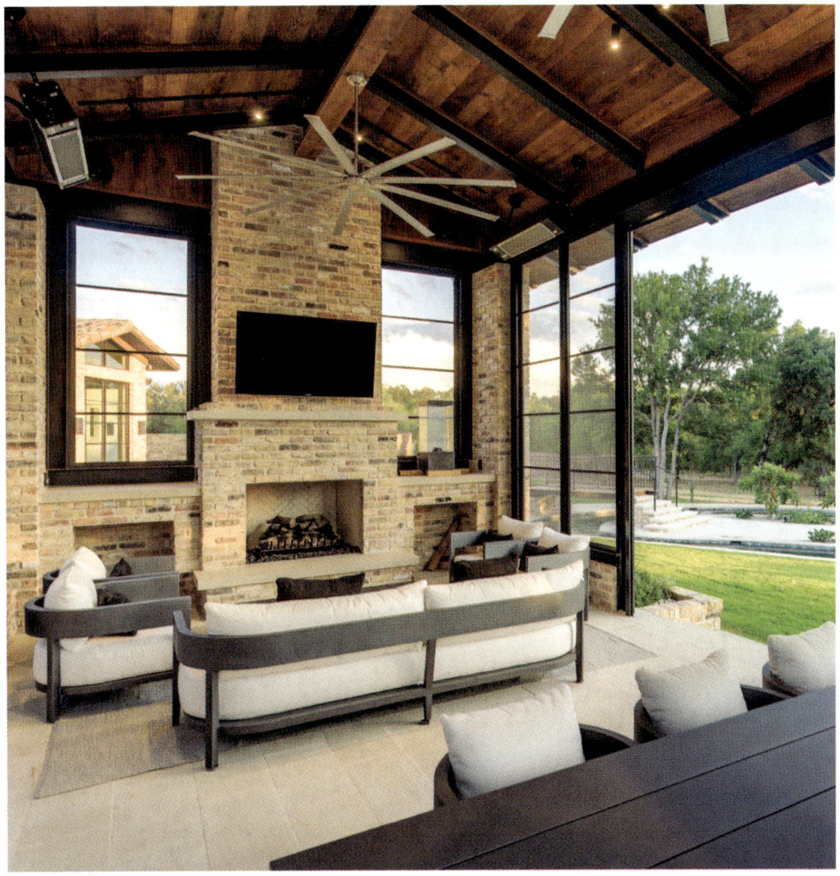

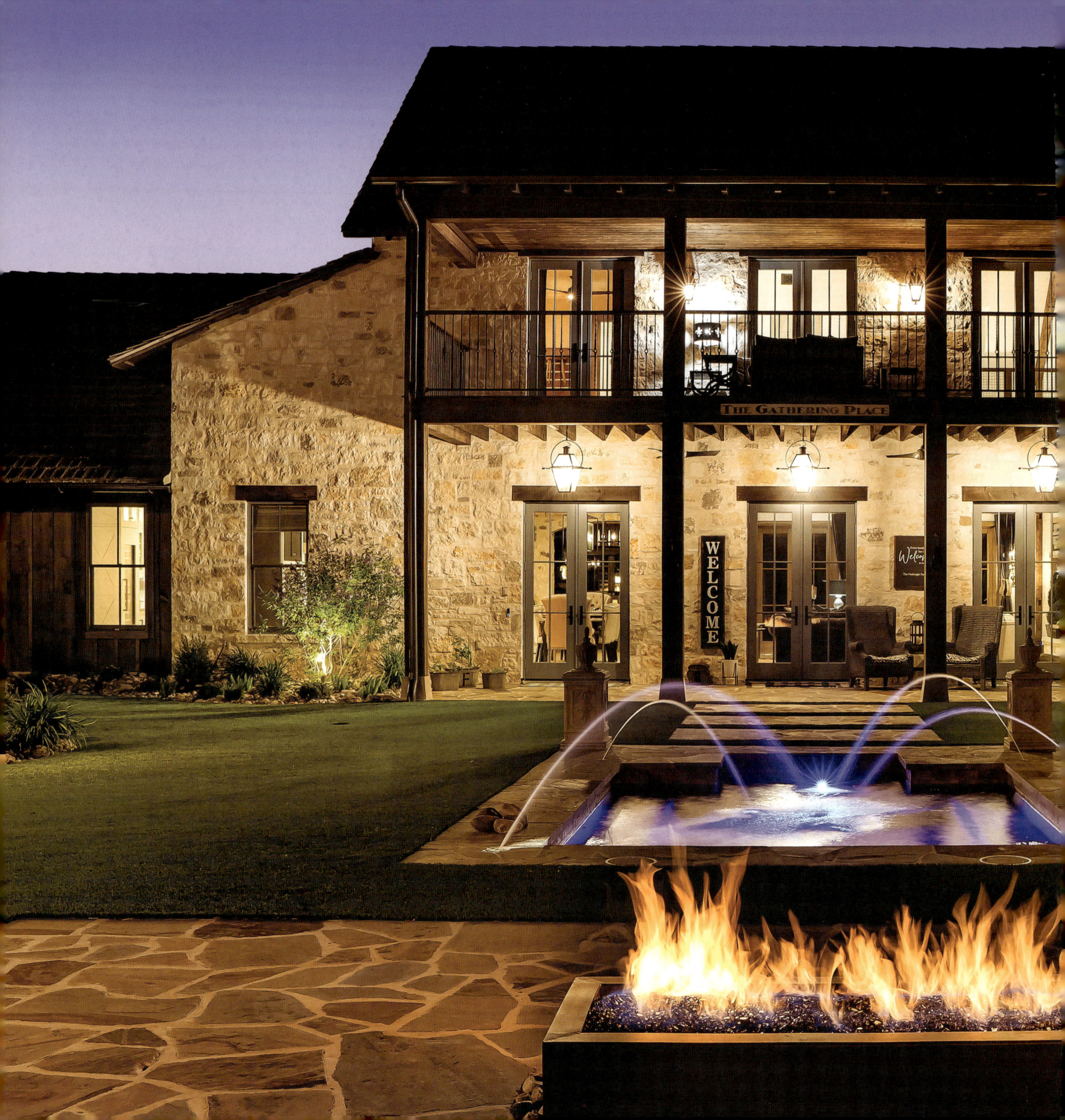
THE GATHERING PLACE
WELCOME

MABERY CONTRACTING

A homeowner's excitement to build a dream property, along with the process of creating something amazing from the ground up, is what inspires Matthew Mabery of Mabery Contracting the most!

Matthew believes quality comes first and achieves this goal by personally visiting each homeowner's job site daily. High standards of quality are further enhanced by performing all their own carpentry work including framing, siding, door and window installation, and trim work. This allows them to construct luxury homes that are more cost-efficient without having to sacrifice the quality and features discerning clients expect. Their distinctive style, attention to detail, and workmanship is visible in every home they build. It's this approach that has earned Mabery Contracting the status of Preferred Luxury Home Builder in the acclaimed Golf Course Community of Boot Ranch. This resort-like community is located in the town of Fredericksburg. Matthew also works closely with architects to make sure that the building process flows smoothly and in a timely manner. Having built and completed more than 35 homes in Boot Ranch, he is well-versed in the build requirements of the developer. A typical build takes 10 to 12 months, depending on how quickly information is received from the homeowners or designers. Fredericksburg happens to be where Matthew calls home, so he takes special pride in building beautiful properties in his own backyard. Besides building quality, luxury homes, the Mabery Contracting team views every project as an opportunity to develop lifelong relationships with their clients.

FACING PAGE: A glowing firepit and soothing water feature welcome guests in the magnificent courtyard of this modern farmhouse, a one-of-a-kind property located in the Texas Hill Country which was completed in 2020 for owners Gary and Joan Freiburger. Photography by Jeremiah Dearinger.

"I respect and value all of my clients and it's truly rewarding when the same is given back to me. Gary and Joan Freiburger were one of those, and I feel fortunate to be part of their amazing project. They will be great friends forever." —Matthew Mabery

ABOVE LEFT: This stunning, inset freestanding tub is highlighted by reclaimed barnwood and candle niches. The penny gap wall features stained wood windows and marble shower, which both make this bathroom a showstopper.

ABOVE RIGHT: The property has two, two-bedroom guesthouses. Shown here is the one finished rustically for the homeowner's son with reclaimed log and stone chinking. The other bedroom for the daughter features painted penny gap walls and marble tiles.

FACING PAGE: These homeowners were very thoughtful of every space; it was so rewarding to bring this sophisticated and sleek, farmhouse-style aesthetic to life.
Photography by Jeremiah Dearinger.

333

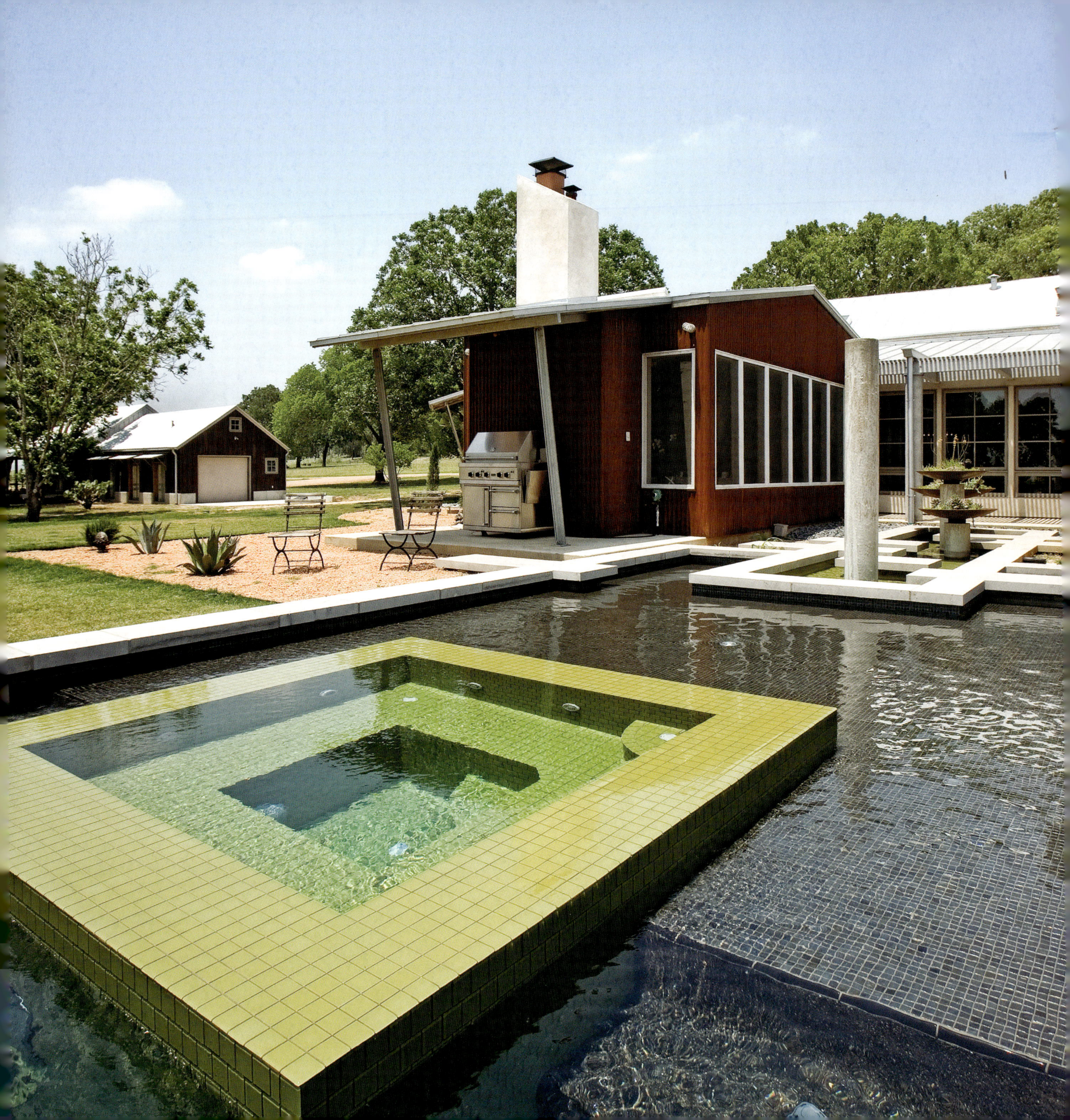